Love, Dad:
Letters from a Father
to His Daughters

Chris Palmer

Bethesda Communications Group

Published by the Bethesda Communications Group
4816 Montgomery Lane
Bethesda, MD 20814
www.bcgpub.com

ISBN-13: 978-1-7321501-5-7
ISBN-10: 1-7321501-5-X

The cover photo shows Cory, Jenny, Kim, and Tina in front and Gail and Chris in back.

Dedicated to my three extraordinary and wonderful daughters:
Kim, Tina, and Jenny

Contents

Preface

By Chris Palmer
June 1, 2018

I was 12 years old in 1959 when my parents sent me to an austere English boarding school in southeast London. Dulwich College was a renowned, boys-only "public school" like Harrow and Eton. My parents made a great financial sacrifice to send their four sons to Dulwich. They did it because they believed this school produced proud, capable, and self-confident men. Many famous men had attended Dulwich, including the writer P.G. Wodehouse and the explorer Ernest Shackleton.

My three older brothers and I found the school intimidating and tough. Many of the boys came from wealthy backgrounds and had amazing self-confidence, something my brothers and I lacked. Bullying and corporal punishment were common.

I remember being incredibly homesick and feeling lonely, scared, and abandoned. I deeply yearned for the warmth and security of home. My most frequent daydream was sitting at home in front of a roaring fire in the family room feeling content, secure, and peaceful.

When my father took my brothers and me back to boarding school after Christmas one year, I remember sobbing uncontrollably for the entire three-hour train ride.

There was, however, one ray of comforting sunshine in this misery – the letters we received from my mother. She wrote long, chatty letters to her four boys once a week. She would type them laboriously on legal-sized paper and make three carbon copies, so she could send a copy to each boy. The last copy was faint and barely readable. We would each receive the top, most readable copy one week in four, so each would feel treated fairly. On the bottom of each letter, my mother hand-wrote a personal note to each of us, giving us her individual attention and affirming each one of us with words of love and affection.

How we loved receiving those letters! How precious they were! My heart would leap when I discovered a new one had arrived, and I would devour it eagerly.

My mother's letters mainly contained news of what my parents were doing, the parties they were attending, and whom they had met. But what was so magical about them was that they took her a long time to write and therefore it stood to reason (at least, to my young mind) that I was deeply loved.

The letters conveyed the unmistakable message that there was a place in the universe where I was special, where I could always go for comfort and security, and where the threats and vagaries of the outside world could be walled off and forgotten about. In short, my mother's letters gave me reason to hope and to have confidence in the future.

* * * * *

Letters have played a big role in my life as an adult, too. When our three daughters were babies, my wife, Gail, was so competent as a new mother that I was in danger of being left out of the family bonding. I sometimes felt jealous and angry because I was not part of the rest of the family's intimacy.

The girls would prefer Gail over me and this sometimes drove me nuts.

Exacerbating this situation were my diligent efforts to build my career as a wildlife filmmaker. I traveled extensively, spending a lot of time away from my family. At home, I wanted to be a capable, loving, and effective father, but the girls sometimes kept me at a distance. I recall one night when Gail and I put our daughters to bed and I tried to cuddle with each one.

"Would you like to snuggle?" I asked my girls, all of them under 10 years of age and each of them adorable, loving, and beautiful in her own way. "No," they answered, one by one, unknowingly inflicting wounds to my heart. They would only snuggle with their mom. It hurt to be left out.

I yearned to be a father who wasn't simply an awkward appendage to the nuclear group, but a pivotal and integrated member. The feelings of rejection roiling inside me prompted me to start thinking of innovative things I could do to play a more significant and meaningful role in my daughters' lives.

Thus I became a student of what makes an effective parent. I resolved to learn all I could about what it means to be a loving and capable father. I undertook a deliberate, self-imposed program of study, reading book after book on parenting, and later wrote my own book on the subject: *Raise Your Kids to Succeed: What Every Parent Should Know* (Rowman & Littlefield, 2017).

Inspired by my studies of parenting, and with Gail's support, I introduced new traditions to help build a strong family and set up our kids to succeed.

One "tradition" I initiated, inspired by my mother's example, was to write letters to my daughters every night when I was away traveling and making films. I invested a lot of time and effort in these letters and wrote scores of them over the years. I saw that my daughters really liked them and got a lot out of them. The letters were a way I could build a meaningful connection with my children.

When I was away from home, my nightly letters were an attempt to get the attention of my daughters and not be "out of sight, out of mind." I soon realized that my letters were also an effective way for me to tell my daughters things I wanted them to know and to convey my love for them.

So this book has its origins in my extensive travel as a wildlife film producer at the National Audubon Society and the National Wildlife Federation. When our oldest daughter, Kim, was a baby (she is now 37) I started leaving simple letters to her for each night I was away, expressing my love for her. I wanted Kim to know I was thinking about her even when I was away from home. I wanted to matter to her.

These letters soon became a family tradition, but I didn't attach a great deal of significance to them until one Christmas when our daughters were still little. I noticed an unusual mood of excitement in Gail and the girls as we were opening gifts. When I thought all the gift-giving was over, Gail brought out a special gift for me, and the four of them looked at me in eager anticipation as I unwrapped it.

Inside was a book. But it wasn't from a bookstore. It was a book that Gail and the girls had put together themselves and had beautifully bound. It was called *A Father's Love* and it contained all the letters I had written to the girls up to that point. Gail, without my knowledge (so the book would be a surprise) had surreptitiously collected my letters and painstakingly typed them all out. She wrote the following preface in the book:

Perhaps the hardest part of fatherhood for Chris has been the separation he has faced because of his frequent overnight trips away from home. I will never forget his first trip away as a father, when Kimberly was just a few months old. He was due to spend most of the week in Denver, Colorado – but he couldn't bear being away from her for that long and cut the trip short!

Chris has helped Kimberly, Christina, and Jennifer bear the separations by leaving a letter for them each night that he must be away. The letter reminds them of his love for them, sometimes with philosophical ideas, sometimes with challenging questions for them to answer, always with supportive thoughts, humor, and love. The letters have served as a focal point for our evenings without him – a treat to look forward to as soon as the kitchen is cleaned up. The girls will cheer "Daddy's letter! Daddy's letter!" with great anticipation!

I have put these letters into print (a surprise Christmas present) as a way of helping us all remember the love that Chris sends the girls, even when he must be away from them!

I was deeply moved by this gift and it made me realize that the letters I was writing to my daughters were an important part of our family life. From then on I began to take my responsibility to write these letters even more seriously, and I would never depart on a trip without leaving the girls a letter for each night I was away, even if it meant staying up half the night before a 6 a.m. flight the following morning. It became an obligation, but it was a self-imposed obligation that I relished.

If I was going to be away for, say, 12 nights (as happened now and then), I would write 12 letters (addressed to all three girls) before I left, many of them more than a page long. I remember once going to Africa for a 14-day photo shoot; before I left I wrote 14 letters!

The topics ranged from the qualities desirable in a husband to how to prepare for meetings, from family history to why having a sense of humor is important, from discussions on what constitutes success and happiness to stories about Abe Lincoln and George Washington, from how to give a dinner party to how to tell a good joke. My letters gave me a chance to talk to them about issues that deeply mattered to me.

*   *   *   *   *

In 1983, columnist Maureen Dowd wrote an article for The Washington Post in which she told the moving story of how her relationship with her mother, at one time strained and stilted, had been transformed when her mother started writing letters to her, especially as the letters became more intimate. Dowd's mother could say things in letters that she couldn't say on the phone or in person.

Writing "love letters" to your child is rich with positive long-term consequences. It is a chance to compliment your child, affirm her, tell her how she has enriched your life and how much she means to you, thank her, give her encouragement, and tell her you love her.

Email, FaceTime, text messaging, and other communication technologies help families stay in touch, but they have also led to fewer thoughtful, reflective letters from parent to child. This is a significant loss today when everybody is so busy that it is even a challenge for families to get together over dinner.

I found that leaving letters for my daughters when they were growing up was a very special gift to them. Writing letters is one way to strengthen the bond between parents and kids that can be frayed and weakened by busyness.

Many parents, like me, are not skilled at expressing their feelings. Their children may not even realize how much their parents love them and are proud of them. Because they don't express their feelings, some parents, especially dads, can become emotionally distant from their kids. This deprives their children of parental love and nurturing. It can result in long-term damage to kids, such as ingrained feelings of inadequacy.

As a professor, I like to call the parents of the top half dozen outstanding students in my class at the end of the semester to tell them how well their son or daughter has done in my class. (I get permission from the student first, of course.) Once the student gives me permission, I call the mom and dad and tell them that they can be very proud of their son or daughter for, to use a few examples, the diligence, creativity, or tenacity he or she has shown in my class. The parents are always delighted to receive this call from me and invariably respond with how proud they are of their child. This message, in turn, is one that I convey to the student the following day. I am amazed by how many students respond wistfully, "I've never heard them say that before."

Writing expressive letters or notes—leaving them in your child's lunch box, under her pillow, in her backpack, taped to the steering wheel, wherever—can go a long way toward strengthening your parent-child relationship.

There is one letter to your children that is particularly important, and that is the letter you write to them (or should write them) before you die. This letter will tell them how much you love them, treasure them, and will miss them. That in and of itself is important, but such a letter also gives them a document that they will forever cherish. It will be passed down from generation to generation and become a family heirloom.

We leave our kids our possessions and financial assets, but of far more value are the life lessons, wisdom, experiences, and emotional/mental assets we each accumulate and hopefully pass on. There are many ways of leaving these legacies, including letters, memoirs, and journals, and they all are fruitful. I hope the letters in this book will become one of the non-monetary legacies I leave to my family.

Why did I write them? I've explained that I wanted to be relevant to my daughters as they were growing up, but I want to add this: By writing these letters, I sent some essential messages to my daughters, namely that they are important to me, that I love them, that I'm proud of them, and that I profoundly value them, care about them, and want the best for them in life.

What parents don't long to connect deeply with their children? Sadly, the pressures and demands of daily life conspire to stop this from happening. Writing a love letter to your child is an effective way to strengthen your unique bond with your child and show her how much you care.

Long after I am gone, the letters in this book will remain for my daughters and their families to remember me and the loving relationship we shared. What better way to defeat death?

I hope you enjoy this book of love letters to my daughters.

*   *   *   *   *

Author's Note: My oldest daughter Kimberly (now a journalist and published book author) was born in December 1979. My middle daughter Christina (now a doctor) was born in May 1982. And my youngest daughter Jenny (now a lawyer) was born in May 1987.

1987

January 12, 1987

MEMO TO: KIMBERLY HALLETT SHEARER-PALMER
                CHRISTINA MELLEN SHEARER-PALMER
                BABY-STILL-TO-BE-BORN SHEARER-PALMER

FROM: YOUR 'OL DAD

RE: LOVE

QUESTION: WHAT IS LOVE?

ANSWER:

1. LOVE IS SNUGGLING IN THE MORNING.

2. LOVE IS SOMEONE GETTING YOU A DRINK OF WATER IN THE MIDDLE OF THE NIGHT.

3. LOVE IS A HUG WHEN YOU GET HOME FROM WORK.

4. LOVE IS THINKING ABOUT THE NEEDS OF YOUR SISTER.

5. LOVE IS BUYING SOMEONE A THOUGHTFUL BOOK.

6. LOVE IS SHARING A GOOD JOKE.

7. LOVE IS TRYING TO MAKE THE WORLD A BETTER PLACE.

8. LOVE IS SAVING FOR COLLEGE SO YOU CAN DO SOMETHING EXCITING WITH YOUR LIFE.

9. LOVE IS HAVING A LOVING FAMILY THAT CARES ABOUT YOU.

10. LOVE IS SWEEPING UP THE CRUMBS.

11. LOVE IS ENJOYING KIMBERLY JUMP-ROPE.

12. LOVE IS ENJOYING CHRISTINA ON THE TRAMPOLINE.

13. LOVE IS USING A PENNY WORD.

14. LOVE IS MAKING FRIENDS.

15. LOVE IS WASHING 2 GIRLS IN THE BATH.

16. LOVE IS NOT BOTHERING SOMEONE WHEN THEY WANT TO BE LEFT ALONE.

17. LOVE IS ENCOURAGING SOMEONE TO EAT FRUIT AND FRESH VEGETABLES.

18. LOVE IS LENDING SOMEONE YOUR HAIR BRUSH.

19. LOVE IS HAVING FUN TOGETHER.

20. LOVE IS TELLING THEIR NOSEY MUM AND DAD EVERYTHING THAT HAPPENED IN SCHOOL.

21. LOVE IS TWO GIRLS WHO ARE THE MOST SPECIAL PEOPLE IN THE WHOLE WORLD.

Your 'ol DAD
XXXXXXXXXXX
OOOOOOOOOOO

P.S. Love is flossing 2 little girls' teeth

Saturday, February 14, 1987

To My 2 precious Valentines,

I'm not going to tell you who is writing this letter. It's from a <u>secret admirer</u> of you 2 big girls! You'll never guess who I am. My first name rhymes with FISH (almost), my last name with FARMER, and my middle initial comes right after M in the alphabet. I love to keep fit and especially like doing exercises with 2 girls climbing all over me. I like going to the library with you, and I helped bring you both into the world (with a little help from Mummy!) I sometimes hear you talking with a funny accent like when you say tomato as if it rhymed with potato, and you sometimes spell words wrong like COLOUR! I like to work at my desk and, like both of you, I like to read and study. [Can you guess who I am yet?!!]

Give up? I know it's hard. I'll tell you. It's ME, your old luvable, friendly, and loving Pop, pa, Dad, pops, your old tootin-shootin, hot potato, rarin' to go, zippy zappy, on-your-mark-get-set-go,

DADDY!!
XXXXXXXXX
OOOOOOOOO

March 3, 1987

Dear adorable, delicious, delectable (Kimberly -- pay attention -- I'm talking to you too!!) delightful, dazzling daughters,

QUESTION

What is pink, cuddly, clever, loving, highly intelligent, enthusiastic and creative?
[Answer: KIMBERLY]

QUESTION

What is highly intelligent, cuddly, pink, creative, enthusiastic, loving and clever?
[Answer: CHRISTINA]

For K: If you read one book every day, how many books will you read in 2 weeks?

For C: If you read one book one evening and three books the next 4 nights, how many books have you read?

For K: If one book has 200 pages, another 300 pages, and a third 200 pages, how many in total?

For C: If you do 20 jumps on the trampoline, and then 1 more, how many jumps in total? If you do 99 jumps, and then add one more, what is total?

For K: Can you say these words:

   SYLLABLE
   LOQUACIOUS
   VITALITY
   SOCIETY
   EBULLIENT

For: Find odd one out:

ABCD	ABCD	ABCE	ABCD
4321	4321	4321	4311
CAT	CAT	CAT	CAR
BOOKS	BOOK	BOOK	BOOK

1988

Friday, June 9, 1988
(morning)

Kimberly, Christina, Jennifer,

Have a wonderful day! I hope you laugh a lot, smile plenty, put up your hands in class to show your exuberant enthusiasm, get lots of exercise swimming, playing tennis, and squashing uppity boys in the playground, do a fun show and tell (C), have a great tennis lesson (K), and enjoy the great lives you are blessed with to the hilt.

I ADORE YOU!
DADDY
XXXXXX

1989

February 13, 1989
Valentine's Day

Have lots of fun today. I'll be thinking about you. You are three very special children. You have no idea how much Mummy and I treasure you each. Our lives are deeply enriched by each of you.

Love,
DADDY
XXXXXXX
OOOOOOO

May 2, 1989
My Three Wonderful Daughters:

KIM KIM   TINA   JEN JEN

I'll miss you today. I'll miss your smiles, your laughter, your curiosity, your intelligence, your warm affectionate natures, your hugs and kisses, your athletic prowess, your deep desire to live to your potential. For all these reasons and many others, I can't wait to get home to be with you all again.

All my love,
DADDY
XXXOOO

May 4, 1989
My Darling Kimberly, Christina, and JenJen,

Sorry to have to leave early again before you guys wake up. Have a great day. AND remember, I don't love you, I don't adore you, I don't like you ... I'm CRAZY about you!

I'll be thinking about you.

DADDY/LOONATIC
XXXOOO

July 18, 1989

I know you are looking after each other and that makes me feel good! I' in currently making a list of my values i.e., those things (unifying principles) that are important to me, and out of which my long-term goals grow. Our family is at the top of the list!

I love you.

DADDY
XXXOOO

1990

Saturday, February 3, 1990

My Darling Kimberly, Christina, and Jennifer,

I hated saying goodbye to you today. I hate being away from you, and I know you hate me being away. It seems like I'll be away a long time and you may be feeling sad but it will go fast. Remember you are always in my thoughts.

As you read this, I'm in the plane going to Frankfurt in Germany. I'll land there for a few hours in the early morning (before you wake up). Then -- even before you wake up on Sunday morning (tomorrow), I'll be on another plane leaving Frankfurt and flying to Nairobi in Kenya (on the equator). I land in Kenya at about 11:00 p.m. Sunday night -- or about 3:00 p. in. Sunday afternoon your time. We have to go through customs, get our baggage and then get to our hotel. As soon as I get there, I will call you. It could be <u>any time</u> Sunday evening, even after you're in bed because there are often long delays on international flights.

It will be exciting to be in a country I've never been to before. The smells, the sites, the architecture, the people, the air, the noises and so on will all be completely different from anything I've ever seen before (I remember when I first came to America in 1972, just before I met Mommy, how observant and "alive" I was because everything was so new. After a few months, your mind tunes out a lot of the everyday things around you because they are not important, but for the first few weeks one is sensitive to so much.)

Tomorrow Peter Berle and I are having dinner at the American Embassy with the Ambassador.

I love you each of you with all my heart. Next Sunday will come quickly.

DON'T BE SADISH, EAT A RADISH!!

> DADDY
> XXX
> OOO

Sunday, February 4, 1990

My loves -- Kimberly, Christina and Jennifer,

I know I must seem a long way away. As you read this, I am probably fast asleep in Nairobi. (I'm staying at the Hilton Hotel) exhausted after the long flight. I bet you, I'm dreaming about you all <u>right now!!</u> Bet I'm feeling homesick. Bet I'm thinking next Sunday, when I'll be home in TOO FAR AWAY! Bet I'm feeling sad to be so far away from you. Still, however many miles there are between us, you are all right there in the center of my being, and wherever I am, my thoughts about you come right along with me.

Tomorrow we are giving a press luncheon and briefing reporters on what we're doing. I'll also be going "on location" and watching the making of our film. And tomorrow evening (Monday) we'll be having dinner with the Ambassador.

I am 8 hours ahead of you! So if you ar reading this at, say, 7:00 p.m. in the evening, it will be 3:00 a.m. in the morning in Kenya and I'll be fast asleep.

Later this week, we'll be going to the Mara Maasai National Park. I'll tell you all about it -- and some of the great wildlife I'll probably see, in my letter tomorrow night.

You are three wonderful girls, and I miss you terribly.

love,

DADDY
XXX

Monday, February 5, 1990

My Precious Treasures: Kimberly, Christina and JenJen,

How I miss you. I think of you all the time and am comforted knowing you are being "buddies" and looking after each other.

On Wednesday I am going to the Maasai Mara National Reserve. This is considered by many to be the best animal reserve in Kenya. With any luck I should see zebras, giraffes, buffalos, wildebeests, elephants, hyenas, jackals, ostriches, and prides of lions! I wish you could all be with me. It'll be exciting!

Between July and November, there is an annual migration of millions of wildebeest through the Maasai Mara! What a sight that must be.

When I first arrive, I will probably be awed by the realization that I am among real, uncaptured wildlife. I will take some photos to show you!

I love you so much.

DADDY
XXXXXXXXX

Tuesday, February 6, 1990

Kimberly, Christina and Jennifer,

Tomorrow we go into the bush -- Yes, that's what they call it! The Maasai Mara National Reserve is huge! 700 sq. miles. No houses or development are allowed in it. (People can visit it, of course, as I'm doing). There is an outside area where local Masai (tribesmen) are allowed to pasture their cattle but which is otherwise undisturbed.

As I said in my letter to you last night, the Mara country is world famous for its vast assemblages of plains game together with their associated predators. It is perhaps the only region left in Kenya where visitors can see animals in the same super-abundance as existed a century ago. In every direction, there are seemingly endless herds of game animals.

Mara possesses the largest population of LIONS to be found in Kenya -- Do you want me to bring one home?!! (Answer written by Kim: YES!! Jen wants a kitty and Tina also wants a rabbit, I don't mind).

My loves, will you please do your diaries tonight? Thanks.

All my love,

DADDY
XXX

Wednesday, February 7, 1990

My Darlings Kimberly, Christina and Jennifer,

Did you write in your in your diaries? I'm looking forward to reading what you write when I get back on Sunday. Write down anything that comes to mind -- how you are feeling, what made you laugh in school, a compliment paid to you by your teachers, games you played with JenJen, things you want to remember to tell me when I get home, interesting things you've learned, why you enjoy Mathnet, your favorite book, a good word you've just learned, how your parents can do a better job of bringing you up(!), what you want to be (and do) when you grow up, an outline for your first novel, science discoveries you would like to make , what you would do about drugs if you were President Bush, the weather, how you would like to change the design of the house, the number of press ups you did during your morning exercises, where you'd like to travel, what you dreamed about last night, why it's nice not having brothers, why it would be nice to have brothers, what you would do if you were the Principal of BE to improve the school, why girls are smarter and work harder than boys (!), why our family is so precious, etc.

I ADORE YOU

DADDY
XXXXXX

Thursday, February 8, 1990

My treasures Kimmie, Tina, and JenJen,

I don't like you. I don't love you. I <u>adore</u> you! Enjoy Bill Cosby tonight. I love the way Bill Cosby finds humor in the nooks and crannies of day- to-day life. My twin brother, Uncle Jon, is the same way. It takes a special sort of creativity which I greatly admire.

How was school today? I know you both did well and were enthusiastic and engaged, and <u>enjoyed</u> yourselves. So many kids don't enjoy school, hate learning and dislike the discipline of work, and Mummy and I are so glad you are not among them. Love of learning is much more important than passing of exams but if you love to learn, love to ask questions and discover things, then you'll pass exams and tests with top grades.

I hope you like all the things I'm leaving you every evening. They come with all my love to each of you.

Have a <u>great</u> day tomorrow.

Buckets of hugs and kisses,

Yer old, very own DAD
XXX

Friday, February 9, 1990

My Loves -- A TEST!! Stand - By for <u>the</u> test of the century! Test your brains against these and you will become SUPER - BRAIN!

For K: What is 2/3 of 99?
            What is 1/2 of 550?
            What is 1/4 of 1/2?
            What is 0.5 x 4 +

For C: What is 75 + 25 =
            What is 1/2 of 50?
            What is $5 + $60?
            What is 1/2 + 1/4 + 1/4?=

For J: Fill in the blanks:

A	_	C	D
1	2	_	4
1	_	3	4
A	B	_	D

CONGRATULATIONS!! <u>I adore you and I miss you!</u>

                        love,
                        DADDY

Saturday, February 10, 1990

Darling Kimberly, Christina, and Jennifer,

        Tomorrow, I'll be home! Can't wait to see you ! Have you done your diaries? I'll be eager to read them and catch up on everything I missed.

        How was Marvatots this morning? And, Jen Jen, how was Me and My Shadow? I missed seeing you all today doing your gymnastics -- I love to see how strong and agile each of you is (are?).

        Here are a few of the things that I love about each of you. I love it when you smile -- you light tip the whole room; I love it when you ask questions -- you push me to think; I love it when you crack jokes -- laughter is so important; I love it when you eat well -- good food is fundamental to a fulfilled life; I love it when you exercise, play tennis or do anything athletic -- fitness is fundamental to living up to your full potential as a person; I love it when you write and read -- loving language and being able to express yourselves lucidly is so important; I love it when you get excited by a new venture or new challenge (e.g. the 260 foot slide, or new computer software) -- rising to challenges is how you grow and relish life; I love it when you enjoy learning something new like biology (K) or American Presidents (C) or colors and numbers (J) -- yearning to learn and discover is what makes people so special; I love it when you take care of each other and enjoy each other (although quarrels are to be expected occasionally) -- caring for each other is one of the few things that make life worth living and give our lives meaning; I love it when you have fun with your friends— friends are very important; I love it when you are assertive and stand up for yourselves -- to flourish in the world, you have to be strong, have self-confidence and high self-esteem; and finally I love it when you are just you -- three incredibly special, talented (I should say multi-talented) gifted, hard-working, fun loving, beautiful and devoted daughters. Never were a mother and father as lucky as your Mummy and Daddy!

All my love -- I can't <u>wait</u> to see you!!

Kisses galore.
DADDY
XXXXXX
OOOOOO

February 21, 1990

My Darling Kimberly, Christina and Jennifer,

Hi my three precious loves! I'll be home tomorrow. Enclosed are some things I hope you'll enjoy!

Kimberly -- don't forget your diary!

Christina -- did you laugh in school today?!

JenJen -- I adore you too!

Answer: **<u>MAYBE</u>**

Do Mummy and I wish you three were different in any way at all?
Answer: **NO SIR**.

See you tomorrow.
Enjoy the enclosed!

love, DADDY
XXX

April 17, 1990

My Darling Kimberly, Christina and JenJen,

Didn't we have a great vacation last week? I loved spending so much time with you. You are wonderful companions. Do you know that some parents actually enjoy getting AWAY from their children?!! Not Mummy and me!

Here's what I enjoyed most about last week. Being with Mummy and you guys, seeing you have fun together, playing tennis with you, doing lots of things with you like clearing up the kitchen, playing smashball, sharing good jokes with you, seeing your creative artwork, listening to you talk and ask questions, swimming with you in the pool, and giving you kisses and hugs. I'm sure there are other things I've forgotten!

I wonder how school went for you both today. Undoubtedly you both had a great time. Well done! Enjoy tomorrow at Brookside, Christina -- wish I was coming with you. Kimmie -- is your foot OK now? JenJen -- well done for using the potty today!

Hope you enjoy the enclosed. Kimmie -- I love you; Christina -- I love you. Jenny -- I love you. Gail -- I love you too!!

> All my love
> Yer 'ol DADDY
> XXX

Friday, December 7, 1990
PEARL HARBOR DAY!!

Imagine you're an American kid on Dec. 7, 1941 and you've just got up. You're feeling sleepy, you know the Brits under Winston Churchill are battling valiantly against Nazi Germany led by the brutal and ruthless dictator Adolph Hitler. America is unsure whether to join Britain in its brave and lonely fight, or whether to stay out. If they enter the war, tens of thousands of American lives might be lost. If they stay out, Hitler might conquer Europe and dominate and destroy the European democratic nations.

Suddenly the radio crackles into life. You hear the unmistakable voice of Franklin Delano Roosevelt. His tone is grave and you notice your parents have stopped puttering about the house and are listening with taut and drained expressions. You ask your Dad what's happening. He whispers, "The Japanese have attacked Pearl Harbor -- scores of American ships have been sunk and destroyed -- we are declaring war against the Japanese. All people in the US of Japanese descent are being rounded up and contained in camps." You don't fully understand but you have this sense that something of major historical importance has just happened.

> DADDY
> XXX

1991

January 13, 1991
My Precious Loves -- Kimmie, Tina and Jennie,
REMEMBER:

1. We (i.e., Mummy and I) know with a deep certainty that you can all be trusted to become responsible and independent.

2. How YOU feel about yourselves and your own efforts is the most important thing (not how Mummy and I or your teachers, or anybody else feels).

3. You DON'T have to be perfect. What are important are your efforts and improvements.

4. You are learning to feel glad for successes of others as well as for your own successes. And Mummy and I appreciate this learning in you.

_____

Have a super, delicious, nutritious, muscle-building, brain-enhancing, personality-enriching pneumonia-resisting*, vitality-increasing BREAKFAST! I adore you!!

DADDY
XXX

Have a great day tomorrow. I can't wait to get home.

I love you each profoundly.

DADDY
XXX
OOO

Friday, March 22, 1991
My Darling, Precious, Super, Tremendous Kiminie, Tina and Jenny,
There are some things I keep forgetting to tell you:

- I love the way you wake up in the morning, each with your own unique rhythm and style.

- I love the way you enjoy exercising with me, climbing on my back, doing flips, standing on your hands, jumping on one foot (Jenny!) and so on.

- I love the way you enjoy playing with your friends, and that you pick good people for friends.

- I love the fact that you enjoy school so much, relish the challenge of learning, enjoy (sort of!) your homework, and find your teachers fun to be with.

- I love the self-confidence you all have with regard to creative projects. No timidity or tentativeness do you show when thinking about drawing, painting, gluing, cutting, building, writing, and coloring.

- I love the way you tackle jobs you have to do -- you show determination, alacrity, competence, and energy.

- (This should have gone much earlier). I love the way you laugh, the way you make jokes, your sense of humor, your wonderful smiles which light tip our lives.

- I love the way you (Kim & Tina) show competence in managing family meetings, and how you (Jenny) join in and participate.

- I love the people you are -- curious, fun loving, highly intelligent, athletic, loving, generous, caring of each other, gentle <u>and</u> tough at one and the same time, sensitive <u>and</u> strong -- all three of you destined for great success in whatever unique way you define it yourselves. The key is to invent the future (rather than drift into it), and this is what you are doing.

All my love,
DADDY
XXXOOO

Monday, March 25, 1991

My Darling Kimberly, Christina, and Jennifer,
(A.K.A. Kimmie, Tina & Jen Jen)

I feel bad about being away <u>again</u> when I have just been away from you last Friday and Saturday. I was away on Friday and Saturday because I had to attend an Audubon Board meeting in San Antonio, Texas. I'm away tonight and tomorrow night in New York City because I have a breakfast tomorrow morning with Ted Turner, followed by meetings with GB (our corporate underwriter) and then with various colleagues. On Wednesday morning, I have a meeting with a big foundation (the Rockefeller Brothers) and then I have to look at a fine cut of our film on toxics in the Great Lakes.

My job consists of creating new ways to reach non—environmentalists with the need for a clean, healthy environment -- one that does not injure people's health, and which allows wildlife and natural areas to remain in their pristine (untouched) condition. To do this job, I create programs (films, books, computer software) that the general public will enjoy. And in order to achieve success, I create innovative partnerships with people and organizations (e.g., TV networks, book publishers, software designers, authors and celebrities) with whom Audubon can have synergistic (1+1=3) relationships.

Our family is a synergistic entity! The sum of the whole is far greater than the sum of the parts! I love you.

DADDY
XXXOOO

Wednesday, June 5, 1991

My Darling Kimberly, Christina, and Jennifer,
I'll be home tomorrow!

Mummy and I are very pleased how the family biography is developing. Would you like me to read you the more interesting stories one day? Every time we go back to England, we learn more about the people we descended form Why is this important? In the old days, people didn't move away from the place of birth. Children, grandchildren, aunts, uncles and parents all lived in the same village. So family wisdom and stories were passed down verbally from generation to generation, and kids gained a sense of their history, their place in the world, and where their roots were. It helped them to understand themselves and each other better because they could become better observers of the historical discourses which produced them -- and so better able to design or invent their futures instead of drifting into a future designed for them by others.

And besides, it's fun learning about your parents, grandparents, great-grandparents, etc. One day, you three will be grandparents!

All my love,
DADDY
XXX

Sunday, July 21, 1991

My Darling Kimmie, Tina and Jenny,

In two weeks or so, I am moving offices from 801 Penn Ave to 666 Penn Ave. So on Friday -- which is why I was late home -- I started taking down things from the wall and packing files in boxes.

One thing I took down from the walls were all your zillion drawings and pictures and photos. All and each of them is so special. They have been accumulating on my wall over the years, and I guess that because Kimmie has been going at it longer, there are a few extra from K and a few fewer from Jenny.

Each of them glows with imagination, creativity and joy. As I've told you before, Hope Babcock, our general counsel, once came into my office, observed all your drawings for the first time, and exclaimed, "don't you have <u>happy</u> children!"

So thank you for all your pictures over the years. They have warmed my office, made me happy and proud, and constantly reminded me of how special and unique you each are.

I love you,
DADDY

P.S. All my love to Mummy!!

September 26, 1991

Kimmie, Tina and Jenny,

How I love you! You each are so special and unique each in your own special way. (oops--too many "eaches" and "specials" in that sentence!) Mummy and I are very proud of you. Sometimes it probably seems to you that we complain a lot (make the bed! sweep the floor! Don't jump on the bed! Stop putting tomato sauce in your ears! etc etc) but when you're asleep and we are going to bed, we often say to each other how lucky we are, and what super kids you are.

Each of us is "thrown" to do things. Our history and biology builds our actions into our nervous systems and bodies, so that we don't really <u>choose</u> the way we react but get "thrown" that way. Sometimes the way we are thrown to act is not effective. I notice this in myself at home. I'm thrown to believe there is a certain "right" way to do things. Often there's no grounding for this but I am blind to that and act like it's true. For example, the kitchen being clean. With three creative, productive, fun-loving kids in the house, I shouldn't have such strict standards. Anyway, I can't change overnight so I ask you to be patient!

I <u>love</u> you and send you kisses, hugs and tickles galore. Can't wait to get home tomorrow.

love,
DADDY
XXX

Tuesday, October 15, 1991
My Darling, wonderful three daughters Kimmie, Tina and Jenny,

I miss you terribly tonight. I will be away til Friday night. It is far too long, and I miss so many things so much. For example, doing exercises with Jenny, reading to Kimmie and Tina, seeing you work so enthusiastically and with determination your homework, admiring all the creative work Jenny brings home from school, seeing all three slowly wake up in the morning, hearing all about your plans with your friends, having fun and playing with each other, you running and jumping to me when I get home, Kimmie practicing her jazz steps, Tina practicing her poem, saying goodnight to you, getting you iced water, seeing the mess around the house and realizing I wouldn't have it any other way, discussing things with you, listening to your ideas, and seeing you grow into three happy, creative, loving, successful and determined people.

I love you.
I miss you.
I wish I was at home with you.
I can't wait til Friday.
BUCKETS OF LOVE
MOUNTAINS OF KISSES
DADDY
XXX

Wednesday, October 16, 1991
My Treasures,

Today I have been in back-to-back meetings in New York City. It is a grubby, crowded, uncomfortable city, and I can't wait to get to the exercise place and work up a sweat -- yes, sir, that's what I need.

I hope school went well today for you all. Do your teachers know how special each of you is? Hope they do! Mummy and I do.

Would you like to come and visit NYC one day? We'd love to take you. There are so many places we want to take you! Hawk Mountain, Disney World, skiing at Round Top, rafting in Colorado, pony-trekking in Montana, another visit to the Maine camp, a canoe/camping trip. So much to do -- so little time (or at least it sometimes seems that way!)

I adore you.

All my love,
DADDY
XXX

Thursday, October 17, 1991
My loves: Kimberly -- Christina -- Jennifer (in a circle!)

I'll be home tomorrow! I have missed you more than I can tell you. I hate being away from you.

Thanks for caring for each other while I've been away. Our family is the most important thing to me in the whole world. We're like 5 sticks (6 including blue baby!). One stick can break but put 5 sticks together, and nothing can break it. That's called SYNERGY: the sum of the whole is greater than the sum of the parts.

Remember to come up with something interesting to teach me this weekend. I'm an avid learner!

See you tomorrow my loves.

> Hugs and kisses galore,
> Yer ol' Dad
> XXX
> OOO

1992

March 3, 1992
My loves,

Remember, Edison said: 'We do not know one millionth of one percent about anything" and "Success is simply a matter of luck. Ask any failure" and "Children are a great comfort in your old age -- and they help you reach it faster."

I love you. Have a happy, energetic, friendly, fun, learning day!
Daddy
XXX

March 12, 1992
My Three loves -- Kim, Tina & Jen
I love you.

Here is something I've been thinking about: Do we demand perfection from you? -- And if we do, is that a mistake? I think I sometimes (often?!) forget that the goal is not perfection but rather acquiring skills. This requires <u>taking risks</u> i.e., having a go at something even tho' you risk rejection, a bad grade, or whatever. We should all be tolerant of failure -- even be <u>proud</u> of it! -- because it shows you are taking risks, and doing something active. If perfection is the goal, we'll all be so terrified of failing we'll be afraid to take risks. All three of you have so much **ability** AND you have capability of hard work and **effort** -- & that combination should give you the self-confidence to tackle anything.
I love you.
I miss you.
Daddy
XXXOOO

Saturday, March 14, 1992
My Treasures,

I can't <u>wait</u> to get home to be with you tomorrow. Here are some witty comments for you to think about:

Dancing -- the art of pulling your feet away faster than your partner can step on them.

Etiquette - learning to yawn with your mouth closed.

A teacher -- a person who tells students how to solve life's problems which he/she has avoided by becoming a teacher.

Consult -- to seek another's approval of a course already decided on.

Genius -- the perception of the obvious which nobody else sees.

Failure -- the path of least resistance.

Television -- radio with eye-strain.

A bargain -- something you can't use at a price you can't resist.

A bore -- a person who talks when you wish him to listen.

Diplomacy -- the art of letting someone have your (sic) way.

A perpetual holiday -- a good working definition of hell.

Television -- it's very educational because when someone turns it on I go to the study and study.

And finally -- He who laughs, lasts.

I love you so much.

Daddy
XXXOOO

Thursday, March 19, 1992

Darling Kimmie, Tina & Jenny,

Well I'm sad tonight. As you read this, I'm on the plane to England. I don't like being away from you all -- after all you & Mummy are the most important people to me in the whole world.

Here is me in the plane. (sketch). That's me in the window thinking about you.

And here's me in the plane reading and writing (sketch).

Here's a story about me growing up in England: We lived in Dulwich, a suburb of London from when Jon & I were 5 to when we were 12. In the winter, the house was FREEZING & so we used hot water bottles to warm the beds. Getting out of a snug bed on a cold winter morning was TOUGH! Then Jon & I would walk together through Dulwich Park to our school -- about a mile walk. We used to wander aimlessly home, taking our time. But once, I remember, Jon & I had a project we were really excited about. I wish I could remember what it was. What sticks in my mind is the incredible energy in my body because we had a goal to achieve. At the time I was amazed at the contrast with how I usually felt at that time of day -- tired, lackadaisical & bored. I loved the feeling of purposefulness, direction & energy, & try to recapture it as often as possible.

I miss you.
You are so important to me.
I love you.
Daddy
XXXOOO (Jen -- this time I didn't forget the hugs.)

Friday, March 20, 1992

MY LOVES: KIMMIE, TINA & JENNY

Here's another story from England: When I was 11, my father (Grandpa) was promoted and got a high-level job in Bath. We lived in Dulwich. My parents were faced with a difficult decision: Should the whole family move back to Bath & put the 4 boys in new schools in Bath, or should the 4 boys become boarders so they could continue at Dulwich College (one of England's preeminent schools). My parents asked what we wanted and we opted to become boarders. This meant we wouldn't see my parents for 6 weeks at a time. We were horribly homesick -- miserable -- & I used to yearn -- crave -- to be home with a roaring fire in the grate.

Looking back I realize that my mother probably suffered more than we did. After all, she suddenly had no role. From being a busy mother with 4 rambunctious kids, she suddenly had virtually nothing to do. Remember she didn't work. Mummy used to type long letters to us every week -- Each letter had 3 carbon copies and we each took it in turn to receive the top copy. (The child who received the bottom copy received a letter that was barely readable.) This was in the days before word processing & laser printers. Those distinctions didn't even exist back then! At the bottom of each letter my mother would handwrite an additional P.S. to each one of us. Boy did we love getting those letters!

So -- in a sense -- these letters to you are carrying on a family tradition. And family traditions are important -- very very important.

> I miss you so much.
> Thanks for taking care of each other.
> All my love
> DADDY
> XXXOOO

Saturday, March 21, 1992
My Darling Precious Loves
> Kimmie -- yeah!
> Tina -- yeah!
> Jenny -- yeah!

Here's another story from my childhood. I was about 12. An important exam was coming up in which I had to write an essay. I had never much enjoyed writing -- hadn't had much practice -- never got particularly good grades -- it was always an effort & gave me little enjoyment. So I was anticipating this breakdown (i.e., another mediocre performance) when I decided I wasn't going to let that happen. So I resolved to go into the exam and take a risk. I would break a few rules & write with gusto instead of cautiously as I normally did.

I went into the exam, saw the list of topics we were asked to write on, quickly selected the "swim meet", i.e., my participation in a swim competition, & did a quick outline, quickly generated a whole bunch of ideas, sorted them out, & then started writing.

Instead of worrying about what anyone would think, I became totally focused on presenting the feelings & excitement of the day & wrote in a way which broke all the conventional ways of writing e.g. "The whistle blew, quick, fling myself off, breathe carefully, go straight, how are the others doing? Faster, faster, my lungs bursting, I lunged at the water, willing myself faster & faster That sort of thing.

I wasn't sure if I was going to get a B or a D but I felt good about myself & proud of the result. Even if it got a D, it was the first time I'd ever written something that was fun to read!

> All my love
> Your Loving Daddy
> XXXOOO

P.S. I got an A grade and the best marks of anyone!

Sunday, March 22, 1992

My Treasures Kim/Tina/Jenny (arranged in a circle with rows of hugs and kisses inside)

I love you! And I miss you. Thanks for taking care of each other, & of our family.

Here is a sad story from my childhood. Every November 5 in England is called Guy Fawkes night to celebrate the defeat of Guy Fawkes several 100 years ago who attempted to blow up the Houses of Parliament. Kids & families buy fireworks & let them off. I remember one year, all of us 4 boys bought a few fireworks, & then my parents came outside to watch them with us, but none of us wanted to let them off because we resented the other three enjoying them too.

Now that shows kids who haven't learned how to "coordinate action" -- in other words, how to cooperate & enjoy life. I remember at the time it made me sad that we behaved that way.

And here's a happy story: I was about 13 or 14, & a big science exhibition was coming up in school. I had recently been reading this book on science "tricks," and decided (even tho' it "broke the rules") to do about 20 small science experiments that people could participate in (instead of just watch). I remember how doubtful everyone was it would work but I was sure people would enjoy it, & it turned out that on the day, there was constantly a small crowd of people around it, & my teachers were delighted. I won the prize for the best exhibit!

I love you and miss you. You are so extraordinarily special to Mummy & me.
Your old Daddy
XXXOOO

Monday, March 23, 1992

My Precious Loves Kim, Tina & Jen Jen
(Tomorrow I'm home! !XXXOOO)

Here are some thoughts that help guide me in my life[1] and which you also may find useful:

1. Find people doing something right (not wrong).

2. Always set goals so you design the future and don't just drift into a future someone else foists on you.

3. Human relations are everything in life, not just an important aspect. In a sense, the are life.

4. Exercise and eating nutritious food are fundamental to a good life. They are the first building blocks. You can't care properly for others if you can't care for yourself.

5. Nobody can take away the freedom and ability you have to respond to any situation in the way you want.

6. Never talk negatively about someone behind their back. It's a false way to compliment yourself and never works.

7. Laughter is the shortest distance between two people.

---

[1]   I fall short in living up to them, needless to say, but I try!

8. However bad a situation seems, there is <u>always</u> some action you can take.

9. Learning takes place in the body. Real learning only takes place when it shows up recurrently.

10. Saying to someone "I love you" doesn't mean a thing unless it shows up inactions.

11. To succeed, we must never stop learning, and learning means having the ability to take new actions (i.e., make an offer, promise a request).

12. Everything is said by somebody. Anything said by somebody is an interpretation.

13. Pay attention to language. How we use it is not trivial. (Compare: "I'll write you" vs. "I'll try to write you") It is distinctions in language (e.g., assertion vs. assessment) which allow us to make sense of the world.

   WHEW! That's a lot to think about! I love you!
   Dad
   XXXOOO

P.S. Can't <u>wait</u> to get home tomorrow.

Tuesday, April 7, 1992

My Darling Treasures Kimmie, Tina and Jenny,

   As you read this, I am in Los Angeles, about 3000 miles west of Bethesda. It is an ugly, sprawling, polluted city, made bearable by the knowledge I'll be home again with all of you the day after tomorrow! Today I have had meetings with the Disney Channel. They have agreed to buy an environmental TV special we are doing with Kenny Loggins called <u>Don't Drop the Ball</u> (The "ball" being the earth). The special will air in September and it will be accompanied by a print insert in consumer magazines. The purpose is to teach environmentalism to an audience far larger than just members of environmental groups like Audubon. Tomorrow we are doing a shoot with Kenny Loggins and I have more meetings with key Disney people. In the evening I fly to San Diego to meet with a donor.

   I love you. I hope you are having a satisfying week in school. Remember a key rule: Continuous and Never-Ending Improvement. Make every day better than the one before. And have <u>fun</u>!

   I adore you.

               love,
               Daddy
               XXXOOO

Monday, April 20, 1992

My Darling Kimmie, Tina and Jenny,,

   I can't wait to see Kimmie & Tina tomorrow morning, and Jenny the day after! Hope you are having a great time at the seashore (that's what the English call the beach!) Do you miss school?! Here are the best things which happened to me last week:

1. Kimmie voluntarily showing me her homework on endangered species.

2. Tina making me feel wanted by saying she'd like me to be at home on Friday.

3. Jenny asking me to play games with her and read to her.

   I was thinking this morning about how Kimberly is now practically a teenager, & how you, Kimmie, are growing up and maturing and, quite rightly, are different from how you were as a child. I know you are going to be a wonderful teenager (even tho' your parents will continue to make errors of judgment!) but these 12 years with you that are now just memories were unbelievably precious and special, just as they are now for Tina & Jenny. Mummy and I thank you each for bringing such joy and fulfillment to our lives.

I love you
Daddy
OOOXXX[2]

Monday, April 27, 1992

My Darling Kimberly, Christina and Jenny,

   I've been reading a lot about Isaac Asimov recently. He has always fascinated me. He wrote almost 500 (sic) books during his life. He died a week or so ago at age 72. He wrote incredibly fast and only revised once. He loved to write. The more he wrote, the easier he found it. He was a scientist by training -- Ph.D. in biochemistry. His first books were science fiction but over his lifetime he wrote about science, archeology, the bible, Shakespeare, humor and many other subjects. His mother was very dominating, and his father humorless and moralistic. Isaac Asimov was brilliant. But he also had a lot of common sense -- enough common sense to recognize that his brilliance was in only certain domains -- science, the humanities, and writing. My favorite books of his are his 2 books on humor, the latest of which you have seen me reading.

   You might ask how anyone could write almost 500 books -- that is an incredible number. I feel sad that someone of his caliber and creativity would die at a relatively early age. He was an atheist incidentally.

I love you.
DADDY
XXX
OOO

April 30, 1992

My Darling Kim, Tina & Jenny,

   Here are 2 stories. The first is an example of where I used poor judgement (i.e., I made an ungrounded assessment, yet acted as though I was certain I was right). And the second is something that I'm proud of:

1. Jenny had gone to bed last Saturday. Kim & tina were enjoying -- relishing -- a good read on our bed -- something we're constantly encouraging you to do. I wanted to read to you both. You were both absorbed by your books (which was super!) I felt we should have been doing something together and so got upset. What I should have done was get my book and read on the bed with you. Instead I stupidly told Kimmie she was being "destructive" -- which was nonsense. And then you, Kimmie, and the graciousness to apologize to me when it should have been me saying sorry to you!

2. On Wednesday morning, Tina and Jenny were arguing over a piece of sea glass. Jenny thought

---

2   Jenny, I remembered.

it belonged to her and Tina thought it belonged to her. Back and fro the bickering went, driving Mummy nuts. Finally I had an idea. I told them about win-win solutions, versus zero-sum games or win-lose solutions. (Ask Mummy to explain). After some thought, Tina and Jenny agreed that the sea glass would belong to Tina if Tina gave Jenny 10 cents. Satisfaction all around!

_____

I love you my treasures. I will see you tomorrow. And I will give a nickel to whoever knows the year Christopher Columbus discovered America.

> I love you & I adore you
> Your loving Daddy
> (with apologies to Kimmie)
> XXXOOO

Thursday, June 25, 1992
My Darling Kimmie, Tina & Jenny,

I love the way you have started your summer vacations: Jen with camp & a visit to Daddy's office! Tina with tennis camp & lots of fun activities with Emily! Kimmie with earning $$, having fun with friends and tennis. You all seem determined to have a fun summer and not just waste it in front of the TV. Did you read Catherine O'Neill's article this week in the Washington Post on how to make the summer enjoyable? It was an excellent article buy you are already way up that learning curve! I am particularly eager for you to get into some really exciting books this summer that hold you enthralled or make you laugh your head off. And each of you should set a goal of learning at least one new skill e.g., improving your touch typing speed from 10 wpm to 25 wpm.

I think you are three super girls. By the way, I want to revisit the idea of dates with me. Once a month you choose to do something with me and it can be anything. Just 2 of us at a time. Jenny & I had a date on Tuesday, when we went to my office. It could be a meal out, a movie, game of tennis, softball, shopping, bookstore visit, Kennedy Center -- whatever (MacDonald's swim, bowling smashball, canoeing, cycling). I ask you each to think of something for July & to let me know at the next Family Meeting what you'd each like to do.

I love you!

> Daddy
> XXXOOO

Monday, July 13, 1992
To Kim at Camp Letts
My Darling Kimberly,

I love you. Hope you are having a super time. A "care package" should arrive in a day or two!

Becoming a father was the best thing that ever happened to me (after marrying Mommy, that is!). It made me into a complete human being and opened up a whole new world I didn't know I could have. You, Tina and Jenny have done far more for me than I have done for you. I adore you.

> DADDY
> XXXOOO

Wednesday, July 22, 1992

My Darling TINA and JENNY

I'm writing this in a cab so my writing is untidy – <u>most</u> unlike my usual writing!

Do you realize how much I hate leaving you? It's the only bad part of my job, even tho' it's exciting to see different parts of the world & meet interesting people. But much more exciting is to see you & be with you, and play with you, and read to you, and see you grow up so beautifully in mind, body and spirit.

I've been reading about Gandhi, and watching a movie about him too. He was an extraordinary man. He was small and weak as a child -- and very timid. he thought of himself as cowardly. And yet through the force of his character, he led India to freedom and defeated the British. He had no army, wasn't an artist, owned no land, had very little money, and wasn't born into influence -- and yet, any sign of injustice and untruthfulness was so unacceptable to him, he taught himself new ways of 'moving' so he mastered his fear. He was incredibly brave and inspired courage in others. His guidelines in life were honesty, simplicity and justice.

> I love you.
> DADDY
> OOO
> XXX

I love you! See you tomorrow!

> Yer 'ol Dad
> XXXOOO

September 8, 1992

My Darling KIMMIE, TINA AND JENNY

I will be thinking about you today:

- Having fun, smiling and laughing

- Concentrating in class

- Being in a mood of serene ambition

- Learning and thinking and growing

- Deeply enjoying yourselves

- Taking your work seriously, and yourselves lightly

> I love you
>
> DADDY
> XXXOOO

Thursday, September 10, 1992

My Darling Kimberly, Christina and Jenny,

Last night at Back-To-School night at Westland made me realize what a <u>great</u> opportunity you have there, Kimmie. The same is true for you at BE, Tina, and you at Bethesda Montessori, JenJen. Those teachers are eager to do well and have their students succeed. They <u>want</u> lots of participation and enthusiasm, and they want you to learn how to be efficient and organized (e.g., not waste time looking for misplaced papers). These are all skills you need to succeed in life in your careers, whether you become poets, politicians, writers, doctors, lawyers, teachers, or whatever. It's sad when an adult says (as so many of us do) "I wish I'd worked harder/concentrated/done better/learned more in school when I was young." I am confident that you three will never have reason to say that.

You have a challenging year ahead of you, Kimmie, and I know you'll <u>thrive</u>! You too Tina and Jenny. Remember this: ALWAYS ask for help when you get puzzled or stuck or frustrated. And don't forget to <u>celebrate</u> your successes!

I love you. I wish I wasn't away. (I'm in the ADIRONDACKS in NY State at an Audubon Board Meeting).

All My Love
DADDY
XXXOOO

P.S. TINA -- I am so sad to be missing BE's school picnic on Friday night. I'll be thinking about you all. (Kimmie -- enjoy the dance). Daddy X

JENNY -- How was your first day in school?!!! XXX

September 22, 1992
DARLING, PRECIOUS KIMMIE, TINA & JENNY
How I love you! I hate being away like this, but it's only 2 days and I'll be back on Friday afternoon so we can play tennis before dinner.

Tonight I'm at a big dinner in L.A. It's the Environmental Media Association's Awards Dinner, and Audubon is up for 2 awards (i.e., we have 2 nominations). First for <u>Battle of the Great Plains</u>, and second for our Marvin Gaye Music Video. If we win, I will have to go up in front of hundreds of people and give a short speech (2 if we win both!) -- I <u>may</u> even mention you guys!! Will you be embarrassed if I talk about you in front of all those people??! Wish you were there. Do you think we'll win?!

Then on Thursday I'm meeting with Fox Television, Disney and various Hollywood types to have conversations about movies and other environmental projects.

I adore you. Mummy and I are so proud of you. You are -- each of you -- such self-confident, <u>together</u> kids.

All my love & hugs & kisses
Yer old Daddy
XXXOOO

Friday, October 9, 1992
My Precious Loves: Kimmie, Tina & Jenny

1. Kimmie --   I'm so proud of you <u>asking</u> for coaching from Mummy and me before your interview on Wednesday. Some people -- maybe most people -- are blind to the fact that in

certain domains they are beginners. <u>Declaring</u> that you're a beginner and that you want coaching and a coach, is the first step in learning. And remember, we are <u>all</u> beginners in some domains -- nobody is competent in all domains.

2. Tina --   I'm proud of you for the great progress you're making in many areas of your life -- <u>reading, tennis, friends</u> to mention just a few. You show great determination to succeed. And remember, Mummy and <u>I don't care</u> about your <u>grades</u>. Learning and curiosity are much <u>more</u> important.

3. Jenny --   I'm proud of you for the way you have started to enjoy and relish more grown up books like <u>Charlotte's Web</u> and <u>The Little House on the Prairie</u>. And Mummy and I love your colorful and inventive drawings and paintings!

You are three very special, unique people.

> All my love
> DADDY
> XXXOOO

Saturday, October 10, 1992

My loves: Kimberly, Christina, and Jennifer,

I miss you. I wish I was at home. I am in Boston learning about management, effectiveness and how to coordinate action with other people. Why am I doing it? Because I want to be more ambitious (i.e., achievement in my career), and at the same time spend more time with Mummy and you three. (A paradox: then why am I away this weekend?!)

This is a <u>new</u> problem for most men, but an <u>old</u> problem for a lot of women. In my father's generation, men were not expected to have much of a role in bringing up kids, and women were expected to stay at home all the time. The women's movement (feminism), which I strongly support, started to break up people's preconceived notions of these inflexible roles for men and women, and more women started getting better educations and taking on responsible jobs (e.g. Hillary Clinton, Gail Shearer ...). This led to tremendous internal conflicts for women as they wanted <u>both</u> careers and family -- and why shouldn't they? Now men are doing more to support their families emotionally and they are feeling the same tension -- and that's good too. Because we can all work on the problems together and get more flexible hours, longer maternity leave, longer vacations, better baby care, more respect for being a full time mother, etc. etc.

> I LOVE YOU!!
> DAD
> XXXOOO

Tuesday, October 20, 1992

My Darling Kimmie, Tina and Jenny,

I wish I was at home with you! I'm in New York for a senior staff meeting, meetings with producers and writers, and meetings with colleagues. Why do grown-ups have so many <u>meetings</u>??! Well, meetings are a way to coordinate and bring about action. Everything a person does in life is done with other people. Relationships just aren't important -- they **are everything**. Some meetings are not run very well -- people get in negative moods (resigned, resented, unambitious, angry), tell stories, wander off the point, forget why they're there and so on. The best meetings are those that result in offers, requests and promises (i.e., <u>action</u>), that put people in positive moods (ambition, joyful, engaged, peaceful), which start and finish on time, and which have a clear purpose. You are getting competent at leading and participating in meetings thro' our family meetings (Jen -- it won't be long before <u>you</u> will take turns being chairperson!)

Anyway -- I'd much rather be at home with all of you than even be in an enjoyable meeting!

I love you with all my heart. Mummy and I are so lucky to have three such wonderful children!
Yer 'ole DADDY
XXX
OOO

Friday, November 13, 1992

My Darling Kimberly, Christina, and Jenny,
I love you. I'm in Tucson, Arizona now but I wish I were home with you and Mummy.

Granny and Grandpa will be with us soon. We'll have a great time with them. They are lots of fun. Can you think of some fun things to do with them? Here are 33 ideas to get you started:

1. Go to the movies with them.

2. Play checkers with them.

3. Ask them what they did in the War.

4. Ask them what it was like to be in school.

5. What is their favorite joke?

6. What is the best advice they ever received?

7. Play hide and seek.

8. Watch your favorite TV show with them and tell them why you like it.

9. Ask them what was the bravest thing they ever did.

10. Ask Granny why she's so good at languages.

11. Ask Grandpa why he's so good at maths and science.

12. What was the hardest thing about being a parent?

13. Play catch.

14. Play tennis.

15. Talk French with them.

16. Plan our trip to England and Ireland next summer.

17. What was the thing they appreciated most about their parents?

18. Is it better to be a child now -- or when they were growing up?

19. Read a book together.

20. Go to the library together.

21. Compare English cons with American coins.

22. Tell them something which happened in school.

23. Ask their advice about a problem or challenge you face.

24. What was the best year of their lives? Why?

25. What is their secret of a successful and happy retirement?

26. Tell them why you wanted Clinton/Perot to win?

27. What is the thing they are proudest of in their lives?

28. Ask Grandpa to tell you some stories about Little Granny.

29. Show them your drawings/paintings/artwork.

30. Play smashball.

31. Snuggle in bed.

32. Ask Granny to show you her make-up box.

33. Tell them your future plans -- what you want to be when you grow up.

Granny and Grandpa are very special. They made me what I am today (but don't hold it against them!)

All my love,
Yer old Daddy
OOOXXX

December 1, 1992
My Darling Kimmie, Tina and Jenny,
I love you! And I can't wait to see you this evening when I get home from NY!
Here's an idea to think about: Be an observer of how -- as kids -- you tend to be rewarded in school for conforming and for being obedient. You are typically rewarded as being "good" almost directly in proportion to how well you stay tuned in to the voice of authority -- parents, teacher, coaches, etc. What do you think about that?! Just something to think about. The main thing today is to HAVE FUN and be full of energy, zest, creativity, smiles, questions, laughter, curiosity and vitality! (Like Granny and Grandpa).

I adore you.
Yer Old Dad
XXXOOO

December 3, 1992

HALO KIM! ! HALO TINA!! HALO JEN! !

Today I've been meeting with Board members, giving presentations, showing some of our videos, demonstrating our new interactive multimedia software, and thinking about how lucky Mummy and I are to have three unique and beautiful children like you -- and so well-behaved ALL the time (Ahem!).

Remember that everything said is said by an observer. So if someone says "church is boring," or "I love learning" or "the movie was exciting" or whatever, it is simply an assessment from one person. This is useful to remember when people like me starting talking as though we KNOW the truth. Always be suspicious of certainty. That's what I like about science -- it demands proof without certainty, whereas religion demands certainty without proof. And remember (and please keep reminding me!) never take yourself too seriously. Take issues/creativity/relationships/goods or whatever seriously, but not yourself. I made that mistake for years.

You are each so special. And, believe it or not, Mummy and I learn so much from you. Have you ever noticed how children are full of energy all day whereas grownups slump down in front of the TV exhausted and drained. I believe one reason is because grownups have forgotten how to play and have fun, whereas children instinctively know to play.

I adore you! See you tomorrow.
DADDY
XXXOOO

December 15, 1992

My Darling Kimme, Tina and Jenny,

TOMORROW IS MOMMY'S BIRTHDAY!! I'm very sad I won't be there but we'll celebrate it on Sunday with a cake, treasure hunt and gifts! (Not Saturday because it'll be a busy day with the shower and wedding.)

Thank you in advance for making Mommy feel very special tomorrow. She IS very special!
Today -- as you read this, I'm at Greenwich in Connecticut at a senior staff retreat. We are thinking DEEP thoughts! (or trying to). It's good every so often to step back, pause, and ask yourself if you're heading in the right direction. Here are some ideas for you to think about:

1. "Most of the things worth doing in the world had been declared impossible before they were done." (Louis Brandeis)

2. Do not follow where the path may lead. Go instead where there is no path, and leave a trail.

3. Be ready not only to take opportunities, but to make them.

4. "In the pursuit of great and noble causes, it is not enough to do our best. What is essential is that we do what is necessary for success." (Churchill)

Enough seriousness! ! Have a super day tomorrow. Mummy and I, and Granny and Grandpa are so proud of each of you. And from now on, the grownups outnumber the children (4 to 3) so everything will be decided by vote!

> I adore you. Yer old greying, aging but still-ever-so-fit and strong
> DADDY
> XXXOOO

December 16, 1992
Treasures! HI KIM! HI TINA! HI JEN!
This is Dad calling you. All together now (sing with vivacious gusto)

> HAPPY B'DAY TO YOU
> HAPPY B'DAY TO YOU
> HAPPY B'DAY DEAR GAIL
> HAPPY B'DAY TO YOU

I remember when it was Mummy's b'day in 1972. We'd know each other for about 3 months and had become inseparable (so to speak!). I was going home to England for Xmas to see Granny and Grandpa and my brothers, and I remember buying all kinds of gifts[3] (so she wouldn't forget about me while I was away!) . It was tough to leave. While I was in England, the mail was slow because of all the Xmas mail, and so no letters arrived -- until the last day or 2, and then about 4 or 5 arrived! I expect my parents guessed we were pretty serious. I can't remember now why you three didn't write to me while I was away!

Meeting Gail made my life complete and whole (and you three made it completer and wholer!) . I couldn't have met anyone so special as Mommy -- BOY, was I the lucky one!

I love you. Can't wait to get home tomorrow. Hope you are all coming to my office party!

> Buckets and spades of kisses and
> hugs
> DAD
> XXXOOO

---

3   Actually it was probably about 3 inexpensive ones because I was an impoverished student.

1993

January 25, 1993
My Darling darling loves

    KIMME   TINA   JENNY

I love you! Here are some ideas to think about:

"Luck is the residue of design." (Is there such a thing as luck?)

"The best gift you can have in life is to be comfortable in your relationships with other people."

"True education is the habitual vision of greatness."

"It is easier to act your way into a new way of feeling than it is to feel your way into a new way of acting."

In 1899, the Commissioner of the US Patent Office said, "Everything that can be invented has been invented" --!!

I can't wait to get home tomorrow. Buckets of love and hugs and kisses.

                      Yer old DAD
                      XXXOOO

February 8, 1993
My Darling Kimberly, Tina and Jenny,
I love you! I hope you enjoy these "spoonerisms":

1. Tom, Tom, the siper's pon
   Pile a stig and away rid dien

2. Peorgie Gorgie, pudding and pie
   Gissed the kirls and made them cry;
   When the boys plane out to cay
   Peorgie Gorgie ran away

Editorial comment: Not very funny so far. Can't find a good "gowering flarden," "floyal ramily" or "Dood for his Fonkey"!

Here's a silly joke:

Q: Where do farmers leave their pigs when they come into town?
A: At porking meters.

Q: What is brown, hairy and limps?

A: A coconut with blisters.

Q: What do you do with a sick wasp?

A: Take it to the waspital.

Q: How about the author who made a fortune?

A: He was in the write business.

Q: What happens when you cross a hen with a poodle?

A: You get pooched eggs.

Have a great day tomorrow. Remember -- it's important to celebrate failures as well as successes: It's the EFFORT that always counts ---- not the winning or losing. Failures show you tried, and being determined and enthusiastic is more important than always succeeding. There are lots of times in my life I didn't succeed.

> All my love,
> Yer old DAD
> XXXOOO

P.S.: See you tomorrow!

February 9, 1993
Morning letter: There MIGHT be one tonight <u>IF</u> you're lucky!
> XXX

My Loves,
I hope your day is fun, exciting, sublime, magnificent, grand, glorious, intense, relaxing, funny, vital, prodigious, boundless, amusing, delightful, zestful, cheerful, exhilarating, playful, invigorating, stimulating, energizing, vivifying, healthful, wholesome, enlivening, motivating, inspiring, rousing, thrilling, uplifting -- in short, I hope you design today to be everything you want it to be.

> I love you!
> DAD
> XXXOOO

TINA: Ahem, Ahem -- I never saw your Friday folder!!
> XXX

March 8, 1993
My Darling Kimme, Tina and Jenny,
Now here are some things for you to think about:

1. "What is unexamined has power over you." (Plato)

2. What we dislike most in others is generally what we dislike most in ourselves. But it is easier to see these negative traits in others than to see them in the mirror.

And, finally -- remember, we all make lots of mistakes -- EVEN me!! And there's nothing wrong with losing (say a game of checkers) . Nobody wins 'em all. It's good to practice losing as well as winning. We are proud of you (and, much more importantly, you will be proud of yourselves) when you simply try. Perseverance and tenacity -- those are the things which matter. So I hope you'll fail a lot in your lives! That will show that you are trying to do things -- that you are being proactive.

> Lots of love,
> DADDY
> XXXOOO

March 9, 1993

My Precious Loves.. KIM   TINA   JEN

Here are some things to think about and to see what possibilities show up for you by reflecting on them:

1. Q: How do you go about finding your purpose in life? A: You don't <u>find</u> your purpose in life but rather it is better to <u>invent/design/make</u> your purpose in life.

2. I've always had the problem of taking myself too seriously. I need to learn how to laugh at myself more and take myself more lightly. I have a lot of flaws and foibles (as you know!), so there's a lot of material to laugh at. It would be painful but I should ask you each to <u>impersonate</u> me!

3. "Nobody makes a greater mistake than he who did nothing because he could only do a little." (Edmund Burke, British statesman and orator)

4. Dreams (visions) are simply the outer boundaries of what is actually possible. It's important to let your imaginations soar.

5. "To know and not to do is not to know." (Saint Ignatias Loyalo)

6. "Comedy is simply a funny way of being serious." (Peter Ustinov)

7. Being a father to you three fulfills a part of me I never knew existed before you came along. I love it because it makes me feel like a whole human being.

> All my love,
> DADDY
> OOOXXX

March 14, 1993

My Darling

IMMETIN
JENNY

52

Kimme: Thanks for remembering to turn off the water and lights in 3rd floor bathroom last night.

Tina: Thanks for being assertive yesterday afternoon during your tennis lesson with Richard.

Jenny: Thank you for saying you won't eat any junk food today so you'll eat a good dinner.

I LOVE YOU! Have a super day!

> Yer old Dad
> OOO

March 18, 1993

My Darling Kimberly,

Even though I think confirmation is not important, I feel sad I'm missing your confirmation. Any and every event in your life is important. And anything that's important to you is important to me. Besides, my assessment in this matter doesn't matter. It's your assessment that matters.

I'll be thinking of you. Religion is important if only because it is a powerful force in the world and has to be reckoned with. Whether it's good or bad, or a mixture of both, is an assessment that is hard to ground. And whether you want to pray to or worship a god is totally your decision and no one else's business, including mine. Whatever you do, I will always love you.

Enclosed is a gift. It has some symbolism, but I'm struggling to articulate it. Something about the more you put into life, the more you get back (boomerang -- get it?) .

We all live in narratives and stories. Mine is that organized religion produces no possibilities for me. This is not the "truth" or "reality". It's a story or interpretation which can be redesigned and changed. And it is a story which should be judged by its usefulness in living effectively, in my view.

Other people have different stories -- such as Auntie Yvette. One of my challenges is to see the integrity in other people who have different stories from my own, and not to dismiss them arrogantly.

Anyway -- enjoy the boomerang (watch out it doesn't hurt anyone) . And thanks for being such a special teenager.

> I love you.
> Yer old Dad
> XXXOOO

April 20, 1993

KIMME,   TINA,   JENNY,

I'm constantly amazed at how much fun it is to have you three as children. If someone had told me in the BC era that it is possible to have children and not be in recurrent moods of despair, anger, frustration, resentment and anxiety, I would have said they were naive and had both feet firmly planted in the air. What you three have shown me -- despite parenting mistakes I make (and for which I thank you for forgiving me!) -- is that children can be fun and be the source of tremendous joy, laughter and insight. Mommy and I are so grateful we were blessed with three such special and unique children

-- each of you with your own special powers and strengths. We know that you will all grow up to be strong, independent, fun-loving, serious (but not solemn) hardworking, relaxed, intelligent, well-educated, resilient, assertive, loving, tough and wonderful adults in recurrent moods of ambition, acceptance, serenity and gratitude, with a lot to contribute to the world community.

I love you!

Yer old PREACHY! Daddy
XXXOOO

May 2, 1993
My LOVES,
    LOOK 8 FEET BELOW WHERE YOU USE "LEFTY LOOSY, RIGHTY TIGHTEE" TO SHED NEW LIGHT -- but where you look is in the shadows!

DAD
XXXOOO

May 2, 1993
My Darling Kim, Tina and Jenny,
    You found it! Well Done!

Tonight I'm in IOWA with Pat and Bill Heidenreich. Today I explored the Upper Mississippi Refuge for a film we're doing with Mariel Hemingway on the National Wildlife Refuges.

And you having a great summer?! I think you are but what matters is what you think. And when you make an assessment like that, it is always against some set of standards. Have you written in your summer notebooks what your goals are for this summer with:

- your family
- your friends
- reading
- exercising
- FUN (very important!)
- new skills
- computer
- typing
- weight lifting
- tanning
- giving Dad hugs and kisses.

ETC. ETC.!

I love you so much. You are each so very special to me.

DADDY
XXXOOO

May 5, 1993

My Darling Jenny,

I love your class! And I think Ms. Van Pool is a <u>GREAT</u> teacher.

Where is the photo of you among the new kids at the school entrance?

I like the body and head you left on your chair! And I like your SEPTEMBER sign! And I like your letters I hope you don't mind the additions I made!

I think you are super, and I adore you!

> DADDY
> XXXOOO

May 11, 1993

Darling Jenny, Tina, Kimme, Kimme, Tina, Jenny,

I remember an incident which happened to me when I was about 17. I had just joined the Navy (mainly because I wasn't sure what else to do) and had been sent to Plymouth to the Royal Naval College at Manadon. One of my assignments was to study a small ship (I think it was a tugboat) and give a report on it orally to the whole class (about 30 people my age some a year or two older). I worked hard at this, wanting to give a good impression. (Remember that my father was very high up in the Navy so I was conscious that I was conspicuous.) Eventually, it was the day to give my presentation. The first minute or so went fine. And then I did something (I can't remember whether deliberately or not) which made them laugh. After that, I was off and running. Soon they were roaring with laughter at my jokes. I remember some of them were holding their stomachs in <u>pain</u> because they were laughing so much. Everything I said seemed to come out of me with effortless hilarity. I loved it. I wish I knew how I did it. It was partly the circumstance the formal uniforms, the son of the boss, the sudden release from boredom, the shear joy of laughing your head off, especially when it is the last thing on earth you expect after all, I was talking about a tugboat!

> All my love,
> DAD
> XXXOOO

P.S.:   Have you heard the one about the Irishman, the Italian and the....zzzzzzzzzzz

June 4, 1993

My Darling Tina, Jenny and Kimme,
 (Putting Tina first for a change!)

What a great year of accomplishment for all three of you each succeeding in your own unique ways. Mummy and I are very proud of you! You succeeded not just academically and in your school work, but in many other equally important domains:

> ➤ Socially, e.g. making friends.

> ➤ In your artwork at home.

➢ As members of this very important family.

➢ In athletics and sports.

➢ In learning wisdom 'bout how to live a life full of serenity, laughter and ambition.

➢ In learning how to handle disappointments and breakdowns, which are really usually opportunities in disguise.

➢ In developing your sense of humor and learning to laugh at yourself.

And lots of other areas. So...

WELL DONE!!

Though remember, what matters is your own assessment of yourself, <u>not</u> mine or Mummy's.

*   *   *   *   *

By the way, did you hear about the cannibal who had a wife and ate/eight children?! (GROAN__!)

And do you know what the Spanish Fire Chief named his new twin sons? (A: Jose and HoseB.)

I love you!
DADDY
XXXOOO

P.S.:   I'm in Hidden Valley near Pittsburgh at an Audubon Board Meeting. Will be home on Sunday by dinner.

June 5, 1993
My Darling Treasures,

KIMME   TINA   JENNY

Hope you had a great time today. I'll be home tomorrow.

If you were locked in a room and told you couldn't come out until you made a pun, what would you say? [Answer: OPUN THE DOOR!]

When I was growing up, I'd always know when my father was trying to be funny. His nostrils would flare. I don't know where he learned this, or whether he realized he did it, and I don't know why he did it. In recent years, I've noticed my father has become a very good story teller. He's worked hard to gain this competence. Like everything else (tennis, standing on your head, or learning mathematics), it takes practice, and Gapo practices a lot.

Sometimes my father would start telling a story or joke, and Granny would in her natural exuberance butt in and finish telling the story, and this would irritate my father no end.

When you're my age, I wonder what memories you'll have of your childhoods.

You are three very special children.

> Love,
> Yer old Dad
> XXXOOO

June 16, 1993
My Darling TINA and JENNY,

As you read this, Kimme and I are in a plane on our way to Orlando. When you both finish 8th grade, I'll take you on an exciting trip too. Tomorrow we are going to be at EPCOT getting a "behind-the-scenes" tour of the *LIVING SEAS* exhibit which focuses on whale and dolphin communication. And then in the afternoon we are getting another VIP tour, this time of Sea World where they have a famous manatee tank and exhibit.

We'll be back on Sunday. Can't wait to see you! Thanks for looking after each other and for looking after Mummy. We are so proud of you and the unique person each of you is (are?).

And remember this: Humor isn't for everyone. It's only for people who want to have fun, enjoy life, and feel alive! As the French proverb goes: "The most completely lost of all days is the one on which we have not laughed."

I adore you!

> All my love,
> Yer old DADDY
> XXXOOO

June 17, 1993
HI <u>TINA</u>! HI JENNY!

I MISS YOU! Tomorrow Kim and I will spend time at the MGM/Disney Studios, or EPCOT, or Disney World, or Sea World, and then drive to Key Largo to get ready for our swim with dolphins on Saturday morning!   It'll be exciting! We'll also learn a lot about dolphins how they communicate, what they eat, how they reproduce, how they socialize and interact, how they defend themselves against sharks, what they wear (just a wee joke to check you're paying attention!).

*   *   *   *   *

Remember Don't take things too seriously, because by tomorrow they may not be important!

Q: Why are lawyers buried 20 feet deep?

A: Because deep down they're good people.

*   *   *   *   *

| Lawyer to client: | "Have you ever been up before the judge?" |
| Client: | "Well, I don't know, what time does she get up?" |

*   *   *   *   *

I love you both (AND MUMMY too <u>of course</u>) so much.

> See Ya'!
> LOVE Ya'!
> ADORE Ya'!
>
> DADDY
> XXXOOO

June 18, 1993
My Darling Treasures

> TINA -- Yeah!! Yeah!!
> JENNY -- Yeah!! Yeah!!
>
> I <u>LERVE</u> YOU!

Tomorrow Kim and I swim with dolphins! In the morning we'll be at Dolphins Plus and, in the afternoon, 50 miles further south at the Dolphin Research Lab. It'll be exciting!

Now here are some puzzles:

<u>For TINA</u>:

> What is ½ of ½?
>
> What is 100% of 20.56?
>
> What is 3/4 of 2?

<u>For JEN</u>:

> What is 8 + 4 + 2 =
>
> What is 4 - 5 + 1 =
>
> What is 100 + 200 - 50 =
>
> What is ½ of (50 + 50) =
>
> Well done!

I love you with all my heart.

DADD-I-O
XXXOOO

June 19, 1993

HALLO HALLO HALLO TO

TINA!!! (Fans scream)
JENNY!!! (More fans scream)
(Pandemonium breaks out, police called to restore order)

Phew! How are you doing?

Tomorrow, Kim and I snorkel 3 or 4 miles off the coast of the John Pennekamp Coral Reef State Park and the Key Largo National Marine Sanctuary. We will be looking at the only coral reef in the Continental US. We'll have to watch out for (drum roll and heart-thumping drum beat) SHARKS AND BARRACUDA! Danger! Bravery! Courage! Bravura! Nature up close and face to face! Actually, we'll be with experts and will be well looked after. What do you think I'm stupid?! It'll be lots of fun.

And then we'll fly home. Our flight gets in at 6:40PM, so we should be home by 8:00PM if plane isn't delayed.

Can't wait to see you tomorrow!

All my love and buckets of kisses and hugs.
DAD
XXXOOO

June 29, 1993

DARLING KIMME, TINA AND JENNY,

I was so proud of Kim and Tina playing tennis yesterday (you both showed determination, tenacity and good humor and enjoyment) and Jen swimming three times from the side to the red divider! Well done to each of you.

Tomorrow I give a speech at the UN, and I'm going up tonight for a "rehearsal." Also, tomorrow I'm bringing together about a dozen people from Audubon and Turner to look at the "fine cut" of our film on the anti-environmental backlash in the country (led by people like the one who wrote in a book that I have "a battery" missing)!!

A request: Please write your diaries! You are each having such fun and learning so much and doing so many different things, and have such interesting observations and assessments about your world that I ask you each to keep up writing your diaries. You should do it daily! It's great practice at writing (which is a vitally important skill you need to have) and your children and grandchildren will be eternally grateful to you. Thanks!

All my love,

DADDY
XXXOOO

July 13, 1993
Darling TINA and JENNY,

I love you! And I miss you! But while I miss you and Mommy, I'm also having a super time in New England with all my friends at work. About 150 Audubon staff (roughly ½ of the staff) the most senior ones are meeting for a 3-day staff retreat. We are going to discuss our goals, talk about team-building, have workshops on subjects like environmental racism and how to avoid libeling people, and enjoy the time together (e.g., get to know staff who we rarely see because they are in different parts of the country). Audubon is quite disaggregated (i.e., spread out).

On Thursday night, we are having a roast of Susan Martin, and I am one of the speakers. A roast is when you are playfully rude about someone in an affectionate way. Susan is leaving Audubon, after 6/7 years, to start her own company advising non-profits (like Audubon) on how to raise money. Anyway, I've worked hard on my speech, and I hope everybody thinks it's funny!

I adore you!
DADDY
XXXOOO

July 14, 1993
My Precious Loves <u>TINA</u> and <u>JENNY</u>,

How is your reading going? And your drawing on the computer? (I love what you invent there.) And tennis camp, Tina? And swimming lessons, Jen? I know you're having lots of un, and that's important (and I KNOW, ahem, you are doing your diaries everyday and practicing your writing and improving your competence at expressing yourselves!

Did you know that Uncle Jon and I were born in Hong Kong? In 1946, Granny went to Hong Kong after World War II ended to join Grandpa who had been sent out there in 1945 to repair the Hong Kong dockyards. They had been badly bombed by the Japanese. (In WWII, Great Britain and America fought Germany, Japan and Italy.) Jon and I were born on August 25, 1947, 45 minutes apart. Granny was deeply upset neither of us were girls she longed for a baby girl. We lived in comparative luxury in Hong Kong but, after four months, my father was told to come home and we took a month long sea journey back to England. Conditions were very tough. There was still rationing and the country was in a mess after the war. Can you imagine how tough it must have been for my mother to have four kids under 6? And no dishwasher or laundry!

I love you so much.

DADDIO
XXXOOO

July 15, 1993
DARLING LOVES   TINA -- Yeah!!

                  JENNY -- Yeah!!

I'll be home tomorrow! Can't wait to see you.

Did you know that I started my career (when I was 17) studying engineering and how to design warships? I did that for about 6-7 years and then resigned to come to America on a John F. Kennedy Scholarship. While I was in the Navy, I got my first two degrees (Bachelors and Masters) from London University. When I was 17 I had no idea what I wanted to do with my life. I was good at math and science and so drifted into engineering. What else was open to me? Not much. And I was familiar with engineering from observing my father work. I never liked it much I really didn't see it as having any power to change and improve the world. When I came to America (where I met Mummy!) I was so excited to have the opportunity to study economics and the softer sciences like political science. My degree at Harvard (an MPA) gave me the opportunity to jump out of naval engineering to energy and environmental policy work. But more changes were in store... (to be continued).

I <u>LOVE</u> YA!!
DAD
XXXOOO

July 27, 1993

My Darling Kimme, Tina and Jenny,

Most of TV and films are passive pop crud junk which stops you being active and energetic just like junk food does. Please limit your doses of it. It's easy to live lives (especially for you when you live in such luxury with everything given to you) which are lethargic and self-indulgent instead of disciplined and pro-active. Please lend your weights in the right direction. You are wonderful children, but Mummy and I need more help managing the house, and we want to see more appreciation of the good things you've been given and have worked for. The more you're given, the more obligation you have to <u>give</u> of yourselves. Materialism and consumption must be balanced off against idealism and service to others and service to <u>yourselves</u> (healthy food, being strong and fit, being well-rested, having high self-esteem, being playful and relaxed, etc.).

ENOUGH LECTURING!

Love,
DADDY
XXXOOO

P.S.: I love you.

September 9, 1993

My Darling Treasures Kimme, Tina and Jenny,

I'm in San Francisco on the other side of the country! I'll be back in 3 days and I apologize for having to be away. While I hate being separated from you, I want you to know that I also love my job and am immensely enjoying myself but I still miss you.

I'm out here for an Audubon Board meeting. The Board consists of 35 men and women of them distinguished and some of them famous who oversee how Peter Berle and his staff (which includes me) manage Audubon. Sometimes there are conflicts between the Board and staff. For example, this meeting will be tense, even tumultuous. Our membership numbers are way down. Also, Orsino (head of Membership) has been fired for incompetence (she used to work at CU and came with superb references!) and the Board is upset by the financial crisis facing the organization. (Don't worry my job is fine because Audubon Productions produces a surplus of funds, i.e. a "profit".) So it will be a lot of fun. They are all wonderful people and all have the best interest of Audubon at heart. It's just hard to build a consensus on what actions should be taken. All the Board members, as well as Peter Berle and all the staff out there are very good friends of mine, and I enjoy being with them. Can't wait to see you on Sunday.

> All my Love,
> Yer 'ole Daddy
> XXXOOO

September 10, 1993

My Loves   Jenny, Tina and Kimme
                 Tina, Kimme and Jenny
                 Kimme, Jenny and Tina

                 (We treat you equally y' know!)

     I wonder how your week is going Kim at HA; Tina at Westland; and Jen at BE. Somehow I just know that you are all doing well. Not that you won't occasionally have setbacks, disappointments and breakdowns of various descriptions. This is where courage and tenacity play such an important role in your lives. What matters is <u>how you respond</u> to breakdowns. Different people respond different ways to the identical breakdowns. Some responses (reactions) bring about better results than others. (My typical reaction to a spill in the kitchen AAAGGHHAH!! is an example of an effective response <u>NOT</u>!) Breakdowns are constituent of life they go with the territory so to speak, and it's important to try to turn them into valuable experiences form which you learn something.

     I love you so much. Thanks for looking after each other and for looking after Mummy.

> BUCKETS OF KISSES AND HUGS,
> DAD
> XXXOOO

September 11, 1993

HEH YO! KIM, TINA, JEN, LISTEN UP!
I'm home tomorrow night and it will be super to be home and together again.

     Georgina's disappointment over her exam results reminds me of something that happened to me shortly before I came to America. I had always done well in school got top marks, etc., so I was <u>used</u> to excelling. I won a 1st Class Honors degree in Engineering and got top marks way ahead of even the small handful of people who also got a 1st. Then I won two prestigious and hard-to-win scholarship (Kennedy and Harkners) to America, decided to study economics/public policy type issues, and realized I needed to line up a job for when I came back (little did I know....!). So I took the exams to get into the elite corps of the civil service, expecting to do well. Was I in for a humiliating shock! When the results came out I barely passed. I felt crushed. I wasn't supposed ever to do badly. Luckily for me, my father used his influence in the government and got me accepted (whew was I relieved!) into the top part of the civil service. It turned out of course that once I got to America, I fell in love with Mummy and the rest you know about.

I love you more than I can say. And Mummy and I feel so lucky to have such three wonderful daughters.

Love,
DADDY
XXXOOO

September 27, 1993

My precious loves   Kimberly (KIMME)
                      Christina (TINA)
                      Jennifer (JENNY)

I love you!

Yesterday I read a beautiful thought in an article. It went something like this: "Children approach life without rancor, meanness (sp?) or deceit. The greatest gift that raising children give us is helping us to see the world again through children's eyes." I found the quote: "A child looks out toward life without prejudice or deceit or meanness, and all through a child's growing years we are given the most precious gift of all -- a chance to feel like a child again ourselves."

I read and re-read those sentences.

Tonight I'm at a big dinner in Los Angeles. VP Gore is here with lots of famous Hollywood people. We have been nominated for an award for *This Island Earth*. So, if we win, I'll have to go up in front of all these people and give a few remarks.

You are each so precious. Mummy and I are so proud of you. Each of you is unique and so special. Mummy and I are so lucky to have you as our children. Don't even think about changing families!

All my Love,
Yer old DAD
XXXOOO

September 28, 1993

My Loves, Tina (1st for a change), JENNY, KIMME,

I'll be home tomorrow and I can't wait to see you. I've had a very exciting day seeing lots of people in Hollywood about movies, children's TV programs and things like that. I hope you had a satisfying day at school with lots of fun with your friends and lots of PRO ACTIVE PARTICIPATION! (Secret: It only happens with planning and preparation.)

JOY LISTS. We'll work on these. When you start, you might only be able to think of a couple of ideas. But gradually you'll accumulate hundreds (literally!) of ideas and thoughts. It's a way to remind you of how glorious life can be, and it will help you become a more astute (perceptive) observer of what lifts your spirits and makes you feel you're fully alive. Sometimes I get so caught up in life's details the hum drum routines which have to get done that it is easy to forget that life has so many high points. Your joy list will constantly remind you to look for the best life has to offer. And your list will be unique to you.

I LERVE YOU!
DADDY
XXXOOO

October 4, 1993

My Darling Loves,

KIMME   TINA   JENNY

Tonight, I'll be with Ted Turner and Jane Fonda and lots of other celebrities for the world premiere of a new film called *Gettysburg*. It'll be a lot of fun!

By the way, I took your advice and mowed the lawn without first raking the leaves and blow-me-down-with-a-crooked-flagpole you were <u>right</u>! It worked fine! While it doesn't necessarily follow it will work with a <u>heavy</u> covering of leaves, I deduct something valuable from this incident. NEVER BE AFRAID TO CHALLENGE AUTHORITY because it is often wrong as in this case, when my assessment was not grounded.

Have a super evening. I'll be home after you are all asleep and zzzzzzzzz....

I LOVE YOU! I ADORE YOU!

Yer 'ole DADDY
XXXOOO

October 12, 1993

My Darling Kimme, Tina and Jenny,

Now here are some questions for you to write answers to this is an <u>INTERACTIVE</u> letter!

QUESTION 1

WHAT THINGS WOULD YOU (AS YOUR ESTEEMED DAD!) LIKE ME TO DO DIFFERENTLY?

ANSWERS

<u>Kim:</u>   1. Don't yell at me when we play tennis.
             2. Buy a normal bathing suit.

<u>Tina:</u>   In the letters, give us clues to where things are, so we can find them.

<u>Jenny:</u>   Do math problems (Jenny only!) in letters.

<u>Gail:</u>   Get some good party clothes.

QUESTION 2

WHAT THINGS DO I DO WHICH YOU LIKE AND YOU WOULD LIKE ME TO DO MORE OF?

ANSWERS

Kim: Go running with me more (even though I say I'm busy!).

Tina: Play football with me outside and soccer.

Jenny: Play more tennis with me.
            Read to me more.
            Play catch with me.
            Play games with me more.
            I want you to play more exercise games/athletic games like football that make you
            strong.

QUESTION 3

WHICH THINGS HAVE YOU SEEN OTHER EFFECTIVE DAD'S DO WHICH YOU WOULD LIKE ME TO
DO? AND WHICH NEW THINGS WOULD YOU LIKE ME TO DO?

ANSWERS

Kim:

Tina: Bring us to amusement parks, canoeing, hiking.
            And go shopping with us.

Jenny: Ditto for Jenny.

I thank you in advance for your replies (remember "Feedback is the breakfast of champions").

                        I ADORE YOU!
                        DADDY
                        XXXOOO

December 1, 1993
My Darling Kimberly, Christina and Jennifer,
    I'm in San Francisco! I'm meeting with donors, film-makers, software designers, and venture capitalists. It will be lots of fun! I hope the three of you will have jobs you relish where the distinction between "work" and "play" fades so that you find every moment (well, maybe not every moment!) fulfilling and challenging, and where you are constantly learning. Mummy and I have jobs like that. It's rare, and so you could say we are "lucky" but luck comes to those that make opportunities happen, and who work hard and intelligently as you three do and will.

    One key to success is to make offers. In a sense, you are the offers you make. People who make lots of offers are by definition frequently failing, but they enjoy life, make a difference to the world, and have power. So don't be afraid to "fail" (e.g., answer a question incorrectly). All successful people fail and learn from their failures and become stronger because of them. (Phew, what a sermon! but one last point. Definition of success: Achieving your goals). I love you!!

> I adore you!!
> Yer old DAD
> XXXOOO

December 2, 1993
My Treasures, what I ADORE!

> Yea for Jen!
> Yea for Tina!
> Yea for Kimme!

I miss you and can't wait to see you tomorrow. I should be home for dinner if my plane gets in on time.

I remember my time at school with a mixture of feelings. I wasted great gobs of time not really understanding the work, but learning it by rota, and then regurgitating it for tests (and then promptly forgetting it after the test). It was only when I wrestled with an issue, and argued about it, and discussed it with friends and teachers and (most importantly, tried to teach it to friends who were even more lost than I) did I begin to understand stuff and begin to enjoy real learning (real learning being when you learn something in your body so you know it through and through, and not just so you can remember and recite something). Mummy and I want you girls to get a real <u>education</u> (to some extent I say to hell with grades), which means you have an <u>insatiable</u> curiosity, and are constantly challenging the conventional wisdom and status quo. All of us need to keep asking <u>WHY</u>? (Phew, another boring sermon! sorry. Where's my sense of humor gone?!)

I LOVE YOU. You are <u>so special</u>.

> Love,
> DADDY
> XXXOOO

December 9, 1993
My Specialist Treasures: the KIMME, the
> CHRISTINA, and the
> JENNY

As you read this, I am attending a big dinner in New York City, dressed in "black tie" (although mine is red!). It is Audubon's Annual Dinner. Can you imagine the electricity when Lila Berle (Peter's wife) says halo to Laura and Bill Rlley (who are leading the effort to oust Peter)?! I'll tell you all about it. HIGH DRAMA!! Incidentally, the head and founder of The Body Shop, Annita Roddick, is this year's winner of the Audubon Medal.

The Board meeting is on Friday, and that's where the SHOWDOWN will occur. Flurries of words, PAINED expressions, inner wrestling, should they? Shouldn't they? What about this? What about that? Peter will have the say and then the VOTE! My guess is 296 against. But DON'T COUNT PETER

OUT TILL THE FAT LADY SINGS ___ LA LA LA, AND SHE AIN'T SUNG YET. Showdown in Audubon corral the best Westerns had nothing on this! I love you too much for words.

DADDY
XXXOOO

December 10, 1993

DARLING Kim, Tina and Jen,

What is success? The most obvious answer is someone who achieves their goals (e.g., getting all A's or getting on the tennis team, or whatever). (For grownups, you might answer having a "good" job, earning a certain income, living in a certain kind of house, sending your kids to the best school, whatever). Everybody will have their own unique and idiosyncratic answer to the question, and different people will have different criteria (e.g., compare Mother Teresa with Donald Trump, both of whom one assumes assess themselves as successes). Here is a distinction you might find useful as you think about what it means to succeed in life: Private success v. public success. Private success are the successes you achieve inside yourself being proactive, developing and achieving goals, having vision being honest, designing yourself (i.e., choosing) to be in moods of serenity, ambition and forgiveness, keeping fit, and so on. Public victories are the victories you achieve with other people (e.g., Mummy's success at CU) or mine at Audubon ('scuse me tootin...!). Here's the point (roll of drums). I don't think you can ever achieve real, enduring public victories unless you have already won the private victories over self. Love yer, adore yer, miss you. See you tomorrow buckaroos.

DADDY
XXXOOO

1994

January 11, 1994

My Darling Kimme, Tina and Jenny,

You are the greatest kids parents could ever wish for. Mummy and I are so lucky. I think you'll have great memories of your childhoods (yes, even you Kim!) and you deserve them and you <u>earn</u> them by being responsible, caring, funny, ambitious and self-confident. And Mummy and I have earned them in a way too -- we've not been afraid to be parents. A lot of parents, sadly, don't want to do anything (e.g., set limits) which might make them unpopular with their kids. Well, in my view, parents aren't there to be popular but to do everything they can to help their children grow up to be everything they can be, and that sometimes means saying "no" to things.

You are each so incredibly special. And what you may not realize is how much you do for <u>us</u>! You enrich our lives in so many wonderful ways, and open new possibilities for us all the time. (I don't think, Kim, that learning about organella, nucleopoops and RNAAAAAAGH is one of them tho'!).

I LOVE you! I ADORE you! I MISS YOU! Hugs and kisses,

DADDY
XXXOOO

February 8, 1994

Darling KIM, TINA and JEN,

Thanks for taking care of each other and of Mummy while I'm away. It constantly amazes me how little you fight sure you have spats like all sibling do[4] but have you observed the venom and coldness in other sibling relationships?[5] It can get bad! I think if we had a boy, then that can sometimes exacerbate (good word) it, but I know that isn't really the explanation. For some reason (I give a lot of the credit to Mummy) you three are basically happy, content, friendly kids. I remember in my family the fights were vicious. My poor mother was traumatized (another good word!) by them. No one had ever coached her on how to handle them effectively. (In those days, parents were just parents -- they never realized parenting is a skill you can get better at through training, study, coaching and practice.)

Anyway, just remember that if you have kids, they may not get along as well as you three! It may be hard to realize but you will always be each other's best friends always there for each other, through thick and thin, whatever the circumstances. That's a wonderful thing Mummy and I will always be grateful for.

I love you,
DADDY
XXXOOO

February 9, 1994

MY TREASURES:

---

4   If you didn't, it would mean you'd need a psychologist!
5   Which, in later years, can turn back to warmth and friendship.

Kimme -   good luck this week practicing for the Talent Show. It is <u>terrific</u> you are willing to do it. The world grows thru offers.

Tina -   good luck in asking good questions this week in class. I like your incentive system, and your body (i.e., YOU) will enjoy the power you gain. The world will be a better place if you are powerful (i.e., can do things and make offers that others cannot).

Jenny -   good luck in Little Feet tomorrow, show and tell tomorrow and Brownies with Mummy on Saturday. It's great when you participate so actively in things. The world is enriched when you threw yourselves into fun activities like these.

Tonight I'm hosting a dinner at Peter Berle's apartment for all the "Captains" of the Staff Birdathon (which I chair). The Captains are the Staff Birdathon Leaders in each Department. It should be a lot of fun, and I know I will enjoy being "Leader of the band"!

I love you. I adore you. I miss you. I think you each are very, very special and unique. This is no one else in the world like you! And Mummy and I are so incredibly lucky to have children like you.

> All my love,
> Yer half-blind, half-dead old DADDY/POPPS
> XXXOOO

February 16, 1994

My Treasures: <u>KIMME</u>   <u>TINA</u>   <u>JENNY</u>

Have I ever told you how extraordinarily <u>special</u> each of you are (is?)? Well I'm telling you now! Mommy and I are incredibly lucky to be blessed with such delightful and loving children. <u>HOW DO YOU DO IT</u>?? Parents all over America, who regularly curse the day their kids were born, would like to know the answer!

I hope you enjoy the enclosed designed to entertain <u>and</u> stretch your minds!

> I love you.
> I adore you.
> Yer 'old DADDY
> XXXOOO

March 3, 1994

My Darling, Darling, Darlings

> KIMME   TINA   JENNY

I love you! As you know, I'm in the LA area (watch out for earthquakes!). Visited Warner Brothers, The Disney Channel and Walt Disney Pictures today. Then went on to Audubon Board meeting close by.

Here are some things I've recently added to my joy list:

- Laughing uproariously (sp?).

- Listening to you guys say something funny.

- Running with weights in my hand til I get tired but elated.

- Eating buttered toast and banana.

- Getting an unexpected hug from Gail (as well as an expected hug!).

- Doing ANYTHING with you three.

- A hug from anyone.

- Falling asleep quickly after I get into bed.

- Hearing wonderful music.

- Doing a good tennis serve.

- Cooking a meal which everyone says is delicious.

- Hearing you guys laugh uncontrollably.

- Listening to you ask good questions.

- When you remind me about doing "Tables Turned."

- Family meetings.

- When the 5 of us go out for a meal together.

- Seeing a rainbow.

- When you guys get a good grade.

- Seeing a superb and life-enhancing movie.

- Being told I did an excellent job by my peers.

- Hearing a hilarious joke.

- Reading a profound and life-changing book.

- A beautiful sunset.

I adore you! All my Love,

DADDY
XXXOOO

March 4, 1994

My Treasures - Kimme, Tina and Jenny,

I miss you! <u>AND</u> I'm having a great time. I don't want you to think I'm sad! We're in a beautiful part of the world about 50 miles South of Los Angeles. Today we visited one of our sanctuaries (called * * * * * Ranch) on which we have <u>mountain lions</u>!

Recently, I've been rewriting (really recreating) my personal mission statement (PMS). Just like America has a Constitution which helps keep the country strong and healthy and heading in the right direction, so my PMS helps to guide me every day and helps me keep learning and improving. Continuous, relentless improvement is the key. I wish it went like this:

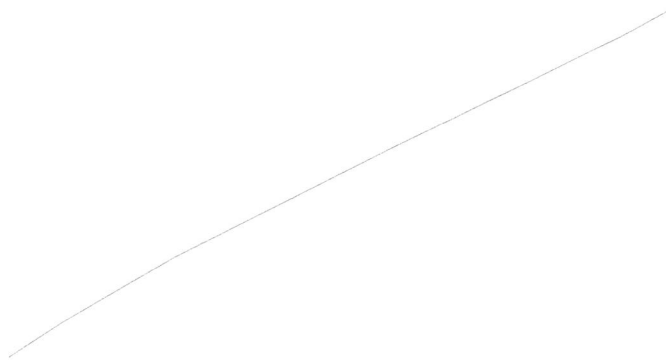

In reality, it goes more like this:

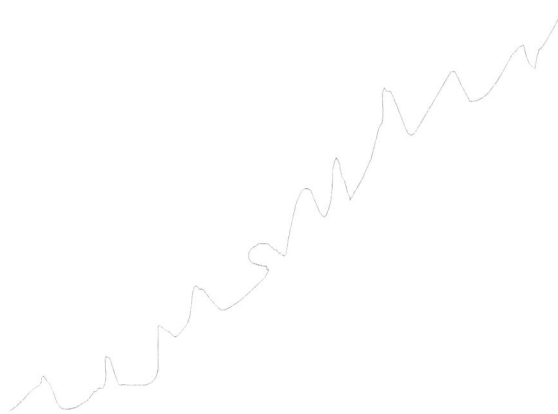

As you know, I'm not perfect! When I've finished writing it (I rewrite it afresh every year or so when I put aside some time to think deeply about my life and what I'm doing). I'll show it to you (YAWN, YAWN!). I think most people would suffer less and feel happier if they had a PMS.

I ADORE YOU!
DADDY
XXXOOO

March 5, 1994

My loves: Kimme, Tina and Jenny,

Memories from my childhood:

1. Listening with Jon to a funny song on the radio (Danny Kaye?) and laughing so hard we couldn't stand up. (Age 10)

2. My mother smacking our hands with a wooden spoon when she couldn't get us to behave (it hurt!). (Age 4-8)

3. Climbing a big oak tree near Aunty Yvette's house, everyone on the ground admiring how far I'd climbed, and then getting scared trying to come down. (Age 9)

4. The four boys cycling to school together on the 1st day of school at Dulwich College. Jon and I were 9, Jer was 13, and Tim 11. That was the last day we ever cycled together. We left our house at 20 Dulwich Common and cycled 1 mile to school along a very busy road. (Age 9)

5. Age 6-8: Leaving Dulwich Hamlet (our school) with a bunch of friends, finding a penny in my pocket, going to a sweetshop and buying aniseed balls. Then taking 1 or 2 hours to wonder home (or 2 miles), often getting home with Jon after dark (I remember my father once came looking for us).

6. Discovering a book, at age 7, called the Schoolboy's Pocketbook, and finding all the facts in it fascinating. And finding a book, age 10, called Shadow The Sheepdog, which so gripped me that I couldn't put it down.

7. Age 8-15: Playing with my 3 brothers in our garden in Dulwich -- a never ending invention of games -- cricket, digging holes, running and on and on (we didn't have TV so we invented games together). Jer never really joined in. He had his own thoughts.

8. Age 8: Watching my father come out in the garden and see him bowl to my brother Tim just once or twice, and then it suddenly dawning on me how he never comes out in the garden and plays with us and wondering why not and feeling saddened.

9. Age 8-9: Observing with incredulity how, seemingly suddenly at about age 14, my older brother started treating my mother with contempt and disrespect, and my mother letting them get away with it.

> I love you,
> Daddy
> XXXOOO

P.S.: Please keep a journal! I wish I had.

March 6, 1994

Jenny, Tina, Kimme Darling My

> (I've written it backwards so Jenny's
> name goes 1st for a change!)

Today I read a book, and the dedication went as follows:

It would not have been possible to get this book done without my sister, Shannon Williams. I thank you so much, Shannon, for all you do for me. I love you.

That touched me. It's the kind of dedication I can imagine one of you girls writing one day in a book you've written.

The same book had this quote from Diane Sawyer:

There is no substitute for paying attention.

And this one:

You can't let the seeds stop you from enjoying the watermelon.

And these, too:

Experience is what you get when you don't get what you want.

Experience teaches us to recognize a mistake when we've made it again.

Today, I went out to sea to see migrating grey whales. They are bottom-feeding, baleen (cf. toothed) whales which spend their summers in the Arctic and their winters in the warm, shallow waters near Baha, California. What a privilege for me!

I can't wait to see you tomorrow. I love you all so much.

DADDY
XXXOOO

March 23, 1994
My Loves: KIMME, TINA (a.k.a. CHRIS!), and JENNY,
I love you! We are going to have a great vacation this summer in New England. We'll stay at the Audubon Maine Camp, hike and canoe in the Adirondacks, maybe see the Niagara Falls, go whale-watching, and do lots of other fun things together.

And I'm looking forward to this coming weekend at Berkeley Springs together.

I love it when we do things together as a family whether it's going on vacation, or clearing up the kitchen after a meal, or watching Dr. Quinn.

Children who grow up in healthy, vibrant families (like ours) are so lucky -- as are the parents!

I hope we will always be a close and warm family.

I love you,

Yer ol' Daddy
XXXOOO

P.S.:   Kim, thanks for coming to the office last Monday.

Tina and Jen, I'm so pleased you are going to visit my office next week. Which is the best day?

May 10, 1994
My Darling Three Treasures: KIM, TINA, and JEN,
Mummy and I are so proud of you and much more important than that, we are glad that you are proud of yourselves. All three of you are self-assured, self-confident and at peace with who you are. Not to say that you are complacent. You're not everyday you learn more about the world and yourselves.

Now here is something to always remember. You can't always control everything that goes on around you -- in fact, you really can't. You can influence it and occasionally control things, but things happen, like getting caught in an unexpected thunderstorm. BUT you can <u>totally</u> control how you react to whatever happens.

And here is an "opener" I might use in my next talk: "Some of you at the back might not be able to hear me. Those of you in the front may want to go back and join them."

I adore you. Have a great day in school tomorrow. Be alert in class don't drift off. And ask questions keep asking yourself "WHY?".

<u>I love you</u>,
Yer 'ole DADDIO
XXXOOO

Sunday July 17, 1994
My Darling Kimme,
It was wonderful to see you yesterday! You looked great -- so full of life, exuberant, buoyant and happy. I enjoyed seeing your friends too. My heart went out to Bianca without her Mom and Dad there. 1 sense she felt let down.

Somehow this seems like your last hurrah of childhood -- not really because you might to to Camp Letts again next year. I think -- despite stupid errors of judgment I've made periodically as a father, that you've had a fantastic childhood. This is a tribute to you more than a pat on the back for Mummy and me. It's you who have made the choices and decisions -- and they were invariably wise and smart ones (such as going to Holton, going in for swim team, reading widely, keeping fit, keeping off drugs, etc.)

Well we did get much of your time yesterday (Hmmm!) and you didn't invite me to go with you on the sea raft (Hmmm!) but it was great to see you and to see where you were sleeping and so on.

Hope my last letter has arrived by now. Did you find the 3x5 card I left for you in your trunk?!

I just read an article on actor Alec Baldwin. I'm going to work with him and his wife (Kim Basinger) on an Audubon Special on the illegal and ghastly trade in wild birds. (By the way, his new film, The Shadow, sounds good.) Anyway, in this article, he says his father (now dead) tried to teach him to distinguish between what really matters and what doesn't matter in life. I hope I can do the same for you.

I love you so much.
Daddy
XXXOOO

June 20, 2004 (10 years later)
Happy Father's Day, Dad! You have taught me what things really matter in life!
Love, Kim XOXO

September 8, 1994
My Darling, Darling Darling

      KIMME!   TINA!   JENNY!

I love you! And I miss you! I haven't been away for some time so this is the first letter you've received for some time. Kimme I hope you have a great first day at school tomorrow. Mommy and I have absolute confidence that all three of you will take whatever it takes to enjoy learning, enjoy your friends, participate actively in class and get good grades. (Note that LEARNING is more important than GRADES. In fact, learning to love learning is more important than learning!)

We had a great summer together. And next summer will be fun too, with our trip to England (and Ireland??!).

Tonight I'm hosting an important dinner with the key people on our IMAX film on whales. (Across town in NYC is a big EMMY dinner where one of our films is up for a nomination, but I'm not going to that.) Then I meet on Friday morning with various colleagues and producers before coming home. So I'll see you tomorrow! We are so proud of you. Each of you is unique and <u>very</u>, <u>very</u> special.

                  I love you!
                  Yer 'ol Dad
                  XXXOOO

September 13, 1994
My three precious loves Kim, Tina and Jenny,
I had lunch today with three top executives of the World Wildlife Fund. One of them, a woman called Debbie Hechinger, asked me about my family and I told her I had three daughters, age 7, 12 and 14. It turns out she has a 16-year old daughter and she said to me something like: "So you've found out how awful a 14-yr old can be" or words to that effect. I replied, Well, no actually, Kimberly is delightful to have around and we enjoy her enormously." She had a hard time believing this! She had no comments on 7 or 12 year olds!

Tomorrow I have a senior staff meeting. Like I tell you to for school, I prepare carefully for this meeting, with a list of questions and points to make. If I'm making a presentation, I write out beforehand the 10 worse questions I might be asked and prepare my answers. Of course, things come up I don't anticipate, but this way I can relax, enjoy the meeting, be totally focused on what others are saying, crack jokes (if I can think of any), knowing that I'm fully prepared and will do a good job. So....

Be Prepared, as we Girl Scouts say! Lots of lots of buckets of Love.

I LOVE YOU,
DADDY
XXXOOO

October 17, 1994

My Darling Kimme, Tina and Jenny,

Tonight I'm accepting the "Frank Wells Award" at a big (1,000 people) dinner in Hollywood. An edited version of the awards event will be broadcast next Sunday on TBS. I'll give a short (under 30 second) acceptance speech.

Suppose I walk on stage to thunderous applause and trip over a wire?! That would be great -- it would even be better than the "Craig/Table" story! Think of the fun you'd have telling that to your grandchildren!!

Good luck tomorrow, Tina, in your play rehearsal. Good luck, Jen, with your Brownie investiture (sorry I'm missing it), and good luck, Kim, in your tennis match (sorry I'm missing that, too).

While I'm in L.A., I'm meeting with The Disney Channel, Sony, Walt Disney Pictures and a dozen or so other "movers-and-shakers" in Hollywood about movie ideas I have. Trying to get my work at the NWF off to a fast start!

I love you. I miss you. Granny, Grandpa, Mummy and I think you three are the cream of the crop, the cat's pajamas, the tops, the corps delight, the creme de la crème, the salt of the earth, the piece de resistance, and we love you so much.

Love,
Yer old Dad
XXXOOO

October 18, 1994

My Three Treasures

KIM Yeah!
TINA Yeah!
JEN Yeah!

I'll be home (I think) early tomorrow morning. My plane gets into Dulles at 5:35 AM so I should be getting home round about 6:30 AM (but planes are often late).

Did you know that Grandpa almost had to flee to America in 1940 when Nazi Germany was about to invade England? The invasion never came, but ask Grandpa and Granny what they had to do to prepare for what was a very likely Invasion of hostile German soldiers. If Hitler had ordered an invasion, then Grandpa had secret instructions to abandon his family (Jon and I weren't yet born) and find his way to Liverpool, and board an English warship and escape to America. There, he, along with other British military personnel, would continue the fight against Hitler's tyranny.

Pretty exciting, eh?!

I love you.

DADDY
XXXOOO

November 14, 1994

My Three Treasures   KIMME!!!
                            TINA!!!
                            JENNY!!!

I love you with all my heart. And I'm so proud of you. (As I've mentioned before, that's nice, but what's really important is that you be proud of yourselves.) Here are a few reasons I'm proud of you (going backwards in age for a change):

Jenny: For loving to read (what a guy that Henry Hudson was!); for wearing your head gear so diligently; for enjoying school and your friends so much (P.S.: Enjoy the BE Book Fair this week!); for making Granny and Grandpa laugh so much.

Tina: For asking Grandpa to read Tom Sawyer with you (that's a sure sign of one smart kid); for working daily (Ah'em!) with Granny on Spanish; for eating well (yes, I've noticed!); for trying to think of ways to have a civilized relationship with Sheila; and for being courageous, and telling Sheila how you felt. PLUS your "A" grade on your Humpback whale paper!

Kim: For going in for that swim team (Yeah!); for having the boldness to hold a super surprise B'Day party for Sarah; for picking such great friends; for working regularly with Granny on Spanish; for working so tenaciously this past weekend on your sophomore paper.

You are three precious, wonderful daughters, and Mummy and I, and Granny and Grandpa and Nana ARE SO LUCKY!

DADDY
XXXOOO

November 15, 1994

My Three Precious Loves Kimme, Tina and Jen,
    Here are some jokes for you to enjoy with Granny and Grandpa:

1. While sitting in the clubhouse, an old friend asked Dave why he no longer played golf with George. Dave said, "Would you play golf with a guy who's always improving his ball position, occasionally slips a tee under his ball in the fairway, and regularly lies about his score?" The answer from his old friend was obvious, "Certainly not!" Dave said, "Well, George won't play with a guy like that either!"

2. Definition of CONFIDENCE - that uplifting feeling you have before you truly understand the situation.

3. It's 1927. A secretary came running into her boss' office. "It's Lindbergh! He did it! He crossed

the Atlantic!" The boss looked up, "So what? He was alone right?" "Yes," she cried. "He did it all by himself!" "Humph," sniffed the boss. "One man alone can do anything. Let me know when it's done by a committee!"

4. Many years ago, a large American shoe manufacturer sent two sales reps out to different parts of the Australian outback to see if they could drum up some business among the aborigines. Some time later, the company received telegrams from both agents. The first one said, "No business here. Natives don't wear shoes." The second one said, "Great opportunity here - Natives don't wear shoes!"

Ha ha ha!! I love you!!

> Yer old Dad
> XXXOOO

November 25, 1994
My Three Treasures

> KIM   TINA   JEN

Have a day that you will look back on with pride and say, "I did my best, I fulfilled my potential, I loved my family and friends, I laughed and played, I worked hard, met my goals and fulfilled my promises (or at least managed them)."

BRAVO!!

I love you so much!

> Yer 'ol DADDY
> XXXOOO

1995

February 20, 1995

My Precious Darling Kimme, Tina and Jenny,

It has been some time since I've left you a letter because I haven't done much traveling recently. When I was young (i.e., late teens, 20s), I used to love to travel. Now I'd rather be home with you and Mummy. One of my favorite parts of the day is family dinner because we all get together. When I was growing up, families had meals together all the time -- breakfast, lunch and dinner. Not that they were always fun and friendly, but at least the opportunity was there to talk. There was no television (virtually), no video games, no computers, few books, few movies (at least, we didn't often go). Nowadays, all those things seem to make it harder for families to spend time together. But I suppose the main thing is <u>parents</u> both working, and working long hours. When I was young, almost all mothers stayed at home.

After dinner when we lived in Dulwich (I was 7-10), the 4 boys sat around the "round table" (our dining room table was round!) and did our homework which my father sat there sternly, making sure we did it, reading our comics! (We subscribed to *The Eagle, the Swift, and the Robin*).

As we rushed off to school every morning, leaving all the breakfast dishes in a mess, I remember wondering what my mother was going to do all day (laundry? washing? see friends? clean? cook?).

I love you each so much. See you tomorrow.

> Hugs & Kisses Galore
> Yer 'ole DAD
> XXXOOO

February 27, 1995

My Three Loves: KIM!   TINA!   JEN!

After attending the Parent Peer Group meeting last Thursday night at Holton Arms, I came away marveling at how lucky Mummy and I are with you three. Do you realize the pain, humiliation and suffering that most(?) children cause their parents[6]?!! Yet in you three, Mummy and I have a constant source of delight and wonder and joy. How does one explain that? We know other parents who seem -- as far as one can tell -- to be conscientious, dedicated, sensible, and aware, and have kids who are hooked on drugs (and alcohol) of one sort or another or who are repulsive in some other way! Of course, we shouldn't count our chickens too quickly! You can get in with the "wrong" crowd where drinking and drugs and smoking is seen as cool and hip, and peer pressure can push you down the road to failure pretty quickly. But we have enormous faith in each of you that you'll resist that path and take another based on hard work, self-discipline, joy, friendship, compassion, caring and laughter (i.e., the <u>good</u> life).

We adore you, and we are so proud of you, and proud of the fact that each of you takes pride in your own accomplishments and growing abilities.

> DADDY
> XXXOOO

March 7, 1995

My Darling Precious Treasures KIM! TINA! JENNY!

---

6   And Jeremy caused my parents.

Do you ever wonder why I minimize the time I spend watching the national TV news, and never watch the local news broadcasts, and minimize the time I spend reading the newspapers (except for very specific articles)? One reason is that I try to stay within my "circle of influence" (i.e., deal with things I can change and influence) and stay away from things within my "circle of concern" (i.e., those things I'm concerned about but cannot influence or change).

This distinction between "influence" and "concern" is a valuable one. In my opinion, far too many people spend time on things (e.g., watching the OJ Simpson trial) which they have no role in and cannot influence. Better to spend time on things (e.g., doing a scientific experiment with your kids) which you can have a direct impact on. And the more time you spend in your circle of influence, the bigger it gets, and the more powerful you become.

I adore you. I love you. See you tomorrow!

> Yer 'ole DAD
> XXXOOO

March 22, 1995
My Darling Kim, Tina and Jen,
    I'm in California -- fund-raising, meeting with Hollywood studios, The Disney Channel, Hanna-Barbera, film producers, environmentalists and other people with whom I have "strategic alliances." It is a lot of fun and I hope to achieve a lot.

I'm glad you are all better after your sickness of last week. Eating well and exercising are your best defenses against disease. And if you eat healthfully and exercise rigorously and regularly, then on the rare occasions you might get sick, you will recover more speedily and with less suffering.

One of the things I do is build exercise into my daily schedule. So you'll notice how I welcome (even look for) reasons to climb up and down the stairs because climbing stairs is great exercise. I walk up and down the Metro stairs; and, even when at my desk will occasionally roll my neck and do other stretching exercises. Actually, I wish I did more exercise. Here is what I'd like to do ideally: Run for 30 minutes daily. Lift weights for an hour four times a week. Play tennis with one of you or running four times a week.

Also remember what a wonderful effect exercise can have on your alertness, mood and academic performance!

I love you! I adore you!

> Yer old DAD
> XXXOOO

March 23, 1995
My Treasures,
    I wonder how your game went today, Kim? And I hope you had a wonderful day yesterday at the Chesapeake Day, Tina! And, Jenny, good girl for working hard on your homework this week you've done a whale of a job! (Get it?!)

I'm often amazed at how "automatic" I am -- all of us are. In other words, we face situations all the time, and before us are hundreds of possible "moves" we could make but, in fact, we can predict pretty much (not always) what we're going to say or do. Observing how predictable I am -- and how much of what I do and say is inherited rather than chosen proactively by me -- is useful because it opens the possibility of redesign and reinvention. The moods we get in, the choices we believe we face, how we behave in relationships, how we react to other people, the offers we make to others, and so on, are all situations where we benefit if we observe that we have far more choices of "moves" to make than we often realize.

> I adore you!
> DADDY
> XXXOOO

April 12, 1995

My Darling daring KIMME! TINA! JEN!

I love you! If my writing is EVEN worse than usual (ahem -- no comments please!) it's because I'm writing this in a cab going to Laurel Ridge.

Now I'm writing it in a cab going from Laurel Ridge <u>to</u> home. I stopped writing at the end of the last paragraph because I wanted to practice the presentation I gave this morning at the so-called Senior Leadership Team meeting.

It's funny this business of "practice" -- per our conversation the other day, Tina -- people generally have an easy time acknowledging that you have to "practice" in order to learn the piano, but they have a harder time recognizing how universal this is. I believe learning <u>is</u> practice, and that applies as much to the domain of people's relationships, say, than to tennis or playing the piano. That's why it's important to "practice" <u>declining</u> offers, giving gifts (ahem!), being affectionate -- these things won't be done competently unless you practice.

I love you.

> Yer 'ol GRUMPS Daddy
> XXXOOO

P.S.: Tina, dying to know how you did in your science experiment. It doesn't matter if you got a B. In my book, you get an A+ for effort, and that's what matters.

April 13, 1995

My Three Loves, **KCJ**,

Today I've been visiting donors in Florida trying to get them to support my work with a large gift of mullah ($$). It is an interesting process. The key is to let them see that this is an opportunity for <u>them</u>, and gives <u>them</u> new, exciting possibilities in their life.

I work for a nonprofit, educational organization, and a lot of what I do by its very nature of being for a <u>cause</u> and aimed at social reform -- is not economic to do, so environmental group like NWF, along with other nonprofits who fight for women's rights, children's rights or other causes, raise money from wealthy individuals (also foundations and corporations) who share their values and want to participate in exciting and worthwhile programs which help society become more just, equitable and decent.

Jen, I'm looking forward to our camping trip. Tina, have a <u>super</u> time this weekend. And Kim, I hope you get the job you want on *The Scribbler*.

I adore you!
Love DAD
XXXOOO

June 16, 1995

My darling Tina and Jenny,

I miss you! It's tough being away from all of you, but it is made a lot easier by having Kimberly with me, of course. I wish we were <u>all</u> going on this dolphin trip!

When I was young and went away to boarding school, it would often get homesick, and it is quite painful. You may experience this a little when you first go to Camp Letts, Tina. Just remember that you will survive it, and the best thing is to join in actively with things going on around you and look out for ways to help other people.

I often remember that grandpa left my family in 1945 for <u>18 MONTHS</u>! Can you imagine?

I love you both with all my heart.

Lots of love,
Daddy XOXO

June 17, 1995

To my two treasures, Christina and Jennifer,

I hope you are both doing well! Kimberly and I are out at sea swimming with dolphins! I have just been reading a new book by Dr. Roger Payne called <u>Among Whales</u>, and he tells marvelous stories about dolphins and what wonderful animals they are. I feel very lucky to have the opportunity to go on this trip (that wording does not seem quite right, since I was the one who created the opportunity but you know what I mean), and to be able to go out for a week into the Atlantic Ocean and see these extraordinary animals in their own habitat is a wonderful privilege.

Take care of each other and of mommy. I love you with all my heart and I cannot wait to see you next Friday.

Love,
Dad XOXO

June 18, 1995

My darling Tina and Jenny,

Did you know that Mark Twain once said that, at the age of 14, he was convinced that his parents were among the stupidest people on the face of the earth. When he reached 21, he was amazed at how much they had learned in only seven short years!

It is a good story because, of course, it is he who has changed -- not his parents.

While I love the humor in that story, the thought that always occurs to me is that parents should constantly learn and change, too.

You both love dogs, so here is a dog joke for you:

> A professional dog-walker was leading her charge towards the entrance to the park. A man walked up to her and said, 'that's a beautiful dog. Does it have pedigree?' She raised her eyebrows. 'If this dog could talk,' she said, 'he wouldn't speak to either of us.'

Get it?!

I love you. I hope you have a great week.

Love your old dad XOXO

June 19, 1995

Darling Tina and Jen,

Did you yet have a chance to look at my Journal? You may want to read what I wrote about all of you and mommy. It's in the last few pages. I know you saw a rough draft, but I added some more things since then about you both. I hope you like what I wrote. As I said in my Journal, mommy and I feel so lucky we have three such wonderful children.

You know I love humor, so here are some things that people have said about humor:

➢ Comedy is simply a funny way of being serious.

➢ Everything is funny, as long as it is happening to somebody else.

➢ You can pretend to be serious, but you cannot pretend to be witty.

➢ Man thinks; God laughs.

I love you!

Daddy XOXO

June 20, 1995

My darlings,

Here is a joke:

> A fisherman was carrying his gear from his cabin to his car, getting ready for the Sunday-evening drive home. A friendly looking man ambled up and asked, 'Any luck today?'
>
> 'No,' the fisherman said. 'Today was bad. But yesterday! I caught 16

trout before lunch, then another dozen in the afternoon. Best fishing day I've ever had.'

'No kidding?' The stranger said. 'Do you know who I am?'

'Why, no, I don't,' the fisherman answered.

'I'm the Game Warden,' the stranger said.

'Oh. Well, do you know who I am?' The fisherman asked.

'No, I don't.'

'I'm the biggest liar in the United States.'

Pretty funny, eh?

All my love. I love you both so much, and I miss you.

Daddy XOXO

June 21, 1995
My darling Christina and Jenny,
    Here's a good story:

'Names, names!' The crusty editor insisted to his young reporters. 'No story is complete without the names of everyone involved.'

The newest member of his staff filed the following report on a local disaster:

Three farms in our area were effected by the severe lightning storm that struck Thursday night. Mr. and Mrs. Alva Todd reported a fire in their barn. Michael Arlington said several trees were knocked down by the violence of the storm. And Fred Morse reported that three of his cows were struck by lightning. Their names were Bessie, Gilda, and Plug.

And here is another good joke:

The doctor handed her overweight patient a bottle of pills. 'Don't take these pills,' she said. 'Spill them on the floor three times a day and pick them up one-by-one.'

I love you!!

Dad XOXO

Thursday, June 22, 1995
To my precious Tina and Jenny,

Kimberly and I will be home tomorrow! I hope you've had a great week with lots of sports and exercise, lots of good eating, lots of smiles and laughs, lots of good friendship, lots of reading, lots of writing, lots of drawing, and lots of love. Thanks for looking after each other and mommy while Kimberly and I have been away.

I cannot wait to tell you all about our trip and to hear what you've been doing while we've been away. I love you both with all my heart.

From your loving Dad XOXO

September 7, 1995
My darling Kimme, Tina and Jenny,

I will be back early Saturday morning! I fly this evening to Los Angeles, where I will spend tomorrow all day in meetings. Then, I will return on the "red eye," which is the plane that leaves at about 10:00 PM at night on the west coast and arrives back at about 6:00 AM the following morning on the east coast.

It is called the red eye, because everybody gets off the plane with red eyes! You basically lose a night's sleep.

I am enclosing with this a copy of the journal I wrote while we were on vacation this August in England, Ireland and Wales. Would each of you please read it and mark it up with changes you want in it. I will put in those changes before finalizing it.

I hope you enjoy it!

I love you guys so much. See you Saturday morning! Buckets of love...

Daddy XXXOOO

September 8, 1995
My loves: Kimberly, Christina and Jennifer,

See you in the morning! I will be flying back overnight, and you will hear me ring the front doorbell when I get in at roughly 7:00 (unless the plane is late, which often happens). I might go straight to bed, because I will be tired!

Would you please read more of my August journal and try and finish reading it, so you can give me all your changes? Thanks a lot.

You have each gotten off to a great start in school. Mummy and I are very proud of you.

Daddy XXXOOO

September 14, 1995
My darling Kimberly, Christina and Jennifer:

How I miss you! I will be away until tomorrow week (?), which seems like an awfully long time, but it will go quickly. The good news is that you will all be busy, working hard and having fun in school, and I will be busy, working hard and enjoying my work first at an IMAX conference in Galveston,

Texas, and then in a film-making conference in Jackson Hole, Wyoming (where Bill and Hillary recently vacationed!).

I will miss you very much while I am away, but I will be thinking about you all the time and will be greatly comforted knowing that you are looking out for each other and living honorable and loving lives.

Since we are all feminists in our family, here is a joke for you to enjoy: Perfect Man, Perfect Woman, Santa Claus and the Easter Bunny were driving down the street together and got a flat tire. Who fixed the flat tire? Answer: The Perfect Woman because the other three are mythical characters! Ha Ha Ha! Good joke.

I love each of you so much and with all my heart. Mummy and I are incredibly proud of each of you, and we like it that you are proud of yourselves, too.

All my love,

Daddy XXXOOO

September 15, 1995
My three precious loves, Kimme, Tina and Jenny:
I love you! I am in Galveston, Texas, on the Gulf of Mexico with about 1,000 important people from around the world who own and run IMAX theaters. I will be working hard to convince these people that our IMAX film on whales is worth leasing.

Recently, I read a very interesting article called, "Notes On An Unhurried Journey." Part of it went as follows:

> When we adults think of children, there is a simple truth which we ignore: Childhood is not a preparation for life, childhood is life. A child isn't getting ready to live; a child is living. The child is constantly confronted with the nagging question, 'What are you going to be?'. Courageous would be the youngster who, looking the adults squarely in the face, would say, 'I am not going to be anything; I already am.' A child is an active participating and contributing member of society from the time she is born. Childhood isn't a time when she is molded into a human who will then live life. She is a human who is living life. No child will miss the zest and joy of living, unless these are denied her by adults who have convinced themselves that childhood is a period of preparation.

> How much heartache we would save ourselves if we would recognize the child as a partner with adults in the process of living, rather than always viewing him as an apprentice. How much we would teach each other... adults with the experience and children with the freshness. How full both our lives could be. A child may not lead us, but at least we ought to discuss the trip with her, for, after all, life is her journey, too.

Isn't that wonderful? How many times have I made the mistake described in that short essay?!

Thank you for being such wonderful children. Mummy and I are so lucky.

I love you. I will be home in a week. All my love,

Daddy XXXOOO

September 16, 1995

My precious loves, Kimme, Tina and Jenny:

How are you all doing? I think of you every moment I am away and, although I am very happy and I know you are very happy, I cannot wait to get home so we are all together again.

Have you read the family history recently? Do you remember that wonderful story about Granny during the war? In 1939, at the beginning of World War II, she joined the Women's Auxiliary Police Corp (WAPC). She was an interpreter. Part of her duties in the WAPC was to man (uh hmm, woman, I mean) the telephones whenever an air raid warning sounded. Plymouth (where we recently were with John Coles) was heavily bombed -- vast areas were devastated. Granny would run up to the Police Station as the bombs were dropping. At the Police Station, she handled calls about the bombing until the raid was over, often for several hours. Once the raid was over, Granny would go out with a mobile canteen to help victims and helpers alike.

One night, she had to save her own house first. Two incendiary bombs came through the roof. Her father helped her climb through to the attic, handed her a bucket of sand, which she used to smother the bombs! Granny once told me, "Looking back at myself racing up to the Police Station in the pitch black (no lights were allowed because they would show the Germans where to bomb) with incendiary bombs falling relentlessly all around me, it amazes me I wasn't scared to death."

By the way, Granny remembers being stirred beyond measure by Winston Churchill's oratory.

Have you written to Granny and Grandpa recently? They would love to hear from you, even if it is just one line. Also, Hannah and Ross I know would love to hear from you (again!).

I love you all beyond words.

Your old Daddy XXXOOO

September 17, 1995

Darling Kimme, Tina and Jenny:

Tomorrow starts a new week back at school. In the morning, I will fly to Jackson Hole for a big film conference, where I will be giving talks to large groups of people every day.

My one big sad regret about this week is that I will not be at Bethesda Elementary for the back-to-school night on Wednesday night. That, I think, is the first time I have ever missed it. It is always one of my favorite nights, not only because we get to know your teachers and get to learn about the work that you are doing, but also I get a chance to leave you notes in your desks and I get a letter back the next day from each of you!

For the last two years, I have turned down going to this conference, even though there was tremendous pressure on me to go because there are always school events that have such a higher priority for me and Mummy. But, this year, I decided that I just had to go.

Did you all read about Cal Ripken, Jr.? Last week, America celebrated his breaking Lou Ghrig's "Iron Man" record by playing in his 2,131st consecutive game.

David Broder wrote a very good article about him last week in *The Washington Post*. He wrote, "Ripken is a great athlete. But the record he set to such acclaim last week was achieved, not by his mechanical perfection, or by some sudden burst of brilliance, but by the more pedestrian practice of keeping himself so mentally and physically tuned so well-prepared and well-disciplined that he was ready to start every single game, without exception, for more than 13 years.... His workmanlike habits were instilled by his parents, and Ripken was surrounded by three generations of his family on his record-breaking night. When he stripped off his #8 jersey to reveal the T-shirt with the legend, '2,130-plus. Hugs and kisses for daddy,' and scooped up his two children in his arms, America cheered and wept with him.... His work ethic was instilled in him long before he had any idea of the stardom he might achieve.... These qualities doing the job to the best of your ability, every day, out of respect for yourself and your occupation, and respect for the parents who taught you that work is a value in itself are so precious to Americans and so rare that they took Ripken to their hearts."

I admire someone like that.

I love you all so much. All my love,

Daddy XXXOOO

September 18, 1995

My precious loves, Kimme, Tina and Jenny:

In my letter last night, I wrote about Cal Ripken. Another American hero is Collin Powell, who may run for the presidency and could conceivably win. He is a retired former Chairman of the Joint Chiefs of Staff. Like Cal Ripken, he showed up for work everyday for 35 years of his military career, for much of which he was as anonymous as anyone could be. Like Ripken, his splendid character was formed by hard-working parents. The senior Powells were Jamaican immigrants in the Bronx the mother sewing dresses in the apartment, the father working six days a week as a Garment District Shipping Clerk, determined that their children get an education and get ahead.

The family prospered for the same reasons many other immigrants have: Strong families, discipline, hard work, high standards, and attaching a huge importance to education.

A year ago, in a memorable commencement address at Howard University, Collin Powell told the graduates, "You have been given citizenship in a country like none other on earth, with opportunities available to you like nowhere else on earth.... What will be asked of you is hard work. Nothing will be handed to you. You are entering a life of continuous study and struggle to achieve your goals."

Food for thought. (And, by the way, in case we are getting too serious in these letters, don't forget it is important to smile and laugh as well as be reflective!)

All my love,
Daddy XXXOOO

September 19, 1995
Darling Kimme, Tina and Jenny:
Here are some maxims for you to enjoy:

1. An informal survey shows that what most people want for Christmas is two more weeks to prepare for it.

2. If you cannot make a mistake, you cannot make anything.

3. You have to start knowing yourself so well that you begin to know other people. A piece of us is in every person we can ever meet.

4. We all have enough strength to bear other people's woes.

5. Now and then, an innocent man is sent to the legislature.

6. It's good when you can learn from the mistakes of others, but it is even better when the others are your competitors.

7. Overheard: "My brother finally decided to marry. He said he had to -- he couldn't hold in his stomach forever."

Jenny, I am so sorry to be missing your back-to-school night tomorrow. Mummy will take notes and brief me in detail.

All my love,
Daddy XXXOOO

September 20, 1995
My three treasures, Kimme, Tina and Jenny:
It won't be long until I am back! In fact, I will be home the day after tomorrow.

I wonder how school is going for each of you? I hope you are asking a lot of questions, politely challenging what is said in class, and constantly asking yourself the question "why?".

I also hope you are smiling a lot, laughing a lot, enjoying the jokes, making people laugh (when appropriate!), and generally having a great time.

I notice that each of you have very good social skills. You know how to get along with other people, and each of you is excellent at picking good friends.

Here are some things for you to think about and enjoy:

1. Perseverance is the hard work you do after you get tired of doing the hard work you already did.

2. It is easy to sit up and take notice. What is difficult is getting up and taking action.

3. Success is more a function of consistent common sense, than it is of genius.

4. When you teach your daughter, you teach your daughter's daughter.

5. Nothing is so good as it seems beforehand.

6. To show a child what once delighted you, to find the child's delight added to your own -- this is happiness.

7. And, finally, a quote from Aristotle: Moral excellence comes about as a result of habit. We become just by doing just acts, temperate by doing temperate acts, brave by doing brave acts.

8. Oops, one more: Education is a lifelong journey, not a destination.

9. Oops, another one: So much time, so little to do. (From the Dalai Lama.)

10. Oops, one final one: Do not follow where the path leads, rather go where there is no path and leave a trail.

I adore you! All my love,

Daddy XXXOOO

September 21, 1995

My darling, darling, darling, Jenny, Tina and Kimme (I will reverse the names on the last night I am away!):
I will be home tomorrow! I cannot wait to see you all.

Thanks for looking out for each other so well and lovingly while I have been away. Knowing you were looking out for each other made it easier for me to be away for so long.

See you tomorrow. All my love,
Daddy XXXOOO

September 30, 1995

My darling, darling, darling Kimberly, Christina and Jenny:
I am on my way to Patagonia in Argentina! I wish we were all together and you were coming with me because it is going to be very exciting. We will be filming Right whales which congregate in the bay in Patagonia to breed. After a few months, they leave and go to their feeding grounds. We know so little about these whales that we do not even know where their feeding grounds are.

There is one species of whale we do know a lot about, and that is the Humpback. We know the Pacific Humpback feeds in Alaska and then migrates 4,000 miles to breed in Hawaii. We will be filming them in Hawaii next spring, and our film crew (led by Dave Clark) was in Alaska for four weeks last month filming them in their feeding grounds in Alaska.

Dr. Roger Payne, who I will be joining in Patagonia, is one of the world's leading whale scientists, and he has been studying the Right whales in Patagonia for over 20 years. He has a camp right on the beach. He brought up his family there. He recently published a book called *Among Whales*, which talks a lot about his experiences in Patagonia. He is wonderful guy, and I hope I will have a chance one day to introduce you to him.

One of the play behaviors that the Right whales exhibit there is that, sometimes when it is windy, they put their tails up in the air and let the wind push them along as if they are a sailboat. I hope, next week when I am in Patagonia, to get in a zodiac and go out to see them. They will often breach just a few feet from the zodiac!

I will be thinking of you all the time when I am away. I will not be able to call very much, if at all, because it is difficult to phone from Argentina (which is a poor third world country). If I can call, I certainly will. I will be flying back on Wednesday night, arriving on Thursday morning. So, I will be away for a total of five nights.

Do not forget, next Wednesday at 8:00 PM, there is *Scientific American* on with Alan Alda on PBS. Please don't miss it!

Thanks for looking after each other and have a great week in school! I love you with all my heart.

Daddy XXXOOO

October 1, 1995
Darling Kimme, Tina and Jenny:

How is your arm doing, Jenny? I hope it is not too painful for you. I am very proud of you going to school right away and keeping going with your studies, even though you are in discomfort.

Ann Landers said something good the other day. Someone wrote a letter to her regretting that they had spent so little time with their parents before they died, and regretting not taking enough time to spend with them and expressing their appreciation to them. She replied to the letter, "Children tend to treat their parents the same way they see their grandparents treated. What goes around, comes around."

I am writing this to you because sometimes I realize that I am not nearly appreciative enough of my parents and of Nana and all they have done for Mummy and me. I tend to take them for granted and not do nearly enough for them. I tend to be too critical and ignore all the good and wonderful things they do.

I had an interesting experience recently. You remember the journal that I kept when we were in England, Wales and Ireland in August? Well, I sent a draft of it to my parents for review, and they were quite upset by some of the things that I had written in it. I am going to make, of course, all the changes that they wanted. Which reminds me to ask you each please to throw away the draft copy that I gave to each of you. I will give you a new copy when I put the changes in. Thanks.

Anyway, I hope the five of us will continue to have fun together as Mummy and I get more and more ancient.

When I get back next Thursday, I will tell you all about the Right whales in Patagonia. By the way, do you know why they are called <u>Right</u> whales? It is because they were the "right" whales to hunt. The whalers found them slow so they could catch them and, after they had been harpooned, they did not sink. Thank goodness they are no longer hunted now.

I adore you and cannot wait to get home to be with you all.

Love,
Daddy XXXOOO

October 2, 1995

My three darlings, Kimme, Tina and Jenny:

You know how we always encourage you to read. It is so important. It is important because it helps you with language and makes you more eloquent and articulate.

But it also helps you on a whole other level, and that is on the level of living. Reading stories (or, in fact, reading anything of quality) provides a sort of lexicon and grammar of possibilities -- ways of being, acting, and moving through the world. It adds to the range of "moves" that you can think of taking under various circumstances. Some of these you may remember consciously, but most will remain submerged until you need them.

Under any condition you find yourself, there are dozens and dozens of different ways you can act and things you can say. Most people can only think of a few, and when you are living, you tend to automatically just to do one or two things things that you are used to doing, or accustomed to doing, or have been trained to do, or have watched other people do. One of the benefits of reading is that you learn that, in fact, there are scores of new possible moves that you can take, and this is very empowering.

Good stories work on metaphoric and symbolic, as well as literal levels. And they also work on a moral level. For example, the simple story of *The Little Engine That Could* ("I think I can, I think I can, I think I can") illustrates the importance of courage, determination and tenacity.

Anyway, all of this is only to say that reading is so important, and much more important than simply a valuable way of increasing your grades and getting better jobs in the future. It can make you a fuller and more rounded human being, and a person with many more possibilities, and many more offers to make to friends and colleagues.

So, keep reading! And I urge you also to read with a pen in your hand and paper nearby so you can jot notes, mark up the book (if it belongs to you) so that the whole exercise of reading becomes much more physical and active.

Sometimes it is good to read when you are standing up because this improves your concentration, because your body is alive and your muscles are not slack.

And, as you have heard me say before, when you read, make it a conversation. In a very real sense, you are in conversation with somebody (the author), and the conversation you have today will be different from the conversation you will have in a week's time when you reread the piece because in that week you have changed and grew.

Before you read anything, ask yourself why you are reading it and what relevance does it have to your concerns. Ask yourself (before you start reading) what do you expect to find in what you are about to read. Are you looking for something in particular? And, when you finish reading, you can ask yourself what new actions can you now take that you were not able to take before? What new ways do you have of dealing with the world?   What new words have you learned? Was it a good use of your time?

Of course, one of the special delights of reading to the three of you as you have grown up, is it gives Mummy and I a chance to have a quiet time with you. Speaking to children with kindness, patience and respect can easily get lost in the day-to-day blur of deadlines, to do lists and errands.

Kimme, Tina and Jenny, you are all so very, very special. Have a great day in school tomorrow and ask lots of good questions!

> I love you,
> Daddy XXXOOO

October 3, 1995

My precious loves, Kimme, Tina and Jenny:

Remember I talked to you about this last week. They call it the marshmallow test. A researcher gives this choice to a four-year old: "I am leaving for a few minutes to run an errand and you can have this marshmallow while I am gone; but, if you wait until I return, you can have two marshmallows."

Researchers at Stanford University ran that test in the 1960s. A dozen years later, they restudied the same children and found that those who had grabbed the single marshmallow tended to be more troubled as adolescents. Astonishingly, the one-marshmallow kids also scored an average of 210 less on SAT tests.

To me, this shows the importance of early character training, and it is an excellent reminder as if any more were needed of just how critical the early home years are in the life of a child.

Mummy and I have done our best to give you the best possible childhood, and judging by how well each of you are doing, we feel we have done a pretty good job! I know you don't always agree! I cannot help thinking though that you three would have done well whatever happened to you. Each of you work hard, show determination, pick friends well, get along with people, and are successful in everything you try to do. Mummy and I are very proud of you.

> I love you!
> Your old dad XXXOOO

October 4, 1995

My darling Kimme, Tina and Jenny:

Do you remember the wonderful story grandpa tells of how one day in 1940, the Superintendent at Haslar (Dr. Gawn) sent for grandpa (who was working at Haslar) and told him that the British government had made emergency plans for certain key people to go to America if the Germans secured a foothold in England. At the time, England was at war with Germany and was fighting Germany alone. America had not yet entered the war (this was before Pearl Harbor), and Hitler had defeated virtually every other country in Europe, except for England.

My father was ordered to say nothing to my mother or to anyone else. The emergency plans were top secret. He was told he would have to make his way (by car, bicycle, walking or whatever) with a small package of microfilms on German mines to a certain quay in Liverpool docks where a cruiser would be standing by ready to flee to America. Luckily, thanks to Winston Churchill's leadership and the courage of the British people, the Germans never did invade, and so my father never had to abandon his family.

Can you imagine what went through my father's mind?!

Don't forget to watch *Scientific American* at 8:00 PM tonight on Public Television with Alan Alda. I hope you enjoy it!

I love you.

> Love,
> Daddy XXXOOO

October 5, 1995

My three loves, Kimme, Tina and Jenny:
I will be home tomorrow morning and cannot wait to see you. I love you and I am so proud of you. All my love,

> Daddy XXXOOO

October 23, 1995

My darling Kimme, Tina and Jenny:
I am so sorry I have to be away for a few days this week. As you know, I left early this morning (Monday) to go to the Saw Tooth Mountains in Idaho. I am going to camp out for a night with a pack of wolves! This is to plan an IMAX film on wolves.

I am taking out with me five or six people, who are part of the team on this project. They include Richard James (the distributor), Mose Richards (the writer), T.C. Christian (the Director of Photography), Lynn Christofferson (Accountant), Jim Dutcher (the Director, actually Jim's already out there because this is where he lives), and one or two other people.

It will be pretty exciting, even though it will be bitterly cold -- in the low teens.

Jim Dutcher has had this pack of wolves for five years and, in fact, he is a "member" of the pack. The wolves know him, and behave quite normally around him.

As you know, wolves are like dolphins, they are extraordinarily social animals. To survive, they must work together, and different pack members take charge during travel, hunting, feeding, "baby-sitting," and guarding the territory.

A wolf standing with his tail up and his ears pointed forward is showing power. A wolf crouching with its tail between its legs and its ears turned down is showing submission.

Adult wolves, like pups, enjoy chasing, wrestling, and tumbling on the ground. When a wolf is looking for a playmate, it may approach another wolf, bow down low with its front legs flat on the ground, and wag its tail vigorously. If the invitation is not accepted, it will be repeated and sometimes alternated with leaping about in a zig-zag fashion. If the other wolf is willing to play, the two will engage in mock fights or take turns chasing each other until both are worn out and ready to rest.

So, on Monday and Tuesday, I will be seeing a lot of wolves up close! We will be camping in a 25-acre enclosure where these wolves live. I will tell you all about it when I get back in the middle of the week!

I love you, and I miss you. But I am comforted knowing that you are all doing well, getting the most out of life, enjoying your friends, and looking out for each other.

I will be home very late tomorrow night at about midnight after you are all asleep, so I will see you Wednesday morning.

I love you,
Daddy XXXOOO

October 24, 1995

My three precious darlings, Kimme, Tina and Jenny:
I will be home late tonight -- after you are asleep. My plane does not land until about 11:00 PM. So, I will see you on Wednesday morning. I am going to work that day, and then I have an important dinner in the evening with a potential donor called Peter Stent. So, I won't see you then either. I will get home around about 10:00 PM. Then, on Thursday, I leave the house very early to fly to Los Angeles. I will be in Los Angeles for about 36 hours of constant meetings and speeches before I fly back on the Red Eye on Friday night. I will get in around about 6:30 AM on Saturday morning while you are all sleeping, and I will probably go straight to bed!

I am sorry to be away so much this week. Even though I am sleeping two nights at home (Tuesday night and Wednesday night), I will hardly see you because I will be out at meetings most of the time. I hope you are all having a great week, working hard, and enjoying moods of serenity and ambition!

I adore you. You are each so special. All my love,

Daddy XXXOOO

October 25, 1995

My three treasures, I am out tonight having dinner with an old friend, Peter Stent, who I am trying to persuade to invest in our IMAX film on wolves.

Here is something interesting: The other day, Ruth Thomas wrote me a memo saying that Kathy Pearce had mentioned to her that I am "chronically over-scheduled," meaning that I over-book myself for meetings and calls. Ruth pointed out that, in doing that, my meetings and calls are often too rushed to accomplish things, and the person I am meeting with often does not have enough time to discuss the matters they want to discuss.

I very much appreciated Ruth telling me this. It is helpful to me when people tell me things that they observe which I may not observe myself. Ruth went on to say in her memo, "This memo is just an FYI to you that other 'customers' of yours may be feeling the way that Kathy Pearce is feeling." My feeling (said Ruth) is that this could create tension or possibly "hurt" a deal, a relationship, or a negotiation that you are working on if the other party feels they are being rushed during your meetings, or if they, too, feel that you are "over-scheduled" or have cut yourself too thin to effectively work on their projects or show.

Ruth ended her memo by saying, "I have also noticed that you sometimes do rush people in a conversation and I have often thought the person you were talking to could have been offended by your rushing."

Ruth knows, like I do, that with a lot of people it is good to rush because, otherwise, they waste a lot of time. But I really appreciated Ruth's point. This kind of constructive feedback helps me do my job more effectively. One of the axioms that I put in the Search For Wisdom book that I gave you a year or two ago was "busyness destroys relationships." That is what Ruth was getting at. She is not recommending that I waste time or dilly dally, but only that I give people enough time to "dance" in conversations so that they feel they are being listened to (and are listened to!) and have an opportunity to make the points they want to make.

Both Delores and Ruth are wonderful colleagues in this way. Both of them will talk to me privately and tell me when they think I can do a better job at something.

Well, my loves, I hope you are having a great week and, even though I am away a lot this week sleeping with wolves and deal-making in Los Angeles, remember that I think so highly of each of you and I love you deeply with all my heart.

Love,
Daddy XXXOOO

October 26, 1995
My darling, darling, darlings, Kimme, Tina and Jenny:
Today, I am in Los Angeles! As you know, I left early this morning, after an exhausting first three days of this week, to go to Los Angeles for a series of meetings with film producers, Hollywood studios, agents and other people like that. I am also giving a speech on Friday morning to a big conference. I will be coming back on the Red Eye on Friday night and will probably be asleep in bed by the time you wake up on Saturday morning.

One of the things that I am trying to be better at is listening to other people really trying to understand their concerns when they are talking which may not be clearly reflected in the words they use but may have to be divined from the look in their eye and their body language. Listening well helps build solid relationships, and getting along with others is one of the most single most determinatives of success. It is funny how no one ever gets training in how to listen. I believe it is a skill that you can learn, and I am trying to increase my ability to listen -- really listen -- when people talk. Part of listening effectively means not jumping to conclusions and not making ungrounded assessments. This is very hard for me to do! I tend to be judgmental (I know you will find that hard to believe!), and this really impedes my ability to listen and understand people. One of my New Year's resolutions this year was "Seek first to understand, then to be understood. Learn to listen without making judgments or giving advice." Hey, what are you smiling at??! Give me a chance, I'm just a beginner you know!

I love you. See you on Saturday morning!

Your old dad XXXOOO

October 27, 1995
My darlings Kimme, Tina and Jenny:

I will be home early tomorrow morning! I hope you have had a great week, and I cannot wait to see you. Let's go to the pumpkin patch on Saturday to get pumpkins!

All my love,
Daddy XXXOOO

December 6, 1995
My darling Kimberly, Christina and Jennifer:

I am in San Francisco today and then flying up to Oregon tomorrow. I have lots of important meetings with interesting people, and I will be having a lot of fun -- just as you will be (I hope!) in school.

Here is an interesting way to relax that I read about recently in *The New York Times*: Stand with both arms hanging naturally at your sides. Keeping in place, shake your hands as fast as possible. Your whole body, including your toes, should shake. Stop shaking your hands and remain quietly in this position. The goal is to be in a state of complete relaxation. Try it!

Here is another thing I read recently about ways to simplify ones life. I am constantly trying to rid myself of clutter and unimportant things in my life and in my mind. There is a book called *Simplify Your Life*, which was published in 1994, which I have not read, but which apparently contains the following ideas:

> ➤ Get rid of the clutter in your house. (We're trying!)

> ➤ Leave your shoes at the front door: It cuts down on dirt and turns your home into a sanctuary.

> ➤ Pack your own lunch.

> ➤ Get up an hour earlier.

> ➤ Keep a journal.

> ➤ Watch a sunset.

I am sure you can think of lots more things along those lines that can simplify and enrich your lives.

I thought you might be interested in the seven "roles" I have currently selected for my personal mission statement. They are:

> ➤ Husband.

- ➢ Father.

- ➢ Extended family and friends.

- ➢ Humor.

- ➢ Student/teacher.

- ➢ NWF.

- ➢ Raising funds.

By analyzing these roles and thinking about them, it helps me to keep my life in balance. It is amazing how simply writing something down like this can help you reshape your life. I am a big believer in mastering life by setting goals and achieving them. Everyday is full of goals -- big ones, little ones -- to be fulfilled.

Each of you is so special, and Mummy and I love you very, very much. You are each unique and have so much to offer the world, your friends, your family and all the communities you live in.

Also, I noticed how all three of you constantly strive to improve. Just in the last day, I have noticed how you, Tina, are really striving to read more and raise your competence in language; and you, Kim, how you are really making a daily effort (and the regularity of it is the important thing) of keeping fit and running; and you, Jen, I noticed how creative you are when it comes to your school projects. In fact, that is characteristic of all of you -- your enthusiasm and creativity.

Mummy and I are very, very proud of you.

See you on Friday! I adore you. All my love,
Daddy XXXOOO

December 7, 1995

My darling, darling darlings: Kimme, Tina and Jen:
It often amazes me how little I know about my own childhood. I have almost no notes or special information about it. In some ways, it is just one big blank, except for the occasional memory here or there.

But what I have come to realize is that every day is full of special memories. It is not just the vacations. Looking through our family photo albums, they are filled with wonderful photos that commemorate the big events and grand occasions. I think it also important to remember and cherish those special moments of daily life that are too quickly forgotten.

This is why I encourage you to keep a journal, keep a joy list, write letters and, generally, become an observer of special moments and special memories.

I cannot wait to get home and see you all. I miss you! I love you!

Daddy XXXOOO

1996

January 18, 1996

My darling Kimme, Tina and Jenny:

I will be away for six nights, and I don't like it at all! I hate being away from you, even though I love my job and I will have a wonderfully productive, enjoyable and professionally rewarding trip. I know that you think I work all the time (and I do love my work), but the most important thing in my whole life is Mummy and you three. You will notice how, in my New Year's Resolutions, you guys came first and my work at NWF came last!

Anyway, I hate being away from you, but it is part of my job. I am spending the first four days at the Sundance Film Festival where I will be meeting with a lot of people and viewing a lot of films. Then, on Monday, I will go to Las Vegas for what is called the National Association of Television Programming Executives (NAPTE) Conference. Again, I will be meeting with a lot of people and looking for ways in which I can use television and the mass media to promote conservation, environmental protection, and biological diversity.

I cannot wait to get home next Wednesday. I am rushing home on that day (even though the NAPTE Conference will not have finished) in order to attend the Holton Arms event that evening at 7:00 PM. That is something I do not want to miss.

One major regret I have about being away is being away next weekend and not being around for your soccer clinic, Jenny, or your basketball, Tina, or just being around to be with you.

Mention of my New Year's Resolutions reminds me that one of them was to help you guys build up your vocabularies. So, every letter this week is going to contain some good words for you:

➢ Adumbrate: To sketch in outline; to indicate faintly.

➢ Atrophy: To slowly die through lack of food or lack of use (His arm atrophied from lack of use.).

➢ Anarchy: Disorder, without rule (There was anarchy in the classroom.).

➢ Allude: Refer (He alluded -- hinted at -- to his wife's first marriage.).

➢ Animosity: Hostile (Her attitude was full of animosity.).

➢ Assiduous: Diligent, unremitting (She worked assiduously for her exams.).

➢ Arduous: Hard, strenuous, energetic (The climb up the mountain was arduous.).

➢ Abstemious: Sparing, moderate in food, drink, and so on (Ghandi was abstemious.).

Try and use these words in your writing and in your talking.

Thanks so much for looking after each other while I am away. I miss you terribly, but you are in my thoughts every second. Mummy and I love you so deeply, and we will always love you.

Have a great week -- have fun with your friends, work hard, exercise vigorously, and live life to the hilt.

I adore you.

Daddy XXXOOO

January 19, 1996

Darling, darling Kimme, Tina and Jenny:

I was so proud of you last weekend, Tina, when you asked me to review your essay on the medicinal value of rainforest plants. When you ask somebody to review something, you make yourself vulnerable, and open yourself up to criticism. It takes great maturity to do that, and then to listen carefully and openly to the feedback. To ask me to review your writing took courage, and you should feel proud of yourself. The more you practice courage, the more courageous and brave you become. And, as you heard me say before, one of the characteristics of successful people is that they are not afraid to constantly ask for help because they recognize that, in almost every domain in life, there is someone who is better than they are and that they can learn from. So, they become successful by constantly asking other people for coaching.

So, well done, Tina! You have also worked relentlessly and tenaciously on your report, and I am proud of you for that as well. And you have shown great competence in coordinating action with both Nina and Lizzie. And you were great on television!

Something that all three of you are exceptionally good at is choosing friends, and creating warm and mutually satisfying relationships with them. I don't think you realize how good you are. It is a wonderful asset and will help you all through your lives. Relationships underline everything in life and, if you know how to get along with people, build on their strengths, tolerate their weaknesses (we all have them, even me!), and have fun, even when the issues are serious, you will reap deep satisfaction for yourselves and for your friends.

I was very proud of how thoughtful your New Year's Resolutions were this year. Each of you thought deeply about what you wanted to achieve.

Okay, here are today's words to learn:

➢ Malevolent: Wishing evil to others (The evil witch was malevolent.).

➢ Mitigate: To reduce the severity of, to alleviate (The medicine mitigated the symptoms of the disease.).

➢ Meager: Lean, scanty, insufficient (The prisoners were given meager rations.).

➢ Mundane: Worldly, earthly, ordinary (The comments of the Pope were mundane.).

➢ Mute: Silent, dumb.

➢ Mendacious: Lying, given to lying (The fired teacher was mendacious.).

➢ Militant: Combative, engaged in warfare (The extreme environmentalists were militant.).

➢ Maladroit: Bungling, tactless (He was a maladroit poet.).

➢ Malign: To slander or misrepresent (She was unfairly maligned.).

➢ Meretricious: Showily attractive, flashy (His party clothes were tawdry and meretricious.).

I started this out by writing about Tina, so now a word about Kimme and Jenny. Kimme, good luck working for exams this week. You have been working hard and you are doing your best, and that is all that matters. Jenny, well done for going (and wanting to go) to the soccer clinic on Sunday. You did great. (Love those baggy pants!!)

I adore you and I miss you. All my love,

Daddy XXXOOO

January 20, 1996

My precious three loves, Kim, Tina and Jen:

One of my favorite maxims in the book I gave you, *A Search For Wisdom*, is #275. Did you know that a Chinese bamboo tree does not grow at all for its first four years? It just develops a massive root structure, while the bulb barely shows. In the fifth year, it grows 80 feet. Many things in life are like that Chinese bamboo tree. You may not see any initial evidence of what you are about; but, if you just persist on the basis of correct principles, eventually a tremendous harvest will result. The Chinese bamboo tree is an excellent metaphor of our growth, and the importance of patience, diligence, consistency and persistence in the nature of our work.

One fundamental principle is keeping your word, and always telling the truth. Honesty eliminates the need to engage in covert behaviors and cover-ups. When we are true to our conscience, when we keep our word consistently, when we strive to harmonize our habits (i.e., our behavior) with our values, then our life is integrated.

The writer, Stephen Covey (who I greatly admire), writes, "Integrity is the root of all goodness and greatness. The security which emerges from it eliminates the need to live for impression, to exaggerate for effect, to drop names, to borrow strength from credentials, possessions, fashions, affiliations, associations, or status symbols."

If you always tell the truth, it will give you incredible strength.

Now I want to tell you about something which is a great source of happiness for me, and that is Mummy's unconditional love of me. One reason I am so happy is that Mummy loves me and believes in me, even when sometimes I don't believe in myself. She is so inwardly anchored and rooted that I can depend on her utterly. Mummy knows me, cares about me, her love is unconditional, and I know that she would stay with me when everyone else deserts me. I am so lucky! What a wonderful gift. I am incredibly blessed.

I miss you and I love you. All my love,

Daddy XXXOOO

January 21, 1996

Darling Kimme, Tina and Jenny:

Here are the words for tonight (I forgot them last night!):

➤ Foible: Weak point in character (The author described the protagonist's foibles.).

➤ Facetious: Cheeky, insolent (The schoolboy got in trouble for being facetious to the teacher.).

➤ Fastidious: Hard to please, squeamish, carefully selective (The woman washed her hands fastidiously.).

➤ Futile: Useless, frivolous, ineffectual (Their efforts to find the lost contact lens were futile.).

➤ Fallible: Liable to error, unreliable (The Pope claims he is infallible.).

➤ Frugal: Economical (The woman had a low income and so lived frugally.).

➤ Fatuous: Silly, senseless (The ignorant person's remarks were fatuous.).

➤ Flagrant: Glaring, scandalous (The boy who got a D grade made flagrant mistakes in his exams.).

➤ Fiasco: Failure, breakdown (The snow removal in DC this week has been a fiasco.).

➤ Flamboyant: Florid, colorful (The mayor's incompetency is matched by his flamboyancy.).

➤ Fortitude: Courage in pain or adversity (She showed great fortitude in not giving up.).

➤ Frenetic: Frantic (With three kids, family life is frenetic.).

Number 19 of my maxims on page two is Goethe's expression: "Whatever you can do, or dream you can, begin it. Boldness has a genius, power and magic in it." Goethe was a famous German philosopher. What he says is worth thinking about. There is nothing like action to transform yourself (i.e., moving from thinking about something to actually doing something, even if it is a small beginning).

Another quote I like (#91 on page nine) is: "A child looks out toward life without prejudice or deceit or meanness, and all through a child's growing years we are given the most precious gift of all a chance to feel like a child again ourselves." This is something that you three have done for me and for which I can never thank you enough.

I hope you have a wonderful week, full of learning, full of fun, full of adventure, full of friendship, full of love, full of laughter and full of good, healthy, nutritious food!

I love you each more than I can ever tell you.

Daddy XXXOOO

January 22, 1996

Darling Kimme, Tina and Jenny:

     I am now in Las Vegas. The very words trigger a negative feeling. When I think of Las Vegas, I think of everything that I loathe, such as people wasting their lives on gambling, and filling their lives with inane, pointless activities. I have never been there, so I don't know what I am talking about and maybe I'll get a different view. But somehow I don't think so. I am here for a big meeting of the television industry and, since I loathe most of what I see on television, I am not expecting to find much which will inspire me. There will be some quality people here from places like The Discovery Channel and A&E, and I will have useful conversations with them.

     Here is what Stephen Covey says about meditation and contemplation: "Take time each day for private meditation, contemplation, prayer, and a study of the wisdom literature. Many people are bored when they are by themselves or retired, because their lives have been a merry-go-round of activity, almost always with other people. Cultivate the ability to be alone and to think deeply, to enjoy silence inside you, to reflect, write, listen, visualize, ponder, relax, prepare and plan. These activities are vital to your sense of personal worth and security."

     And here is what he says about physical and mental exercise: "Regular, vigorous exercise is vital to radiant health. Cultivate the habit of regular exercise in stretching, aerobic, and toning exercises. For mental exercise, I suggest cultivating the habit of reading widely. Take a college course now and then to add external discipline and accountability. Read history, biography, autobiography, good fiction all the great literature. When we continue our education, our economic security is not dependent upon our jobs, but rather is based upon our ability to create and produce."

     In my opinion, what he says is very wise.

     Here are some good words:

> ➢ Prolific: Producing much, fruitful (Isaac Asimov was a prolific writer.).

> ➢ Plutocracy: A country in which power belongs to the rich (The United States Senate is in one sense a plutocracy.).

> ➢ Pernicious: Destructive, injurious (She told pernicious lies about him.).

> ➢ Patent: Obvious (His motives were patent.).

> ➢ Paltry: Petty, contemptible, trifling (The results were paltry.).

> ➢ Perspicacious: Having insight, penetrating (Her comments were perspicacious.).

> ➢ Philistine: An uncultured, imaginative person (His taste in music is Philistine.).

> ➢ Propensity: Inclination or predisposession (Rich people sometimes have a propensity to spend their money carefully.).

> ➢ Protagonist: The chief person in a drama (The main protagonist was the villain.).

- ➢ Petulant: Given to small outbursts of temper, touchy (When I get exhausted, I get petulant.).

- ➢ Platonic: Confined to words, harmless, not issuing in action (Their friendship was platonic.).

- ➢ Pristine: Unspoiled by modern tendencies, ancient, primitive (The beautiful countryside was pristine.).

I hope that is helpful. Having a large vocabulary can give you enormous power and confidence.

Being able to ask significant questions is a great skill. Think about this, and try these types of questions:

- ➢ If you were in my shoes, what key area would you focus on?

- ➢ What two things should we do to work towards being a great school/organization/whatever?

- ➢ What do you mean by...?

- ➢ Why?

- ➢ How?

- ➢ Can you be more specific?

- ➢ What are we trying to accomplish?

We tend to get agitated just before we learn something new. Recognize these signs of perturbation in yourself and in others as a sign that something new is about to present itself and stick with the questioning.

I love you so much. I hope you are having a great week. All my love,

Daddy XXXOOO

January 23, 1996
My darling Kimberly, Christina and Jenny:
I will be home tomorrow! I cannot wait to see you all and to be home again. I have missed you so much, but I have been very serene because I know that you look after each other and look after yourselves with tremendous competence. See you tomorrow! Love ya'!

Daddy XXXOOO

February 20, 1996
My darling Kimme, Tina and Jenny:
As you are reading this, I am in Los Angeles! Yesterday, I was in Atlanta, and next week I will be

in Florida. Too much travel! I don't like being away from you and from home, but at least there is the compensation that I love my work and find it challenging and satisfying.

Mummy and I were so touched by all your valentine good wishes, cards and gifts to us. Thank you! I love every time I think of your note to me, Kimme: "Dear dad, even though you're repressive and authoritative, I still love you! You are a great dad." I am trying to think of a way I can use that in a speech I am giving to the NWF Board on Friday, March 1.

Did I ever tell you of the time I experienced a huge disappointment in my exam results? I was about 18, and had always done quite well in school in my exams. Then, I took some exams to help me move from Naval Engineering into an elite organization which manages and runs the British government.

There was a heavy emphasis in this exam on writing, reasoning, thinking with words, assessing the strengths and weaknesses of fairly dense exposition, and so on.

I remember when the results came out. I was at sea with the Royal Navy, and I received a call from my father. (Don't ask me how he knew the results before I did -- I don't know.) Anyway, Grandpa called me and said that I had only gotten a C grade (or something like that -- whatever the grade was that was barely a pass). Boy, was I depressed! I was not used to failing things, and it stunned me.

Luckily, Grandpa used his influence (he was high up in the government), and got me into the organization that I was applying to anyway. And you know the rest of the story -- when I got to America, I fell in love with Mummy and I did not want the job anyway (because I wanted to stay in the US)!

Anyway, all this prompts me to remind you of something that you know already but it amazes me. Most people already know that the way we feel emotionally influences the way we feel physically. For example, if you are under pressure at work, you get a headache. If you are depressed, your whole body hangs low, your shoulders are bent, your eyes on the ground, and so on. If you get a good exam result, you are strutting!

What few people realize is how powerfully the reverse is true: When we are moved physically, we are moved emotionally, too. The two cannot be separated. Emotion is created by motion. (Good heavens, I am sounding like Jesse Jackson!) The way we move changes the way we think, feel, and behave. Movement affects our body's chemistry, including everything from more physical activities (such as running, clapping, or jumping) to the smallest movement in the muscles of the face. This is one reason why you may have noticed that, when I get up in the morning, I deliberately smile in the mirror, even if I don't want to.

We all know that we smile when we feel good or laugh. But I also believe that smiling and laughing set off biological processes that, in fact, make us feel good. They increase the flow of blood to the brain and change the level of oxygen, the level of stimulation of the brain's messengers, and so on. In sum, put on a happy facial expression and that is how you will feel.

This sounds trivial and silly at one level; but, at another level, I think it is profound. Remember the story of Teddy Roosevelt and how he overcame his fear in the west by "acting" fearless.

I think it is a good idea for you to look for "mentors" on which you can model yourselves. Find people who you regard highly and then notice the way they gesture, they move, and the way they speak. It will change what you expect from yourself and help you become more dynamic, powerful, self-confident and positive.

So, my sweethearts, here is the wisdom of the day: Change the way you move and you will change your lives!

Mummy and I love you each so much. You are each unique and different from anybody else in the whole world. We are incredibly proud of you.

All my love and kisses,
Daddy XXXOOO

February 21, 1996
My darling, darling Kimme, Tina and Jenny:
I am on my way home! I am coming back tonight on the Red Eye, and you will hear the doorbell ring at about 6:00 or 6:30 (if my plane is on time, which it often is not) when I get in. I will probably go straight to bed!

See you in the morning! Love ya! Cannot wait to see ya!

Yer ol' dad XXXOOO

February 27, 1996
My darling Kimme, Tina and Jenny:
I will miss you so much this week! The only compensation is that I will be working hard in Florida, raising lots of money, giving speeches, and generally having a very productive time.

Aren't you proud of Mummy using the treadmill so much? I am really proud of her, and I am proud of you, Kimme, for your articles in *The Scribbler* and the *Bethesda/Chevy Chase Almanac*. And I am proud of you, Tina, for playing in that basketball team and for the reading you are doing. And I am proud of you, Jenny, for getting on the soccer team and for your enthusiasm for science experiments.

Did I ever tell you that I was very argumentative when I was younger? I would argue with anybody about anything. Now, I try to listen more to people, although I often don't do that very well. Here is a good joke about listening:

> It involves the story of two psychiatrists, one old, one young. They both show up each day for work scrubbed, immaculately dressed, and alert. But, at the end of the day, the youngster is frazzled and disheveled, the old man fresh as ever. One day, the young psychiatrist asked, 'How do you do it, stay fresh after hearing patients all day?' The old psychiatrist pauses and then says, 'I never listen.'

Here is another joke:

> Two rival businessmen meet in the Warsaw train station. 'Where are you going?' says one. 'To Minsk,' replies the other. 'To Minsk, eh? What a nerve you have! I know that

you are telling me that you are going to Minsk because you want me to believe that you are going to Pinsk. But it so happens that I know you really <u>are</u> going to Minsk. So, why are you lying to me?'

Get it?!

George Burnett Shaw said, "When a thing is funny, search it for a hidden truth." And I love what William Thackeray said, "A good laugh is sunshine in a house." And I also like what Eugene Ionesco wrote, "To become conscious of what is horrifying and to laugh at it is to become master of that which is horrifying."

And here are some good words to use. Mummy will tell you what they mean: Succulent, staid, sycophant, sublime, transcend, tawdry, truculent, and tenuous.

My treasures, I adore you and I hope you have a great week. I know you will give Susie and Erin a warm welcome tomorrow.

I love you with all my heart.

Daddy XXXOOO

February 28, 1996

My precious loves, Kimme, Tina and Jenny:

I hope Susie, Erin and Steve arrived safely! Please give them my love. Tina, good luck this week with your confirmation, and I hope the rehearsal and dinner go well on Thursday. Good luck, Kimme, with your softball tryouts. And I am dying to know, Jenny, how your Helen Keller performance went. I am sure it went well because you did such a good job when you were practicing.

Here is a story that I once read which is especially for Susie:

> A young woman from Los Angeles once wrote to a newspaper about a very embarrassing moment in her married life: 'It was 3:00 AM, the baby was pressing on my bladder and I had to urinate. I didn't want to wake my husband, so I crept out of bed and felt my way to the bathroom without turning on a light. I backed in, sat down and landed on something warm and hairy -- my husband's legs. He'd been dosing, eyes closed, on the seat. He screamed and jumped so high that I thought he was having a heart attack. I was so embarrassed I almost had the baby right there.'

Here is another good story:

> Harry Cohn, Head of Columbia Pictures, was approached by his brother, Jack, who wanted to do a Bible picture. 'What the hell do you know about the Bible?' growled Harry. 'I'll bet you don't even know the Lord's Prayer.' Jack wagered $50 that he did know the prayer. 'Okay, say it,' said Harry. 'Now, I lay me down to sleep...,' Jack began. 'That's enough,' said Harry, handing over his $50.00. 'I didn't think you knew it.'

That story is funnier when you realize that studio bosses were generally a crowd of louts and ignoramuses who knew how to give the general public what they wanted.

Tina, we are so proud of you getting into Holton Arms. I came across this story the other day which, Kimme, you might want to find a way to put into *The Scribbler*.

When frozen feet threatened to keep Admiral Robert Peary from reaching the North Pole, he wrote on the wall of his makeshift shelter, 'I shall find a way or make one.'

As you know, this is the spirit of those who make history; it is the spirit certainly of those who design their own lives, rather than get pushed around by circumstances. They won't be deterred by the "shouldn't-be-dones" and "can't-be-dones."

Jenny and I watched *Sister Sister* last Sunday night and found it funny. But waiting for it to come on and watching the ads reminds me how much trivial junk there is on television. It is really quite shocking. It makes it difficult for people to separate stuff that matters from stuff that doesn't matter. Here is a story to bring that point to life:

> A woman is wheeling her baby through a park. A man stops the carriage and looks inside. 'What a beautiful baby!" he says. 'Oh,' says the mother, 'that's nothing. You should see her picture.'

And here are some good words to use: Judicious, jargon, juxtapose, juggernaut, idiosyncracy, incipient, inexorable, infringe, invective, irrevocable, and impotent.

My treasures, say hi to Susie, Erin and Steve from me. I hope you are having a great week. I think of you all the time. Mummy and I are so proud of you.

I love you.

Daddy XXXOOO

February 29, 1996

My darling, darling, darling Kimme, Tina and Jenny:

Tina, I am sorry you are going to miss your basketball game at the weekend. And, by the way, I am proud of you for getting involved as a stagehand in the school play. Kimme, how did the softball tryout go? (Or is it tomorrow?) And Jenny, I hope you enjoy pottery tomorrow. And Kimme and Susie, if you go to Alex's band tomorrow night, I hope you have a great time!

Steve will be here tomorrow night. Please give him a big hello from me. I am sorry I am not there to be with you all.

Mummy's wonderful t-shirt, "My next husband will be normal" reminds me of this joke.

> A woman I know is making some interesting plans for the future. She says that, when her husband dies, she is not going to have him buried. I said to her, 'What are you going to do?' She said, 'I am going to have him stuffed, mounted and put on the living room couch. Then, I will turn on the TV to a baseball game, talk to him -- and he won't answer. It'll be just like he never left.'

One of the things I am doing in Florida is raising money. Here is a story about fund-raising:

> I once knew a man who was asked to become the chairman of a small town charity. And he found that a certain citizen of the town with a six-figure income had never contributed. So, he went to this man and said the record showed that 'you have this

big income, but you have never contributed a cent.' And the man said, 'Do your records show that my brother was wounded in the war, permanently disabled and never to work again? Do your records show my mother lost everything she had in bad investments and has thousands of dollars of debt hanging over her head? And do they show that my sister was widowed with ten children and there was no insurance and no way to make a living?' Abashed, the Chairman said, 'Well, no, the records don't show any of that.' And the man said, 'Well, if I don't give anything to them, why should I give to you?'

Actually, a better punch-line for that joke is: "Well, why should I give to you if I don't give anything to them?"

Sweethearts, I love you.

Here are a few good words: Hypothesis, hagiography, hone, halitosis, gawky, geriatric, gauche, frenetic, ennui, feign, and frugal.

Treasures, I love you so much and I miss you.

Daddy XXXOOO

March 1, 1996

My darling, darling Kimme, Tina and Jenny:

First, a big welcome to Steve to our home! I am so sorry that I am not there to be with you, Susie and Erin, but I know that Gail and the girls will look after you well.

Here is a poem that I saw in an ad for one of your competitors, Steve (The Prudential):

There's a house
Whose rooms
I know by heart,
Where I tended the garden
And read my books,
Where dreams were dreamt
And memories made,
Where children grew up
And I grew old.
There's a house
Where life was lived.
A house
Where I belong.

And that lovely poem reminds me of another of my favorites, this time from Shel Silverstein. It goes as follows:

Said the little boy, "Sometimes I drop my spoon."
Said the little old man, "I do that too."
The little boy whispered, "I wet my pants."
"I do that too," laughed the little old man.

114

Said the little boy, "I often cry."
The old man nodded, "So do I."
"But worst of all," said the boy, "it seems
grown-ups don't pay attention to me."
And he felt the warmth of a wrinkled old hand.
"I know what you mean," said the little old man.

Here is another story I like:

> Some years ago at the Savoy Hotel in London, there was a banquet attended by most of the notables of Britain, including the Prime Minister, Sir Winston Churchill, and his wife, Lady Churchill. It was a tradition at this particular banquet to put on some sort of public charade before the main address by the guest speaker. The game that night was: 'If you couldn't be who you are, who would you like to be?' Each of the dignitaries at the head table answered the question in their own way; but, of course, the audience was breathless with anticipation as to how Churchill would respond. After all, a Churchill wouldn't want to be a Julius Caesar or Napoleon. When Churchill, as ranking member of the occasion, rose as the last speaker, he said, 'If I can't be who I am, I would most like to be' and then the 78-year old Sir Winston turned to touch his wife's hand 'Lady Churchill's second husband.'

I can relate to that story, because that is how I feel about Gail.

And here is a good riddle from *Ranger Rick*:

> Question: What does a moose get when it lifts weights?
>
> Answer: Big mooscles!

Well, my loves, I miss you terribly and I cannot wait to see you on Sunday. Good luck tomorrow, Tina, with your confirmation.

I love you all so much. You make my life what it is.

Buckets of hugs and kisses.

Yer 'Ole Dad

March 2, 1996
My darling, darling, darling Kimme, Tina and Jenny:
I cannot wait to see you tomorrow. I should be back in the early afternoon if my plane gets in on time.

You know, humor can be used as a way to diffuse situations. There is a story about President John F. Kennedy that goes like this:

> When he decided to appoint his brother, Robert, Attorney General, he was asked how he was going to make the announcement. Boldly and forthrightly, Kennedy said. He would open the door to his Georgetown home in the middle of the night, look both ways and whisper, 'It's Bobby.' Everybody laughed and the crisis passed.

Here is a joke that President Reagan used on the leaders of the Democratic party in 1986 to show that they had lost touch with the rank and file:

> Three guys came out one day to get the car and found that it was locked. One says, 'Give me a coat hangar, I can straighten it out and get in.' But the second guy declares, 'You cannot do that. Somebody will think you are stealing the car.' Then, the third fellow pipes up urgently, 'Well, we better do something pretty quick because it's starting to rain and the top's down.'

See you tomorrow! All my love.

Daddy XXXOOO

March 17, 1996

My darling Kimme, Tina and Jenny:

I am off on an exciting trip! As you know, I am in Hawaii with my film crew shooting Humpback whales and other wildlife for our IMAX film on whales. By the way, the title of the film is going to be *Whales: Voices Of The Deep*. We tested several options with several IMAX theaters, and they favored this. Do you like it? I hope so!

Hawaii is in the middle of the Pacific Ocean, roughly halfway between America and Asia. It is the most remote island chain in the world. About seven million tourists visit there each year! People use the word *Aloha* a lot. Aloha breaks down as *Alo* which means "to face," and *ha* which means "the breath of life." I think people use it there to say hello or goodbye. Loosely translated, it means love.

Have you heard of Pearl Harbor? Early on Sunday morning, December 7, 1941, two waves of Japanese aircraft -- 360 planes in all -- dropped below cloud cover and attacked every major military installation on Oahu, which is one of the major islands. Japan had been expanding its control in Asia for half a century; now the Pacific was on its agenda, including Pearl Harbor, a naval station on Oahu since 1908 and home of America's Pacific naval fleets.

The Japanese attack devastated America's Pacific naval forces. It was probably the greatest military and naval disaster in America's history. Nearly 200 planes were destroyed and nearly 20 battleships, cruisers, destroyers, and other vessels were lost or severely damaged.

The same day as the attack on Oahu, President Franklin Roosevelt declared war on Japan. On the American mainland (i.e., where we live), Americans of Japanese ancestry were confined in desert internment camps, a policy entirely racial and not substantiated by claims of national security. That action is now viewed by historians as a great injustice.

I have never been to Hawaii before, and I am excited to be there. I wish you were with me! I miss you all very much and look forward to seeing you on Friday when I get home.

I love you with all my heart. You and Mummy are the most special people to me in the whole world. All my love,

Daddy XXXOOO

March 18, 1996

Hello my treasures, Kimme, Tina and Jenny:

Do you remember the book Mummy recently bought all of us called *Character Above All*? It explores the relationship between the President's character and the President's leadership. I have started reading it and it is a marvelous book. The first chapter is about Franklin Roosevelt, who was President from 1933 to 1945. The chapter is written by a well-known writer and historian called Doris Kearns Goodwin.

Goodwin points out the most amazing thing about Roosevelt was his absolute confidence in himself and in the American people. He had this inner well of serenity. In tracing the roots of his sublime confidence, biographers are invariably drawn to Hyde Park on the River Hudson, the boyhood home which remained for Roosevelt a powerful source of strength all the days of his life.

"All that is in me goes back to the Hudson," Roosevelt liked to say, meaning not simply the peaceful, slow-moving river, and the big, comfortable clapboard house, but the ambience (good word!) of boundless devotion that encompassed him as a child.

He was the adored only son of a young mother and an aging patriarch, so he grew up in an atmosphere where affection and respect were plentiful, where the discipline was fair and loving, and the opportunity for self expression abundant. From his position of primacy in his family home, he seemed to develop what Freud has called "the feeling of a conqueror, that confidence of success that often induces real success." The sense of being loved wholeheartedly by his parents taught him to trust that the world was basically a friendly and agreeable place.

Goodwin says that no experience stretched Roosevelt more, both intellectually and emotionally, than his bout with polio, which left him, at the age of 39, paralyzed from the waist down. This was what his wife, Eleanor, later called his "trial by fire." She said that "the thing that took most courage in his life was his mastery and his meeting of polio. I never heard him complain." Goodwin writes, "Anyone remembering how athletic and strong he had been as a young man could not fail to realize what a terrific battle must have gone on within him. He just accepted it as one of those things that was given you as discipline in life."

After his struggle with polio, he seemed less arrogant, less smug, less superficial, more focused, more complex, more interesting. Far more intensely than before, he reached out to know people, to understand them, to pick up their emotions, to put himself into their shoes. No longer belonging to his old world in the same way, he came to empathize with the poor and the underprivileged, with people to whom fate had dealt a difficult hand.

It is a wonderful book which I hope we will all read together.

Jenny, good luck tomorrow with the science fair! I am proud of the science experiment you did. And, Kimme, good luck this week with your studying and with softball. You had a rough week last week with your history and biology tests, but I love the way you don't let struggles like that get you down for too long. And, Tina, good luck with softball starting soon and with all your reading. I noticed you are reading more and more. That is so important and so good.

Talking about reading reminds me to give you some good words: Rabid, renaissance, renovate, regurgitate, rococo, resuscitate, reminiscent, radical, and reticent.

I love you and I miss you. Mummy and I are so lucky having three such wonderfully accomplished, loving, beautiful and special children.

Have a great week in school. All my love,

Your ole' Dad XXXOOO

March 19, 1996

My darling Kimme, Tina and Jenny:

Have you all seen the film, *Dead Poets Society*, with Robin Williams? I think Kimme has, but I am not sure if Tina and Jenny have. It is a very good film, and I think you will enjoy if you have not seen it. There are lots of interesting things about the film, but one thing is that it is set in a school which has the motto *Carpe Diem*. The protagonist in the film, played by Robin Williams (he plays the character of an innovative and inspiring teacher), marvels at this motto and finds in it the seeds of self transformation.

Literally, the term means "Seize the Day." Latin scholars say that it may also be translated accurately as "seize the moment," or "seize the opportunity." All these definitions are excellent.

To seize the day, to grasp the opportunity in reality is to embrace the whole of life. For those people who seize the moment earnestly, eagerly, persistently, creatively, and with zeal it is those resolute men and women who realize the greatest achievement and the highest fulfillment and reward in their work and in their lives.

Note how I talk about not just work, but a successful life. For to "seize the moment" personally is the essence of living the full life the kind of life so many desire, and so few know how to achieve. As the character that Robin Williams plays in the film points out, those two words -- *Carpe Diem* -- unlock the secret of just how to live that kind of life. Perceive the opportunity, wage war on it.

I know *Carpe Diem* sounds almost antithetical to strategic planning; but, in my view, good planning gives people even greater opportunity to live spontaneously.

A saint once wrote, "The present moment is eternity." Ah, he (or, more likely, she, since the saint was so wise!) understood life. And Seneca, who desired above all to live life to the brim, admonished us to "dispose of each day in such a way that it consumes our life."

Carpe Diem! The inspiration for personal growth and professional development. Words to guide and fire our imperatives. A term to underline the vigor and enterprise necessary to achieve great victories.

Remember that opportunities may not come again. You must engage the day, ravish the moment, wring and wrest from it all that is good and all it will yield. This is, indeed, the time, your mighty moment.

Great opportunities surround us, but escape all but the most vigilant and diligent. There are no trifling moments, no days without unending return. The genius of life and professional success is to capture the precious opportunity. *Carpe Diem*. That says it all.

And one of my greatest opportunities in my life was to meet Gail and have a wonderful family. Now <u>that</u> is a transforming experience!

I adore you. All my love,

Daddy XXXOOO

March 20, 1996

My precious three loves, Kimme, Tina and Jenny:

We are having a marvelous time in Hawaii filming whales. Whales, dolphins and porpoises are known collectively as cetaceans, from the Latin *cetus* (a large sea animal) and the Greek *ketose* (sea monster). There are about 80 species currently recognized, and we may discover more in the future. They come in a variety of shapes and sizes, ranging from tiny dolphins just over three feet long to the Blue whale, which is typically over 80 feet long and is one of the largest animals ever to have lived on earth.

Cetaceans probably evolved from furry land mammals with four legs. The first real whale-like animals, called Archaeocytes, appeared about 50 million years ago. They were not the direct ancestors of modern cetaceans, but were probably very similar. They are believed to have lived in coastal swamps and shallow seas. They had torpedo-shaped bodies and their forelimbs had turned into paddles. Archaeocytes died out around 30 million years ago.

As you know, at first glance, whales, dolphins and porpoises resemble fish, particularly sharks. They have remarkably similar body shapes, and both have dorsal fins, flippers, and huge tails. In fact, the similarities are so striking that, for many years, whales and all other cetaceans were thought to be "spouting" fish. However, as you know, they are mammals and more closely related to people: They are warm-blooded, breath air, and give birth to live young.

The best way to distinguish a cetacean from a fish at a glance is to look at the tail: A whale's tail is horizontal and moves up and down, while a fish's tail is vertical and moves from side to side.

If you are still awake, I'll go on!

As you know, there are two main types of whale: Toothed whale, which possess teeth; and Baleen whales, which do not. The Toothed whales include the Beluga, all the dolphins and porpoises, Sperm whales, and Beaked whales. They feed mostly on fish, squid and, in a few cases, marine mammals, and normally capture one animal at a time. The Baleen whales include most of the larger whales, such as the Rorquals, Right whales (the ones I saw in Patagonia), and the Gray whales (which migrate up and down the west coast). The Baleen whales have baleen plates, instead of teeth. Their vast jaws enable them to catch thousands of shrimp-like crustaceans or small fish at a time.

Cetaceans have shed most external traces of their terrestrial ancestry and are all supremely adapted to underwater life, as Kimme and I know from swimming with them. Their body shape has become streamlined, and they have lost most of their body hair, improving hydrodynamic efficiency. They have short, stiff necks, which are essential for swimming at high speed. Their forelimbs have turned into flippers, and their hind limbs have disappeared. They have muscular tails, providing a powerful means of propulsion. And, over aeons of geological time, their nostrils have moved to the top of their head for easy breathing at the surface.

There are also many other, less obvious adaptations. For example, they have excellent hearing, which compensates for a poor -- or entirely lacking -- sense of smell and for the uncertainties of visibility underwater. They have a high tolerance to carbon dioxide, to help with lengthy dives, and are two to three times more efficient than land mammals at using oxygen in inhaled air. Their rib cages are collapsible for deep diving. And they have layers of insulating fat to keep them warm.

This week in Hawaii, I hope to see whales breaching (this is where whales launch themselves into the air head-first and fall back into the water with a splash), flipper-slapping (where they roll over at the surface to slap their flippers onto the water with a splash), lob-tailing (this is the forceful slapping of the flukes against the water while most of the animal lies just under the surface), and spy-hopping (many cetaceans periodically poke their heads above the surface of the water, perhaps to have a look around).

I want to teach you one other word echolocation. Most whales, dolphins, and porpoises are able to build up a "picture" of their surroundings with the help of sound. This is called echolocation. They make noises that bounce back from nearby objects and alert the animals that something else is in the water. Bats use a similar system to find their way around in the dark. In fact, Dr. Roger Payne, who is with me out here in Hawaii, first started doing research on bats and sound before moving about 25 years ago to start studying whales and sound.

A few centuries ago, there were probably more cetaceans in the sea than there are today. Whaling and other forms of hunting, incidental capture in fishing nets, competition with fisheries for food, human disturbance, habitat destruction, and marine pollution have all taken their toll. No cetacean has become extinct in modern times, but some species are now in serious trouble, and others have all but disappeared from many of their former haunts.

Our director of photography here, Al Giddings, tells me that he is amazed at the number of whales that he has been able to approach and the closeness he has been able to achieve.

You may remember the name Al Giddings because I mentioned him before. He once held the record for holding his breath (over 11 minutes!) and was in the *Guinness Book of Records*. Apparently, his record has now been exceeded by someone who has held their breath for 13 minutes! The way Al is filming Humpback whales out here is that he dives to 60 feet plus, breath holding without a scuba tank (the bubbles scare the whales) and filming, and then leaving the monstrous camera (it weighs about 300 pounds) and sprinting to the surface for air. The camera, with slight positive buoyancy then finally rises to the surface about a minute later. This is a technique that probably only Al Giddings could ever accomplish!

Well, my treasures, I wish you were out here with me, but I know you are all flourishing at home and living life to the full. *Carpe Diem*!

I love you and I cannot wait to see you on Friday. All my love,

Daddy XXXOOO

March 21, 1996

Darling Kimme, Tina and Jenny:

You will hear the doorbell go at about 7:00 AM tomorrow morning because my plane arrives in Dulles at about 6:00 AM. I will be very tired! So, I look forward to seeing you all at breakfast time and waking you up. I might go straight to bed -- I will see how I feel. I hope to spend the day in the office catching up on everything I missed during the week.

I love you.

Daddy XXXOOO

April 30, 1996

My darling Kimme, Tina and Jenny:

I love you so much. I was in Utah for several hours today for meetings on our IMAX film on wolves. Then, late this afternoon, I flew to Los Angeles for a meeting with The Disney Channel, followed by a dinner for the American Oceans Campaign (where I will be meeting with people like actor Ted Danson). I have several more meetings in Los Angeles tomorrow before flying home tomorrow -- I will not be home until after midnight. I have very specific goals I want to accomplish on this trip, so wish me luck!

Mummy and I are very proud of you. I know sometimes it may not seem that way because we are all so extraordinarily busy -- too busy! We are so busy that we barely have time to appreciate each other. Old people are often nostalgic -- they look back on the past and think that the past is far better than the present. Let's not wait for years to pass before we realize how wonderful our lives are now!

We live wonderfully blessed lives, full of purposeful work, love, affection, and joy. Again, I know that it sometimes does not seem that way because of life's little frustrations; but, I, for one, feel incredibly lucky to be in the same family as all of you.

I like the opportunity to write these letters because it gives me a chance to tell you how much I value you all, how much you mean to me, how much you enrich my life, and how much you teach me. Again, this may seem nuts when it must seem to you that the first thing I do when I come home is complain that the house is a mess. I do complain too much! I know that and I am sorry. I am trying to teach myself to observe that the glass is half full rather than half empty. You may find it hard to believe, but I am much better than I used to be -- I am much better than I used to be at seeing the good things people have done, rather than just the things they have not done or the errors I think they have made.

Tina

I am going to start with you, Tina, because you are the middle child, and people sometimes say the middle child feels ignored or neglected. I am putting you first for a change because, as you know, you are as important as anybody else in this family. Well done on your grades last week. Don't worry about the B grade in English. I see you working hard and reading more and more. I encourage you to reduce the time you spend watching TV so you can read more. I know you are talking more in class, and I want to encourage you to do that more. The more you can practice talking in public, the better you will get at it. Your note to Kimme the other day was wonderful -- the one expressing your appreciation to her because she lent you her shoes. And I know you study the *Time* magazines that Jenny brings home from school. That is a good idea, because it can give you material to talk about in world affairs (or whatever that course is called that you take). I am also proud of you for going to the library. I see you going to the library more and more, and using that as a resource. You have also been doing more exercise recently. A few weeks ago, you were doing three-mile runs. That is great. Try and use the tread mill if you can. (I am disappointed how none of us are using it much.) It is great what you and Lauren are doing at the nursing home. Thanks for the terrific help you gave me planting the tomatoes and flowers last Sunday. And I noticed -- despite what I said to you on Sunday evening, which I regret -- that you are asking me more and more questions. For example, just recently, you asked me two good questions about colonization. Keep pushing yourself to ask more and more questions. And congratulations again on getting into Holton Arms that is a big victory for you. I am proud of you for being part of the stage design team, making the design setups for the school play, and I love the fact that you are deeply relishing the drama course you are taking with Mrs. Cosby. Well done! And you are working hard on your Irish project and the family history project for school. Good luck with them both. By the way, Tina, I hope you write for the new editor-in-chief of *Scribbler* at Holton next year!

Jenny

Jenny, it was so much fun going camping with you last weekend! I think you are mature for your age, as well as being lots of fun and enthusiastic. I know last week you were struggling a little bit with some of your math at school, but you asked Mummy and me for help, and you quickly learned the new subject matter. Well done. I think you show great discrimination in what you watch on TV, but I still want you to try and cut it down to give yourself more room for reading, writing, and your artwork. Do you know what Migul, my barber, said to me on Saturday when I had my hair cut? He said that his children (ages 8 and 11) were not doing very well in school, so he and his wife decided to cut out all television. Since then, he said, their grades have gone up to all A's, they are talking as a family much more, they are reading more books, they are much happier, they are not frightened by scary rubbish they see on TV and, all together, they are simply delighted by the change. I like your resolve to get stronger and fitter. You are, like Tina and Kimme, athletic, and I encourage you to use more weight-lifting to build up your strength even more. I am so glad you and Julie came to the environmental fair at Laurel Ridge on Saturday. Thank you! You are doing very well in school (your report reflects that), but you want to be careful not to be complacent (that means assume the work is easy and you can do it without really having to work very hard). Keep pushing yourself, and always try and do twice the amount of homework that Mrs. Stone actually asks you to do.

Kimberly

Congratulations on your recent successes at school, being elected the President of Model UN, and being selected to be the next editor-in-chief of *Scribbler*. Wonderful accomplishments! You pack your life with so many great activities -- friends, exercise, reading, work, new experiences -- you are constantly pushing yourself to learn more, do more, and gain experiences that will help you make an even more substantial contribution to the world. Like me, you have to be careful to keep some kind of balance in your life so that you do not get worn out and exhausted. Trying to cut back on some television might help a little bit! (Although I do not think you watch very much.) I am so glad you played tennis with Mummy a few days ago. Will you play with me? Please! And I was so pleased you wrote to Granny and Grandpa recently asking them about their experiences in World War II. That was not only helpful to you, but did you realize how much profound pleasure you gave to Granny by reaching out to her in that way? And, like Tina and Jenny, I am very proud of the way you keep fit, strong and healthy. You deserve to get into any college you apply to, and we will be proud of you whatever college you get into (whether it is Princeton or some other college). I appreciated your generosity when you lent Tina your shoes the other day. A lot of older sisters would never do that. And well done for the scholarship you have won for your work at the scientific lab this summer. That must give you a very good feeling.

*   *   *   *   *

You are three wonderful girls, and Mummy and I are very proud of you. I am sorry if it sometimes seems as though we don't appear that way because we are complaining that the house is in a mess. I know you forgive us and that you understand that being a parent is not always easy, and that I especially (as opposed to Mummy) sometimes make errors of judgment in parenting. I have this wonderful feeling that you girls appreciate that we do our best and forgive us for the mistakes we make.

One mistake I have been making recently, which I very much regret, is not always getting home for our family dinners. That is a direct violation of one of my New Year's resolutions, and I feel ashamed that I keep breaking it because of my workload. Please help me with this by telling me how important it is to you that I get home and spend time with you at dinner. If I know it is important to you, then I will make a greater effort to get home. I love my work so much that I could easily spend 16 hours in the office and get home very late every night.

I have started to read the marvelous book that Mummy discovered for us called *Reviving Ophelia: Saving The Souls Of Adolescent Girls*, by Mary Pipher. She writes:

> As I looked at the culture that girls enter as they come of age, I was struck by what a girl-poisoning culture it was. The more I looked around, the more I listened to today's music, watched television and movies, and looked at sexist advertising, the more convinced I became that we are on the wrong path with our daughters. America, today, limits girls' development, truncates their wholeness, and leaves many of them traumatized. --- What can we do to help them? We can strengthen girls so that they will be ready. We can encourage emotional toughness and self-protection. We can support and guide them. But, most important, we can change our culture. We can work together to build a culture that is less complicated and more nurturing, less violent and sexualized and more growth-producing. Our daughters deserve a society in which all their gifts can be developed and appreciated.

Finally, to fulfill another New Year's resolution, here are some words to enrich your vocabulary:

1. To deploy: To spread out as if in battle formation; use effectively; as, "Would a lower tax rate encourage investors to deploy capital more efficiently?"

2. Compromise: To reach an agreement in negotiations, each side giving up some demands; as, "The budget impasse (another good word) ended when the two parties began to compromise."

3. Litigation: Lawsuit; legal proceeding; as, "Many people believe the amount of litigation is out of control."

4. Potent: Having great power, authority, influence; as, "The capital gains tax became a potent

symbolic (another good word) issue."

5. Tenacity: Determination; persistent; firmness; as, "Do the Russian people have the tenacity to maintain democracy?"

6. Cyberspace: An environment generated by computers in a network, such as the Internet, that has no physical existence.

7. Punitive: Inflicting punishment; as, "Attempts in Congress to cap punitive damages in lawsuits."

8. Intrusion: Interference; uninvited intervention; as, "Many ranchers resent federal intrusion in their daily lives."

9. Fiscal: Related to financial matters; as, "Fiscal responsibility by the government."

10. Toxic: Poisonous; as, "The resistance of towns to local toxic dumps."

11. Dysfunctional: Impaired or abnormal in functions; as, "The children's behavior reflected their dysfunctional family life."

12. Pervasive: Widespread; as, "The pervasive violence in action movies."

13. Ethnic: Relating to nationality, race or common heritage; as, "The tragedy of ethnic conflicts."

14. Clandestine: Secret; concealed; surreptitious; as, "Illegal drug production in clandestine labs."

Kimme, Tina and Jenny, I love you so much. See you late tomorrow night (or, more realistically, Thursday morning when you wake up). Have a great couple of days, and I will be thinking about you all the time. Work hard, play hard, be creative, and have lots of fun -- and don't forget to smile and laugh! It is important!

I love you. All my love,

Daddy XXXOOO

Thursday, June 27, 1996

My darling Kimme and Jenny:

As you know, Tina and I left this morning for Tahiti! We flew to Los Angeles, arrived in the afternoon, and then tonight we are flying to Tahiti. It will be a long flight -- eight hours! Los Angeles is three hours behind east coast time, and Tahiti is three hours behind Los Angeles time. In other words, if you are reading this at 8:00 PM on Thursday night, it is 2:00 PM in the afternoon in Tahiti!

We will be exhausted, so we will sleep late in the morning (on Friday). Then, tomorrow afternoon, we will take a catamaran ferry to Moorea. It is all pretty exciting! During this week, we will learn a lot about the marine life here. We will be swimming with whales and dolphins, meeting some very interesting people, and going to some interesting places (such as an island, owned by Marlon Brando, famous for its birds, which apparently one can get very close to because they rarely see humans and are not afraid of them).

As you know, I am taking about 20 friends and donors with me -- two less than we expected because, at the last moment, Deb Ahrendt and Jayne Fenton both could not come unfortunately because of unexpected surgery.

Tina and I miss you both and Mummy very much. We will be back in about a week with lots to tell you about.

Kimme, good luck in your job this week. I am so proud of you for having a summer job of such challenge and quality. You are doing so well and, at the same time, you are doing a wonderful job of keeping your life in balance. Most people have to learn how to "compose a life," but you seem to know about these things at a very young age.

Jenny, I hope you are enjoying Creative Summer at Holton Arms. I got such a kick out of two of your answers to the questions about "your dad" the other day on the Mini Page. They gave you questions and said, "How do you think your dad would answer these questions?" One question was, "What hours do you work?" Your wonderful answer was, "You don't have any. You work whenever you want." Another question under "Current Favorites" was "friend." Your answer was, "You don't have any friends!"

This reminds me of something I read the other day in a magazine I get about humor:

1. How do people in love behave? Answer from Wendy (age 8): "When a person gets kissed for the first time, they fall down and don't get up for at least an hour."

2. Why do people fall in love? Answer from Mae (age 9): "No one is sure why it happens, but I heard it has something to do with how you smell. That's why perfume and deodorant are so popular."

3. What is falling in love like? Answer from Glen (age 7): "If falling in love is anything like learning how to spell, I don't want to do it, it takes too long."

4. Why do lovers hold hands? Answer from Gavin (age 8): "They want to make sure their rings don't fall off. They paid good money for those rings."

5. What qualities do you need to be in love? Answer from Robbie (age 8): "Sensitivity don't hurt." (sic) Also, another answer from Ava (age 8): "One of you should know how to write a check because, even if you have tons of love, there are still going to be a lot of bills."

6. Is it okay to kiss someone not in your family? Answer from Tammy (age 10): "It's never okay to kiss a boy. They slobber all over you and that's why I stopped doing it."

7. What makes love last? Answer from Natalie (age 9): "Don't say you love somebody and then change your mind. Love isn't like picking what movie you want to watch."

I don't know whether somebody made up those answers or whether they are real answers from real kids. They sound like real answers from real kids. Aren't they precious?

Here are some good words to learn:

1. Piety. This means devoutness in religious beliefs, as in "Kimme, Tina and Jenny's touching display of piety in church." (Ahemm)

2. <u>Bogus</u>. This means false, not genuine. It means fake or spurious.

3. <u>Fiasco</u>. This means failure, complete and usually ignominious. For example, "The fiasco of trying to explain away the obvious deception."

4. <u>Furtive</u>. This means secretive, stealthy, as in "He gave a furtive glance at the confidential document."

Kimme and Jenny, I love you so much and miss you. Have a great time while Tina and I are away, and thanks for looking out for each other and Mummy. All my love.

Daddy XXXOOO

Friday, June 28, 1996
My darling Kimme and Jenny:
Tomorrow morning, we will go on a half-day boat trip to watch spinner dolphins and, possibly, whales. Then, in the afternoon, all of us are boarding two large four-wheel drive Land Rovers for a land tour of the interior of Moorea. We will visit some ancient archeological sites (temples), pineapple plantations, and apparently a wonderful waterfall. We will also see some ancient petroglyphs that the inhabitants of Moorea carved in larva boulders centuries ago. It will be a great day!

In my letter to you yesterday, I told you those stories about what kids said about love. This reminds me of the wonderful letters you received recently from your fellow students, Jenny, when you were "student of the week." I know that you are a little cynical about the letters because you know that the kids in your class "have" to do them and that Mrs. Stone would not allow anyone to say anything rude, but I still feel there is a wonderful freshness and sincerity to them. Here are some of my favorites:

> From Thomas: "Hi, Jenny. Colin likes you. You may not think I am telling you the truth. But I am! Do you like Colin?" (His diagram above the letter has two 'love zones' with a don't enter sign, and a 'big kiss' coming out from behind the door!)

> From Julie: "Dear Jenny, we've been best friends for a long time and I want it to stay that way. Let's not fight anymore, okay?"

> From Cecilia: "Dear Jenny, I hope you had a happy birthday. Do you like being 9? Your birthday party was really fun. I also like to watch *Step By Step*. I hope you are in my class next year."

> From Michael: "Dear Jenny, happy late birthday! Do you like your sisters? Do you know square roots? I don't."

> From Joe: "Dear Jenny, you are a very smart person in math. I hope you can be in the top group in math in the fourth grade. Well, got to go."

> From Katherine: "Dear Jenny, I am glad you are my friend. I hope you will be in my class next year. You are a good friend."

> From Rebecca: "Dear Jenny, how come you always say 'cool'? I also like art. My favorite

TV show is *Wishbone*! How old was your hamster when she died? I wonder how it feels to have two older sisters?"

> From John: "Dear Jenny, what is it like being one of the smartest kids in the class? Is it fun or bad? Are you popular or not? Is everything easy or not? What's it feel like?"

> From Daniel Levine: "Dear Jenny, I heard you might move right next door to me. Are you still thinking about it? If so, I dare you to write a 300-word essay on it. Do you take my dare? Do you? Yes or no? Remember, it's your choice."

> From Miranda: "Dear Jenny, I second your opinion of being nice. In other words, I think you're nice, too. Would you like to have a dog? I would really like to have one. I am very glad you're my friend."

Now, here are some good words to learn:

1. Finite. This means limited, having fixed and definite boundaries as in "The earth's resources are finite."

2. Homage. This means honor or public display of respect, as in "The country radio station paid homage to Patsy Cline."

3. Equate. This means to consider to be equivalent or similar, as in "The novelist mistakenly equated anarchy (no laws and free of any civilizing constraints) with freedom."

4. Wanton. This means unjustifiably malicious or ignoring justice or morality, as in "The wanton excesses of local party bosses left the City nearly bankrupt."

5. Raconteur. This means a skilled storyteller, as in "President Reagan enjoyed his role as raconteur."

Kimme, you remember in my letter to you yesterday I talked about how you keep your life in balance. As you know, there are certain things that are fundamental to human fulfillment. If these basic needs are not met, we feel empty, incomplete. Whether or not we fully acknowledge or address these needs on a conscious level, deep inside we know they are there. And they are important. These needs have been recognized in the wisdom literature throughout time as vital areas of human fulfillment. (By "wisdom literature," I means that portion of the classic, philosophical and religious literature of our society that deals specifically with the art of living.)

The essence of these needs is captured in the phrase, "To live, to love, to learn, to leave a legacy." I found this phrase in the book, *First Things First*, by Stephen Covey. The need to live is our physical need for such things as food, clothing, shelter, economic well-being, health. The need to love is our social need to relate to other people, to belong, to love, to be loved. The need to learn is our mental need to develop and to grow. And the need to leave a legacy is our spiritual need to have a sense of meaning, purpose, personal congruency, and contribution.

I love you both and Mummy so much. Tina and I miss you very much, but we are having a wonderful time.

All my love,
Daddy XXXOOO

Saturday, June 29, 1996
My darling, darling Kim and Jen:
Kimme, how is your job in the lab going with Neal? Don't forget to give us a tour of the place before you finish. Jenny, how is Creative Summer going? I hope you are enjoying the swimming! Shall we get you some new goggles? How is the writing you are doing (everyday?) for your summer school writing project?

A friend recently sent me a list of "thoughts for a vital life," and here are some of them:

> Honesty isn't the best policy -- it is the only policy.

> Admit when you are wrong.

> Do the right thing -- do things right.

> Don't settle for anything less than the very best.

> Show respect for others.

> Maintain impeccable integrity.

> Revere your heritage and roots.

> Listen before you speak. Listen. Listen!

> Be childlike, not childish.

> Courtesy is contagious -- start an epidemic.

> Keep your word.

> Show appreciation, often and spontaneously.

> You don't have a second chance to make a first impression.

> Take time to enjoy life.

> Apologize, and mean it.

> Don't get angry.

> Practice humility.

> Welcome challenges.

- In life, when one door closes, another door opens.

- Blaze a new trail, seek the unexplored.

- Be a roaring optimist.

- Stay fit -- work at it daily.

- Count your blessings, think about them everyday.

- Seize the moment.

- Enjoy a hearty belly laugh.

- Stand firm for what's right.

- Laugh -- especially at yourself.

- Follow through.

And here are some good words to learn:

- Trumpet. This means to proclaim or praise loudly, to celebrate, as in "Congress trumpeted its roster of sweeping reform legislation.

- Rampant. This means unchecked, unrestrained, flourishing, as in "Rampant flood waters."

- Apex. This means highest point, the top, the summit, as in "Winning the tournament was the apex of his sports career."

- Libido. This means sensual or sexual desire and instinct, as in "The editor turned the magazine into a journal of libido and slick fashion."

- Enigmatic. This means puzzling, mysterious or difficult to understand, as in "The foreign minister's enigmatic statements left the press core speechless."

In my letter to you yesterday, I talked about something I found in a wonderful book by Stephen Covey called *First Things First*. I have recently been listening to him as I drive to work (in my effort to use that time productively, rather than just wasting it sitting in the car). On this tape, he told the following story:

Years ago, as I was wandering between the stacks of books at a university library, I chanced to open a book in which I encountered one of the most powerful, significant ideas I have ever come across. The essence of it was this: 'Between stimulus and response, there is a space. In that space is our power to choose our response. In our response lies our growth and our freedom.' That idea hit me with incredible force. In the following days, I reflected on it again and again. It had a powerful effect on my paradigm of life. I began to discover in that space my own ability to make a consciously chosen response.

I study "wisdom literature" because I am trying to redesign my life so I put the important relationships in my life (the most important of which are with Mummy and with you both and Tina) ahead of everything else. I want to lead a life of meaning and contribution. I want to live, to love, to learn, and to leave a legacy with balance and joy.

This requires real learning, and this brings me to another quote from a book by Peter Senge, called *Fifth Discipline*: "Real learning gets to the heart of what it means to be human. Through learning, we re-create ourselves. Through learning, we become able to do something we never were able to do. Through learning, we extend our capacity to create, to be part of the generative process of life. There is, within each of us, a deep hunger for this type of learning."

It is my experience that, almost without exception, everything people identify as really important has to do with others. Even those who list something such as "health" or "economic security" generally do so because they want to have the resources to enjoy life with their family and friends. Our greatest joy -- and our greatest pain -- comes in our relationships with others. It is interesting that, if you look at the seven "roles" I have defined currently for myself (husband, father, extended family, humor, student/teacher, NWF, and raising money), every one of them involves relationships with other people.

Incidentally, you might be interested to know how I plan each week: I look at my Personal Mission Statement, look at my seven roles (which are not fixed, by the way -- every so often, I redesign those roles and change them) and decide what are the key goals I want to achieve in the coming week.

I have noticed that you girls, especially Tina, hate it when people quarrel. I hate it, too. I remember when I was young listening to my parents and Jeremy fight, and it filled me with feelings of fright, powerlessness and pessimism. Yet, the paradox is that it is best to let kids fight and work out their problems, rather than intervene. Easier said than done!

Here are some more good words:

> Reprobate. This means a bad person, an immoral and unprincipled person, as in "At the movie's conclusion, the reprobate becomes the good guy."

> Cartel. This means monopoly, or a group of business firms controlling prices, as in "The foreign drug cartel made illegal contributions to the politician."

> Bipolar. This means two opposing qualities, as in "The compulsive gambler's bipolar world of mania and depression."

> Recuse. This means to withdraw from a position of judgment because of a conflict of interest, as in "The federal judge recused himself."

> Boon. This means to benefit, a blessing to be thankful for, as in "Lower mortgage rates are a boon to house buyers."

Darling Kimme and Jenny, I love you and I miss you. All my love,

Daddy XXXOOO

Sunday, June 30, 1996
My darling treasures, Kimme and Jen:
This afternoon, we went on another dolphin/whale watching trip. And, tomorrow, we are going on an all-day boat tour wrapping up at the end of the day with a picnic feast on one of the islands. We will be swimming and snorkeling. Boy, what a tough life!

On Tuesday, we are going to an island called Tetiora, which was once the ancient holy refuge for Polynesian royalty, but is now owned by Marlon Brando.

Here are some more "thoughts for a vital life":

> ➢ A good loser is still a loser.

> ➢ Reach for the stars.

> ➢ If you believe you can, you will.

> ➢ Think audacious dreams.

> ➢ Keep a daily journal.

> ➢ Think about what is really important in life, and not just what is urgent.

> ➢ The cheapest is not always the least expensive.

> ➢ Mistakes can be your best friends if you learn from them.

> ➢ Allot your time as if it were the most precious possession you have -- it is.

> ➢ The harder you work, the luckier you get.

> ➢ To achieve the impossible, attempt the unthinkable.

> ➢ Take someone's hand.

> ➢ Each day do something that tests your mettle.

> ➢ Insist on excellence.

> ➢ Be passionate about something.

> ➢ Always compete with those better than you.

> ➢ Nothing worthwhile comes easy or cheap.

- Live each day as if it were your last.

- Make someone happy.

- You should have more dreams than memories.

- Keep trying and never give up.

- It's okay to cry.

- Do something special for someone.

- Pat a back.

- Prejudice stinks.

I love you and I miss you. You both and Tina are such precious children. Mummy and I are so proud of you, and we adore you totally. All my love,

Daddy XXXOOO

Monday, July 1, 1996

My darling, darling Kimme and Jenny:

How are you doing without us? I hope you are having a great week. Thanks for looking after Mummy and keeping the house going. I know you are doing jobs around the house like emptying the dishwasher, and I appreciate that.

My hopes for you both and Tina are that you live happy, loving, and fulfilled lives. That your hearts are full of tranquility and that, while you have an inner peace and serenity, you are also ambitious to fulfill your potential. I also hope that you will constantly look at disadvantages, setbacks and breakdowns as opportunities to turn a lemon into lemonade. And always remember the freedom that is represented by the gap between stimulus and response.

I think you can tell a tremendous amount about a person from the books they read. If you want to learn more about me and what matters to me, you only have to look at the books in the study.

And here are some more "thoughts for a vital life":

- Worry about details.

- Don't be a bystander -- get into the fray.

- Surprise someone with a letter.

- You only fail if you don't try.

- Have pride in yourself.

- Find shoddy work repugnant.

- Be the best that you can be.

- Lead, follow, or get out of the way.

- Plan ahead.

- Work hard.

- Don't put things off.

- Take time to watch a sunset.

- Have fun -- life is glorious.

- Make promises and keep them.

- Abhor the common place and reject stuff (e.g., TV, food) which is junky and trash.

- Reach out to someone who needs help.

- Strive always for quality.

- Say something kind.

- Look for the best in others -- catch them doing something right.

- Have towering standards.

- It's not too late to become what you might have been.

- Say please.

- Plant a tree.

- Smile always, laugh often.

- Be thankful.

- Say thanks.

- Have soaring expectations.

- Love without qualification.

Kimme and Jenny, you are two wonderful daughters, just like Tina. We are so proud of you. All my love,

Daddy XXXOOO

Tuesday, July 2, 1996
My darling, darling Kimme and Jenny:
Tomorrow will be our last day in Moorea! We are getting up early in the morning to go on yet another dolphin/whale watching trip and, hopefully, to swim with them as well. Then, about lunchtime, we are going to enjoy a beach-side Tama'ara (a Tahitian feast). We will experience authentic Tahitian food, cooked in a pit filled with heated volcanic stones. We will also snorkel and swim, and Polynesian dancers from one of the local villages will entertain us. In the late afternoon, we will return to Tahiti for a few hours before leaving for the airport.

I am longing to see spinner dolphins. Apparently, they hurl themselves out of the water and spin with incredible acrobatics. What a sight it is going to be.

Most of all this week, I am looking forward to spending a lot of time with Tina and having a great time with her.

Jenny, are you remembering to use those green weights in your exercise routines?? (Ahmmm!!!)

Well, as one of Jenny's friends said to her recently, "got to go"!!! I love you both so much. All my love,

Daddy XXXOOO

Wednesday, July 3, 1996
My darling, darling, darling Kimme and Jenny:
Cannot wait to see you on Friday morning! I love you. All my love,

Daddy XXXOOO

September 10, 1996
IMPORTANT MEMO!
TO: KIMME, TINA AND JEN
RE: QUESTION ONE FROM YOUR DEVOTED DAD

Here is the question for you to answer below:

What would you like me to continue doing as a father that I am already doing? Please put your answer below. Thanks very much.

Dad
XXXOOO

September 10, 1996
IMPORTANT MEMO!
TO: KIMME, TINA AND JEN
RE: QUESTION TWO FROM YOUR DEVOTED DAD

Here is the question for you to answer below:

What would you like me to stop doing as a father that I am now doing? Please put your answer below. Thanks very much.

> Dad
> XXXOOO

September 10, 1996
IMPORTANT MEMO!
TO: KIMME, TINA AND JEN
RE: QUESTION THREE FROM YOUR DEVOTED DAD

Here is the question for you to answer below:

What would you like me to start doing as a father that I am not now doing? Please put your answer below. Thanks very much.

> Dad
> XXXOOO

Thursday, September 12, 1996
My darling Kimme, Tina and Jen:
I am on my way to Barcelona, Spain, where I will be meeting with hundreds of people involved in the IMAX industry, and giving various speeches and presentations about our new IMAX film, *Whales* -- which is due to be released in November -- and working on two new IMAX films on wolves and bears.

I will be away for about a week, and I will miss you very much. I am comforted by knowing that you will all look out for each other and that you will be having a great time enjoying school -- both your friends and your learning. I am also comforted by knowing that I will have an exciting and challenging time in all my various meetings and presentations.

Next Monday, I will leave Spain and fly directly to Jackson Hole in Wyoming for another big conference (the Jackson Hole Film Festival), where I will be making another presentation and having several meetings with film producers and television executives.

I am not going to leave you long letters on this trip, because I am enclosing the first 40 or so pages of the journal I have started to write to celebrate Kim's last year at home. Would you please, while I am away, read this over and mark up your copies with any changes you want in it? I may well have written about things that you don't want me to write about, or miss things that you do want me to write about, and I will gladly make any changes you want. No one has seen this yet, except you, and I have written it for you. I don't want it to contain anything that you don't want it to.

So, here is your assignment! Please read over the enclosed draft journal before I return on Wednesday, September 18. Thanks very much! I hope you enjoy it, and I hope you will learn something from it. Please be uninhibited in your criticisms and feedback because I want this journal to be as good as possible.

Please start work on this right away because I have another big assignment for you <u>tomorrow</u> night!

And here are some important words for you to learn:

1. **Infomercial**: A TV presentation that is really an extended advertisement. A combination of *information* and *commercial*.

2. **Wuss**: Wimp; a cowardly or ineffectual person.

3. **Mommy track**: A career path that allows a mother flexible or reduced work hours, but tends to slow or block advancement. (Kim -- a good topic for *Scribbler*!)

4. **Hot button**: An emotional, often controversial issue or concern that triggers an immediate, intense reaction; as, "The reporter pushed the ball player's *hot button* when he asked about a past drug conviction."

5. **Grunge**: A person who is untidy, shabby or obnoxious. Also, rock music incorporating elements of punk rock and heavy metal.

6. **Reality check**: Clarification of the facts, often by correcting a misconception; as, "The over-confident candidate got a rude *reality check* when she saw the latest poll results."

My precious loves, please take care of each other and Mummy. You are the most important people in the world to me, even though sometimes I don't always act like it -- you know, those <u>rare</u> occasions when I get a little <u>GRUMPY</u>!!

I adore you.

Daddy
XXXOOO

Friday, September 13, 1996
My darling Kimme, Tina and Jen:
How are you doing reading my draft journal?! I hope you are getting through it and enjoying it. Don't forget to mark it up with all the changes that you want. Please also circle any grammatical and spelling errors you catch.

Again, I am going to keep this letter short tonight because I have another <u>big</u> assignment for you. Please find enclosed a sheet of paper with a very important question on it, which is as follows:

What would you like me to continue doing as a father that I am already doing?

You each have a sheet of paper enclosed. Please take your copy and scribble on your answers. Please take this request seriously! The more detailed your answer, the better.

This is what one calls an exercise in listening to the "customer," or customer feedback!

I look forward very much to receiving your responses.

Tomorrow, you will have another BIG assignment!

I adore you. All my love,

> Daddy
> XXXOOO

Saturday, September 14, 1996

Darling Kimme, Tina and Jen:
How are you doing reading and correcting my journal? And how are you doing answering the important question I had for you last night?

Tonight, you have a <u>new</u> assignment! This assignment is, as you can see from the enclosure, to answer the following question:

What would you like me to stop doing as a father that I am now doing?

Again, please take this seriously and give me your honest and candid feedback. Just scribble your answer on the sheet of paper with your name on it.

I request that you do this by the day I get back, which is Wednesday, September 18.

Thank you very, very much.

Here are some important words for you to learn if you don't already know them:

1. **Torrid**: Scorching; intensely hot; as, "Lawns turned brown during those *torrid* summer weeks." Also, ardent; passionate (as in Jenny's feeling towards her multiple boyfriends!!).

2. **Maelstrom**: Large or violent whirlpool. Named after a famous and dangerous whirlpool off the northwest coast of Norway.

3. **Inclement**: Rough, stormy or harsh; as, "*Inclement* weather forced them to land at another air field."

4. **Inundate**: To flood; cover with water; as, "The overflowing Mississippi River *inundated* adjacent farmlands."

5. **Erosion**: A wearing away or gradual destruction of something; as, "Many shorelines suffer from *erosion*."

Kim, Tina and Jen, you are so very special. As I told you last week, about 11 billion people have lived on this planet over eons of time, but no one has ever existed on this earth who has been like any of you. You are unique.

I hope you are having a great time in school, having fun, enjoying yourselves, learning all you can, and indulging your curiosity.

I adore you. All my love,

> Daddy
> XXXOOO

Sunday, September 15, 1996

My darling Kimme, Tina and Jen:

Now, we come to the final question, as you can see from the enclosed:

What would you like me to start doing that I am not now doing?

As I have said in my earlier letters, please take this request seriously! Please take the sheet of paper enclosed with your name on it, and do your best to answer it to the best of your ability.

The deadline for doing this is this coming Wednesday, September 18, when I return home. Thank you very much for your help with this! Feel free to get Mummy's ideas and incorporate them with yours.

Tomorrow, I leave Spain to fly to Jackson Hole in Wyoming for another round of speeches, presentations and meetings. It will be fun!

I hope you all have a great week in school. Remember this week will never come again, so make the most of it!

A few good words to learn:

1. **Literate**: Educated; well-read; as, "She spent the evenings in civilized, *literate* conversation."

2. **Imprudent**: Rash; lacking judgment; as, "The actor's *imprudent* remark was widely reported in the London press."

3. **Copious**: Abundant; plentiful; as, "Samuel Johnson's work is not only *copious*, but remarkably consistent."

4. **Irascible**: Very irritable; easily angered.

5. **Farcical**: Ludicrous; absurd; as, "The actor's behavior was *farcical*."

6. **Deference**: A yielding to another's judgment; as, "She acted in *deference* to her mother's wish."

7. **Resplendent**: Dazzling or gloriously brilliant; as, "Kimberly looked *resplendent* in the new clothes she bought last Sunday."

By the way, Samuel Johnson came from a modest background, yet he became known as one of the most brilliant people of the 18th century. As I have mentioned to you before, in 1775, he created the first comprehensive English lexicography, setting the standard for all dictionaries. He was an extraordinary person and well worth studying.

I love you all so much. All my love,

Daddy
XXXOOO

Monday, September 16, 1996

My special treasures Kimme, Tina and Jen:

I will be home in two days! That means you have two days to finish reading my journal and scribbling on it all your changes and suggestions, and two days left to complete the three-part questionnaire about what you would like me to do or not do as a dad. Thank you for doing them!

Kimme and Tina, tomorrow you have your first varsity tennis match. I am sorry I will miss it, but I will be thinking about you. I hope you have lots of fun. I hope you win, but that is not important. It is great that you are both on the team.

Here are some good words for you to learn if you don't already know them:

1. **Veneration**: Deep reverence, respect or devotion; as, "John wrote of the scientist, 'No man ever looked upon her without *veneration*.'"

2. **Prowess**: Exceptional ability or valor; as, "People at Edgemoor Club admired the Shearer-Palmer girls' *prowess* at tennis."

3. **Deductive**: Reasoning that moves logically from the general to the specific; as, "All humans are mammals; you are human; therefore, you are a mammal."

4. **Mutable**: Changeable; variable; as, "He brooded on the *mutable* circumstances of life."

5. **Tactile**: Pertaining to touch; as, "*Tactile* contact to the earth was important to him."

6. **Milieu**: Surroundings, especially of a social nature; as, "Similarities in their social *milieu* linked Olivier and Tina."

7. **Redress**: To set right; remedy a wrong or injury by compensation; as, "He had no legal way to *redress* the wrong."

8. **Uncouth**: Awkward; without manners; strained; as, "As an old man, I will probably have an *uncouth* appearance."

9. **Gusto**: Keen pleasure; as, "With *gusto*, Jenny began to eat her peanut butter and jelly sandwich."

Giving you these words reminds me of something that happened to me when I was about 13 or 14. I became intensely frustrated with my lack of ability to write and talk. My vocabulary was limited and, as you already know, I started keeping a list of every new word I came across. And, over the next ten years, this did a lot to expand and enrich my vocabulary. I did one other thing, which I don't think I have ever told you. I created my own *Roget's Thesaurus*. I did this because, when I was writing or talking, I often got stuck because I could not think of a good word, or the precise word, that would satisfy me.

So I started focusing not only on new words, but on <u>ordinary</u> words. For example, if I thought of the word "happy," in order to give me more options when I was writing, I began to collect all the words that I could use instead of "happy" so I could introduce more subtle shades of meaning into my writing. So, in my own *Roget's Thesaurus* book, I would write "happy," and then I would start to collect words which were synonyms, such as delighted, glad, pleased, contented, gratified, satisfied, elated, thrilled, chuffed, euphoric, buoyant, optimistic, positive, carefree, merry, hilarious, smiling, laughing, joyful, jubilant, exultant, exhilarated, fortunate, auspicious, prosperous, successful, thriving, flourishing, fruitful, and so on.

I found this was very helpful because, when I was writing or talking, I would have many more words at my command. This gave me more confidence and helped me be more articulate.

You might ask: Why do this when books of synonyms already exist? The answer is that the physical act of writing down the word helped me to learn it.

Advice, advice, advice! Do dads ever stop giving advice? It is so BORING!

I love you so much I cannot tell you how much I love you. All my love,

Daddy
XXXOOO

Tuesday, September 17, 1996
My darling Kimme, Tina and Jenny:
I will be home tomorrow! I am racing home to get to the BE back-to-school night, as well as the Holton Arms 12th grade dinner. Both events are terribly important, and I cannot miss them.

See you tomorrow, my treasures! All my love,

Daddy
XXXOOO

Monday, October 14, 1996
My Darling Kimmie, Tina and Jen:
        I am in Los Angeles tonight at a big Hollywood awards dinner. This is the dinner where, two years ago, I received an award from the head of Disney, Michael Eisner. It will be fun!

        I have an intensive round of meetings today and Tuesday with producers, reporters, and various other people, and then I fly home on Tuesday night on the Red Eye, arriving at about 6:00 AM on Wednesday morning.

        I love you. Each of you is so incredibly special. Kim, I am longing to know how Princeton went! What (or who) was the Orange Key Guide? How did the Admissions Office interview go? And how was the talk with the Neuroscience Department?

        Tina, how did your lunch with Jacqui at the Thyme Restaurant go? Here are some things you might want to discuss in your article: The quality of the food, the quality of the service (for example, the politeness of the waiters, how long you had to wait to be served, etc.), the ambiance (intimate? noisy?), was the place clean, what did the place look like (spacious? light? dark?), would it be good for kids or is it better for older people or families, the location, etc., etc. I am very proud of you for writing for *Scribbler*. And thanks for solving the problem of the broken key in the front door! Let's play tennis on Wednesday evening. I enjoyed our game last night very much.

        Jen, how did Spanish go this morning? You were very self disciplined in getting up so promptly this morning. Where are you going to on your school field trip on Wednesday? How did your tennis lesson with Richard go today? I am enjoying the biography we are reading together of Stonewall Jackson. How would you like to have a dad like Stonewall?! No sirree Bob, I don't think so!!

Kimmie, Tina and Jen, enclosed is my current Personal Mission Statement for your review and comments. I hope you like it. It helps me keep on track and focused.

I adore you. See you on Wednesday.

> Love,
> Yer Ol' Dad
> XXXOOO

Tuesday, November 12, 1996
My Darling Kimmie, Tina and Jenny:

As you know, I left this afternoon for Boston for the world premiere tomorrow of our IMAX film, *Whales*. This is the fruition of six years of work! I wish you and the whole family were with me to celebrate because it will be an exciting event and lots of fun. Two hundred to 300 influential people will be there, including the press and, as the producer of the film, I will have a lead role in the press conference and various other events that are happening.

So, tomorrow will be an intensive day of giving speeches and answering questions. Then, after a final talk to about 300 people in the evening (at a second showing of *Whales*), I will head home by plane and, hopefully, will be with you by about 10 or 11 o'clock in the evening. I regret very much that I will miss the parent peer meeting at Holton Arms tomorrow night.

My loves, I have told you in the past (and I am sure not often enough) that I have learned so much from you. One of the things I have learned from being a parent is the importance of accentuating the positive -- catching people doing something right. It is quite common in some families and some organizations to do the reverse of this -- catching people doing something wrong. This is the way I tend to behave towards people and towards myself. But I cannot tell you enough how important it is to catch people doing something right -- and to praise progress. It is a mistake to wait for perfection until one praises.

This is something that I am still learning. I only began to learn it in the last few years or so, and I still have not fully learned it. (By learning it, I mean that this new behavior becomes transparent and happens naturally.)

Of course, this is one reason why we instituted in our family meetings the agenda item, "Encourage each other." This is to encourage all of us to catch each other doing something right.

You might have heard me say that I believe that parenting is a skill (like playing tennis or playing the piano) which can be learned. One specific parenting skill that can be learned is praising -- a key component of catching people doing something right. When I was growing up, the idea of learning "parenting skills" would have seemed quaint. Over the years, I have been trying to teach myself some of these skills. Again, I am not there yet, but I am getting there slowly (as I hope you have noticed!).

As I say, there is a skill in praising people, and it is a skill that people can learn. There is a similar skill in reprimanding people, in apologizing, and in goal-setting; but, in this letter, I am only going to focus on what it takes to give an effective praising.

Of course, I am assuming that there is clarity in the goals and purposes surrounding the situation. Here are the four keys to praising somebody in an effective way:

1. <u>Do it immediately</u>: A lot of people save giving praise until a later period, but that is a mistake. The time to praise somebody is <u>immediately</u>.

2. <u>Be specific</u>: To fulfill this part of the praising needs homework. To go to somebody and say they do a terrific job is not nearly as meaningful as saying, "You did an excellent job organizing your desk because I can see now that you can find any papers you want on it right away." Or "Thanks for getting your report in on time -- the summary at the end was concise and accurate, and was particularly helpful to me in the meeting I had yesterday afternoon." In other words, the key in this part of the praising is to be specific in <u>describing the behavior</u>. This is not the time to be evaluative (that comes next). Instead, be specific about the behavior that you are praising. As I say, this needs homework.

3. <u>Share your feelings</u>: At this point of the praising, you want to tell the person how you feel. Now is the time to be evaluative. For example, you might say, "I feel so proud of you that you wrote that editorial on drunkenness." Or "I am so pleased that you wanted to get to school at 7:30 so you could prepare for your test on mythology." Or "I am proud of you for taking Grandpa's idea and going to the computer and coming up with a mental puzzle of your own which is so challenging." You get the idea -- share with the person how you feel. This could be pride, joy, excitement, amazement, delight, or whatever.

4. <u>Encourage future good performance</u>: Here is where you end the praising by saying something like, "Keep up the good work" or (for a child) "You are a great kid" or whatever is appropriate.

So, that is one way to praise effectively. The whole thing might typically take anything from 15 seconds to a minute or so. You will be amazed how many people have not mastered this basic skill.

When you combine the skill of praising with the understanding of the importance of finding people doing something right (instead of finding them doing something wrong), you can become a powerful and effective parent, manager, leader or whatever.

Finding people doing something right is a key to a successful marriage, career, family, or operation of any kind. As you all know, I have a lot to learn in this area; and because I am conveying this information in this letter, I am not claiming I have learned how to do it myself yet. I am just a beginner in this area. I will become competent if I keep practicing.

One footnote to this: Some people have positive thoughts, but forget to express them. This is sad because positive thoughts not expressed aren't worth diddley squat. Again, that is why we instituted the "encouragement" agenda item in our family meetings, and why recently we have added the agenda item of "rocks" in the family meetings so that all of us have a chance to express deep and joyful thoughts. I was fascinated the other night when you, Kimmie, came down (as part of your psychology homework) and asked us all what our major concerns were. What a wonderful question!

Now, here are some important words for you to be familiar with:

1. **Tranquility**: Calmness, serenity, peacefulness; as, "The tranquility of the music that Daddy played at dinner attracted his three daughters to a new level of listening."

2. **Intercession**: Petition, prayer or entreaty on behalf of another; as, "The doctor's intercession helped Granny get over her illness."

3. **Atone**: To repent and make up for a previous wrong; as, "Daddy atoned for his grumpiness by apologizing and being cheerful!"

4. **Millennium**: Period of joy and peace; The anticipated thousand-year reign of holiness under Jesus Christ; as, "According to Auntie Yvette, sin will be greatly reduced in the Palmer-Shearer family during the millennium."

5. **Charitable**: Kind, loving and generous; as, "Daddy should make a bigger effort to be charitable to nutty, unintelligent morons who believe in astrology."

6. **Rapture**: Ecstasy, intense joy in a religious or other experience; as, "The rapture of Kimmie and Tina watching a Brad Pitt movie."

7. **Solicitous**: Showing care or anxious concern; as, "Grandpa is solicitous about Granny's comfort."

8. **Magnanimous**: Noble-minded; generous in feeling or conduct; as, "Daddy is over-magnanimous when it comes to giving out allowances to his children!"

9. **Mantra**: Sacred phrase, word or sound repeated continually while meditating to help focus one's attention.

10. **Humility**: Showing modesty in attitude and behavior; as, "St. Francis of Assisi exemplified humility, for he was free of self-importance."

11. **Sanguine**: Cheerfully optimistic; confident about the future; as, "As Mummy and Daddy have sanguine expectations about their daughters' futures."

12. **Nirvana**: A time of peace, bliss and enlightenment. For Hindus and Buddhists, freedom from suffering, desire and earthly attachments when the soul is absorbed into the Supreme Being; as, "A happy family dinner is like Nirvana for me."

13. **Congenial**: Compatible; having similar natures; as, "The girls were congenial sisters in our family." It also means social and pleasant.

Finally, I am enclosing the latest draft of my Journal celebrating Kimmie's last year at home. There is an extra copy for Granny and Grandpa. Please give it to them. Would you all (including Granny and Grandpa) review it and mark on any changes you want on it? No one else has seen it yet. Thanks very much.

I love you so much. You are all flourishing this year in school. (I will leave out the specifics of that praising for now!) And Mummy and I, as well as Granny and Grandpa and Nana, are all extraordinarily proud of each of you.

All my love,
Daddy
XXXOOO

Enclosures

1997

Monday, January 6, 1997

My Treasures Kimmie, Tina and Jen:

This will be short, as I have run out of time! Have a great three days when I am away in Seattle. As you know, we are opening our *Whales* IMAX film there and it should be a lot of fun.

Kim and Tina -- good luck preparing for your exams! Jen -- good luck with your science experiment! I know you will all do well.

Enclosed is an important book by Bonnie Parsley entitled *The Choice Is Yours*. It was recommended by Margarita Kelly in *The Washington Post*. I hope you all read it. I would like to read it after you.

See you Wednesday. I adore you. All my love.

Dad
XXXOOO

Tuesday, January 7, 1997

My Precious Loves: Kimmie, Tina and Jen:

Thanks for reading my journal, Kimmie, and giving me your feedback. You want more information to be in there about what you are doing -- NO PROB! Tina and Jen -- have you read it? Please read it if you haven't and give me your changes, corrections and feedback. Thanks!

Here is what could happen if you are a little deaf like me:

When God gave out brains, I thought she said trains -- and I missed mine!

When she gave out good looks, I thought she said books -- and I didn't want any.

When she said noses, I thought she said roses -- and I ordered a big red one.

Boy! Am I a mess.

I told you I'm a funny guy!

Love ya', adore ya',

Dad
XXXOOO

Tuesday, January 14, 1997

My Three Loves,
KIMMIE!! TINA!! JENNY!!

You each are so incredibly special to Mummy and me. You each have enriched my life beyond words. I am one lucky dad to have three such wonderful daughters. Each of you is unique. Thank you for being you, and for giving Mummy and me so much love and joy. No parents could be prouder.

I love you!! See you Wednesday.

Daddy
XXXOOO

P.S.: I am New Orleans for a huge TV convention. Do you remember I met Jane Seymour last year?!

Wednesday, February 12, 1997

My darling Kimmie, Tina and Jenny:

As you know, I will be in Los Angeles for a couple of days for the premiere of *Whales* at the IMAX theater in Los Angeles. I wish you were going to be with me! It will be a big event and lots of fun. Hundreds of invitations have gone out to "movers and shakers" in Los Angeles with my name on the invite as the "special guest." Boy, am I important!!!

I will be back late Friday evening (probably around 10:00pm if my plane gets in on time) and I look forward to seeing you very much then Jenny (and you will be home late that night yourself because you have a birthday party to attend), but I won't see you Tina until you get back from your ski trip with Lizzie on Sunday, and I won't see you Kimmie until Sunday after lunch when you get back from your Model UN Conference.

Mummy and I love to see you all relishing life so much and having so much fun!

Here is a story from my childhood. When I was about 11 years old, for reasons I cannot now remember but which may have been connected to my starting at boarding school and being away from home, I started struggling with math and falling behind. (In England we call this subject "maths" not "math" as you do here in America.)

Luckily for me, my father saw this happening and arranged for me to have some private tutoring from a teacher named Mr. Booth. What was extraordinary about this situation is that I only had four or five lessons from him and I remember being conscious that he was teaching me little. Nevertheless, the impact of these tutoring sessions was immense. My marks started to go up and my self-confidence was restored. From then on, I always did well in math.

Without my father's intervention, I probably would have found math a colossal headache and a source of much frustration for the rest of my school career instead of a pleasure and a source of much success.

So here is the lesson I learned from that: whenever I am in trouble of any kind, it is important to reach out and get help. That is one of the secrets of success -- not being afraid to ask questions and ask for assistance. The most successful people do it constantly and do it relentlessly.

I love you more than I can say and I think of you every moment of the day. Each of you is so incredibly special.

All my love,
Daddy
XXX OOO

Thursday, February 13, 1997

My darling, darling three treasures, Kimmie, Tina and Jenny:
    Here is a memory: As you know, there were six of us in our family when we were growing up.

Granny and Grandpa plus the four boys: Jeremy, Timothy, Jonathan and me.

I remember thinking one day when I was about 8 or 9 years old and washing up in the kitchen with the counter crowded with dirty plates that how much easier everything would be if there were fewer children in the family. (Of course, if there had been fewer children, I wouldn't have been around to think this!)

The house just seemed too crowded for comfort and I remember being struck forcefully with the notion of how much easier everything would be if we were a family of say four instead of a family of six. (Incidentally, I think the size of our family is just perfect.)

In poor countries in the Third World, parents often think the reverse of this -- the more children they have, the more hands there are available to work in the fields. So you often find large families in the developing world. (Let me just say in passing that researchers have discovered that probably the best way to reduce the world's population and persuade people to have smaller families is to empower women. The more educated and empowered women are in the Third World, the fewer children they tend to have.)

Here is another memory from my time at the Royal Naval College Manadan in Plymouth when I was about 17 or 18. A local priest came to give a talk to all the Naval officers at the college. I don't remember the topic but what I do remember is that he looked unimpressive and of little consequences as he stood being introduced waiting to give his talk.

However, when he got up to the podium, he turned out to be immensely funny and his whole talk had the audience, including me, in fits of laughter.

This experience reminded me of the power of humor. I had already noticed from my time in the Navy that many great Naval leaders I knew or knew of, had this ability to make people laugh, especially in tense situations.

When people laugh together, they trust each other more. Sometime I will try to work out in my own mind why that is the case.

Incidentally, one of the funniest remarks I ever heard was said by a very earnest and serious guy in a standup comedy class I once attended. He said: "What if everybody else thinks you're funny but you don't think you're funny?" When I heard him say this, I convulsed with laughter but I noticed that no one else in the class found it funny. I felt like saying to him : "You're not saying that seriously are you?!"

Each of you has a wonderful sense of humor and you have enriched the lives of Mummy and me so much with your jokes, smiles, humor and laughter. Thank you!

I love you so much. Jenny -- see you on Friday evening. Tina -- see you on Sunday at about 5:00pm. And Kimmie -- see you on Sunday when we pick you up from Holton Arms at about 1:00pm.

I love you.

Daddy

XXXOOO

Tuesday, March 25, 1997

My Darling Kimmie, Tina and Jenny:

I am writing this letter to Kimmie as well, even though she is not at home! The reason I am doing that is that, as you all know, I am going to have breakfast with Kimmie in Florida tomorrow, and I will hand-deliver this letter to her!

I hope you are having a wonderful weekend in Florida with Nana, Kimmie. I am sure you are. That is a wonderful idea of yours to help Nana write a book about what it is like to be a widow. I hope you are having lots of fun also with Erin, Suzy and Steve. Please give them all my love.

Tina, you are enjoying a well-deserved break from school this week. You have been working hard and doing well at school. The work is tough, but you are rising to the challenge and, if you remain as determined, diligent and tenacious as you have been since you arrived at Holton Arms, your grades will remain high and even get better. And we love how well you are doing in sports. Well done this week for volunteering with Lauren at Suburban Hospital and getting some of those community hours under your belt. It is a great experience.

Jenny, your school vacation is next week when, sadly, I will be away in Tucson for the NWF annual meeting. I hope you have lots of fun with your friends at soccer camp.

Kimmie, Tina and Jenny, please find enclosed the latest entries from my Journal celebrating Kimmie's last year at home. No one else has seen this yet. I will make any changes you want in it. Please look it over and mark the things you want deleted or added. I welcome all changes. I want this to be something that you will enjoy reading with your children and grandchildren. So think about what else in your lives you would like me to write about, and I will do my best to do it. Kimmie, you wanted more about your activities. Am I doing better in that regard? The most likely mistake I have made is that I have put something in my Journal which embarrasses you. Let me know if you see anything like that and I will delete it. Anyway, I hope you enjoy reading it, and I look forward to getting your changes.

Incidentally, I never received any feedback from any of you from my Journal entries from January 1-5 (pages 100-133). It may be that you never got around to reading it, or you read it but forgot to tell me that you had no changes. Will you please check around your desks to see if you can find it? Thanks.

Jenny and I have read some wonderful biographies recently which I want to tell you about in this letter.

The first one was a biography of Leonardo DaVinci. What I learned from this book was how important Leonardo's father was to Leonardo's development. His father encouraged Leonardo to pursue whatever interests he had, and Leonardo was interested in literally everything. He was consumed with curiosity about the whole world, and loved to experiment and explore. His father had a very dull job as a notary and was eager for his son to do better. At one point, as Leonardo grew up, his father thought that he was fickle and would start lots of different things and never finish them, and he was worried that his son would end up becoming a notary after all.

His father worried about Leonardo and did not know what would become of him. As he continued to pursue his multiple interests, his father suddenly understood that his son was not fickle and not half-hearted in his interests. Leonardo was, in fact, interested in everything and had an extraordinary ability for everything. Of course, as we now know, he grew up to become everything his father thought he would engineer, architect, botanist, painter, inventor. He became all this and more because he was one of the greatest thinkers and creators of all time. He lived from 1452 to 1519.

Jenny and I read another book called *The Beagle And Mr. Flycatcher -- A Story Of Charles Darwin*. One thing I learned from this book is how a father can so easily misunderstand a son. Charles Darwin was born in England in 1809 (in fact, the same birthday as Abraham Lincoln). He came from a family of successful intellectuals (both his father and grandfather were doctors of medicine). However, Charles Darwin seemed to be a misfit in this family of energetic and successful people. He liked an easygoing life -- taking solitary walks, collecting beetles, and romping with his dogs. His father got very frustrated and angry with him. Then, at the age of 23, Charles Darwin got the opportunity to go on a five-year voyage around the world aboard HMS Beagle. As the ship's naturalist, he was affectionately called "Mr. Flycatcher" by the crew. This journey changed Darwin's life and led him to develop his theory of evolution, one of the most important theories of modern scientific thought. When Darwin returned from his trip on HMS Beagle, his father finally became proud of him.

Jenny and I also read a biography of Robert E. Lee, the great Southern Civil War general, who was born in 1807. His father was a failure as a father and abandoned his family and spent their money unwisely. But, despite this, Robert E. Lee turned out not only to be a brilliant and courageous general, but also a wonderful father.

Robert E. Lee's duties as an engineer in the Army took him away from home for months at a time. During these absences, he wrote long letters telling his seven children about his adventures and how much he missed them. He was also a stern disciplinarian who had strong opinions and expected to be obeyed. His sons, he believed, must be kept to a high standard so they wouldn't become failures like their grandfather. He demanded reports on their progress on everything from mathematics to swimming. He made regular room inspections, as in an Army barracks, to make sure everything was neat and clean. The children were constantly lectured on their reading habits. The word "can't" was banned from the children's vocabulary. By all accounts, he was very happy as a husband and father.

I love you each so much. Mummy and I are so lucky to have three such wonderful children.

I love you.
Daddy
XXXOOO

Monday, March 31, 1997
My Darling, Kimmie, Tina and Jenny:

I miss you! And I love you! I am on my way to Tucson for the NWF annual meeting. I will be back very late next Saturday night -- I will be racing back in order that we can all go to the Kennedy Center on Sunday to see the dance performance.

Jenny, I am so sorry to be away this week while you are on vacation. I hope you have a wonderful soccer camp on Monday, Tuesday and Wednesday. I wonder if you will go to Mummy's office on Thursday? Anyway, have a great time.

Kimmie and Tina, good luck getting back to school. I hope you have both had a restful and relaxing break. I am so sorry I am going to miss your softball games this week. You are both playing on Saturday, aren't you? Good luck!

Here is a memory from my childhood: Jon and I were about 7 or 8. We had invented a project that we were wildly excited about. I wish I could remember what it was. Perhaps it was something we were building or making. Whatever it was, it was something we had created and were deeply interested in. Normally, we would wander back from school, taking about 45 minutes to walk from Dulwich Hamlet to our home on Dulwich Common. Our energy was low and we were not motivated in any way to speed up the process of getting home. But the day we had this project, we were just brimming with energy, overflowing with excitement, and totally focused on this project. It was a wonderful feeling that I will never forget. It was as though the world had suddenly become alive and life had purpose. We raced home from school, bubbling with excitement, our bodies filled with energy, determination and excitement. In some ways, I have spent my life trying to recapture that sense of purpose, meaning, focus and delight. I think the secret has to do with serving other people, doing something bigger than yourself, and somehow transcending ones own little clod of petty interests. It is important to serve a cause which is going to leave the world a better place.

You have probably already thought of this, but if you would like to drop a note to Grandpa encouraging him to get better, I know he would appreciate it.

Did you read the extracts from my Journal which I left you to review last Wednesday when I was in Florida? I hope you enjoy it, and I am eager to get your changes.

I love you each so much. You are so unique and precious, and I love you with all my heart.

Daddy
XXXOOO

Tuesday, April 1, 1997

My Darling, Darling, Kimmie, Tina and Jenny:

I mentioned yesterday that Grandpa was not well. Here is a lovely poem by David Meuel I recently came across which relates to Grandpa:

When it was time to climb the stairs that night,
dad went first, like he always did.
He put his right hand on the railing, then dragged each stone foot up
in slow and strained, supremely careful moves.
And together we inched our way along.

As we climbed, I thought
of the pack trips we used to take.
He was in front then, too,
his strong, stocky legs guiding us
over smooth white passes
that held the sky like open hands.
He was in front then, too.

But now his legs were thin and weak,
dry sticks still clinging to the ancient oak.
Now his high country was a room one story up
where craggy ledges hung
in wooden picture frames
and plants and flowers grew in round red earthen pots.

So, to the room we climbed.
And, as we did, I saw in his eyes
an evening calm.
This was not a time for tears, they said,
simply a time for less.

Getting old is no fun, but if anybody can "do it" with courage, humor and dignity, it will be my father. All my love,

Daddy
XXXOOO

Wednesday, April 2, 1997

My Precious Three Loves, Kimmie, Tina and Jenny:

I hope soccer camp is going well, Jenny! And I hope school is going well for you, Kimmie and Tina! Yesterday, I gave two big presentations -- one to the National Wildlife Federation Endowment Trustees, and a second to the National Wildlife Federation Board.

I know you are going to a concert this coming Saturday, Kimmie. Are you going, Tina? Please take care of Mummy's concerns with regard to your safety. Thanks.

I have been reading a wonderful book recently, called *The Fifth Discipline -- The Art And Practice Of The Learning Organization*, by Peter Senge. He uses the term "personal mastery" to talk about the discipline of personal growth and learning. He says that people with high levels of personal mastery are continually expanding their ability to create the results in life they truly seek.

Here is an extract from his book:

Personal mastery goes beyond competence and skills, though it is grounded in competence and skills. It goes beyond spiritual unfolding or opening, although it requires a spiritual growth. It means approaching one's life as a creative work, living life from a creative, as opposed to reactive, viewpoint.... When personal mastery becomes a discipline -- an activity we integrate into our lives -- it embodies two underlying movements. The first is continually clarifying what is important to us. We often spend too much time coping with problems along our path that we forget why we are on that path in the first place. The result is that we only have a dim, or even inaccurate, view of what is really important to us. The second is continually learning how to see current reality more clearly. We've all known people entangled in counterproductive relationships, who remain stuck because they keep pretending everything is alright. Or we have been in meetings where everyone says, 'We're on course relative to our plan,' yet an honest look at current reality would show otherwise. In moving toward a desired destination, it is vital to know where you are now. The juxtaposition of vision (what we want) and a clear picture of current reality (where are relative to what we want) generates what we call 'creative tension,' a force to bring them together, caused by the natural tendency of tension to seek resolution. The essence of personal mastery is learning how to generate and sustain creative tension in our lives.... People with a high level of personal mastery share several basic characteristics. They have a special sense of purpose that lies behind their visions and goals. *For such a person, a vision is a calling, rather than simply a good idea*.... They have learned how to perceive and work with forces of change, rather than resist those forces. They are deeply inquisitive, committed to continually seeing reality more and more accurately. They feel connected to others and to life itself. Yet, they sacrifice none of their uniqueness. They feel as if they are part of a larger creative process, which they can influence but cannot unilaterally control.... People with a high level of personal mastery live in a continual learning mode. They never 'arrive'.... Personal mastery is not something you possess. It is a process. It is a lifelong discipline. People with a high level of personal mastery are acutely aware of their ignorance, their incompetence, their growth areas. And they are deeply self-confident. Paradoxical? Only for those who do not see that 'the journey is the reward'.... Truly mature people build and hold deep values, making commitments to goals larger than themselves, are open, exercise free will, and continually strive for an accurate picture of reality. They also have a capacity for delayed gratification, which makes it possible for them to aspire to objectives which others would disregard, even considering 'the impact of their choices on succeeding generations.' It is a deficiency in modern society's commitment to human development that we do not pursue emotional development with the same intensity with which we pursue physical and intellectual development. This is all the more unfortunate because full emotional development offers the greatest degree of leverage in attaining our full potential.

Isn't that great? I like all that very much, and I hope you do. I miss you and I love you all so much. I can't wait to get home and see you on Saturday. All my love,

Daddy
XXXOOO

Thursday, April 3, 1997
My Treasures, Kimmie, Tina and Jenny:
I hope your week is going well. I was reading the magazine, *Family Fun*, recently and there was an article under the generic heading "My Great Idea" called *Table Topics*. It was subtitled "To Add Spice To Your Family's Next Meal, Try Serving Up A Basketful Of Tantalizing Questions."

Here is the idea. Let me know what you think of it. I would love to make it a mealtime tradition for us all. Supposing I am in charge at dinnertime of "Table Topics." I would place six folded strips of paper in a basket in the center of the dinner table. On each one would be a question or a topic to discuss. You can either answer the question <u>or</u> talk about something of your choice. It's a game! The idea is to give the speaker undivided attention. There would be two rules to keep things running smoothly: We may choose to talk about whatever we wish, rather than the question drawn; and we would allow the speaker uninterrupted time (within reason) until she/he requests comments. The writer in *Family Fun* ends her article as follows:

As the children have grown older, I have slipped in topics for which we must draw on current events and our opinions on local and international issues. We have learned interesting facts about the kids' school subjects and laughed long and loud at our foibles. Best of all, our practice of regular communication has made it easier for us to share disappointments and difficulties that otherwise might have been masked beneath tantrums or silence. We have discovered a lot about each other.

I like this idea a lot, and so I started to think of examples of questions. Here are a few I thought of:

➢ Discuss something fun you have done in the last few days.

➢ Discuss a good book you have read lately.

➢ Describe something embarrassing that has happened to you.

➢ If you could be an animal, which one would it be?

➢ What is the best, worst thing you have ever eaten?

➢ What is something you would like to be doing in ten years?

➢ What is your earliest memory?

I think a great source of further questions is in those two books I (or one of you) once gave Mummy called *If... Questions For The Game Of Life*.

I cannot tell you how much Mummy and I love each of you -- more than all the grains of sand in the world and more than all the stars in the sky. All my love,

Daddy
XXXOOO

Friday, April 4, 1997
Darling Kimmie, Tina and Jenny:
I will be home tomorrow night, and I cannot wait to see you!

One of the books I have been reading recently is called *School Girls -- Young Women's Self Esteem And The Confidence Gap* by Peggy Orenstein. She wrote it in association with the American Association of University Women. That organization, in 1990, had conducted a ground-breaking poll that highlighted how, as young girls reached adolescence, their self-esteem plummets. The conclusion of this study (an investigation that involved over 3,000 girls and boys between the ages of 9 and 15 and cut across ethnic and regional lines) was alarming: There is a crisis in this country regarding the way we educate our daughters.

In spite of the changes in women's roles in society, many girls still fall into traditional patterns of low self-image and self-censorship. I am glad to say that you three do not. Some girls begin first grade with the same levels of skill and ambition as boys, but, all too often, by the time they reach high school, their doubts have crowded out their dreams. They emerge from adolescence with reduced expectations of life, and much less confidence in themselves and in their abilities than boys have.

Orenstein's book is shocking. It shows that by sixth grade, both boys and girls have learned to equate maleness with opportunity and femininity with constraint. Again, I am so proud that you three have not learned this. Too often, though, girls have learned to see boys as freer, with fewer concerns, and ultimately more powerful. Girls' diminished sense of self means that, often unconsciously, they take on a second-class accommodating status.

Here is an extract from Peggy Orenstein's introduction:

Without a strong sense of self, girls will enter adulthood at a deficit: They will be less able to fulfill their potential, less willing to take on challenges, less willing to defy tradition in their career choices, which means sacrificing economic equity. Their successes will not satisfy and their failures will be more catastrophic, confirming their own self-doubt. They will be less prepared to weather the storms of adult life, more likely to become depressed, hopeless, and self-destructive. In order to raise healthier girls, we must look carefully at what we tell them, often unconsciously, often subtly, about their worth relative to boys'. We must look at what girls value about themselves -- the 'areas of importance' by which they measure their self-esteem -- as well as the potential sources of strength and competence that, too often, they learn to devalue.

I was shocked in reading this book to see how our schools tend to subdue girls into a "disengaged silence."

I am so pleased that you girls go (or, in Jenny's case, will go) to Holton Arms. I just wish every girl in this country had the same opportunity that you have. Mummy and I are incredibly proud how you, Kimmie and Tina, have taken advantage of the opportunities that Holton Arms has offered you, and we know that Jenny will do the same when she gets to ninth grade.

I cannot wait to see you tomorrow night! I adore you more than I can say. All my love,

Daddy
XXXOOO

Sunday, June 15, 1997
Darling Jenny:
How did your softball game go today? I hope you had some terrific hits and some great catches. I wish I had been there to watch you. As you are reading this, Kimmie, Tina and I are on our way to Alaska. We will miss you and Mummy very much while we are there, but I know you will have a great time at home (and at the shore), and we will have a great time in Alaska.

We are flying into Anchorage, which is a frontier city founded in 1915.

Here is a joke for you:

The two ladies were sitting in the living room, waiting for their hostess, who was slightly delayed. The daughter of the family was with them, on the theory that she would keep the visitors occupied during the wait. The child was, perhaps, six years old, snub-nosed, freckled, buck-toothed and bespectacled. She maintained a deep silence, and the two ladies peered doubtfully at her. Finally, one of them muttered to the other, 'Not very pretty, I fear,' carefully spelling the key word. Whereupon the child piped up, 'But awful smart!!'

Jenny, you are very, very special, (and <u>both</u> pretty <u>and</u> smart!) and I cannot tell you how much I love you. Have a great day in school tomorrow -- your last week in fourth grade!

Love and kisses,

Daddy
XXXOOO

Monday, June 16, 1997

Hi Jenny!

I love you! And I miss you! Today we are in Anchorage and we will have a big dinner tonight with all the people joining us on the trip. It is an exciting and interesting group of people, and the dinner will be a lot of fun.

Tomorrow we go to the small fishing town of Homer. The first settlers of this area were Dena'ina Indians, an Athabascan tribe who lived in this area undisturbed for thousands of years. Then, in 1786, came Russian fur traders, who organized trading posts along the rivers. In 1948, gold was discovered, and the Alaskan wilderness was opened.

Jenny, here is a joke:

> There is a tale (not to be found in the pages of Conan Doyle, you may be sure) concerning Sherlock Holmes and John Watson on board a train. They passed a herd of sheep, and Watson said, 'A sizeable herd, Holmes, eh?'
>
> 'Exactly seven hundred and eighty-four in number, my dear Watson,' said Holmes sleepily.
>
> 'Good heavens, Holmes,' said Watson, 'Surely, you can't have counted them.'
>
> 'Not directly,' said Holmes. 'I made use of a simple trick any schoolchild knows. I merely counted the legs and divided by four.'

Jenny, I adore you. Have a great day in school tomorrow. All my love.

Daddy
XXXOOO

Tuesday, June 17, 1997

My Darling, Darling Jenny!

How was school today? I hope you had a great day.

You know we are putting solar energy on our house? Here is a joke about solar energy:

> On the glorious day of July 20, 1969, when the first human being stepped onto the surface of the moon, an Englishman said to an American friend, 'That is a great achievement, but we English will do much better. We are planning a manned expedition

to the sun.'

'To the sun?' exclaimed the astonished American. 'But the heat? The light? The radiation?'

The Englishman chuckled. 'Do you think we English are fools? We will send the expedition at night.'

Today, we arrived at the Kachemak Bay Wilderness Lodge which overlooks a commanding sweep of mountains, sea and sky. This lodge offers unparalleled opportunities for wildlife viewing. Seals bask on outlying sandbars, otters play in the tide, and bald eagles circle overhead. I wish you and Mummy were here!

Jenny, I love you so much. You are a wonderful, wonderful girl and so incredibly special. All my love,

Daddy
XXXOOO

Wednesday, June 18, 1997
My Darling Treasure Jenny!
How are you doing? Tomorrow is your last day of school! I hope you have a super day. Here is a joke in case any of your friends are sad about the end of school:

Anderson and Johnson sat silently over their beers, each sunk in misery. Finally, Anderson heaved a sigh and said, 'I wish I were dead.' Johnson sighed in his turn and said, 'If only I felt that good.'

And here is another joke:

Robinson, who stuttered badly, said with impassioned earnestness, 'I t-t-tell you, nnnations must ab-b-bandon all s-s-selfish cons-s-sideration and c-c-come togethgether in wwworld union if cha-cha-chaos is to b-b-be prev-v-vented.' Williams, listening skeptically, said, 'Sure, that's easy enough for you to say.'

Either today or tomorrow, we are going to spend a day at remote Chenik Camp where brown bears (grizzlies) gather to gorge on the salmon the spawn in the streams. One of the largest carnivores in the world, these bears can reach nearly one thousand pounds in weight and stand nine feet tall!

Jenny, I adore you. All my love,

Daddy
XXXOOO

Thursday, June 19, 1997
My Darling Jenny!
Today was your last day of school! And tomorrow you go to the beach to be with Erin, Suzy, Steve, Nana and Henry. I hope you have a wonderful trip and a wonderful time at the shore.

Here is a joke:

Little Johnnie, aged 5, was bending over a sheet of paper, guiding his pencil with most meticulous thoroughness. His mother, smiling at him fondly, said, 'What are you drawing, Johnnie?'

'A picture of God,' said Johnnie, without looking up.

'But, Johnnie, nobody knows what God looks like,' said his mother.

And Johnnie said, 'They will, once I am finished.'

I think of you and Mummy all the time. I know you are having a great time. Kimmie, Tina and I are having a great time in Alaska. I hope you enjoyed the celebration tonight at the Sugrues. All my love,

Daddy
XXXOOO

Friday, June 20, 1997
My Darling Jenny:
I hope you had a safe trip up to the shore today. Please give my love to Nana, Suzy, Steve, Erin and Henry.

Here is a joke:

Bill and Joe, neither noted for vast erudition, had found the perfect fishing spot, had done well, and now found it was time to turn their rented motorboat back to shore.

Bill said, 'Gee, if we could only find this place tomorrow.'

Joe said, 'Mark it, let's carve a notch right here on the side of the boat, right where we have been casting the line.'

Bill said, 'Oh, you jerk, that won't work. Suppose they hand us a different boat tomorrow?'

And here is a knock-knock joke (in case you're facing an audience of chemists):

Knock knock!
Who's there?
Ammonia!
Ammonia who?
Ammonia bird in a gilded cage.

Jenny, have a wonderful time at the beach! I adore you. All my love,

Daddy
XXXOOO

Saturday, June 21, 1997
My Darling, Darling, Darling Jenny:
I hope you enjoy the following joke:

The Rosenthals had an outstandingly happy and successful marriage, and Mr. Rosenthal was once asked to what he attributed this remarkable situation.

'It's simple,' he said. 'Division of labor. My wife makes all the small, routine decisions. She decides what house we buy, where we go on vacation, where the kids go to private schools, if we should change my job, and so on.'

'And you?'

'I make the big, fundamental decisions.' I decide whether the United States should declare war on China, if Congress should appropriate money for a manned expedition to Mars, and so on.'

Here is a variation on that:

The husband has explained the division of decisions, small ones to his wife and large ones to himself, as the method for making marriage happy. He describes his wife's small decisions, and the questioner says, 'And what kind of big decisions do you make?'

The husband answers, 'I don't know. Big decisions haven't come up yet.'

All my love,

Daddy
XXXOOO

Sunday, June 22, 1997
My Darling Jenny:
I admire Winston Churchill, the great British statesman. Here is a story about him:

It is said that a hostile voter once accosted Churchill after an election in which the latter had retained his seat in Parliament. The voter said with a sneer, 'I presume we may expect you to continue to be humbly subservient to the powerful interests that control your vote.'

To which Churchill replied with a growl, 'I'll thank you to keep my wife's name out of this.'

I miss you!! All my love,

Daddy
XXXOOO

Monday, June 23, 1997

Jenny, My Darling, Darling Daughter:

Here is a joke for you:

On one occasion, the Jones' were having a fight. Mr. Jones had managed to make his way into a closet just one step ahead of the pursuing Mrs. Jones. He locked the door and stood there panting. Mrs. Jones banged peremptorily on the door. 'Come out of there, you worm!'

'I will not,' shouted Mr. Jones from within.

'Do as I say,' thundered Mrs. Jones.

'I won't,' yelled her husband. 'I'll show you who's master of the house.'

Jenny, I adore you. I cannot wait to see you when we get home. All my love,

Daddy
XXXOOO

Tuesday, June 24, 1997

My Darling Jenny:

See you tomorrow! I love you! Love and kisses,

Daddy
XXXOOO

Tuesday, July 1, 1997

My Darling, Darling Kim, Tina and Jenny:

What three wonderful daughters you are! One reason I love to write these letters is that it's easier for me (with my inherent limitations by virtue of being male!) to express my feelings in writing than face-to-face. I have so many things to thank you each for. Here are just a few of them:

➢ Thank you for the opportunity you have given me to love you.

➢ Thanks for the opportunity to play with you.

➢ Thanks for the opportunity just to be with you.

➢ Thank you for uncovering parts of me (relating to responsibility, feelings and nurturing) that, without you, would have remained dormant within me.

➢ Thank you for the opportunity to write to you and to talk with you through these letters and through my journal.

➢ Thank you for being so loving and for forgiving me for my many foibles (e.g., my occasional grumpiness!), and forgiving me when I sometimes fail to do as well as a father as I should do.

- Thank you for having the most exceptionally wonderful, loving, devoted and dedicated mother in the whole world!

- Thank you for enriching my life in ways that are deep and immeasurable.

- Thank you for being you.

At the dinner that Mummy and I went to on Saturday night, given by Steve and Janice Lee, I sat next to Lynn Heinz. I was telling her about this journal and about Sharon's biographies. I told her that I can write in these letters things that I would never get around to saying, and this is one of them: All your lives you will face exciting challenges, adventures, adversity, and trauma. Here are some of the things that I want for you as you live your lives with courage, honesty and energy:

- I want you always to love, cherish and support each other.

- I want you to make a difference to those around you and to be a source of inspiration and leadership.

- I want you to live your life according to the deepest principles you can find.

- I want you to have a written personal mission statement.

- I want you to renew yourselves daily with exercise, reading, reflection, laughter, love and friendship.

- I want you to have a network of wonderful, trustworthy, trusting and loyal friends.

- I want you to know you have Mummy's and my undying love and unwavering commitment.

- I want you to relish learning and be deeply curious about the world and to avoid any kind of pseudo-science (like astrology or channeling).

- I want you to be loyal to people who are absent.

- I want you to have careers which give you a great sense of fulfillment and which leave the world a better place.

- I want you to be bold and ambitious, but to have a deep inner sense of tranquility, joy and peace.

Kim, Tina and Jenny, I love you so much. I'll be home tomorrow. All my love,

Daddy
XXXOOO

P.S.:   FYI, I am in New York City to meet with Nikon, The Outdoor Life Network, the consultant who works with me on movies (Betsy Stahl), several film producers, several major donors, and with the PBS station in New York City, Channel 13, for whom we are producing a one-hour documentary on bison.

September 5, 1997

Darling Kimmie:

Have you recovered yet from last night's party??! I hope you had fun and didn't drink too much water!

Your $500 check from Nana arrived safely yesterday.

Glad you enjoyed Ruth's gift to you of virtual flowers!

I was relieved to see in your P.S. that you have a lot of work "but not too much." I hope you are not getting too exhausted from too little sleep.

And I was delighted that you enjoyed English class today. That was such a funny story about the professor accidentally writing down the author of the book you reviewed instead of your name! And that is excellent that you are participating a lot in all of your classes. That is critically important. I know you will never let anyone intimidate you, especially any aggressive male students!

By the way, is Professor Townsend a man or a woman? I would love to learn more about your English class, what books you are using, and the kind of things you are learning. Come to think of it, I would like to take that class!

Today, Christina has her tenth grade retreat and, fortunately, the weather is wonderful. Jenny had a soccer practice last night and scored two (or was it three?) goals.

Jenny told me this funny story yesterday. She and Julie were listening to two boys arguing at lunch. Eric said to Roger, "You're a roach." Roger replied, "You're a black-headed roach." Eric responded, "Well, at least I am not a roach!"

We received a letter from Granny yesterday, and she wrote about Diana as follows:

Here today all is gloom because of Princess Diana's tragic death. The BBC canceled all Sunday programs and have talked of the day. It has been amazing and proves she WAS the most famous face in the world. Thousands of flowers have been left around every house connected with her life. I have always been on her side, whereas a huge number of our friends (women especially) deemed her a 'great actress.' The Prince of Wales didn't treat her well -- he should have known, as a much older person, how to help her become a successful 'royal,' but Camilla Parker Bowles remained in his life and made it an impossible 'ménage-a-trois.' Perhaps you have been hearing on TV about the shock and grief affecting everyone here, tears being shed openly, and so many lovely words being spoken. She will NEVER be forgotten, especially when William and Harry are on public view -- what a wretched start their young lives have gone through already. Prince Charles must be wishing none of it happened at all -- such regrets for him.

Did I tell you the great news on Grandpa that his doctor has told him that he is one of the "lucky ones," and that his prostate cancer is a mild case.

Jenny's new teacher, Miss Horowitz (apparently she likes to be called Miss rather than Ms.) asked Jenny to articulate her goals for fifth grade, and Jenny wrote the following:

In fifth grade, I want to learn a lot of things. I especially want to improve on my math and reading skills. I'd like to write a lot and do fun science experiments. I have some other goals also. I'd like to do Math Olympiad, and I also want to do service core and help people. I think this year I will achieve many things.

Kimmie, call us as often as you like. We will never think you call too much.

I will hold on to the binoculars until you tell me you need them. No problem.

You mentioned in a recent letter that one of your professors recommended possibly doing a science writing internship next summer? Did I get that right? Sounds great. We look forward to hearing more about it.

Your frisbee friends sound great. It's great you like being part of a team. Learning to be an effective member of a team (and also learning to lead them) is one of the great secrets of a successful life.

Good luck with your article on the Career Counseling Office for *Amherst Student.* I look forward to reading it! I am glad we have taken out a two-year subscription to *Amherst Student.*

Your camping trip with those new friends sounded fantastic, and you mentioned you might go again which would be wonderful.

I am trying to find a way to send you a box! I went to Fresh Fields last night hoping that they do "boxes" but they don't. I'll keep trying!

Just to confirm, here is the information you gave me about Amtrak. The information number to call is 1-800-USA-RAIL. I will call them to find out about the train from Amherst to Union Station for Friday, November 21 (leaving after 4:00 PM) or Saturday, November 22 (in case you decide to leave early on that Saturday). Then I will find out about the return train on Sunday, November 30. Did I get all that right?

Mummy and I think that the four classes you are doing this semester are perfect. Chemistry, Economics, Adolescence in America, and English. They are all foundational, and the principles you learn in them will be useful in whatever career you choose to follow.

Kimmie, I am going to repeat back your schedule here so that Mummy, Tina and Jen have it:

Monday: 10:00 Chemistry, 12:30 Economics, 1:00 Chemistry Lab.

Tuesday: 8:30 English, 11:30 Adolescence Seminar, 1:00 Economics.

Wednesday: 10:00 Chemistry, 12:30 Economics.

Thursday: 8:30 English, 11:30 Adolescence Seminar.

Friday: 10:00 Chemistry, 1:00 Chemistry Lab.

Did I get that correct?

I am really enjoying sending e-mails to Tina. I regret now that I wasn't using e-mail last year when you were at Holton Arms.

Kimmie, we adore you and we are so proud of you.

All our love,

Daddy
XXXOOO

September 9, 1997
My Darling Kimmie:
Mummy and I loved talking with you last night on the phone. Your full life of friends, frisbee, work, writing, parties and everything else sounds great. We loved your note on September 7, "Life is wonderful."

We know you are working hard (you said last night that especially Monday, Tuesday and Wednesday were jammed because of your three classes each day) but you are also having the best fun. That's wonderful! Occasionally you may feel overwhelmed with papers you have to write, e-mail you have to answer, and so on. Don't feel you have to write long letters to us. An occasional phone call and brief e-mail is just great. Whatever you can fit in.

Are you getting used to the coed bathrooms?! Sorry the three fat envelopes from me arrived on the same day. I mailed them on different days deliberately so they would arrive on different days! I don't mean to add to any sense of "overwhelm" that you may be having.

Well done for getting your article done for *Amherst Student.* Please send Mummy and me a copy because I am not sure when our subscription to *Amherst Student* will begin.

I hope you do use the Writing Center -- it seems like a great resource.

I wish we could have watched your ultimate Frisbee game on Sunday, and especially seen your "lay-out." (Am I using that word in the correct way?!) We will be watching Jenny at soccer on Saturday at 10:20 AM and watching Tina at tennis at Holton Arms at noon.

Nana and Mark enjoyed seeing you on Sunday morning for breakfast. They said you looked wonderfully happy, but your room was untidy!! (As Mummy says, Nana has very high standards when it comes to tidy rooms!)

Glad you are using your bike. Your ride with Lauren to Northampton last Sunday sounded great.

I wonder if you'll ever find it useful to take your laptop to classes.

We saw Neil Grundberg at the BE picnic last Friday. He sends you his love. He was delighted to hear how happy you are.

Here are the details about your train to and from Amherst at Thanksgiving. A big question: Do you want to go first class, or are you happy with coach? First class (they actually call it "custom class") costs an extra $34 each way. The advantage is that it gives you a little more room and a little more privacy, but the disadvantage is that it may cut you off from friends riding in coach. At the moment, I have put you in coach as follows:

Friday, November 21, train #55 (called the Vermonter) leaves Amherst at 12:49PM and arrives at Union Station at 9:47PM (the train fare is $76).

Sunday, November 30, train #56 (also called the Vermonter) leaves Union Station at 7:30AM and arrives at Amherst at 4:00PM (the train fare is $90)

The reservation number is 688392. The tickets are coming to me and I will send them on to you. Let me know as soon as possible if you want us to spend the extra $68 on "custom class," and I will see what I can do.

Tina has started driving! So far, she has only hit one curb! She is doing great.

Kim, we love you and we miss you, but we are so happy that you are so happy.

All our love,
Daddy
XXXOOO

September 15, 1997
My Darling Kimmie:
It was wonderful when you called on Thursday night. You sounded great, and I enjoyed the three-way chat we had with you, Tina and me. I told Mummy about it, and we think we will get a cordless phone (as part of the sophisticated telephone system we will install in our "new" house) so that, when you, Tina or Jenny call, Mummy and I can talk with you at the same time.

Good luck with the economics professor who disappointed you. You are quite right to find a way to get coaching in economics from someone else (in addition to whatever that professor can give you).

We will be looking out for your book review in October in *The Washington Post* educational supplement.

Dave Andrews (who was my Best Man when Mummy and I got married in 1975) had dinner with us on Thursday night. Dave and I will always be friends, but we have become a little less close over the years as our careers have diverged and we live in different countries. However, I realized on Thursday night that he was important to me because we went through formative years together (between the ages of 18 and 25) where we did virtually everything together. He is a person of great integrity and I am very fond of him.

Rebecca (18 years old) is now dating a 36-year old man whom Dave likes very much.

After dinner, Dave made a funny remark which caught my attention. He was describing Rebecca and saying how focused she was and how, when she has a goal, she zooms in on it and will not be distracted even though her efforts may inconvenience other people. When he said this, he looked at me with a smile and said, "like someone else I know" (meaning me!). I was not sure if Dave meant this as an insult or a compliment!

Kimmie, thanks so much for reading the last part of my draft journal celebrating your last year at home. I appreciate your warm comments about it and I am glad you like it.

Do you remember that Tina challenged me to finish the journal in a "good" way? Well, when she read what I had written at the end, she wrote on the draft in big letters, "AWESOME! Great ending -- I'm impressed!! You met the challenge! !" That meant a lot to me because I don't often get praise from Tina.

Other people who have read my journal (for example, Jon or my parents) don't seem that impressed by it, but one person who really did seem to have a grasp of the amount of work and creativity it takes was my brother, Tim. I was thrilled to talk with him yesterday and hear him say how much reading my journal meant to him. He asked me if I was going to continue my writing in this area, and I told him I was going to do the same thing for Tina and Jen to celebrate their last year at home.

Mummy and I thought that was a lovely thing for you to do when you went to the Campus Center and spent several hours reading Virginia Woolf s *A Room Of My Own.* What a lovely relaxing (and enriching) thing to do.

I am writing this on Sunday night. We had a typical Saturday yesterday. I got up, showered, and went to my 8:30 AM two-hour exercise class with Lin. Jenny had a soccer game at 10:20, but we decided as a family that I would miss that because it was half an hour away and I had to leave at 11:00 to take Tina to her tennis match at Holton Arms. I was sad to miss Jenny's soccer game (her team won, incidentally), but Mummy said she looked great and played well. Their team has given themselves the name "Women in Black" because their uniform is black!

I got back from the exercise class at about 10:30, had a quick breakfast and left with Tina for Holton Arms. I spent several hours there watching her play (she had a very close game and just lost -- as did everybody else on the Holton Arms team!), with Jenny and Mummy joining us halfway through after they returned from Jenny's soccer match.

Last week, Tina was frustrated with herself in a match. She was playing cautiously and getting annoyed at herself about it, and she was losing 7-0. Then she said to herself, "To hell with this, I'm going to lose anyway so I might as well play more aggressively." She started playing harder and she won three games and then lost 8-3. When I watched her on Saturday, she did not seem to play cautiously at all, and hit some hard shots.

On the way back from the tennis match at Holton Arms, Tina and I stopped at St. Bart's and Tina practiced driving in the big parking lot there. She is great at going 30mph in first gear! I'm only joking, she is a good driver.

As soon as we returned home, Mummy went to get her hair done at 2:30, I grabbed a quick lunch, found some articles for Tina on how to use the Internet (Tina is writing an article on this subject for *Scribbler),* and then I drove Jenny and Martha to Summit Hall in Gaithersburg to play miniature golf.

After that, we rushed home in time for Mummy to take Jenny and Tim to church. Then we had dinner with Uncle Bob and Aunt Judy. Do you remember them? Judy is Pop Pop's sister. Their two children, Debbie and Bruce, have had a tough time with their marriages and children.

Today (Sunday), Tina volunteered at a hospital with Lauren, Jenny played with Martha, Tina and I had a good game of tennis, and then we all went to a goodbye party for Chris and Lynn Kelly (did you know they were moving about a mile away?).

Early this morning, after doing my yoga exercises, I went running on the Crescent Trail and went as far as River Road. It's a beautiful path on which to run. Tina said she wanted me to run with her and Lauren on that trail next weekend which I am looking forward to doing. (Oops! I can't -- I'm leaving on Friday for a ten-day trip to Canada and Wyoming, so I will be away.)

You just called us! It was wonderful to hear from you. Ahemm -- out until 4:00 AM last night! And now you are going to be a deejay and have to take a night shift between 2:00 AM and 4:00 AM -- we hope you don't get too exhausted! After we said goodbye to you on the phone, Mummy expressed concern to me that you will get too tired, but I said you were exploring lots of things and I would be doing exactly the same thing if I was in your situation. It is a great time in your life to try some things (like being a deejay) that you might never have another chance to do in your life.

I talked to Granny and Grandpa last night. There is a hot rumor going around Bath that Jon has a new girlfriend, but I talked to Jon today and he said that speculation was "premature"!

Granny and Grandpa leave tomorrow for ten days in France and are looking forward to it. Aren't they great to do that kind of thing at their age?!

As I mentioned already, I had a great talk with Tim today. We have never in our lives enjoyed each other so much as in the last year or two as we have become closer. This is a result of a deliberate effort I have made to call him regularly and frequently. He told me he has been keeping a journal for years and years which no one has ever seen. He said that he liked what I had written so much in my journal that he was going to "dedicate" his journal to me -- the word "dedicate" may have a different meaning in England than in America -- I think what Tim meant is that he is going to, at some point, give me his journal, which I would like very much.

Tina is doing It's Academic at school, and she also went to a meeting of the National Organization For Women. Every night at dinner, Tina studies five to ten new vocabulary words. If she keeps this up, she is going to have a wonderfully rich and powerful vocabulary.

Last Friday evening, I was playing tennis with Jenny on court 8. On court 7 was Alex Lowe's father, Bill. He said that Alex was happy at college.

I think I mentioned to you that I got a lovely thank-you letter from Lauren's mom, Jeannine.

I sometimes think that you, Tina, and Jenny think that everything I do turns to gold. This is not the case.. Here is a small example that happened to me last week. I received a call from somebody called Ken Leonardo at Animal Planet asking if they could meet with me and perhaps a few others at NWF to talk about ways in which Animal Planet and NWF could mutually help each other (e.g., with us telling our members about Animal Planet, and Animal Planet telling their audiences about NWF).

Since I like Animal Planet very much and we are producing programming for them, I told Ken that I would be delighted to help. I set up a meeting with about five or six people throughout the organization, including Jaime Matyas (our Vice President for Cause-Related Marketing and an excellent person). We had the meeting. However, after the meeting, I received a constructive but critical memo from Jaime saying that the meeting would have been much more effective had we had a pre-meeting in which we could have planned what our approach was going to be to Animal Planet, what the mood of the meeting was going to be, and what outcomes we hoped to obtain. I sent Jaime's memo on to everybody who attended with an apology and acknowledgment that Jaime had a good point and that I would learn from this experience.

When you make an error of judgment like that, the best way to handle it is just to acknowledge it and apologize. Jaime and I have a very high regard for each other and I appreciated her being straightforward and telling me how she felt. I tell you (and Tina and Jenny) this story to show you that, like anybody else, I make lots of mistakes.

Here is a quote I recently read from Erica Jong. She said, "You see a lot of smart guys with dumb women, but you hardly ever see a smart woman with a dumb guy." This is one of those quotes which strikes me as saying something very important; but, for the life of me, the exact meaning (at least to me) is elusive and just beyond the capacity of my brain to completely grasp. Can you please give me your interpretation?

It's rather like the quote from the Buddha who cryptically summed up his teaching to his disciples this way "Be a light unto yourself." I found this quote in a wonderful book on meditation by Jon Kabat-Zinn entitled *Wherever You Go There You Are -- Mindfulness Meditation In Everyday Life*. I'm reading this book because I have just finished listening to the companion tape and was so impressed by it. I think what the Buddha meant was that waking up is ultimately something that each one of us can only do for ourselves.

What Kabat-Zinn teaches in this book is that, in essence, mindfulness is about wakefulness. Henry David Thoreau said in *Walden,* "Only that day dawns to which we are awake." Kabat-Zinn writes as follows:

Our minds are such that we are often more asleep than awake to the unique beauty and possibilities of each present moment as it unfolds. While it is in the nature of our mind to go on automatic pilot and lose touch with the only time we actually have to live, to grow, to feel, to love, to learn, to give shape to things, to heal, our mind also holds the deep innate capacity to help us awaken to our moments and use them to advantage for ourselves, for others, and for the world we inhabit.

He says we fall into a robot-like way of seeing, thinking and doing. And he says not knowing that you are even in such a dream is what the Buddhists call "ignorance" or mindlessness. He says being in touch with this not knowing is called "mindfulness," and he says the work of waking up from these dreams (or automaticity) is the work of meditation, the systematic cultivation of wakefulness, of present-moment awareness.

This waking up goes hand in hand with what he calls "wisdom," seeing more deeply into cause and effect and the interconnectedness of things, so that we are no longer caught in a dream-dictated reality of our own creation. Mindfulness provides a simple but powerful route for getting ourselves unstuck, back into touch with our own wisdom and vitality. It is a way to take charge of the direction (says Jon Kabat-Zinn) and quality of our lives, including our relationships within the family, our relationship to work and to the larger world and planet, and, most fundamentally, our relationship with our self as a person. He says, through careful and systematic self- observation, we may be able to live lives of greater satisfaction, harmony, and wisdom. Mindfulness, he says, is the direct opposite of taking life for granted.

I have never been able to meditate, but perhaps this book will help me.

Kimmie, sorry this letter is so long. Your letters and phone calls to us can be very brief because we know how busy you are, especially on Mondays, Tuesdays and Wednesdays when you have three classes a day (and you are still recovering from getting to bed at 4:00 in the morning!).

Your train tickets for Thanksgiving have arrived. I will hold on to them and bring them to you when we see you at the end of October.

We love you and we miss you and we think about you constantly, and we are happy knowing how happy you are. All our love,

Daddy
XXXOOO

P.S.: Now it is Tuesday, September 16. I am going to Holton Arms at 4:00 PM today to watch Tina play tennis in a match against Madeira, and then tonight Mummy and I are going to Holton for a tenth-grade dinner meeting with other parents.

September 30, 1997

My Darling Kimmie, Tina and Jenny:
I am so sorry that I failed to leave you nightly letters last week when I was away in Vancouver and Jackson Hole. I think that was the first time I have not done that since Kimmie was born.

As you know (or at least as Tina and Jen know), my plan had been to take my laptop and then to send you letters every day from my hotel rooms in Vancouver and then Jackson Hole. What happened when I got to Vancouver was that I could not get my e-mail to work because I was in Canada (there is some kind of access charge across the US-Canada boundary which mucked up the telephone connection). Then, when I got to Jackson Hole, I often found that my modem in my laptop would not connect and it became very frustrating. I also found it difficult to do e-mail because I was busy from early morning to late at night giving speeches, running workshops and in meetings.

So I wanted to send you this note of apology. You were in my thoughts the whole time, and I was often talking about the three of you with people.

Here is one story I had noted down to write to you about had I been able to do letters to you last week by e-mail. It is a story about Mummy and me, rather than Jenny, although at first blush it looks like a story about Jenny.

Jen was at a soccer training session and she lacerated her knee. The coach, Jeff Wagner, was making the team run to build up their endurance and he could see that Jenny was in pain with her cut knee, but made her run anyway. Mummy's reaction to Jenny afterwards was to be very sympathetic (and I suppose to imply that, if she had been in Jeff's position, she would not have made Jen run with her cut knee); whereas I said that, if I had been Jeff, I probably would have done the same thing because as the coach you are trying to toughen the team up and increase their endurance.

So Jenny got these quite different reactions from us both -- which I think is just great. I think that, if Mummy was not there, I probably would have been more sympathetic, and if I had not been around, Mummy probably would have shifted her position a little closer to mine. My interpretation of this story is two parents are better than one!

I love you,

Dad
XXXOOO

P.S.: Mummy made me laugh with her e-mail last week to Kim when she wrote at the end, "My, this health world is complicated...somebody should do something to simplify things...oh, that's my job, better get back to work!"

October 3, 1997
My darling Kim:
I spent the whole day smiling yesterday because of the two e-mails I received from you! When Jenny was in my office for the day yesterday, we called Mummy to read them to her. (Of course, she already had them on her own e-mail.)

Kimmie, sorry to be dozy, but what is a type B personality? I know what type A is (or at least I think I do -- someone who is intense, works hard, is ambitious and does not find it easy to relax). But what is type B? I don't believe it is necessarily the exact opposite of all those things, is it?

Your camping trip to the Catskills sounds great! Tell us more what you mean when you say you are leading it.

I didn't know you were writing an article on religion. Who is that for? Anyway, it sounds great.

I look forward to reading it. So far, we have received four issues *of Amherst Student,* but I have not seen your by-line anywhere. Did your article get published?

I am so impressed that you are not feeling totally stressed. And I felt even more admiration for you on this score when we arrived home last night and found a delicious box of apples from Mary and Brent Bohlen (Will's parents) with a note saying, "Kimberly and Will are doing a great job with their letters -- we're trying to store them all so they can put the book together, but we are also gaining a lot of insight from them." As an aside, Mummy and I were envious that Mary and Brent had seen your letters but we hadn't! But the point I'm trying to make is that I am so impressed that you are managing all your commitments -- to Will, to Keith and all your friends, to Frisbee, to your professors, to your various writing projects (and many other activities/commitments I don't even know about). So, well done, sweetie pie -- it's wonderful that you have free time and hardly ever need to rush. I liked your sentence:

"This is how I like to live -- I can be more thoughtful and appreciate people more."

I love e-mail! Yesterday, I was copied on two sweet notes which flew back and forth between Mummy and Tina. Mummy wrote to Tina wishing her good luck at her tennis match today and joking that she hoped that she would not get too "distracted by any BOYS that might be watching!" Tina responded, "Thanks, mom! It's so nice of you to send me notes all the time!! I love you!"

I am reading a new book by Dr. Blaine Lee called *The Power Principle: Influence With Honor*. He says that the principles we live by create world we live in. If we change the principle we live by, we can change our world. He defines power as the ability either to act or produce an effect or to influence others. He talks about different types of power (for example, coercive power -- the power to do something to someone, or utility power -- the power to do something for someone). But the type of power he recommends is principle-centered power -- the power to do something with someone.

He defines principle-centered power as based on honor extended to you from others and by you to others. This power asks an important question: What can we be together? He says principle- centered power leads to lasting influence, lasting relationships, trust, synergy, respect and interdependence.

Blaine Lee says that principle-centered power, based on what you can do with others, is the positive power created when individuals perceive that their leaders are honorable. Because these leaders are honorable, individuals trust them, respect them, are inspired by them, and believe deeply in the goals communicated by them. Consequently, individuals desire to willingly follow such leaders. In short, the more we are honored, respected, and genuinely regarded by others, the more power we will have with them. To have honor is to have unquestionable integrity, dependability, deference, homage, reverence, and veneration. It includes being patient, gentle, kind and consistent.

I like this book very much because it goes to foundational issues -- fundamental principles which never change.

He tells one story about the great Indian leader Gandhi who was a skinny, almost shriveled person, never held elective office, but had incredible power and, in fact, he led the revolution which evicted the British from India after World War II. He did not wait for anyone to tell him what to do, he just "got up and went." A leader knows what she has to do and just goes ahead and does it.

As Blaine Lee is telling this story, he tells a specific story about a fast that Gandhi undertook to stop the fighting and killing between Muslims and Hindus. He went on a fast knowing that he could die from it. We now know, of course, that his fast led to the stopping of the fighting (at least temporarily); but, when he was on the fourth or fifth day of the fast, he had no idea what would happen. Then Blaine Lee writes the following, which I kept rereading, rereading and rereading because it resonated with me so powerfully. He wrote:

> When we put our foot onto an honorable path, we know the outcome before the results are in, because the commitment to worthwhile things is itself a worthy thing to do.

Isn't that a fascinating thing for him to say? I was riveted by the notion that you can "know the outcome before the results are in."

Kimmie, I love you. You are very special. Mummy, Tina and I are so happy that you are having such a great time at Amherst.

All our love,

Daddy
XXXOOO

P.S. October 8: Good luck on your DJ test today! And good, good luck on your Chem mid-term Thursday night -- we'll be thinking of you. Have a wonderful time camping this weekend.

Sunday, October 12, 1997

My Darling Kim:
As I write this, you are out camping in the Catskills with lots of friends, and I bet you are having the time of your life.

Congratulations again on your article, "A View From College," in *Scribbler*. I read it with great fascination and admired how good it was. It has a freshness to it that I had not seen in your writing before. It was authentic and original. I loved the total lack of pretentiousness. Mummy and I are proud of you. I am going to reproduce it below because I want a record of it in this journal (this letter will go in my journal), so here is your *Scribbler* article:

You may not realize it, when you get a C -- and your teacher doesn't understand why you can't take three tests on one day, or when you get yelled at for cutting in line in the cafeteria, but Holton is warm and fuzzy.

You can come to school wearing sweat pants and an old sweat shirt (as long as it comes in some shade of blue) and not think about who is going to make fun of you or what you are going to do if you feel sick.

Your classmates will generally be polite to you, at least after the cliques of Middle School disintegrate, and you go home every night to privacy and a parent that will give you drugs for your menstrual cramps and assure you that your life will be more fun than it is now.

Well, college is certainly fun, but not warm and fuzzy. Warmth and fuzziness is what I miss most about Holton and living at home.

I dance until three o'clock in the morning every Thursday and Saturday night. Perhaps you have found a social oasis at Holton that I missed, but I never found a night life that interested me enough to keep me out that late last year. At the same time, no one is waiting up for me to welcome me home or make me tea when I am tired at the end of the day.

A big difference that exerts a strong influence on my "warm and fuzzy" scale is the presence of males. They can be mean as well as fun stimulators. Guys like to make fun of you -- I never go through a day without being hounded for not being rebellious enough, ("Hey Kim, I bet you can't bring yourself to put your fork in the knife chute," or "I can't believe that you have done your chemistry reading for tomorrow!") They don't make fun of people they don't like, but my male hallmates love to joke around.

It took me a couple weeks to understand that I should take the attention as a compliment and not as an insult.

Being surrounded by rowdy boys 24/7 can make you feel like you want to crawl under flannel sheets and not see anyone for a day.

Since I usually only have three hours of classes each day, I could do this if I wanted to, but I have developed an alternative coping mechanism. I have figured out how to feel good without the affections of my parents.

I have become my own parent. I buy my own grape chewable Tylenol for my cramps, I make myself tea, and I tell myself to go to bed when it gets close to 2:00 AM. I learned how to feel affection from other people when it isn't obvious at first. My roommates and I hug each other often, and my hallmates stop teasing me when I look like I need a hug.

So as time goes on, I learn to have fun and feel happy at the same time. Of course, I do not think it is right to always feel satisfied; it is important to get out of your comfort zone and take risks. But after taking risks all day in classrooms, on the field, and in the newspaper room, it feels good to receive a hug and feel loved. Especially if that hug is coming from an attractive male.

Kimmie, I think your writing is getting stronger and stronger. Writing is so important and I am glad you love to write. Are you getting coaching on your writing from the Writing Center (is that what it is called?)? Being able to write well is going to help you enormously in whatever career you pursue.

I had a funny reaction reading your essay. As I read it, I found myself saying, 'Oh, this writer likes her parents." It took me a second to remember that I was one of those parents!

Kimmie, would you like to run in the Turkey Chase this Thanksgiving? It would be fun for all five of us to run it together as we traditionally do.

This afternoon, we went to the Big Apple Circus and enjoyed it a lot. I love the circus because of the humor (the clowning) and the athleticism -- I love to roar with laughter at the clowns, and I love admiring the incredible gymnastic feats of the performers.

I went to Barnes and Noble on Saturday and bought the following books:

Finding Flow: The Psychology Of Engagement With Everyday Life by Mihaly Csikszentmihalyi.

Give Me A Moment And I Will Change Your Life by Allen Lakein.

Built To Last. Successful Habits Of Visionary Companies by James Collins and Jerry Poras.

Managing By Values by Ken Blanchard and Michael O'Connor.

I have also been reading three other books I recently bought:

Masters Of Change: How Great Leaders In Every Age Thrived In Turbulent Times by William Boast.

Trail Of The Wild West: Rediscovering The American Frontier by Paul Robert Walker.

Yesterday, I called Granny and Grandpa to see how they were doing. They are both doing very well. Grandpa was delighted because he had received a letter from Tina telling him that she had met somebody in her volunteer work at Suburban Hospital who knew him from the Navy. Grandpa says he is going to write back to Tina.

I have speeches coming up on October 19 (in New York City), the 26th (in Myrtle Beach, South Carolina), and on November 14 (in Roanoke). Please send me any funny stories, jokes or anecdotes about you or Amherst that I can use in these speeches! You have been a great source in the past.

I am reading Jenny a wonderful biography on Albert Einstein. It is totally engrossing. He didn't do particularly well in school, but he had this incredible curiosity. He would not asking why.

This weekend, I played tennis twice with Jenny (she is getting good), and we also played soccer yesterday. Jenny is eager to earn money, so Mummy and I have been looking for jobs around the house for her to do such as washing the filters and folding laundry.

Yesterday morning, Tina did crew on the Potomac. The day was glorious and she loved it. I think she might do crew next semester, instead of playing tennis. After crew, she went into Georgetown and then came back by bus. She spent Saturday evening at Olivia's house. She volunteered at Suburban today, and she said tonight that she and Lauren would come with me in the morning to my two-hour exercise class with Lin. I am delighted.

Mummy and Tina had an argument today over going to the Youth Mass. Tina did not want to go, and Mummy wanted her to go, and I felt an obligation to take Mummy's side.

Jenny listened to the discussion closely. Tonight, when she was going to bed, she dug something out of her Sunday school lesson and presented it to me triumphantly. It was a quote from the Old Testament which goes as follows: "To the woman he said, 'I will greatly multiply your pain and childbearing; in pain, you shall bring forth children, yet your desire shall be for your husband, and he shall rule over you." Jenny presented this to me knowing full well that I would totally agree with her that it is hogwash.

When I went food shopping this afternoon for the family, I saw Carol Beach at the Giant, and she said she had just heard from you because you had called her to get advice on NPR internships. Well done, Kimmie -- you are very smart to call people like Carol to get advice, counsel and help. That is exactly what successful people do -- they are always reaching out to people asking for help.

Tonight, the four of us went to Clyde's for dinner and had a delightful time. We had our family meeting during dinner, and it went very well. When we came to "rocks," I said that my rock was to make a greater effort to make a distinction between "issues" and "nuisances." Issues are things which matter and which are worth arguing about, whereas nuisances should just be ignored. Tonight, when I started gently complaining to Jenny about the mess in her room, she piped up, "Dad, is this a nuisance or an issue?"!

Kimmie, with regard to Parent's Weekend, if we arrive by about 6:30-7:00, is that too late? Tina does not want to leave until 11:00 AM when her chemistry class finishes. We hate to miss seeing you on

Friday afternoon, but Tina says she cannot afford to miss a chemistry lesson. What do you think?

Kinimie, we adore you and think about you all the time. We are glad you are so happy, although reading your essay in *Scribbler,* I realize that sometimes you miss being at home. Incidentally, Pat Sugrue called the other day and told us that Kerry started off unhappily at her school in the south (apparently she did not take to the southern girls), but she is doing better now.

Kimmie, we love you!

Daddy
XXXOOO

P.S.: We have sent you an "organic fruit assortment" which should arrive in early November. We hope you, Lauren and Kristina enjoy it!

October 15, 1997
My Darling Kimmie:
Mummy and I were so delighted that you called last night. Thank you! I'm sorry that Tina and Jen couldn't talk with you because they would have loved that -- they were both asleep.

As I mentioned on the phone last night, I thought your front-page article, "Entry To Seligman Limited To Residents," in the October 1 issue of *Amherst Student* was excellent. Well done!

As you know, I was away at a senior staff retreat on the first two days of this week at Harper's Ferry. It was a lot of fun, and I will write to you more about it in another letter later on. As part of the retreat, I took the *Myers-Briggs Type Indicator Test.* Have you ever heard of it? It tells you about your preferences and how you like to live your life. It turns out I am an ESTJ, in case that means anything to you.

I did something before this retreat which I do for every important meeting I have. I write down all the words which are triggered in my mind when I ask myself the question: How do I want to appear to others in this meeting? By asking this question and then jotting down words, it helps me to create a vision of what I want to accomplish at the meeting.

So here is the list I wrote down as I was preparing myself for this two-day retreat: Attentive, totally focused, smiling, empathic, engaged, listening, constructive, articulate, courageous, learning, open to new ideas, not defensive, encouraging, playful, laughing, physical, good posture, good team member, bold, unpretentious, modest, productive, building on the ideas of others, grounded, wise, mountain-like, outgoing, energetic, helping others, action-oriented, driven to closure, successful, balanced, honest, honorable, collaborative, responsive, cheerful, dedicated, positive.

Occasionally, during the meeting, I would go back to this list to remind myself of my goals. It helps me do better and reach my potential more. Of course, a list like this does not deal with the substantive issues of the meeting (e.g., for this particular retreat, coming up with a vision statement for NWF) -- I prepare for that separately.

Anyway, I have found this process helpful and perhaps you, Tina and Jenny might as well.

For this retreat, I was away both on Sunday night and Monday night and I left letters for Tina and Jenny.

They were handwritten. In my Sunday letter, I wrote:

My Darling Tina and Jen, I'll be back on Tuesday at about 6:00 PM. Jen, let's go for a run then and play soccer. Tina, like to drive? Also, Tina, good luck at your tennis match on Monday, and good luck on your tests this week (especially chemistry on Monday). I believe you can do almost anything you want in this world if you try hard enough.

Here are some good words for you both to know (and then I gave definitions of eulogy, euphoric, hindrance, inculcate, incurable, lurid, Machiavellian, and obstreperous)

Tina, good luck in your vocab test on Tuesday!

I love you both so much.

> Daddy
> XXXOOO

And my letter on Monday evening went as follows:

My Precious Loves, Tina and Jen, as I said in my letter to you yesterday, you guys can do anything you want in this world if you are determined enough.

Here is something you already know: People would much rather live lives dedicated to an idea or a cause that they believe in, than lead lives of aimless, frivolous diversion. People need meaningful purpose in their lives. That's why we live. With a purpose, with goals (and the more specific the better), you can achieve anything. I love you!!

> Daddy
> XXXOOO

Kimmie: Mummy, Tina, Jen and I love you so much. We will be thinking about you camping this weekend. Have a wonderful time.

Buckets and oodles of love,

> Daddy
> XXXOOO

Sunday, October 26, 1997
My Darling Tina and Jenny,
As you are reading this, I am in Myrtle Beach giving a speech about *Whales* to about 300 people and, according to the invitation, I am the "special guest." It should be a lot of fun and I am looking forward to it. I will be back tomorrow in time for our family dinner.

Wasn't that a lovely letter that Grandpa wrote to you, Tina? You deserve it because you evidently wrote a lovely letter to him. I am reproducing Grandpa's letter to you below so we have a record of it in my journal:

My dear Tina,

Thank you for your interesting letter about meeting in hospital a man who had known me some years ago. I don't remember him by name but might remember his face if we met.

I was in a job and at a time when things were very different from the way they are today. When I was 28, just after Granny and I married, I was sent to Portsmouth Dockyard and given about 2,000 men and told to keep all the minesweepers and other small ships (hundreds of them) in good running order. I have never worked harder, and I loved it, but your friend is right, I was strict; strict with myself and with everybody else in the business.

I am sure these people in hospital love seeing a beautiful and intelligent young girl like you coming around their wards, so you are doing a fine thing to help them feel happier. Little Granny spent the last 10 years of her life in a retirement home for old people -- she refused to live with me and Granny because, she said, we would be out all the time and she would be left home alone. Well, young girls from a local school used to come to Little Granny's home, just like you are doing, and she loved it -- probably much more than the kids realized, and she would talk to me about it for days.

But I must tell you that these visits were not quite the very best visits that Little Granny liked. The number one favorite was a big brown dog whose owner used to come in to visit his mother. This dog would bounce around the room, so pleased to see so many people, and then he would come and rub against, and make friends with, every single person there.

Your Granny is a bit like that dog. She just loves meeting people and if she goes into a crowded room her instinct is to go from one to the other and make friends with them and embrace them. I was not like that when I was young, perhaps because I felt I was too important or perhaps because I was a bit shy. But I am not like that now. Granny has taught me that it is far better to like everybody and to show it, and now I am nearly as bad (good?) as she is.

In my last job I had about 4,000 men working for me in Bath and I prided myself in remembering their names. Sometimes I would be walking down a corridor and be coming towards a chap whose name escaped me but, nearly every time, at the very last instant his name would come to me and I would say, "How do, Jim" or Tom or whatever. Perhaps I made mistakes, which would have made them laugh when I went away.

Bless you, my darling, and please give our love to all the family. We love you all so much.

Grandpa

When I was growing up, I observed my father writing to his mother (Little Granny) every Sunday telling her about the family activities and what was going on. I remember admiring the fact that he had the character to know that writing to his mother was important.

And talking about character, I want to commend you both on how you are managing through the awful mess in the house. It is not easy living in all this dust, confusion and limited facilities, but you are both showing grace under pressure and retaining your intrinsic serenity and good nature. Well done!

After the *Whales* opening at Myrtle Beach on Sunday, I leave early on Monday morning to visit Shirley McGreal. She is a British woman who stumbled into the world of endangered wildlife smuggling and, with the help of a smuggler-turned-witness, she managed to capture the world's most notorious primate smuggler. Primates including wonderful creatures like orangutans and monkeys. I have optioned Shirley's life and I am looking forward very much to meeting her.

Tina, thanks for asking me for my advice about how to structure and organize the topics for your ebola virus term paper. And thanks for involving me in learning your words for the vocab test on Friday. I loved doing that. I owe you $0.50 because you pointed out two words that I did not know: remonstrate and expostulate!

Jen, I loved listening to you blast away on your trumpet. How did you get so good so fast?! And I love your artwork and I love the fact that you are enthusiastic about school and say that every day there is something interesting, such as the math olympiad. Well done!

Mummy and I are very proud of you both. I often tell people how both of you and Kimmie have made bringing up children so easy for us. Mummy and I often count our blessings -- and we have three very special ones!

I love you.
Daddy
XXXOOO

November 4, 1997

My Darling Kimmie,
I have just finished reading Mummy's wonderful letter that she wrote to you yesterday, and there is not much I can add. I completely agree with her, She wrote almost the identical letter that I was about to write you!

Thank you for the warm welcome you gave us when we arrived in Amherst on Friday. We had a most fantastic weekend with you--enjoyable at so many levels. I liked Keith, and I loved Lauren and Kristina. All the people you introduced us to (Alex, Paul, Katie, and so on) seemed to be very special people and I took an immediate liking to all of them.

Kimmie, good luck in your economic mid-term exam today, and also good luck with your interview with *The Hampshire Gazette* for the internship on Thursday. Remember to check the person out very carefully and get references on him, Also I hope your visit to the Amherst Funeral Home goes well.

Mummy and I will add $100 to your AC account.

It was fun to call you during your radio show, *You Don't Own Me*, this morning. As Mummy asked, did you use what Jenny and I mentioned to you?! Can you send us a tape? I will call you next Monday as well (assuming you want me to!), so don't forget to tell me what the question is!

Your question, "What do you feel passionate about?" was an excellent one. Here are a few others for future shows in case they are helpful: What bugs you? What are the best and worst things your parents say to you? What embarrasses you? What do you miss most about home? What emotion do you love experiencing the best? Is politeness important?

Also, may I make a request? Can you play *Hit The Road Jack?* Also *Georgia On My Mind* by Ray Charles. Great music to wake up to!

We thought the *a cappella* performances were hugely enjoyable, and the Woman In Science panel was good as well.

Kimmie, you are a very special person. I liked everything Mummy put in her letter to you today and endorse it totally. You have two equally wonderful sisters, and Mummy and I are so proud of all you three girls.

Thanks again for a great weekend. I love you.

> Daddy
> XXXOOO

November 9, 1997
My Darling Kimmie:
Congratulations on getting the internship with the *Daily Hampshire Gazette*! I am delighted for you. It will be a great experience, and now you can relax knowing that you have an excellent way to spend your interterm in January. Getting there and getting back will be a drag.

It was great talking with you today (Sunday). Mommy and I love it when you tell us all the things you are doing. The ballroom dancing on Friday and all your writing and jogging sound great. You really know how to live a good life.

I am looking forward to calling you on your radio show tomorrow morning!

Good luck this week in your chemistry exam.

As we discussed today, I will send you some grapefruits. And I will send you the book *The Fairest College.*

I smiled when I went into the bathroom this morning because someone had put an adhesive calking tube (which is the same shape as a tube of toothpaste) where the toothpaste normally is. Just imagine if someone used that instead of toothpaste!

Kim, you have not met Don yet. He is one of our contractors and we like him. He told me the other day that he had found our family meeting books, and I told him they were terribly valuable and would he please give them to me. Sometime later I saw the books on the dining room table, and on them were some nails. Gail was on the portable phone at the table, Don was sitting at the table working on the speakers, and he saw me asking Gail if I should throw away the nails. But, because Mommy was on the phone, I was asking by pointing. When Mommy nodded, I took the family meeting books with the nails on top over to the garbage and was about to toss the nails away when Don shouted out, 'No, no, they're the family meeting books!" He thought I was going to throw away the family meeting books and did not realize that I was only tossing away the nails on top! This was amusing to us (and very sweet) because Don had evidently internalized how important these books were to us and he thought I was about to do a terrible thing and throw them away!

I am reading a wonderful book by Stephen Covey called *The Seven Habits Of Highly Effective Families.* It contains the following story about a father and son which brought tears to my eyes:

I have a dear friend who once shared with me his deep concern over a son he described as being 'rebellious,' 'disturbing,' and 'an ingrate.'

'Stephen, I don't know what to do,' he said. 'It's gotten to the point where if I come into the room to watch television with my son, he turns it off and walks out. I've tried my best to reach him, but it's just beyond me.'

At the time I was teaching some university classes around the 7 Habits. I said, 'Why don't you come with me to my class right now? We're going to be talking about Habit 5 -- how to listen empathically to another person before you attempt to explain yourself. My guess is that your son may not feel understood.'

'I already understand him,' he replied. 'And I can see problems he's going to have if he doesn't listen to me.'

'Let me suggest that you assume you know nothing about your son. Just start with a clean slate. Listen to him without any moral evaluation or judgment. Come to class and learn how to do this and how to listen within his frame of reference.'

So he came. Thinking he understood after just one class, he went to his son and said, 'I need to listen to you. I probably don't understand you, and I want to.'

His son replied, 'You have never understood me -- ever!' And with that, he walked out.

The following day my friend said, 'Stephen, it didn't work. I made such an effort, and this is how he treated me! I felt like saying, 'You idiot! Don't you realize what I've done and what I'm trying to do now? I really don't know if there's any hope.'

I said, 'He's testing your sincerity. And what did he find out? He found out you don't really want to understand him. You want him to shape up.'

'He should, the little whippersnapper!' he replied. 'He knows full well what he's doing to mess things up.'

I replied, 'Look at the spirit inside you now. You're angry and frustrated and full of judgments. Do you think you can use some surface-level listening technique with your son and get him to open up? Do you think it's possible for you to talk to him or even look at him without somehow communicating all those negative things you're feeling deep inside? You've got to do much more private work inside your own mind and heart. You'll eventually learn to love him unconditionally just the way he is rather than withholding your love until he shapes up. On the way, you'll learn to listen within his frame of reference and, if necessary, apologize for your judgments and past mistakes or do whatever it takes.'

My friend caught the message. He could see that he had been trying to practice the technique at the surface but was not dealing with what would produce the power to practice it sincerely and consistently, regardless of the outcome.

So he returned to class for more learning and began to work on his feelings and motives. He soon started to sense a new attitude within himself. His feelings about his son turned more tender and sensitive and open.

He finally said, Tm ready. I'm going to try it again.'

I said, 'He'll test your sincerity again.'

'It's all right, Stephen,' he replied. 'At this point I feel as if he could reject every overture I make, and it would be all right. I would just keep making them because it's the right thing to do, and he's worth it.'

That night he sat down with his son and said, 'I know you feel as though I haven't tried to understand you, but I want you to know that I am trying and will continue to try.'

Again, the boy coldly replied, 'You have never understood me.' He stood up and started to walk out, but just as he reached the door, my friend said to his son, 'Before you leave, I want to say that I'm really sorry for the way I embarrassed you in front of your friends the other night.'

His son whipped around and said, 'you have no idea how much that embarrassed me!' His eyes began to fill with tears.

'Stephen,' he said to me later, 'all the training and encouragement you gave me did not even begin to have the impact of that moment when I saw my son begin to tear up. I had no idea that he even cared, that he was that vulnerable. For the first time I *really* wanted to listen.'

And he did. The boy gradually began to open up. They talked until midnight and when his wife came in and said, 'It's time for bed,' his son quickly replied, 'We want to talk, don't we, Dad?' They continued to talk into the early morning hours.

The next day in the hallway of my office building, my friend, with tears in his eyes, said, 'Stephen, I found my son again.'

As my friend discovered, there are certain fundamental principles that govern in all human interactions, and living in harmony with those principles or natural laws is absolutely essential for quality family life. In this situation, for example, the principle my friend had been violating was the basic principle of respect. The son also violated it. But this father's choice to live in harmony with that principle -- to try to genuinely and empathically listen to and understand his son -- dramatically changed the entire situation. You change one element in any chemical formula and everything changes.

Kimmie, we love you!

Dad
XXXOOO

P.S.: Kim, last night (Tuesday evening), there was a Parent Peer meeting for parents of tenth grade students at Holton Arms, and they asked me to be the "Peer Facilitator." I enjoyed doing this very much. About 15 parents attended. The issues that came up included driving, drinking, dating, parties and summer jobs. These are the same things I remember parents discussing when you were in tenth grade!

November 13, 1997

My loves: Gail, Kim, Tina and Jen:

It is time to rethink and redesign our Family Mission Statement! We wrote our first one in November 1990 (attached), and I love it. I suspect it has had a more profound influence on our family than we realize. It has acted as our constitution -- the DNA of our family life. I believe it helped to create a shared vision and purpose for all of us, and the benefits of this accrue not only to us, but to future generations. In raising you three girls, Mummy and I are, in a sense, raising your children. There is a high chance that they also will be responsible, optimistic, resilient, capable, successful and fulfilled.

In a sense, that November 1990 Family Mission Statement was our second one. The first was our wedding ceremony that Mummy and I wrote together in 1975. I did not realize it then, but, in effect, we were envisioning the future and articulating our purpose. We were "beginning with the end in mind" -- attempting to create a clear, compelling vision of how we wanted to live and what we were all about.

The opposite of having vision is to have no envisioning of the future, no mental creation --just let life happen to you, to be swept along with the flow of society's values and trends without having any sense of purpose. It is simply living out the scripts that have been given to us by our genes, upbringing and environment.

Our family is so important to me, and families are so important to society. They are the most important, fundamental organizations in the world, the literal building blocks of society. No civilization has ever survived the breakup of the family. If families fail, society fails. No other institution can fulfill its essential purpose. No other institution has had its impact for good or ill.

Nonetheless, in most families, members do not have a deep sense of shared vision around its essential meaning and purpose. I want one of our legacies to be a strong family with family members who love each other, care for each other, respect each other, laugh together, have fun together, grow together, and who enjoy rich, meaningful relationships with each other.

The creation of a Family Mission Statement is, in my opinion, crucial to achieving that legacy. Other activities are too (for example, family traditions, weekly family meetings, family vacations, one-on-one bonding experiences), but a Family Mission Statement is the most important activity because it is the foundation. It governs everything else.

The purpose of this letter is to initiate a new conversation between all of us which will lead us over the next six months or so (or however long it takes -- there is no hurry) to create a new Family Mission Statement. It is possible it may end up looking similar to the one we created together in 1990 -- or it may end up as a poem, a picture, a phrase, a sentence, a full-page essay, or whatever. It doesn't matter. What does matter is that it is meaningful to each one of us and capture our deepest desires about the kind of family we want to be and the kind of lives we want to live.

We already have a wonderful family. Mummy and I often reflect on how lucky we are. We love being together and enjoy each other's company We have fun together Our lives, however, are slowly changing. Kimmie is now in college. In two or three years, Tina will leave home to go to college. Jenny is growing up. Mummy and I are beginning to think about what we might do as we get older It is time for us to revisit fundamentals and recommit to things we feel are of enduring value and importance

Our new house is another thing that has triggered my thinking along these lines. We are building a beautiful home, and I want to make sure we all realize that far more important than living in a beautiful house is creating a wonderful family where we all feel affirmed, loved and appreciated and where we live fulfilled, productive and purposeful lives which contribute to making the world a better place.

The New Year's Resolutions we each write at the beginning of every year are a sort of "Family Mission Statement" -- or at least serve a similar kind of purpose. Appropriately, they tend to focus more on goals rather than on timeless purposes Isn't it fascinating to review them periodically during the year to see how one is doing?

As you all know, I have a Personal Mission Statement which I revise every year Both a Personal Mission Statement and a Family Mission Statement are powerful ways for us to keep our eye on what really matters in life -- especially when the milk gets spilled! I was proud of Tina recently when she told me she had written her own Personal Mission Statement.

I don't believe happy, fulfilled families just happen. It takes planning, dedication, daily work, and constantly learning new skills You have to do daily the things which dysfunctional families fail to do. Often, we will be off course; but you just keep coming back to what matters -- building a beautiful and enduring family culture as envisioned m the Family Mission Statement .

Over your childhoods, I have blown it many times as a parent. I lost my temper, lost perspective, misunderstood, judged before understanding, did not listen, acted unwisely, was impatient, acted grumpy, and stayed too late in the office. But I have also tried to learn from my mistakes. Having a Personal Mission Statement and a Family Mission Statement helped me do that more effectively. I apologized (I hope), shifted my values, went back to fundamental principles, learned to laugh at myself, and kept learning, learning and learning some more.

One thing that I am still learning is the reality that all true and lasting change occurs from the "inside out." In other words, instead of trying to change the situation or the person I am dealing with, I have come to realize that the important thing is to go to work on myself. It is my own deep interior work that eventually creates fundamental change in the world. By consistently applying the principles contained in my Personal Mission Statement and our Family Mission Statement, I have realized I can bring about positive change in any relationship or situation. I can become an agent of change. This is why I keep -the words "work on myself' in front of me at all times in my organizer.

As you know, the basic idea of having a Family Mission Statement is to create a vision that is shared by us all so we have a clear destination. In fact, the journey is really part of the destination. They are inseparably connected. How we travel is as important as where we arrive. A Family Mission Statement can provide a guiding purpose and keep pulling us back onto the right path.

So the purpose of this letter is to ask each of you to give some thought to this issue and to write back with your ideas and thoughts. Please ponder the following types of questions:

1. What is the purpose of our family?

2. What are we all about in life?

3. What is our identity as a family?

4. What kind of a family do we want?

5. What kind of a home do we want to invite friends to?

6. What makes us feel comfortable at home, and uncomfortable?

7. What makes us want to come home?

8. What makes you feel drawn to us as parents so that you are open to our influence? How can we as parents be more open to your influence?

9. What are the things that are truly important to us as a family?

10. What are our family's highest-priorities, goals?

11. What are our unique talents, gifts and abilities?

12. What are the priorities we want our family to operate on (such values as trust, honesty, kindness, service, etc.)?

13. What is our responsibility in caring for aging parents?

14. What is our responsibility in caring for extended family (such as brothers and sisters)?

15. What competences do we want Kim, Tina and Jenny to develop as they grow up? (These should deal with the five basic needs in life: to live, to love, to learn, to leave a legacy, and to laugh -- or, to put it another way, the five dimensions of the physical, the social/emotional, the mental, the spiritual, and the need for perspective.)

16. How do we want to make a difference in our community and to the world?

Another way to think about this is to envision Mummy's and my 50th wedding anniversary and the family gathering to celebrate it. Who is there? What is the feeling'? What is quality of the relationships? How are problems worked out and overcome?

Based on the ideas I receive from all of you, I will draft a new Family Mission Statement for everyone to review and think about. I think e-mail is a great way to do this together. Please copy everybody else on your responses. Can you send me your initial thoughts by the end of the year? Feel free to respond earlier! You may have some much better ideas of how the process should work. We will discuss this together over Thanksgiving, too. Let's make it fun!

The reason that I think it is important to put our Family Mission Statement in writing is it helps bring self-discipline to the process. Lord Bacon wrote, "Reading maketh a full man, but writing maketh an exact man."

Finally, let's keep in mind the miracle of the Chinese bamboo tree. After the seed for this amazing tree is planted, you see nothing, absolutely nothing for four years, except for a tiny shoot coming out of a bulb. During those four years, all the growth is underground in a massive, fibrous root structure that spreads deep and wide in the earth. But then in the fifth year, the Chinese bamboo tree grows up to 80 feet!

Many things in family life are like the Chinese bamboo tree. You work and you invest time and effort, and you do everything you can possibly do to nurture growth, and sometimes you don't see anything for weeks, months, or even years. But, if you are patient and keep working and nurturing, that "fifth year" will come, and you will be astonished at the growth and change you see taking place. A Family Mission Statement which is vibrant, alive and owned by each one of us will help us reach that "fifth year."

I look forward to hearing from all of you! hove you.

Dad/Chris
XXXOOO

Attachment

SHEARER PALMER FAMILY MISSION STATEMENT

The mission of our family is to create a nurturing place of love, laughter, warmth, security, and happiness, and to provide opportunities for each of us to meet our full potential so that we can each make a positive contribution both to our own family life and to society.

Among our goals are to love each other, to help each other, to believe in each other, to encourage each other, and to wisely use our time, talents and resources.

We want to live our lives with integrity, courage, humility, love, justice, patience, humor, trust, loyalty, self-confidence, hard works and self-discipline.

We want our home environment to be warm, and to provide a place where not only do we all feel related and happy, but also to be a place that warmly welcomes our friends and relatives.

We want our children to gain from their family not only their roots but their wings. We want them to feel the special bond that pulls them back home to spend time with their family, but also to understand who they are, based on what we know and can learn about grandparents and relatives who went before them. We want them to develop faith in themselves so that they will work hard in school and know that with hard work and self-confidence, the world is theirs and they can achieve great things.

Bringing these goals to a day-to-day level:

We want to have time to be with our friends, but also to save time to spend together doing things as a family. And we should have some relaxed time to just do things around the house;

We want to always be loving to each other;

We want to be happy;

We want each of us to have a love of learning;

We want each of us to remember people who are not as fortunate as we are, and to find concrete (even if small) ways to help them;

We want to exercise wisdom in what we choose to eat, react, see, and how we spend our time;

We should remember to be generous with our hugs (everyone needs at least ten a day!);

No matter how pressing our work or school challenges, we should always remember that a happy family life is of prime importance, and demands a lot of our time and attention. "Quality time" isn't enough!

We will have weekly family meetings, plan memorable and exciting vacations, and keep fit and healthy;

We should all be patient with each other;

We should all be sensitive to each other's feelings.

We are lucky to have each other . . . we should remember this each day!

Thanksgiving Day
November 22, 1990

1998

Wednesday, January 28, 1998

My Darling Kimmie, Tina and Jenny:

I will send this to Kim as well, even though she is up at Amherst! As you read this, I will be approaching Mexico City. It is about a five-hour flight, and this will be my first visit there. The language is Spanish because, for many years, it was a Spanish colony. Sanitation practices are poor, and travelers often get diarrhea (which is commonly known as "Montezuma's Revenge" -- Montezuma was a leader of the Aztecs!).

My loves, I will miss you. I will be away for three nights, and will fly back on Saturday morning, arriving for dinnertime. I will be glad to get home, not only to be with you, but also to get out of the bad air pollution in Mexico City. Apparently it is terrible!

I am looking forward to going to Mexico. It is a fascinating place. Mexico is the most populous Spanish-speaking country in the world, and the second-most populous country in Latin America after Portuguese-speaking Brazil. About 70 percent of the people live in urban areas. Some people estimate that the population of the area around Mexico City alone is about 20 million, which makes it the largest concentration of population in the world anywhere.

Do you know much about the history? It is so interesting. As you know, highly advanced cultures, including those of the Mayas and Aztecs, existed long before the Spanish conquest. The Spanish conquest was led by Hernando Cortes, who conquered Mexico during the period 1519-21 and founded a Spanish colony that lasted nearly 300 years. This is why about 90 percent of the people in Mexico are Roman Catholic. They proclaimed independence from Spain in 1810, and that launched a war for independence (rather like the Declaration of Independence in America in 1776 launched the Revolutionary War). An 1821 treaty recognized Mexican independence from Spain and called for a Constitutional monarchy. The planned monarchy failed, and a republic was proclaimed in 1822 and established in 1824.

I have just been reading about the conflict between Mexico and Texas, and it is also fascinating. A prominent figure in Mexico's war for independence from Spain was General Antonio Lopez de Santa Ana. He went on to control Mexican politics from 1833 to 1855, and he was Mexico's leader during the conflict with Texas.

Texas declared itself independent from Mexico in 1836. I think that was the date of the Alamo ("Remember the Alamo!"). The Mexicans annihilated a small group of Texans and other Americans who were defending a small mission called the Alamo. I think John Wayne starred in a movie about it. Mexico fought the United States between 1846-48 and lost. Texas became independent of Mexico and later became a state belonging to the United States.

Tina, I know you are studying the American Revolution at the moment. History is so important. Jenny and I recently read part of a book on the American Revolution. I was amazed to learn what a tough fight George Washington had against the British. In the eight years he fought the British (1775-1783), he lost more battles than he won but always managed to keep his army together even though the suffering and deprivation were almost crippling. In 1781, at Yorktown, he captured an entire British army and secured American independence.

Thomas Jefferson said about George Washington, "Never did nature and fortune combine more perfectly to make a great man." Washington is called the "father of his country" because he was Commander of the Colonial Army during that Revolution, Chairman of the Constitutional Convention, and first President. In fact, he was the only President to be elected without opposition. In 1789, and again in 1793, he was the unanimous choice of the Presidential Electors. He died in 1799. As you know, his home was at Mount Vernon, close to where we live.

Here are some good words to know:

- Crestfallen: Dejected, dispirited, as, Many pop music fans were crestfallen when the Beatles broke up in 1970. (Apparently, this name comes from a bird's crest that falls after backing down from a rival.)

- Bovine: Dull, slow, ox-like, as, A bovine mentality in the organization led to them losing the contract.

- Bullish: Optimistic about the future, as, Bullish about the stock market. Bullish can also mean impetuous and aggressive.

- Red herring: Something misleading or diverting attention from a more serious matter. It comes from pulling a smoked herring across a trail to distract hunting hounds.

- Queasy: Uneasy, nauseating, as, The queasy motion of the waves.

- Opaque: Allowing no light through, hard to understand, as, Their motives are opaque and difficult to decipher.

- Epicenter: The focal point of an earthquake or of any activity, as, The university was an epicenter of originality and free thinking.

- Undulate: To move with a wave-like motion, as, The great river undulated across the beautiful countryside.

- Apprehension: Feeling of anxiety or fear, as, Apprehension, as if an undertow, tugged at him.

- Peerless: Without equal, unique, incomparable, as, Teddy Roosevelt was a peerless and brilliant President.

- Redolent: Fragrant, reminiscent of, as, One redolent spring morning.

Kimmie, I hope things are going well for you up at Amherst. Tina and Jenny, I hope things are going well for you at the hotel and in school. I love you all very much and miss you.

All my love,
Daddy
XXXOOO

Thursday, January 29, 1998

I love this quote from Margaret Thatcher: "In politics, if you want anything said, ask a man; if you want anything done, ask a woman." And I like this one, "Behind every successful man is a surprised woman." (That is a spoof of the old cliche, "Behind every successful man is a woman.") And I love this from Gloria Steinem: "I have yet to hear a man ask for advice on how to combine marriage and a career."

And here is another one from Gloria Steinem which I don't understand, but it has a good ring to it: "Some of us are becoming the men we wanted to marry." What do you all make of that?

In my letter last night, I talked a little about history and mentioned Thomas Jefferson. He was a man of countless talents and interests. He was one of the founders of the United States, he wrote our nation's first and, perhaps, most famous document – the Declaration of Independence. He served as Governor of his home state of Virginia. He traveled to France to represent the new US government and, in 1800, he was elected our country's third President. During his 83 years, Jefferson was many other things as well. He was a farmer, lawyer, law-maker, architect, inventor, archeologist, and musician. He enjoyed studying weather, plants, human and animal bones, and fossils. He was also a loving son, husband, father, and grandfather. He could read books in seven languages. Amazingly, Thomas Jefferson thought of himself as an ordinary man.

From an early age, Thomas Jefferson lived by the advice he later gave his own daughter, "It is wonderful how much may be done if we are always doing." Even as a young boy, Tom Jefferson was "always doing."

As you know, it was Jefferson who sent Meriwether Lewis and William Clark to explore the Louisiana Territory and look for "objects worthy of notice." They discovered 200 new species of plants, and Clark shipped back 300 fossil bones which Jefferson displayed in the President's mansion. The Lewis and Clark expedition was an extraordinary adventure.

Before his death, Jefferson wrote a letter describing how he wished to be remembered. He mentioned the three things of which he was most proud: Writing the Declaration of Independence, starting the University of Virginia, and writing the Virginia Statute of Religious Freedom. He did not mention being President! What a great life he lived!

Here are some good words for you to know:

- Principal: Foremost, most important, as, Lennon and McCartney were the Beatles principal composers. Also, as a noun: Invested money; head administrator of a school.

- Principle: General truth or doctrine used as a guide to action or conduct, as, A principle of democracy.

- Gibe: To taunt, jeer, make scoffing remarks, as, The hockey fans booed and gibed at the referee.

- Vile: Highly offensive, as, Vile slander or language.

- Reek: To stink, smell strongly. Also, to be connected with something bad or unpleasant, as, The business deal reeks of payoffs.

- Saga: Usually a long story of heroic achievements and adventures, as, Laura Ingalls Wilder's *Little House* books are sagas of frontier family life.

- Innuendo: Subtle put-down, derogatory hint, as, The innuendos regarding the athlete's ability.

- Repugnant: Distasteful, offensive, repulsive, as, I find certain daytime talk shows repugnant.

- Reticent: Uncommunicative, taciturn, reserved, as, The reticent scientist disliked social functions.

- Literally: Actually, truly, as, The prisoner was literally starving to death.

- Stigma: Impression or mark of disgrace or shame, as, Political corruption today seems to carry less of a stigma than in the past.

My treasures, if you can drop get well notes to Granny and notes of encouragement to Grandpa, I now they would appreciate it.

I love you, Kimmie; I love you, Tina; I love you, Jenny; and I look forward to being home on Saturday.

> All my love,
> Daddy
> XXXOOO

Friday, January 30, 1998

My Three Treasures: Kimmie, Tina and Jenny,

Here is a funny remark that came from Linda Ellerbee: "If men can run the world, why can't they stop wearing neckties? How intelligent is it to start the day by tying a little noose around your neck?"

Have you heard of Zsa Zsa Gabor? She has often gotten married and divorced, and she once said this: "I am a marvelous housekeeper. Every time I leave a man, I keep his house."

Here is the basis for a possible article that Kimmie or Tina might want to write. Tina, for *Scribbler*, you could do an article based around the idea that you would go to various teachers and say to them: "Looking back, if you could change one thing about the way you balanced your teaching career, personal, family and community activities over the years, what would it be?" It would be fascinating to see what they would say, and I think the readers of *Scribbler* would enjoy it. You could do a similar thing, Kim; but, obviously you would reword the question to fit the audience you are going after.

I recently saw an article along those lines in *The Wall Street Journal* by Sue Shellenbarger, who writes a regular column called "Work & Family." People who are professionally successful, when asked to reflect on their lives, will often say things like:

- I wish I had known sooner that, if you miss a child's play, performance or sporting event, you will have forgotten a year later the work emergency that caused you to miss it. But the child won't have forgotten that you weren't there.

- I wish I spent more time with my children.

- I don't want to be defined solely by the boxes I happen to occupy on organizational charts. As important as that may be, I want to be defined as the father of my children, as someone who made my community a better place.

Of course, if you don't have a successful career, then you might have slightly different answers.

If you were to ask me who I competed against in my work, my initial answer would be to say things like National Geographic, the BBC or other competitors like that. But that really is not right. My real competition is all the other things in my life which compete for a part of my attention. If I do not get those things in the right order, then it does not matter what is happening with the outside competition because I am not going to succeed because I won't be happy and fulfilled.

Thinking through what your goals are in life, what precise activities you want to undertake to accomplish those goals, setting schedules to achieve those goals, and writing all this down with specificity, are all very important things to do, in my view. It simply amazes me how many people do not articulate their goals, and then they wonder why they aren't more focused and successful.

Here are some more great words for you to know:

- Oxymoron: Contradiction in terms, combination of two words opposite in meaning, as, Cheerful pessimism; sweet sorrow.

- Pliant: Flexible, bending or twisting easily, as, Pliant molding clay.

- Tepid: Lukewarm, half-hearted, as, The candidate received only tepid applause.

- Quintessence: Refined essence or most important part, as, The lawyer's summation got to the quintessence of the case.

- Implement: Activate, put into effect, as, Donations to implement the building of a new church.

- Finicky: Fussy, overly particular, as, Our cat is a finicky eater.

- Analogy: A similarity seen between certain features of two different objects, as, The analogy between the computer and the human brain.

Well, my loves, I will be home tomorrow, and I will be pleased to get out of the air pollution in Mexico City. I love you each deeply and thank you for all you do to enrich Mummy's and my life.

I love you!

Daddy
XXXOOO

Tuesday, March 3, 1998
My Darling Kimmie, Tina and Jenny:

As you know, I left for England tonight to visit Granny and Grandpa. They have not been well, so it will be great to see them and, hopefully, my visit will cheer them up. I will be away for three nights and return on Friday. My flight gets in at about 3:00 PM on Friday afternoon, so I should be home by 5:00 if my plane is on time. Often planes are delayed, so I may be late. I will be very tired when I get home because I will have had little sleep for three days and, when I get home at 5:00 PM on Friday, it will be 10:00 PM in England!

As you know, flying to England is exhausting. My plane leaves at 6:40 PM tonight (Tuesday) and arrives at 6:30 AM tomorrow (Wednesday) morning. I will get a lot of work done on the plane. Of course, 6:30 AM on Wednesday morning in England is 1:30 AM in the middle of the night in America. You guys will be sound asleep! Uncle Jon is very generously going to pick me up from Heathrow Airport tomorrow morning. I might fall asleep in the car as he drives me to Bath!

As you know, on Thursday Mummy is going to drive to Princeton for a health conference and will return on Saturday afternoon. So there will be one night (Thursday) where I will be in England and Mummy will be in Princeton. Isn't that rare for both of us to be away at the same time? Normally, we design our lives so we are not away at the same time in order that one of us is always at home to take care of the family.

On this coming Thursday night, Tina will be at Laura's and Jenny will be at Sara Wipfler's house. I hope you both have a great time! I know you will remember to help clean up the kitchen, say thank you, and things like that. Being a gracious and welcome guest is a great social skill to develop. On Friday, Jenny is going to go to Rebecca's house and participate in their Shebat. Have a great time!

Tina, enjoy the tennis team this week! This is your first week and I hope you enjoy your new coach. Remember to be enthusiastic. If you enjoy it, you will help everybody else enjoy it. I know you will do whatever you can to build up the team spirit.

Jenny, your trumpet playing at the old people's home on Sunday was terrific. Those elderly people really enjoyed it, and I am sure the presence of all you vibrant, energetic children cheered them up enormously. And, Tina, I am so proud of you for playing on your basketball team. It does not matter that you lost. What <u>does</u> matter is that you all had a good time and you showed great sportsmanship.

I want to tell you about two episodes in American history which showed people at their best. The first is the Declaration of Independence which was the document announcing America's separation from England. As you know, it was adopted on July 4, 1776 in Philadelphia, Pennsylvania. In 1776, the 13 American colonies were at war with England, their mother country. The members of the colonial Continental Congress wanted the world to understand why they had revolted and why they wanted the colonies to be free and independent states. As you know, they asked Thomas Jefferson of Virginia to write a "Declaration of Independence" to explain why they were fighting. The first person to sign the Declaration of Independence was John Hancock of Massachusetts. The rebels who signed the Declaration of Independence put their lives on the line for freedom and democracy.

Another person who showed great character was Thomas Edison, who invented the light bulb, the phonograph, and a movie camera. He was born in 1847 and died in 1931. During his lifetime, he was awarded more than 1,000 patents! His lifelong motto was, "There's a better way to do it." Like Benjamin Franklin, he was born in poverty and had very little formal schooling. But he read widely to satisfy his enormous curiosity. The list of his inventions and achievements was staggering, and it made Edison one of the most admired men of his time. Sadly, I read recently that he was not a very competent family man.

Kimmie, Tina and Jenny, I love you so much. There <u>might</u> be another letter for you tomorrow!

All my love,

> Your 'ole Dad
> XXXOOO

P.S.:   Jenny, good luck tomorrow morning on your math exam at Westland!

Wednesday, March 4, 1998

My Darling Kimmie, Tina and Jenny:

I spent the day today with Granny and Grandpa. I will talk with you on the phone and tell you how it went. I very much regret missing the Parent Information Night at Westland tonight. I am dying to know, Jenny, how your math exam went at Westland this morning. And I hope you enjoyed your art class this afternoon. Tina, I hope tennis is going well, and I know you are asking good questions in class.

I discovered something which fascinated me recently. I am rather ashamed I didn't know this before. Did you know that the potable water that comes out of our faucets is drawn from the Potomac River? The raw water is drawn from the river, it enters a water treatment plant where coagulants are added, causing small particles to adhere to one another, making them heavy enough to settle out of the water in a sedimentation basin. The settled water is then filtered through sand and anthracite to remove remaining fine particles. Chlorine is added to kill harmful bacteria and viruses, and lyme is added to minimize the potential for dissolving the lead used in older household plumbing. Fluoride is added as a dental prophylactic. The treated water then is delivered to our house. Isn't that amazing? We drink water from the Potomac!

Here are some good words for you to know:

1. <u>Mogul</u>: An influential or powerful person (as, Ted Turner is one of the world's most successful entertainment moguls.)

2. <u>Nirvana</u>: State of great bliss or peace (as, Nirvana for the monk came after many days of intense meditation.)

3. <u>Pundit</u>: Expert who makes authoritative pronouncements or comments (as, Political pundits quickly weighed in with their opinions after the President's State of the Union Address.)

4. <u>Kamikaze</u>: Wildly reckless person (as, The bus driver was a highway kamikaze. Also, A Japanese kamikaze fighter plane deliberately crashed into an enemy target during World War II.)

5. <u>Boondocks</u>: Remote, rural area; tough backwoods or marshland.

6. <u>Pariah</u>: Outcast; despised person (as, The artist's outrageous behavior made him a social pariah.) Also, a member of a low social caste in India.

7. <u>Garble</u>: Confused explanation, either accidental or intentional, that creates distortion or misunderstanding (as, A garbled telephone message.)

8. <u>Brood</u>: To worry about; focus on a subject obsessively and silently (as, Don't brood over a missed field goal.)

History fact: Did you know that Thomas Jefferson (our third President) and John Adams (our second President) both died on July 4, 1826, the 50th anniversary of the Declaration of Independence. Isn't that amazing? They were political enemies for many years and wouldn't speak to each other; but, in the last years of their lives, they renewed their friendship and exchanged many letters.

Kimmie, Tina and Jenny, have you ever observed that what you dream about and focus on you get good at and achieve? Anything you focus on you will be able to do, and your possibilities will be endless (especially for you three girls because you are each so determined, focused and competent).

You three girls and Mummy have given me an incredible happiness and sense of fulfillment for which I will be forever deeply grateful. My life feels complete. I hope I am not complacent, but my life feels complete. As you know, I am forever pushing myself to learn more, to do more, to achieve more; but, if I die tomorrow, I will die happy and what more can one ask for?

My treasures, live tomorrow with energy, passion and enthusiasm. Don't waste a day!

I love you!

> Daddy
> XXXOOO

Thursday, March 5, 1998
My Darling Kimmie, Tina and Jenny:
Today I will be at an IMAX conference in London, and it will be a lot of fun. Then, at the end of the day, I will meet up with Uncle Tim (who is about three and a half years older than me), and we will drive to Bath to see Granny and Grandpa. Uncle Jon will join us, and then Tim and I will sleep at Jon's house tonight (I think Hannah and Ross will be there as well). Then, tomorrow morning (Friday, March 6), Tim will drive home to Wimbledon and, on the way, drop me off at Heathrow Airport. Then I will fly home to America, arriving at about 3:00 PM on Friday (if there is no delay).

Here is some interesting history for you: You've heard about the Lewis and Clark expedition (1804-1806). It was the greatest exploration in American history. When Lewis and Clark reached the Pacific Ocean on October 7, 1805, Meriwether Lewis wrote in his journal, "Ocean in view! Oh! The Joy!" A Shoshone Indian woman named Sacagawea served as a guide to Lewis and Clark and translated the language of the Indian tribes that the party encountered.

More history: It was June 1863, the Civil War had been raging for more than two years, and General Robert E. Lee, Commander of the Confederate army, decided to gamble everything on one battle that he hoped would gain independence for the south. This was the Battle of Gettysburg. More than 51,000 men in the two armies at Gettysburg were killed, wounded or captured. It was the largest battle ever fought in America. On July 3, the third day of the battle, Lee staked everything on one massive attack on the center of Cemetery Ridge. Most of the troops were led by General George Pickett, and the attack was called Pickett's Charge. In some of the most terrible fighting of the war, Pickett's Charge was driven back. Lee's great gamble had failed.

And one final historical fact: Did you know that, in 1849 when the gold rush began, there were 14,000 people in California. Three years later, there were 250,000! Isn't that amazing? People came by ship and they came by wagon train, and they were called Forty-Niners. Gold was found all through the California mountains, and many Forty-Niners became rich.

Kimmie, Tina and Jenny, we have a very interesting person coming to have dinner with us on Sunday night: Manuel Arango. He is a Mexican businessman and philanthropist and a very interesting person whom you will enjoy. I am so sorry, Kimmie, that you will miss meeting him.

Tina and Jenny, I cannot wait to see you tomorrow. Kimmie, I love you and miss you.

All my love,

               Daddy
               XXXOOO

Thursday, March 26, 1998

My Darling Kimmie, Tina and Jenny:

I am on my way to Montana to join our crew shooting the *Wolves* IMAX film! I will be back in three days on Sunday. I am sorry Tina was unable to come with me, but maybe next time.

Wolves are fascinating. They are hunters, and an individual wolf is so strong that it can pull down prey ten times its own weight. Stone Age people took wolf pups and tamed them, and all our domesticated dogs are descended from them. Indeed, the very characteristics we most admire in dogs — loyalty, intelligence and courage — are precisely the characters that the wolf has to have to survive in the wild.

As you know, many wolves, for much of the time, operate as a pack. They have such an extraordinary degree of intuition that their understanding of one another's intentions often seems beyond normal explanation. Younger members learn from the older, more experienced ones so that the whole group operates as a unified and highly skilled team.

Some packs can be 15-strong. The pack is dominated by an adult pair who are often together for life. Offspring from the previous three years make up the rest of the group. These pups look fully grown, but they are still learning from their parents. Their schooling is long, and their family life intense. Wolf packs are no more than highly organized and mobile nurseries, and it is this extraordinary mobility which makes them so difficult to observe at close range, and explains why we will be using primarily captive packs in the film. This disappoints me, but we have no choice. A wolf has a loose-limbed trot that is so effective and economical of energy that it can cover 50 miles in 24 hours, and do so for day after day after day.

When I get back, I will tell you more about my experiences with wolves in Montana and Yellowstone National Park.

Here are some good words for you to know:

➤ Altruistic. This word means unselfish, generous or large-hearted.

➤ Obsequious. This word means excessively submissive; too eager to please; as, "Obsequious waiters at a celebratory party."

➤ Droll. This word means amusing in an odd or whimsical way. You might say, "My father attempted to be droll at the office Christmas party."

More words in tomorrow's letter -- you lucky things!

I adore you and miss you and hope you have three great days while I am away.

Your devoted Daddy
XXXOOO

Friday, March 27, 1998

My Darling Kimmie, Tina and Jenny:

This is my second day in Yellowstone National Park working on our IMAX film on wolves. I will tell you all about it when I get home on Sunday!

Whenever I come out West, I always think about Native Americans. In the last century, a few people (like Dorothy on *Dr. Quinn*) viewed them as friendly, courteous and even hospitable to the initial invaders of their lands. In this view, they were seen as having great stamina and endurance, exhibiting great calm and dignity in bearing and in conversation, being brave in combat and tender in love for their families and children. According to this view, the Indian (as symbolized by Cloud Dancing on *Dr. Quinn*) lived a life of liberty, simplicity, innocence, and relished in the wholesome enjoyment of nature's gifts.

On the other side, most whites in the last century saw Indians as naked and lecherous, living lives of polygamy and constant warfare, with habits and customs which were brutal and loathsome. Cruelty to captives, human sacrifice, and incessant warfare all were seen as reasons for justifying the Indian's elimination. Filthy surroundings, inadequate cooking, and certain items of diet repulsive to white taste confirmed a low opinion of Indian life. Indolence, rather than industry, improvidence in the face of scarcity, thievery and treachery added to the list of traits buttressing the view of Indians as vermin.

Here are some good words for you to know:

➤ Squander: To fritter away; waste; as, "The lottery winner squandered his fortune."

➤ Divulge: To reveal, disclose something private or secret; as, "The traitor divulged his country's military plans."

➤ Demure: Shy, modest or reserved; as, "The actress played a demure country girl."

➤ Elusive: Slippery; hard to grasp; as, "An elusive thought."

> Debunk: To expose false or pretentious claims; as, "Copernicus debunked the belief that the sun revolved around the earth."

> Implacable: Relentless; cannot be pacified or appeased; as, "The frustration of negotiating with an implacable enemy."

> Cordial: Friendly and gracious; as, "The queen gave her subjects a cordial smile."

> Impinge: To trespass; intrude; as, "A hacker can impinge upon someone's privacy on the Internet."

My loves, I have given each of you another section of my latest journal for Tina for you to review for errors of grammar, fact and judgment. Please mark it up with all your changes so it can be as good as possible. Thanks very much, in advance, for your help.

Mummy and I love you each so much, and we feel so lucky to have you as our children. You are each so uniquely special and precious.

Yer 'ole Dad
XXXOOO

Saturday, March 28, 1998

My Darling Kimmie, Tina and Jenny:

I will be home tomorrow! I cannot wait to get back and be home with you all again.

Jen and I have been reading a most fascinating biography of Benjamin Franklin written by Thomas Fleming.

When he was almost 21, Ben Franklin did some thinking about his own life. He decided it was time to reflect upon his life experiences so far and draw some conclusions from them. Thus far, he decided, his life had been like a bad play — "a confused variety of different scenes." He felt he was now entering upon a new scene, and he decided to make some resolutions:

1. He decided it was necessary for him "to be extremely frugal for some time, til I have paid what I owe."

2. He decided it was critical for him "to endeavor to speak truth in every instance; to give nobody expectations that are not likely to be answered, but aim at sincerity in every word and action — the most amiable excellence in a rational being."

3. He decided that it was important "to apply myself industriously to whatever business I take in hand, and not divert my mind from my business by any foolish project of growing suddenly rich; for industry and patience are the surest means of plenty."

4. He resolved "to speak ill of no man whatever, not even in a matter of truth; but rather by some means excuse the faults I hear charged upon others, and upon proper occasion speak all the good I know of everybody."

This biography says that if a single word had to be chosen to describe Benjamin Franklin, "paternal" would come close to saying it all. Thomas Fleming writes:

> This burly, broad-shouldered man seem to fulfill himself most when he was in his fathering role, sharing his strength, his wisdom, his generosity, and his humor with other people.

He had a special relationship with his only son, William, who was illegitimate.

Ben Franklin was an extraordinary man — extraordinarily proactive. One can learn so much from studying his life.

Kimmie, Tina and Jenny, I love you each so much.

All my love,
Daddy
XXXOOO

Wednesday, April 8, 1998

My Darling Kimmie, Tina and Jenny:

I am in Montreal tonight getting ready for a packed day of meetings starting early tomorrow morning. I will return tomorrow evening, I hope in time for our family dinner. One reason I am visiting Montreal is to review the footage we have shot so far on our IMAX film on wolves.

Here are some jokes that have made me smile recently. I hope you enjoy them, too:

1. Two men were sitting in a doctor's office. "What are you in here for?" asked one. "Circumcision," came the reply. "I had one of those done the day after I was born," the first man commented. "Afterward, I couldn't walk for a year."

2. A woman answered her front door and found two boys holding a list. "Lady," one of them explained, "we are on a treasure hunt, and we need three grains of wheat, a pork-chop bone and a piece of used carbon paper to earn a dollar."
   "Wow," the woman replied. "Who sent you on such a challenging hunt?"
   "Our babysitter's boyfriend."

3. At the County Clerk's office where I work, a couple applying for a marriage license complained that they were having a hard time finding a clergyman who would tie the knot without requiring premarital counseling. "What do I need counseling for?" the groom-to-be moaned. "I have already been married three times!"

4. You may be addicted to the Internet if:

   ➤ You wake up at 3:00 AM to go to the bathroom and stop to check your e-mail.

   ➤ You decide to stay in college another year or two, just for the free Internet access.

   ➤ Half the plane trip is spent with your laptop beside you and your child in the overhead compartment.

5. To prevent our dog, Lacy, from pestering visitors to our house, my mother often massaged her as she lounged beneath the kitchen table, her favorite resting spot. One day, a

199

contractor came over to talk about a home improvement project. As he and my mother sat across the table discussing the renovations, my mother slipped off her shoes and mindlessly soothed Lacy with her feet. My mother had been talking for about a half-hour when, to her great embarrassment, she heard Lacy bark outside the front door.

6. With our aircraft carrier underway on an important exercise, the Admiral called all of the pilots together to discuss safety. He sternly lectured the group, then glared at them and asked gruffly, "Any questions?"
No one said a word, so he asked a second time. Still no takers. "No one is leaving," he demanded, "until I get a question."
"So," came a weak voice from the back, "where you from?"

7. During Passover, a Rabbi is so overwhelmed with religious fervor that he drops to his knees, puts his forehead to the ground and says, "Before you, Lord, I am nothing."
Not to be outdone, the Cantor, too, gets down on his knees, puts his forehead to the floor and says, "Before you, Lord, I am nothing."
Moved by their humility, a man in the fourth row steps into the aisle. He falls down on his knees, puts his forehead to the ground and says, "Before you, Lord, I am nothing."
The Cantor, noting the gesture, elbows the Rabbi. "So," he whispers, "look who thinks he's nothing."

8. "I told my doctor that every time I look in the mirror I get sick," says Rodney Dangerfield. "He told, 'at least your eyesight is good.'"

My three precious loves, I love you all so much. One of my greatest joys is to see you smile and laugh.

Buckets of love.

Your Devoted Dad
XXXOOO

Monday, April 13, 1998

My Three Precious Loves, Kimmie, Tina and Jenny:

I miss you! I am on my way tonight to the International Wildlife Film Festival in Missoula, Montana. I wish I had never accepted this invitation. The Festival has been asking me for years to come, and I have always turned them down in the past. This year, Mummy and I agreed that I would attend, and it was only after I made the commitment to go that I found out it was in the same week as Jenny's Easter vacation. AAARGHHHH! I was so upset when I found out! I was slightly comforted by the thought that at least Jenny would be busy with soccer camp this week, but then I found out last week that she did not even have soccer camp. There is nothing I can do about it; and what I can't change, I have to accept and make the most of.

I am also sorry I am going to miss your two tennis games, Tina, tomorrow and Thursday. Good luck!

I have been reading a fascinating book by Edward de Bono on "lateral thinking." This is thinking where you dream up alternatives, rather than trying to find the one "correct" answer. Lateral thinking is closely allied to creativity and humor, and can be contrasted with "logical" or "vertical" thinking.

I think it is an important concept, and I hope you get the chance to study lateral thinking one day. Lateral thinking is a good antidote to arrogance and rigidity, two weaknesses from which I suffer (cries of "no way!" and "impossible!").

Here are some good words:

1. Discretion: Showing good judgment and caution; as, In giving advice, counselors need a keen sense of discretion.

2. Delegate: To give responsibility or authority to other people; as, Key executives know how to delegate work.

3. Corollary: Natural consequence or results; as, Her success was a direct corollary of intense ambition.

4. Wane: To decrease; grow gradually less; as, The school's good reputation began to wane.

Kimmie, Tina and Jenny, Mummy and I love you each so much. You are so very special to us. All my love,

Dad
XXXOOO

Tuesday, April 14, 1998

Darling Kimmie, Tina and Jenny:

I came across these funny bloopers in *Reader's Digest* the other day which were taken — they claim — from actual medical transcriptionists' records:

➢ Experienced mood swings because she suffered from PBS.

➢ Since the patient stopped smoking, his smell is beginning to return.

➢ The patient is a 65-year old woman who fell, and this fall was complicated by a truck rolling over her.

➢ She Is quite hard of hearing. As a matter of fact, she cannot hear at all in the left eye.

➢ She has no rigors or shaking chills, but her husband states that she was very hot in bed last night.

➢ She is to refrain from sexual intercourse until I see her in the office.

My treasures, here are some words:

1. Larceny: Theft; as, Better store security reduced the incidence of larceny.

2. Allege: To assert without proof; as, The letter to the newspaper alleges the Mayor is corrupt.

3. Mediator: One who settles a dispute; as, Henry Clay was a skilled political mediator in the 1800s.

4. <u>Taut</u>: Tight; as, The plunging steer inadvertently helped the cowboy by keeping the lasso taut.

5. <u>Churn</u>: To stir or agitate violently; as, The raging storm churned the sea.

Kimmie, Tina and Jenny, I am happily enjoying my work in Missoula, Montana, but I miss being with you.

I love you each so much. All my love,

Your devoted Dad
XXXOOO

Wednesday, April 15, 1998

My Darling Kimmie, Tina and Jenny:

Don't forget there is a wonderful TV documentary on PBS tonight — another in the *Scientific American* series. I hope you can watch it.

Tina, you have been asking me some good questions recently about relaxation versus work. I don't know if what I have been saying has been helpful or not, but you have been helpful to <u>me</u> because your questions have reminded me that this is an important area to think about.

It is important to work hard and it is important to relax, but what exactly does all that mean? Good questions to ask are, "What is 'work'? What do we mean by it? What needs to show up so that we recognize something as 'work'? How would one know when one isn't 'working'?" Does work always have to be "hard?" Can work be joyful? What is the opposite of work? All of us create meaning for words, so that when we use or hear a particular word, our nervous systems are triggered into giving us an automatic assessment of what that word means. There are many words in the language that we use so often that their meanings have become cliched and, in a sense, forgotten. We take for granted words like work, relaxation, education, success, courage and listening. What do these words mean exactly? Is there one meaning, or do each of us create our own meaning for them? And is there only one useful interpretation, or many useful interpretations?

In my opinion, it is a good idea to "deconstruct" these words i.e., take them apart, analyze them, examine them in fresh ways, challenge the assumptions underlying them, and redesign our understanding of what they mean. This is one way to clear away mental clutter from our lives, and remind ourselves of fundamental principles. Having said all that, my opinion is that work is deeply satisfying.

Here are some good words:

➢ <u>Zeal</u>: Fervor, intense, tireless, an enthusiastic devotion to a cause or goal; as, The premiere's zeal for a peace agreement.

➢ <u>Bane</u>: Cause of misery, distress, harm or death; as, Crime is the bane of society.

➢ <u>Gig</u>: A short-term job, especially for a jazz musician; as, He played a gig last night at a hotel.

➢ <u>Preen</u>: To dress up with fussy, painstaking care; as, She preened for hours before her date.

This is also said of birds to smooth or clean feathers with their beak.

➢ Perjury: Lie; false testimony under oath; as, Kenneth Starr accused President Clinton of perjury.

➢ Mitigate: To make or become less severe; as, The judge mitigated the trespassing fine.

My three precious loves, you are three wonderful daughters, and Mummy and I feel so lucky to have you.

I love you!

Dad
XXXOOO

Thursday, April 16, 1998

My Dear Kimmie, Tina and Jenny:

The following are actual statements found on insurance forms where car drivers attempt to summarize the details of an accident in the fewest words possible:

1. Coming home, I drove into the wrong house and collided with a tree I don't have.

2. The other car collided with mine without giving warning of its intentions.

3. I thought the window was down, but I found out it was up, when I put my head through it.

4. I collided with a stationary truck coming the other way.

5. A truck backed through my windshield into my wife's face.

6. A pedestrian hit me and went under my car.

7. The guy was all over the road. I had to swerve a number of times before I hit him.

8. I pulled away from the side of the road, glanced at my motherinlaw and headed over the embankment.

9. In an attempt to kill a fly, I drove into a telephone pole.

10. I had been shopping for plants all day and was on my way home. As I reached an intersection, a hedge sprang up, obscuring my vision and I did not see the other car.

11. I had been driving for 40 years when I fell asleep at the wheel and had an accident.

12. To avoid hitting the bumper of the car in front, I struck the pedestrian.

13. An invisible car came out of nowhere, struck my car and vanished.

14. I told the police that I was not injured, but on removing my hat, found that I had a fractured skull.

15. The pedestrian had no idea which direction to run, so I ran over him.

16. The indirect cause of the accident was a little guy in a small car with a big mouth.

17. I was thrown from my car as it left the road. I was later found in a ditch by some stray cows.

18. The telephone pole was approaching. I was attempting to swerve out of its way, when it struck the front end.

And here are a few good words:

➢ Mesh: To coordinate; combine; as, The couple made an effort to mesh their careers.

➢ Bleak: Dreary; without hope; as, A bleak future.

➢ Litigate: To sue; contest; as, Pet owners decided to litigate the town's leash law.

➢ Affidavit: Written statement made under oath for use as legal evidence; as, According to his affidavit, he never received payment.

➢ Coercion: The use of force, often through threats and intimidations; as, He resigned from the job under coercion.

I will be home tomorrow! And I cannot wait. I hope you are each having a great week in your own unique ways. Remember how very special you each are.

I adore you! Love,

Dad
XXXOOO

Tuesday, April 28, 1998
My Darling Kimmie, Tina and Jenny:
I am in Fort Lauderdale to give several speeches about our IMAX work. It is a series of very important meetings for me, and one reason why I felt under such pressure last week. I had so much going on and I had to get ready for this trip as well!

I feel under such pressure when I have so much to get done, and I just cannot do it all without staying up all night and getting exhausted. This last week has not been good for me because I have not spent enough time with the family, and I have just not been the source of joy and happiness that I want to be for you all. I apologize to you all for not being as good as I can be.

Laughter is a great way to release tension and to see the funny side of things. Often the funny side of things only shows up years later — by why wait for years to see the funny side of things? Why not see it right away, and laugh at some of the ridiculous things we now think are important but which really aren't?

Here are some recent jokes, quotes, and one-liners that I have enjoyed:

➢ There cannot be a crisis next week. My schedule is already full. (Henry Kissinger)

- Cordless phones are great. If you can find them.

- Some people's idea of "roughing it" is not having cable.

- My neighborhood is so dangerous, American Online won't even deliver e-mail here.

- Do you know what the letters in "DELTA" stand for? "Don't Expect Luggage To Arrive."

- Airplanes are the ultimate in consolidation. Flight attendants instruct: "We have a floatation device, but actually, it's your seat!" I am paranoid to throw anything away, I might need it later. For all I know my empty peanut bag is my life raft.

- I think airline flights should be cheaper. At the airport, they always make you walk at least halfway to your destination before you even get on the plane.

- Of course, America had often been discovered before Columbus, but it had always been hushed up. (Oscar Wilde)

- What a hotel we're staying at! The towels are so big and fluffy, you can hardly close your suitcase.

- My wife thinks I am too nosy. At least that's what she keeps scribbling in her diary.

- I am thinking about getting married. I looked up the word "engaged" in the dictionary. It said, "To do battle with the enemy." Then I looked up mother-in-law, "See engaged."

- I would like to go to an assertiveness training class. First, I need to check with my wife.

- Husband: "Darling, will you love me when I am old and feeble?"
    Wife: "Of course, I do."

- The book *Men Are From Mars, Women Are From Venus* explains that men and women are from different planets. For example, women like to verbalize their feelings on relationships. It's difficult for a man to even admit he is in a relationship.

- High heels were invented by a woman who had been kissed on the forehead.

- I am a marvelous housekeeper. Every time I leave a man, I keep his house. (Zsa Zsa Gabor)

- For a man, getting dressed up is anything that requires underwear and socks. Whereas a woman gets her hair done, puts on make-up, tummy toner, a short skirt, and high heels, and then says she wants to "find a man who loves me for *me*."

- Our doctor is an eye, ear, nose, throat, and wallet specialist.

- He must have had a magnificent build before his stomach went in for a career of its own.

- How come people who are always late wear it like a badge of honor? They will brag about it, "I am always running late." How can you be "running late"? If you were running late, you should have made it! If you're running, you're doing it quickly! Which means some people want to be late "as fast as they can"!

- You go to the ballet and you see girls dancing on their tiptoes. Why don't they just get taller girls?

- A hospital surgeon told his patient, "I have some good news and some bad news. Which do you want to hear first?" The patient said, "Give me the bad news." The doctor said, "We are going to have to amputate both of your feet." The patient said, "Oh, that's terrible! What's the good news?" The doctor said, "The patient in the next bed wants to buy your slippers."

- I looked at the TV guide last night. The "Best Bet" was the off button.

- Television enables you to be entertained in your home by people you wouldn't have in your home.

- On cable TV, they have a weather channel — 24 hours of weather. We had something like that where I grew up. We called it a window.

- Television — a medium, so called because it is neither rare or well done.

- I find television very educational. Every time someone turns on the set, I go into the other room to read a book.

- If I see one more horror movie, I'm gonna scream!

- The brain is a wonderful organ; it starts working the moment you get up in the morning and does not stop until you get to school.

My treasures, don't forget to smile. When you smile, you bring so much joy into the world.

I love you each so much, and I miss you. All my love,

Daddy
XXXOOO

Wednesday, April 29, 1998

My three precious treasures, Kimmie, Tina and Jenny:

I love you! And I miss you! I will be home tomorrow — which is where I love to be. When I was young, I used to love to travel. Now, I love to be at home.

I hope, by the time you read this letter, I will have gotten my life back into a better balance between all the various pressures that relentlessly bear down on me. It isn't easy being a good dad, a good husband, an effective professional who can earn enough money to support his family, and an effective executive who can run a nonprofit organization devoted to conservation. I am not saying all this so you will feel sorry for me — I am saying all this because, however good life is, there are constant challenges and constant learning to be done. Whenever I get overwhelmed with things I have to do, I go back to fundamentals and try to sort out what really matters to me. There is always time to do the things that really matter.

One of the difficulties when one is so busy is that busyness sometimes can prevent one from appreciating how lucky one is and how grateful one should be. I should be incredibly grateful for the wonderful family I have, that you three have the most wonderful mother in the whole world, that I have a wonderful wife, a great job, loyal and devoted colleagues, superb health, and so on — yet it is easy for me to forget, in the rush and hassle of daily life, how grateful I should be for my good fortune. Of course, to some extent, I have earned this good fortune by working hard and exercising -- for the most part -- good judgment in my decision-making over the years. Nevertheless, I am incredibly lucky, and I owe so much to so many people for helping me achieve the kind of life I live — and at the top of the list would be Gail, you, and my parents.

I have become acutely conscious in the last few days of how lucky I am because I have been listening in the car to a book that I have read in the past and think very highly of (and which I gave to Tina for Christmas one year) called *Man's Search For Meaning* by Viktor E. Frankl. Frankl was a distinguished psychiatrist who recently died. In this book, Frankl gives a moving and poignant account of his life amid the horrors of the Nazi death camps, chronicling the harrowing experience that led to some of his discoveries in psychiatry. He stresses man's freedom to transcend suffering and find a meaning in his life, regardless of his circumstances. This is a book which has had a tremendous influence on me because of the lesson it teaches that one is always free to choose one's attitude and response to circumstances, however bad. (But let me just say how lucky we are to live in America in a thriving democracy!)

In order that you don't go to bed too solemn, and remembering that laughter is the best medicine of all, here are some more jokes and one-liners that I have recently enjoyed:

> ➢ I went to a bookstore and I asked the woman behind the counter where the self-help section was. She said, "If I told you, that would defeat the whole purpose."

> ➢ My friend thought he was not gonna make it. Then he started thinking positive. Now he is positive he is not gonna make it.

> ➢ He has turned his life around. He used to be depressed and miserable. Now, he is miserable and depressed.

> ➢ Why is it that lemon pie filling and lemonade are made with "artificial lemon flavoring," but dish soap and furniture polish are made with real lemon juice?

> ➢ Cured ham? No thanks, pal. Cured of what? What if it has a relapse on my plate?

> ➢ As for evolution, I have a hard time believing that, billions of years ago, two protozoan bumped into each other under a volcanic cesspool and evolved into Cindy Crawford.

- Epitaphs on gravestones:

  - If you can read this, you're too close; get off my grave!

  - I told you I was ill.

  - Looked up the elevator shaft to see if the car was coming down. It was.

  - Keep the line moving.

- I am not afraid of dying. I just don't want to be there when it happens. (Woody Allen)

- Dads are born without the sympathy gene. You can break your leg, hobble into your house, and all your dad will do is look over the paper and grumble, "Shake it off!"

- My son has taken up meditation — at least it's better than sitting and doing nothing.

- My father used to tell me, "When Abraham Lincoln was your age, Abraham Lincoln had a job. When Abraham Lincoln was your age, he walked 12 miles to get to school." I said, "Dad, when Lincoln was your age, he was President, okay?"

- As a kid, I thought my dad was blind and deaf. He would sit for hours in his recliner moaning, "I can't see! I wish I could hear what's going on!" Finally, my mom told me to quiet down and to stop playing in front of the TV.

- Bill Cosby says of golf, "You got the ball. You had it right there. Then you hit it away! And then you go and walk after it again! It's a dumb game!"

- Jim was just beginning to make a putt when a funeral procession drove by the golf course. He bowed his head, holding his hat over his heart until the procession had passed, then he began putting again. His golf buddies said, "Wow, Jim, we had no idea you were a religious person... that was very sensitive!" He replied, "Well, after all, I *was* married to her for 28 years!"

- Middle age starts to show around your middle. (Bob Hope)

- My doctor said I looked like a million dollars — green and wrinkled. (Red Skelton)

- Have you gotten your income tax papers yet? They have done away with all those silly questions now. There are only three questions on the form: (1) How much did you earn? (2) How much do you have left? (3) Send it in.

- I fear that one day I will meet God, He'll sneeze, and I won't know what to say.

And, finally, here's a poem by Judith Viorst called *Father Doesn't Want A Dog*:

Father doesn't want a dog.
Father says they smell,

And never sit when you say sit,
Or even when you yell.
And we to go back out because
The dumb dog has to go.

Father doesn't want a dog.
Father says they shed,
And always let the strangers in,
And bark at friends instead,
And do disgraceful things on rugs,
And track mud on the floor,
And flop upon your bed at night,
And snore their doggy snore.

Father doesn't want a dog.
He's making a mistake,
Because, more than a dog, I think
He will not want this snake.

Kimmie, Tina and Jenny, I love you so much. I want to be a warm, close, affectionate, and supportive father to you. I don't always succeed, and I apologize for that. It's not always easy to know when to listen, when to advise, and when to butt out. I am sure I should but out more and listen more, and I am sure that I spend too much time offering superfluous and ridiculous advice. Anyway, as long as I live, I hope to continue improving my ability to be a competent and effective father to you. It's a wonderful job — the most wonderful job in the world. Before you three came along, I was very worried that I would make a complete mess of being a father, and so I got lots of books out of the library on how to do the job. I soon realized that there were skills that a Dad needed that I didn't have, but that, if I learned them, I could be more effective (such as learning how to praise a child effectively). Of course, I have made a lot of mistakes, and one thing that has always amazed me is how forgiving you three are of my mistakes. (A mistake, in my view, would be yelling, not listening, not understanding, embarrassing you, neglecting you, and so on.) When I come to the end of my life, I hope that you will consider me to have done a half decent job as your father. Nothing would give me more profound pleasure. You are each so special and deserve the best. You certainly have the best in Mommy.

I love you so much.

Daddy
XXXOOO

Wednesday, May 13, 1998

My Darling Kimmie, Tina and Jenny:
As you read this, I am in Los Angeles for a meeting of the so-called "Large-Format Cinema Association" — which is a three-day conference of the IMAX industry, including IMAX film producers like me. I am giving several presentations and will have many meetings on our six IMAX films: *Whales*, *Wolves*, *Water*, *Bears*, *Dolphins*, and *Bison*. I feel very lucky to be doing a job which I care about and which I think does some good for the world.

I hope you three loves are having a wonderful week. I know, Kimmie, that you are working hard on your exams and papers. Isn't it amazing that you have come to your last week of your freshman year at Amherst? Tina, good luck in all the preparation you are doing for your exams. And I am so proud of you and Mara last Friday for fighting back from being down 1-4 in your ISL tennis championship, and then going on to win 75! Jenny, I am glad you had such a good time with Henry, Leigh and Erin last weekend. They were so lucky to have you to play with and I know how much you miss them.

I am writing this letter to you on Mother's Day (May 10), and I am thinking what an incredible, wonderful mother you three girls have. When Gail and I fell in love in the early 70's and decided to spend our lives together, I never once said to myself what an incredible mother she would make; but, now as I think back on it, that was one of the many qualities that made me realize what an extraordinary person she was.   I wish all the children in the world could have a mother as devoted, competent and caring as Gail. I know you three girls appreciate her as profoundly as any children could appreciate a mother, and that is yet another reflection of how special she is, that she would have the love and competence to raise three children as loving, capable, optimistic, and emotionally intelligent as you three.

How extraordinarily special Gail is as a mother has been driven home to me recently because I have been listening in the car to one of the best books I have ever read called *How To Talk So Kids Will Listen And Listen So Kids Will Talk* by Adele Faber and Elaine Mazlish. I read this book years ago when I first became a father because I was concerned about my incompetence in the domain of fathering. This is one of the many books I studied, and I found it immensely helpful.

It is a "how to" book on communication skills for parents. It gives parents instructions on how to talk to their children, and it gives hundreds of examples of helpful dialogues so that parents can learn new skills in order for them to learn how to talk so their kids will listen and listen so their kids will talk.

As I "reread" the book in the car last week, I was reminded of how these are skills that Mommy has automatically — while I had to learn them and, indeed, am still learning them. Mommy feels good about herself and she helps other people, especially those she loves, feel good about themselves. She tries to live without blame and recrimination. She is sensitive to other people's feelings. She expresses her irritation and anger (on the rare occasions she feels that way) without doing damage. She is respectful of other people's needs (and of the needs of you three girls), and she is respectful of her own needs. She has brought up three children to be caring and responsible. She has broken any cycle of unhealthful talk that might have been handed down from generation to generation, and passed on a different legacy to you three.

I think, because of Gail, you three will find (and have found) ways of communicating that you can use for the rest of your lives with your friends, your co-workers, with us, with your families, with your own husbands (if you decide to get married), and one day with children of your own (if you decide to have children of your own). These communication skills that you learned and continue to learn from Mommy will be a great legacy that you will pass on to future generations.

Faber and Mazlish say that some of the methods most commonly used by adults to get their children to cooperate include ones which are ineffective, such as:

> Blaming and accusing ("Your room's a mess again! Why do you always do that... what's the

matter with you anyway? Can't you ever do anything right?.... How many times do I have tell you to clean up your room? The trouble with you is you never listen.")

➢ Name calling ("It's freezing today and you are wearing a light jacket! How dumb can you get? Boy, that really is a stupid thing for you to do.")

➢ Threats ("Just you touch that lamp once more and you'll get a smack." "If you are not finished dressing by the time I count to three, I am leaving without you!")

➢ Commands ("You still didn't take out the garbage? Do it now!.... What are you waiting for? Move!")

➢ Lecturing and moralizing ("Do you think that was a nice thing to do — to grab that book from me? I can see you don't realize how important good manners are..... You wouldn't want anyone to grab from you, would you? Then you shouldn't grab from anyone else. We do unto others as we would have others do unto us.")

➢ Warnings ("Watch it, you'll burn yourself." "Careful, you'll get hit by a car!" "Don't climb that! Do you want to fall?")

➢ Martyrdom statements ("Will you two stop that screaming!? What are you trying to do to me... make me sick?... give me a heart attack?" "Do you see these grey hairs? That's because of you. You're putting me in my grave.")

➢ Comparisons ("Why can't you be more like your sister? She always gets her work done ahead of time." "Lisa has such beautiful table manners. You'd never catch her eating with her fingers.")

➢ Sarcasm ("You knew you had a test tomorrow and left your book in school? Oh smart! That was a brilliant thing to do." "Is this the homework you are bringing to school tomorrow? Well, maybe your teacher can read Chinese; I can't.")

➢ Prophesy ("You lied to me about your report card, didn't you? Do you know what you're going to be when you grow up? A person nobody can trust." "Just keep on being selfish. You'll see, no one is ever going to want to play with you. You'll have no friends.")

I am embarrassed to admit that I have probably used every one of these approaches, and every one of them is wrong in the sense that they produce feelings in children that lead them to have negative feelings about themselves and to produce the very opposite of their intended effect. The goal is to get the child to cooperate, but these ten ways of talking produce actions and feelings in a child which push them in the opposite direction of cooperation.

Anyway, the point I am making is that Mommy has an instinctive knowledge that the methods that are commonly used by adults to get children to cooperate are ineffective, and she has much better and more effective ways of communicating with all of you (and with me).

The book by Faber and Mazlish deals with helping children deal with their feelings, engaging cooperation, alternatives to punishment, encouraging autonomy, praise, and freeing children from playing negative roles. (The latter point refers to labeling kids with words like "stubborn," "aggressive," "selfish," and so on.) Mommy is skillful in communicating in all of these areas, and I have learned much from observing her and using her as a model.

So, on this Mother's Day in 1998, let's celebrate one terrific Mom!

> I love you,

> > Daddy
> > XXXOOO

Thursday, May 14, 1998

My Darling Kimmie, Tina and Jenny:

> Oh, my goodness! The last episode of *Seinfeld*! What will we now do on Thursday nights?!

> Here are some good words:

> - Befriend: To act as a friend to; as, "Jerry befriended Kramer."

> - Adjunct: Addition or enhancement; as, "Lifting weights is an adjunct to aerobic exercise."

> - Entourage: Attendants to someone important or well-known; as, "Jerry arrived with his entourage of three friends."

> - Motivate: To incite someone's interest; as, "Knowing yourself means knowing what motivates you and what you like or dislike about yourself."

> - Confidant: Trusted friend; as "Elaine and Jerry were confidants."

> - Discern: To see clearly with the mind or eye; as, "Jerry and George were discerning, but not always about their own faults."

> My treasures, did you read the interview with Diana Beebe in the May issue of *The Washingtonian*? It was an excellent interview. She stressed the importance of accomplishments over popularity, and stressed the importance of strength and health for girls instead of looks. She emphasized that the way for a girl to feel good about herself is not to go on a diet, go shopping or watch mindless television, but rather to be "involved in all sorts of fascinating pursuits — whether it's building a robot or being in a play or singing in a chorus or being on an athletic team or the debating team."

> In a recent essay for *Highlights*, the newsletter of HAPA, Diana Beebe wrote:

> > ...Girls do better in single sex settings because of increased self-esteem and confidence... Girls feel free to take risks that they were unwilling to take in classes where boys were present... What research tells us about girls is that they learn best when they are in a place that develops their confidence, their competence and their sense of connectedness. It stands to reason that a school such as Holton-Arms, which has a clear mission, high standards, small classes, individual attention, a sense of community, strong

adult role models, and focuses on the special needs of girls, will foster not only strong academic achievement, but also the skills and the confidence that contribute to life's success.

Hey, Kim and Tina, I have just noticed in that same issue of *Highlights* that there is a recommendation in an article on teens and driving that adolescents should be financially responsible for the privilege of driving — that they should pay half of the cost of lessons, at least one-half of the car insurance, and the cost of any increases in premiums due to accidents. What do you think?! Sounds like a good idea to me!

Kimmie, Tina and Jenny, I love you and miss you!

Dad
XXXOOO

Friday, May 15, 1998
My Darling Kimmie, Tina and Jenny:
Mommy recently asked me when I was going to retire and when we could relax and take it easy. I have been thinking about that and also remembering how some people when they retire seem to fall apart because they suddenly lose purpose. This is particularly true for men. Stephen Covey believes that one reason why women live seven years longer than men, on average, is because from their point of view, a woman's work is never done. He writes:

Women learn to multi-task. They may have career activities, but they never give up on their families. In contrast, many men become primarily focused and single-minded around their careers. They don't multi-task as much, and they feel that when they retire, they essentially lose that which gave their life its meaning. They then begin to degenerate and deteriorate, since the lack of meaning for their lives weakens the immune function of the body.

I mentioned to you the other day that I have been rereading Victor Frankl's book *Man's Search For Meaning*. He thought hard about the challenge of how to live life without negative stress. His ideas on stress contrast sharply with today's popular, but, in my view, superficial approaches which are based on relaxation and meditation exercises. Frankl knew that the core cause of destructive stress is a life devoid of meaning, contribution, and service — and, conversely, that the greatest way to remove negative stress is to have meaningful life work and to make a lifelong contribution.

So, even if I retire, I hope to have meaningful projects, to contribute service, and to make a difference. Frankl's life was saved in the death camps of Germany because he learned from hard experience a simple truth: We all need to have meaningful projects to give our lives meaning and strengthen the *why* and the *will* to live. He learned from his death camp experiences that meaning alone could keep people alive and relatively well, even in the harshest of conditions.

The strong temptation when people retire is to live off the legacy of the past, to enjoy the ease and comfort of home, and to surround yourself with friends and family only — rather than continue to accomplish things that help the world to be a better place. The thing that keeps people strong, healthy, vital, vibrant, and alive is that they keep learning and keep contributing.

My view is that, along with my many family commitments, after I "retire" I will have many projects that get me up in the morning that keep me "young" with passion and enthusiasm for life. I hope that key words for me will be: family, friends, learning, passion, vitality, contribution, achievement, commitment, leadership, insight, empowerment, wisdom, education, influence, opportunity, integrity, courage, action, clarity, abundance, performance, vision, focus, impact, intelligence, freedom, autonomy, discovery, purpose, meaning, gratitude, rigor, self-discipline, relaxation, ambition, compassion, fulfillment, quality, strength, triumph, communication, renewal, boldness, and tranquility.

The last word is interesting to me because I want to have projects, even when I am retired, that I feel passionate about; but, at the same time, I want inner peace, and for most people it is not easy to be both passionate and peaceful at the same time. This goal — of being both passionate and, at the same time, inwardly tranquil and serene — was impossible for me when I was younger. I hope as I get older I will gain more wisdom and be able to have both.

The underlying key to having an extraordinary quality of life, I believe, is to lead a life of one's own design, rather than one scripted for you by your environment, your history, your parents, your biology, your genes, society, or anyone else.

Kimmie, Tina and Jenny, you three girls are learning the skills you need to lead lives of joy, impact, achievement, contribution, love, and distinction. All it takes is constant learning!

I love you!

Yer 'ole Dad (who is basically a boring preacher at heart!)
XXXOOO

Wednesday, May 20, 1998

My Darling Kimmie, Tina and Jenny:

I am in Montreal tonight to look at the footage we have so far for our IMAX film on wolves, and to hold a series of meetings connected with our wolves film such as meeting with book publishers to work out a deal for producing a companion book. I am squeezing this trip in between two very important events: Your birthday, Tina, on Tuesday; and your birthday, Jenny, on Friday! It is hard to believe you guys are now (or will be) 16 and 11, respectively. Each of you three girls is growing up so beautifully, and Mummy and I love you so much and are so proud of you.

I recently came across the following four thoughts that seem to have some merit.

1. If someone betrays you once, it's her fault; if she betrays you twice, it's your fault.

2. Great minds discuss ideas; average minds discuss events; small minds discuss people.

3. Beautiful young people are accidents of nature, but beautiful old people are works of art.

4. Learn from the mistakes of others. You can't live long enough to make them all yourself.

I am trying to decide if these deserve to go into my book of maxims. What do you think?

Did you have a chance to read all the letters I gave you from people who commented on the article Kim wrote in *The Washington Post* about my journal? There were some wonderful letters there.

I hope you enjoy them. (And, Kim, I think there is raw material for another article!)

And, finally, here are some good words for you to know:

1. Ramification: Consequence; as, "The ramifications of my father's long hours on our family life."

2. Tangent: A branching off; divergence; as, "My daughter's talk was very focused and did not go off on a tangent."

3. Resilient: Flexible; springing back into a former shape; recovering quickly; as, "Our three daughters are resilient, which is good because the world out there is tough."

4. Segue: To continue without interruption; as, "After my father gave his speech, he intended to segue into questions and answers."

5. Regimen: Way of life, especially for promoting health; as, "A daily regimen of stretching, aerobics and weight-lifting will give our daughters life-long health."

6. Provocative: Stimulating or exciting; as, "As a family, we should think of more provocative subjects to discuss at family dinners."

7. Charisma: Magnetic appeal or charm; as, "Daughters very rarely feel that their fathers have any special charisma at all."

8. Density: Thickness, solidity and compactness; as, "Weight-training for women helps them to maintain bone density."

My treasures, I love you so much and cannot wait to get home tomorrow. Kim, it will be wonderful to have you home this weekend. Tina and Jenny, the birthday girls, it's always lovely to have you at home.

You are each very special. I love you!

Daddy
XXXOOO

Friday, June 12, 1998
My Darling Kimmie, Tina and Jenny:
As you know, I am on my way to England to celebrate Granny's 80th birthday! Actually today (June 12) is her 80th birthday, but we are celebrating it with a big dinner party tomorrow night on June 13. It will be a lot of fun and I am looking forward to it. I have my toast prepared, and I thank you for your help in preparing it.

I will land in England tomorrow morning at 6:30 AM, and Jon is kindly coming to pick me up and drive me back to Bath. I will only be in England for two days before flying home on Monday arriving at Dulles at about 3:00 PM. Then I will be home for about 36 hours before flying to Alaska for eight days. I am sad that none of you are with me for either of these two trips, but that is just the way it is. I will be thinking about you all the time, and I will be happy knowing that you are taking care of each other and leading good, healthy, happy lives.

Since this is Granny's birthday, I have been thinking about her family history. You have some amazing ancestors! It will be super when Mommy takes a three-month sabbatical and gets her book written on her family history. It is going to be fascinating and it will become a family heirloom. On my side of the family, we have the 100+ book that Mommy and I wrote to celebrate my parents' 50th wedding anniversary in 1991. It contains lots of fascinating information about the people from whom you are descended. As I wrote in the Preface, one of the purposes of that book was:

> To remember those who have died. We want them to remain for each new generation to enjoy. In a very real sense, a person does not die until they are forgotten.

Your great grandparents on Granny's side of the family were Richard Thomas Hallett and Agnes Mary Stratton. Richard Thomas Hallett was born in 1843 and died in 1903. Agnes Mary Stratton was born in 1848 and died in 1937, ten years before I was born.

Richard and Agnes were married in England in 1870 and — what I considered to be a courageous act — emigrated to Nottoway County in Virginia in 1871, soon after the end of the Civil War. The land he bought was situated in the rural area between the two townships of Crewe and Blackstone. He bought 420 acres of land for $3.85 an acre.

Agnes was a farmer's daughter from Perth, Scotland, and was used to living in comfort. (Her father discovered coal on his property and this made him wealthy — he was once decorated for his bravery in rescuing miners when an explosion occurred and many miners died.) Agnes came to Virginia with a trousseau of taffetas, good linen, and lovely dresses. She thought she and her new husband were going to live in a grand ante-bellum plantation. The reality was a shock to her. Their house was a mud log cabin. She found the conditions very primitive and, although their house in Crewe was named "Walnut Grove," she always called it "Purgatory." We think she may also have given the road its existing name — Stingy Lane!

So Agnes returned to England in 1877, soon after her fourth child Jerry (Granny's father) was born. Richard bought a farm at Five Head in Taunton, and spent half of each year in each country. He made the trip between America and England about 20 times after 1877. Just think about that — and remember how tough that trip was. I wish I knew more about him.

Agnes was known as the "Angel of Mercy" in Nottoway County because she rode side-saddle around the county bringing "custard" and other help to the sick and to new mothers. She helped to establish the first school for blacks. By all accounts, Agnes was a strong, dominating personality. She could still jump rope at age 89, shortly before she died. She was an accomplished pianist and loved to go for walks. Granny remembers her very fondly.

So, my treasures, you are descended from people who were adventuresome, tough and resilient. Life was not easy for them.

One of the biggest responsibilities that Mommy and I have as parents is to make sure that you have the skills, knowledge, and values you need to thrive and succeed in a very tough, competitive world. You need both ambition and serenity in equal proportions, but I sometimes worry that so many kids today — brought up as you three are in unbelievable luxury and ease with no physical deprivations of any kind — are not prepared to live lives which will leave a legacy of any kind. The big danger for kids today is that they will lead passive lives of quiet suffering and disappointment, instead of lives of rigor, joy, self-discipline, love, and accomplishment.

Children are given so much in a material sense that they get easily bored and can suffer from a destructive ennui. Parents mistakenly allow them not to do chores; they are allowed to watch too much TV; and the parents themselves perhaps do not set a good example of what a powerful, pro-active, caring, and vigorous life can be.

So kids are not prepared for life — they are soft, careless, passionless, lazy, and live without a sense of mission or purpose.

In my view, it is a big mistake to live life as though it is one big carnival. I use the word carnival because I associate carnivals with loud vulgar music, faint temporary amusement, and forgettable thrills — a place where hard work, laughter, long-range thinking, creativity, joy, accomplishment, and postponing gratification are alien.

Some children have almost come to feel a sense of "entitlement" to a life that consists of playing Nintendo, watching sitcoms, and listening to pop music. They feel they have some sort of "right" to an easy life. Anything which takes them away from the life of luxury and being waited on is perceived as a deprivation! A "peak" experience to them is an essentially passive experience, and not one brought about by one's own wits, hard work, skill, imagination, bravery or good judgment.

Anyway, that is enough preaching! Here are some good words for you to know:

➤ Quandary: Perplexity or uncertainty; as, "In a quandary, Tina asked her teacher for advice on the test."

➤ Articulate: Fluent; expressing oneself effectively; as, "Her superior abilities in writing an articulate speech."

➤ Spontaneity: Act of impulsiveness or instinct; as, "Her spontaneity sometimes brings on surprises."

➤ Parameter: Limit or boundary; as, "Our daughters' ability to bond with people goes beyond everyday parameters."

➤ Inhibition: Self-consciousness or anxiety that holds back action; as, "She has no inhibitions and does not worry about her image."

➤ Transcend: To rise above; excel; as, "She has the ability to transcend difficulties and unfair-ness."

Kimmie, Tina and Jenny, I adore you. I will call you from England. Buckets of love,

Yer 'ole Dad
XXXOOO

Saturday, June 13, 1998

Darling Kimmie, Tina and Jenny:

Tonight is the party and birthday celebration for Granny! About 35 people are coming, and I will tell you all about it. I hope my toast goes well! It does not contain a lot of humor (although I expect I will make more jokes as I go along). I have been looking for humor, and here are some basic ideas that I might be able to use in some way tonight at the dinner:

- No matter how old a mother is, she watches her middle-aged children for signs of improvement.

- The first half of our lives is ruined by our parents, and the second half by our children.

- Have children while your parents are still young enough to take care of them.

- My parents have been visiting me for a few days. I just dropped them off at the airport. They leave tomorrow.

- If you don't want your children to hear what you are saying, pretend you're talking to them.

- The thing that impresses me most about America is the way parents obey their children. (Edward VIII)

- Parents are the last people on earth who ought to have children.

- Never raise your hand to your children — it leaves your mid-section unprotected.

- I'd get pregnant if I could be assured I'd have puppies.

- When my kids become wild and unruly, I use a nice, safe playpen. When they're finished, I climb out. (Erma Bombeck)

- The reason grandparents and grandchildren get along so well is that they have a common enemy.

- I lived in Miami for a while, in a section with a lot of really old people. The average age of my apartment house was dead.

- I stay away from natural foods. At my age, I need all the preservatives I can get.

- You don't stop laughing because you grow old. You grow old because you stop laughing.

- You know you're getting old when you stoop to tie your shoes and wonder what else you can do while you're down there. (George Burns)

- My grandmother started walking five miles a day when she was 60. She is 80 now, and we don't know where the hell she is.

- A friend of mine was asked how she liked having her first great grandchild. "It was wonderful," she replied, "until I suddenly realized that I was the mother of a grandfather!"

- We are continually faced with a series of great opportunities brilliantly disguised as insoluble problems.

- The greatest use of life is to spend it for something that will outlast it. (William James)

- I don't want to achieve immortality through my work. I want to achieve it through not dying. (Woody Allen)

My loves, I love you! I adore you! I miss you!

> All my love,
> Dad
> XXXOOO

Sunday, June 14, 1998

My Darling Kimmie, Tina and Jenny:

I will be home tomorrow! I will barely see you before I am off again to Alaska early on Wednesday morning.

It is interesting to observe people's reaction when they see I am reading Stephen Levine's book, *A Year To Live — How To Live This Year As If It Were Your Last*. Most people react, as Tina did, by saying, "What a depressing subject!" But not at all! If you only had one year left to live, what would you do? It is a very good question because we never know the day when our last year will begin. Thinking about this question can lead to some radical life changes like quitting dead-end jobs, opening up to love, healing relationships, and acting on plans that have been postponed for years. Thinking about this question can help you live your life with a vivid fullness and vitality which is what we should do anyway.

This is the second book I have read by Stephen Levine, and one thing I have learned from him is to make a distinction between pain and suffering. I had never observed that distinction before, but I think it is a useful one.

Recently, I was looking at some old journals, and I came across these funny stories about Jenny when she was about 5 years old. I am sure that, if I looked, I could find similar stories about Kim and Tina. Anyway, here they are:

1. On February 15, 1993, Gail said to Jenny, "Are you ready to go, Jenny, to pick up Tina?" Jenny replied, "I don't want to go. I want to continue to work at the computer. I know you'll be sad." (She laughs, knowing she is being amusing.)

2. On February 24, 1993, Jenny came up to me with a Valentine's Day card she had designed and produced for Nana. She immediately said to me, "Dad, don't get all upset because I am going to make one for Granny and Grandpa."

3. On February 14, 1993, Jenny asked me how to write, "Granny and Grandpa." I said, "Jenny, you can do that, have a go.... Here's some scrap paper. Have a go and show me what you can do."

A few minutes later, Jenny came back. On the piece of paper, she had written, "GRANE and GAPO."

4. On March 7, 1993, Jenny said, "I need a tissue." As she came over to me to get the tissue, I said to her, "May I have a kiss, too?" Jen replied, "I'll skip that!"

5. I was writing Jen's diary for her (this was before she could write herself), and I suggested that we write, "Today I had a doughnut in church." Jenny immediately said, "No, no, no, I don't want to give a bad habit to my children when I grow up!"

6. On March 23, 1993, Jenny said to me, "If I was 100 and I was dead, how old would you be if you were dead?"

7. On May 20, 1993, Jen said to Gail while they were shopping, "I want that watch" (pointing at a watch). Gail responded, "If you spent money on everything, you won't have anything left." Jenny replied, "If you spent money on everything, there's nothing left to want."

8. On May 18, 1993, I arrived home and Tina was hugging me. Suddenly we heard a 5-year old shout out, "GET OFF MIMAN!"

9. In July 1993, Gail was hugging Jenny as Jenny was waking up. I entered her bedroom to give her a hug, and Jenny said, "Hug blue baby — I'm already busy!"

10. In July 1993, I am carrying Jenny into the waves on the beach at the shore. The waves are big and scary, and Jenny yells at me, "Hug me as though you really cared!"

11. This happened with Jenny early in first grade when she was 6. I said to her when I returned home, "Jenny, did you eat all the lunch at school that I made for you?" Jenny replied, "Yes, I ate everything — the cheese sandwich, the raisins, the applesauce, the cucumber, and the orange juice." I said, "Well, that's great, well done, Jen." About ten minutes passed and we were chatting, and then I said to Jen, "Jen, I can't find your lunch bag, do you know where it is?" Jen replied, "Oh, I'll get it." Jenny went to get it and she starts heading for the garbage. I said to her, "Jen, let me see." I looked inside the lunch bag and I find most of her lunch in the bag!

And, finally, here is a line I wrote down that made me smile: "A dad like me is hard to find — but the couch is a good place to start."

Kimmie, Tina and Jenny, I cannot wait to see you tomorrow. I love you!

Dad
XXXOOO

Wednesday, June 17, 1998
My Darling Kimmie, Tina and Jenny:
I am in Alaska! I wish you were with me, but it just did not work out. Next time! Tomorrow we start four days in Denali National Park, one of the world's greatest nature preserves. We are staying at a lodge set deep in the interior of the park, and the experience will not be dissimilar from the lodge we stayed in last year with Diane and Mike McBride. We will do lots of hiking, exploring and learning.

Then, after four days in Denali (in which, by the way, is Mount McKinley, the highest mountain in North America), we will travel to the tiny Afognak Island, just off the coast of Kodiak, where we will track the legendary Kodiak Brown Bear, the largest of the grizzlies. Some get over 1,400 pounds and stand 12 feet tall. There are also eagles, seals, sea otters, and some of the largest sea lion haul-outs in Alaska. We might even see orcas and porpoises.

While the ostensible reason for the trip is to visit Alaska, my main agenda will be to bring my group together to learn, to experience, and to discover more about themselves. We will learn about nature, about the cultures that other people come from, and about the work that we do at NWF and NWP. It will be a marvelous, memorable, life-enhancing trip, and the only thing missing is going to be you three and Mummy.

Tonight, as you are reading this, we are gathering at the Anchorage Hotel in downtown Anchorage, where everybody will meet each other, and Johnny Bushell and I will give an orientation about the trip. We will then have a wonderful dinner together, and I will introduce everybody in some detail so that they can start getting to know each other.

When I was in England a few days ago, I left you a letter which talked about some of Granny's grandparents. Now, let me tell you a little about Grandpa's grandfather. His name was William Palmer, and he was born in Llangwm, Wales in 1849. He died in 1934. He was married to Ellen Letitia Rees, who was born in 1852 and died in 1928. William and Ellen were married in 1873. They had six children, and the fifth one was Grandpa's father.

William Palmer was the oldest of five children. He had an uncle who went to America and died, leaving some money which all the family shared. William served "his time" (i.e., an apprenticeship) at a local shipyard as a blacksmith. Many of his ancestors had worked in the local shipyard. It is funny to think that when I trained as a Naval architect when I began my professional career, I was carrying on a long family tradition, although I had no knowledge of it at the time.

When William was about 20, he went to work as a blacksmith at the Pembroke Naval Dockyard. In those days (around 1870), the blacksmith's trade was one of the most skillful and respected in shipbuilding. Those were the days of iron ships, with each plate and frame bent hot by the smith to the required shape.

William (remember we are talking here about Grandpa's grandfather) worked in the dockyard until he retired at age 60 — the usual age for retirement. He then helped his son, Edwin (my father's father's elder brother) who had a shop and bakery in Llangwm. You have been there several times — it is where my cousin, Chris Palmer, lives, but the shop is now closed.

Whenever my father went there as a child, his grandfather (William was then in his late 60's) would make Grandpa a special little loaf in the big bread oven.

William played the violin and read his Bible daily. For the 40 years he worked in the dockyard, he was up at 4:00 AM every morning. He walked four miles to the ferry, then, with others, rowed in a dinghy about two miles to the yard. He worked six days a week from 7:00 AM to 5:00 PM, then returned the same way, washed and had supper, read his Bible, and played his violin for an hour, and then went to bed. My father was told that his grandfather never missed a day.

William Palmer was a good gardener, and finally he simply dropped dead in his garden at the age of 84 in 1934. About five years earlier, Grandpa's grandmother, Ellen Palmer (nee Rees), died at the age of 74. Ellen was born in Pembroke Dock in 1852 and died in 1928. My father remembers her as a handsome woman, hard working, with a great sense of fun, and very affectionate with all her family. My father says that they all adored her, and he says that William and Ellen Palmer did a good job of bringing up their family.

Grandpa remembers his grandfather as a rather remarkable character: upright, handsome, extremely hard working, consulted by his contemporaries as an intelligent and wise advisor, and known as "doctor." My father thinks that he was called "doctor" because people came to him for advise about their illnesses and other problems. My father remembers William as a severe but just father to his family.

My guess is that William and Ellen Palmer would have liked the following quotes. They come from an organization called The Caring Institute, which is a nonprofit organization (i.e., a charity like NWF and Consumer's Union), dedicated to the promotion of "caring, integrity, and public service." They publish posters under the title "In Search of the Great Secrets of the Universe," and here are some of the people they quote on those posters:

➤ Aristotle (384-322 B.C.) said, "What is the essence of life? To serve others and to do good."

➤ Moses (about 1200 B.C.) said, "Whatever is hurtful to you, do not do to any other person."

➤ Confucius (551-471 B.C.) said, "What you do not want done to yourself, do not do to others."

➤ Hillel (110-10 A.D.) said, "If I am not for myself, who is for me? But if I am only for myself, what am I?"

➤ Aesop (620-560 B.C.) said, "No act of kindness, no matter how small, is ever wasted."

➤ Benjamin Franklin (1706-1790) said, "Doing nothing for others is the undoing of ourselves."

➤ Buddha (563-483 B.C.) said, "Let go. Why cling to the pain and the wrongs of yesterday? Why hold onto the very things that keep you from hope and love?"

➤ Socrates (470-399 B.C.) said, "The surest way to live with honor in the world is to be in reality what we appear to be."

➤ St. Francis of Assisi (1181-1226) said, "Lord, make me an instrument of thy peace. Where there is hatred, let me sow love. Where there is injury, pardon. Where there is despair, hope. Grant that I may not so much seek to be consoled as to console, to be loved as to love, for it is in the giving that we receive."

My loves, aren't those wonderful thoughts? I love you each so much, and I miss you. Take good care of each other and Mummy. I know you will. All my love,

Daddy

XXXOOO

Thursday, June 18, 1998

My Darling Kim, Tina and Jen:

This morning we are driving north from Anchorage to Talkeetna, a small town of about 450 people in the interior of rural Alaska. The town is set against a backdrop of some of the most spectacular scenery in Alaska. If we are lucky, we may have beautiful views of Mount McKinley and the entire Alaska Range. Later this afternoon, we will continue north to Denali National Park, watching for wildlife and stopping to admire the scenery along the way.

Oh my goodness, it is Thursday and no *Seinfeld*! Do you know that the average person watches almost four hours of television a day (three hours and 44 minutes to be exact). Spending so much time sitting idly when we could be exercising and enriching our relationships with friends and family has become, in my view, almost a public health issue. The easiest way for people to get more daily physical activity (which is one of the key ways to remain healthy and free from disease) is to turn off the TV.

As you know, the key with television is to be incredibly selective. And if, for some reason, you watch something that you know deep down inside you is a waste of time, at least watch it critically and recognize what a poor reflection most TV shows are of reality. Actually, this makes them an ideal point of origin for initiating discussions about truth and values. This is called turning lemon into lemonade! Oh no! Now I have given you an excuse to watch lots of television! Actually, I am very impressed how selective and discriminating you three are. Even you, Jenny, while you like to watch TGIF on Friday nights, are selective in what you watch, and all the programs you watch are basically good. I have actually been impressed by some of the "messages" that are being conveyed in programs you watch like *Boy Meets Girl*. Do you remember the one recently about drinking? I thought it was excellent.

Here's a joke for you:

'I was relaxing in my favorite chair on Sunday,' said one office worker to another, 'reading the newspaper, watching a ball game on TV, and listening to another on the radio, drinking beer, eating a snack, and scratching the dog with my foot — and my wife has the nerve to accuse me of just sitting there doing nothing!'

And here's another:

'My Mary is so smart, she walked when she was eight months old,' bragged one woman. 'You call that intelligent?' challenged her companion. 'When my Cindy was that old, she let us carry her.'

And here's another:

Horace grabbed his plate and walked up to the party buffet for the fourth time. 'Aren't you embarrassed to go back for so many helpings?' asked his wife. 'Not a bit,' Horace replied, 'I keep telling them it's for you.'

Kimmie, Tina and Jenny, I love you and miss you. Buckets of love,

Daddy
XXXOOO

Friday, June 19, 1998
My Treasures: Kimmie, Tina and Jenny:

How are you doing? I think about you and Mummy all the time and wish that I wasn't so far away from you. Today we are going for a long journey through the whole of Denali National Park. We will be learning about the plants and animals, birds, history and geology of Denali. We will drive the entire length of the park (which is a 90-mile, six hour journey) learning about the natural history of this magnificent ecosystem, while we watch for grizzly bears, moose, caribou, Dall sheep, ptarmigan, arctic fox, and wolves along the way. Eventually, we will reach the base of the mighty Denali Mountain itself and arrive at Kantishana Lodge where we will be staying for a few nights.

Do you remember in my letter to you two nights ago, I gave you some quotes pulled together by The Caring Institute in response to the question, "What are the great secrets of the universe?" Here are some more:

➢ Mother Teresa said, "There is joy in transcending self to serve others."

➢ Edwin Markham said, "There is a destiny that makes us brothers. No one goes his way alone. What we send into the lives of others comes back into our own."

➢ Ella Wheeler Wilcox said, "So many gods, so many creeds, so many paths... while just the art of being kind is all the world needs."

➢ Albert Einstein said, "Only a life lived for others is a worthwhile life."

➢ Frederick Douglass said, "I will unite with anyone to do good, but with no one to do harm."

➢ Martin Luther King Jr. said, "Life's most persistent and urgent question is, 'What are you doing for others?'"

➢ Millicent Fenwick said, "The greatest source of happiness is forgetting yourself and trying seriously and honestly to be useful to others."

➢ Margaret E. Kuhn said, "We can only survive when we have a goal — a passionate purpose which bears upon the public interest."

➢ Dorothy Height said, "Progress comes from caring more about what needs to be done than about who gets the credit."

➢ Esther Peterson (whom Mummy knew quite well) said, "Have I done any good in the world today? Have I cheered up the sad and made someone feel glad? If not, I have failed indeed."

➢ Victor Frankl said, "Love is the ultimate and highest goal to which one can aspire. The salvation of humanity is through love and in love."

> Sir Winston Churchill said, "We make a living by what we get. We make a life by what we give."

> Elisabeth Kubler-Ross said, "Each of us has within us a Mother Teresa and a Hitler. It is up to us to choose what we want to be."

Well, my loves, I hope you are doing well and I hope you have a great weekend. Tina, enjoy your work at the club party tomorrow night! Kim and Jenny, I hope you enjoy the Sugrues' party tomorrow night.

I love you and miss you.

Dad
XXXOOO

Saturday, June 20, 1998
My Darling Kimmie, Tina and Jenny:

I wonder how the club party went for you tonight, Tina? And I wonder how the Sugrues' party was? I hope you all had a lot of fun.

If the weather permits, we will make a flight today around Mount McKinley, a spectacular landscape of massive glaciated peaks, towering granite walls and jagged spires that rise nearly a mile above the surface of Ruth Glacier. Scientists say the glacier may be over a mile thick in places, making this the deepest known gorge on earth. Mount McKinley rises to a height of 20,320 feet, and it is North America's tallest peak and the showcase of Denali National Park. The park's remaining six million acres are made up of magnificent glaciers and mountain landscapes, surrounded by a wild array of low-growing tundra vegetation characteristic of this sub-arctic environment. During the summer months (and also in the spring), a wide variety of wildflowers cover the hillsides in a riot of color.

From our base at Kantishana Lodge, we will be looking for moose in the forests of birch, aspen, and spruce; caribou and grizzly in the tundra-covered hills or along the bars of braided rivers; Dall sheep and marmots on the steep slopes of Igloo Mountain; beavers and loons in the tundra ponds; wolves, golden eagles and other wildlife wherever we can find them.

There is plenty to do and see here and, of course, the days are 20 hours long. So we have lots of daylight. We may also go mountain-biking, horseback riding, and we may even pan for gold!

Here are a few lines that have made me smile recently:

> When a person with experience meets a person with money, the person with experience will get the money. And the person with the money will get the experience.

> In high school, I never understood why I had to take Economics from a teacher who made less than $14,000 a year.

> Can I put my Visa bill on my American Express card?

> I joined a health club last year. Spent $400. Haven't lost a pound. Apparently, you have to

show up.

- ➤ My wife and I have been together so long, I know we'll never break up. Yes, there's love and commitment, but the main reason we'll always be together is that neither one of us can imagine having to retrain somebody new.

- ➤ If a woman has to choose between catching a fly ball and saving an infant's life, she will choose to save the infant's life without evening considering if there are men on base.

- ➤ T-shirt: My wife says I never listen to her. At least I think that's what she said.

- ➤ Outside of a dog, a book is a man's best friend. Inside of a dog, it's too dark to read.

- ➤ The Heimlich Maneuver works on house pets. My pit bull was choking on his dinner. I squeezed his stomach and the neighbor's cat shot right out.

- ➤ When you go into court, you are putting your fate into the hands of 12 people who weren't smart enough to get out of jury duty.

- ➤ Too bad all the people who know how to run the country are busy driving cabs and cutting hair. (George Burns)

- ➤ Bill and Hillary Clinton were at a restaurant. The waitress asked Hillary for her order. She said, "I'll have the chicken and a baked potato." The waitress said, "What would you like for your vegetable?" Hillary said, "He can order for himself."

- ➤ What gets me is that estimated tax return. You have to guess how much you're gonna make. You have to fill it out, fix it up, sign it, and send it in. I sent mine in last week. I didn't sign it. If I have to guess how much I'm gonna make, let them guess who sent it.

Kimmie, Tina and Jenny, you are so very, very special, and Mummy and I adore you. All my love,
Daddy
XXXOOO

Sunday, June 21, 1998

It is Father's Day! Oh how awful not to be with you! Can we celebrate it when I get home? Take away my role as a dad, and I would have an unbelievably huge hole in my life. In fact, it is just unimaginable to me.

Two weeks ago, there was an article by Sue Shellenbarger in *The Wall Street Journal*. She writes an excellent article every week under the generic title of "Work and Family." This particular article was entitled, "Would Your Team Give You High Marks On Career-Handling?". Sue Shellenbarger interviewed a bunch of 15-17 year-olds to find out how they would grade their parents' approach to work and family, and how they planned to combine their work and family lives, and how they managed stress.

These teenagers described their family lives as nearly barren of relaxed time together, and said that they wished for more leisurely time spent talking with their parents as peers. Though they expect it to be difficult, most of them vowed to find a way to spend more time with their own children.

They voiced a nearly unanimous wish for more relaxed time with parents, not to hear rules, but to share stories and experiences. One girl recalled a three-hour talk with her father one night at a coffee shop: "He listened to what I had to say. I listened to what he had to say. We didn't get into a fight if we had conflicting views. I learned a lot about him that night and it was great. I will remember that for a long time."

As you know, I am always looking for ways to be a better dad, and I am constantly learning new things about how to be an effective father. One reason I am constantly learning is that I have so much to learn! I have been reading a wonderful book by Paul Lewis called *The Five Key Habits Of Smart Dads* and, through the book, he sprinkles a number of ideas which I think are excellent. Here are some of them:

➢ Mail a short note to each of your children's teachers. Express your appreciation for their dedication to education, and assure them of your support at home.

➢ A hundred years from now, the size of my bank account won't matter, nor the size or style house that I live in, nor the model car I drove, but the world may be different because I was deeply involved in the life of my children.

➢ If your child is off to college or on an extended trip, send along a special pillowcase on which every family member has written (with permanent markers) words of love, respect, and encouragement. It's a great refuge at the end of a lonely day.

➢ On your next family car trip, give each child a responsibility to manage — purchasing gas, cleaning the windshield, throwing out trash, directing roadside stretching games, etc. Devote 30 minutes of each hour to a good book on tape.

➢ Here is how to put your child in the news when she wins an honor or does something interesting. Write a brief account of the event; then take it (with photo) to the feature, sports, business, or religion editor of your community paper.

➢ Write a letter to your soon-to-be-born child (or create an audio cassette). Express your joy, anticipation, and hopes for the child — and your commitment to fathering. Then tuck it away in your safe-deposit box to be pulled out and read again on the child's 12th birthday.

➢ How long has it been since your child has heard you say you were wrong? That you've failed? Communication is enhanced when you admit your faults and errors and seek forgiveness.

➢ If you leave in the morning before your kids are up, write your affection and good wishes on some Post-it™ notes. Stick them to their bedroom door, bathroom mirror, in their shoe — even on their sandwich in their lunch bag.

➢ List the names of the five best dads you know. Then create an opportunity (a note, phone call, lunch together, etc.) to ask each of them these two questions: What key ideas guide you as a father? What three family activities do you most enjoy?

- Take a poll tonight at dinner: What's the most fun we've had as a family in the past month? In the past year? Ever? Look for the reasons why and put a date on the calendar to do each again.

- "Monday Night Interviews" keep kids talking. Make a 20-minute recording of their answers to your reporter-style questions about weekend activities, the day at school, pets, hobbies, friends, dreams, latest fads, etc. Send a copy to grandparents, and archive the original.

- Take your appointment book to dinner tonight. Show each family member your schedule for the next two weeks, and write in a date with each of them at the time you agree on. Then turn to the two weeks after that, and do it again.

- Reminisce with your kids about your own childhood favorites: Games, toys, teachers, play-mates, foods, pets, clothes, candy, vacations, hobbies, subjects in school, adult friends, TV shows, rewards for good behavior, etc. Recall your least favorites, too.

- Preschoolers and grandchildren love to wiggle through the holes you create when you lay on the floor and join your hands into a circle, raise your knees, bow your legs to join the bottoms of your feet, arch your back, etc. Add some traps and tickles.

- Play Balloon Volley Ball in the living room on a moment's notice. Lay a center line on the floor with masking tape, then two back lines — and maybe tape between two chair backs for a net. Blow up a balloon, review the rules, and play!

- On your business card, under your occupation or title, consider adding "Father of Kimberly, Christina and Jennifer." The card will launch conversations, as well as make your children feel that they get equal billing with your career.

- The most productive fathering time of your day may be the five minutes you stop along your route home, close your eyes, and determine your family agenda for the evening — especially your first 30 minutes.

- How would you finish the sentence: "One thing my dad always said was...." How will your children finish the sentence?

- Take photos of your kids doing things right — daily chores, cleaning their rooms, doing homework, helping mom, dad, a sibling. Set aside special pages in the family album for these snapshots.

- Tonight at the dinner table, switch places — everyone sits in someone else's customary chair — with this assignment: During the meal, they must behave like the family member whose chair they are sitting in. If you don't die of laughter first, you will learn a lot.

Aren't those great ideas? You can see how much I have to learn!

Jenny, how did your softball game go today at 3:00 PM? I love watching you play and I am so sorry I missed it today.

Kimmie, Tina and Jenny, I can feel your love being transmitted to me on Father's Day, even though I am 4,000-5,000 miles away from you. Your love is that strong!

Have a great week and I adore you.

Dad

XXXOOO

P.S.: Tina, good luck in your job tomorrow at Creative Summer; and, Jenny, good luck starting at Creative Summer tomorrow! I hope you both have a great day.

Monday, June 22, 1998

My Darling Kimmie, Tina and Jen:

Tina, how did your day go today at Creative Summer? I hope you had a good time. And, Jenny, how was your first day at Creative Summer? I hope you are enjoying the courses you selected. And, Kimmie, I hope your job is continuing to go well at PRI.

Recently, Ruth found something on the Web for me that was entitled, "Seventeen Questions That Could Change Your Life." The author was "unknown," and the subtitle of the article was "Take A Moment To Reflect On Your Life." Here are a few of the questions:

➤ If I had to wear my philosophy as a motto on a T-shirt, what would it be?

➤ When was the last time I felt joy? Not just pleasure, but joy. That soaring feeling still lives inside me. What can I do to wake it up?

➤ Am I inhibited by a fear of failing? What can we do to embrace and welcome rejection and failure? In order to make progress, we have to fail. Paradoxically, failure is a triumph, not a shame. It shows that we tried.

➤ If I could take a six-month sabbatical from my job, what would I do? Travel around the world? Perform good deeds? Put my butt in a chair and nose in a book? Figuring out the answer can help us figure out what our dream is.

➤ How do I envision myself at age 60? What would I like to look like? What would I like to know that I don't know now? What should I be doing now that I will happily look back on then?

➤ Am I as healthy as I want to be? If I imagine myself in ten years' time, how would I like to feel, physically and mentally? What steps should I be taking now to make sure that my ideal becomes reality?

And Ruth found another thing on the Web for me which was entitled "Forty Valuable Lessons I Have Learned" by somebody called Jewel Diamond Taylor. Here are a few of them:

➤ Practice every day saying and/or doing something that is loving, helpful and purposeful.

- Most people are not bad or mad, they are just sad and don't know how to get the love and attention they deserve.

- Fear and procrastination are the major enemies to success.

- Don't ignore or mistreat people. Everyone is important.

- Good health is so valuable, fragile and a blessing. Drink a lot of water.

- Don't take everything so seriously, have a sense of humor.

- People like to help or do business with people they already know, so networking is critical. Meet and serve as many people as you can.

- Stay away from negative, critical, judgmental, gossipy people.

- Spend as much time as possible around nature and beautiful environments.

- Acknowledge your shortcomings and work to improve them. Acknowledge your strengths, be humble but don't diminish or deny them.

- Stay focused to get a job done. Either do it, delegate it or dump it.

- I didn't die from the painful times in my life, they made me stronger.

- Don't let a fool kiss you. Don't let a kiss fool you. Kisses aren't promises.

- Have a life, don't depend on others to make you happy and fulfilled.

- Marriage and parenting are serious commitments, don't be in a hurry.

- Find ways to show appreciation to those you love and care about, not just on holidays or birthdays.

- Pay attention to details and keep good records.

- If you take it, return it. If you break it, fix it. If you know it, live it. If you want it, ask for it. If you use it, clean it. If you wear it, hang it up. If you made a mistake, take responsibility for it. If you have some, share it. If you own it, protect it. If you love someone, show it. If you believe it, you can achieve it.

- Time is precious, live every day to its fullest, and every day is a special occasion.

- Learn to enjoy your own solitude.

Kimmie, Tina and Jenny, I adore you each so much and I miss you. Thanks for taking care of each other and of Mummy. I love you.

Dad
XXXOOO

Tuesday, June 23, 1998

My Darling Kimmie, Tina and Jenny:

We are returning to Anchorage today to board a flight to Kodiak Island. From there we go to Afognak, a mountainous and densely forested island just off Kodiak.

Newly designated as a state park, Afognak Island offers an unusual combination of land and sea mammals that are rarely found together elsewhere. In addition to the legendary Kodiak Brown Bear, the largest of the grizzlies, Afognak is also home to the only herd of elk in Alaska. There are deer, fox, eagles, puffins, sea otters, and some of the largest sea lion haul-outs in Alaska, and we may even see killer whales and porpoises.

We are staying at Afognak Wilderness Lodge, set along the towering Sitka spruce on the edge of a pristine saltwater cove. We will have the lodge and the whole island virtually to ourselves.

Here are some more of those great "fathering ideas" from Paul Lewis' book, *The Five Key Habits Of Smart Dads — A Powerful Strategy For Successful Fathering*:

➢ If a child on your block is receiving too little parental attention, include him in one of your family activities, even if it is just a short trip to the store or the park. Make it a point to tell his parents what good characteristics you observed in the child.

➢ I cannot do anything about my ancestors, but I can do a lot about my descendants.

➢ On your next business trip, if you cannot take one of the children with you, tape record yourself reading a few bedtime stories for your children to listen to while you are gone. Leave the books with them so they can follow along as they listen to your tape. Spice up your recorded readings by making a funny or unusual noise when it is time to turn the page.

➢ Whatever your children's ages, they always enjoy back rubs and foot rubs — plus they create an excellent climate for honest communication.

➢ Read your high schoolers' textbooks. You'll never be at a loss for a good conversational topic.

➢ Make a habit of taking your child to breakfast once a month.

➢ Next holiday when the grandparents visit, videotape an interview with them, during which each of them reminisces about their childhood experiences, their own parents, what their best and worst choices were, etc. The video will become an instant family heirloom.

➢ After dinner one night this week, haul out the photo albums or videotapes and relive your best family vacation.

- Collect in a folder, shoe box, or notebook all the quotes, clippings, anecdotes and stories that best express your beliefs and favorite axioms. Label it "Ideas I Want My Kids To Remember," and organize the material as a going-away gift when they leave home. (This is one that I can safely say I did!)

- Secretly tape-record your family's breakfast table conversation next Saturday or Sunday morning. Then play it back that night as a dinner surprise.

- A person's last thoughts of the day remain in the subconscious all night. It's a good reason, as you say goodnight to your child, to praise her for a character strength you admire or an act or word of hers that made you proud of her.

- As you are tucking your child into bed, get crazy. "Hey, let's camp out in the living room tonight!" Grab two sleeping bags and a flashlight. Make shadow animals on the ceiling, talk about your day, and plan a real camp-out together in the near future.

- Hugs are therapeutic. Would your family become better at expressing love if each member made a point of hugging the others at least once a day? And don't let a week go by without a "family hug."

- Children can create wonderful stories. Take dictation from your child, then read the story back to her. Keep her stories in a special notebook; they make great reading years later, too.

- Help shape your older child's growing independence by presenting on each birthday a roster of new privileges and responsibilities. Talk over last year's list and celebrate the areas of significant growth.

- There is probably a magazine devoted specifically to your child's hobby or interest. Check the library for such lists of periodicals. Then give your child a personal subscription to the most suitable one — and read the issues together.

- Once in a while, surprise your family by coming home a day early from a trip. Or cancel a whole day of work (or even just a morning) to be with them. If your wife works, coordinate schedules so that everyone can be together.

- Ask another dad to tell you the fathering mistakes he wants to avoid and the fathering examples he hopes to emulate.

- Manage TV viewing time. Balance it with reading, chores, music practice, homework, friends, exercise, whatever. Track a child's TV time with a jar of marbles on top of the tube: A marble is deposited in the jar for each half hour of reading, chores, etc. A glance at the jar lets people know how much TV watching the child has earned.

- Discern where it is that you and your wife or children most easily talk — your bed, their bed, the couch, the car, the backyard, wherever — and return to that setting often.

- Discipline yourself to write to your out-of-the-nest children every week. It may be only a cartoon clipping, a two-sentence greeting, or a "what's up with you?" question — but the frequency will keep your relationship growing.

- Encourage a habit of critical thinking and activism in your kids by keeping postcards or stationery and a supply of stamps by your TV. When a program, newscast segment, or political report pleases or annoys you, express your sentiments in writing.

- A famous man is one whose children love him. (French Proverb)

- Challenge your family to take a vacation from complaining. Dare them to go 24 hours without a complaint. It's not as easy as it sounds; you'll all discover how easily complaining becomes a habit.

I am grateful to Paul Lewis for writing a superb book. On page 161, he writes the following paragraph which I can identify with:

> I'm famous in my house for recognizing what good fathering means to my kids, framing a plan, putting it in writing — and then gliding along on the strength of my good intentions. Meanwhile, a dangerous gap grows between my great plan and my actual performance. In fathering, as in most aspects of life, it's performance that counts, not wonderful intentions.

Well, my loves, I apologize for the gap between what I say I want to do and what I actually do; but the truth is that it is an incredible privilege to be the dad to you three extraordinary girls. I feel so lucky. All my love,

Dad
XXXOOO

Wednesday, June 24, 1998
My Darling Kimmie, Tina and Jenny:

I say goodbye to everyone very early this morning and leave from a remote part of Kodiak Island on a postal plane (sic!) to get me into the official airport on Kodiak Island. From there, I take another small plane to Anchorage; and, from there, I fly to Victoria, British Columbia, to give a speech tonight to a large number of people for the premiere of *Whales* at the new National Geographic/Destination IMAX theater there. Then I will get up early tomorrow morning to fly home. I cannot wait!

My loves, here are some one-liners and jokes which made me smile:

- Women who seek to be equal to men lack ambition.

- Can you imagine a world without men? No crime and lots of happy, fat women.

- If they could put one man on the moon, why can't they put them all?

- I have yet to hear a man ask for advice on how to combine marriage and a career. (Gloria Steinem)

- The trouble with some women is that they get all excited about nothing — and then marry him. (Cher)

- Many men die at 25 and aren't buried until they are 75. (Benjamin Franklin)

- It's not the things we don't know that get us into trouble; it's the things we do know that ain't so. (Will Rogers)

- You are going to call him 'William'? What kind of name is that? Every Tom, Dick and Harry is called William. Why don't you call him Bill? (Samuel Goldwyn)

- Question: What happens if you play country music backward? Your wife returns to you, your dog comes back to life, and you get out of prison.

- Be nice to your children, for they will choose your rest home. (Phyllis Diller)

- If your parents did not have any children, there's a good chance that you won't have any.

- My mom is a clean freak. She vacuums so much, the guy downstairs went bald.

- There are three ways to get something done — do it yourself, hire someone to do it, or ask your children not to do it.

- If Abraham's son had been a teenager, it wouldn't have been a sacrifice.

- If you are going to tell people the truth, be funny or they will kill you.

- If you ever need a helping hand, you will find one at the end of your arm. (Yiddish Proverb)

- If you don't agree with me, it means you haven't been listening.

- Patient: 'This hospital is no good. They treat us like dogs.'
  Orderly: 'Mr. Jones, you know that's not true. Now, roll over.'

- A woman accompanied her husband when he went for his annual checkup. While the patient was getting dressed, the doctor came out and said to the wife, 'I don't like the way he looks.' 'Neither do I,' she said. 'But he's handy around the house.'

Well, my treasures, I love you so much and I cannot wait to see you tomorrow. I adore you.

Daddy
XXXOOO

Tuesday, July 7, 1998

My Darling Kimmie, Tina and Jenny:

As you know, I am in New York City for one night for a bunch of meetings to do with raising money, finding investors for our *Dolphin* IMAX film, and meeting with reporters from *The Wall Street Journal* and *Business Week*.

Wasn't that a wonderful trip to the Bahamas?! "Dan, Dan the party man" — I won't forget that in a hurry! It was so much fun to have all of us together and to spend time with you. I especially treasure the dance that I had with each of you. I thought the comedy was excellent, and I loved the exercise classes in the morning. And I enjoyed snorkeling, although I wish I had had my own equipment with me so I would not have gotten so much salt up my nose! And I loved the banana boat ride! Wasn't that generous of Janet to give us that wonderful treat?

I was also pleased with the reading that I did on the ship. I finished *Tuesdays With Morrie* and read a lot of three other books:

➢ *Time And The Soul: Where Has All The Meaningful Time Gone?... And How To Get It Back* by Jacob Needleman.

➢ *You Can Go Home Again: Reconnecting With Your Family* by Monica McGoldrick; and

➢ *Family Man* by Calvin Trillin (the book you guys gave me for Father's Day).

I relished reading these four books, especially *Tuesdays With Morrie* and *You Can Go Home Again*.

See if you can complete the following well-known proverbs:

➢ A stitch in time....

➢ Better be safe than....

➢ Strike while the....

➢ It's always darkest before....

➢ You can't teach an old dog new....

➢ The pen is mightier than the....

➢ An idle mind is....

➢ A penny saved is....

➢ Laugh and the whole world laughs with you, cry and....

As you know, a proverb is a short pithy saying that expresses a basic truth or practical precept.

I love you! I can't wait for our week away at a cottage on the New Jersey shore.

Buckets and oodles of love,

Daddy

XXXOOO

July 9, 1998
Darling Tina and Jenny:

I never heard back from you on my November 13, 1997 letter about the Family Mission Statement!

So rather than repeat my request to respond, I want to ask you some very specific questions. Please e-mail back to me your answers to these questions, and then I will be able to use that as raw material for a new Family Mission Statement. Here are the questions. As I say, please type in your answers and get them back to me. Can you do that by July 25?

1. What is the purpose of our family?

2. What kind of family do we want?

3. What kind of a home do we want to invite friends to?

4. What are the things that are truly important to us as a family?

5. What are our family's highest priority goals?

I look forward to getting your responses to these questions! Thanks very much! I love you,
Daddy
XXXOOO

Wednesday, July 29, 1998
My Darling Kimmie, Tina and Jenny:

Here are a few of the things that have given me joy in the last few days. I share these with you because I want to encourage you to keep adding to your own "joy lists." The list is not comprehensive, nor complete, but rather a quick brain-dump:

1. Having weekly dinner dates with Gail.

2. Hearing one of you three girls laughing out loud.

3. Hearing Kim and Tina wanting to share confidences.

4. Doing <u>any</u> activity with any of you three girls.

5. Talking about <u>anything</u> at <u>any</u> time with any of you three girls.

6. Tina asking me what a word means from a book she is reading.

7. Seeing Tina read a book (and you've been reading a lot).

8. Receiving a letter from Jenny from Camp Carysbrook.

9. Kimmie submitting a new article to *The Washington Post*.

10. Buying books and/or software for you three girls.

11. Jen walking on my back to massage it.

12. Going food shopping with Jenny and throwing her food for her to catch.

13. Hearing you girls say that you have set goals and reached them.

14. Finding an insightful article and realizing you girls will benefit from and enjoy reading it.

15. Finding a joke that makes me laugh out loud.

16. Looking at our new house and enjoying the order, serenity, and uncluttered beauty of it.

17. Enjoying the esthetic delight that Mommy and Nylene have designed into all our new rooms.

18. Entertaining friends and enjoying substantive discussions with them on issues we all care deeply about.

19. Composing a speech designed to make an audience roar with laughter.

20. Meeting a boy that you girls might like who I think is good son-in-law material.

21. Coming across an amusing story that I instinctively know will be something I could use in an upcoming speech.

22. Writing my journal (designed to be read by you, your children and grandchildren in the future).

23. Inventing the future, looking 20 years ahead.

24. Planning the next month so I am perfectly prepared to fulfill every commitment that I have made.

25. Closing a deal on an NWP project.

26. Exercising rigorously, and exercising in all three dimensions equally — stretching, weight-lifting (strength exercises) and aerobics.

27. Reading a book that I assess as being profound, and knowing that I will return to it over and over again to drink more fully from it.

28. Holding family meetings.

29. Enjoying family rituals like treasure hunts on birthdays.

30. Going out to dinner as a family.

31. Seeing you girls do something thoughtful and considerate towards each other or to other people.

32. Learning or re-learning a new word (like obfuscatory) — one that rolls around deliciously in my

mind, tossing off possibilities like a dog shakes off water after a swim.

33. Reading our Family Mission Statement.

34. Reading your (and my) New Year's Resolutions.

35. Making people laugh.

36. Receiving a donation to NWP.

37. Looking at and admiring the paintings of you three girls when you were five years old.

38. Seeing you use the treadmill.

39. Seeing Jenny use weights.

40. Running on the bike path.

41. Sending e-mail.

42. Learning more about our family history and seeing behavioral patterns.

43. Discovering a great book in Barnes & Noble.

44. Getting up early and getting a lot of work done before breakfast.

45. Discovering anything that makes me laugh out loud.

46. Discovering a profound and far-reaching maxim.

47. Having a good talk with my parents, Tim, or Jon.

48. Writing a letter that I think will have some enduring value.

49. Seeing a magnificent mountain (most recently, Mt. McKinley in Alaska).

50. Discovering other parents who share our ideas on the best way to bring up children and who share our values.

51. Throwing out junk and clutter.

52. Learning something new that fascinates me.

53. Returning safely from a trip and being reunited with the family.

54. Seeing Jay Leno skillfully telling a good joke.

55. Not watching television.

56. Seeing a cardinal or, for that matter, any bird.

57. Seeing a gorgeous tree and admiring its beauty.

58. Seeing a film that makes me cry with joy.

59. Realizing I may be 50, but that my life is not yet over.

60. Watching Tina hit a superb forehand.

61. Anticipating the front door being put on and the porch being finished.

62. Sweeping the floor in the house so that I can pad around barefoot and be comfortable.

63. Seeing positive articles in the press about NWP and my work.

64. Having a shower when I feel sweaty and dirty.

65. Realizing my lower back is better, and crediting it to the new stomach strengthening exercises that I am doing.

66. Enjoying the respect and admiration of my colleagues at NWF.

67. Eating All Bran with loads of fresh blueberries for breakfast.

68. Rapidly getting through seven days of newspapers (*The Washington Post*, *The New York Times* and *The Wall Street Journal*, as well as local papers) in under 15 minutes, and still finding two or three articles that contain nuggets to enrich me or you girls.

69. Having our security system.

70. Discovering or rediscovering any underlying principle of human success that transcends circumstances, the environment, genes or dogma.

71. Operating my life around completions.

72. Planning my life around commitments (rather than "jobs to do").

73. Having family dinners. (I should have said this much earlier.)

74. Learning more about the American Civil War and the history of the American West.

75. Seeing a beautiful evening sky streaked with red, multicolored clouds.

76. Finding an elegant, fresh, pithy, Churchillian English sentence.

77. Admiring all the books I have.

78. Listening to an excellent audio tape in the car and learning a lot from it.

79. Swimming with wild dolphins.

80. Having money.

81. Seeing a beautiful flower.

82. Working for a mission-based charity and realizing that I enjoy my work so much that I would do it even if I were paid only a fraction of my current salary.

83. Going to Lin's two-hour exercise class every Saturday morning.

Kimmie, Tina and Jenny, I adore you. I will be home from Montreal tomorrow night. You are each having a great summer and accomplishing a lot.

Buckets and oodles of love,

Your 'ole Dad
XXXOOO

Tuesday, September 1, 1998

My Darling Kimmie, Tina and Jenny:
As you know, I will be in Mexico City for two nights working with my friend Manuel Arango on our two IMAX films on water and dolphins. I will be back for Thursday dinner. (Kim, you will be on your camping trip with the freshman!)

Kim, good luck this year at Amherst. It was fun taking you back and we loved meeting Alison. Tina, good luck at Holton Arms this year. I have been so pleased to see you enjoying your work on Scribbler. And Mommy and I are looking foward to getting to know Mauro better. Please invite him to dinner one night. Jenny, good luck at Westland this year. Anyone who can start sixth grade knowing how to solve $x+3y=4$ and $3y-2x=-2$ is going to do really well!

You each had a great summer and are well prepared for the challenges of the coming year. Since Mommy and I are gradually having to (and want to!) give each of you more autonomy and freedom as you grow older, here is a poem which celebrates that idea. It is called *To Let Go Takes Love:*

To let go does not mean to stop caring.
It means I can't do it for someone else.
To let go is not to enable, but to allow
learning from natural consequences.
To let go is to admit powerlessness,
          which
means the outcome is not in my hands.
To let go is not to care for, but to care
                about.
To let go is not to judge, but to allow
                another to be him or herself.
To let go is not to be in the middle
                arranging all the outcomes
but to allow others to determine their
                own destinies.
To let go is not to be less protective, it is
                to permit another to face reality.
To let go is not to dominate but to be
                willing to let things happen.
To let go is not to betray the past, but to

> have faith in the future.
> To let go means to fear less, and love
> more.

Kim, Tina and Jenny: Mommy and I love you each so much and feel so incredibly lucky to have you as our daughters.

All my love,
Daddy
XXXOOO

Wednesday, September 2, 1998

My Darling Kimmie, Tina and Jenny:

In my letter yesterday, I left you a serious poem. Here is a lighter poem I first heard when I was very young. I rediscovered it when I was grownup (i.e. sometime in the last few years!) and, as you know, love reading it aloud to you. It is called *Puppy and I:*

> I met a Man as I went walking;
> We got talking,
> Man and I.
> "Where are you going to, Man?" I said
> (I said to the Man as he went by).
> "Down to the village, to get some bread.
> Will you come with me?" "No, not I."
>
> I met a Horse as I went walking;
> We got talking,
> Horse and I.
> "Where are you going to, Horse, today?"
> (I said to the Horse as he went by).
> "Down to the village to get some hay.
> Will you come with me?" "No, not I."
>
> I met a Woman as I went walking;
> We got talking,
> Woman and I.
> "Where are you going to, Woman, so early?"
> (I said to the Woman as she went by).
> "Down to the village to get some barley.
> Will you come with me?" "No, not I."
>
> I met some Rabbits as I went walking;
> We got talking,
> Rabbits and I.
> "Where are you going in your brown fur coats?"
> (I said to the Rabbits as they went by).
> "Down to the village to get some oats.
> Will you come with us?" "No, not I."

I met a Puppy as I went walking;
We got talking,
Puppy and I.
"Where are you going this nice fine day?
(I said to the Puppy as he went by).
"Up in the hills to roll and play."
"I'll come with you, Puppy," said I.

My loves, didn't we have a good summer? It was fun and each of you accomplished so much, each in your own unique ways. Thanks you again for my lovely birthday gifts which were extraordinarily special.

Kim, have a wonderful time camping with Allison and Joshu. Tina and Jenny, I can't wait to see you for dinner on Thursday night.

I love you,
Daddy
XXXOOO

Tuesday, September 8, 1998
My Darling Kimmie, Tina and Jenny:

I am on my way tonight to Sydney, Australia, to attend a big IMAX conference. One of the things I will do there is explore the youth hostels that you, Kim, and Alison may want to use when you are in Sydney this coming January. I will give speeches and presentations on our IMAX films on wolves, dolphins and water; and I will speak on the educational value of IMAX films. I have been working hard to prepare all my presentations and speeches, and I am looking forward very much to being there.

This trip to Australia reminds me of Grandpa's trip out to the far east right after the war when he was sent by the British Navy to repair the dockyard in Hong Kong. On his way there, he stayed in Australia for several weeks.

As you know, Winston Churchill was the great British statesman and leader who led Britain in World War II against Nazi Germany. Here is a well known story about Churchill which may be apocryphal:

It was in 1959, when Churchill was at the sunset of his life. He was accustomed to spending most of his time in the antechambers where they dispensed liquid refreshments. On one occasion, the bell rang for a division vote, and Churchill, thoroughly fortified, began wobbling toward the door as the 250-pound Laborite from Liverpool, Bessie Braddock, came waddling toward the same door. There was the inevitable collision, and down went Bessie for the count.

Furious, Bessie got herself off the floor and said, 'Sir Winston, you are drunk. Furthermore, you are disgustingly drunk.'

Churchill looked at the obese Bessie and replied, 'Mrs. Braddock, you are ugly. Furthermore, you are disgustingly ugly. What's more, tomorrow I, Winston Churchill, shall be sober.'

Here are some good words for you to know:

- Cavalier: Casual; indifferent; as, "How can you be so cavalier about such a vital issue?"

- Reciprocate: To interchange; give and get in return.

- Condone: To excuse; to forgive; as, "I'm not condoning this man's terrible behavior."

- Tangible: Real; able to be touched; as, "The physical, tangible, practical elements of her life."

- Proclivity: Tendency; inclination.

- Remorse: Deep regret for a wrongdoing; the biting of one's conscience.

- Inherent: Inborn; native; as, "You're just a young person with normal, inherent insecurities."

- Autonomy: (I used this word in a letter to you last week.) Independence; personal liberty; as, "Daughters capable of financial autonomy."

- Metamorphosis: Transformation; as, "The metamorphosis of your Dr. Jekyll boyfriend into a marital Mr. Hyde."

- Inexorable: Relentlessly; unyieldingly; as, "If you feel inexorably drawn in 'what if' directions, we need to talk about your anxieties."

And here is a little history: When Thomas Jefferson became the third President of the United States in 1801, the United States extended only to the Mississippi River. Much of the land west of the Mississippi was owned by France. But in 1803, France sold all this western land to the United States in what was called the Louisiana Purchase. The acquisition more than doubled the size of the US. No one knew much about the territory — how large it was, what the land was like, what Indians and animals lived there. The answers to those questions were provided by Meriwether Lewis and William Clark, who explored the Louisiana Purchase.

Kimmie, Tina and Jenny, I love you so much and I miss you. I am comforted knowing that you are each leading vigorous, energetic, hard working and joyful lives.

I love you,

Daddy
XXXOOO

Wednesday, September 9, 1998
My Darling Kimmie, Tina and Jenny:
Tina, this is your first day of eleventh grade at Holton-Arms! I am sad that I am not there to be with you and to see you off. I am looking forward very much to back-to-school night on the 16th. And

then for you, Jenny, we have back-to-school night at Westland on the 17th. Do you remember that in some previous years I had to miss your back-to-school nights because of conferences that I have had to attend, and missing these vitally important events has caused me great pain.

Here is a story that I once heard someone tell at a Royal Naval dinner. Like the story I told you last night about Winston Churchill, I don't think it is particularly funny, although I suppose I would have to concede it is witty:

In the Revolutionary War the British House of Commons had at least one conspicuous partisan of the American cause. He was the notorious John Wilkes, whose penchant for taking what in England was the opposite view was only exceeded by his passion for the opposite sex. At one point when he openly hailed an American victory, Lord Sandwich of the King's party attacked his treasonable conduct, saying: 'The honorable gentleman from Middlesex will have a limited career in this chamber, for it shall either end on the gallows or by a loathsome disease.'

To which Wilkes replied: 'The Honorable Lord may well be correct. It all depends on whether I embrace his programs or embrace his mistress.'

Here is more history: Do you know the largest battle ever fought in America? It was the Battle of Gettysburg in 1863. More than 51,000 men in the two armies were killed, wounded or captured. It was June of 1863, the Civil War had been raging for more than two years, and General Robert E. Lee, Commander of the Confederate Army, decided to gamble everything on one battle that he hoped would gain independence for the South. Fresh from a victory at Chancellorsville in Virginia, Lee drove his Army of Northern Virginians through Maryland and into Pennsylvania, invading Northern territory and challenging the Union Army.

That Union Army — the Army of the Potomac, led by General George Meade — accepted Lee's challenge. The battle began on July 1, and the Confederates were the winners in the fighting that day. Meade's men retreated to high ground known as Cemetery Ridge near the town. On the second day of the battle, Lee made flanking attacks against both ends of Cemetery Ridge. In very fierce fighting, the Union troops managed to beat off his attacks. On July 3, the third day, Lee staked everything on one massive attack on the center of Cemetery Ridge. Most of the troops were led by General George Pickett, and the attack was called Pickett's Charge. In some of the most terrible fighting of the war, Pickett's Charge was driven back. Lee had to retreat into Virginia. His great gamble had failed.

Please don't forget to review the latest portion of my Journal that I have given you all. Thanks very much! I depend on you to give me feedback on what I have written, to tell me what parts I should change or delete, and to remind me of things that I should write about and have neglected to write about. Thanks again.

Here are some good words you need to know:

➤ Pivotal: Crucial; central; as, "The pivotal role played by Gail in our family life."

➤ Unilateral: Done by one person or group; as, "Her unilateral decision to leave the marriage upset her husband."

> Shunt: To get rid of; move to an alternative course; as, "I became outraged that men would shunt responsibility for their actions."

> Demeanor: Manner or behavior; as, "The three daughters were gracious and poised in their demeanor."

> Intimacy: Closeness; familiarity; as, "There is an intimacy in the family that makes all the members feel very close to each other."

> Coerce: To compel or force; as, "I was coerced by Tina into lending her the family car!"

> Fidelity: Loyalty; faithfulness.

> Onus: Burden; obligation; difficult task; as, "The onus of single parenting."

> Monogamous: (Remember I used this in a humorous remark in my recent speech at Bay Head.) Having one mate or spouse.

My loves, expanding your vocabulary is important. Please keep looking up words in the dictionary and constantly enrich your writing with powerful new words.

I miss you, I love you, and I think about you and Mommy all the time. All my love,

Daddy
XXXOOO

Thursday, September 10, 1998

My precious loves, Kimmie, Tina and Jenny:

Tina, I think you had a tennis match at 4:15 PM today. How did it go? I hope you enjoyed it. I don't care whether you won or not; the important thing is to enjoy it, to support your team members, and to have lots of fun together.

You know how I love you to learn new words and to have rich vocabularies. Well, here is a story about words:

Back in the 1950 senatorial primary campaign in Florida, veteran Claude Pepper was opposed by George Smathers. Pepper was especially strong in the 'Bible belt,' or northern, section of Florida. To shake the hold Pepper had on these people, Smathers developed a special speech making use of the facts that Pepper, a Harvard Law School graduate, had a niece who was a staff member of a Senate Subcommittee, and a sister who acted in New York.

For the county courthouse rallies, Smathers would say, 'Are you aware, my friends, that in his youth Claude Pepper was found — matriculating — in Harvard; that before marriage he habitually indulged in — celibacy. Not only that, he has practiced — nepotism — in Washington with his own niece; and he has a sister who is a — thespian — in wicked Greenwich Village in New York. Worst of all, my Claude Pepper is known all over Washington for his latent tendency toward overt extroversion.'

Here are some words you need to know:

➢ Tweak: To pinch or pull; as, "The clown tweaked the ringmaster's nose." Also, to fine-tune; as, "To tweak a carburetor."

➢ Flout: To disregard with contemptuous scorn; as, "The spoiled young athlete began to flout the terms of her contract."

➢ Prone: Inclined or likely; disposed to; as, "Haste makes everyone more prone to error."

➢ Saw: Proverb; familiar saying; as, "The old saw 'many hands make light work.'"

➢ Cull: To choose, select or pick out; as, "The chef culled the freshest vegetables for his famous dish."

Did you know that, by 1849, when news about the discovery of gold in California reached the East, people by the thousands were hurrying to California from every corner of the country. They came by ship and they came by wagon train, and they were called Forty-Niners. Gold was found all through the mountains, and some Forty-Niners became rich. In 1849, when the Gold Rush began, there were 14,000 people in California. Three years later, there were 250,000!

I wish I wasn't so far away from you all, but I feel very close to you even though I am on the other side of the world. You are so very precious to me.

I love you,

Daddy
XXXOOO

Friday, September 11, 1998
My Darling Kimmie, Tina and Jenny:
I find most of the humor on the Internet to be totally unfunny; but, last week, Ruth found the following for me. It starts off with the sentence, "You know you're having a bad day when...," and these are some of the answers:

➢ Your horn sticks on the freeway behind 32 Hell's Angels motorcyclists.

➢ Your twin brother forgets your birthday.

➢ Your birthday cake collapses from the weight of the candles.

➢ Your parents approve of the person you're dating.

➢ When the doctor tells you that you are in fine health for someone twice your age.

➢ You call your spouse and tell them that you would like to eat out tonight and, when you get home, you find a sandwich on the front porch.

Here are some good words for you to know:

- > <u>Dank</u>: Damp; uncomfortably wet and cold; as, "All the photos stored in the dank basement were ruined."

- > <u>Tick</u>: Twitch; spasmodic contraction of a facial muscle.

- > <u>Skew</u>: To distort; as, "Insufficient data often skew poll results."

- > <u>Vet</u>: To carefully exam or check for accuracy; as, "Experts vet road maps and atlases before they are published."

- > <u>Rogue</u>: Dishonest person; scoundrel. Also, dangerously unpredictable thing or animal; as, "A rogue from the herd."

- > <u>Dearth</u>: Any scarcity or lack; as, "The unexpected frost led to a dearth of citrus crops."

- > <u>Deign</u>: To condescend; to do something considered beneath one's dignity; as, "The best-selling novelist barely deigned to talk to the small-town reporter."

And here is a little history about the Declaration of Independence. As you know, in 1776, the 13 American colonies were at war with England, their mother country. The members of the Colonial Continental Congress wanted the world to understand why they had revolted and why they wanted the colonists to be free and independent states. They asked Thomas Jefferson of Virginia to write a "Declaration of Independence" to explain why they were fighting.

The members of the Continental Congress made some changes to it, and then voted unanimous approval of it on July 4, 1776. The first to sign the Declaration of Independence was John Hancock of Massachusetts. Today, "John Hancock" is an informal expression meaning signature.

Well, my treasures, I will sign off with my John Hancock below. I love you so much, and cannot wait to get home and be with you all (except you, Kim, because you are up at Amherst).

Buckets and oodles of love, kisses and hugs,

Daddy
XXXOOO

Saturday, September 12, 1998

My darling Kimmie, Tina and Jenny:

Today is your Uncle Jeremy's birthday. As you know, Jeremy was my oldest brother and died after undergoing heart surgery when he was about 45. Do you remember him?

I am waiting for one of you to solve the following problem:

Three guys go to a hotel. They tell the man behind the desk that they want three rooms. He says, '$10 per room so that's $30.' So they pay and go up to their rooms. Then the deskman remembers that there is a special for three rooms for $25. He gives the bellhop the $5 change and tells him to take it up to them. On the way, the bellhop realizes that he doesn't know how to split it three ways, so he keeps two and gives one to each man. My question is: If, after the dollar refund, each man paid $9 and $9 times three men equals $27, and the bellhop only has $2, then what happened to the other dollar?

Here are a few things that I try to do in my life which I find helpful. This list is not comprehensive or well-organized. Nor do I claim I successfully do all these things!

1. <u>Set goals</u>. I do this constantly for my life, for the upcoming year, for a plane ride, for a relaxing evening with friends, for a meeting, for virtually everything that I do.

2. <u>Be proactive</u>. By this, I mean take initiative and don't be passive or reactive.

3. <u>Ask for feedback and criticism</u>. I constantly go to people and ask them to review drafts of letters or memos or speeches. I welcome this feedback even when it makes me feel uncomfortable because I know, in the long run, I will benefit from it.

4. <u>Be assertive</u>. It's good to be bold, but it's also good to listen. In fact, in social situations, it is useful to forget your own concerns and think about what are the deepest concerns of the other people.

5. Before any event, <u>visualize</u> how you want to be perceived and what you want the outcome to be.

6. <u>Learn continuously</u>. Keep asking: Why?

7. <u>Constantly use a dictionary</u> to enrich and expand your vocabulary.

8. <u>Never be submissive</u> to anyone.

9. <u>Smile</u>.

10. <u>Never be fearful</u>, and even more important, <u>never act fearful</u>.

11. Create a vast <u>network</u> of friends and contacts.

12. <u>Build on your strengths</u>.

13. <u>Exercise rigorously</u> so your body becomes tough, strong and resilient.

14. Remember that you will never have friends more loving, devoted, loyal or caring than your <u>siblings</u>.

15. <u>Throw yourself into a campaign you care about</u> (for example, women's rights, environmental protection, stopping child abuse, or whatever). This is far more important than money.

16. <u>Never talk about someone negatively</u> in their absence.

17. <u>Work hard and be industrious</u>.

18. <u>Read and write as much as you can</u>.

19. <u>Observe accomplished people, read inspiring biographies</u>, and learn from winners.

20. Create your own <u>personal mission statement</u>.

21. Be totally <u>authentic, genuine and honest</u>.

22. Constantly <u>upgrade your computer literacy</u>.

23. <u>Keep a daily journal</u> and be an observer of something amazing and miraculous: Your ability to design and invent your own life.

24. <u>Seek first to understand, then to be understood</u>.

25. <u>Find the hidden humor</u> in everyday life.

Well, my loves, I could go on and on and bore you all rigid, but those are a few of the guidelines that are helpful to me, and I hope they are helpful to you.

I love you! All my love,

> Daddy
> XXXOOO

Sunday, September 13, 1998
My darling Kimmie, Tina and Jenny:
I miss you! I hope you are all doing well and enjoying each other, your friends, learning, and everything you are doing in school.

Here is a wonderful story I recently read on page 277 of Monica McGoldrick's brilliant book *You Can Go Home Again: Reconnecting With Your Family*:

There is a story of an old Hasidic Rabbi who said, 'When I was young, I set out to change the world. When I grew a little older, I perceived that this was too ambitious, so I set out to change my state. This, too, I realized as I grew older, was too ambitious, so I set out to change my town. When I realized I could not even do this, I tried to change my family. Now, as an old man, I know that I should have started by changing myself. If I had started with myself, maybe then I would have succeeded in changing my family, the town, or even the state — and, who knows, maybe even the world!'

My treasures, here are some good words for you to know:

1. <u>Retract</u>: To revoke a previous promise or offering; as, "The corporation retracted its acquisition bid."

2. <u>Acronym</u>: Word made from the initial letters of other words; as, "MADD is an acronym for Mothers Against Drunk Driving."

3. <u>Reconcile</u>: To make peace or restore friendship; as, "To reconcile the North and the South."

4. <u>Expedient</u>: Temporarily suitable; as, "An expedient repair." Also, advantageous, whether right or wrong; as, "It was politically expedient to lie."

5. <u>Gyrate</u>: To whirl; rotate; move in a circular way; as, "We watched our daughters gyrate on the dance floor."

6. <u>Ideology</u>: Beliefs, often the basis of economic or social systems; as, "Different ideologies separated the two nations."

One of you asked me about Thomas Jefferson the other day. As you know, he is best known as the author of the Declaration of Independence and as the third President. But the tall, red-headed Virginian was also an architect, a musician, an inventor and a scientist — and he loved words! Above all, he was America's foremost champion of freedom and democracy.

A member of one of Virginia's leading families, Jefferson studied at The College of William and Mary and became a lawyer. He was only 25 when he was elected to the Virginia Legislature, where he was an effective spokesman for colonial rights. In 1776, he attended the Continental Congress in Philadelphia, where he wrote the Declaration of Independence proclaiming America's separation from England.

Jefferson later served as Governor of Virginia, Minister to France (where he took over from Ben Franklin), Secretary of State and Vice President. He was elected President in 1800 and his term started in 1801.

The highlight of his two terms was his decision in 1803 to pay France $15 million for the Louisiana Purchase, which doubled the size of the nation.

In retirement at his beloved home, Monticello, Jefferson had time to pursue his many interests. But he never stopped writing and speaking out about the importance of human liberty. He (and amazingly John Adams on the same day) died on July 4, 1926, the 50th anniversary of the Declaration of Independence.

Kimmie, Tina and Jenny, I think we need to put more emphasis on family meals. I read recently about some research which shows that the more narrative and explanatory talk children are exposed to during mealtime conversations, the better their vocabulary scores. Vocabulary is one of the best predictors of reading ability. We should make our family meals special, and we should not start until everyone is present. If one of you is on the phone and we begin without you, we unintentionally send you the message that you are not important enough to wait for. Also, all of us should stick around until the last family member is finished, so that dinner is a family event, rather than a rushed experience.

I worry that we are always too busy and too rushed. I worry that I probably look sometimes to you as though I don't have time to talk to you. To me, the most important thing about our vacation in Avalon last August was that we had time to talk together without being rushed.

Talking and listening together in a relaxed, focused and unhurried way is something that I am not very good at. I regret that I may have unwittingly left you a legacy of "busyness." The way I live my life is dominated by so much "busyness" that relationships tend to take a second priority. It is important that families have time together to talk so there can be a high trust level and discussions of jugular issues (i.e., issues that deeply concern everybody). You will notice in some families how the conversations are inhibited, moody, resentful, uncomfortable, tense, and everybody is in some way or another withdrawn. What we should aim for is to have family meals and conversations where there is a sense of gratitude, appreciation, joy, bonding, hope, optimism, acceptance and serenity. That's my goal!

My treasures, I adore you! All my love,
Daddy
XXXOOO

Monday, September 14, 1998
My precious loves, Kimmie, Tina and Jenny:

I remember when I used to write to you, I sometimes changed the order of your names so that Jenny and Tina would sometimes go first! Tina, do you mind your name always going second?! Jenny, do you mind your name always going third?!

I cannot wait to get home and be with the family again. Of course, you won't be there, Kimmie, because you are at Amherst. But it is great having e-mail because we can easily stay in close touch.

Here are some good words you need to know:

1. Vivid: Bright; glaring; as, "My daughters each used to paint pictures with vivid colors."

2. Acrimonious: Bitingly hostile; as, "The divorce proceedings quickly grew acrimonious."

3. Inequity: Unfairness; as, "Great inequities of wealth."

4. Suave: Polished, pleasing; as, "Your dad is one suave guy!"

5. Reminisce: To recall past events; as, "We will try to persuade Granny and Grandpa to reminisce about their lives when they stay with us this October and November."

6. Casual: Incidental; chance; as, "A casual encounter between old friends."

Here is some history: On the peaceful Sunday morning of December 7, 1941, Japanese planes attacked the American fleet at Pearl Harbor in Hawaii and plunged an unsuspecting America into World War II. Over 2,400 Americans died in the attack. The Japanese attacked Pearl Harbor because it was the major base of the US Navy's Pacific Fleet. Bombers and torpedo planes flying from Japanese aircraft carriers struck at "Battleship Row," where seven American battleships were anchored. All seven were sunk or damaged. One bomb struck USS Arizona's forward magazine, where ammunition was stored, and set off an enormous explosion that broke the battleship in two and sent her to the bottom of the Harbor.

President Franklin D. Roosevelt called that day in 1941, "A date which will live in infamy."

Well, my treasures, I love you so much, and it will be great to be home. I hope you are enjoying your lives!

I adore you.

Yer 'ole Dad
XXXOOO

Thursday, October 8, 1998
My Darling Kimmie, Tina and Jenny:

    I am in Montreal tonight and will return home tomorrow evening. I am looking at the rough cut of our *Wolves* IMAX film.

    Kimmie, what are your plans for this weekend? Whatever you do, I hope you have a great time with Ann.

    Tina, I hope your tennis game went well today. I am very proud of you for diving for that ball at your Tuesday match (and getting it back!), even though you ended up hurting your finger.

    Jenny, I love to see you reading! And playing soccer! And learning how to touch type fast on the computer!

    Kim, Tina and Jenny, have you each reviewed your New Year's Resolutions recently? You will get great pleasure and inspiration from doing that, and I urge you to review them to see what your goals for the year were last January.

    One thing in my New Year's Resolutions was to learn more and to teach you what I was learning. One thing I have been studying recently (as part of my ongoing effort to improve my vocabulary) is idioms. Understanding and being able to use idioms is an important part of having a rich and powerful vocabulary.

    If you have an extensive vocabulary and an understanding of idioms, you won't get cold feet (hesitation because of fear) when it comes to talking in class or in public. You will be able to keep a stiff upper lip (be uncomplaining and courageous) when you talk before an audience. And I know you won't ignore the advice in this letter because that would be looking a gift horse in the mouth (being critical of a present).

    Whenever you get a chance, study *Roget's Thesaurus*, your dictionaries, and any books on words such as *The Synonym Finder* (or the word books that I recently bought you, Jenny, at Barnes and Noble which you are enjoying so much). Study these books so you know the ropes (be fully acquainted with procedures) when it comes to using them. Without a good vocabulary, you will be behind the eight ball (be in trouble).

    At some meeting, you may want to say something on the spur of the moment (on impulse or without thinking). This can be a great experience if you have a good vocabulary, or the experience can be a fly in the ointment (something that spoils or lessens the enjoyment) that ruins what otherwise would be a good meeting. A weak vocabulary is like a Sword of Damocles (any threatening danger). It will lead you to be a wet blanket (a spoilsport) at events where you might be called on to sow your wild oats so-to-speak (lead a wild life) and say something in public!

    You girls are very good at avoiding fair-weather friends (people who are with you only in good times). Instead, you make a beeline (go directly) to people who make excellent friends. It is important not to take the wind out of a friend's sails (remove an advantage). That does not mean you cannot occasionally be tongue-in-cheek (mocking or satirical). The most important thing is not to give a speech with a lick and a promise (in a cursory manner).

A speaker with a poor vocabulary has an Achilles' heel (a weakness or a vulnerable spot). Of course, one could take the attitude that the success or failure of one's efforts at public speaking are in the lap of the gods (out of one's hands), but I reject that attitude. Enough research has now been done to show the handwriting on the wall (a prediction or warning). By pulling your weight (doing a fair share of the work), you can be fully prepared when you talk and be confident of doing a great job.

Studying words can get you out of the doldrums (in a bored or depressed state). Also, having a good vocabulary is a feather in one's cap (something to be proud of), and it helps you lead a full life, tackling challenges lock, stock and barrel (entirely or completely) without wasting time tilting at windmills (fighting imaginary enemies) or on trivia.

Having a prolific vocabulary can also put you on the qui vive (on the alert) to new opportunities that you might otherwise not observe because you might be out of your depth (in a situation too difficult to handle). Being alert and alive in this way can help you perceive quickly if a friend feels like a square peg in a round hole (someone who does not fit the surroundings) so you can take that friend under your wing (become responsible for) and help him or her take appropriate action and say something which will hit the nail on the head (state something correctly).

Maybe this little essay I am writing to you about idioms is gilding the lily (elaborating unnecessarily), and I certainly don't want to steal your thunder (take attention from) by talking about idioms that you would like to talk about yourselves. I just know how a weak vocabulary can take a person down a peg (humiliate), when what they really want is to be lionized (make a big fuss over someone). The most essential thing is not to pass the buck (evade responsibility) and think that someone else can improve your vocabulary for you.

You have to strike while the iron is hot (act at the right time) and make a beeline to a good dictionary! Once in a blue moon (a very rare occasion), you may feel that this goal is not worth pursuing, but let me not split hairs (make a fine distinction). There are few things more important than learning new words, as well as learning new nuances of words with which you are already familiar.

So don't sleep on this (postpone a decision), but decide now to use a dictionary regularly. This way, you will rule the roost (be the boss). I ask you to throw down the gauntlet (offer a challenge) to others who feel differently.

Take the bull by the horns! (face a problem directly). This way, you will avoid jumping out of the frying pan into the fire (going from a difficult situation to a worse one) because you will be able to anticipate problems and, in a nice way, feather your own nest (enrich yourself at every opportunity). You will be in seventh heaven (at the highest happiness). You will also be on terra firma (solid or firm land) and not living in some naive fantasy land.

Having a good vocabulary will also help you to be honest as the day is long (as honest as possible). You will carry the day (win the approval of the majority), and all your efforts will not go up in smoke (end fruitlessly) because you will have done the right thing and made the right decisions. No one will feel obligated to offer you crocodile tears (hypocritical sympathy).

Having a good vocabulary will also help you to wear your heart on your sleeve (make your feelings obvious), and will help you save face (avoid embarrassment) if you have to wash your dirty linen in public (openly discuss private affairs).

Well, the fat is in the fire (the mischief is done) and this little essay is almost over. You are probably on tenterhooks (in a state of suspense) wondering if this is ever going to end! I know you don't want to give me the cold shoulder (snub or ignore me) by not reading to the end; but, unless I quickly finish, you might perceive this essay as being without rhyme or reason (making no sense). That perception by you would be a bitter pill for me to swallow (a humiliating defeat).

I like to think of myself as being like Caesar's wife (above suspicion) and loaded for bear (well prepared). If I don't finish soon, you will get your backs up (become angry), and then I will have to pay the piper (bear the consequences) because you might not read any of my future letters to you! And now I have shown my hand (revealed my plans) by telling you that I might write you future letters! Well, you don't need a grapevine (an informal means of spreading information) for you to know that I like writing you wonderful girls letters!

Idioms are important! I love you. All my love,
                                        Yer 'ole Dad
                                        XXXOOO

Tuesday, October 20, 1998
My Darling Kimmie, Tina and Jenny:
I am on the Eastern shore tonight and tomorrow night for a "retreat." A retreat is a meeting in which people get away from the pressures of their day-to-day professional lives and step back to think more strategically about their long-term goals and what they want to accomplish.

The theme of this particular retreat is Collaboration: What is it? Why is it important? How do we know it when we see it? What is our role as NWF leaders in creating a collaborative work environment for change at NWF? For a break on Wednesday afternoon, we are going for a sail on H.M. Crantz Skipjack, which is a working boat. We will be crew members and help out! We will "drudge" for some "ersters" (that's oysters!). We have been told to leave our fancy duds behind and bring our oil skins!

Isn't it great having Granny and Grandpa here? I'm sorry you, Kim, are not seeing more of them, but all of us (including Granny and Grandpa) are looking forward very much to seeing you at Thanksgiving. Of course, Mommy and I can't wait to see you at Parents Weekend at Amherst the weekend after next.

I was thinking about Granny and Grandpa being here and thinking about the many vacations we have spent with them in England. This led me to re-read my journal in August 1995 when we went on a trip with them to England, Wales and Ireland. I found the following paragraphs on each of you three girls, written on August 11, 1995 (my parents' wedding anniversary!):

Notes on Kimmie: She has mono but fortunately only a mild case of it. She got it, we think, when she was at the NWF Teen Adventure Camp in North Carolina in July. She had a temperature of 101 and could have come home but hung in there (she 'sucked it up and held it in' as the expression went in their camp) and now is on a slow mend. She often feels tired. Other notes: among her best friends are Claire, Alex Lowe, and Emily

Ossinoff (with whom she went to camp). She came in third in the tennis championships. She enjoyed the movie, *Clueless*. She is exercising regularly, especially her butt, stomach and inner thigh muscles. She writes in her journal regularly (I think everyday). She is thinking seriously of getting coaching in Spanish to help her in school. Yesterday, with Ross's help, she sugared her legs to rid them of hair! Tina and Jen were helping. And, of course, Kim and I had a fantastic week swimming with a pod of wild dolphins off the Bahamas this summer, an experience we will never forget. She has also been working in the tennis pro shop this summer earning money with Richard, and enjoying it.

Notes on Tina: She is healthy and strong. Everyday she seems to grow bigger and stronger and more sure of herself. She is putting more and more emphasis on physical fitness, and regularly goes to the pool with friends like Olivia or Lauren and swims 30 or so laps. She also does sit-ups and seems to know that an athletic, fit and lithe woman is intrinsically beautiful. Tina, like both her sisters, is exceptionally good at picking wonderful friends. Girlfriends like Olivia and Lauren are truly special people. Of course, as Gail pointed out today, they are lucky to have Tina as a friend. Tina and Kim have been playing tennis together recently (which I love to see) and enjoying playing with each other. Tina has been reading, and one of the books she has read has been *Lord of the Flies*. She had a superb time at Camp Letts this year. This is the first time she has been away from home to a camp and she adored every moment of it, and made some great new friends. I think she experienced a freedom that she had never felt before - and perhaps a power in her life that was new to her. Anyway, Gail and I were delighted. She has also done tennis camp this summer and she won a tennis trophy. She is also planning to do Camp Christina at the end of August for some local kids.

Notes on Jenny: Jenny has enjoyed doing things with Lily this summer. One reason for this is that Lily has a dog called Mickey whom Jen loves. Jen is eating better and better. I put a lot of pressure on her to eat protein and carbohydrates but it is hard when there is so much tempting junk food around. I am very firm about it and get upset with Gail when she isn't equally firm. I am shocked how many parents let their kids eat anything. Jen has really improved her swimming this year, and her diving too. Recently she (along with Tina and Kim) looked after a tiny little dog next door called Pixie. Jen is writing a school journal at the encouragement of BE. She hated the camp at BE though. Compared to the three week camp at Holton-Arms (Creative Summer) the BE camp was unappealing. (You get what you pay for.) Jen loved Creative Summer at HA. She has been reading with great determination this summer and has so far read fifteen books. She has read all the Beverly Cleary books in the Bethesda library! She has enjoyed a new CD-ROM called Counting on Frank (about math) and she wrote a sweet note to Nana about Ed's funeral. Jen and I both enjoyed the movies *Free Willy 2* and *Apollo 13*. One game we both enjoyed this summer was her racing up the front stairs and me timing her to see if she could beat her own record.

My loves, I hope you enjoy those notes about you which are now over three years old.

Here are some important words that you need to know:

➤ Impede: Hinder or interfere.

- ➤ <u>Cacophony</u>: Unpleasant noise.
- ➤ <u>Vulnerable</u>: Susceptible.
- ➤ <u>Serenity</u>: Peaceful, repose.
- ➤ <u>Compatible</u>: Harmonious.
- ➤ <u>Sedate</u>: Quiet or undisturbed.
- ➤ <u>Disgruntled</u>: Displeased.
- ➤ <u>Equanimity</u>: Composure or calmness.
- ➤ <u>Infallible</u>: Always right (like me!).
- ➤ <u>Propinquity</u>: Nearness in time or place.
- ➤ <u>Bedlam</u>: Uproar or confusion.
- ➤ <u>Irrational</u>: Absurd or unreasonable.
- ➤ <u>Moribund</u>: Dying.
- ➤ <u>Avarice</u>: Greed or passion for riches.
- ➤ <u>Exploit</u>: Use for selfish purposes.
- ➤ <u>Nadir</u>: The lowest point.
- ➤ <u>Conflagration</u>: An enormous fire.
- ➤ <u>Insatiable</u>: Impossible to satisfy.
- ➤ <u>Eradicate</u>: Wipe out completely.
- ➤ <u>Complicity</u>: Participate in a wrongful act.
- ➤ <u>Accomplice</u>: One who helps in wrongdoing.

Kimmie, Tina and Jenny, you are the most three precious daughters in the whole world. Mommy and I love you so much.

Daddy
XXXOOO

Wednesday, October 21, 1998

Darling Kimmie, Tina and Jenny:

I will be home tomorrow! Our retreat finishes late in the afternoon, and then I am going to see my friends Ted and Jenny Stanley. I will be home about 9:00 PM.

As you know, one of the things I am interested in is happiness. Some people are happier than others, and it is intriguing to ask why. Here are some of the conclusions that I have tentatively come to:

1. <u>Think about and act on principles</u>: I discussed this in my New Year's Resolutions this year. I think it is important to think about fundamental principles — principles that are far more meaningful than a lot of what you hear in church. Each one of us should search for the principles of human conduct that have enduring, permanent value, and that are fundamental to living a complete, satisfying and joyful life. These principles include fairness, integrity, honesty, service, courage, patience, self-discipline, responsibility, generosity, hard work, creativity, and tenacity.

2. <u>Find autonomy and control your freedom</u>: A sense of being in control of our own lives, and a sense of having the freedom to make choices, makes us feel happy. We are least happy If we consider ourselves victims forced to react to random, out-of-control occurrences.

3. <u>Be an optimist</u>: People who expect the best seem to be the happiest. Optimists are aware that bad things can happen, but don't dwell on it. They move forward and focus on good things. When you face a difficulty, rejection or failure, instead of feeling defeated and depressed, look

at what has happened and say, "That is fascinating," and then try again and again and again. Never give up. Be persistent and tenacious.

4. <u>Forget leisure and relaxation</u>: Happiness is not a goal, but a consequence of pursuing something meaningful. Relaxing will not bring happiness. While time to re-energize is vital, too much leisure is disastrous. Instead, find a mission that challenges your skills, increases your activity, engages your mind and makes time fly. Commit yourself to something that makes a difference to the world. If you only had two more years to live, what are the most important things you would want to make sure you did? What sort of work or activities really excite and energize you? When do you feel most vibrant and alive?

5. <u>Build relationships</u>: Relationships are everything. Nothing is more important than the key relationships in your life. And family relationships are more important than any others. Build a large support network.

6. <u>Put on a happy face</u>: Smile, find an excuse to laugh, lighten up and communicate with happy mannerisms. No matter what your situation, act happier and you will be happier. Remember the story I have told you repeatedly of Teddy Roosevelt "acting" brave when he went out West as a young man — and how that made him brave.

7. <u>Be patient with pain and suffering</u>: Obviously suffering is to be avoided if possible, but it is a myth that you should avoid pain if you want to be happy. In fact, everything that leads to happiness involves pain (e.g., sacrifice or delayed gratification). This includes marriage, children, and any worthwhile pursuits. You don't want a pain-free life as possible, but rather as life-filled a life as possible. The two are mutually exclusive. "No pain, no gain" is not only true for developing a good body, it is equally as true for developing a good life. Remember there is no realization of dreams and purpose without difficulty, opposition, disappointment and failure. Life is hard — and exhilarating.

8. <u>Find the meaning of life</u>: Thinking about the purpose of life, developing a personal mission statement, and designing a life which is meaningful, are sure ways to achieve happiness. The meaning of life is the meaning you yourself give it.

9. <u>Keep physically, emotionally and mentally fit</u>: Daily exercises to strengthen your body and give yourself endurance and flexibility are fundamental to a happy and full life. Remember what Benjamin Franklin said, "An ounce of prevention is worth a pound of cure." You can learn to be nourished by stress and use normal life stress to toughen yourself. Tough times represent opportunities for getting better and stronger.   Read and write constantly.

10. <u>Forget the money</u>: The basic fact is that, after you get out of poverty, money does not help much. Unless you are destitute, money does not bring happiness.

Well, my loves, there are a few quick thoughts on how to live a happy life. I hope you find it useful. One major contribution to a happy life is constant learning, and increasing your vocabulary is one aspect of that. Here are some good words you need to know:

 > <u>Aegis</u>: Protection or sponsorship.
 > <u>Congenial</u>: agreeable or sympathetic.
 > <u>Initiate</u>: Begin.

- ➤ <u>Awesome</u>: Overwhelming.
- ➤ <u>Deplorable</u>: Pitiable.
- ➤ <u>Puny</u>: Weak or unimportant.
- ➤ <u>Disperse</u>: Scatter or spread.
- ➤ <u>Imbibe</u>: Drink.
- ➤ <u>Doddering</u>: Shaking with old age.
- ➤ <u>Senile</u>: Weak as a result of old age.
- ➤ <u>Longevity</u>: A long duration.
- ➤ <u>Sage</u>: A wise person or philosopher.
- ➤ <u>Revere</u>: Admire or honor.
- ➤ <u>Virile</u>: Manly.
- ➤ <u>Hoard</u>: Accumulate.
- ➤ <u>Rue</u>: Regret.
- ➤ <u>Obliterate</u>: Wipe out or destroy.
- ➤ <u>Detriment</u>: Damage or injury.
- ➤ <u>Debris</u>: Fragments.
- ➤ <u>Eruption</u>: Bursting out.
- ➤ <u>Conflagration</u>: A great fire.

Kimmie, Tina and Jenny, Mommy and I love you so much. You are each unique and so special — each in your own ways. Mommy and I will always love you and always treasure you.

Yer 'ole Dad
XXXOOO

Wednesday, October 28, 1998

My Treasures Kimmie, Tina and Jen:

I am in NYC for one night meeting with all the people working on our *Water* IMAX film.

Jenny and I have recently been reading a joke book together at night before she goes to bed. Here are two jokes I've recently come across that I enjoyed:

Who Won?

About a century or two ago, the Pope decided that all the Jews had to leave Rome. Naturally there was a big uproar from the Jewish community. So the Pope made a deal. He would have a religious debate with a member of the Jewish community. If the Jew won, the Jews could stay. If the Pope won, the Jews would leave.

The Jews realized that they had no choice. So they picked a middle aged man named Moishe to represent them. Moishe asked for one addition to the debate. To make it more interesting, neither side would be allowed to talk. The Pope agreed.

The day of the great debate came. Moishe and the Pope sat opposite each other for a full minute before the Pope raised his hand and showed three fingers. Moishe looked back at him and raised one finger.

The Pope waved his fingers in a circle around his head. Moishe pointed to the ground where he sat. The Pope pulled out a wafer and a glass of wine. Moishe pulled out an apple. The Pope stood up and said, "I give up. This man is too good. The Jews can stay."

An hour later, the cardinals were all around the Pope asking him what had happened. The Pope said, "First I held up three fingers to represent the Trinity. He responded by holding up one finger to remind me that there was still one God common to both our religions. Then I waved my finger around me to show him that God was all around us. He responded by pointing to the ground and showing that God was also right here with us. I pulled out the wine and wafer to show that God absolves us from our sins. He pulled out an apple to remind me of original sin. He had an answer for everything. What could I do?"

Meanwhile, the Jewish community had crowded around Moishe. "What happened?" they asked. "Well," said Moishe, "First he said to me that the Jews had three days to get out of here. I told him that not one of us was leaving. Then he told me that this whole city would be cleared of Jews. I let him know that we were staying right here."

"Yes, yes,... and then???" asked the crowd.

"I don't know," said Moishe,

"He took out his lunch, and I took out mine."

And here is the second joke:

The Private and the Toolbox

A newly promoted colonel had moved into a makeshift office during the Gulf War. He was just getting unpacked when out of the corner of his eye, he noticed a private with a toolbox coming his way.

Wanting to seem important, he grabbed the phone: "Yes, General Schwarzkopf. Of course, I think that's an excellent plan." He continued: "You've got my support on it. Thanks for checking with me. Let's touch base again soon, Norm. Goodbye."

"And what can I do for you?" he asked the private.

"Uhhh, I'm just here to hook up your phone."

My loves, I love you each so much. I often tell people what a delight you are to raise. You make child-rearing seem effortless!

Buckets and oodles of love,

Daddy
XXXOOO

Thursday, November 19, 1998
My Darling Kimmie, Tina and Jenny:

I am in Cleveland tonight for the premiere of *Whales* at the Great Lakes Science Center. I am the guest of honor at the opening and will give three speeches. I have been collecting raw material for these speeches (including stories and jokes) for some weeks now and am looking forward very much to doing the best job possible. I will also be doing radio and television interviews.

Mommy and I treasure you each so much. Everything about you is important to us. I wonder what you will remember vividly from your childhoods and whether they will be the same things as Mommy and I remember. I suspect that what we remember as being important to you may be different from what you remember as being important. In fact, what is important and memorable to you about your life so far may well be things that Mommy and I are blind to.

I read recently of a mother and daughter who wrote a book in 1996 called *The Conversation Begins*. It is a collection of essays by prominent mothers and their daughters on their lives together. Apparently, several mother-daughter pairs dropped out, partly because of differences in memories.

One reason I keep a journal is to help me be more aware of, and better able to observe, the magic in the ordinary day-to-day moments of your lives — and ours, too. Ordinary life can seem so... well, ordinary. In fact, it may not be ordinary at all. Here is a small example: Thanks to Mommy, we have chosen to have our study in the center of the house where we can stay connected to everybody in the house while we work. I think this gives you (I hope) a sense of security. To other people, choosing where we put the study may not seem that important. I know some parents who have deliberately built their studies away from the main house so they are not interrupted by family activities. Ordinary life consists of important decisions like that.

I remember Grandpa telling me the following story from his childhood. When he visited the family bakery in Llangum, his grandfather (William Palmer) used to give him a small bun of some kind to eat straight out of a hot oven. Grandpa loved that! I wonder if William Palmer realized how special his gift to Grandpa was. Maybe he did — we'll never know, unless we discover a journal that he kept!

Obviously, people attach importance to different things. Here are a few things that are important to me:

1. Thomas Jefferson: I have recently been studying the life of Thomas Jefferson. I think there is so much to learn from him. Here is one thing that impressed me about him. When he was 17, he was buying books lavishly and reading constantly. He filled his days with reading. After a year at William and Mary, he left to start a course of self-study. He wrote in his journal that he studied 15 hours a day: "Rise at 5:00 AM, read til 8:00 AM books on agriculture, botany, zoology, chemistry, anatomy, religion. 8-12 read law. 12-1 read politics. In the afternoon read history, then run a mile into the country and back for exercise. And in the evenings read rhetoric, oratory, literature and language." What a guy! He had a lifelong quest for wisdom.

2. Anecdotes that are insightful: Here is one (probably apocryphal): During the heat of the space

260

race in the 1960s, the US National Aeronautics and Space Administration decided it needed a ballpoint pen to write in the zero-gravity confines of its space capsules. After considerable research and development, the Astronaut Pen was developed at a cost of about $1 million. The pen worked and also enjoyed some modest success as a novelty item back here on earth. The Soviet Union, faced with the same problem, used a pencil.

3. <u>Constantly improving one's vocabulary</u>: Here are some good words you need to know:

   ➢ <u>Controversial</u>: Causing argument.
   ➢ <u>Access</u>: Ability to enter or acquire.
   ➢ <u>Landmark</u>: Historic.
   ➢ <u>Paragon</u>: A model of excellence.
   ➢ <u>Alleged</u>: Supposed or reported.
   ➢ <u>Preclude</u>: Prevent.
   ➢ <u>Fetter</u>: Tie or chain.
   ➢ <u>Invalidate</u>: Cancel.
   ➢ <u>Asperity</u>: Bitterness of temper.
   ➢ <u>Epithet</u>: A descriptive name.
   ➢ <u>Accomplice</u>: One who helps another in wrongdoing.
   ➢ <u>Complicity</u>: Partnership in wrongdoing.
   ➢ <u>Culpability</u>: Guilt or blame.
   ➢ <u>Recant</u>: Take back previous statements.
   ➢ <u>Whitewash</u>: Conceal defects.
   ➢ <u>Liquidation</u>: Disposal of.
   ➢ <u>Extrinsic</u>: Coming from the outside.
   ➢ <u>Nomadic</u>: Wandering.

4. <u>Success</u>: There are no secrets to success. Success is the result of showing up, paying attention, hard work, learning from failure, asking questions, and being persistent. Booker Washington (1856-1915) said, "Success is to be measured, not so much by the position that one has reached in life as by the obstacles that one has overcome while trying to succeed." And here is a funny thing about success: You are not judged by the number of times you fail, but by the number of times you succeed. However, the number of times you succeed is in direct proportion to the number of times you fail and keep trying. And remember that if at first you do succeed, then try something harder and more challenging.

Well my treasures, those are a few of the things that are important to me. You each will have your own lists. It goes without saying that the most important thing to Mommy and me is our family — you guys — and your happiness, health, vigor and accomplishments.

It will be great to be all together at Thanksgiving with Kim home again for over a week. I am looking forward to us all being together — and it will be extra special because Granny and Grandpa will be with us. Buckets and buckets of love,

Daddy
XXXOOO

Thursday, December 3, 1998

My darling Kimmie, Tina and Jenny:

As you know, I am in Chicago for 24 hours to raise money. It will be a lot of fun because I love meeting new people. I will be home tomorrow for family dinner.

Here is a poignant story I recently read:

His name is Bill. He has wild hair, wears a T-shirt with holes in it, jeans and no shoes. This was literally his wardrobe for his entire four years of college. He is brilliant. Kinda esoteric and very, very bright. He became a Christian while attending college.

Across the street from the campus is a well-dressed, very conservative church. They want to develop a ministry to the students, but are not sure how to go about it. One day Bill decides to go there. He walks in with no shoes, jeans, his T-shirt, and wild hair. The service has already started and so Bill starts down the aisle looking for a seat. The church is completely packed and he can't find a seat. By now people are looking a bit uncomfortable, but no one says anything. Bill gets closer and closer to the pulpit and when he realizes there are no seats, he just squats down right on the carpet. (Although perfectly acceptable behavior at a college fellowship, trust me, this had never happened in this church before!) By now the people are really uptight, and the tension in the air is thick.

About this time, the minister realizes that from way at the back of the church, a deacon is slowly making his way toward Bill. Now the deacon is in his eighties, has silvergray hair, a threepiece suit, and a pocket watch. A Godly man, very elegant, very dignified, very courtly. He walks with a cane and as he starts walking toward this boy, everyone is saying to themselves, "You can't blame him for what he's going to do. How can you expect a man of his age and of his background to understand some college kid on the floor?"

It takes what seems like years for the man to reach the boy. The church is utterly silent except for the clicking of the man's cane. All eyes are focused on him. You can't even hear anyone breathing. The people are thinking, "The minister can't even preach the sermon until the deacon does what he has to do."

To their surprise they see this elderly man drop his cane on the floor.

Then, with great difficulty the deacon slowly lowers himself to the floor, sitting down next to Bill....just so he won't have to worship alone!

The congregation is choked with emotion.

Once the minister gains control he says, "What I'm about to preach, you will probably never remember. But, what you have just seen, you will never forget."

Isn't that a great story?

My three loves, you have each been so loving and affectionate to Granny and Grandpa during their seven-week stay with us. Mommy and I are very appreciative and grateful to you. Sometimes I lose sight of how special and remarkable you each are because of all the pressure and exhaustion I am under from juggling so many roles and responsibilities. Then I see something like the little note that Tina left for Granny and Grandpa yesterday morning at the top of the stairs, and I realize that Mommy and I are incredibly lucky to have you three as our children.

I love you.

Daddy
XXXOOO

Sunday, December 6, 1998

My Darling Kimmie, Tina and Jenny:

As you know, I am flying to Los Angeles tonight, and then on to Palm Springs. I will get there when you are all fast asleep! At 8:30 AM tomorrow morning (11:30 AM your time), I am meeting with a company called US Filter (which works in the area of clean water) to persuade them to sponsor our *Water* IMAX film. I will ask them to invest $1 million. Then I will drive to Laguna Beach for a day and a half-long meeting on our *Dolphins* IMAX film, where the discussions will focus primarily on the educational and marketing components of the film.

After the *Dolphins* IMAX meeting, I will go to Los Angeles on Tuesday afternoon to meet individually with five writers who are working on various environmental movies we are developing. On Wednesday, I meet with donors, Hollywood agents, and various other people before flying to Dallas, Texas, on early Wednesday afternoon.

In Dallas, I will meet with Mary Kay, Inc., to persuade them (as with US Filter) to underwrite our *Water* IMAX film. I will fly home on Thursday afternoon and arrive exhausted but eager to see you all at our family dinner. The whole trip will be a lot of fun, and I am looking forward to it even though I will miss you.

As you know, I have a high regard for Stephen Covey and his books, including *The Seven Habits Of Highly Effective People*. I want to teach you what I have learned from him:

Habit One: Be proactive. Being proactive is more than taking initiative. It is recognizing that we are responsible for our own choices and have the freedom to choose based on principles and values, rather than on moods or conditions. Proactive people are agents of change and choose not to be victims, to be reactive, or to blame others.

Habit Two: Begin with the end in mind. Individuals, families, teams, and organizations shape their own future by creating a mental vision and purpose for any project, large or small. They don't just live day-to-day with no clear purpose in mind. They identify and commit themselves to the principles, relationships, and purposes that matter most to them.

Habit Three: Put first things first. Putting first things first means organizing and executing around your most important priorities. It is living and being driven by the principles you value most, not by the agendas and forces surrounding you.

Habit Four: Think win-win. Thinking win-win is a frame of mind and heart that seeks mutual benefit and mutual respect in all interactions. It's about thinking in terms of abundance and opportunity, rather than of scarcity and adversarial competition. It's not thinking selfishly (win-lose) or like a martyr (lose-win).

Habit Five: Seek first to understand, then to be understood. When we listen with the intent to understand others, rather than with the intent to reply, we begin true communication and relationship-building.   Opportunities to then speak openly and to be understood come much more naturally and easily. Seeking to understand takes consideration; seeking to be understood takes courage. Effectiveness lies in balancing the two.

Habit Six: Synergize. Synergy is the third alternative — not my way, not your way, but a third way that is better than either of us would come up with individually. It's the fruit of respecting, valuing, and even celebrating one another's differences. It's about solving problems, seizing opportunities, and working out differences — not through compromise (1+1=1 ½), nor even by cooperation (1+1=2), but by creative cooperation (1+1=3 or more).

Habit Seven: Sharpen the saw: Sharpening the saw is about constantly renewing ourselves in the four basic areas of life: physical, social/emotional, mention and spiritual (for me spiritual does not mean religion or church-related activities, but rather the issue of living purposefully and meaningfully). It's the habit that increases our capacity to live all other habits of effectiveness.

My treasures, I hope you find that useful, and I hope you will constantly seek to absorb new wisdom from many different sources. In studying the lives of extraordinarily accomplished people like Ben Franklin, Thomas Jefferson or Abe Lincoln, I notice how over and over again, successful people like them are dedicated to learning and to constantly seeking feedback from others which helps them become wiser.

You guys are already way up on the learning curve when it comes to common sense and "emotional intelligence." Mommy and I love you more than we can say.

Buckets of love,

Daddy
XXXOOO

Monday, December 7, 1998

My loves, Kimmie, Tina and Jenny:

Did you know that, until about 15 years ago, bed rest was the treatment of choice for back pain? Now we know that inactivity is one of the worst things that you can do for your back. A fitness regimen consisting of aerobic exercise, strength training and stretching helps treat and prevent back pain.

Isn't it interesting how common wisdom changes? What I have just written about back pain makes me wonder how many things (which we now perceive as sensible and "common sense") will be wrong in 20 years' time.

One thing that will not change is the importance of constantly improving your vocabulary. Here are some words that you need to know:

- ➢ Inclement: stormy or harsh.
- ➢ Mastiff: a large dog.
- ➢ Recoil: draw back.
- ➢ Desist: cease.
- ➢ Doleful: sad.
- ➢ Premonition: forewarning.
- ➢ Imminent: about to happen.
- ➢ Inert: powerless to move.
- ➢ Symptomatic: indicative.
- ➢ Peruse: read carefully.
- ➢ Persevere: persist.
- ➢ Engrossed: absorbed.
- ➢ Elusive: hard to grasp.
- ➢ Obsess: preoccupy.
- ➢ Frustrate: foil or deny.
- ➢ Salient: most prominent.
- ➢ Pertinent: appropriate.
- ➢ Interject: interrupt.
- ➢ Squeamish: easily upset.

Kim, Tina and Jenny, I love you with all my heart.

Yer ole Dad
XXXOOO

Tuesday, December 8, 1998

My Darling Kimmie, Tina and Jenny:

I love maxims! In a few words, they capture the wisdom of the ages. Here are some that I like:

1. People are always blaming their circumstances for what they are. I don't believe in circumstances. The people who get on in this world are the people who get up and look for the circumstances they want, and if they can't find them, make them. (George Bernard Shaw)

2. The greatest discovery of my generation is that you can change your circumstances by changing your attitudes of mind. (William James)

3. Man is not fully conditioned and determined; he determines himself whether to give in to conditions or to stand up to them. In other words, man is ultimately self-determining. Man does not simply exist, but always decides what his existence will be, what he will become in the next moment. (Viktor Frankl)

4. He who conquers others is strong; He who conquers himself is mighty. (Lao Tsu)

5. I have generally found that a man who is good at excuses is usually good at nothing else. (Benjamin Franklin)

6. A wise man will make more opportunities than he finds. (Francis Bacon)

7. Destiny is no matter of chance. It is a matter of choice. It is not a thing to be waited for, it is a thing to be achieved. (William Jennings Bryan)

8. I don't wait for moods. You accomplish nothing if you do that. Your mind must know it has got to get down to work. (Pearl S. Buck)

9. I think one's feelings waste themselves in words, they ought all to be distilled into actions and into actions which bring results. (Florence Nightingale)

10. One can spend a lifetime of assigning blame, find the cause "out there" for all troubles that exist. Contrast this with the "responsible attitude" of confronting the situation, bad or good, and instead of asking "What caused the trouble? Who was to blame?" asking "How can I handle this present situation to make the most of it? What can I salvage here?" (Abraham Maslow)

11. What you can do, or dream you can, begin it: Boldness has genius, power and magic in it. (Johann Wolfgang von Goethe)

12. We who have lived in concentration camps can remember the men who walked though the huts comforting others, giving away their last piece of bread. They may have been few in number, but they offer sufficient proof that everything can be taken from man but one thing: the last of the human freedoms — to choose one's attitude in any given set of circumstances — to choose one's own way. (Viktor Frankl)

13. You must be the change you wish to see in the world. (Mohandas K. Gandhi)

14. The tragedy of life is what dies inside a man while he lives. (Albert Schweitzer)

15. Nothing contributes so much to tranquilize the mind as a steady purpose — a point on which the soul may fix its intellectual eye. (Mary Wollstonecraft Shelley)

16. Many persons have a wrong idea of what constitutes real happiness. It is not obtained through self-gratification, but through fidelity to a worthy purpose. (Helen Keller)

17. The greatest use of life is to spend it for something that will outlast it. (William James)

18. Happiness, wealth, and success are byproducts of goal setting; they cannot be the goal themselves. (Denis Waitley)

19. Man's main task in life is to give birth to himself. (Erich Fromm)

20. Failing to plan is a plan to fail. (Effie Jones)

21. What is the use of running when we are not on the right road? (German proverb)

22. When there is no vision, the people perish. (Proverbs 29:18)

23. He who lives without discipline dies without honor. (Icelandic proverb)

24. Besides the noble art of getting things done, there is the noble art of leaving things undone. The wisdom of life consists in the elimination of nonessentials. (Lin Yutang)

25. He who every morning plans the transactions of the day and follows out that plan carries a thread that will guide him through the labyrinth of the most busy life. The orderly arrangement of his time is like a ray of light which darts itself through all his occupations. But where no plan is laid, where the disposal of time is surrendered merely to the chance of incidents, chaos will soon reign. (Victor Hugo)

26. If one advances confidently in the direction of his dreams, and endeavors to live the life which he has imagined, he will meet with a success unexpected in common hours. (Henry David Thoreau)

27. At the end of your life, you will never regret not having passed one more test, not winning one more verdict or not closing one more deal. You will regret time not spent with a husband, a friend, a child or a parent. (Barbara Bush)

28. No life ever grows great until it is focused, dedicated, and disciplined. (Henry Emerson Fosdick)

29. If time be of all things most precious, wasting time must be the greatest prodigality. Since lost time is never found again, what we call "time enough" always proves "little enough." Let us then be up and doing to a purpose; so that by diligence we shall do more with less perplexity. (Benjamin Franklin)

30. Men give me some credit for genius, but all the genius I have lies in this: When I have a subject in mind I study it profoundly. Day and night it is before me. I explore it in all its bearings. My mind becomes pervaded with it. The result is what some people call the fruits of genius, whereas it is in reality the fruits of study and labor. (Alexander Hamilton)

31. The shortest and surest way to live with honor in the world is to be in reality what we would appear to be; all human virtues increase and strengthen themselves by the practice and experience of them. (Socrates)

Kim, Tina and Jenny, I hope you relish those maxims and deeply imbibe them! I love you!

Daddy
XXXOOO

Wednesday, December 9, 1998
My treasures Kimmie, Tina and Jenny:
I will be home tomorrow!

Here are some more maxims which I find inspirational:

1. We must not, in trying to think about how we can make a big difference, ignore the small daily differences we can make which, over time, add up to big differences that we often cannot foresee. (Marian Wright Edelman)

2. He makes things easier for himself who makes things easier for others. (Asian idiom)

3. Listen, or thy tongue will keep thee deaf. (American Indian proverb)

4. Great Spirit, help me never to judge another until I have walked in his moccasins. (Sioux Indian prayer)

5. He who knows only his own side of the case, knows little of that. (John Stuart Mill)

6. He that answereth a matter before he heareth it, it is folly and shame to him. (Proverbs 18:13)

7. He that is good with a hammer tends to think everything is a nail. (Abraham Maslow)

8. I have never met a man who was not my superior in some particular. (Ralph Waldo Emerson)

9. People are never so near playing the fool as when they think themselves wise. (Mary Wortley Montagu)

10. The unexamined life is not worth living. (Socrates)

And here are some important words that you need to know:

- Neutralize: make inactive.
- Analogous: comparable or similar.
- Neurotic: having an emotional disorder.
- Decade: ten years.
- Irascible: irritable.
- Susceptible: vulnerable to.
- Mandate: an authoritative command.
- Maladjusted: mentally or emotionally disturbed.
- Catastrophic: disastrous.
- Pedagogue: a teacher.
- Heterogeneous: dissimilar or diverse.
- Introspective: looking into one's own feelings.
- Perpetuate: cause to continue.
- Enunciate: speak clearly.
- Phenomenon: an unusual occurrence.
- Perspicacious: acutely perceptive.
- Gamut: the complete range.
- Inordinate: excessive.

Kim, Tina and Jenny, I hope you are having a wonderful week at school, studying hard, asking good questions, having fun, laughing a lot, and enjoying your friends. I love you so much.

Daddy
XXXOOO

1999

Tuesday, January 5, 1999

My Darling Kimmie, Tina and Jenny:

As you know, I am on my way to Patagonia in Argentina to join our IMAX crew filming the foraging behavior of dusky dolphins! It will be exciting. Kim, you may not read this letter until you return from Australia on January 19. Tina, good luck this week preparing for your exams. Remember in your preparation to simulate the exams rather than just read your notes. And, Jenny, good luck in school this week. Please read extensively way beyond your school requirements. You must set your own goals for learning way above the standards set by the school. My treasures, thank you all for a great Christmas together. Mommy and I love being with you.

We are making this IMAX film on dolphins with Greg MacGillivray who made *Everest*. He is a good person, and I will be with him in Argentina. We are going to be in wild country on the coast. *Dolphins* will have its premiere in February 2000.

As you know, dolphins are among the most intelligent mammals on earth. They adapt quickly to new situations, and in captivity can be taught all sorts of complicated behaviors. There are over 30 species of dolphins worldwide. All dolphins are toothed whales. The biggest dolphin is the killer whale, which may grow to be over 30 feet long. Wild dolphins could easily kill people, but they very rarely even hurt them. And when they do, it is almost always because people have done something stupid like tried to feed them.

I will be with two first-rate dolphin scientists, Kathleen Dudzinski and Alejandro Acevedo. The major area of their investigation is communication. Do dolphins communicate? Have they developed a language? Kathleen and Alejandro are studying dolphins to explore these questions and to understand how dolphins convey and comprehend information. Dolphins can be taught to associate abstract concepts or signs with specific objects or actions. Such symbolism can be said to be the underlying basis of a language.

Can dolphins think without words? Do they think and reason without a formal language? Dolphins are believed to be smart, but how intelligent are they — and how would anyone know they are intelligent? What is intelligence? Scientists have long argued about what intelligence is. Once they agree on a definition of intelligence, then they can design experiments or questionnaires to measure it.

Another interesting question: Can dolphins empathize? In other words, can a dolphin put itself in the place of another dolphin?

So these are some of the issues I will be thinking about while I am in Patagonia. By the way, *Scientific American Frontiers* airs on PBS on January 20 at 8:00 PM and is devoted to an exploration of how smart animals are.

Kimmie, Tina and Jenny: Mommy and I love you totally and are very proud of you.

Daddy
XXXOOO

Wednesday, January 6, 1999

Darling Tina, Darling Jenny, and Darling Kimmie:

I mixed the order of your names up! Do you remember we talked about that jokingly at

Christmas? You are all equally important!

Isn't it funny to think how split up we are this week with Kim and me being in the southern hemisphere (but still being thousands of miles apart) and experiencing hot summer weather?

My loves, you may wonder sometimes where I get the energy to keep a journal. It is partly because I know how much pleasure it will give you and your children when you are older. I read three things recently which helped me to better understand my motivation. The first was from a December 13, 1998 book review in *The Washington Post*:

> One of the primary impulses behind a memoir is the need for order: We seek coherence at the core of our own fuddled selves, and a narrative that makes sense of chaotic and unpredictable events.

The second item was from a May 16, 1997 *New York Times* article about keeping journals:

> 'My journal is that of me which would else spill over and run to waste.' This sentence, written by Henry David Thoreau in a marbled, word-swollen, sun-bleached notebook during the winter of 1841, goes a good way toward encapsulating one of the most rooted and mysterious of human impulses: The need to stop the spillage and make a record of the behavior of the self.

The third item comes from a recent issue of *Reader's Digest* entitled "Tell Me A Story," and subtitled "Those Tales Shared At Special Moments With The Family Have Untold Worth":

> Storytelling is a psalm of praise and thanksgiving for the love and connection of family. Stories are the heart and soul of our culture. They give us hope and help us set goals for ourselves.... Storytelling can also be beneficial to older people. When you allow elderly family members to express their feelings through stories, you give them back the humanity our youth culture snatches away. If we forget to ask for their stories or fail to listen to them when they are told, we set ourselves up for a lifetime of unanswered questions.

My journal keeps a record of our family stories so we don't lose them. That article from *Reuder's Digest* also points out that the time for listening and storytelling is fleeting.

And talking about history, I have been reading voraciously over Christmas, and one of the many books I read was called *Buffalo Nation: History And Legend Of the North American Bison*. I read this book because I want to learn more about the history of the American West. I am also thinking of producing an IMAX film on buffalo. Here is what I read in this book about the war on the buffalo:

> The Indian tribes of the West were completely dependent on the bison.... Extermination of the bison would mean the economic end for Indian people of the Great Plains. So the bison was slated for extermination.... The idea to subdue the Indian tribes by eliminating the buffalo was not original; Sheridan and Sherman practiced a similar 'scorched earth' policy on General Robert E. Lee's Confederate Army late in the Civil War. It had the desired results, but Sheridan's and Sherman's march through Georgia

left more than fame for the Union generals and scorched earth for the Confederacy: It left deep, abiding resentment in the South at the sheer brutality and ruthlessness of the campaign. Thus, when Sherman and Sheridan moved West after the Civil War, they were already hated by Texans. Their anti-Indian policies would soon make heroes of them.... The US government and its Army waged a covert war on Native Americans and the bison by employing a secret army of buffalo hunters. The government simply had to protect the hunters and ensure that their lines of supply was secure.... By 1894, the only free-living bison remaining in the US were found in Yellowstone National Park. Six years later, by 1902, this last wild herd was reduced by poachers to 23 animals.

That is 23 animals down from about 60 million in the 1840s!

Here's a joke to cheer you up before I say goodbye. You can remind me of this when I am an old man!

> Herman, a senior citizen, was driving down the freeway, when his car phone rang. Answering, he heard his wife's voice urgently warning him, 'Herman, I just heard on the news that there is a car going the wrong way on 280. Please be careful!'

> 'Hell,' said Herman, 'it's not just one car, it's hundreds of them!'

Kimmie, Tina and Jenny, I love you so much.

> Daddy
> XXXOOO

Thursday, January 7, 1999
My Darling Kimmie, Tina and Jenny:
I love you! And I love Mommy! I recently read a book by James Autry called *Life & Work: A Manager's Search For Meaning*. On page 245, I came across the following part of a poem which explained beautifully how precious Mommy is to me:

> And I am moved one more time to find the words,
> to bring up from somewhere a sense,
> even a hint,
> of what it is to understand at last
> how the love of one person can deliver us
> into a life we didn't even know we believed in.

> Not a life without pain or anger or hurt or disappointment;
> to the contrary, a life with all of that,
> and yet,
> a life without despair.

Together, Mommy and I have tried to create a family and a family life that is profoundly and deeply satisfying. Ironically, I work in a business — television, although I think of my "business" as being conservation, not television — which seems determined to destroy those values that families need to live by if they are to be healthy, robust, vibrant and successful — values such as self discipline, hard work, consideration for others, honesty, courage, service, responsibility, and tenacity.

I read three things recently which reminded me of how bad television is for our society. The first is from an April 6, 1998 article in *The New York Times* entitled "TV Stretches Limits Of Taste, To Little Outcry":

> Like a child acting outrageously naughty to see how far he can push his parents, mainstream television this season is flaunting the most vulgar and explicit sex, language and behavior that it has ever sent into American homes. And, as sometimes happens with the spoiled child, the tactic works: Attention is being paid. Ratings are high, few advertisers are rebelling against even the most provocative shows, and more and more parents seem to have given up resisting their children in squabbles over television. Often, in a nation of two-income families and single parents, children are left alone to watch whatever they want.

And here is an extract from an essay in *Time* magazine (October 20, 1997) from Lance Morrow:

> 'Nothing human is foreign to me,' is a dictum that floats in to us like elegant driftwood from the second century B.C., when the Roman playwright Terence said it. The line describes the ideal state of today's movie and television audience: A morally promiscuous and passive receptivity, a tolerant consumer's connoisseurship of vice and weirdness.

And the third thing I read came from an essay by the comedian and writer, Steve Allen, in a November 13, 1998 article in *The Wall Street Journal*. He writes:

> We live in an environment bombarded morning, noon and night from messages from films, television, radio, recordings and other modes of mass communication. It is almost impossible to escape encouragement to act in ways that have traditionally been the province of the libertine, thuggish, coarse, and depraved.

One of the worst things about television is that it distracts people from doing more important things, such as exercising, talking with one another, or (and here is something I want to focus on for a minute) studying the lives of great people. Gaining inspiration from the eminent minds of the past by studying biographies of renowned people is a very important thing to do. I recommend borrowing attributes and ideas from trail-blazing champions whenever you find them, and recombining them to create and design your own lives.

When you face a challenge, think about how Golda Meir, Eleanor Roosevelt, Mother Teresa, Ben Franklin, Abe Lincoln, Thomas Jefferson, or Martin Luther King Jr. would advise you. Read books about these people and their lives, keeping your challenge in mind. One of the attributes of the successful person is they passionately explore the lives and work of those before him or her, absorbing bits of genius for recombination into their own lives. Bathe your minds in the traits of the finest characters and people you can find. To the extent that television distracts us from doing this, even good television is detrimental.

Kimmie, Tina and Jenny, I adore you! And I miss you! I wish you were with me in Patagonia

273

swimming with dolphins! (I am writing this before I leave, so I actually don't know whether I will have the opportunity to swim with dolphins.)

I love you!

Daddy
XXXOOO

Friday, January 8, 1999

My Special Loves, Kimmie, Tina and Jenny:

How are you all doing? You Kim, are in Australia; you, Tina are working hard for your exams; and you Jenny, are back in class asking lots of good questions! I hope you are all smiling and laughing a lot. Laughter is so important. None of us laughs enough, especially me.

As *Reader's Digest* says, laughter really <u>is</u> the best medicine. Study after study has shown how laughter helps block pain (by flooding the body with endorphins, the body's own opiate-like painkillers), relaxes muscles, fights infection, and reduces emotional stress. It is important to find out what you think is funny, become more playful, cultivate the laughter habit, find humor in language (I recently read about a sign in a department store that read, "Bras are half off!"), develop your sense of irony and absurdity (especially when something unpleasant happens to you), don't take yourself too seriously, and lighten up during times of stress. These are all areas in which I am a beginner. We often find that, when bad things happen, we look back ten years later and laugh about them. But why wait ten years?

Here is a summary of my religious beliefs (which I have adapted from some literature I have recently read about humanism), but see if you can tell what is missing for me:

I like to call myself a humanist because it includes my agnosticism, but expresses it a lot more positively. Humanism is based on the conviction that the universe is all that exists or is real. Humanism serves for me some of the functions of a religion, but without belief in deities, transcendental entities, superstition, pseudoscience, miracles (using that word in a religious sense), life after death, and the supernatural. Humanists seek to understand the universe by using science and its methods of critical inquiry — logical reasoning, empirical evidence, and skeptical evaluation of conjectures and conclusions — to obtain reliable knowledge. Humanists believe that humans have the freedom and obligation to give meaning, value, and purpose to their lives by their own independent thoughts, free inquiry, and responsible, creative activity. Humanists stand for the building of a more humane, just, compassionate, and democratic society using ethics based on human reason, experience, and reliable knowledge — ethics that judge the consequences of human actions by the well-being of all life on Earth. Humanism thus derives the goals of life from human need and interest, rather than from theological or ideological abstractions, and asserts that humanity must take responsibility for its own destiny.

Okay Kimmie, Tina and Jenny, what's missing? I will give you the answer in tomorrow's letter. Here is a clue though:

Son to his father as they watch television, 'Dad, tell me again how when you were a kid you had to walk all the way across the room to change the channel.'

I love you!

Daddy
XXXOOO

Saturday, January 9, 1999
My Darling Kimmie, Tina and Jenny:

The answer to what was missing from the description of my beliefs is: Laughter! Or, more fundamentally, the value of perspective.

I cannot wait to get home tomorrow to be with you all (and to be ready to meet you, Kim, when you return on the 19th).

Marilyn vos Savant, writing in *Parade* magazine on December 27, had some good things to say about happiness. Somebody wrote to her asking if it was possible for a person to be happy if a person is poor. Marilyn vos Savant replied:

> ...We have trained ourselves to value ease and material goods above all.... For more people to be happy, we must change our prevailing social philosophy. Consider that only 50 years ago, there were surely plenty of happy people. But none of them had a computer, cable TV or microwave. Happiness has nothing to do with cell phones and never did. Rather we must base our happiness on personal success, like skills, artistry, the acquisition of knowledge, the refinement of character, the development of a sense of humor, the satisfaction of helping others, the pleasure of friends, the comfort of family and the joy of love.

I have not left you any words in these last five letters to enrich your vocabularies, so here are a few as I come to the end of this last letter:

- ➤ Methodical: Orderly and systematic. ("He was methodical in his work habits and always met his commitments.")

- ➤ Fantasize: To imagine or daydream (as "He fantasized about superseding Jay Leno.").

- ➤ Therapy: Healing, or treatment for illness or injury. ("Not eating great wads of butter was part of his therapy to prevent himself from getting a heart attack.")

- ➤ Chronic: Constant or ongoing. ("His chronic back pain forced him to rethink his entire life-style.")

- ➤ Pragmatic: Practical or businesslike. ("He was pragmatic in family meetings and didn't waste time.")

- ➤ Orate: To speak, often in a high-flown or stuffy way. ("While their father orated on the subject of ethics, his daughters doodled in a soporific state.")

- ➤ Synthesize: To combine, or to bring parts into a whole. ("His Personal Mission Statement and New Year's Resolutions synthesized his whole thinking about how he wanted to live his life.")

> Phobia: Fear, often irrational. ("He had no phobias about flying in airplanes and so traveled to Patagonia happily.")

> Cataclysm: Disaster, or sudden tragedy. ("The cataclysm of Hurricane Mitch left thousands dead in Central America.")

> Hoi polloi: Common people, or the masses. ("Violence broke out among the hoi polloi attending the rock concert.")

Tina and Jenny, I cannot wait to get home and see you tomorrow. Kim, I cannot wait to see you on the 19th when you return from Australia. I love you all so much.

Daddy
XXXOOO

Wednesday, February 3, 1999

My Darling Kimmie, Tina and Jenny:

I am on my way to Sweden for meetings and talks on our IMAX films. On my way back on Saturday afternoon, I will land in London where, as you know, Tim will pick me up. We will drive to Bath to have dinner with Granny, Grandpa and Jon. Then Tim and I will drive from Bath to London on Sunday morning, and I will get home on Sunday afternoon at about 5:00 PM.

Enclosed with this letter you will find all of our New Year's Resolutions. Please study them carefully. I am so proud of all of us for thinking about our goals for 1999. Your New Year's Resolutions reflect so well on each of you. Remember, "the more goals you set, the more goals you get."

You have often heard me say that teaching is the best way to learn. What I mean is this: If you are listening in class to your teachers, and you listen to what is being taught with the realization that sometime within the next two days you will have to turn around and shift your role to become the teacher or expert and teach a third person (like me) the concept, then the information will be retained better because you will be making a stronger effort to try to understand, comprehend and remember the material. When you teach somebody what you have just learned, your understanding will be significantly increased — both because you have to teach it, and because when you are learning it in the first place, you will pay more attention.

Here are some good words you need to know:

> Gastric: Pertaining to the stomach; as, "His gastric pain came from eating his dad's cooking."

> Thesaurus: Dictionary of synonyms, or words of similar meaning; as, "A Thesaurus can be a writer's best friend."

> Eulogize: To highly praise someone, usually after his or her death.

> Mania: Craze; extreme enthusiasm; as, "Beatlemania began to sweep America in 1964."

> Panacea: Cure-all; remedy; single solution for multiple problems.

> Ostracize: To exclude; shun; as, "In *The Scarlett Letter*, Hester Prynne was ostracized because of adultery."

> Theology: Religion and its formal study.

> Cathartic: Cleansing; purging; as, "Watching the movie, *Saving Private Ryan*, was a cathartic experience for many war veterans."

And finally, my treasures, here is a joke:

> 'Mr. Quinn, I have reviewed this case very carefully,' the divorce court judge said, 'and I've decided to give your wife $775 a week.'

> 'That's very fair, your honor,' the husband said. 'And every now and then I'll try to send her a few bucks myself.'

Kimmie, Tina and Jenny, I love you so much. You are so precious to Mommy and me in every way. You enrich every moment of our lives. Lots of love,

Daddy
XXXOOO

Thursday, February 4, 1999

Darling Kimmie, Tina and Jenny:

I didn't watch the Super Bowl last Sunday, but I saw a couple of the ads in passing. I was impressed by an article about those ads which appeared yesterday in the February 1 edition of *Advertising Age*. It was entitled, "Chauvinist Pigskin," and was subtitled, "Super Bowl Advertisers Set the World Back 30 Years With Naked Appeals to Guys." The article was by Bob Garfield, who is one of their regular columnists, and this is part of what he wrote:

> Now that the Super Bowl is over and the victory recorded for the ages, let's spend a quiet moment thinking about who lost: Gloria Steinem. Also Betty Friedan, Germaine Greer, your mother, your daughter. When all the empties are collected, and all the street rioting is over, and when the Fox pregame coverage finally ends, what will be starkly apparent is that the real Super Bowl loser was the American woman. In a rout... After three decades of gradually weaning itself from naked objectification, advertising has apparently decided that the benefit of crudely impressing men trumps the disadvantages of dishonoring women. It's as if Madison Avenue sneaked into the nation's psyche and absconded with 30 years of feminist awareness.

Food for thought.

Here is a joke I saw recently that made me smile:

> One summer evening during a violent thunderstorm a mother was tucking her small boy into bed. She was about to turn off the light when he asked with a tremor in his voice,

'Mommy, will you sleep with me tonight?' The mother smiled and gave him a reassuring hug. 'I can't dear,' she said. 'I have to sleep in Daddy's room.' A long silence was broken at last by a shaken little voice saying, 'The big sissy.'

My treasures, here are some words you need to know:

1. Repeal: To take back; cancel; as, "The 18th Amendment was repealed in 1933, ending Prohibition."

2. Diplomatically: Tactfully; cautiously; as, "Tina argued diplomatically to stay out after 11:00 PM."

3. Endorse: To support; approve; as, "Most local merchants endorsed him for mayor."

4. Acclamation: Voiced approval, often given loudly; as, "He was chosen by acclamation."

5. Veto: To prohibit; as, "If the President vetoes a bill, Congress can pass it by a two-thirds majority of each chamber."

6. Incumbent: Occupying; holding office; as, "A blitz of TV ads helped reelect the incumbent Senator."

Kim, Tina and Jenny, I love you and miss you.

Daddy
XXXOOO

Friday, February 5, 1999

My Darling Kimmie, Tina, Jenny and Conker:

Everybody makes mistakes. In my life, I have made plenty. Some of them I am aware of, many I am surely blind to — especially if I include "missed opportunities" in the definition of "mistakes." I have been afraid and timid, made dumb decisions, and failed to keep promises. I say all this because I want you to know that nobody is perfect — especially me (as you well know already!).

You three girls seem so far ahead of where I was at your three ages of 11, 16 and 19. I didn't speak up much. I was shy and sometimes fearful. My self-confidence was fragile. I was a mediocre student most of the time, and incredibly ignorant. Not infrequently, I was rude, angry, inconsiderate, impatient, egotistical and obnoxious — all the things one expects from teenagers.

My vocabulary was limited. I had a hard time expressing myself and articulating my views. I only began to read extensively when I was about 15. I was a poor writer, and the few articles I had published in newspapers when I was in my late teens were sometimes naive and childish.

I was overly harsh in my judgment of other people, and I am sure often erroneous in those judgments. I had no close friends.

The only thing that I had going for me was that, at about the age of 14, I suddenly realized that I could start getting good grades through hard work; and, through good grades, I could increase the power I wielded. So hard work, combined with ambition, helped me eventually find a life I could love

— the life you see me leading now.

Many things have helped me, but one of them is the following exercise: Find a quiet time and place where you can be alone. Close your eyes and imagine that you are on your deathbed, with your loved ones gathered around you. Review your life from beginning to end, seeing both yourself and those around you through various stages of your life. As you do, notice what you regret having done and not having done. Ask yourself questions:

➢ What do you wish you had spent more time doing?

➢ What are you proudest of in your life?

➢ What times of your life were the happiest and why?

➢ What were the times or situations in your life where you felt best about yourself?

➢ What has made your life worthwhile?

➢ What do you leave as a legacy?

The answers to these questions reflect what you value most and also reveal whether you are living out your values and principles. This exercise can be very powerful.

And talking about deathbeds, here is a joke I told Nana the other day and it made her laugh. So perhaps it will make you laugh as well:

A man lies on his deathbed, surrounded by his family: a weeping wife and four children. Three of the children are tall, good looking and athletic; but the fourth and youngest is an ugly runt.

'Darling wife,' the husband whispers, 'assure me that the youngest child really is mine. I want to know the truth before I die, I will forgive you if--'

The wife gently interrupts him. 'Yes, my dearest, absolutely, no question, I swear on my mother's grave that you are his father.'

The man then dies, happy. The wife mutters under her breath: 'Thank God he didn't ask about the other three.'

Kimmie, Tina and Jenny, I love you so much, and thank you for all the happiness you bring Mommy and me.

Daddy
XXXOOO

Saturday, February 6, 1999

My Precious Loves, Kimmie, Tina and Jenny:

As you read this, I am having dinner in Bath with Granny, Grandpa, Tim and Jon.

You know all about the alleged healing powers of Bath's hot-mineral water. The fame of these waters started after a six-week visit to the spa town in 1702 by Prince George, Queen Anne's husband. Soon, a trip to Bath became the astute thing to do for anybody seeking a remedy for a wide variety of ailments. During the 18ᵗʰ and 19ᵗʰ centuries, Bath became transformed into an architectural showcase for which it is now world famous.

It was the Romans who first built bathhouses over the springs in the first century A.D. The Romans believed that the goddess Minerva was the patron of these sacred hot springs. (Jen, did you come across Minerva in your recent studies on ancient Greek gods?) Now that Roman world is lost beneath the city that you walk through when you visit Granny and Grandpa. The remains of the original bathhouses lie about 20 feet beneath the streets and shops of modern Bath.

My treasures, I cannot wait to get home tomorrow and be back with you all (although not you, Kim, because you are in Amherst!).

I love you each more than I can say.
                                   Daddy
                                   XXXOOO

Monday, February 22, 1999

My Darling Kimmie, Tina, Jenny and Conker:

As you know, I am on my way to Atlanta for the world premiere tomorrow night of our new giant-screen film, *Wolves*. Ted Turner and Jane Fonda will be there, plus many other important people. It will be a lot of fun, and I am looking forward to it. I have to give several talks while I am there about the film, and so for the last few weeks I have been preparing carefully — collecting ideas, searching for possible jokes and stories, studying up on wolves, and thinking about the purpose of each of the talks that I have to give.

One aspect of all this preparation is telling stories. I want to become better in my speeches at telling stories (especially humorous ones) which can illustrate points that I want to make. In pursuing this goal, I have recently been studying a book on giving effective presentations by a guy called Tom Antion. I enjoyed this book and thought highly of it, so I called a number given at the back of the book in order to buy some additional material by the same author.

When I called the number, Tom Antion himself answered the phone. I introduced myself, congratulated him on his excellent book, and we started talking. I told him about my job and what I did, and he was interested to learn about it. After a bit, he asked me if I would like some free advice, and I said I would. Tom said that, in terms of adding stories to my speeches, the best thing to do is to write my autobiography by jotting down all the incidences and stories that I can remember ever happening to me. He recommended I keep a file on this and, as memories come back to me, make a note of them.

Having done this (Tom said) and developed a number of stories (each of which will hopefully have a humorous angle to them), he then advised me to examine these stories and pick out the points that could be made with each story. The next step would be to practice telling them over and over again until I am able to tell them in an effective way.

Tom Antion's advice sounded good to me, so I made a list of different parts of my life, and now

I am trying to remember something about them! Here is the list that I developed: Birth; being a baby; ages 2-5; Dulwich Village; ages 6-8; living on Dulwich Common; being a twin; my brothers; my parents; my relatives; Dulwich College (ages 9-19); boarding school; University College (ages 18-25); the Royal Navy (ages 18-25); going to America; Harvard; meeting Gail; Booz, Allen & Hamilton; getting married; married life; having children; stories about Kimberly, Christina and Jenny; working on Capitol Hill; working at the EPA; balancing work and family; becoming a United States citizen; National Audubon Society; National Wildlife Federation; and having teenage daughters.

If you guys can think of any funny stories, please let me know!

I have to give several presentations at the NWF annual meeting in Houston, Texas, from March 16-21. I have started preparing for those and collecting (by "brainstorming") a lot of ideas. Since the event is in Houston, Texas, I have been looking for Texas-related stories. Here is one I came across recently in a funny book by Bob Dole called *Political Wit*:

> The late John Connally liked to tell a story about his Texas roots. In boasting of his background, Big John included George Washington in the Lone Star State's pantheon of heroes. As he told the story, young George one day went out into the backyard with a hatchet in hand and chopped down the family's mesquite tree. In due course he was summoned inside by a very angry parent.
>
> 'Did you chop down my mesquite tree?' demanded George's father.
>
> 'I cannot tell a lie, Father,' said George, 'I did chop down your mesquite tree.'
>
> On hearing this, the elder Washington ordered his son to start packing his bags. 'We're moving to Virginia,' he announced.
>
> 'Why, Father? Is it because I chopped down your mesquite tree?'
>
> 'No, George,' came the reply. 'Because if you can't tell a lie, you'll never amount to anything in Texas.'

Kimmie, Tina and Jenny, I love you so much. You are three incredibly special children, and Mommy and I adore you and are so proud of you. You make bringing up children such a delightful and rewarding pleasure.

Daddy
XXXOOO

Tuesday, February 23, 1999
My Treasures Kimmie, Tina and Jenny:
Tonight is the world premiere of *Wolves* in Atlanta, and it will be an exciting event. I wish that you three and Mommy could be there. I will not know until I see the audience's reaction tonight whether we have made a successful film or not. We have worked hard on this for four years, and so I am keeping my fingers crossed!

Even if the film is not a success, wolves themselves are fascinating animals. As you know, tribal cultures in North America coexisted with wolves for generations without serious problems — most likely because the Native Americans had little in the way of domestic livestock.

The more or less balanced coexistence between people and wolves here in the US began to change shortly after the arrival of the first European explorers and settlers. In the eastern part of the country, the introduction of domesticated animals (such as pigs, sheep, and cattle), along with the already present population of wild game that was considered essential for survival, first began to put the wolf against the needs of the white man.

In the western part of the US, it was the arrival and rapid spread of the horse that upset the existing order. Horses, at least after they were adopted by western tribes, altered traditional lifestyles and the hunting methods used to reap the most bountiful source of meat throughout the west — the buffalo.

Mostly stalked and hunted singly before the horse, slain buffalo were used frugally and completely, leaving little edible material for the wolves to scavenge. After the arrival of the horse, tribes expanded rapidly because of their new efficiency at food gathering. Although Native Americans were still conservative at how many buffalo they killed and how much of each buffalo was utilized for food and clothing, there was an increasing number of carcasses scattered across the western regions throughout the seasons, a potent catalyst that prompted the rapid expansion of the wolf population.

The arrival of fur traders, miners, ranchers, farmers, and other settlers from the east in the early 1800s (after the Lewis and Clark expedition) marked the beginning of an unprecedented era of feasting for the plains wolf. By the time widespread buffalo hunting had become a trend, packs of wolves were a constant presence throughout the buffalo's range. Because the white man wanted to force the Indians onto reservations, buffalo hunting became an organized and efficient operation, so thorough and voracious in its appetite that, between 1870-1880, an estimated 20 million buffalo were killed. The buffalo remains left behind by these operations provided a virtually limitless supply of food for the wolf population.

Beginning in the 1870s, western cattlemen began publicly complaining about losses to wolves. At about this time, associations were first formed to provide cattlemen with political influence to deal with railroads, rustling, and natural predators. Although the western territories had already by this time established bounties on wolves, the cattle organizations offered additional rewards for wolves destroyed and also supplied regular supplies of poison — most strychnine — for range riders to use on all available carcasses, including buffalo and livestock.

With a sudden and almost complete destruction of the buffalo herds by the end of the 1880s, the newly-expanded population of wolves was left without its regular diet and an inevitable confrontation began between these predators and the herds of cattle and sheep that settlers had brought with them to the west. Wolves were targeted and systematically eradicated to provide safe pasturage and rangeland for livestock. By the early 1900s, the last wolves had disappeared in most of the west.

Now, of course, thanks to the leadership of organizations like the National Wildlife Federation, wolves have been reintroduced to Yellowstone. That is a wonderful conservation success story which our IMAX film celebrates. I cannot wait for you guys to see the film!

Remember when we all went to see *Whales* for the first time? I remember it because we walked along the road to the theater arm-in-arm, and Kimmie called out, "What are we — the Brady bunch?!"

Here are two jokes I hope you enjoy. Here is the first one:

> **Neighbor:** George, your office has that certain je ne sais quoi
> **George Jefferson:** Not anymore -- I just had it exterminated.

And here is the second joke:

> **What John F. Kennedy meant to say during an impassioned speech at the Berlin Wall:**
> 'Ich bin Berliner!'
> **Translation:** 'I am a Berliner!'
> **What he actually said:** 'Ich bin ein berliner!'
> **Translation:** 'I am a jelly doughnut!'

My loves, I love you so much. You are three wonderful kids. Thank you for making an incredible impact on my life.

I love you,

> Daddy
> XXXOOO

Sunday, March 7, 1999
My Darling Kimmie, Tina, Jenny and Conker:

As you read this, I am flying to Los Angeles. I will land tonight in LAX at about 2:00 AM (ET) when you are fast asleep. I will go straight to bed at the Beverly Hilton Hotel to get rested for an intensive day of meetings all day tomorrow (Monday). Then I will catch the "Red Eye" back tomorrow night so I can see you early on Tuesday morning and then work all day in the office on Tuesday.

On Monday in Los Angeles, my first meeting is at 8:30 AM with Sue Zizzi, my Hollywood consultant. At 9:00 AM, we will have breakfast with Barry Clark and Justin Albert from Peter Guber's office. Then we will meet with Alan Horn, the President of Castle Rock, followed by a meeting with an agent called Glenn Bickel at CAA. This will be followed by a meeting with three writers on a movie project we are developing called *War Against The Greens*. Then we will have lunch at 1:00 PM with Pam Falk and Mike Ellis, who are two writers we are working with on a TV series called *Wildlife ER*.

At 2:30 PM, we are meeting with our Hollywood lawyers, and at 3:30 PM with an executive at Turner Network Television. At 4:30 PM, we are meeting with Robin Palmer (great last name!) at LifeTime, which is a cable network devoted to women's issues. We are trying to interest LifeTime in a film on women conservationists. At 5:30 PM, we are meeting with a Hollywood agent called Garrett Chau (with UTA) who may represent us.

At 7:00 PM, we are meeting with a donor — a wonderful lady called Bernice Park. Then at 8:00 PM, we are having dinner with another writer to discuss a movie we are developing called *Elephant Soldier*. After all those meetings, I will race to the airport to get back on the 10:00 PM "Red Eye," so I will be at home before you wake up on Tuesday morning!

One thing I do when I travel is to use every minute of my time productively. If you want a life (which I don't claim mine is) characterized by terrific vitality, extraordinary relationships, serene ambition, inspired leadership, massive achievements, unstoppable courage, and exuberant joy, then I think one way to help achieve those goals is not to waste "in-between time" when you have a few extra, unstructured minutes at your disposal "between things" that you are doing. Whether you are between classes, appointments, activities, flights, or whatever, incorporating any of the following will turn your spare moments into quality moments and help give you a deeper satisfaction in your life.

1. Unclutter your surroundings: Clean out (or begin to clean out) a drawer, desktop or closet. The act of uncluttering will make you feel lighter and give you a sense of greater control because you decide what you need to keep around you.

2. Pick up a book or magazine that you have stored on your "to read" pile, and incorporate something from it into your knowledge base.

3. Visualize how you want to be perceived at your next meeting or at an upcoming event.

4. Find something good and very specific that someone has done and tell them: Remember that an unexpressed compliment isn't worth squat.

5. Repeat the affirmation, "I am going to be happy no matter what."

6. Stretch, and breath in and out slowly, with a relaxed smile on your face: This will refresh and energize you.

7. Tell someone you love how much you love them.

8. Enhance your vocabulary: Pull out a dictionary or thesaurus. Commit a few words to memory and aim to use them that very day. Your vocabulary is one of your greatest assets.

9. Drink or eat something to support good health and a strong body: Eat a piece of fresh fruit or crunchy vegetable, or drink a glass of water, and listen to your body thank you!

10. Strengthen your personal connections: Call a friend or family member to say hello. Let someone know that they are important to you. Explain that you only have a short time to talk.

11. Practice smiling: Exercise the muscles in your face which enable you to smile. Give them a workout.

12. Engage in a personal brainstorming session: Think about a problem you have or a presentation you have to give. Get out a blank sheet of paper and fill the page with all kinds of ideas (many of which will be deliciously crazy and outrageous). Get your brain cells moving and your creativity active. Stretch your mental muscles and conjure up new ideas of how to do things in a different way. You will be amazed at the new possibilities you can generate.

13. Memorize a maxim and use it as an affirmation: Repeat it and relish it.

14. Think about all the things for which you are grateful: Appreciate all the good things in your life. Allow yourself to feel lucky. Feel the abundance of all the good things that have come your way. One of the biggest mistakes I make is to forget how incredibly grateful I am for all the wonderful things that I have in my life (which include Mommy and you three).

15. Think about your posture and hold yourself with grace, elegance and strength.

16. <u>Add some more items to your joy list</u>: Think of things that make you feel euphoric and fulfilled.

17. <u>Go back to fundamentals and remind yourself of the most important principles in your life</u>: They are simple and very powerful.

18. <u>Read your Personal Mission Statement and your New Year's Resolutions, and feel inspired by them</u>.

My treasures, you are so special to Mommy and me and we feel so lucky to have you. I adore you with all my heart. Lots of love,

Daddy
XXXOOO

Monday, March 8, 1999

My Treasures, Kimmie, Tina, Jenny and Conker:

I am flying back on the "Red Eye" tonight from LAX. I will board the plane at about 1:00 AM (ET) when you are fast asleep, and land at about 6:00 AM tomorrow morning. So I will see you for breakfast!

If someone were to ask me what, in my opinion, are some of the secrets to being an effective parent (and here I humbly acknowledge that I don't always measure up to being an effective parent!), here are some of the things I would say:

1. <u>Marry the right person to begin with</u>! I am not sure Mommy did that, but I certainly did. There is nothing more important than total trust and shared values between parents.

2. <u>Hold weekly family meetings with an agenda</u>: The agenda would include "rocks" (the most important things family members have to do in the following week) and "encouragement" (each family member encourages the other members of the family).

3. <u>Produce a Family Mission Statement</u>: Everybody should contribute to it and feel an "ownership" of it.

4. <u>Develop the habit of catching other family members "doing something right"</u>: The dominant family mood should be one of finding things to praise rather than to criticize.

5. <u>Listen to each other</u>, and prove it by articulating back to other family members what their positions are on controversial issues.

6. <u>Have family dinners every evening to which everybody looks forward</u>.

7. <u>Be respectful of each other</u>.

8. <u>Find ways to have lots of smiles and laughter when you are together</u>.

9. <u>Be at home with the kids</u>: Don't be out playing golf, entertaining, or doing other things which might lead you to inadvertently neglect your children.

10. <u>Set a good example in your own life in terms of behavior</u>.

11. <u>Have lots of family traditions and invent new ones</u>. (We invented a new one recently with "Christmas predictions.")

12. <u>Keep a journal so that family members can observe their family life in all its richness</u>.

13. <u>Apologize quickly when you make a mistake</u>.

14. <u>Set firm limits, but don't be inflexible</u>.

15. <u>Have no favorites among the children</u>.

16. <u>Have high expectations of yourself and of your children in terms of accomplishments</u>.

Oh boy! Just looking at that list makes me see how much work I have to do to become a more effective parent! Please don't think I claim I do all these things. On some of them, I am just a beginner. And this list is not (obviously!) comprehensive. I know there are lots of other excellent ideas about effective parenting of which I am ignorant.

Kimmie, Tina and Jenny, I love you and I miss you. Kim, I am delighted you are coming home on March 25, and we cannot wait to see you. Tina and Jenny, I will see you in the morning when I arrive home from Los Angeles on the "Red Eye." I will have four bags — one in each hand and two under my eyes!

Buckets of love,

> Yer 'ole Dad
> XXXOOO

Tuesday, March 16, 1999
My Darling Kimmie, Tina and Jenny:
As you know, I am in Houston for the NWF Board meeting and annual meeting. I will be here for five days and will return on Sunday. It will be a fun week with lots of meetings and events to attend. I like the NWF Board members very much, so am looking forward to spending time with them.

On Wednesday, I will give a presentation to the Board; on Thursday, a brief presentation to the Endowment; on Friday at 9:00 AM, I will conduct an hour and a half workshop entitled *Lights, Camera, Wildlife!* (which last year was very popular — the room was packed); and, on Friday evening, I will give a brief speech to the NWF Board and to donors when we show *Wolves* at the IMAX theater at the Houston Museum of Natural Science.

As I say, the whole week will be packed with exciting meetings with Board members and colleagues. I will miss you and will be thinking about you, even though I will be happy and busy.

Kimmie, I hope you have a wonderful time this week with Nathaniel in New Mexico. Tina, good luck on Saturday with your SAT exam! Jenny, enjoy your first lacrosse practice, and I hope you have fun at the St. Patrick's Day Dance on Friday night.

Kim, I will see you when I meet you at the airport on the evening of Thursday, March 25. Tina,

I will see you when you return from your college tour with Mommy late on Wednesday, March 24. Jenny, I will see you when I return from Houston on Sunday afternoon, March 21!

Here is a lovely essay by the late humorist Erma Bombeck entitled *If I Had My Life To Live Over*. There is a lot of wisdom in it:

> If I had my life to live over I would have talked less and listened more.
> I would have invited friends over to dinner even if the carpet was stained and the sofa faded.
> I would have eaten the popcorn in the 'good' living room and worried much less about the dirt when someone wanted to light a fire in the fireplace.
> I would have taken the time to listen to my grandfather ramble about his youth.
> I would never have insisted the car windows be rolled up on a summer day because my hair had just been teased and sprayed.
> I would have burned the pink candle sculpted like a rose before it melted in storage.
> I would have sat on the lawn with my children and not worried about grass stains.
> I would have cried and laughed less while watching television and more while watching life.
> I would have shared more of the responsibility carried by my husband.
> I would have gone to bed when I was sick instead of pretending the earth would go into a holding pattern if I weren't there for the day.
> I would never have bought anything just because it was practical, wouldn't show soil or was guaranteed to last a lifetime.
> Instead of wishing away nine months of pregnancy, I'd have cherished every moment and realized that the wonderment growing inside me was the only chance in life to assist God in a miracle.
> When my kids kissed me impetuously, I would never have said, "Later. Now go get washed up for dinner."
> There would have been more "I love yous"... more "I'm sorrys"... but mostly, given another shot at life, I would seize every minute... look at it and really see it... live it... and never give it back.
>
> Don't forget to stop and smell the roses today!
> Take time to tell a loved one how much you love them, do something nice for yourself, and stop to give God thanks for all of it.

Treasures, Mommy and I love you each so much. You are more important to us than anything in the whole world, and we adore you.

Daddy
XXXOOO

Wednesday, March 17, 1999
My Darling Kimmie, Tina, Jenny and Conker:

Happy St. Patrick's Day!

Jenny, I can't wait to hear how the lacrosse practice went. I am so pleased you are playing.

Tina, well done for watching *Schindler's List* last Sunday. Here are the first few paragraphs of an essay by Stephen Covey called *The Freedom To Choose*. It concerns the late Victor Frankl's story in a Nazi concentration camp:

> Victor Frankl's riveting personal story as a Jew in a Nazi concentration camp and his face-to-face encounters with deprivation, torture and cruelty is one of the most forceful examples of what it means to be proactive and to consciously choose our response to situations.
>
> We will probably never find ourselves in such savage conditions, yet many of us still run our lives as though we were helpless to rise above the defeating and discouraging things that others say or do to us. We might seek revenge, lash out emotionally, or harbor resentments for years that destroy our peace and equilibrium. That's what psychologists call the stimulus/response theory — that we are conditioned to respond to events based on genetic coding, environmental factors or our parental upbringing. We're pushed, so we push back. Someone threatens us, and we return the threat.
>
> There is a better way. It's called proactivity, and as Frankl discovered, it's one of the most liberating concepts available to us. Being proactive means that between the stimulus and response is our freedom to choose. Frankl was able to mentally transport himself away from the death camps — not to escape their reality or horror — but to blunt their impact so that he wouldn't suffer twice — once, from the atrocities themselves and second, from the justifiable anger and hatred that his Nazi guards hoped to inflict. This remarkable transformation enables us to have enormous control in shaping our lives and to transcend the convenience of being defensive or reactive. When we choose proactivity we declare that no one can hurt us without our consent. Frankl's guards had more liberty, but Frankl had more freedom, and he became a beacon of inspiration to others in that hellish prison.

One of the keys to being proactive is to identify what lies within your circle of influence in contrast to your circle of concern. All of us have concerns. Some impact us more directly and personally than others. Those that lie within our circle of influence should be preeminent in our lives — such things as what time we choose to rise in the morning, our eating and exercise habits, the time we spend with our loved ones, and the efforts we make to improve our skills and talents. There are many other concerns, such as the threat of war, potential unemployment, the spread of infectious diseases, droughts, floods and other natural disasters. These are things over which we have little control. If we spend time worrying and fretting about those issues, we unwittingly empower those things that control us and, in turn, our feelings of inadequacy and helplessness will grow. Proactive people concentrate on their circle of influence — on the things they can do something about. At the heart of this process is making and keeping promises. As we make and keep promises (i.e., as we practice integrity), our influence and power grows even wider.

My darling treasures, Mommy and I love you so much. All my love,

Daddy
XXXOOO

Thursday, March 18, 1999
Darling Kimmie, Tina and Jenny:
Jenny, have a great St. Patrick's Day Dance at Westland tomorrow night!

I still remember Pop-Pop, Mommy's father, as though he were alive today. One of the things I remember about Ralph is that he introduced me to a little publication called *Bits And Pieces* (subtitled *The Magazine That Motivates The World*). He knew how interested I was in quotations, maxims, aphorisms, and wisdom. I continued to subscribe to *Bits And Pieces* after Ralph died. Here are some examples from the latest issue:

- Two shoe salesmen were sent overseas to scout for new markets. Their first stop was a country where everyone was barefoot. The first salesman sent back a telegram to the home office saying, "Leaving tomorrow. No one wears shoes." The second salesman's telegram was very different. He said, "Great potential market. No competition." (Lair Ribeiro, *Success Is No Accident*, St. Martin's Press)

- Compared with what we ought to be, we are only half awake. We are making use of only a small part of our physical and mental resources. Stating the thing broadly, the human individual thus lives far within his limits. He possesses powers of various sorts, which he habitually fails to use. (William James (1842-1910), Psychologist)

- Wise people learn when they can. Fools learn when they must. (Arthur Wellesley Wellington (1769-1852), British general and statesman)

- Many people aim at nothing — and hit it with remarkable precision.

- If we had no winter, the spring would not be so pleasant; if we did not sometimes taste of adversity, prosperity would not be so welcome. (Anne Bradstreet (1612-1672), Poet)

- The greatest power we have is the power of choice. It's an actual fact that if you've been moping in unhappiness, you can choose to be joyous instead and, by effort, lift yourself into joy. If you tend to be fearful, you can overcome that misery by choosing to have courage. Even in darkest grief you have a choice. The whole trend and quality of anyone's life is determined in the long run by the choices that are made. (Norman Vincent Peale (1898-1993), Clergyman)

- The best thing to spend on your children is your time. (Louise Hart)

- Those who make the worst use of their time are the first to complain of its brevity. (Jean De La Bruyere (1645-1696), Writer and moralist)

- Too many of us are hung up on what we don't have, can't have, or won't ever have. We spend too much energy being down, when we could use that same energy — if not less of it — doing, or at least trying to do, some of the things we really want to do. (Terry McMillan, Writer)

- Every time you wake up and ask yourself, "What good things am I going to do today?", remember that when the sun goes down at sunset, it will take a part of your life with it. (Indian Proverb)

- The better I get, the more I realize how much better I can get. (Martina Navratilova, pro tennis player)

- One neglects to see an important factor in love, that of will. To love somebody is not just a strong feeling — it is a decision, it is a judgment, it is a promise. If love were only a feeling, there would be no basis for the promise to love each other forever. A feeling comes and it may go. How can I judge that it will stay forever, if my actions do not involve judgment and decision? (Erich Fromm (1900-1980), Psychoanalyst)

- Thoroughly to teach another is the best way to learn for yourself. (Tyrone Edwards, Editor and theologian)

- There's more to life than crossing things off your To-Do list.

- When you are inspired by some great purpose, some extraordinary project, all your thoughts break their bounds: Your mind transcends limitations, your consciousness expands in every direction, and you find yourself in a new, great, and wonderful world. Dormant forces, faculties, and talents become alive, and you discover yourself to be a greater person by far than you ever dreamed yourself to be. (Patanjali (Second century B.C.), Philosopher)

I liked Ralph very much. I thought he was a great father-in-law because he always showed great respect for me, which I appreciated.

My treasures, I love you.

> Daddy
> XXXOOO

Friday, March 19, 1999

My Darling Kimmie, Tina and Jenny:

Tina, good luck tomorrow with your SAT exam. I will be thinking of you. I know you will do well.

Here are a few stories I can remember from when I was growing up:

- One day, when I was about 6 years old, my father got a mischievous grin on his face and pulled me aside. He put me in some nice clothes, and told me to go up to my mother (your Granny) and say to her, "Look at me, don't I look posh?!" Posh is an old English word meaning well dressed or fancy looking. A 6 year old would never use it. I was shy and I also stuttered at the time, and so did not do a very good job of delivering my line. I'm not sure Granny appreciated the humor. In fact, I seem to remember having a hard time even getting her attention.

- When Jon and I were 3 or 4 years old, we went to a little school for preschoolers called Oldfield Lodge. This school was across the street from our house on Bloomfield Avenue. From the upper windows of our house, you could see everything going on in the playground. (Sadly, the school has been torn down and houses built in its place.) There was a magnificent tree on the playground with huge gnarled limbs. These huge branches were horizontal as I recall, and little kids could easily climb on them with safety. What fascinated me about this tree was that there were caterpillars on the leaves, and the teachers used to teach us about these creatures and about nature. I sometimes wonder if my interest in wildlife and the natural world doesn't partly come from the pleasure I got as a little boy up in the branches of that big, old tree.

- When I was about 7 years old, Jon and I went to a little school in Dulwich called Dulwich Hamlet. Grandpa was Professor of Naval Architecture at the Royal Naval College Greenwich. Occasionally, Daddy used to come to Dulwich Hamlet to pick us up after school in order to take us home. If he didn't come to pick us up, Jon and I would take an hour or more to wander home, and my parents would sometimes worry about us. We lived about a mile from the school and had to cross a big park to get home called Dulwich Park. (This park was famous for its magnificent rhododendrons, but what I remember most starkly were the incredibly filthy lavatories which were never cleaned and which were unbelievably disgusting.) Anyway, one day Daddy came to pick us up and I didn't know he was coming. I looked across the playground to see my teacher, Mr. Murphy, whom I hero-worshiped. To my astonishment and delight, Mr. Murphy waved to me and I waved back not believing my good fortune that he would acknowledge me in that way. My heart swelled with pride and importance. A few seconds later, I was mortified because I turned around to see that he was actually waving at my father who had entered the playground behind me.

- When I was about 8 years old, I remember Mr. Murphy asked me to run an errand. I was delighted to be of service to him, and I did the job as efficiently and fast as I could. I returned, out of breath from running, with a message to give him. At the time I stuttered, and I remember coming up to him, getting ready to give him the message, breathing hard, and realizing that I couldn't give him the message because I was afraid I would stutter and be unable to do it. I stood there looking at him and breathing hard, trying to get up the courage to give him the message. I was filled with apprehension that I would just stutter and get stuck, so I deliberately kept breathing hard to give me time to recover my confidence. I think he understood what was going on because he waited very patiently until I got my act together.

- I remember one of the first times I ever made people laugh. I was probably about 6 years old. The question came up in a discussion between my mother and Tim about how many people there were in the country who had been awarded knighthoods. I deliberately sat down, put my chin in my hand, and said, "Well, let's count them — first, there is Winston Churchill...." I let my voice trail off, realizing that the adults in the room would find this funny — a little boy trying to count the knights in the country and seemingly not realizing there were thousands of them. I've been using self-effacing humor ever since.

My treasures, I wonder what stories you'll remember from your childhoods? Mommy and I adore you. All my love,

Daddy
XXXOOO

Saturday, March 20, 1999

My Darling Kimmie, Tina and Jenny:

I will be home tomorrow! Of course, when I arrive home, Gail and Tina will have left for their college trip to visit Dartmouth, Williams and Cornell. Kimmie will be back at Amherst from her trip with Nathaniel to New Mexico, and Jenny will be with Sarah. Jenny, I should get home around 3:00 or 4:00 in the afternoon, and will come over to get you. Maybe we will walk to Chicken Out to get some delicious mashed potatoes! Yummy.

Frequently in my life I have not communicated well with people. Because I have not done well at communicating and it is not a skill I was ever formally taught, I have studied the topic in order to become more skillful and competent in my relations with other people.

Here are some guidelines that have helped me — and I hope will help you. They promote deeper, more intimate relationships with other people and encourage authentic communications:

1. Use I/my statements: In other words, "own," or be responsible for what you are saying. Authentic communications is ME telling YOU about ME.

2. To communicate effectively, speak personally and specifically, rather than generally and abstractly.

3. Do not mind read: A "you" statement is a way of analyzing or second guessing, and this can cause misunderstandings or defensiveness. Allow others to be responsible for themselves. Use "I" messages.

4. Listen to your inner voice: Become aware of when you are moved to speak and when you are not moved to speak.

5. Listen carefully and with respect to what another person is telling you: Don't formulate your response while someone is speaking, but wait until the other person has completely finished. Start by articulating back to them what they have just said, and describe their position and feelings even more effectively than they can themselves.

6. Be comfortable with silence in communication: Meditating on what was just said, and checking your motivations for what you are about to say may take a few moments. This is a kind of honoring of both the speaker and yourself.

7. Respect differences: (This one is very hard for me.) People can have other ideas, thoughts and

feelings. Don't try to convert them to your way. Celebrate the diversity. Respect other people's choice of religion, politics and opinions. It is okay to disagree with people, but that is different from assessing their opinions as being wrong or bad. Try not to assume your opinion or belief is superior or better or the only "right" stance. (As you know, I am a complete beginner — or even worse — in this domain.)

8. <u>Be aware of your own barriers</u>: Obstacles to authentic communication include prejudices, expectations, ideologies, judgments, or a need to control.

9. <u>Listen with your eyes</u>: Look and listen for the "heart" of a person behind his or her words. Concentrate on finding the strengths and gifts.

10. <u>Take yourself lightly</u>: Be able to laugh at yourself and with others.

My treasures, listening is a skill we are never taught. So we have to teach it to ourselves. I am just beginning to educate myself in this domain. One thing I have come to realize is that listening is incredibly hard work — far harder than talking. To really listen to somebody is like doing 200 press-ups without stopping. If you really listen to someone — listen with a deep and sincere empathy for the underlying concerns behind the words, concerns that the person to whom you are listening might only dimly perceive themselves — then it is exhausting and hard work, requiring endurance, tenacity, strength, and patience. I don't think I have ever really listened to anyone in my whole life.

Kimmie, Tina and Jenny, Mommy and I think you are so special. You bring incredible joy into our lives, and we are so grateful for your love and affection. We want you to have (and we think you do have) the most special, glorious, and fulfilled lives.

Buckets of love,

Yer 'ole Dad
XXXOOO

Monday, May 3, 1999
My darling Kimmie, Tina, and Jenny,
I am in Toronto for two days to open *Wolves* at the Ontario Science Center. I have prepared my speeches carefully and am looking forward to all the press and VIP screenings with great anticipation.

As you know, there has been a lot in the press about the massacre in Columbine High School. Of course, the issues are complex and there are multiple causes. However, there are things you can do as individuals to help alleviate these social problems. Here are just a few of them:

- Don't watch (and therefore support) violent movies like *The Matrix* which celebrate and glamorize vicious, criminal behavior and which portray suffering as entertainment.

- Support (i.e., watch) films and TV programs that tell engrossing stories which inspire you, and which reflect integrity, courage, tenacity, joy, humor and deep insight.

- Surround yourself with friends who share your values and who you respect and admire.

- Speak up courageously and assertively when friends invite you to do things which you feel intuitively are not healthy. Don't go with the crowd.

- Set an example in your own life of someone who always tells the truth, defends the weak, is loyal to the absent, works hard, and who has an uplifting, ennobling vision for how they want to design and live their life.

- Do whatever you can to oppose those who exploit the worst aspects of people's character in order to make money. For example, don't buy the products of those companies who advertise in TV programs that portray teenage girls as obsessed with clothes, sex, appearance, boys, and as having no interest in academic excellence, athleticism, art, poetry, the environment, women's rights, poverty, the Serbs, and so on.

- Make teachers and school counselors aware of any cruelty or other problems that you witness or know about in school (e.g., bullying).

- Be kind and compassionate to everybody, especially those who are shy, reserved, unpopular, or handicapped in some way.

- Befriend the friendless. I know that you would never participate in any taunting or teasing of another child, but go further and defend those who are bullied.

- **Never** allow yourself to be bullied or harassed. Say 'no' to a bully's demands from the start.

- Stand, walk and hold yourself in a way that commands respect. Never show fear even if you feel fearful.

- Toughen yourself with a rigorous regimen of exercises (including strength, endurance and flexibility exercises) so that you are physically ready at any time for whatever challenges might confront you.

- Look for opportunities to practice the skills of integrity, courage, creativity, tenacity, patience, hard work, reliability and trustworthiness. Yes, they are *skills* you can learn and gain competence in.

Kimmie, Tina, Jenny, those are a few thoughts that occur to me as I reflect on the awful tragedy in Colorado. You will have many thoughts and better thoughts of your own.

I love you. You are so precious to Mommy and me. We are so grateful to have such affectionate, ambitious, socially competent, street-savvy, loving, happy and accomplished daughters!

Yer 'ole Dad
XXXOOO

Tuesday, May 4, 1999
My precious loves, Kimmie, Tina and Jenny,
Work and play. Two important words. What are they? What do they mean? Tina, you sometimes tell me that I work too hard and that you don't want to make that same mistake.

Here is what I think. I don't do any "work." All my "work" is play to me. I enjoy it. I love it. I would do it if I were paid nothing. The reason is that all my activities help to protect wildlife and the environment, and that is deeply satisfying to me.

When I think of the word "work," I think of people doing things which do not excite or inspire them and about which they feel no passion or purpose.

We all grow up with the notion that "work" is something we "have" to do. We think that if we can avoid it, then we will be less stressed.

But here is what I think: We have limited time on earth. It is a privilege to be here. We are extraordinarily lucky. Let's not waste it by watching trivial programs on TV or indulging in other distractions. Instead, I believe each of us should develop a vision for our lives — a vision which is ambitious, serene and balanced — and pursue it with focused intensity. I have tried to develop such a vision for my own life in my January 1999 New Year's Resolutions.

 Don't let the words "focused intensity" fool you into thinking that your brow has to be constantly furrowed. Part of your vision will have to do with joy, laughter and having fun with people you love.

One way to begin to understand all this is to gain a new understanding of the words "stress" and "relaxation." Hard work and making progress towards your goals *relieves* stress, while "relaxing" in front of a TV or distracting yourself in other ways (by drinking, doing drugs, playing bingo, smoking, reading inconsequential magazines, or whatever) ultimately increases your stress level. The word "stress" should be associated with the word "fear" rather than the word "work."

Your goal should not be to avoid "work" and "relax." *Your goal should be to achieve extraordinary results and unparalleled personal fulfillment.*

And don't be enslaved by a "to-do" list. Focus on your *vision*, your *goals*, and the *results* you want, rather than tasks. That way you can simplify your life, throw out the things that aren't important, deeply enjoy yourself, and move towards living the kind of life you feel really good about, without feeling unduly stressed.

Kim, Tina and Jenny, I adore you as only a father can. You are more important to me than I can say. I love you.

Daddy
XXXOOO

Wednesday, May 19, 1999
My darling Kimmie, Tina, and Jenny,
Today is Tina's 17th birthday! Happy birthday Tina! You are a unique, distinctive and very special person, just like your two sisters, and I love you. I am so sorry to leave you on your birthday to go on a business trip to LA. As you know, I am at an IMAX conference where I will be giving brief speeches (to introduce *Wolves*), moderating a panel, having meetings with producers and theater operators, and so on. But I will be thinking of you on your birthday Tina, and I will, of course, be calling you. I hope your AP Bio exam went well this morning.

By the way, we have a documentary on TBS Superstation tonight at 10.05 PM called *Wild City* starring Isabella Rossellini. It is about the importance of maintaining parks and other wild areas in cities, and about the surprising wildlife you find in urban areas. It has taken us about 18 months to make.

Tina, I have a special birthday gift for you — one that I know you will appreciate! If I was you Tina (and I'm not so you can ignore the rest of this!), here is how I would be going about preparing for and planning my internship at NIH. I am not claiming this is the only way, or even the best way. I <u>am</u> claiming that it is better than the typical way people prepare for something like this, which is to say, with little planning except for a "to-do" list. I recommend you not "drift" into the NIH experience and react to whatever shows up on June 21 and the subsequent days. You want to be proactive, not reactive.

Here is the way I would begin to think about how I might proactively design the seven weeks at NIH:

First, capture ideas, commitments, promises, thoughts, anything which could be useful. In other words, brainstorm and collect zillions of ideas, many of which will be crazy -- but later, out of a few of those way-out ideas, might come a winner. This is the first step in any project, whether the project is an internship, a new job, writing an article, renovating a home, or designing your life. Capture any thoughts in any way related to the issue at hand. In this case Tina, your capture list might be several pages long and include references to keeping in touch with friends, clothes to buy and wear, coaching Jen at tennis, earning extra cash, preparing mentally for the first day on June 21, transportation, stress-busters like exercise, reading up on medical issues, staying in touch with Granny and Grandpa, seeing Mauro, doing fun things with Kim and Jen, preparing for 12th grade at Holton, keeping a journal, searching for a college, and a zillion other things I can't even begin to imagine.

Second, articulate in writing the ultimate outcome you want from this seven week experience so you have a vision to aim for. As the book of Proverbs profoundly observes, "Where there is no vision, the people perish." Many people never do this but it is a good idea whether you are preparing to give a speech, get married, start a new job, run for political office, attend a dinner party, or write an editorial.

Visualizing the outcome you want and envisioning the great feelings that come from success will help you drive towards your goal. So in this case Tina, you might say your ultimate outcome is perhaps something along the following lines:

- I am going to have a life-changing, awesome experience this summer at NIH and deeply enjoy learning while making new contacts in the professional world which can help me later on in my career.

- I will learn all I can and be inspired by the privilege of working at one of the leading medical research organizations in the world.

- I will create new standards by which interns are normally judged by doing an outstanding job, working hard and participating actively.

- I will enjoy myself, and help those around me enjoy themselves, and I will be a source of cheerfulness and vitality.

- I will be constantly on the look out for ideas that can feed into the essay I have to write next year to get into college.

It is important that you write out your vision using words that thrill and inspire you. You want to feel juiced and excited.

Third, describe your purpose. Why are you doing this internship? Your answer might include: give my career a leap forward, to help me get into the college of my choice, to see if I would enjoy a career in the medical field, to develop as a person, to practice being assertive and self-confident in an intimidating situation, to wake up every morning feeling excited and juiced, to deeply enjoy myself, to give me interesting things to talk about with other people such as my teachers at Holton-Arms, to be perceived by my supervisor at NIH as enthusiastic, hard-working, focused, smart, curious, responsive, responsible, cheerful, assertive, and bold.

The reason this second and third step is so important in planning (and you can combine the second and third step if you want to simplify the process), is that activity (as represented by typical "to-do" lists) without purpose (i.e., without connecting it back to your vision and ultimate outcomes) is enervating and drains you of fulfilment.

Fourth, list the specific actions you want to take and develop an action plan. Commit to carrying out certain actions, schedule them, do them, and celebrate (I am a real beginner at celebrating my accomplishments).

What you will often find is that if you compare the original "to-do" list (i.e., the one you had prior to doing this planning) with the action plan you now have, some of those original to-dos can be dispensed with because they really aren't that useful and don't contribute that much value. Remember that 80% of results come from 20% of the activities.

Those who succeed (i.e., those who feel totally fulfilled because they have an appealing balance in their lives between playfulness and driving towards some worthwhile goal) always start, as Stephen Covey says, with the end in mind. They are totally clear about the final result they are after. Clarity and focus give you power.

So, now you know my loves why Mommy has a T-shirt which reads, "MY NEXT HUSBAND WILL BE NORMAL!" (I gave it to her as a gift!)

Happy birthday Tina!! I love you Tina, I love you Kim, I love you Jenny.

Daddy
XXXOOO

Thursday, May 20, 1999
My Treasures Kimmie, Tina and Jenny,
Brainstorming and capturing all sorts of ideas is one of the most critically important elements in effective planning and accomplishing what you most want in life. It applies to any project, including bringing up kids, throwing a party, designing a house, painting a picture, giving a presentation, having a conversation, writing a poem, or redesigning your life.

Here is an example from my own life. Mommy and I have recently begun to think about what we want to do and accomplish when we 'retire' — that is, when we stop working at our current jobs at NWF and Consumers Union. This won't happen for a long time yet but it is never too early to start preparing for a major life-change. Here are a few ideas that occurred to me over a matter of five minutes as part of the "brainstorming and capture" component of planning for this new life. These ideas are not organized, prioritized, assessed or judged in any way. Nor am I committed to any of these ideas yet. I will likely reject most of them. I don't claim the list is comprehensive or even particularly good. I am just doing a "brain dump" to help me create new possibilities and to help me think creatively and boldly. By the time I have finished this brainstorming exercise, the list will undoubtedly be five or ten times as long, or even longer.

So here are fifty ideas I tossed out to myself:

1. Revise totally my Personal Mission Statement.
2. Find ways of helping others.
3. Be superbly fit and strong for my age, including endurance, strength and flexibility.
4. Raise money for a cause I care deeply about.
5. Do something about tawdry and family-damaging TV programs.
6. Do another degree, perhaps in psychology or psychotherapy.
7. Volunteer at a hospice.
8. Continue to collect and organize my maxims.
9. Continue to collect and organize my jokes.
10. Join a book club and attend regular meetings.
11. Look into becoming a "voice talent".
12. Prepare for old age.
13. Continue writing a daily journal.
14. Read extensively.
15. Support Gail, Kimmie, Tina, and Jenny in all that they do.
16. Start a fourth or fifth career.
17. Write book reviews for publication.
18. Be mentally, physically and emotionally vigorous and strong.
19. Be in a mood of continuous and never-ending learning.
20. Join a singing group and perform in hospitals and nursing homes.
21. Travel with Gail all over the world.
22. Grow delicious vegetables in the garden.
23. Wake up every day excited, juiced and raring to go.
24. Create and design a set of goals and a new vision for this phase of my life.
25. Learn to manage our financial affairs in case something happens to Gail.
26. Become active in the Ethical Society.
27. Look for mentors, especially people who have "retired" successfully like Jimmy Carter.
28. Write my autobiography, focusing on stories.
29. Give speeches which are funny but have a purpose.
30. Use my laptop to leverage all my projects.
31. Study death and learn about it, and prepare my own funeral.
32. Lead groups on travel expeditions.
33. Entertain and enjoy our friends.
34. Build a network of friends in each domain of my life.

35. Be active in our neighborhood and local community.
36. Run for local office.
37. Offer a workshop on goal-setting, life-planning, and effectiveness.
38. Write a book.
39. Focus on one "work" project, such as an IMAX film.
40. Continue my relentless search for wisdom.
41. Be an inspiring example to others.
42. Deal with health problems with patience and serenity.
43. Help others get what they need.
44. Learn how to listen to other people.
45. Look for and record "magic" moments.
46. Focus on making changes to me rather that to others.
47. Simplify and "de-junk" my life, and focus on what is important even if it is not urgent.
48. Learn the importance of playfulness.
49. Delight in the beauty of birds and nature.
50. Above all, take care of and adore Gail, and show it.

My loves, this process of creating and capturing ideas through brainstorming and "mind-dumping" can be aided though lateral thinking techniques developed by Edward de Bono and others. Talking to friends and colleagues, and reading books, are also good ways to develop new ideas and new perspectives.

I fly back from LA late tomorrow night. I am leaving the IMAX conference early so I can be home for Jenny's birthday on Saturday. I may have to catch the "red eye" but I am hoping to catch an earlier plane. I love you!!

Daddy
XXXOOO

Friday, June 11, 1999
My darling Kimmie and Jenny,
Tina is not in the salutation because she is with me in the US Virgin Islands! However, I am going to write this letter as though I am writing to all three of you.

When Tina and I return next Tuesday, we will tell you all about our trip. We will snorkel from golden beaches, and we will watch leatherback sea turtles, weighing as much as 1300 pounds, struggle up the beach in the middle of the night to lay their eggs.

These letters I leave you when I travel give me an opportunity to talk to you about things which are important to me. Do you remember I wrote in one of my recent letters to you about the importance of capturing ideas and brainstorming? That phase of planning is so important, whether you are writing an editorial, designing your life, planning to climb Everest, getting married, working at NIH, or making an IMAX film.

There is another part of planning which is equally important, and that is developing a <u>vision</u> of the outcomes you want. You could call this "dreaming" but I don't like the lack of rigor that the word "dream" implies.

"If you can dream it, you can achieve it." (Did I just make that up, or did I steal it from Jesse Jackson?!) People rarely have a sudden vision. Instead, they reflect deeply on what matters most to them and what they profoundly care about.

People often lack vision for their lives. If fact, this is a continuing challenge I have had in my own life. My lack of imagination has been a huge drag on my success. I still wrestle with these three questions:

- What do I really want to create out of my life and what is the legacy I want to leave behind?

- What do I care deeply and passionately about and am willing to work really hard to achieve?

- How can I find enduring meaning and fulfillment in a world that bombards me daily with trivial and distracting information?

My treasures, I challenge you not to let these three questions go unanswered in your own lives.

Having a vision and a set of measurable goals is one of the most essential steps to gaining personal mastery — a condition where you are autonomous and proactive, and essentially immune to the insults life throws at you from your parents (if they are incompetent or unloving), your boss, your environment, the weather, or whatever people like to blame for their bad luck.

Having a vision and mission for your life gives you a deep inner peace because you are focused on where you can make a contribution to other people and to society, and you are less likely to be pulled in a hundred different directions by other people's agendas. It makes it easier to decline requests, and to make offers in which others see new possibilities for themselves.

My loves, I love you. You are each so incredibly special and accomplished. Mommy and I are so lucky to have three such wonderful and loving daughters.

Daddy
XXXOOO

Saturday, June 12, 1999
My loves Kimmie and Jenny (and Tina with me!),
It is Granny's birthday today! My mother was born in 1918 at the end of The Great War (or as it came to be known, World War I). So Granny is 81 today. She told me a few days ago that, when she was younger, she didn't expect to live this long.

I sometimes wonder what I will say at my Mother's funeral when I give a eulogy (assuming Grandpa wants me to). And then I wonder why I would wait until she dies to say those things.

Jen, have a great game of softball tomorrow at noon. I'll be thinking about you and rooting for you!

I love you! I am thinking about you!

Yer ol' Dad
XXXOOO

Sunday, June 13, 1999

My darling Kimmie and Jenny (and Tina with me in the Virgin Islands!),

While you are reading this letter, I am giving a speech to an environmental organization in the Virgin Islands. One of the most important questions I put to myself when preparing a speech is: *What are the concerns of the audience?* That is, what are their <u>real</u> concerns, their <u>deepest</u> concerns. This is not always easy to know so I often call people before giving a speech (people who know the audience well) to find out. This pre-speech research is very important.

Another thing I do when preparing a speech is to try to answer the question each audience member will be posing to themselves: *What's in it for me?* The audience needs to perceive that there is something in the presentation which will talk directly to their concerns and needs. A speaker, to be effective, must make a promise early in the speech (e.g., "I'm going to show you how to make dazzling speeches") and then keep that promise.

But the biggest secret of all to giving a dazzling speech is to be totally yourself, and let your passion for the subject shine through.

With practice, you will all become outstanding public speakers. It is a very important skill to have. I am constantly learning how to do it better.

I love you! Please give Conker a big kiss from me!

Daddy
XXXOOO

Monday, June 14, 1999

My four loves, Kimmie, Tina (still with me in the US Virgin Islands!), Jenny and Conker,

Tina and I will be home tomorrow. Jen — your last day in sixth grade is Wednesday!

You will be meeting new people over the summer, especially Tina and Kim. It is important to make a good first impression — sometimes that is the only chance you get to make an impression of any kind. Here are some basic things to remember, although I have observed all three of you do these things already. You each have excellent social skills. Anyway, here are eight tips you might find helpful:

1. Appear appropriately dressed and well groomed.

2. Maintain good eye contact.

3. Shake their hand at the beginning and when parting, and look them in the eye when shaking their hand.

4. <u>Smile</u>! Even if the other person doesn't. In other words, exude warmth.

5. Listen more than you talk. Be interested in the other person, even if you have to force yourself a little.

6. Relax and be yourself.

7. Ask them about their professional and personal life. People love to talk about themselves. This also shows you are not self-centered.

8. Part with a smile, a handshake and a sincere comment or compliment.

See you tomorrow my loves. It will be wonderful to have the family back in one piece again. I love you with all my heart. I am one lucky Dad!

Daddy
XXXOOO

Saturday, June 19, 1999
My darling Kimmie, Tina and Jenny,
I am in Yellowstone National Park! Our IMAX film, *Wolves*, is opening here and we are having a big event to celebrate the occasion. I have prepared my remarks carefully and am looking forward to it very much.

Tomorrow is Father's Day! It is a paradox that although I love being a father to you three wonderful daughters and strive to be loving and competent, I often say dumb things to you. For your amusement, I have collected together a few of my dumber pronouncements. As I wrote them down, some of them made me laugh out loud!

As you will see, several of these statements have earned a place on this list because, even though well-intentioned, they don't elicit the behavior I would like to see — yet they spill out of my mouth anyway. Saying ineffective things is not very smart — hence on the list they go.

You will surely be able to think of many other dumb things that I say. Please let me know which ones you think of — it will help me get smarter and learn what not to say, and what turns kids (and others) off.

So....in the hope that these favorite expressions of mine won't become *your* favorite expressions when (or if) you have kids of your own, I dedicate this list to you three precious girls with all my love:

- When I was growing up, we had chores to do every day.

- You girls should have chores to do in the house every day.

- What are your goals for today?

- We need to have a family meeting.

- Please review your New Year's Resolutions.

- I was so funny.

- Why did you only get 95% in the test?

- Enjoy church.

- Ask questions in church; challenge what you are told.

- I'll be ready in two minutes.

- I'm coming, hold on.

- I'm nearly ready.

- We've got plenty of time; the plane leaves in half an hour.

- You should leave the kitchen ready for the next person to use it.

- PG-13 used to be called X when I was growing up.

- Being organized isn't the same as being tidy.

- Teenagers today think they have some sort of entitlement to have whatever they want.

- Please clean up your room and get everything off the floor.

- Your room is such a mess.

- (When something is lost) You should always keep it in the same place.

- (When something is lost) Where do you normally keep it?

- What's your generation going to produce that's equivalent to my parent's generation fighting and winning World War II?

- If you surround yourself with garbage, you'll become garbage.

- You are what you eat.

- I work all day so I've already done my share of the chores.

- We should all clean up the kitchen together.

- I never get sick.

- Mommy and I would be wealthy if we didn't have children.

- You watch too much television.

- You need to work harder — and I mean really work creatively, not just letting your eyes glance over the page.

- You need balance in your life between all your various roles.

- My parents would never leave food on their plate.

- Spoiled Bethesda brats.....(mutter, mutter, mutter).

- I never had a phone in my room when I was your age.

- I don't care what your friends think.

- You act like Mommy and I are your servants.

- You already have too many CDS.

- We're not lost; I'm just not sure where we are.

- You've just *been* to the bathroom!

- I have just cleaned up the kitchen and now you are mucking it up again.

- This house is a sanctuary; please take your shoes off.

- That breakfast isn't healthy enough.

- Look what I am having for breakfast — All Bran, prunes, a pear, and 1% milk.

- Why do you want a dog? You've got me to play with.

- You've got to get to bed or you'll never get up in the morning.

- Manners maketh women.

- Keep asking why.

- Ask good questions in class today.

- Did you ask good questions in class today?

- You watch too much TV.

- When I took exams when I was your age, I worked right up to the start of the exam.

- How much did it cost?

- Voting is a sacred responsibility of every citizen.

- I couldn't vote today because I was working.

- Please keep adding to your joy list.

- Why did you spill the milk?

- When was the last time you swept the floor?

- The language you use should be more rigorous and disciplined.

Blah, blah, blah........You will probably be able to think of many more dumb and ineffective things that I say!

Talking in such a way that brings out the best in other people, and helps them see new possibilities for themselves, is an area of continuous learning for me.

Kim, Tina and Jenny, I love you! See you tomorrow night. Good luck in your 1:30 PM game tomorrow Jenny!

Yer 'ole Daddy
XXXOOO

Thursday, July 15, 1999

My darling Kimmie, Tina and Jenny,

As you know, I am in Alaska for ten days with some wonderful people (friends of NWF's) to learn about bears, prepare for our giant screen film on bears, get to know the people coming with me, and learn all I can about environmental issues in Alaska. I am sure I will have exciting adventures up there, and will come back with lots of funny stories to tell you.

Kim, have a great weekend in Boston with Alison and Patty. Please remember Mommy and me to them. Tina, thanks so much for agreeing to accompany Mommy and Jenny to Camp Carysbrook (and thanks to Andy too). And good luck with the pigs and rats at USUHS the rest of this week and next. Jenny, have the most wonderful time at Camp! And Tina and Andy, thanks for taking care of precious Conker while Jen and I are away! (And thanks, too, to both of you for watering Carol Beach's flowers while Jen is at camp.)

In my view, the best jokes are those that tell a truth. Here is an old joke I saw recently, which was funnier when Russia was a totalitarian society:

> Moishe is being indoctrinated by the Russian government:
> Government official: "If you had a yacht, what would you do with it?"
> Moishe: "Give it to Mother Russia."
> Government official: "And if you had a palace, what would you do with it?"
> Moishe: "Give it to Mother Russia."
> Government official: "And if you had a sweater, what would you do with it?"
> No reply.
> Government official asks the question again. And still no reply. Finally, he shouts: "Moishe, why don't you reply?"
> Moishe: "Because I have a sweater."

Kim, you have been feeling understandably stressed recently with so much going on in your life. Here are a few general ideas which may help you. The key is to learn how to manage your response to stressful things. It isn't the stressful things themselves which cause us trouble so much as how we respond to stressful things. We know this is true because the people react differently to the same stimulus (say spilled milk in the kitchen), with some people remaining calm, cheerful, energetic, resourceful and optimistic, while others (such as yours truly) becoming uptight, irritable, moody, pessimistic and grumpy!

So here are a few ideas for handling stress, all of which you have heard before:

1. Accept stress, challenge and change as a fact of life and relish it.

2. Commit yourself to lifelong learning. As long as you are learning, you are on the road to an exciting, fulfilling, and meaningful life. You will never have that awful feeling that the world is leaving you behind.

3. Stay in vibrant health through proper nutrition, exercise and rest.

4. Begin to look at stress as an opportunity. In other words (echoing #1) change your attitude to stress. Welcome it as invigorating, strengthening, and life-enhancing.

5. Develop and maintain a strong network and support team. Your talk last Friday with Neil is an example of you already doing that.

6. Find meaning in your life. Create an over-riding purpose for your life so that stress is put into perspective.

7. Engage in warm traditions and rituals. For example, eating dinner as a family, weekly family meetings, keeping a daily journal, weightlifting before dinner, or whatever. This gives you a sense of stability, and a sense of security. You know that some things never change.

8. Rid yourself of the little irritations (and sometimes big ones) that drain you of energy. For example, having a messy desk where you can't find things you need, watching scary movies, watching local TV news, meetings that go on too long, and so on.

9. Keep a daily journal. I already mentioned this but it is so important, I am going to give it its own #! This habit is unbelievably therapeutic.

10. Engage in yoga, meditation or a similar activity.

11. Create your own personal mission statement so that when you are stressed, you can remind yourself what is really important to you.

Well, I hope that is helpful, not only to you Kimmie now, but to all three of you during your lifetimes. I love you so much and miss you terribly when I am away like this, even though I am having the time of my life.

Thanks for being so special, each in your own special ways. I love you.

Daddy
XXXOOO

Friday, July 16, 1999
My treasures Kimmie, Tina and Jenny,
I love you! I hope you are doing OK without me! I miss you!

Here is a lovely story:

> Author and lecturer Leo Buscaglia once talked about a contest he was asked to judge. The purpose of the contest was to find the most caring child. The winner was a four year old child whose next door neighbor was an elderly gentleman who had recently lost his wife. Upon seeing the man cry, the little boy went into the old gentlemen's yard, climbed onto his lap, and just sat there. When his mother asked him what he had said to the neighbor, the little boy said "Nothing, I just helped him cry."

And here is another story that I liked:

> Whenever I'm disappointed with my spot in life, I stop and think about little Jamie Scott. Jamie was trying out for a part in a school play. His mother told me that he'd set his heart on being in it, though she feared he would not be chosen. On the day the parts were awarded, I went with her to collect him after school. Jamie rushed up to her, eyes shining with pride and excitement. "Guess what, Mom," he shouted, and then said those words that will remain a lesson to me, "I've been chosen to clap and cheer."

Kim, Tina and Jenny, I adore you like only a father can. You are so important to Mommy and me. I hope you have a great weekend with all your various travels. I'll be thinking of you!

Yer ol' Daddy
XXXOOO

Saturday, July 17, 1999
It is a big day tomorrow for Jen! Camp Carysbrook is lucky to get you for two weeks! Thanks, Tina and Andy, for helping by going with Jen and Gail tomorrow.

You all three have great potential leadership qualities. I say this because I am a student of Warren Bennis who has spent his life studying leadership and has written some of the best books on this subject. Here is what Warren Bennis says are the characteristics of exemplary leaders. See how you think you measure up:

1. They have passion and purpose.

2. They generate and sustain trust.

3. They are purveyors of hope and optimism.

4. They manifest a bias for action.

5. They keep learning and growing.

Leaders are needed everywhere -- on college campuses, in newspapers, in high schools, in families, in environmental and consumer nonprofit groups, everywhere where important projects get undertaken. And closely allied with the concept of leadership is the issue of power. Understanding why some people have it and some people don't is important so you can learn how to maximize your own power -- the ability to make offers and to deliver on promises, to get things changed, and to get things done. I want the three of you to be powerful leaders in the communities in which you select to live and work.

My loves, I love you and I miss you.

Dad
XXXOOO

Sunday, July 18, 1999

My Precious Loves, Kimmie, Tina and Jenny,

Jen, your first night at camp! I hope you are having a wonderful time and making lots of new friends. Kim, welcome home from Boston! I hope you had a super time. Tina and Andy, welcome home from your long trip today with Gail and Jen. You were great to go. How did you like the University of Virginia?

I am in Alaska on Kodiak Island. The Kodiak Archipelago is home of the world famous Kodiak brown bear. They are recognized as the largest land carnivores (more accurately, omnivores) in the world! Males can weigh up to 1500 pounds! The reason I have chosen to arrange this trip now is that around mid-July bears start to congregate on streams to fish for salmon. This is a very high protein diet for them, and explains why they are so huge. (A male grizzly in Yellowstone might only be 600 pounds.) Bears begin entering their winter dens in late October. Biologists estimate that over 2,500 bears live on Kodiak Island. I will be visiting at the very best time to see them. They fascinate me!

How dangerous are they? Brown bears are potentially very dangerous animals because of their size, strength, intelligence and unpredictable personalities. This is especially true when they are protecting their cubs or protecting their food caches. Fortunately, Kodiak bears rarely live up to their "man-killer" reputations. Bear/people encounters are very common on Kodiak, yet only 7 people were mauled between 1973 and 1992. None of these maulings were fatal and all victims recovered without any serious after effects. No one has been killed by a bear on Kodiak in over 30 years.

They are extraordinary animals. It is increasingly important, as Alaska continues to develop, for the public to recognize that maintaining sufficient amounts of habitat for brown bears to continue to thrive will mean forgoing opportunities for some kinds of economic development in some places.

I send you each a big bear hug! I love you and think about you all the time even though I love being here. Kim and Tina, do you remember our trip together to Alaska two years ago? Wasn't that a great trip?!

This letter comes with lots and lots of hugs and kisses.

Daddy
XXXOOO

Monday, July 19, 1999
My darling Kimmie, Tina and Jenny,
Good luck at *USA Today* Kim! Good luck at USUHS today Tina! And good luck at Camp Carysbrook today Jenny!

When I was growing up, I was often a klutz when it came to relationships. I'd say things that would upset people -- even people I loved -- and not know why. So let me pass on to you some things I am trying to learn to say:

1. I love you.

2. I'm sorry, I made a mistake.

3. I hear you saying...

4. What you say makes sense to me because...

5. I imagine that you must feel... Is that how you feel?

6. What I really appreciate about you is...

7. Thank you for...

8. Would you please....?

9. I'm feeling...

10. I forgive you for...

You three have unconsciously (or consciously) learned so much in this whole area from observing Mommy and seeing how she skillfully takes care of people's needs. Gail anticipates breakdowns so she can prevent them from happening in the first place.

Kim, Tina and Jenny, I love you and send you a big hug and kiss each from Alaska.

Daddy
XXXOOO

Tuesday, July 20, 1999
My loves Kim, Tina and Jen,
Tina, thanks for taking care of Conker and the Beaches' flowers. Jenny and I appreciate your help.

As you know, I love jokes, especially ones which give me an insight into something. Here are some I have come across recently that made me think. I hope you enjoy them too:

1. Two guys are walking down the street when a mugger approaches them and demands their money. They both grudgingly pull out their wallets and begin taking out their cash. Just then, one guy turns to the other and hands him a bill. "Here's that $20 I owe you," he says.

2. My grandfather is hard-of-hearing. He needs to read lips. I don't mind him reading lips, but he uses one of those yellow highlighters.

3. A guy joins a monastery and takes a vow of silence. He's allowed to say two words every seven years. After the first seven years, the elders bring him in and ask for his two words. "Cold floors," he says. They nod and send him away. Seven more years pass. They bring him back in and ask for his two words. He clears his throat and says, "Bad food." They nod and send him away. Seven more years pass. They bring him in for his two words. "I quit," he says. "That's not surprising," the elders say. "You've done nothing but complain since you got here."

4. I was walking across a bridge one day and I saw a man standing on the edge, about to jump off. So I ran over and said, "Stop! Don't do it!"
"Why shouldn't I?" he said.
"Well, there's so much to live for."
"Like what?"
"Well, are you religious?" He said yes.
I said, "Me too! Are you Christian or Buddhist?"
"Christian."
"Me too! Are you Catholic or Protestant?"
"Protestant."
"Me too! Are you Episcopalian or Baptist?"
"Baptist."
"Wow, me too! Are you Baptist Church of God or Baptist Church of the Lord?"
"Baptist Church of God!"
"Me too! Are you original Baptist Church of God, or are you Reformed Baptist Church of God?"
"Reformed Baptist Church of God!"
"Me too! Are you Reformed Baptist Church of God, reformation of 1879, or Reformed Baptist Church of God, reformation of 1915?"
He said, "Reformed Baptist Church of God, reformation of 1915!"
I said, "Die, heretic," and pushed him off.

5. What a hotel! The towels were so fluffy I could hardly close my suitcase.

6. Two old men are chatting. One man says, "My friend, you must try this memory pill I'm taking. I remember everything. It's amazing, this pill." The other man says, "Sounds wonderful. What is the name of the pill?" The first man says, "The name of the pill...let's see.... Hmmm, what is the name of the flower...with the thorns? It's red... You give it on Valentine's Day?" The other man says, "A rose?" The first man says, "Yes, that's right!" Then, calling for his wife, he says, "Rose, what is the name of that pill?"

7. Guy finds a snail on his front stoop. He picks it up and throws it across the street. One year later, he hears a knock at his door. The man goes to the door, opens the door, looks down, and there he sees the snail back on his front stoop. And the snail looks up at the guy and says, "What the hell was that all about?"

8. Skeleton walks into a bar and says, "Give me a beer and a mop."

Ha, Ha, Ha!!! Laughing is one of the most wonderful things in the world. I hope your lives are full of laughter. That is one reason I admire Oscar Wilde.

I love you, and I miss you. I don't like being away from you so long.

Yer ol' Daddy
XXXOOO

Wednesday, July 21, 1999

Kimmie, Tina and Jenny, my three precious lovebugs,
How are you all doing? I have been away from you for so long!

As you know, I am deeply interested in wisdom -- how to make sense of the world and how best to behave in society. As you also know, I read a lot of fascinating books on this subject and learn a lot from all of them. But a lot of wisdom is common sense and doesn't need to come dressed up in fancy words or jargon. For example:

1. If you are at fault, take the blame.

2. If you don't know something, admit it.

3. Always tell the truth. Then you need never be afraid. And you need never have to remember anything.

4. Never act fearful.

5. If you are wrong, apologize.

6. Catch people doing something right.

7. Never gossip. And don't let people gossip to you.

8. Be loyal to those absent.

9. No task in beneath you.

10. Share the credit whenever possible.

11. Ask for help. (In doing this, you will also make a friend.)

12. When you don't like someone, don't let it show. Don't burn bridges you may later need to use.

13. When you are right, don't gloat.

14. Don't harbor grudges. Move on. Let it go. Forgive.

I am still learning the wisdom in many of these ideas.

We have the possibility of at least two stances in life: life is something that we are inventing, or life is something that happens to us and we simply react to our circumstances. The core of a person's identity is the future she/he is committed to invent. And one way you invent the future is in the promises and commitments you make. To make lots of exciting promises, you need to be proactive, bold and imaginative. To make and keep commitments, you need to be trustworthy and reliable.

Kim, Tina and Jenny, I love you with all my heart. And I am so proud of you and all that you do and accomplish.

Dad
XXXOOO

Thursday, July 22, 1999

My darling Kimmie, Tina and Jenny,

I wonder how your week is going for each of you. Here is a little joke to cheer you up in case you have had some disappointments:

> Two elderly ladies meet at the launderette after not seeing one another for some time. After inquiring about each other's health, one asked how much the other's husband was doing.
>
> "Oh! Ted died last week. He went out to the garden to dig up a cabbage for dinner, had a heart attack and dropped dead right there in the middle of the vegetable patch!"
>
> "Oh dear! I'm very sorry," replied her friend, "What did you do?"
>
> "Opened a can of peas instead."

A very good strategy if you feel low about something is to think of people who are worse off than you, and then take steps to help them. Another strategy is to look for ways to encourage other people, especially people who need help. In our weekly family meetings, as you know, we always have as an agenda item "encouragement." Have you noticed that I make a distinction between "praise" and "encouragement"?

Praise evaluates the person: "You are a good artist." It may make a person dependent on external evaluation. It is different from encouragement which acknowledges effort: "You really worked hard on that. You used very strong lines and vivid colors." Even with encouragement, a person is still free to make his or her own evaluations.

My loves, I am very proud to be your Dad. I love being with you, and I love your great sense of humor. Don't forget to smile a lot, drink lots of water, exercise every day, be in awe of nature's beauty, have some quiet time, eat three good meals, say thank you to the people in your life, give something to the world, write in your journal all the things for which you are grateful, and read your personal mission statement to make sure you are spending your time on the things that are most important to you.

I love you.
Daddy
XXXXOOOO (an extra kiss and hug for Conker!)

Friday, July 23, 1999

Darling Kimmie, Tina and Jenny,

I love you! One thing I have been slow to learn during my life is to be grateful, and to acknowledge all the things in my life for which I need to feel a deep appreciation. Here are a few of them:

1.   Gail
2.   Kim
3.   Tina
4.   Jen
5.   Being a Dad
6.   Having a loving family
7.   Being alive
8.   Being healthy
9.   Learning
10. The chance to write these letters to you
11. The natural world
12. Mountains, meadows and meandering rivers
13. Waves at the beach
14. Birds at our bird feeder
15. The warmth of the sun on a cold day
16. Our beautiful house
17. The unique character of each of you
18. The abundant food we have to eat
19. Friends and neighbors we love
20. Living in a democracy
21. Having so much autonomy at work
22. Our family and the love we have for each other
23. Water
24. Conker
25. Sunshine
26. Rainbows
27. Tim's appreciation of my journal
28. Jon's sense of humor
29. My parents' long and happy lives
30. Working for a worthy cause
31. Abe Lincoln, Ben Franklin, Thomas Jefferson
32. The opportunity to make people laugh.

Above all I am grateful for the opportunity to see you grow up and become loving, resilient, resourceful, accomplished and strong.

I love you! And I miss you!
Yer ol' Daddy in Alaska
XXXOOO

Saturday, July 24, 1999
My treasures Kim, Tina and Jenny,
I'll be home tomorrow! Jen, you are half way through your two week camp already! I hope you are having a wonderful time. Tina and Kim, I hope your jobs are going well. I can't wait to see you all again.

Being your Dad gives me a purpose in life. You may think that I do a lot for you, but you will never know how much you do for me.

Life magazine recently had a series of articles on fathering, and it included "The Dad's Test." Here it is. The correct answer to each question is yes.

1. Can you diaper? Do you diaper?
2. Do you play with your child?
3. Are you a partner parent? Do you talk to Mom about meals, food, clothes, friends?
4. Do you teach by example?
5. Do you understand and respect Mom?
6. Does your child know that you love her?
7. When you discipline, does your child know that you still love her?
8. Do you choose her tennis or soccer over your golf?
9. Do you remember, when dealing with your child, that you were not perfect?
10. So are you *there* for your child?

Good questions! Maybe I'm not such a bad Dad after all!

See you tomorrow Kim and Tina! See you in about a week Jen!

I adore you! Thanks for being you!
Daddy
XXXOOO

Monday, August 2, 1999
My Darling Kimmie and Tina,
This letter is not addressed to Jenny because, as you know, she is with me in Florida. We will be away tonight and tomorrow night, and then be home late on Wednesday.

It is five months to Christmas, and now is a good time for us to rethink our gift-giving habits. You might think I am raising this because, as an environmentalist, I don't want to waste resources, money, packaging etc., and that is true. I hate the extravagance and waste. When I first came to America, I couldn't believe what I was witnessing. But an equally important issue is simply that too many gifts (and here I am thinking about storebought gifts) spoil Christmas by forcing us to spend too much time in the mall, thus adding stress and pressure to an already overpacked and stressful period.

Basically, the idea is less material junk and clutter in exchange for the bliss of being thankful for what we already have.

I believe you will be hearing the following types of rallying cries more and more:

*   Voluntary simplicity.

*   Buy less but buy better.

*   Rid yourself of clutter and junk which has nothing to do with expressing your authentic self.

- Outward simplicity, inwardly rich.

All these statements mean opting out of the consumer rat race in favor of more family time, more creative interests, and a more meaningful life.

The Christmas shopping season is the ideal time to downscale our spending, and to put more time into thinking of gifts which really mean something like a personally created letter, poem or painting.

As I say, this is partly about stopping waste, but it is also about new ways to enjoy the holiday and free ourselves from spending so much time at the mall. The goal is more family fun -- saving the earth is a side benefit.

At an upcoming family meeting, we should agree on a cap on holiday spending.

Well, my treasures, I love you. Jenny and I miss you and look forward to seeing you on Wednesday evening. Tina, good luck on your USUHS paper. Well done for working so hard on it last weekend. Kimmie, good luck during these last few days of your internship at *USA Today*. You have made a tremendous success of it.

Buckets of love, hugs and kisses,
Your ol' Dad
XXXOOO

Tuesday, August 3, 1999
My darling Kimmie and Tina,
Driving you to work a few days ago, Tina, you told me you were going with some friends to watch a new horror movie, *The Blair Witch Project*. I had read that it was horribly frightening and so (as you will recall) I urged you not to see it. (By the way, I was pleased when you came home and assessed it as "stupid.")

You will remember how, in the car, I went on to contrast the type of environment in which you and your friends are growing up (e.g., frequently seeing movies with violence, highly sexualized storylines, extreme vulgarity, and humor based on shock value) with the environment teenagers from earlier generations grew up in (e.g., playing games, reading books, games in the garden, listening to radio comics, singing, playing musical instruments, and dinner conversations about the day's news). Entertainment was something people actively created rather than passively absorbed.

All these negative influences in our present culture are bound to have an impact. Some people may claim it won't. In fact, Tina, I think I have heard you make that claim yourself. But then why does Madison Avenue spend billions on advertising if it doesn't affect viewers' behavior? I do think, however, that both of you are exceptional and not easily influenced by things you recognize as being intrinsically bad for families and for society as a whole.

It isn't just degrading movies which can negatively affect teenagers. They can also be affected by the stressful, time-stretched life styles of parents like Mommy and me. It is easy for a Dad like me, with all the pressures from work and from trying to balance work and family responsibilities, to lose sight of how remarkable you three girls are. I am sure I don't tell you enough how proud we are of you, how much we believe in you, how much you mean to us, and how much we trust you.

With all five of us being so busy, it is a challenge to keep to our Family Mission Statement, and be a family characterized by love, affection, hugs, closeness, mutual support, sharing, and smiles, as opposed to a family characterized by distance, frowns, and isolation.

By the way, changing the subject, I have been meaning to talk to you both about sexual harassment. It is important for you to be knowledgeable about this issue now that you are both working. I am enclosing for your interest NWF's Sexual Harassment Policy. You need to be prepared to say, when appropriate, things like:

- "I consider your behavior sexual harassment and intend to talk to my/your supervisor about what you are saying/doing to me."

- "I feel extremely uncomfortable with the way you are behaving."

- "I feel sexually harassed by you."

Knowing what to say and when to say it is crucially important. If you ever attend a training workshop on sexual harassment (which I hope you will so you get some coaching in this area) you will learn how to speak effectively and powerfully to stop any situation before it gets out of control. Remember that sexual harassment has nothing to do with romance and everything to do with bullying.

Kimmie and Tina, I adore you! You are both (along with Jenny here with me in Florida) so incredibly special, and Mommy and I are so proud of you and how you are designing and living your lives.

See you tomorrow when Jenny and I return from our adventure in Florida!

I love you.
Daddy
XXXOOO

Thursday, September 9, 1999

My darling Kimmie (in Amherst), Tina and Jen,
As you know, I am in New York City tonight for the start of the six day GSTA annual meeting (GSTA stands for Giant Screen Theater Association). I will be very active there, giving speeches, various presentations, meeting people, closing deals, winning leases for our films, forming new strategic alliances, and developing new ideas in scores of different conversations. It will be hard work but lots of fun too.

One reason I am confident that it will be enjoyable is that I have prepared very carefully and feel ready for everything. In fact, I am eager to get started. Tomorrow I am giving a paper to a high level group on what has to show up in a film for it to be considered "educational."

Kimmie, I hope your ankle is mending sweetie-pie. And I hope your new classes got off to a good start the day before yesterday. We are so glad you have loving friends around you.

Tina, Holton-Arms opened yesterday! Good luck with school, with tennis, with *Scribbler*, and with all your other activities treasure.

Jen, you love-bug, good luck to you too with your classes, trumpet and soccer.

You will undoubtedly (as has already happened to Kim vis-a-vis Nathaniel and her ankle) face challenges and even suffering. Mommy and I have absolute confidence in you that you will master the challenges you face, learn from them, become stronger because of them, and find ingenious ways to turn "lemon" into "lemonade". (Do I sense an article in the making about the actions of a certain Nathaniel?!) Remember that every problem is an opportunity in disguise (and often the disguise is distressingly convincing at first).

I was recently clearing out some old files and found the following stories. I had completely forgotten about them!

> 1. June 17, 1986: Christina (who had just turned four) announced during dinner that Christina had gone to the beach, and that she was Christine coming to spend the night. Christina said that Christine was from another country called Bethesda, Maryland where they speak a different language called Unos-Dos-Tres. Christina told us that Christine talks all the time, she never stops talking, and she is never shy at school.

> 2. July 17, 1986: I gave Kimberly (who was about six and a half) a nature magazine designed for young children. She said, "Is this mine?" I replied, "Yours and Christina's." Kimberly said, "I want it just to be mine." I responded, "But you are so good at sharing." Kimberly replied, "Maybe I'm good at it but I hate it."

> 3. July 17, 1986: Christina (age four) asked Gail, "Do you go to the bathroom after you are dead?" Gail said, "No." Christina replied, "That's good because you couldn't get up to go."

Aren't they priceless stories?! You guys are such characters. I remember last year I wrote you a letter which contained similarly wonderful stories about Jen.

My loves, Mommy and I adore you. We had such a great summer, even though it didn't contain a three week "family vacation." For me, every day was special and memorable in its own unique way.

As you know, I collect maxims (a maxim is a succinct formulation of a fundamental principle, general truth, or rule of conduct). I love discovering maxims which stir my blood because they offer some piercing insight. Here is one I discovered recently, and I mention it because of the last sentence in the preceding paragraph:

> How we spend our days is, of course, how we spend our lives. (Annie Dillard)

I love this comment because it reminds us to live in the moment, and that days wasted in trivia, lethargy or indulgence are days spent squandering our lives, not just time. And that reminds me of three other maxims that I love:

- The future is that time when you'll wish you'd done what you aren't doing now.

- Every man dies. Not every man lives. (Tim Robbins in *The Shawshank Redemption*)

- Dost thou love life? Then do not squander time, for that is the stuff that life is made of. (Benjamin Franklin)

Do you remember I gave you each for Christmas once (about ten years ago perhaps) a book of maxims that I had lovingly and painstakingly compiled for you? Well one day I plan to give you another one which will contain an even more spectacular collection. I collect them all the time. Seeking wisdom and collecting wise sayings is one of my hobbies. (At last I have a hobby! When I was growing up, grownups were always asking me what my hobbies were. Other kids collected stamps, or car numbers, but those things never interested me, so to my embarrassment, I never had any hobbies. Now I have one at last — the relentless search to find out what makes a great life!)

Kim, Tina and Jen, you are the most special daughters in the whole wide world, and Mommy and I adore you.

Yer ol' Dad
XXXOOO

Friday, September 10, 1999

My precious loves, Kimmie, Tina and Jenny,
Tomorrow at 10:00 AM, I am holding a creative meeting about our giant screen film, *Bears*. With four key members of our team (including Goulam), we will start making decisions about the content, story, and characters which will shape the film.

I love books for children. Jenny and I have just finished *Harriet the Spy*, and we are now starting *On the Banks of the Bayou*. Non-fiction books for children often reduce an issue to its essential elements, and frequently this is what I am searching for.

Here is a good example: Recently the Mini Page has an issue on character. I thought it was excellent. It said that we sometimes look to athletes and music, film and TV stars as heroes and heroines because they are rich and famous celebrities. But it is their life off the stage or field that really counts. True greatness is based on doing good. The more you practice good character traits, the better person you become. People with good character traits (the Mini Page went on) are usually happier and lead fuller lives than people with bad traits.

The Mini Page then listed the following as examples of good character "building blocks": respect (i.e., showing consideration for others), responsibility (i.e., taking care of your duties in a dependable way, being accountable for your own actions without blaming others), fairness, cooperation, caring, honesty, courage, service, self-control, trust, perseverance, tolerance, and integrity.

Being great starts from within. As with any skill, you have to practice, practice, practice. Every little good thing counts toward building strong character.

You guys have wonderful characters, and you will become ever wiser, stronger and more perceptive as you grow older. I love you!

Daddy
XXXOOO

Saturday, September 11, 1999

My darling Kimmie, Tina and Jen,

What is life all about? What is the purpose of life? I often ask myself this and love to read what the great thinkers, leaders and philosophers of the past and present have to say about it.

I am reading *The Art of Happiness — A Handbook for Living* by the Dalai Lama, who is the spiritual and temporal leader of the Tibetan people. He claims the purpose of our existence is to seek happiness — the kind of happiness which is stable and persistent, and that remains, despite life's ups and downs and normal fluctuations of mood, as part of the very matrix of our being. He writes:

> But isn't a life based on seeking personal happiness by nature self-centered, even self-indulgent? Not necessarily. In fact, survey after survey has shown that it is *unhappy* people who tend to be most self-focused and are often socially withdrawn, brooding, and even antagonistic. Happy people, in contrast, are generally found to be more sociable, flexible, and creative and are able to tolerate life's daily frustrations more easily than unhappy people. And, most important, they are found to be more loving and forgiving than unhappy people.

The Dalai Lama goes on to make a distinction between happiness and pleasure. He writes:

> Every day we are faced with numerous decisions and choices. And try as we may, we often don't choose the thing that we know is "good for us." Part of this is related to the fact that the "right choice" is often the difficult one — the one that involves some sacrifice of our pleasure.

But is the purpose of life to seek happiness? Personally I am not totally satisfied by that formulation. There is no right or wrong answer of course. Everyone's life is unique, and designed by themselves in a unique way. Here are some other ideas that might intrigue you:

- To leave a legacy which has never existed before and which benefits future generations.

- To have loving relationships.

- To produce happy grandchildren.

- To save the environment from being destroyed.

- To be part of, and help create, a wonderfully happy, fulfilled family.

You will be able to think of other, perhaps richer, ideas for the fundamental purpose of your own lives. This is a subject worth pondering more and more deeply. It can help anchor your lives when times get tough.

Kim, Tina and Jen, I love you so much! And I miss you! I hope you are each having a super week filled with laughter, joy, accomplishments, learning, and deep satisfactions.

Buckets of love, hugs and kisses,
Dad
XXXOOO

Sunday, September 12, 1999

My loves, Kimmie, Tina and Jenny,

Today is Jeremy's birthday. He would have been 57 today. He was five years older than Jon and me. As you know, he died tragically about ten years ago after undergoing heart surgery. I felt I never really knew him very well, but I still remember how I cried when Jon called me with the unbelievable news that he had died.

One of the great joys of Mommy's and my life is how close you three sisters are. It is an incredible blessing for all five of us.

Life is sometimes tough, unfair, and challenging. But you will always have each other for support, love and encouragement. (That was so sweet when both Tina and Jen called Kim to comfort her after the Nathaniel incident.)

It is special lifetime experience to know that you can always count on each other to be a cherished, loving and loyal friend.

The following is from the book I lent you all the other day entitled *The Joy of Sisters* by Karen Brown:

> Selfless
> Inspirational
> Supportive
> Trusting
> Encouraging
> Reliable
> SISTERS

Here are two other quotes from the book:

- Sisterhood is a club with a lifetime membership.

- Diamonds are nice, but a <u>sister</u> is a girl's best friend.

Kim, Tina, and Jen, you are so incredibly special, and I love you more than I can say.

Daddio
XXXOOO

Monday, September 13, 1999

My darling Kim, Tina, and Jen,

I have recently finished listening with great fascination to a biography of the great Sioux warrior, Crazy Horse. It was written by Larry McMurtry. Crazy Horse was a seminal figure in American history, was a leader against Custer at the battle of Little Big Horn in 1876, but we know surprisingly little about him. What I would do to have a chance to meet him!

Another book I've been enjoying recently is *Unweaving the Rainbow — Science, Delusion and the Appetite for Wonder* by Richard Dawkins. The author is a professor at Oxford University, and the book is a brilliant and trenchant attack on pseudoscience like astrology and telepathy.

Dawkins writes at one point about the challenge of understanding geological time. We pick up a fossil and are told it is, say, 500 million years old. It is very hard to comprehend such an age even though "there is a yearning pleasure in the attempt." He writes that our brains have evolved to grasp the time-scales of our own lifetimes. Seconds, minutes, hours, days and years are easy for us. When we come to millennia — thousands of years — it is more difficult. Yet, on the time scale of a fossil, vaunted antiquities like the epic myths of Homer, the deeds of the Greek gods Zeus and Apollo, and the Jewish heroes Abraham, Moses and David, are "scarcely yesterday."

Richard Dawkins has an analogy that I have not come across before but which I think you will find, as I do, very helpful. Fling your arms wide in an expansive gesture (go ahead, do it!) to span all of evolution from its origin at your left fingertip to today at your right fingertip. Remember the earth was formed perhaps four billion years ago (and the universe started perhaps 15 billion years ago with the so called "Big Bang").

All the way across your midline to well past your right shoulder, life consists of nothing but bacteria. Many-celled, invertebrate life flowers somewhere around your right elbow. The dinosaurs originate in the middle of your right palm, and go extinct around your last finger joint (65 million years ago).

The whole story of *Homo Sapiens* and our predecessor *Home erectus* is contained in the <u>thickness of one nail-clipping</u>! As for recorded history — the Jewish patriarchs, the Pharaohs, the legions of Rome, Jesus Christ, the dark ages, Henry VII, Napoleon, Hitler, the Beatles, Bill Clinton, and the Spice Girls — they and everyone that knew them are blown away "in the dust from one light stroke of a nail-file." Think about that!

By the way, did you know that the people behind the recent Kansas decision (to minimize evolution in the school curriculum) believe that people and dinosaurs existed at the same time? Oh my!

My treasures, I love you. Remember always to be curious and to ask, "Why?" And always be skeptical of what people, including me, tell you. Don't believe anything unless there is evidence to prove it.

I adore you! I hope you are each having a great start to the week. And I hope the "Last Splash Party" last night at the Club, Tina and Jen, was fun.

All my love,
Your very own Dad
XXXOOO

Tuesday, September 14, 1999

My precious loves, Kim, Tina and Jen,
I'll be home tomorrow from GSTA! As you know, I will be at home for four days, and then I leave again on Monday for six days at the Jackson Hole Wildlife Film Festival in Wyoming.

I am so pleased that I will be home for the Westland Back-to-School night on Thursday. I very much want to meet all your teachers Jenny. And I am so upset, Tina, that I will miss the Holton Back-to-School night on the 22nd (I will still be in Wyoming).

Tina, good luck with your tennis match on Thursday at 4:15 PM, and again on Friday afternoon at the same time. I am looking forward to watching your games this fall.

Kim, Tina and Jen, when you write out your goals (and it is very important that you write them out and not just carry them vaguely in your head), remember to use words that excite you, that raise your horizons, and that get you juiced up and energized. Many people forget how powerful words can be and how they can effect results.

For example, in my own case, one of my goals at work might be "to produce engaging films about conservation." There would be nothing ostensibly wrong with that, but I see a lot wrong with it because it produces in me a "blah" reaction.

Suppose instead that I said my goal is to become known as "the Stephen Spielberg of conservation films", or to produce films that "absorb, thrill and electrify" viewers, or that "inspire viewers to create new, exciting possibilities for themselves in grassroots political activism as it pertains to conservation", or....well, you get to idea. Lethargic and insipid words drain life of zest and vitality. I am always looking for words or phrases that inspire me with renewed determination, elan, and verve in the pursuit of my goals. Creative use of words is one of the ways Churchill rallied the people of Great Britain early in World War II when we stood alone against Hitler.

My loves, I can't wait to get home tomorrow!

I love you more than all the grains of sand in the world multiplied by total number of water molecules in the universe. Whew! That is a lot of love!

Daddy
XXXOOO

Monday, September 20, 1999
My dearest loves, Kim, Tina and Jen,
I am off again, this time (as you know) to the Jackson Hole Wildlife Film Festival. I have to give several important (to me!) speeches and presentations, and I will have scores of meetings with film makers, networks executives, and others with whom I work or might work in the future.

Kim, I hope your new classes are going well, including the journalism one at Umass for which you can't get credit. How is your ankle? I hope you can get back to running soon because I know how much you love to do that.

Tina, good luck with all your classes at Holton, with *Scribbler*, tennis and all your other activities. Your idea for your college essay (about the letters and poems you have written over the years) is very good I thought. One possible theme could be the importance of fundamentals (love, kindness, generosity, decency, appreciation, listening, affection, and so on) in an age when our popular television programs celebrate and legitimize cynicism, vulgarlty, deception, disloyalty, and stupidity.

Jen, good luck, lovebug, with your classes, friends, soccer and trumpet, and please give our wonderful Conker a big kiss from me.

I am enthusiastic about the ideas we are beginning to discuss in our family meetings for helping to share the jobs in the house more equitably. This is more important to you than you might at first think. During your lives, you will be inundated with subtle, societal messages aimed at women that say, in effect: A worthwhile woman is praised and extolled as one who single-handedly takes care of her family, one who *does* for her family — gives, sacrifices, always goes out of her way to make a good home for them.

Many an otherwise-quite-decent man is happy to spend the weekend playing golf while his wife does everything required to make the house function comfortably for the family. Today, many women, instead of being "liberated", now feel obligated to be almost superhuman. They feel compelled to try to successfully be all things to all people — mother, wife, partner, full-time careerist, family social secretary, cook, shopper, cleaner, launderer, family organizer, and on and on. It isn't fair! No one member of the family should have to carry this burden alone. Every family member should be assigned daily tasks, and understand that privileges and responsibilities go hand-in-hand.

I have been reading Stephanie Winston's new book, *Getting Out From Under — Redefining Your Priorities in an Overwhelming World*. She writes:

> ...until fairly recently, the expected levels of cooperation within a family were radically different from the laissez-faire attitude that has sprung into being seemingly in just the last half century. (In the old days) children were obligated, trained, conditioned, and expected to make a meaningful contribution to the family's well-being.

This no longer happens. Winston asks, "What happened? When did the experience of being part of a family in which every member shared some responsibility for the functioning of the household shift to a completely *different* paradigm of total childhood exemption from responsibility? <u>When did the concept of complete entitlement become the norm?</u>"

Nowadays, many parents (and I don't want Mommy and I to be one of them) have a hard time making any demands on their children. They believe that the role of a parent is to make sure the kids are happy all the time — that the children don't feel too much stress, and that they are not burdened by responsibilities or by tasks they don't like. In my view, this creates chaos, alienation, unfairness and disconnect because the kids do not feel a happy grounded connection to the family or feel a sense of being part of a unit of which they are a vitally important part.

Winston concludes that addressing this epidemic of childhood entitlement Is urgently required, and I agree with her. In the new novel Jen and I have just started reading (set at the turn of the century), Rose leaves home at age 16 for nine months, and her biggest worry is the burden her leaving will place on her parents because they will now have to do all the jobs that Rose routinely does (fetching the water, feeding the chickens, and so on).

As you know, I am developing a new system for getting jobs done in the house so that no one person feels unfairly put upon. Stand by for the next draft! (Kim, see what you are missing by being away at Amherst?!)

Please take care of each other while I am away. I know you will. I love you!

Daddy
XXXOOO

Tuesday, September 21, 1999
My loves, Kim, Tina and Jen,
Tina, I am so upset that I am missing Back-to-School night tomorrow night at Holton-Arms. Kim, I hope your ankle is feeling better. And Jen, good luck at soccer practice tomorrow.

For years I have been fascinated how people are so gullible when it comes to believing in UFOs, ghosts, astrology, and other pseudoscientific, paranormal garbage. And there was one particular activity — walking barefoot over burning hot coals without getting burned — that intrigued me. I first read about this so called "fire walking" in the late 1950s when I was a boy — I think it originated in Ceylon. For many years, unscrupulous people have tried to use this phenomenon to persuade the gullible that something "paranormal" or "psychic" was going on.

Well, I have been reading an excellent new book called *Why People Believe Weird Things — Pseudoscience, Superstition, and Other Confusions of Our Time* by Michael Shermer. For years people have assumed that extraordinary psychic powers were needed to do fire walking without getting burned. Afterall, the temperature in the middle of the raked out path of burning coals is about 800 degrees Fahrenheit!

It turns out that fire walking has nothing to do with the powers of positive thinking and everything to do with physics. You don't need to meditate, chant or have paranormal mental powers. You do need courage because it isn't obvious that you won't get burned!

Here is the explanation: When you bake a cake in an oven, by way of analogy, the air, the cake, and the metal pan are all at 400 degrees, but only the pan will burn your skin. Hot coals, even at 800 degrees, are like cake — they do not conduct heat very quickly — so as long as you stride across the burning coals without delay, you won't get burned. The person you have to admire in all this is the person who, years ago, first had the courage to try it!

Now you can challenge your friends to firewalk and impress them with your courage and psychic powers!

I miss you, and I love you. I think about you all the time.
Dad-the-skeptic
XXXOOO

Wednesday, September 22, 1999
My darling darlings, Kimmie, Tina, and Jenny,
Good luck this year with *Scribbler*, Tina. I am so pleased that you are so proud of the last issue. I can't wait to read it! Undoubtedly you will have some challenges this year with people who don't deliver drafts when they promise, who act in irritating ways, who usurp your and Mara's authority, who fail to do their share, and so on. Those kind of things go with the territory.

I know you will do a superb job as co-Editor-in-Chief. I am not sure if you will find the following ideas annoying (since you already know all this stuff and already do it) or helpful. If the former, then don't read any more! Kim and Jen, I hope you find this useful too. Anyway, here are a few of the things, Tina, to keep reminding yourself to do as the year goes on — especially when you hit the middle of the year when the excitement perhaps has gone but duty calls on you to keep going. (People sometimes forget that the middle of a project is often the hardest part. The beginning and end each have their own special *frisson* which helps you persevere.)

1. Always be cheerful and smile. The staff will take their lead from you. When the going gets tough, rally the troops with your 'can-do' spirit.

2. Never talk negatively about anyone who is not there. In other words, don't gossip, and don't allow others to gossip.

3. If you have a complaint, raise it directly and privately with the person who is causing the problem. Tell others to do the same (see #2 above).

4. Start and end meetings on time.

5. Welcome the opportunity to be the sole leader when Mara is busy.

6. Keep asking the question: *How can we do whatever we are doing in a different, more fun and productive way?*

7. Look at other school newspapers for inspiration and ideas, and plagiarize creatively! (In the professional world this is called "bench marking".)

8. Constantly collect ideas for new themes, articles, issues, layouts, photos etc., and be a relentless source of stimulating ideas.

9. Show your enthusiasm, both verbally and physically.

10. Be the example you want to see.

11. Make clear requests, and always include mutually agreed upon deadlines.

12. Think of new ways to make *Scribbler* "must reading" for all the Holton "stake holders" (including the students, and Diana Beebe and the teaching staff).

13. Praise your *Scribbler* staff liberally and be as specific as possible.

14. Give quick feedback — don't delay giving your comments to people, especially if a rewrite is required.

15. When someone submits a draft which is below par, say to them (sincerity is essential here as in all communications) that this is not up to their usual standard, and you remember (and here tell a true story) how they had written an article five weeks ago and did an excellent job by creating a powerful first sentence which drew the reader in….(or whatever the issues are).

16. Always say please and thank you.

17. Create your own set of "standard operating procedures" (or SOPs), perhaps inspired by

some of the ideas in this letter, get Mara to buy into them, and then ask the staff for their input before posting it on email. People flourish when there are clear ground rules and they know what is expected and what isn't. The goal is less bureaucracy and more creativity.

Tina, I hope that is helpful to you! Good luck! I know you are doing a great job, and I know it isn't easy.

Kim, Tina and Jen, I love you and miss you!
Yer ol' Daddy
XXXOOO

Thursday, September 23, 1999
My treasures, Kimmie, Tina and Jen,
On this day in 1972 — 27 years ago! — I met Mommy at Harvard. I was wearing a purple shirt and a green suit that I had made for me by a Japanese taylor on a British warship when I crossed the Atlantic with the British Navy a few months earlier. I thought that I looked pretty sharp. I think Mommy had other views!

What an incredible blessing to meet Gail! How extraordinarily lucky I was! Gail has brought profound happiness, stability, and purpose to my life — and, of course, together (actually I did it all by myself but Mommy helped a little!) we produced you three wonderful, remarkable, marvelous, fabulous, miraculous, phenomenal, unique, and awesome daughters!

We love you!

Here is a story I like and I hope you will too:

> One day a father and his rich family took his young son on a trip to the
> country with the firm purpose to show him how poor people can be. They spent
> a day and a night in the farm of a very poor family. When they got back from
> their trip the father asked his son, "How was the trip?"
> "Very good, Dad!"
> "Did you see how poor people can be?" the father asked.
> "Yeah!"
> "And what did you learn?"
> The son answered, "I saw that we have a dog at home, and they have four.
> We have a pool that reaches to the middle of the garden, they have a creek
> that has no end.
> We have imported lamps in the garden, they have the stars.
> Our patio reaches to the front yard, they have a whole horizon."
> When the little boy was finishing, his father was speechless.
> His son added, "Thanks, Dad, for showing me how poor we are!"
> Isn't it true that it all depends on the way you look at things?
> If you have:
> 1. love
> 2. friends
> 3. family
> 4. health
> 5. good humor

6. a positive attitude toward life, you've got everything!

You can't buy any of these things. You can have all the material possessions you can imagine, provisions for the future, etc., but if you are poor of spirit, you have nothing!

My loves, I love you! I adore you! I awindow you!
Your loving and devoted Dad
XXXOOO

Friday, September 24, 1999

My loves, Kim, Tina and Jen,
Well, I had a letter all planned out to write you but I am exhausted from writing you so many letters (I am away for a total of twelve nights so that is twelve letters to write before I leave!) so I have decided to tell you a joke instead because it is less work!

> Grandpa is driving down the M4 to London on his way to pick up Mommy, Kim and Jen at Heathrow. Suddenly his cell phone rings. It is Granny: "Darling, wohooo, darling, Sidney John, darling, I have just heard on the news that there is a car going down the M4 in the wrong direction. Please be careful!"
>
> "It's true," Grandpa replies. "But not just one car — there are hundreds of them!"

Ha, ha, ha! That'll make Granny and Grandpa laugh too! They always love a good joke.

Tomorrow night I am giving a talk in Yellowstone National Park to a small group of NWF friends, including one of my favorite couples, Sloan and Anna Marie Hales. I am looking forward to introducing them to you one day soon. Remember they came to Alaska with me. Anyway, I hope I will do a good job on my presentation to them all. Mark Van Putten will be there too.

I will save for another trip the letter I had planned to write to you for tonight.

Kim, Tina and Jen, you are each so very, very special. I love you.

One-tired-letter-writing-Dad
XXXOOO

Saturday, September 25, 1999

My loves, Kim, Tina and Jen,
I will be home tomorrow! I have been away far too much — six days in New York City, and six days in Wyoming. I have had a wonderful time — a time of great personal and professional growth — but I have been away from home and each of you to much, and that has been a sacrifice.

Tina, I look forward to dinner at Holton-Arms next Tuesday night!

Kim, Tina and Jen, I adore you!

Oodles of love and affection,

Your-travel-weary-Dad
XXXOOO

Wednesday, Sep 29, 1999

Tina wrote:

Dad,

I don't understand what is wrong with you. Why do you not care at all that I'm upset? How come you don't apologize?

I can't believe you said that. Why do you constantly bring this up? I know I am quiet and I don't talk that much in psychology class, but that does NOT mean I hate myself. I've realized that it is YOU who hates me, it is YOU who can't accept it. I am happy. Of course there are some things I'd like to improve, just like you have things to improve. It does not mean I hate myself. I do so many things that show how much I've grown since I was younger, yet you never praise me for that. You expect too much, when you should be happy with me for who I am. My father should not make me feel bad about myself, and should not make me hate myself. Yes, you should encourage me, but the way to do that is definitely not doing what you do.

Your middle daughter,
Christina

September 29, 1999

My darling Tina,

I am so sorry. I feel terrible about what I said to you. I've been talking about what happened with friends, and every one of them said that I was horribly mean and unfair to appear to question whether it is worth our while to spend all that money on your Holton-Arms education just because you tend to be reserved (so far) in psychology class.

I didn't mean to say it in the way you heard it. What I meant to say is that I would love to see you taking full advantage of the wonderful opportunities at Holton to get comfortable with speaking in public. Practicing now at Holton will help you so much at college where you will be expected to speak up, despite the often rude, loud-mouthed and overly-assertive males in the class who will attempt to dominate the discussions.

Tina, I appreciated your email. I love you. And I admire you. I don't tell you that enough. It was a very loving act on your part that you would have the strength and courage to write me that note. Thank you. I have always had a tendency (in the observation of myself as well as others) to focus on what needs to be improved rather than focusing on what has been accomplished and achieved. One reason I invented the "encouragement" agenda item in our weekly family meetings was to help trigger in me (and all of us) a focus on what is "right" in the family rather that what is "wrong". In my view, too much parenting revolves around the idea of catching children doing something "wrong". I am often guilty of this, as you know.

All your life I have been worried about you being too reserved and not assertive enough. (I forget how wonderful and unique you are just as you are.) I have worried about you not sharing your rich, wonderful thoughts with other people and with Mommy and me. So when you told me the other night that you were participating only a little in psychology class, it triggered a flood of anxiety in me. Stupidly I let this concern show up as anger and disappointment, hence my thoughtless comment on

328

whether the huge fees we pay at Holton were worth it. That was mistake #1 for which I am truly sorry.

Then you understandably responded, "I hate you!", and I, in an immature fit of pique, said erroneously, "No you don't, you hate yourself!" That was mistake #2. What I said was a glib verbal riposte which I immediately regretted. (FYI — I said it because I have noticed over the years that when I am tempted to criticize somebody, deep down I am guilty of the very thing that I am criticizing, and in fact, that reality is what triggers the criticism. Which reminds me to tell you, if I haven't before, that I was quite shy when growing up and terrified of speaking in public.)

Now, Tina, we haven't talked for two days, and I feel sad, guilty and miserable.

Your note says, "Why do you not care at all that I am upset?" I do care. I have been trying to gather the courage to apologize to you. I was so pleased when I received your email because it gave me the excuse I have been looking for to say I am sorry.
I am very sorry for what I said. Please forgive me.

It isn't easy being a Dad. I am often lonely because you don't talk to me. I often feel unimportant. Sometimes I don't feel respected. As you know, being a father is the most important thing in the world to me (after my role as a husband). I try to be a loving and competent Dad. I sometimes fail badly as I did this week.

I don't want you to be upset. I want us to be close. I love it when you share things with me. I know this last point is tricky for you because if you share something with me (especially a vulnerability of some kind), then it must seem to you that instead of helping you and empathizing, I turn the issue against you, and criticize you for the very thing you confided in me about. So you naturally then wish you had never talked to me. My intention is to help, but it comes across to you (understandably) as almost an attack.

Your email is perceptive. You write, "It is YOU who can't accept (me being quiet)." I wonder where I get this Calvinist or Puritan attitude from? — this desire to change perfectly good people into some version closer to the way I am. (Aunty Yvette has the same problem!) I have to learn to appreciate people the way they are, and to be grateful for people's uniqueness and diversity.

Tina, you are unique and extraordinarily special, and, in my arrogant and blundering way, I sometimes forget that. Please forgive me.

Of course you don't hate yourself! I know that. There is nothing to hate. Everything about you is to love. You are a wonderful person — loving, intelligent, gracious, forgiving, thoughtful, responsive, prudent, empathic, and considerate. You are doing really well in school. You have lots and lots of friends, and they love you dearly. You hold high positions of responsibility at Scribbler, tennis and other activities. Your SAT scores are exemplary. You HAVE done (as you say) so many things that show how much you have grown since you were young. I apologize for not praising you more for that.

I should not make you feel bad about yourself. Tina, I am sorry I did that. In a relentless drive to root out complacency in my own life, I am sometimes driven to make misjudgements about other people. One of my biggest goals is to prepare you three girls for the real world so that when you leave home you feel so strong, so powerful, and so optimistic, that you have the self-confidence to handle any situation, however challenging. In my pursuit of that goal, I sometimes make mistakes, as I did with you earlier this week.

One of my greatest pleasures in life is when you three girls ask me for advice and help. Then I feel important. I feel needed. I feel life is worth living. I have a purpose in being here. I feel respected. I feel loved. My life means something. I know it isn't always easy to ask me for help and advice because I respond full of ideas that sound critical of you. I need to learn how to provide ideas which, instead of threatening, boring or intimidating you, are received by you with joy. I know this is possible for me to achieve because Kim (although I shouldn't speak for her) enjoys getting feedback from me on her articles and other things.

Tina, I do so hope that you will eventually come to see me as someone you can always count on to help and support you at any time and whatever the circumstances, and that you will seek out my help frequently. I was so thrilled a week or so ago when we worked together so well and constructively on your college essay.

Tina, I don't want us to drift apart. We have never talked much but that doesn't mean I don't love you. I do love you, with all my heart. Everybody expresses love in their own unique way. The wonderful poems, essays and letters you have written to me on birthday occasions over your lifetime are incredibly special to me. I treasure them (and can't wait to share them with your children!).

Darling Tina, let's try and get along better. I am sorry for being so mean-spirited two nights ago, and for saying those things. I want to be a deeply loving father to you. You deserve it! Look at the email you sent me! Only someone with tremendous maturity could have written such a letter, and I am very, very proud it was my middle daughter. The fact that you wrote it shows how much you love me. I am very, very lucky to have you as a daughter.

I love you more than I can say.
Your loving Dad
XXXOOO

October 4, 1999
Hey Dad and Jen!
Here is my essay.
I love you!!!
Love,
Tina

"FAMILY MEETING" my dad yells throughout the house Sunday morning. My sisters and I roll our eyes as we walk into the study where my mom and dad are. We sit on the blue carpeted floor in the space between their desks. My little sister Jen sits at the computer and clicks on America Online. Kim looks at her watch. "This has to be quick," she says, "I have a lot of work to do and I'm meeting Clare at one. "Do you all have a pad of paper and a pen?" my dad asks. I reach up and take a pen off his desk ready for him when he says in his English accent "Tina you should come prepared to the meetings."

"Okay, first thing on the agenda is to plan today," my dad says as he opens up our family meeting notebook and gets out a red pen. Sometimes he even has a mallet, but not today. Jen starts im-ing her friends on-line. My dad notices: "Jen, pay attention." We plan the day, then my dad says, "Gail, what chores do the girls have to do today?" This is one of his weekly complaints.   There really aren't any chores, but he makes my mom think of a list anyway.   "When I was growing up we worked for hours doing chores for the family. This isn't fair. Mummy and I end up doing everything." It's not my fault his family didn't have a dishwasher or washing machine when he was growing up. "Who wants to do the food shopping today?" he asks. No one answers. "I guess I'll be doing it again." He says this every week too. He always ends up doing it. "Who's going to make dinner tonight?" No one says anything again.

 My mom will end up doing it.

"Plan the week" he says, as he moves down the agenda. We go through each day of the coming week, saying what each person has on, and who needs the car when. "I need the car this afternoon to go to Lizzie's," I say. This always gets my dad going. "How are you going to pay for it?" he says. I roll my eyes. "Can you afford it? Why do you think you're entitled to our car that Mummy and I paid for?" Jen pops in "This really has nothing to do with me so can you discuss it later?" My dad finally gives in saying I can have the car as long as I do my jobs first.

"Next item: Girls, we need to have more family outings. We never do anything together." We all shift in our seats and I look at my watch. "Do you want to go to the circus?" he suggests. We all have our own excuses of why we're too busy. "We're going to start making it a weekly thing to go out to brunch every Saturday," he says. That's fine, I like the Pancake House. "Can we move on? This is a waste of time" I interrupt as I think of all the things I have to do today. My sisters and I are all slouched down against the wall doodling on our paper. "Okay, okay" he says. "Tina, you need to learn to balance your time better. You seem to have time for everything but your family."

"Alright, now, next item on the agenda is Mummy's birthday. Next year is her 50th birthday. We should do something special." We talked about this last meeting, and the meeting before. "Dad," I say trying not to yell, "we've talked about this every meeting. It's more than a year away. We don't need to keep bringing it up." He marks a star next to it to remind himself to bring it up next week.

"Next: Plan this summer." We talked about this one last week too. "I still don't know my plans yet Dad. Things haven't changed in a week." My sisters say the same. He marks a star next to that one too and moves on.

"Next thing is Rocks." This is when we go around the room and we all say the biggest thing we have this week. My dad got this from one of his many self-help books he reads. That's also where he got the idea of these family meetings, not to mention our family mission statement. Today, and recently, my dad's rock has been to get along better with me. He still hasn't made much progress. Jen's rock is the same as usual -- "school" since she can't think of anything else. Kim's is to work on one of her articles. Mine is my college applications. My mom's is to work on her family history book.

"Next: Encourage each other." This is the one we're supposed to come already prepared with. My dad goes first, with a list of things to praise each one of us for. I go next, thinking them up as I go along. "Mom for working so hard on your book, Kim for your article, Jen for being such a good little sister (that's what I say when I can't think of anything else), and Dad for . . . uh . . . come back to me."

Next is when we raise any issues we might have. Jen brings up her allowance policy. She wants a raise. My dad doesn't wait for her to finish and says, "Jen, write down as one of your commitments to write up a proposal and show it to the whole family. Then we can all sign it if we agree." Jen's writes it down on her doodled on paper. She's only 12, but she's used to this kind of thing.

I have something to bring up. "I think it's ridiculous that no one of the opposite sex can go into my room," I say. I've brought this up before, but now I have a legitimate reason: "When I go to college I'm going to go crazy with all my freedom. I should have more independence now so I don't take advantage of it at college--where I can to anything. You don't want that to happen, do you?" They aren't convinced. Maybe if I wrote a proposal too and had everyone sign it then they'd let me.

We start getting antsy. "DAD, hurry up, we don't have all day," Kim says. "Okay, now, does everyone know their commitments?" "Yes" we say in unison. I start walking away, "Hey where do you think you're going? We're not done yet" my dad yells to me. "Bye!" I say as I walk away laughing.

October 7, 1999

My Darling Tina and Jenny:

As you know, I have flown up to see Kim in Amherst to take her out for dinner this evening. We'll also have breakfast together tomorrow morning, and then I'll fly back to the office.

I was planning on writing you a letter about the importance of living purposefully and strategically (instead of drifting around) but then I found the following four jokes and decided you would enjoy them more! So here they are:

- Bella was terribly upset. Her fiancee, Marvin, had been to a clinical psychologist, and the results were not entirely consoling.

  She said to her mother, "I'm not sure the marriage would be happy, Ma. The psychologist says Marvin tests out to have a pronounced Oedipus complex."

  Her mother shrugged and said, "Don't listen to that fancy talk. I've watched Marvin and I tell you he's all right. Look how he loves his mother."

- How many lawyer jokes are there? Only three. The rest are true stories.

- A mother was preparing pancakes for her sons, Kevin 5, and Ryan, 3. The boys began to argue over who would get the first pancake. Their mother saw the opportunity for a moral lesson.

  "If Jesus were sitting here, He would say, "Let my brother have the first pancake. I can wait."

  Kevin turned to his younger brother and said, "Ryan, you be Jesus."

- The man told his doctor that he wasn't able to do all the things around the house that he used to do.

  When the examination was complete, he said, ""Now, Doc, I can take it. Tell me in plain English what is wrong with me."

  "Well, in plain English," the doctor replied, "you're just lazy."

"Okay," said the man. "Now give me the medical term so I can tell my wife."

Ha, ha, ha! I love you! I miss you!
Your ol' Dad
XXXOOO

Thursday, October 14, 1999

My darling Kimmie, Tina and Jenny,

As you know, I fly to Louisville tonight for the premier of *Wolves* tomorrow night at the Louisville Science Center. I have worked hard on my speech and hope to do a good job. My plan is to entertain the audience as well as inform and inspire them. The reason I have to leave tonight is that I have been invited to appear on a television show tomorrow morning at 6:30 AM (so I will have to get up at about 4:30 AM!)

I am very sorry to have to miss the big celebration tonight at Holton of the opening of the Centennial Garden.

I will be racing home on Saturday morning to get back in time to go to Jen's soccer game at 3:40 PM in the afternoon.

My loves, I have been absorbed of late in a new book entitled *Remembrances and Celebrations: A Book of Eulogies, Elegies, Letters, and Epitaphs*. This deeply enjoyable book is about a powerful and primitive need all people in all societies seem to have — a need to honor and celebrate those who have died. Mommy's 400-page book about her family history, and the 120-page book I wrote eight years ago about my side of the family, are examples of ways to satisfy this need.

It is deeply consoling to say goodbye to loved ones with a meaningful and graceful farewell that expresses sorrow, love, and gratitude. Giving a eulogy is the first time for some people that they make the opportunity to say how rich, full, and meaningful one particular life can be.

As the introduction to this book wisely says, if we are willing to love (and we must be), we must also be willing to grieve. (I am adding that to my list of maxims.) The introduction also points out that delivering a eulogy is a self-defining act because you learn something rare about the eulogist. Too many eulogies simply fulfill what is proper or socially prescribed, without doing justice to the uniqueness, the distinct allure, and the Idiosyncratic essence of the person who has died. I will never forget the poignant service you girls put together for Houdini when he died.

Grief is one of the most difficult emotions with which we have to deal. I can still remember the agony my mother went through when her father, and then three years later her mother, died. I was only a small boy at the time.

I admire those who write about the dead so eloquently, so movingly, so deeply, so perceptively, do tenderly, and so lovingly. Here you see people in their best light — both the eulogist and the person being eulogized. One eulogy I read in the book (S.J. Perelman on Ogden Nash) made me laugh out loud.

My loves, I love you. I will always love you. You are so very, very special. You are each unique and different from each other. I am so lucky to be your Dad. Mommy and I are incredibly proud of you.

Yer ol' lovin' Dad
XXXOOO

Friday, October 15, 1999
My precious loves, Kim, Tina and Jen,
I am the main speaker tonight at the Louisville Science Center where *Wolves* is opening. I always love these events!

Here are some good words that you need to know: tantalize, cynicism, melee, imperil, hackneyed, expiate, detrimental, charlatan, accessible, derelict, culpable, laudatory, usurp, perjure, recidivism, carnivore, placid, epigram, eulogy (see last night's letter!), oleaginous, nettlesome, harass, and intimidate. If you don't know the meaning of any of these words, please look them up in a dictionary!

Those last two words (harass and intimidate) remind me to tell you that I have always been pleased (and relieved) that none of you (so far) has been the victim of a bully (or at least, as far as I know). My guess is that the reason for your success in that domain of your lives is that you all look self-confident and you don't look vulnerable. Bullies (and the world is full of them) are drawn to attack people who they perceive as weak.

One of my biggest goals as a father is to teach you each to be strong, to be proud, to stand tall, to be fearless (or at least to have the courage to act fearless), and to never show weakness or vulnerability. In other words, I want you to always act like you have a phalanx of body guards at your immediate disposal. If you are proud of yourself, bullies will not find you a tempting target. It is to your great credit that you have never needed this advice. You each have strong social skills and have taught yourselves how to get along well with people.

I love you! I miss you! Being your Dad is the second best thing that ever happened to me (meeting and marrying Gail was the first).

Buckets and oodles and piles of hugs and kisses,

Dad-advice-is-my-second-name-dy!
XXXOOO

Wednesday, October 20, 1999
My adorable loves, Kimmie, Tina and Jenny,
As you know, I am at the Liberty Science Center in New Jersey tonight for the opening of *Wolves*. I am delighted that Janet, Gordon, Suzy and Steve will all be there. I hope they don't fall asleep during my presentation!

I have been so interested to observe how you, Tina, and you, Jenny, have recently expressed your desire one day to have children. When I was your age, nothing was further from my mind!

Anyway, your comments have made me reflect on the kind of man I hope you will marry one day. Of course, you may decide never to marry, which is just fine.

In no particular order, your future husband should:

- Have competent, loving parents.

- Work hard because you want to marry someone who knows how to earn a living.

- Have superior "people skills."

- Be patient and forgiving.

- Be playful.

- Not be attracted to the pursuit of frivolous or inane activities.

- Understand that love is a verb, not a noun. Love is something that you do, a sacrifice that you make. It is not a feeling — that notion comes from Hollywood and is selfish and immature. The feeling of love is the result of the action of love.

- Attach little importance to physical beauty, realizing that this is genetic (in other words, mere chemistry), and that inner beauty is the only thing that really matters.

- Have a humility and an uncertainty when it comes to religious matters. Marrying someone who is arrogantly dogmatic can be very unpleasant if you don't share their views. It is good to be skeptical of all dogma and authority.

- Have values very similar to your own.

- Be profoundly serious (but not solemn) about making his life mean something. He should want to leave the world a better place for his passage through it, to leave his footprints in the sands of time.

- Be ambitious, but at the same time, have an inner tranquility.

- Be optimistic, cheerful and positive.

- Attach great importance to the concept of families being the basic building block of all healthy and vibrant societies.

- Value family traditions and rituals.

- Be responsible. By this I mean that your future husband should believe that his life is ultimately his responsibility, however many "bad" things happen (or have happened) to him.

- Be able to take care of himself, and manage his time, space, commitments and health well, so that he has more to give and share with you and the children.

- Have the capacity and ability to keep promises and honor commitments he makes to you and others.

- Be dedicated to lifelong learning.

- Have a good sense of humor and enjoy laughing out loud.

- Be absolutely reliable and trustworthy.

- Be physically fit.

- Be courageous, fair, honest, loyal, devoted, compassionate, generous, creative, tenacious, and a person of sound judgement and wisdom.

- Be relentless in his examination of his life to see how to redesign it so it is more effective, purposeful, and loving.

- Be a highly competent and empathic listener.

- Be ruthless about getting rid of clutter and have a strong desire to simplify his life so he has room for what really matters to him (you).

- Not speak negatively of others when they are not present.

- Be skillful in coordinating his actions with those of others.

- Focus his efforts on things he can do something about rather than on things beyond his control.

- Have a written plan for his life which he enjoys sharing with you.

- Want to make you look good in front of other people.

- Catch you and the children doing things right. And if he does criticize you, he should do it in private and in a loving way.

- Be affectionate and loving, and want to "coddle" you (to use Granny's word).

It goes without saying that when I married Mommy nearly 25 years ago, I measured up poorly against virtually every one of these criteria.

My loves, I do not claim this list of desirable attributes in a husband is complete, comprehensive, well organized, or even particularly insightful. I am sure it can be improved a lot. It is just what occurs to me as I sit writing this letter to you. By the way, he doesn't have to wear booty shorts!

Somerset Maugham said that, "American women expect to find in their husbands a perfection that English women only hope to find in their butlers." Don't expect too much of men, otherwise they are bound to disappoint you. Ann Landers said it best: "A successful marriage is not a gift; it is an achievement."

When I was young, someone silly told my fortune and claimed that I would be married three times. I still remember the revulsion I felt at that possibility and I resolved that I would be free of the dreary, painful banality of divorce.

So there, my treasures, are some quick thoughts on your future husbands! Whomever they turn out to be will be very lucky to marry you!

I adore you.

Dad (aka Mrs. Bennett!)
XXXOOO

Thursday, October 21, 1999

My darling Kimmie, Tina and Jenny,

You have often heard me say that life is tough. One of my goals as a father has been to make you resilient, bold, tenacious, optimistic, strong, self-confident, determined, enthusiastic, energetic, irrepressible and fearless. Mommy and I want you to lead happy, fulfilled lives despite (or even because of) disappointments, challenges and frustrations (and even possibly tragedies) that life will inevitably throw at you.

In my view, too many children today don't have a thorough grasp of reality, and are destined to live lives of disappointment and frustration. Here are my "20 Laws of Life for the Naive." You are unlikely to learn these in a classroom.

1. Accomplishing real results is more important than nurturing your self-esteem.

2. You are responsible for the quality of the relationships you have with other people.

3. You are accountable for your own life.

4. Life is tough, and you have to learn to be tough and resilient.

5. Blaming, criticizing and complaining are the activities of losers.

6. The experiences you have in life are your own creation.

7. The first and often the hardest step to solve any problem is to openly and bravely acknowledge it.

8. Action is what finally counts. Trying to do something, or thinking about doing something, or deciding about something, is not good enough, and can sometimes be worse than taking a bad action.

9. Virtually everything in life is subjective. You observe the world through your own unique lens. You see the world as you see it, not as it is.

10. Only when you write a goal down does it become real and serious for you.

11. If you don't take charge of your life, someone else will.

12. Anger, frustration and resentment are damaging emotions, and best avoided.

13. Life is often unfair. Face up to that fact, and deal with it courageously.

14. The only money worth having and which gives you real satisfaction is the money you have worked hard yourself to earn.

15. The real world does not have grade inflation. Poor performance will be penalized once you leave

school.

16. Television gives a misleading view of reality. In real life, people postpone gratification and attach value to work, sacrifice, self-improvement, and service to family, friends, and the community at large.

17. Babies, pets and children often bring stress to a marriage (although that wasn't at all true in the case of you three girls).

18. A successful marriage is hard work (and shouldn't be confused with Hollywood fueled images), and running a home is often grinding.

19. Learning in life occurs predominantly outside of schools.

20. Never take political stability, freedom and democracy for granted.

So there you have it — twenty rules to help ground you in reality. Not that you three need them. Mommy and I think you have a good grasp of what is required in life to succeed. Anyway, I hope you enjoy them.

My treasures, I love you. In fact, I adore you! And I can't wait to get home.

All my love,
Daddy, the list maker
XXXOOO

Wednesday, October 27, 1999

My precious loves, Kimmie, Tina, and Jenny,

As you know, I am away at a senior staff retreat in Cumberland, Maryland. It will be a lot of fun, I will learn a lot, and I will have a wonderful opportunity to get to know my colleagues on the NWF staff.

I remember the first time I ever gave a speech. I was about eight years old. One day at our school, we had an outside speaker. Just before the speaker arrived, my teacher, Mr. Murphy, who I liked enormously, asked me to give a "vote of thanks" when the speaker finished his presentation.

I was terrified! I had no idea what to say or do. My stomach churned and knotted. I would have done anything to escape the agony I was feeling. The last thing on earth I wanted was to feel hundreds of eyes on me as I struggled to say something vaguely coherent.

The time came. I was suffering. I felt barely conscious, yet I also felt horribly self-conscious. I scrambled to my feet, face crimson, blurted out something, realized I had no idea if what I said was OK or not, and quickly sat down. My "speech" lasted no more than five or ten seconds. I heard applause for the speaker as though through a mist. My mini nightmare was over.

Every experience holds a vital lesson. Painful experiences teach us (if we are wise) to grow. The worst thing is to suffer and not learn from it.

Bumps in life's road are often blessings in disguise. If everything was smooth sailing, we might become complacent. Always look for the lemonade in the lemon. Always learn and grow. Never be a victim. I am still trying to learn this!

My treasures, I love you more than I can say. You are so important to Mommy and me.

Buckets and oodles of love, hugs and kisses,
Daddy
XXXOOO

Thursday, October 28,1999
My darling Kimmie, Tina, and Jenny,
I'll be home tomorrow! Can't wait!

One of my greatest pleasures in life is doing things with you girls. Driving you to school, going to the library, watching a memorable movie with you, watching one of your games, giving you a hug, cooking with you, cleaning up the house with you, talking, arguing, admiring something you have created, helping you with an essay, telling you the meaning of a word, sharing a joke, telling you a story, making you laugh, giving you useful advice (I'm not sure that ever happens!), shopping with you, trying a new exercise with you, pointing out an interesting article in the paper to you, and so on.

Having fun with you could involve going to the Kennedy Center or something big like that, but I get deep satisfaction and pleasure from doing small, simple things with you. Here is a lovely poem a friend recently sent me that I like very much:

If I Had My Child to Raise Over Again

If I had my child to raise all over again,
I'd finger-paint more, and point the fingers less.
I would do less correcting and more connecting.
I'd take my eyes off my watch, and watch with my eyes.
I would care to know less and know to care more.
I'd take more hikes and fly more kites.
I'd stop playing serious, and seriously play.
I would run through more fields and gaze at more stars.
I'd do more hugging and less tugging.
I'd build self-esteem first, and the house later.
I would be firm less often, and affirm much more.
I'd teach less about the love of power,
And more about the power of love.

By Diane Loomans
from Condensed Chicken Soup for the Soul
Copyright 1996 by Jack Canfield, Mark Victor, Hansen & Patty Hansen

My loves, I thank you for all you have taught me and all the lessons I have learned from being your Dad. I adore you!

Dad

XXXOOO

Tuesday, December 7, 1999

My darling Kimmie, Tina and Jenny,

I am in Los Angeles tonight for 36 hours of intensive meetings before flying back late on Wednesday night. I am meeting with producers, writers, business partners, donors, Hollywood agents, and others about giant screen films, movies, and other conservation-related projects. It will be a productive and enjoyable trip. I always love meeting new people and seeing old friends. And I love the long flights because I will get an enormous amount of reading and studying done.

Recently, I have been studying a book about time management which really should be called self-management. This book recommended that I keep a time log, i.e., a record of how I spend my day, so that I could better observe where my time goes. As Tina and Jen know, for about a week, I came home after work and read aloud my time log to the family over dinner. This triggered lots of laughter because so much of my time was spent on low priority tasks. With email relentlessly piling up all day, and interruptions occurring constantly, it was obvious from my time log that I was not focusing the bulk of my time on long term strategic goals.

I came to realize that a better way to start my day (instead of jumping to my email immediately) is to start with a blank piece of paper, write down a strategic goal, develop an operational plan to tackle what needs to be done first (or next), and allocate a block of uninterrupted time to work on that goal.

One of my long term strategic goals in my personal life is to let you girls know how special you are. This gets neglected partly because of the flood of "email-type" tasks, like cleaning up the kitchen and taking out the garbage, which we all have to do when we are at home. Also men are often not very good at expressing their feelings. They feel it is unmanly and wimpish. What this means for many daughters is that their Dads never express their feelings to them so it is hard for a daughter to know how much their father loves them and is proud of them. This means that fathers sometimes unintentionally burden their daughters with emotional pain and feelings of inadequacy. I don't want to make that mistake.

One reason I love writing these letters to you when I travel is that they give me a chance to tell you what I would be embarrassed to tell you face to face — which is that you are three incredible children and I am so deeply proud of you. You have enriched my life in extraordinary ways, and I have learned so much from you. You have anchored my life and given it purpose and meaning. You are gifted, purposeful, determined, spirited and hard working. Mommy and I are the luckiest parents in the world!

Everyday I feel so profoundly happy and fulfilled. That is partly due to my job which I love, but it is due primarily to belonging to this family — this family which is so important to me.

Kimmie, Tina and Jenny, I adore you. You are so very special to Mommy and me.

Buckets and oodles of love, hugs and kisses,
Your very own ol' Daddy
XXXOOO

2000

Thursday, January 27, 2000

My darling Tina and Jenny,

As you read this, I am flying across the Atlantic Ocean to see Kim, as well as Granny and Grandpa, Jon, Hannah, Ross, and Tim's family. I know you will look after each other and Mommy while I am away. I know you'll do that because you look out for each other when I am there!

In fact, I am often astonished how you three girls care so much for each other and enjoy each other's success and each other's company. Your loving and comforting letters to Kim while she has been struggling in London are one example of how you look after each other.

This is not my memory of how I grew up with my three brothers in England. We were combative, pugnacious, competitive, argumentative, aggressive, and preferred to be on our own. If fact, we behaved more like grizzly bears (who, for the most part, live isolated lives) than brothers! May be it was just a "boy thing", I don't know. Words like love, intimacy, warmth, friendship, brotherly love, trust, and sharing, were all vaguely foreign to me.

But you girls cherish, respect and admire each other, and you each know how lucky you are to have such precious sisters. However tough the world becomes for you – and there will undoubtedly be times for each of you that will test every ounce of your resilience, courage and strength – you can always count on each other for support and help.

Tina and Jen, I love you, and I miss you.
Your loving Daddy
XXXOOO

Friday, January 28, 2000

My darling Tina and Jenny,

Good luck tomorrow, Jen, in your 2 PM basketball game at Pyle! And good luck, Tina, as you finish up the next issue of *Scribbler*!

In my letter to you yesterday, I mentioned how loving and supportive you three girls are to each other compared to the way my three brothers and I behaved towards each other when we were growing up.

But there is more to it than that. You are not only more loving and respectful to each other, but you three are also (or so it seems to me) better all around than I was at your age. You are more confident, better educated, more creative, more interesting, better at expressing yourselves, wiser, more mature, socially more astute, and with a far greater ability to make and keep friends of high caliber.

One problem I had was that I was always trying to change and improve others instead of myself. More about that in my letter tomorrow night.

Tina and Jenny, you are so precious to Mommy and me. Thanks for all the profound joy you bring us.

I adore you and I window you.
Yer ol' Dad
XXXOOO

Saturday, January 29, 2000
My darling precious Tina and Jenny,
Tonight Kim and I are in Bath with Grandpa and Granny, Jon, Hannah and Ross!

Yesterday I wrote to you about how one thing I have learnt in my life is that it is more important to work on myself than to try to improve others. In other words, it is better to become the change I want to see in the world than lecture other people about what I see as their faults. Any influence I have on others will come from the example I set.

This reminds me of another important life principle for you to remember: You are responsible for your own lives. This is the essence of being proactive. (Now I am going to slightly digress for a moment to tell you something truly profound: True proactiveness comes from seeing how we contribute to our own problems. People often take initiative, thinking that taking action is being proactive, but in fact they are simply being "reactive" and are blind to their own seminal contribution to the difficulties they are facing. Understanding how we ourselves unwittingly contribute to the difficulties and pain we face in our lives, and then taking action to solve the problem, is to reach a new and unusually high level of wisdom. An example might be a parent who takes his child to a therapist because of behavioral problems.)

Anyway, as I say, you are responsible for your own lives. Nobody is going to take care of you. Some people are deluded into thinking that a knight in shining armor will come and rescue them and take care of them for the rest of their lives. This is the hidden (or not so hidden) message in some TV programs and novels. I admire you girls for knowing better than that – for knowing that it is up to you what you make of your lives and what you do and what you accomplish. Don't depend on anybody else either financially, emotionally, or in any other way.

In a way, you each run your own company: Kim Inc., Tina Inc., and Jen Inc. You are the President and Chief Executive Officer of that company, responsible for setting and achieving goals, forming strategic alliances, and undertaking continuous learning to relentlessly build up your intellectual capital. It is up to you to invent and design your own lives so that you live full of joy, optimism, vitality, enthusiasm, love, beauty, learning, loving relationships, and satisfying accomplishments.

I love you!
Daddy
XXXOOO

Sunday, January 30, 2000
My darling Tina and Jen,
I wrote yesterday about the importance of designing your own lives, not playing a role that is imposed on you, and not relying on others in a way which makes you totally dependent on them. However I don't want to leave the impression that other people aren't important.

As you pursue your own unique dreams and compose your own unique lives, your relationships with other people will be pivotal. There is compelling evidence that people who enjoy strong personal ties with friends, family, neighbors and colleagues also enjoy a greatly reduced illness rate. Kim got a visceral sense of the importance of companionship when she started in London by herself a few weeks ago. You only really appreciate something once you lose it (look how we take oxygen for granted).

Positive social encounters, a feeling of "connectedness" with other people you care about and who care about you, and having a variety of relationships (marriage, work, sisters, parents, friendships etc.) will make you less vulnerable to disease, and give you enormous self-confidence. Never rely on any single relationship to meet all your emotional needs.

You girls have very good social skills and have shown sound judgement in picking boyfriends and girlfriends. You are warm and graceful, listen to others, want to help others who need help, smile when you greet people, shake hands and look people in the eye, and are good company. We are very proud of you!

Tina and Jen, I love you and miss you. Can't wait to see you for family dinner on Tuesday evening.

Daddy
XXXOOO

Monday, January 31, 2000
My precious loves, Tina and Jen,
I'll be home tomorrow! I am sad to leave Kim but it will be great to get home.

At Christmas over a family conversation, I promised to send you the following in one of my letters, so here it is (from the United Nations):

If we could shrink the earth's population (1996) to a village with a population of precisely 100 with all the human ratios remaining the same, it would look like this:

1. There would be 57 Asians, 21 Europeans, 14 North, Central, and South Americans, and 8 Africans.

2. 51 would be female; 49 would be male.

3. 70 of the 100 would be nonwhite, 30 white.

4. 70 of the 100 would be non-Christian, 30 Christian.

5. 50 % of the entire village's wealth would be in the hands of 6 people, and all 6 would be citizens of the United States.

6. 70 would be unable to read.

7. 50 would be suffering from malnutrition.

8. 80 would live in substandard housing.

9. 1 would be near death, 1 would be near birth.

10. Only one of the 100 would have a university education.

11. No one would own a computer.

These numbers make you pause and think.

Tina and Jen, I think you are so special, so very, very special. See you tomorrow for dinner! I'll tell you all my adventures in England!

Buckets of hugs and kisses,
Daddy
XXXOOO

Thursday, February 3, 2000

My darling Kimmie, Tina and Jenny,
I am in Pittsburgh for two days to participate in a giant screen film conference focused on education. I will be very active there, and will cement my ties with my many friends and colleagues in the IMAX industry.

I want to encourage all three of you to keep a journal. This can be one you show to friends and family (like the one I keep), or it can be completely private. Today few people (outside therapists) seem to recognize the value of keeping a journal. Here are some of the reasons I think it is important:

1. A journal reminds you that your life is unique, precious and open to redesign.

2. A journal allows you to leave something of immeasurable value to your children and their descendants.

3. A journal helps you quiet your mind, focus your thoughts, and ease anxiety.

4. A journal helps you to know yourself better, and this can help you find inner serenity.

5. A journal simplifies your life by reminding you what you shouldn't be wasting your time on.

6. A journal helps you to express yourself, to write well, and to communicate more powerfully.

7. A journal helps to clarify your goals and to sort out the important from the unimportant, as well as the important from the merely urgent.

8. A journal helps you generate ideas for taking action to solve problems and improve relationships.

9. A journal affirms the reality of your life and gives it meaning and power, and helps you see that your life is an extraordinary and wonderful experience, despite (or perhaps because of) the tough times.

10. A journal reminds you of your accomplishments, which are easy to forget as you relentlessly surge forward to the next challenge once a task is completed.

11. A journal helps you speak out because it provides a safe "nursery" for words and ideas to grow into sentences and paragraphs.

My loves, I do not claim this list of benefits is comprehensive, but I hope you find it persuasive.

I love you. You are so important to me and Mommy. Our lives feel complete with you three in the world with us.

Hugs and kisses,
Dad
XXXOOO

Friday, February 4, 2000
My darling Kim, Tina and Jen,
I will be home tomorrow and can't wait to see you (or at least Tina and Jen because Kim is still in London of course.)

Remember always to act towards others as though this is your last day on earth. My life would have been even more successful if I had learnt this before I was 52! It may take me another 25 years to learn it fully!

I love you more that I can say.
Your ol' letter-writing Dad
XXXOOO

Wednesday, March 15, 2000
My darling Kimmie, Tina and Jenny,
Kim, I hope your week is going well after your lovely four days last weekend in Bath with Granny and Grandpa. Tina, good luck this week finishing up the next issue of *Scribbler*. And Jen, I hope your first soccer practice this season went well tonight.

Today is Uncle Tim's birthday. He is 56.

Last week I received a postcard from Dulwich College asking for financial support. I was there from the ages of nine to eighteen (1956 to 1965). On the back of the postcard was an aerial photo of the school taken on a beautiful fall day. So much happened to me at Dulwich, and as my eyes poured over the details in the photo, memories flooded back, not all of them pleasant.

People from my parents' generation must experience something similar when reading Tom Brokaw's book, *The Greatest Generation*. As you know, I have been listening in the car recently to Tom Brokaw's sequel, *The Greatest Generation Speaks*, which Mommy gave me for Valentine's Day. It is based on letters that Brokaw received after his first book was published. The letters are incredibly moving and poignant. They often brought tears to my eyes. They speak of honor, duty, sacrifice, deprivation, suffering, bravery and accomplishment.

My loves, study history all you can. It will teach you so much about life and how to live. I love you and miss you.

Dad
XXXOOO

Thursday, March 16, 2000
My precious loves,

Kim, you leave today for four days in Paris with Allison's parents. Have a wonderful time! Tina, I hope tennis and *Scribbler* are going well. Jen, enjoy the St. Patrick's dance tomorrow.

Tina, you wrote to me last week that, "so many women give up so much to take care of and raise their kids." You are so right.

I love you.
Dad
XXXOOO

Friday, March 17, 2000
My three loves, Kim, Tina and Jen,
Tina, enjoy your Spring Fling dance tomorrow evening!

Life seems complicated but the things that really matter are simple. I don't claim they are easy or that I am effective at doing them! Anyway, here are a few important things to remember among the seeming confusion and banality of our everyday lives:

1. Not getting what you yearn for is sometimes a wonderful stroke of luck.

2. If you make a mistake, take immediate steps to correct it.

3. Live a good and honorable life so you can look back on your life with pride (and thereby enjoy it a second time).

4. Nothing is more important than a loving atmosphere at home, so make that a priority.

5. Always be honest and courageous. Those are "muscles" that grow stronger the more you use them.

6. Communicate requests, offers and promises clearly.

7. Show people you care about them. Make it a goal to really connect with people and listen to them. Find them doing something right and tell them.

8. Cherish and honor the extraordinary beauty of the natural world.

9. Keep strong and fit through a regular regimen of strength, endurance and flexibility exercises.

10. Develop a good sense of humor and laugh often.

11. When you have a problem, ask, "What did I do to contribute to this problem?" Focus on how you can change yourself rather than looking for fault in others.

12. Maintain detailed goals and constantly reinvent them in new and imaginative ways.

13. Work hard so that you can turn your goals into real accomplishments.

14. Practice extreme self-care so that you are always there for people, especially the people you love

who bring meaning to your life.

15. Eliminate trivia from your life. Focus on what really matters to you.

16. Relentlessly network!

17. Read voraciously and teach yourself to be curious and to ask questions.

My loves, I am maybe ten percent up the learning curve on these ideas!

I love you and adore you, and think you are each so unique and special. I am forever grateful to have such talented, beautiful, loving, hardworking, determined and successful daughters. Thank you for being you.

Dad
XXXOOO

Saturday, March 18, 2000
To my three wonderful daughters, Kim, Tina and Jen,
I LOVE YOU AND CAN'T WAIT TO GET HOME!!!

Buckets and oodles of love, hugs and kisses,
Your own ol' Dad,
XXXOOO

Wednesday, May 17, 2000
My darling Kimmie, Tina and Jenny,
As you know, I am in LA for two hectic days to speak at an IMAX conference and to have a slew of meetings with producers, directors, investors, and donors. They are all super people and I am looking forward to the trip with great anticipation. It will be fun! I have prepared very carefully for a panel that I am moderating on Thursday morning. My goal is to do the best job possible so that the audience not only learns something useful but enjoys the experience too.

Tina and Jen, thank you for last week. You were a delight to look after and to be with while Mommy was in London with Kim. Caring for you like that fulfills one of my greatest goals – to be a good Dad.

You might sometimes wonder how being a good Dad fits into everything else going on in my life. Enclosed is my life plan to answer that question. I used to call this document my Personal Mission Statement. Throughout my life I have prepared plans like the one enclosed. This is just the latest draft. It is never "finished" or "complete", but rather a "work in progress". Hey, I'm a work in progress too!

I am not satisfied with my life plan, but I see it as a good start. I am constantly improving it, strengthening it, revising it, and polishing it. I welcome your thoughts on it. Thanks.

I urge you to develop your own life plans. I think you will find the process enormously helpful. It will help give your lives focus, power, enthusiasm, and direction Your life plans will likely look different from mine, and that is great. You are each unique and will create your own distinctive and singular lives.

I was going to tell you the steps in creating a successful life plan but you can deduce those yourselves by reading mine. And, of course, there isn't only one right way to do it. Part of any life planning process is to identify the areas in your life you are going to continually focus on and make improvements in (such as health and fitness).

The most important thing to realize (and I am still learning this) is that a daily "to do" list is hopelessly inadequate. You can only plan your day if you know what you are planning it for. That is why it is so important to articulate your fundamental purpose in life, and to describe in writing why you are here on earth. Every day you want to make massive progress on achieving your goals and fulfilling the compelling vision you have for your life as described in your life plan. If you don't do that, you will find yourself frequently filled with ennui, frustration, and lethargy.

One of the baffling enigmas about people is that there is often a mismatch between what is most important to them and how they spend their time. A life plan can help them close the gap. It can also help people to focus on results instead of getting hung up (as I so often do) on a "to do" list.

The goal is to achieve a life of amazing results and extraordinary fulfillment, and to thrive on the challenges and difficulties that will inevitably be thrown at you. You want to lead lives that are characterized by exuberance, autonomy, enthusiasm, love, and deep friendships. You are each well on your way to doing that, and to leading lives that allow you to discover everything of which you are capable.

My loves, I adore you. Have a great two days while I am away. There *might* be a letter for you tomorrow night!

Your greying, balding, advice-giving, old fossilized fogey of a doufus Dodo bird Dad.
XXXOOO

Enclosure

Thursday, May 18, 2000

My precious treasures, Kimmie, Tina, and Jenny,
HAPPY BIRTHDAY TINA FOR TOMORROW!!!!!!!!!! I'll be racing back from Los Angeles so I can be home for your birthday, even though I know you have a self-defense class and will be out in the evening. (I am so proud of you for taking that class.) I am going to leave the IMAX conference early but you are worth it Tina! We will celebrate your birthday on Saturday (along with Jen's) with brunch at the Pancake House, a treasure hunt, and a hunt for dollars (wow, 18 of them!)

And Jen, have a super birthday party tomorrow night with your friends! I'll be there!

Last night I left you the latest draft of my life plan. Some people looking at that document might say, "What is the point of doing that? There is so little I control. I am just trying to survive while being buffeted by all the events around me. I cannot do anything about my genetic makeup, my environment, my parents, my siblings, the weather, the traffic, my boss, my job, my coworkers, world events, volcanoes, hurricanes, what's on television, urban sprawl, logging, gun violence, the demands of other people on me, other people's behavior, the American Constitution, history, geography, and so on."

Good point. It is useful to make a distinction between what you can control and what you can't, and focus on the former. In life, there are many things you are concerned about but cannot control or do anything about (such as disastrous flooding in Bangladesh). One of the keys to a successful life is to focus your energies in areas where you can make a difference i.e., where you have control and influence. After reading the above paragraph giving that long list of things you have no control over, you may be wondering what you *can* control. It is a longer list than you might at first realize. For example:

–What you think, say and do: You are totally responsible for what you think, say or do.

–The values you choose to live by: Your ideals and your beliefs are for you to choose. They are not (or should not be) imposed on you or selected for you.

–Your mood, attitude, and state: You can choose the mood you want to be in, regardless of what is happening around you.

–The friends with which you spend time.

–Your essential physical health: Sure, some health issues are a matter of genetics, or exposure to industrial toxics. But much of our health is heavily influenced by things we <u>do</u> control, such as strengthening exercises, endurance conditioning, stretching, breathing well, drinking enough water, eating healthy foods, keeping away from drugs and alcohol, getting enough sleep, having regular check-ups, not smoking, and so on.

–Your financial situation: You can control whether you spend less than you earn so you are constantly building up your savings for a rainy day.

–Your time: You choose how to spend your time and how much to allot to various activities. People who watch television mindlessly, shop at malls for hours, spend time on astrology, sunbathe for long periods, watch pointless movies, or read trashy novels, have no right to complain of being overwhelmed with commitments they cannot meet.

–Your legacy: You control the way you lead your life, your actions, the knowledge and wisdom that share with others, and the example you give to others. This is the gift you leave those you love when you die.

–Your work: You have much more control over this than you realize, assuming you perform in your job and work hard and effectively. If you are good at what you do, people will bend over backwards to give you what you want so they won't lose you.

–Your goals: You choose your own goals and can control this completely. It is true that if you don't have a clear set of goals, it is most likely that you will end up working to achieve someone else's goals, and that isn't healthy unless it is a choice you have freely made.

I do not claim that the above list is comprehensive. It is just what occurs to me as I sit here writing this letter to you. You control many other things, including how you dress, whether you are clean and well groomed, whether you are organized and can quickly retrieve key documents, the clarity and vigor of your writing, your presentation skills, and so on.

A life plan helps you focus on what you can control and influence, and thus where you can make massive improvements *without needing permission from anyone else*. We are truly free when we focus on those areas. And I believe that when we work on those areas where we have control, then we gain influence. This makes it more likely that we will be able to influence situations that before we thought we had no influence over.

Kim, Tina, and Jen, you are so special. Mommy and I love you each so much. You give so much to us (such as the opportunity to write these letters to you) and we feel so incredibly lucky to have you as our daughters.

Happy 18th birthday again Tina for tomorrow!!! Hugs and kisses to all of you. Kim, see you on June 1!! Good luck getting those papers completed. And give our love to Cat and Alison.

Yer ol' Dad
XXXOOO

Tuesday, June 20, 2000

My darling Kimmie, Tina and Jenny,

We are all over the place! Kim is at home working for the Washington Post. Tina is in Maine on her Outward Bound course with Serena. Jen is with me in Florida. Mommy is at home taking care of everything. Granny comes home today from the hospital. When we are all over the place like this, it reminds me how precious the last few days have been when we have all been together...especially the family meetings and the meals we have shared together.

I am going to be working this week while in Florida with Jenny. None of you girls have ever asked my why I have devoted my life to working in the non-profit environmental arena protecting the natural world. But I expect you sometimes wonder why I didn't become a naval architect (the discipline in which I was initially trained) or some other more conventional career like businessman, lawyer or accountant. Well, first of all, it is a lot more fun. Secondly, I wouldn't be happy unless I was working for a noble cause, and I believe fighting for an unpolluted environment and to protect the wonders of nature is a noble cause.

Some people become environmentalists because they have a special encounter of some sort, or a parent who passes on their love of the outdoors to them, or some situation which encourages them in that direction. In my case, I always wanted to do something that would improve society, even if it meant earning less money. Social change was my goal. That idea got me fired up. Earning big bucks never did, and the idea of working 9 to 5 in some bureaucracy filled me with ennui and disdain.

I might have ended up (and still might, who knows) working to prevent child abuse or to fight for women's rights, but my training in engineering (at University College London and in the Royal Navy) and public policy (at Harvard), led me to energy conservation and environmental protection. And energy conservation was a hot topic in the 70s because of the 1973 Arab oil embargo, so there were new job opportunities in that area.

I love the natural world (wildlife, trees, mountains, birds, flowers) and preserving the planet for future generations is vitally important. I don't want you and your children to live in a world with degraded ecosystems that cannot sustain you. I want you to have clean air and water, abundant wildlife, and a healthy and decent environment. Global warming, the depletion of the ozone layer, the spread of toxic chemicals, the destruction of forests, wetlands and oceans...all these things are going on and need to be stopped and reversed. That is the mission of the National Wildlife Federation, and that is why I love working there.

My loves, I love you. Good luck this week, Tina, enduring the rugged challenges of Hurricane Island. Good luck tonight, Kim, at the White House state dinner. And Jen, I hope you are having fun with me down here in Florida!

Buckets of love, hugs and kisses,
Dad
XXXOOO

Wednesday, June 21, 2000
My precious loves, Kim, Tina and Jen,
Jen and I are enjoying water parks, Sea World, and Discovery Cove in Florida. Tina, I am dying to know how you are enjoying Outward Bound. And Kim, how did your story in today's Washington Post turn out about the State dinner last night at the White House?!

All your lives you will face new challenges. The more you face, the more skillful you will become at handling them with grace and courage. It is almost like a muscle. The more you practice exercising meeting new challenges, the more you will enjoy the experience and realize that you can become good at it. Tina, you have set for yourself many new challenges this summer, and have risen to all of them, showing great focus and determination. One huge new challenge coming up for you will be starting at Dartmouth this September. You will find that all the new experiences you have recently put yourself through (skydiving, self defense, Outward Bound, singing in public) will help you enormously at Dartmouth.

Kim can tell you about how she felt starting at Amherst three years ago. It is likely that one of the first negative feelings you will experience is panic and incompetence as you get to know your fellow students. They will bowl you over with their self-confidence, huge talents, assertiveness, and knowledge. What you won't see is that they perceive you in the same way.

By the way, I am going to focus in this letter on the traumas of becoming a freshman, not the excitement, pleasures, and enormous fun that you may also experience. Another negative feeling you may have is loneliness, homesickness, and even a sense of being abandoned. You will sometimes feel frightened and depressed. One thing you will never know is the full extent of the suffering of all the other freshman. They are having more difficulties than you can ever imagine. One of the ways to surmount your own challenges is to help those around you whom you discover (beneath the facade of self confidence and the veneer of control) are in pain.

At Dartmouth (or is it Princeton?!) you will have to learn new jargon, new buzz words, and new idioms. You will have to find new friends, and have to get used to being at the bottom of a new hierarchy after being at the top at Holton. You will have to decide what to eat, when to study, when to sleep, whether to ask your roommate to turn off her raucous music so you can sleep, and scores of other decisions that can be draining and make you yearn for the comfort, security, peacefulness, privacy, luxuries, and rituals of home.

In short, Tina, being a college freshman can be overwhelming and scary. Virtually every freshman goes through periods of panic. On top of all this, the academic work can be extremely challenging. You will frequently ask yourself whether you will be able to get through it all. Well, Tina (and you, Jen, when it comes to your turn to go to college) you <u>can</u> and you <u>will</u> survive. In fact, you will flourish, and emerge from the experience all the stronger and with an even bigger intrinsic capability to handle new situations with dignity, courage and verve.

Each of you has tremendous determination, and Mommy and I have total confidence that you can meet any challenge thrown at you and succeed. There is <u>nothing</u> that you cannot do. You can handle <u>anything</u> that comes your way.

By the way, a little technique I use when I'm in new situations where I want to produce an outstanding performance from myself, is that I write down key words that summarize how I want to be perceived by other key players who are interacting with me, and the key outcomes I want to achieve from whatever the situation is. So, for example, when I went to England last February for a few days to see Kim (before Granny became sick), I scribbled in a notebook the following:

> Be alert, fun, attentive, energetic, tell stories, collect stories, be affectionate, keep fit, read extensively, do email, spoil Kimmie, listen deeply and actively, be totally present and "in the moment", use humor and be funny, get plenty of sleep, keep a journal, have a good posture, radiate inner peace and life mastery, be in a mood of humility and also serenity, reflect authority and total self-confidence, learn all I can and keep notes, be cheerful, smile easily, be enthusiastic, take photos, be warm, praise others, expand my network, be a leader, make contacts, help others.

These were just quick notes to myself as I flew across the Atlantic to see Kim, my parents, my brothers, friends and business colleagues. They were not for any one's eyes but my own.

Kim, Tina and Jen, I adore you and am so grateful for everything you have given me in my life. You will never know the full extent of that gift.

I hope you are having a super week!

Yer ol' greying, over-the-hill, balding father.
Dad
XXXOOO

Thursday, June 22, 2000
My darling daughters, Kim, Tina and Jen,
Jen and I will be home tomorrow from Florida! Can't wait to see Mommy and Kim, and can't wait to see you, Tina, on Saturday week when I pick you up from Dulles!

In my letter yesterday, I wrote about the challenges of being a college freshman. There are lots of traumas you will have to face, from drunk colleagues to selfish roommates to freezing cold weather, but one of the most essential challenges to master is the central one of successfully getting through the rigors of the academic courses. Being a successful student is simply a matter of following some basic principles. It has little to do with intelligence or IQ, but everything to do with <u>how</u> you work. Knowing how to make the most of your innate abilities is the real key to success.

You will probably expect me to say that hard work is the key because I have always urged you to work hard and not waste time. But it is important to qualify this term. Working hard is good, but working smart is better. Sometimes people think they are working hard because they spend long hours at their desk, staring at a book. What really matters is what you actually do when you are sitting at your desk.

Here is a ten-point guide to being a successful student (at Westland, Dartmouth or Amherst):

1. When you work, make it your top priority: Don't let yourself get distracted by a colleague dropping by, or by a frivolous TV show. Nothing is more important to you at that time than focusing on your work. (And when I say "work", I am including vital "work" like writing to your lonely parents who are pining for news of their middle daughter!)

2. Put aside time every day to work, ideally at the same time so you become accustomed to it: In other words, study consistently. Whatever you focus on consistently, you will become good at. This is how I learned to stand on my hands, and why I have a big vocabulary. I focused on those areas over periods of twenty or thirty years, and eventually became competent.

3. Learn all the time: Even though you might be jogging with a friend, or having dinner with someone, don't ever lose the chance to discuss your work (or their work) with them. Learn something every day. Never miss an opportunity to explain things to other people. If you want to learn something, then teach it to someone else.

4. Be an active reader: You will retain a lot more from a book if you ask yourself questions before you start to read it. I learned this in a speed reading course I took in my early twenties in London. Glance over the contents page, the index, the cover and the back page. Why are you reading this book? What are you looking for? What do you hope to learn? What else does it relate to that you have already read? Spend a few minutes thinking hard about the answers to these questions, jot down your thoughts in writing, and you will be amazed to find how that changes the experience of reading that book, and how it makes it much more valuable. And then as you read the book, constantly ask yourself questions. If you can't think of any questions, simply keep asking yourself Why?

5. Participate in class: At first you may participate in class because you know it will impress the professor or teacher, and you do it because you want to get good grades. Whatever motivates you to start participating in class is fine, but your fundamental goal is to gain a deep understanding and to make yourself intellectually curious. Participating in class will help to give you a dedication to, and love of, lifelong learning. And in the short term, participating in class (which primarily means asking penetrating questions) will give you mastery of the material being taught (which hopefully will lead to good grades).

6. Do more than is requested of you by your teacher: One reason I consistently got the highest marks in exams when I was studying engineering at London University, is that I did more work than anyone else. For example, there were two classes studying stress mechanics. I was in one of them. I soon found out that the professor gave different assignments to the two groups. Because I was determined to do better than anyone else (probably partly to try and impress my father who was then Head of the Royal Corps of Naval Constructors), I resolved to do both sets of homework. When the exam results

354

came out, everybody thought I was brilliant because my marks were way above even the second scoring student. I knew better of course. I had just worked smarter. The point is that if your teacher asks you to read twenty pages, read double that number.

7. Don't procrastinate when assigned a challenging paper: Everybody procrastinates to some extent (and in fact, knowing when it is useful to "put things off" is a key skill in managing your time wisely). But when you have a paper you know you have to write, immediately break it down into doable subtasks, and set deadlines for those mini-projects. Draw up a timetable so you can complete the project early and give yourself time to review and polish it. Freshmen go through agony when a paper is due in less than a week and they haven't started on it. Don't let that pain and suffering happen to you! Feel the glorious liberation which comes from "breaking the back" of a project and knowing that you are going to get it done and that the professor is going to be delighted. Procrastination can also be overcome by incantations in which you forcefully remind yourself of the pleasure to be experienced from getting the project finished, and the pain of not starting immediately.

8. Be a skillful note-taker: What your teacher emphasizes in class is what you are most likely to be tested on in the exam.

9. Simulate the exam when reviewing the work: When you are preparing for an exam or test, don't just look over your textbooks and notes. Instead, simulate the test in the most realistic way possible. For example, make up possible test questions and try to answer them in writing.

10. Be organized: File everything with a eye towards retrieval. You don't want to waste any time searching for missing papers or information. As the great Ben Franklin said, have a place for everything and put everything in its place.

If you follow these fundamentals, then you will not only succeed in your studies, but there is nothing stopping you succeeding in your social life, in sports and athletics, in giving presentations, and in every arena of your life in which you want to excel.

My treasures, I hope you can put the advice in this letter to work for you to help you achieve everything you want in your lives as you continue your journeys of becoming ever more responsible, loving, resilient, optimistic, capable, strong, successful, fulfilled and contributing members of society.

I adore you! I love you! I love you more than all the atoms in the world and more than all the specks of sand in the universe!

Dad
XXXOOO

Sunday, July 9, 2000
My darling daughters, Kim and Jenny (and Tina too, even though she is with me!),
As you know, Lauren Bregman, Tina and I are in Jackson Hole, Wyoming, looking up at the magnificent, rugged peaks of the Grand Tetons. The three of us are 7000 feet above sea level and staying at Lost Creek Ranch. The area is noted for its beautiful scenery and abundance of wildlife – bison, antelope, mountain sheep and goat, elk, deer, mountain lion, wolf, black bear, and grizzly bear. We will be horseback riding, rafting on the Snake River, hiking in Yellowstone, learning about the history of the wild west, watching a rodeo, and much more.

It is one of the special privileges of being your Dad that I can take you girls on trips to show you the world. My goal is to create great childhood memories and experiences for you that you will treasure, and which will enrich your lives.

Ever since Mommy suggested -- over twenty years ago -- the idea of having children (a notion that was bizarre and alien to me at the time!) I have been studying what it means to be an effective father. The job requires a set of skills that I largely lacked when you, Kim, arrived on December 12, 1979. As a Dad, I have made mistakes, but hopefully will continue to become better and better at being a competent father.

Nothing else I will ever do will have the transforming impact on me that you three girls have had. Having children has taught me how to have complete responsibility for another person and to learn how to love and bond in the deepest way.

My goal as a father is to be an outstanding Dad, and to give you everything of myself that I can. I always want to be there for you whenever you need me, to express my love for you (so that I am not, like some Dads, "emotionally distant"), to give you all the support you deserve, to catch you doing things "right", and to encourage you to solve your own problems. I am still working towards these goals!

Kim, Tina and Jen, Mommy and I love you so much.
Daddy
XXXOOO

Monday, July 10, 2000
My darling Kim, Tina and Jenny,
As you know, Granny is home, and Grandpa is devotedly looking after her. I will visit them later this month. Granny is 82 and Grandpa is 86.

When I was about eight years old, I couldn't sleep one night. I was very worried about something (I can't remember what.) I desperately needed comforting and some kind of reassurance that I could handle whatever was troubling me. Granny instinctively knew something was wrong and that I needed attention. This wasn't easy for her because she was distracted with her own concerns. Her acknowledgment of my needs was comfort in itself. Then she snuggled with me in her bed (Grandpa must have been away), and then tucked me into my own bed, all the time saying soothing words that brought me comfort. Granny put my pillow comfortably around my head and shoulders, and I quickly fell asleep, my worries (whatever they were) blissfully extinguished for a few hours.

Mothers are incredibly special. You three girls are so lucky to have Mommy as your Mom. No children could have a more loving, devoted, caring and effective mother. Mom is the best!

I love you more than I can say. I hope you are having a great week!
Daddy
XXXOOO

Tuesday, July 11, 2000
My precious loves, Kim, Tina and Jen,

One of the best books I have read recently is *Tuesdays with Morrie: An Old Man, A Young Man, and Life's Greatest Lesson* by Mitch Albom. Morrie is Professor Morrie Schwarz, who was Mitch Albom's teacher and mentor in college. Mitch rediscovered Morrie in the last months of the older man's life, and wrote this moving book about their relationship and about Morrie's wisdom. I enjoyed the book so much that I found myself deliberately reading it slowly, relishing it word by word, prolonging the tingling pleasure I was getting from reading it.

As Morrie lay dying, he and Mitch Albom talked about death, regrets, emotions, aging, crying, love, marriage, fear, forgiveness, the meaning of life, happiness, suffering, compassion, grief, the importance of the family, and saying goodbye. Morrie was intent on proving that dying need not be a useless, joyless, and draining experience. It doesn't have to be embarrassing, undignified and humorless. (Of course, sometimes, sadly, it does have to be this way.)

One of the things Morrie did was to have a "living funeral" which I think is a grand idea. A "living funeral" means you celebrate the person while they are still alive.

Tuesdays with Morrie is also about the transformation of Mitch Albom from a self-absorbed workaholic whose prime goals were earning lots of money and acquiring all the material trappings of success, to a person with a much deeper understanding of what really matters. Throughout the book, Mitch asks himself again and again, *What happened to me?* What he meant by this question is what happened to all the ideals and dreams he had when he was young, and to the ideas he and Morrie discussed at such length when he was a student in college.

Kim, Tina and Jen, this letter comes with all my love. You are so very special to me. I love you.

Dad
XXXOOO

Wednesday, July 12, 2000
My darling Kimmie, Tina and Jenny,
I have noticed that learning is never a smooth, linear, upward sloping line. Learning involves starts and stops, and progress is mixed in with many setbacks and regressions. This is why persistence is one of the hallmarks of a successful person. The unsuccessful person gives up after a setback because they think they are failing to make progress. In fact they are not failing but rather experiencing the reality of what learning is. It is not a smooth upward slope, but rather a jagged up and down line with an overall upward slope. You know this from learning tennis, and I know it from spending twenty years learning how to stand on my hands. Persistence and the determination never to give up are crucially important if you want to succeed.

Learning is rarely easy. One of the things I am learning is the importance of feeling grateful. My life is blessed in so many ways. Yet I so often breezily take those blessings for granted. Here are some of the many things I am profoundly grateful for:

—My wonderful, loving and irreplaceable wife Gail.

—My extraordinarily accomplished, beautiful and loving daughters.

—Living in a society based on the values of political freedom, liberty, economic opportunity, the right of the individual, the rule of law, and equal justice.

—The beauty and wonders of the natural world.

—Being in perfect health.

—Having a fulfilling career working for a noble cause.

—The opportunity to constantly learn and improve.

If ever I feel depressed or dejected (which is very rare nowadays) I think of all the things I am grateful for. The list is massive.

Taking things for granted is one of my major weaknesses. It was this observation which made me incorporate "encouragement" into the agenda for our weekly family meetings. As you know, this is where we take turns to catch each other doing something "right." Otherwise it is too easy to focus on what is wrong.

When Jen and I were in Orlando recently at Discovery Cove, we learned how they train dolphins. There is nothing magical about it, although the end results are astonishing. When a dolphin does something the trainer wants, the trainer rewards it ("reinforces the behavior") with food and affection. When the dolphin does something the trainer isn't looking for, the trainer simply ignores the dolphin.

I found this fascinating because it is precisely the reverse of what many parents (including me) do. When a child does something right (for example, makes their bed, wipes the kitchen counter, argues constructively, closes the door quietly, comes to a meal on time, does her homework, is loving to a sibling) parents will often ignore the child. When a child does something wrong (for example, leaves their bed unmade, spills milk on the kitchen counter, talks back disrespectfully, slams a door, is late for family dinner, doesn't do her homework, is mean to a sibling) parents will start yelling at the child. I have made this mistake many times and continue to do so.

My loves, your Dad is a slow learner, but I will keep on learning all I can!

I adore you!
Dad
XXXOOO

Thursday, July 13, 2000
My darling Kim, Tina and Jenny,
I am so proud of each of you. Kim, you are doing so well at the *Washington Post* in a very challenging job. Tina, you showed courage, nerve and self-discipline during your recent two week Outward Bound course on Hurricane Island. Jen, you have made a great start to a memorable summer with a lovely mix of tennis, travel, friends, exercise, earning money, and reading. I love the way you are using your summer notebook to maximize your enjoyment and sense of fulfillment.

Each of you shows a remarkable maturity and strength of character for your age. You have achieved success and will continue to do so, experiencing along the way success's three companions:

disappointments, frustrations and setbacks. And you will also experience how apparent failures can often be turned into new opportunities for growth and learning.

The reason you will have great success in your lives is that you each set goals, are determined to achieve them, and you have learned to delay gratification in order to achieve important long term goals. And you have each learned that all great achievements, whether it is building a family, raising children, writing a book, getting all A's, producing a film, or sending a man to the moon, require incredible hard work and self-discipline over a long period of time. That sounds old fashioned in this age of instant gratification, but I don't care. Without an outstanding work ethic, meaningful, lasting success is impossible.

Beyond hard work, other keys to success, not in any particular order, are:

—Set demanding goals for yourself.

—Have a purpose for each day.

—Have a positive attitude, free of toxic anxieties.

—Communicate clearly, especially requests, offers and promises.

—Constantly learn.

—Avoid frivolous, non-essential activities.

—Keep your commitments, and be totally reliable and dependable.

—Learn from role models, and find mentors in each of the different domains of your life.

—Thrive on pressure, and don't confuse pressure with stress.

—Be relentlessly persistent.

—Rid yourself of clutter and relish the feelings of liberation which come with being organized.

—Share credit.

—Learn to be an effective public speaker.

—Be enthusiastic.

—Accumulate power.

—Read relentlessly.

—Be driven by your values, goals and commitments, rather than your moods, circumstances or family history.

–Build on your strengths.

–Keep a journal because a life worth living is worth recording.

–Implement the Pareto Principle (the so-called 80-20 rule): 80 percent of the value comes from 20 percent of the items, while the remaining 20 percent of the value comes from 80 percent of the items. Concentrate on the high value 20 percent and master them.

–Work in a profession which you feel is honorable and contributes to healing and helping society.

–Be fiercely creative and audaciously imaginative in your vision for what you plan to achieve, whether it is for a particular project or for your five year goals.

–Strive for excellence in everything you do.

–Learn from challenges and setbacks.

–Keep on reminding yourself of the fundamental values that are the bedrock of a good and glorious life: integrity, self-discipline, fairness, honesty, service, courage, patience, compassion, responsibility, generosity, hard work, creativity, persistence, tenacity, passion, joyfulness, serenity, love, meaning, adventure, and purposefulness.

Kim, Tina and Jen, you three loves are well on the way to understanding the basic keys to success and putting them to work for you. Success in life can be achieved by consistently applying these fundamental principles. There is no short cut or quick fix.

You are so precious to Mommy and me! We love you more than all the tea in China!

Dad
XXXOOO

Friday, July 14, 2000
My adorable lovebugs, Kimmie, Tina and Jenny,
Last Friday, I took Kim out for dinner to Mongolian BBQ. Jen was at the shore with Mommy, and Tina was still at her Outward Bound Course. During dinner, Kim asked me if I had ever felt insecure in any of my jobs. In other words, had I ever experienced self-doubt and questioned whether I was up to the task. The answer is yes.

It is true that now I am incredibly lucky: At NWF, I have remarkable autonomy, huge resources, significant power, an ennobling cause, and wonderfully supportive colleagues. But it hasn't always been that way. You see me now as supremely self-confident, and it is natural for you to think that I have always been that way. I haven't. I have had to work hard and have had to strive relentlessly for continual improvement. What you observe is the result of my learning from making lots of mistakes.

When I was younger, I occasionally suffered from depression, ennui, anxiety, self-doubt, loneliness, purposelessness, and melancholy. I was sometimes insecure, uncommunicative, self-conscious, bored, and withdrawn. And you can be quite sure that I had lots of people and circumstances to blame for these afflictions! (Of course, I only had one person to blame, and that was me.)

Over time, I discovered one sure-fire solution to my suffering, and that was to find and articulate the purpose of my life. Without doing this, my life seemed like it was drifting and anchorless. Without thinking deeply about the purpose of my life and writing it down, my mood could become disagreeable and even obnoxious. On the other hand, when I searched for meaning and purpose in my life, then that process of actively designing my life began to bring me some inner peace.

Because of this, every year since I was a young man, I have put time aside to articulate the deepest driving force in my life in order to rediscover my passion for living. The goal was always to describe in writing my ultimate vision for my life. Here are some of the questions I grapple with:

–What is the purpose of my life?

–What is my mission?

–Who do I want to be?

–What do I want my life to stand for?

–What do I want to accomplish?

–What do I want to give?

–What do I want to create?

–What do I want from my life?

–What are my specific dreams for the future?

–Why do I want to do this?

–Why do I want to be this kind of person?

–What will it give me and what will it give my loved ones?

Of course, falling in love and marrying Gail, and then having you three girls, gave my life a transcendent and revitalizing purpose and meaning that transformed me.

Being able to clearly envision your passions, dreams, and purposes in life is the foundation for leading a fulfilled, energetic, and vital existence. I have found no better way to chase away feelings of lethargy and melancholy. Without a focus on a central goal, a life can be squandered on small things. Try getting up on a Saturday without a plan. By the end of the day, you will feel lethargic, uncomfortable, and depressed. Nothing has been accomplished. What is true for a random Saturday is true for life because each day is like a mini life.

In *Tuesdays with Morrie*, Morrie asks Mitch, "What if today was your last day on earth?" Morrie then goes on to say;

> Our culture doesn't encourage you to think about such things until you're about to die. We're so wrapped up with egotistical things, career, family, having enough money, meeting the mortgage, getting a new car, fixing the radiator when it breaks – we're involved in trillions of little acts just to keep going. So we don't get into the habit of standing back and looking at our lives and saying, Is this all? Is this all I want? Is something missing? You need someone to probe you in that direction.

Kim, Tina and Jen, you are the most special people to Mommy and me in the whole world. We love you!

Yer ol' Dad
XXXOOO

Saturday, July 15, 2000
My precious loves, Kim and Jenny,
Tina and I will be home early tomorrow morning, may be even before you are up!! I can't wait to see you!! If our plane is on time, we should be home around 10 or 10:30 AM. We will be tired because we will have been up all night flying home from Salt Lake City vis Atlanta.

Buckets of love, hugs and kisses,
Cowboy Dad
XXXOOO

September 4, 2000

DAD'S 70 RULES FOR SUCCESS

by Chris Palmer (a.k.a. Dad)

September 4, 2000

Work hard
Set goals
Pursue excellence
Discern fundamentals
Show up
Live passionately
Take risks
Smile easily
Pay attention
Help others
Make friends
Battle injustice
Obtain feedback
Love deeply
Write daily

Keep healthy
Stand tall
Study relentlessly
Get help
Be indomitable
Cherish sisters
Ask questions
Don't quit
Make offers
Stay focused
Laugh often
Have vitality
Be bold
Have fun
Read voraciously
Find meaning
Keep promises
Avoid TV
Find mentors
Be indefatigable
Enjoy jokes
Be honorable
Take initiative
Delay gratification
Listen actively
Welcome failure
Get coaching
Anticipate breakdowns
Manage moods
Practice courage
Show affection
Be considerate
Acquire role models
Practice self-discipline
Spend wisely
Show enthusiasm
Feel gratitude
Seize opportunities
Nurture friendships
Be joyful
Avoid gossip
Relish humor
Act fearlessly
Invent happiness
Appreciate nature
Dream big
Drink water

Exercise daily
Seek power
Have integrity
Value family
Celebrate success
Rebound quickly
Speak effectively
Praise specifically
Call home!!

Tuesday, September 12, 2000
My darling Kimmie, Tina and Jenny,
It is Uncle Jer's birthday today. He would have been 58.

Didn't we have a good summer?! So many great memories! Your help with my book, Lost Creek Ranch and the Grand Tetons, Erin and Leigh, Outward Bound/rock climbing/the solo, Orlando/killer whales/dolphins, Clinton's eyes staring through the thick glass bottom, Sara's camp, all of you earning money, book agents calling, Washington Post articles, tubing, time with wonderful friends, Sunday brunches at the Pancake House, Cape May, Jen's 30 books, zipping along on the scooter, jogging on the bike path, lots of ex-boy friends, Kim's return from England, Tina's graduation from Holton, tennis camp at Edgemoor, toddler Jake, skydiving, weekly family meetings, celebrating my birthday, and many more delightful things recorded in my journal.

Thanks so much, my loves, for making the summer so enchanting for Mommy and me.

As you know, I am off to Frankfurt, Germany to attend (and be very active at) the Giant Screen Theater Association Annual Conference. I will give several presentations there and I am looking forward to it with great enthusiasm.

Tina, good luck at Orientation tomorrow! Kim, good luck with your exciting thesis! Jen, good luck with getting on the Westland softball team!

You are the most wonderful daughters in the world, and Mommy and I feel so lucky to have you as our children. You bring us unbelievable joy and happiness.

Have a super week!

I love you!
Yer 'ole Dad
XXXOOO

Wednesday, September 13, 2000
My precious loves, Kimmie, Tina and Jenny,
A good friend of mine (and business partner), Greg MacGilivray, who is a renowned film maker (for example, he made the giant screen film *Everest)* recently gave me a book. It was called *The Simple Abundance Journal of Gratitude* by Sarah Ban Breathnach. Greg inscribed the book with a lovely note to me. By the way, Greg has a daughter who is looking at colleges now and may come and visit you at Dartmouth or Amherst.

Anyway, I read this book with great interest because as I get older, I realize how much I have to be grateful for. Another thing I was reminded of by receiving this book from Greg is the enormity in the ordinary (I just made that up!). In other words, small, seemingly unimportant things, can actually be very important. Good manners (which help take care of other people) are an example.

I experience renewal, reflection, reverence and reconnection from reminding myself of all the wonderful things I have in my life. And that includes our family at the top of the list!

I am so deeply grateful for you three girls. Without you and Mommy, my life would be like a drum with no drumsticks, a canoe with no paddles, a balloon with no air, or a kite without wind.

I love you so much!
Daddio
XXXOOO

Thursday, September 14, 2000

My darling Kim, Tina and Jen,
Thinking more about my letter to you yesterday, here are a few of the many things for which I am deeply grateful (I think I wrote a letter along these lines on July 13 earlier in the summer):

1. The warmth and security of our home.

2. The yellow liquid sunshine that streams in the front windows early in the morning.

3. Unexpectedly hearing a Beatles record that I like.

4. Cracking a good joke that everybody enjoys.

5. Receiving an unexpected compliment.

6. Finding a perfect gift for Mommy or for one of you.

7. Waking up to a beautiful day and going running.

8. Rediscovering old family photographs.

9. Friends who make me feel that I matter.

10. Having a deep, long sleep and waking refreshed.

11. Meeting a self-imposed deadline.

12. Laughing so hard my sides ache and I can't stand up.

My loves, are you still collecting ideas for your Joy Lists? I hope so! It's important to remember how much is good in our lives.

I adore you!
Dad
XXXOOO

Friday, September 15, 2000
My precious loves, Kim, Tina and Jen,
I think I was a grown man before I learned that I was not the center of the universe. Even now, when I am not thinking, I have a tendency to slip into that delusion. I know it's a delusion because...well, I just know!

Still, as I finish writing this letter to you, I have this niggling feeling that the center of the universe is at the tips of my fingers as I tap in these words of love and affection on my laptop!

I hope you are each having a wonderfully rewarding and fun week!

Buckets of love and kisses and hugs,
Daddy
XXXOOO

Saturday, September 16, 2000
Darling Kim, Tina and Jen,
One reason I have always encouraged you to read, write and enrich your vocabularies, is that competence in using language underlies success in so many endeavors, from building relationships to running an organization to raising a family. At one level, this means having the competence to write a clear sentence (subject-verb-object) so that another person understands you.

On another level, competence at using language means having emotional mastery, and being in control of your moods. Try this experiment: Say in a loud voice:

> LIFE IS HOPELESS. NOTHING WILL HELP. NO ONE CAN HELP ME. THINGS WILL GET EVEN WORSE. MY LIFE IS WRETCHEDLY BLEAK. NOTHING WILL EVER CHANGE.

Most people are amazed at the effect this has on their body. Their shoulders slump, eyes go to the floor, their mood becomes heavy, and they feel surrounded by huge problems. What actions are they likely to take or not take in this mood? Even though this is just an exercise (and they know that), it is likely that their natural creativity, determination and drive will wither. They will feel like crawling under a log.

How can the words you speak have such a powerful effect on your body, your mood, and your possibilities for action? The fact is that the way you "language" can have a huge impact on you.

I encourage you to become a better observer of how you and others use language. If you catch yourself saying things like:

> —He makes me so mad
> —I can't do it. I don't have time
> —I have to go to that class even though I wish I didn't

pause and ask yourself if you are being "reactive" and (unintentionally through your use of language) giving the responsibility for the choices in your life to someone else. By the use of this reactive language (as opposed to proactive language), a person shifts the responsibility away from themselves to someone else.

So use proactive language as much as possible:

--Say "I will…" instead of "If only…";

--Say "I choose…" instead of "I can't…";

--Say "Let's look at our alternatives" instead of "I have to…";

--Say "I can choose a different approach" instead of "That's just the way I am".

I love you so much!
Daddy
XXXOOO

Sunday, September 17, 2000

My darling darlings, Kim, Tina and Jenny,

Our lives our shaped by the language we use. The better observer you are of distinctions in language (requests, offers, promises, declarations, assessments and assertions) then the more satisfaction you will achieve from your life, the more power and effectiveness you will acquire, the more possibilities will become available to you, and the better moods you will enjoy.

Habitual incompetence with language will cause you lifelong suffering. For example, you can gain huge power by having the capacity to make effective requests.

One of my recurrent linguistic weaknesses has been to be blind to the fact that my assessments are not universal truths. I am gradually learning that assessments are never the truth. Everything that is said is said by someone. That may sound self-evident but my interpretation of it is that my assessments (or judgements) are a function of my history and the standards for satisfaction that I embody. There is no "truth" to my assessments. It is simply what I say.

When I hold my assessments as the truth, then I become rigid and arrogant. You have seen this in me! It invites a mood of intolerance and unease. Everything is either right or wrong.

A better interpretation is: I am the observer that I am, and the observations I make are based on my history. I have certain eyes through which I view the world. With my eyes, I have made the following assessment. My assessment is not the truth, but it could be helpful to me and to others. It is not a question of right and wrong.

I say that I am learning (as opposed to have learned) that assessments are never the truth because my interpretation of learning is knowing something so well that it becomes embodied in me. This takes time and practice. I am still a beginner in this domain. I am still learning.

My treasures, you are so incredibly special to Mommy and me. We love you.

Dad
XXXOOO

Monday, September 18, 2000
Kimmie, Tina and Jenny,
How are my loves doing? I hope you are having a great week!

One very important linguistic skill is to learn how to decline requests. Grandpa is good at this! It is an especially important skill for women because historically they have trouble saying no. I know it is a generalization, but women in our society are taught to be nice, to be pleasing, to be good, and not to upset others. As a result, women tend to end up doing a lot of things they don't want to do. Such passive compliance with others (which I know you three would never be guilty of) can produce moods of resentment, anger and helplessness, all of which can lead to ill health.

A person's inability to say no is not a problem of intelligence or character, but rather of an embodied tendency (or conditioned linguistic tendency, or learned behavior) to say yes.

Learning to say no when you want to say no is a very important skill for everyone to have. If you don't have it, you will end up damaging your relationship with others. As with all skills, it takes practice, and practice means repetition. Remember how, when you were younger, I used to teach you to practice saying, "No, I decline your request but I am open to further conversations with you"! You three used to tease me about that!

Kim, Tina and Jenny, I have enormous confidence that you will spend your lives loving to learn, and that as a result, you will become an invaluable friend and colleague to all who have the privilege of knowing you.

I love you.
Dad
XXXOOO

Tuesday, September 19, 2000
My darling Kim, Tina and Jen,
Jim Rohn is a speaker and author who has written extensively on success and failure. He writes, "Failure is nothing more than a few errors in judgement repeated every day." In other words, failure is not one big event but rather the inevitable result of an accumulation of poor choices.

One of the challenges in recognizing failure is that a minor error of judgement seldom has an immediate negative impact. The consequences of poor habits (e.g., eating the wrong food, or not getting enough exercise) don't show up until later. In the same way, the really important things in life seldom pay dramatic immediate dividends.

It is this lag or delay in feedback which throws people off. When people think something doesn't matter (because there are no immediate consequences) then they make damaging choices which, when repeated, result in major disappointments and suffering years later. If you don't read or make time for exercise, nothing immediately shows up to have an impact on your life. But the pain of these errors in judgement have only been delayed to a future time.

Success is the same way. Do the small right things every day (a written life plan will help you to do this) and success is inevitable. In fact a successful life is just living one successful day after another.

My treasures, you are so special. Thanks for being you. I love you.
Dad
XXXOOO

Wednesday, September 20, 2000
My Loves, Kimmie, Tina and Jenny,
Today I am flying from Frankfurt to London so I can spend a day with Granny, Grandpa and Jon. Then I will fly home tomorrow! Can't wait to get home to see Mommy and Jenny.

Kim, how is your thesis going?

Tina, how are classes going? I know you have just started.

Jen, did you get on the Westland softball team?

My treasured loves, remember the wise fortune cookie saying (yes, occasionally there is a good one!): "It is the hopes and dreams that we have that make us great."

Inspiring hopes, visions and dreams are where a great life starts.

I love you more than I can say.
Dad
XXXOOO

September 23, 2000
Subject: Your philosophy essay on what you feel passionate about

My darling Tina,
Your assignment is not an easy one! One challenge is that the word "passionate" triggers images of a person on a soapbox gesticulating forcefully and working up a crowd as the speaker inveighs trenchantly and vehemently for or against some great cause.

But that is not a body image that sits comfortably with you (yet).. .or for that matter with most people. So I suspect that the assignment seems a challenge to answer.

Here are several approaches that might give you some ideas:

1. I would start by rephrasing the question so it resonates with you (and tell the professor in your essay that this is what you are doing...he will appreciate your candor, boldness and directness). Here are two questions that will lead you into more fruitful areas: What would you have to witness to make you feel deeply moved or upset? What really matters to you? The point I am making is that you don't have to vent in order to feel strongly about something. You can feel strongly about something but keep it inside you. Or you can feel strongly about something and not know how to express your feelings. Or a person may not have the linguistic skills to articulate appropriate actions to take. Passion can show up in all kinds of different ways. My

basic point is to rephrase the question so it becomes more meaningful to you.

2. Put yourself in the shoes of someone you admire. What would they say or do in this situation?

3. Brainstorm: get out blank sheets of paper, give yourself no more than three minutes, and write non-stop. Keep writing even if you write the same thing over and over again. Do the same exercise but design it a different way: sit for 30 minutes, snap yourself into a resourceful and playful mood, and generate lots of crazy ideas (perhaps 10 percent of which you might be able to use in your essay). Be completely uninhibited. The self-editing comes later.

4. Look back at your college essays for ideas.

5. Visit an adviser or a friend (Andy would be good, but anybody whom you like would be good) and tell them you have this assignment, and you want their help in generating ideas. Ask them how they would answer the question. (This is what you did last night when you asked me for my ideas...and look what you are getting!)

So there are a few approaches or techniques for generating ideas. Aim to be fresh and totally yourself.

Now here is an idea that you may or may not like but it may stimulate further ideas of your own: Tina, think about the following events:

hunting
animal abuse
child abuse
parents who mess up their children's lives by doing drugs
innocent victims of vicious criminals
Hollywood studios who market R rated movies to 10 year olds in order to make money

If you think about these things, you are likely to soon find yourself feeling passionate about stopping these sort of ghastly happenings. What is common to all of them is that they involve cruelty and injustice. Now I know you won't want to appear overly virtuous (and you can overcome that by talking about how little you have contributed to solving these societal problems to date) but I believe that what you feel passionate about is injustice and you would be honored to devote your life to doing something to alleviate suffering and cruelty. You have led a fairly protected life so far because Mommy and I gave you the best childhood we knew how to give you, including protecting you from the horrors of the world, but as you get exposed to society's problems, I think you will find yourself wanting to contribute to alleviating distress. You have always been a very empathic and loving person.

My treasure, good luck with your essay. Let me know what else we can do to help. I'll copy Mommy, Kim and Jen in case they have any ideas to add.

I love you!

Dad
XXXOOO

September 24, 2000
wow, dad, thank you so much for all of that advice!! it is very helpful! I did brainstorm a little, and I wrote a rough draft yesterday, on self-defense class when one woman, Molly, who is physically

disabled, was attacked. I think it'll be pretty good after I work on it a bit more.

(by the way, my professor is a WOMAN! . . . you assumed it was he. . .interesting)

anyway, thank you so much for taking all that time to write me that. You're the best!!

I'll write more later in the family meeting email.

I love you!
Love,
Tina

Wednesday, October 25, 2000
My darling Kimmie, Tina and Jenny,
Today I left for an NWF senior staff retreat at a resort in Western Maryland. We will be thinking about the strategic shape of NWF's future. It should be a lot of fun because I will be with colleagues whom I like a lot.

The retreat lasts two days. It ends at 3 PM on Friday afternoon. I will then drive to BWI to catch a plane to Hartford where I will join Mommy and Kimmie at Amherst to celebrate Parents Weekend. I am so sorry not to be seeing you, Tina, but I am so glad Mommy is driving up to see you on Sunday night.

I am writing this letter to you late on Saturday night (October 21). Kim is very tired but back at Amherst after a successful two day trip to Dartmouth (where she saw Tina of course!); Tina is in Boston this weekend with all her old Holton buddies and I'm sure is having the time of her life!; Jen is with Henry, Leigh, Erin, Suzy and Steve in New Jersey, and watching the big baseball game between the two NY teams (as if I know what I am talking about!); and Mommy is at the big NYC retirement dinner for Rhoda Kapatkin, and, I am sure, having the best time with all her CU colleagues and friends. I have talked to each of you today by phone (except for Tina, whom I talked to yesterday evening).

As for me, I am here at home alone, successfully fighting off loneliness by focusing with great energy on my priority tasks (such as writing this letter), and getting them done one-by-one with mounting personal satisfaction. In this way, I not only start next week incredibly well prepared for all my meetings and discussions, but I also feel that my solitude and temporary isolation is worth it. I was at my desk virtually all day working productively, after spending the first two hours exercising.

I periodically go in to Jen's room to say hello to our precious Conker and to check she is OK. She is sleeping in her little self-made nest and breathing steadily with no sign of discomfort.

When a pet dies, it is very sad because they have become part of a family, just like Conker has become part of our family. To lose them is to lose a part of our family. The world seems a little less secure. When Conker does die, Jen and I will be very sad and heavy-hearted as we grieve over her. Conker's death will have quite an emotional impact on us. For me, I think it is exacerbated because it unconsciously reminds me that my own parents are slowly coming to the end of their lives. Grief is a painful but therapeutic process that is important to open yourself up to. Psychologists warn against "unresolved" grief, i.e., grief which is bottled up inside a person and suppressed.

Death is the natural ending of life. All of us are mortal. That is a hard thing to face up to. As I say, I am having to face up to this fact with Granny and Grandpa.

In the old days, when people were well-intentioned but often unenlightened, grown-ups used to use euphemisms about death in an attempt to shield kids from the pain of reality. A child might be told, "Grandmother is sleeping," or "We have lost Grandmother," (oops, I'm a hypocrite because I used that idiom myself above...6th para, 2nd line), or "Grandmother is walking in the valley of the Shadows."

But in my view, these euphemisms are confusing for a child, and it is best to use correct and honest language instead of using language that attempts to deny the reality of death. Death is a natural part of life and needs to be accepted as such. The dead cannot be brought back to life. It is OK to feel sad and cry.

I love Conker for lots of reasons (one being that Jenny loves her of course), but now I have one more reason to appreciate her. Conker has given me this opportunity to tell you a little about my views on death and dying. Thank you Conker. You are a very special hamster and we love you.

I send all my love to each of you. You are our three most wonderful and treasured daughters.
Daddy
XXXOOO

P.S.   Jen, good luck tomorrow in your 3:15 softball match. I will be thinking of you.

Thursday, October 26, 2000
My darling Kim, Tina and Jen,
Jen, how did the softball game go today? I am dying to know. And good luck with your soccer match on Saturday at 1:30 PM.

Do you all remember the rejection letter I received last week from Gail Ross, the book agent? Gail said that my book proposal was too "personal," and "will not find a market." I was disappointed, of course, to receive her rejection letter, but Gail may be correct. I will naturally do everything in my power to show that her assessment is wrong.

Anyway, the reason I am telling you this is that I came across the following advice which I found very encouraging. It helped me regain my resolve to succeed:

> A sky-diving instructor was asked, "How many successful jumps
> must a student make before he or she can become certified?"
>
> He answered, "All of them!"
>
> Sky-diving, however, is the exception. Most of life isn't built
> on a series of successes. We usually do not attempt something new
> and immediately succeed, then succeed again and again. More
> likely, we may find that it is the other way around. Our
> successes are often built on smaller failures. We fell off the
> bike a few times before we learned to ride. And we produced a few
> culinary failures before we baked a successful layered cake or
> prepared a satisfactory omelet.

Tom Hopkins said, "The number of times I succeed is in direct proportion to the number of times I can fail and keep on trying." And <u>Winston Churchill stated, "Success is going from failure to failure without a loss of enthusiasm." They both agree that discouragement, rather than failure, is the enemy of success. Those who can remain hopeful and focused, though they fail, are those who will eventually succeed.</u>

In all, Emily Dickinson is said to have written more than nine hundred poems. Though only four were published in her lifetime and the first volume of her poetry was not published until four years after her death, Dickinson's success is attributed to the fact that she kept on writing.

Where would we be today had Emily Dickinson lost her enthusiasm for writing? Because she kept her desire alive, we now remember her as one of the great poets of all time.

<u>It's good to remember that success may be just beyond the next failure, and you'll get there, not because you're destined to, but because you're determined to.</u>

Isn't that inspiring? I have noticed that all three of you have a remarkable capacity to "bounce back" from disappointments and to quickly regain your natural resourcefulness and determination when things go wrong. That is an important skill and capability to have.

Jen, don't forget Matt is coming on Sunday at 4:00 PM to give you a trumpet lesson. I should be home by about 3 PM if my plane is on time.

You are each very special, and I send you buckets of love, hugs and kisses. I love you!

Daddy
XXXOOO

November 5, 2000
Subject: Virtual Family Meeting #4

My rock this week: Put all the changes in Tina's journal and make massive progress towards getting it to the printer.

Encouragement:

Gail: Well done for the super job you did speaking to Kim's class last Monday at Amherst. And well done for walking the 3K race yesterday.

Kim: Great article in Post last Friday! And thanks for being the only family member who responded to Family Meeting #3!

Tina: That was wonderful of you to write to Granny and Grandpa. Well done for getting an A- in that English essay! And your goal to become tougher is outstanding. We should all have that goal.

Jen: Well done for that magnificent catch at your last softball game! And thanks for staying in better touch with Kim and Tina. Thanks, too, for running the Edgemoor Classic 3K race with me yesterday morning. You could have lazed in bed but you didn't.

Other items:

1. Kim's 21st birthday dinner: What about Wed Dec 27, Thursday 28, or Friday 29? RSVP.

2. How shall we celebrate Mommy's 50th birthday???? It is a big one. We need ideas!

3. Tina, if you would like me to include your recent letter to Granny and Grandpa in my family journal, please email it to me. Totally up to you.

4. Jen and Gail: When shall we go to NYC to visit and have fun there exploring before Cory arrives? Jen, please look at your calendar and see what dates work for you.

5. Would everyone like a family outing on Friday November 24 to visit Cory? It is about a 2 hour drive.

Why don't we plan on leaving late morning, and stop for a nice lunch somewhere? I know Mommy would much prefer to hike the Billy Goat Trail, but that is tooooo bad!! I wonder if we could take our family Christmas photo when we visit Cory so she could be in the picture?

I love you!
Dad/Chris
XXXOOO

November 12, 2000
Subject: Virtual Family Meeting #5

My Rock: To make massive progress with Jen on planning for Cory's arrival (in less than a month!)

Encouragement.

Gail: for your super quote in the WSJ; for sweeping the leaves together from the driveway and suggesting we also sweep the Stevenson's; for all the delicious meals you make for us; for being a fabulous person in every way; I am so lucky!

Kim: for turning lemon into lemonade at your Luce interview, for getting through to the national level; for dealing proactively with HA and not falling into "a story" about him in your own mind that wasn't empowering or helpful to you; for making good progress on your thesis.

Tina: for making good progress on finding a summer job and not just letting it slide until in becomes a crisis; for participating in the "shadowing" program and being open to new learning; for managing the Noah/Mauro thing with great maturity.

Jen: for working hard to prepare for the SSAT this week; for allowing Mommy and me to come to Westland on Friday to sit at the back of some of your classes; for evidently making a excellent impression on Mrs. Hagen, your wonderful world studies teacher; for being such a joy to have at home.

For discussion and decisions:

1. What is the best date for Kim's dinner to celebrate her 21st birthday? December 27, 28 or 29? Kim, should we informally call a few of the guests to check that they are free on one of those dates?

2. How shall we celebrate Mommy's 50th birthday?????????!!!!!!!!!!!!!

3. Jen, we need to prepare (as you have been doing) for Cory's arrival. Let's finish up the list you have started of everything that needs to get done, be bought, etc.

4. We all need to contribute to jobs that need to be done in the house over Thanksgiving, including cleaning out the garage, putting firewood by the back door, sweeping up the leaves, organizing the pantry, and putting some of the shoes in the mudroom in our bedrooms. I'm sure you three girls can think of lots of other communal jobs in the house that you just can't wait to do! Please reserve Friday morning (before we leave to see Cory) to help out on these jobs. Thanks.

5. Big request: Cory is our big gift to ourselves this Christmas. Let's limit all our other gifts. And I really do mean limit. Anybody have any suggestions on how to do that? Gail, I think you have an idea, don't you? Anyway, with Cory in the house, we need to radically cut down on clutter (and the house is already over cluttered in places.) So let's consider Cory our gift to the family, and give very little else. Mommy reminded me the other day that you have all received early gifts already (except maybe Jenny?). Reducing gift giving will reduce the stress on all of us (as well as the expense) and that is very important. How about one small gift per person and each gift under $10 and hopefully less?

I love you!
Daddy/Chris
XXXOOO

December 3, 2000
Subject: Virtual Family Meeting #6

A big welcome to Cory, who doesn't yet have an email address!

My Rock: To have a highly successful NWP Board meeting on Tuesday, and to get up in the night for Cory so Jen can sleep and so be alert in class.

Encouragement:

Gail: for putting up the Christmas lights. Yeah!!!

Kim: forgetting the job offer from the Oregonian. Yeah!!!

Tina: for getting her 15 page paper in and for wrestling with the issue of what it means to lead a successful life. Yeah!!!

Jen: for taking care of Cory so lovingly and so competently. Yeah!!!

Info: The women-only dinner party to celebrate Kim's 21st birthday will be on Friday, December 29.

I love you!!!!
Dad/Chris
XXXOOO

December 10, 2000
Subject: Virtual Family Meeting #7

My Rock: To be more loving to Tina.

Encouragement:

Gail: Thanks a lot for doing a great job on the family Christmas letter, and for doing the labels for our Christmas cards.

Kim: Well done for thinking so creatively and resourcefully about your thesis. I know it is a challenge, albeit an exciting one.

Tina: Well done for getting through your first semester successfully. You should feel very proud because Princeton is one of the best colleges in the country.

Jen: Well done for not neglecting your school work even though Cory is endlessly fascinating.

HAPPY BIRTHDAY TO KIM ON HER 21ST BIRTHDAY ON Tuesday!!!!!!!!

AND HAPPY BIRTHDAY ON Saturday TO MOMMY/GAIL ON HER 50TH BIRTHDAY!!!!!!!!

Remember we are trying to limit our self-indulgence this holiday (except when it comes to gifts for yours truly!)

I love you!

XXXOOO

PS Gotcha! Princeton was a joke!

2001

January 21, 2001
Subject: Virtual Family Meeting #8

My Rock: To completely rewrite my San Diego speech for Feb 17 so it goes from good to outstanding.

Encouragement:

For Gail: Good luck this week with the Board. Thanks for finding me a great new outfit at Lord and Taylors. Well done for finding some great new outfits for yourself. Well done for having Peggy for dinner.

For Kim: Well done for all your hard work on your book and for making great progress. Congratulations on your article in tomorrow's USA Today. That is great you went skiing. Well done for meeting with the Dean of Public Affairs. Your grades last semester (A, A, and A-) were outstanding.

For Tina: That is great you went snowboarding. Well done for mastering the chem quiz. Good luck with, and well done for, the EMT course. I am glad you are exercising with your girlfriends on your floor. Well done for being so happy and having the wisdom to know that happiness is a choice, not something you wait to happen to you.

For Jen: Good luck with your exams this week! You are very good at choosing special friends like Sara and Emma. Well done for working steadily on Spanish. Thanks for all the love and care you give Cory. Thanks for being a wonderful teenager.

Other points:

Tina, do you have your laptop back?

Thanks to everyone for doing their predictions and New Year Resolutions for 2001.

Gail, how about one of us taking Jenny to NYC on her spring break?

Kimmie, I will see you for dinner in Amherst on Monday Feb 19 (and breakfast on the 20th).

Tina, I will see you for dinner in Hanover on Tuesday Feb 20 (and breakfast on the 21st).

Kim, I expect John forgot to put a stamp on his thank you letter!

Keeping planning your summers. June will be here before you know it!
Cory sends Kim and Tina a big woof and lick. She was so adorable this morning romping around in our backyard with Cody!

Everybody please participate in this virtual family meeting!

I love you!
Daddy/Chris
XXXOOO

January 28, 2001
Subject: Virtual FM non-responsa!!!

Hey, you out there in cyberland! I was just about to compose Virtual Family Meeting #9 when I realized that no one (except Mommy) had responded to VFM #8! That is unacceptable! Please take this email as registering a formal complaint to the VPs for Human Resources at Kim Inc., Tina Inc., and Jenny Inc.! This is a breakdown!

I love you anyway!

Daddy
XXXOOO

PS There were questions on VFM #8 that I want answers to. For example, Tina, I've been worrying about your laptop. Did you get it back? Is it working?

Please note that my email will be inoperational from 5 PM Jan 31 to sometime on Feb 5.
As of Feb 5, my new work address and phone numbers will be:

Christopher N. Palmer
President and CEO
National Wildlife Productions
National Wildlife Federation
11100 Wildlife Center Drive
Reston, VA 20190-5362
703 438 6077
fax 703 438 6076
email: palmer@nwf.org (no change)
www.nwf.org

Until Jan 31, my address remains:

Christopher N. Palmer
President & CEO
National Wildlife Productions
National Wildlife Federation
8925 Leesburg Pike
Vienna, VA 22184
703 790 4077
fax 703 790 4076
palmer@nwf.org

February 24, 2001
Subject: Virtual Family Meeting #9

My rock for the week: To make massive progress on writing my book...a preliminary manuscript is due at the publisher, New Market Press, by March 15. Yikes!!

Encouragement:

For Gail: Great job finding a house for the family vacation this August. You were very tenacious in your search. And fantastic job planning the graduation celebration for Kim and all her friends and their families.

For Kim: Congratulations again on winning the Luce Scholarship in the face of intense national competition. And thank you for your sweet Valentine's Day letter to Mommy and me.

For Tina: It reflects so well on you that despite (or perhaps because of) all the challenges, you are making a success of Dartmouth. If you can succeed there, you can succeed anywhere. Thanks, Tina, for your sweet Valentine's Day email to the whole family, overflowing as it was with affection, love and zest for life. Well done, too, for enjoying EMT and learning so much by doing it.

For Jenny: I am so proud of you for not only getting the top score on your trumpet playing (and thus getting through to the state competition) but for the focus, determination and tenacity you showed in achieving your success. You are so mature for your age. And thanks, Jenny, for saying on the phone to me the other night when I called from the office to say I was running late, "We miss you!" Finally, while Mommy is sad about your decision not to get confirmed, we respect your decision totally.

Other notes:

Kim and Tina, I had the best time with each of you this past week when I visited you in Amherst and Dartmouth respectively. Thanks for the great warm welcome! And I loved seeing all your room mates.

Re book: Esther Margolis, the founder and President of New Market Press would like you three girls to write an epilogue for my book on fathering daughters. Would you like to? If so, start collecting ideas for it. Esther needs it by the end of the summer. You can be as rude as you like!

Canine news flash: Cory is the most adorable puppy in the world!

I love you.
XXXOOO

March 11, 2001
Subject: Virtual Family Meeting #10

My Rock this week: Submit five sections of my book to New Market Press!

Encouragement:

Gail: For doing the taxes. I am SO grateful!!!! And for looking after everybody when they were sick (which of course excludes me because I never get sick because I have no psychological problems!)

Kim: For your wonderful article in USA Today last week. Actually, I want to praise you for the self-discipline, focus and hard work that produces these published articles.

Tina: For your paper on extraterrestrial life. I didn't see the final version but I am sure it was outstanding Actually, I want to praise you for the courage, maturity and wisdom you showed in asking someone (it happened to be me but it doesn't matter who it is) for their advice. You would be amazed at how much of my day is spent asking people to assist me.

Jen: For scoring a #1 in the solo ensemble. Actually, I want to praise you for the dedication, diligence and tenacity you show in learning the trumpet. Those are the qualities of every winner.

Cory: For providing endless entertainment, which reached new heights this afternoon when you played with Cody and displayed lavish exuberance, high-spirited playfulness, and zestful vivacity. You were a joy to watch.

Other points:

1. Jen and I are going to Barbados June 22 to 27 to celebrate her graduation from 8th grade!

2. Tina, good luck this Monday on your exams!

3. Please keep collecting ideas for your epilogue for my book. You can be as rude and funny as you like!

I adore you!!
Dad/Chris
XXXOOO

April 9, 2001
Tina wrote:
Dear Mom and Dad,

I was feeling kind of sad and lonely today, I'm not sure why, I guess just one of those days. So I was going to lunch by myself and on the way checked my mailbox, and I got the package of fruit from you guys and it made me so happy and feel so loved, you guys are the best!

Thank you so much!!! It will be so nice. I definitely don't eat enough fruit here.

Have you heard anything about Grandpa?

I love you both so much.

Love,

Tina

I replied:
My darling Tina,

Don't be saddish, eat a raddish!

If you can't find a raddish, find someone else who needs help, and you'll soon stop feeling sad and lonely!

I never have lunch by myself. I always use it as an opportunity to strengthen my friendships with people or extend my network of contacts and friends. Every morning as I put together my list of commitments for the day, I include "call someone to have lunch with." Did you find someone to have lunch with after you found the fruit in your mailbox? Hope so!!

If I am unable to book a lunch with someone, I walk into that lunch room with the absolute conviction that virtually every table in the room would be honored and delighted to have me join them. And because of that conviction, it turns out to be true.

So glad you liked the fruit! I'm sure you are sharing it with Greta and Kerri.

Grandpa is doing OK. I'll be leaving tomorrow to go to England to visit him and Granny. I will give them your love.

Look out for people to say hello to and smile at. When you get up in the morning, do what I do: practice smiling! It is a learned art. Your face has about 100 muscles. Most people only use a fraction of them.

Every morning, say out loud the incantation: "I am a popular, respected, warm person whom people flock to for fun, leaning and enrichment. I am liked by everybody. I will reach out warmly to everyone, knowing with absolute certainty that others will respond in like manner." Say it over and over with passion and energy. Feel your self-confidence rising as you do this.

Finally, give people what they want. If you do this, they will help you get what you want. I made the mistake of not doing that at Audubon, but I have been careful to follow this rule at NWF, and I am having incredible success there.

Tina, you are very, very special, and you are having great success at Dartmouth. I know it isn't easy to be surrounded by people who act like they are God's gift to humanity! (like me!) Everyone has ups and downs. Keep doing what you are doing.

I love you.
Dad
XXXOOO

I received this reply two days later:
Dad, I can't believe I forgot to write you back for your email on how to feel not lonely. I printed it out and put it on my bulletin board right when I got it, but I totally forgot to write you back! It was such a good email, I loved it. Thank you! You're in England right now, how is it going? That must be so hard.

I love you Dad,
Love,
Tina

April 11, 2001
I arrived in England to see Daddy. He has declined badly in the last week. His prostate cancer is ripping through his body and he is very deaf. I thought he was going to die quickly and that I wouldn't arrive in time to see him before he died. Two days ago, he held Jon's hand and told Jon he was ready to go.

Mummy gets very upset every time she thinks of losing Daddy. They are devoted to each other.

April 23, 2001
Subject: Virtual Family Meeting #11

My Rock: to see the silver lining in the unexpected rejection letter I just received from New Market Press! And to react with equanimity and increased resolve!

Encouragement:

Gail: Thanks for all your wonderful support while I was away for Daddy's death and funeral, and thanks for keeping the house going, and for taking care of Jenny and Cory! Thanks for your excellent advice on the eulogy for Daddy. Well done for getting your letter published in the NYT.

Kim: Congratulations again on getting that job in Japan with the International Herald Tribune for next year. And well done for doing those recent articles on smoking and on Bridget Jones. Have a joyful last month or so at Amherst!

Tina: Congratulations again on those superb grades you got last semester! That was so nice that you and other friends gave Greta such a happy birthday. Well done for making the most out of your commitment to deliver papers in the morning. And good for you for earning money. That's important...not for the money so much as for the autonomy and power money can give you. Good luck in working out your semester abroad (go to Japan!!!!), and the term off (go to England and work with Susy and Clare!!!!). Good luck in finding out the best way to pay for medical school (you can be confident you will find a way), and for balancing your life goals of family and professional success. Finally, good luck on your decision on whether to take the UGA job. Remember with all decisions, once you have made them, then change your mind set and attitude completely. Focus not on whether you made the right decision or not, but rather on how to make a success of whatever it is you have committed to. I think you are making a big success of your time at Dartmouth.

Jen: Well done for winning in softball yesterday. But much more important, well done for playing. A lot of success in life rests on just having the gumption just to "show up". I am so glad you had a great time in Philadelphia with your class. Keep up your daily strength training. I encourage you to set specific numerical goals. Well done for reading "Death Be Not Proud" by John Gunther. Thanks for introducing Cory to Henry, Anna and Marshall. I feel like I am a Granddoggy!

Note: I felt all of you with me during the last two weeks. Thank you. It was a wonderful goodbye to Grandpa. He was very special. It was sometimes hard to always remember how special he was when he was alive. It is important to cultivate a deep feeling of gratitude for the blessings we have and sometimes take for granted. This is something I am working on in my life. I never want to take any of you for granted.

I love you.
Daddy
XXXOOO

May 04 2001
Gail wrote:

To my wonderful family,

First, I must start by saying what a fantastic weekend I had with Tina and Kim at Dartmouth's family weekend. It made me SOOO happy to see Tina so happy and settled at Dartmouth, surrounded by lots of friends, and busy learning in so many ways. And it was so special that Kim went to lots of trouble to join us for the weekend!

My rocks: cook a nice dinner for Serena's parents on Saturday, work on organizing my life!

Encouragements:
Chris -- for all the loving care you give Cory every day, and for your adventure to Baltimore driving the wonderful quartet to their competition and Jenny of course to her solo!

Kim -- for getting such EXCELLENT GRE scores -- 730 to 760 on all 3!!!! -- and for the excellent planning skills necessary to actually TAKE them before you graduate. It wasn't easy! But it would be even more complicated later!! This may make the difference in not having to delay grad school by a year! Tina -- for being such a wonderful hostess last weekend! And for your loving care and concern for Daddy and his aching (but almost better) shoulder. And for enjoying your EMT class!

Jenny -- for getting a 1 on your trumpet solo and for leading the effort of your quartet! And for being so tough this week after being sick, going to school for your testing!

Daddy and I think that we have the most wonderful daughters in the world!!!!

love,
Mommy
XXXOOO

May 6, 2001
Subject: Re: Virtual Family Meeting #12

Thanks, my love, for initiating this virtual family meeting!

My Rock: working on getting my priorities right and making massive progress on the rocks in my life rather than the pebbles. Give two superb speeches (making them funny and substantive) in LA at LFCA May 16 to 20.

Encouragement:

Gail: Well done for making a delicious and elegant dinner last night for Serena's parents. And thanks for all the work you have done to prepare for Kim's graduation weekend at Amherst. And thanks for going to visit Tina and Kim last weekend.

Kim: Well done for skillfully managing your life and taking the GRE exams last week, and then topping off that success by doing so well in them. Well done in getting through your thesis interview (though I haven't heard any details on it), and I am so proud of all the many articles you have written recently.

Tina: Congratulations on being selected to be a UGA next year. I am so proud of you for that accomplishment, especially for having the judgement and wisdom to seize the opportunity and put yourself forward like that. Making yourself vulnerable (in this case, risking rejection) takes courage. Thanks for hosting Mommy and Kim last weekend at Dartmouth and giving them such a good time. Well done for all you are learning at your EMT class, and for having the wisdom and self-discipline to take the course in the first place. I think you would make a superb doctor. And thanks for your love and caring concerning my sore shoulder, which is now better.

Jen: I am so proud of you for setting up a goal of learning to play the trumpet, and then pursuing that goal with self-discipline and focused determination. You topped that success of last week by also scoring a "1" at the state level! Icing on the cake! I am also proud of you for rebounding so quickly from your sickness this week. That is a sign of fundamental, vibrant good health. I am also proud of you for the reading you do, and the strength training you do.

Notes

1. IMPORTANT BIRTHDAYS COMING UP!!!! How shall we celebrate? Tina will be 19, and Jen will be 14!!!! Have you both thought what Mommy and I can give you? We will have to do your treasure hunt, Tina, and the search for 19 dollars, when you get home in June. Jen, how about if we invite a bunch of your friends around, and I will organize party games for you like chasing the dragon's tail? (just kidding!)

2. IMPORTANT DAY NEXT SUNDAY!!! MOTHER'S DAY!!! Is there a better Mommy in the whole world? I don't think so! No sirreee Bob!

I love you.
Dad/Chris
XXXOOO

June 17, 2001
Subject: Virtual Family Meeting #13

My Rock: To have a wonderful time with Jenny in Barbados! (We leave on Friday.)

Encouragement:
Gail: You did a fantastic job on Thursday night entertaining John Coles and his girlfriend Janet. I don't know how you did everything, considering you worked all day. Your potato soup is the best! Thanks for the Greatest Generation tape. That is the very opposite of Moulin Rouge in terms of meaning and value.

Kimmie: Magnum Cum Laude! Go Kim! And those two awards! And your GREs, and all the articles you have drafted. Japcwyuzwkeesolmiunahahah!
That means well done in Japanese!

Tina: Well done for having a great trip so far. I know it isn't always easy, but you are hanging in there and making a great time for you and Serena, and having one heck of an experience! We'll miss you at the Burgess's barbecue on June 30. Well done for your wonderful freshman year at Dartmouth! You surmounted many challenges and did very well academically.

Jen: Do we take how good you are for granted?! Especially your outstanding academic results. You make it look easy, although I know you work hard and in a very focused manner. We are very proud of how well you do. And I am proud of you, too, for the caliber of the friends you pick to spend time with. The concert was great. Congratulations on being #1 trumpet.

I love you!!! I am so proud to be the father of Kim, Tina and Jen on this Father's Day. You three are my life's biggest accomplishment.

Daddy/Chris
XXXOOO

July 17, 2001
Subject: Virtual Family Meeting #14

My Rock: To make massive progress on my wildlife film making book proposal, and to continue having a wonderful summer with Gail, Tina and Jenny.

Encouragement:

Gail: Thanks for updating all our assets. And thanks for having the great idea of suggesting the four of us play tennis together last Sunday. And thanks for being you!!! I love you.

Kim: Thanks for calling Tina and Jen on Saturday. It is so important to stay in close touch with each other. Well done for talking with Kathleen Dudzinski. Hope you are OK with the Will situation. Well done for learning Japanese and being very focused about it. And that Washingtonian invite is exciting! I love you.

Tina: Welcome home from your adventures in Europe! And well done for getting the job at Dr. Peebles and hanging in there even though it is often tedious. I am proud of you for using the Bethesda library and especially for getting out the book on organic chemistry. The more you study organic chemistry now, the more you will enjoy the course next semester. Thanks for visiting Granny and being so loving to her. I am so glad you enjoyed Jon so much. Your grades at Dartmouth last semester were great! Thanks for playing tennis with me. And thanks for the most enjoyable jog on the bike path last Saturday and for the bagel breakfast! I love you.

Jenny: You are reading and that's so important. Try and read five books a week if you can, or set yourself whatever goal makes sense to you. I encourage you to keep a journal so you practice writing too. I am so glad you are enjoying tennis camp. You are becoming a good tennis player. I love playing with you, even though you beat me! Congratulations on winning the tennis trophy yesterday. Thanks for coming to Barbados with me. I loved every moment of it. I encourage you to weight train so you become even stronger than you are. I love you.

Cory: I encourage you not to bring mud into the house. Well done for trying not to drip all over the floor after you have drunk from your bowl of water in the kitchen. I encourage you not to be so scared when you go out for walks. I love it when you snuggle up under the kitchen table when I am having breakfast and you put your beautiful head on the cross bar under the chair. Thanks for being so loving to Jen at night. It makes me laugh the way you woof "You're the man" when I pick up your poop! I love you.

Can't wait for our family vacation in August!

I adore you. You are the most precious family in the whole world.

Daddy/Chris
XXXOOO

Monday, August 27, 2001

My Darling Kim, Tina and Jenny,

I am in England with Granny and Jon! Kim, you are in San Francisco! I love you all and miss you. I'll be home on Friday.

Thank you for my wonderful birthday on Saturday! Thanks for calling, Kimmie, and for the poem and aftershave. Tina, thanks for the gift of the tennis balls, and the game with you with new tennis balls. Tina and Jen, thank you for the ENORMOUS tennis shorts! And Jen, thank you for the beautiful collage and the bath wash. I loved all Mommy's gifts to me as well. And thanks for the treasure hunt, birthday cake and delicious family dinner. I loved our birthday tennis match too, even though Mommy's partner looked like tennis shorts "with nobody inside them"! Kimmie, you should have seen me! The tennis shorts Tina and Jen gave me are so large I could have dinner inside them!

Kim, Tina and Jen, you are so incredibly special to Mommy and me. Thank you for being who you are and for being so delightful, each in your own unique ways.

Remember how important it is to dream big and to envision. Get away to a quiet place (the top of a mountain is ideal, or the beach is a terrific place for this too) and reflect deeply on what you want to do with your life. It is important to dream. Many people don't do this and then find they lead lives of quiet sadness because they never feel passionate about anything. Their lives feel humdrum, mundane and unexciting. You can only live with purpose and passion if you care deeply about what you are doing and have projects that excite and challenge you. You feel more alive, focused and happy when you work on what you care about.

Ask yourself these two questions: What makes my heart sing? What would I like to do if I was unafraid of anything? Write your answers down. Without the discipline of writing in a private journal, it will be difficult to translate your dreams into action. The very act of writing your dreams down on paper is the first step in achieving them.

I love this quote from Anais Nin: "And the day came when the risk it took to remain tight in the bud was more painful than the risk it took to blossom."

My loves, you are each doing so well and Mommy and I are so extraordinarily proud of you. You are each so very special.

I love you.
Daddy
XXXOOO

Tuesday, August 28, 2001

My darling treasures Kimmie, Tina Betweena, Jenny, and Cory,

Whoever thought I would have FOUR daughters?!

Kim, I am so proud of you going to Japan. Tina, I am so proud of you going to Europe, working in the pastry store and at Dr. Peebles office. Jen, I am so proud of your determination to improve your tennis game.

Tina, are you enjoying the book by Ann Crittenden, *The Price of Motherhood?* Maybe you'll devote your life to lobbying for the enactment of a Mothers Bill! Such legislation would help to repay the debt the country owes mothers for doing the vital work of raising productive, fulfilled and decent children. It would compensate mothers for the professional marginalization and loss of status that they experience for devoting themselves to building and sustaining families, the fundamental building block of a thriving society. Tina, please lend the book at some point to Kim and Jen.

When I was growing up, I thought acting was basically trivial. I have come to have a different perception of acting now. To learn how to be brave, act brave. To learn how to be charming and confident, act charming and confident. Before you act in those ways, visualize yourself acting in those ways. FEEL the good feelings you will generate in yourself and others. EXPERIENCE in your mind the kudos, applause and good things that will come from your new found behavior. Then go out and act in those good ways, and you will find those behaviors (courage, self-confidence, making other people feel good, assertiveness, vitality, alertness, interest in others, public speaking, whatever) will become a natural part of you. As they say, fake it 'til you make it.

Kim, Tina and Jen, I adore you and miss you.
Daddy
XXXOOO

Wednesday, August 29, 2001
Kim, Tina and Jen,
Oh my goodness! Kim, you are in Japan! Tina, you have one week and one day to go before you go back to Dartmouth! Jenny, your tennis tryouts at Holton start tomorrow! Good luck to each of you!!!!

I hope you will all keep reading voraciously. I was so pleased at how much you all read while we were on vacation in North Carolina. Constant learning is something that every successful person does day-in, day-out. To me, one of the most extraordinary thing about the Founding Fathers is how each one of them (including George Washington who one tends to think of as a man of action) relentlessly imbibed knowledge. Ben Franklin, Thomas Jefferson, John Adams, and the rest of them read hungrily, absorbing all they could. Partly as a result, they were extraordinary human beings.

I hope you all keep (as I do) a private "learning" journal in which you constantly write down interesting things you learn, topics you want to learn more about, your dreams, your wild and crazy ideas that later might get transformed into something wonderful, issues you want to discuss with other people so you can see what others think, great movies which dazzle you, and whatever other ideas you come across that excite and enthrall you. Such a journal allows you to capture great ideas, fascinating statistics and facts, great quotes, and inspirational thoughts that otherwise would get lost and forgotten in the rush and banality of everyday life.

Your private journal will become an invaluable resource for articles, papers and essays, for dinner conversations, and for class discussions.

So please continue to read voraciously. And remember it is perfectly OK (and probably smart) to start a book and not finish it. When you read a book, you are often looking for the key ideas in it, and this doesn't mean you have to read every word of it. Who has time for that?!

I adore you. Mommy and I feel so lucky that you are so close and loving to each other. You will always be each other's best friends.

Your loving old Daddy
XXXOOO

Thursday, August 30, 2001

My precious loves, Kim, Tina and Jenny,
I will be home from England tomorrow! Kim, you have now been in Japan a couple days and I so hope you are doing OK. Can't wait to visit you in November!!

Tina, one week to go!! We are going to miss you so much when you go back. What a great summer you've had!

Jenny, I am dying to hear how the tennis tryouts went today!

Tina and Jenny, at dinner tomorrow night, I will tell you and Mommy all about my adventures in England this week!

You all face big challenges this year. Kim in Japan, Tina as an UGA and picking her major, and Jen at Holton-Arms. Remember to keep working on your bodies. Your bodies are the first line of strength against stress. If you are fit and strong, and if you eat wisely, then you are giving yourself every advantage to combat challenges and come out victorious. Keep your shoulders back, walk tall and proudly, run like athletes, pump your muscles so you feel powerful, and run long distances (or play rigorous tennis matches) to build up your endurance. Apart from ridding your lives of duplicity, there are few better ways of fighting negative stress than exercising and being in superb health. I am very proud of how you each strive to eat well and exercise every day!

My loves, you are so special to me and Mommy. Becoming a father transformed me and gave me something worthwhile to do with my life. I am forever grateful to you. You have given me far more than I could ever give you.

I love you.
DAD
Yer ol' greying, balding, and brimming-with-health Daddy
XXXOOO

September 8, 2001
Subject: Virtual Family Meeting #15

To My Dispersed and Incredibly Precious Family!
My Rock: To be understanding of Jenny when she doesn't want to talk to me.

Encouragement:

Gail: Thanks for all the delicious and healthy meals you have made for us recently! Well done for your appearance on Fox TV and for that great quote in USA Today. Well done for planning the now aborted trip to see Tina next weekend. Thanks for all you do for each one of us!

Kim: We are very proud of you for courageously going to live in a strange apartment in an unfamiliar city in a foreign land far away, and for doing all this with serenity and a sense of excitement and adventure. So much change and so much inner peace! Well done. Good luck in getting on top of your job while you are not yet fluent in Japanese. Thanks for staying in close touch with us.

Tina: What a great success you have made of the first few days back at Dartmouth! It was great to get your happy emails. I am so proud of you for being in the top 15% of your class (don't forget to make a note of that for your resume) and for getting the UGA job. You are going to be so good at that. Thanks for the scrumptious meal you made for us on Tuesday night (Kim, you missed tofu stir fry and mashed sweet potatoes!), and thanks for driving Jen SIX (sic) times that day! It was great playing tennis with you on your last full day here...hey, I forgot, that was one of your birthday gifts to me!! Thanks!

Jen: You are terrific to be (or appear to be...and who can tell the difference?) so self-confident starting off at Holton, and feeling so at home there so quickly. That says a lot about your skills to socialize and know how to get the most of any social situation. Well done love bug. Mommy and I love being back there too! And that was so great Betsy Purcell giving you a hug! I am very proud of the way you set yourself a goal of getting on the JV team. You worked hard all summer to improve and improve you did. Thanks for playing doubles with Mommy, Tina and me. That was the best fun!

I think our vacation at Nags Head was the best vacation I have ever had. The whole summer was wonderful. You three girls did rewarding, challenging, and constructive things...all things that will help you do well in the future, and help you prepare for a very competitive world out there. I encourage you to learn all you can about computers and how to use them.

Thank you for your notes to Granny. She really appreciated them.

And well done to all of you for all the fabulous reading you did this summer. Please continue to read voraciously, it is so important. I visualize the process of reading as building up your intellectual capital so that you can take on any job with confidence, knowing that you have the educational resources to do it.

Kim, please send me the dates ASAP on which I should avoid coming to Japan. I want to start planning my trip to see you.

Tina, is the best time for me to visit you in March? Or is there be a better time?

Jen, don't we need to buy you a watch? (a late birthday gift). And do you want me to search for Spanish software?

I love you. I adore you. I awindow you!
Daddy
XXXOOO

September 20, 2001
Subject: I love you!

My darling Kimmie, Tina and Jenny,
I am in Chicago as you know, at an IMAX meeting and wishing I wasn't so far away. I am very busy here with lots of meetings. Attendance is down 15% from an expected 900 people from all over the world.

Kim and Tina, Mommy says she has talked with both of you and says that you are both so happy and both doing so well. Jenny, your initial test results at Holton are wonderful, and you have a great attitude on the biology challenge you are facing.

I love the way all three of you keep challenging yourselves to be the best you can be at everything you do. Mommy and I are so proud of you and we love you so very, very much.

This comes with all my love, hugs and kisses.
Daddy
XXXOOO

September 21, 2001
My precious loves, Kimmie, Tina and Jenny,
How I miss you! I feel out of touch with you all. Are you all OK? Let me know please!

I am still in Chicago. I will be here until Sunday when I take the train over-night to Denver, and then on to Jackson.

I had a learning experience today. Before I presented Bears, a good friend of mine, Andy Gellis, introduced his new film on pandas, and also announced that he was leaving IMAX. When I started my presentation, I said, "I'd like to ask you all for a moment of silence (pause) while Andy gives out his resume." It fell flat because some people thought it was mean to Andy, and others thought that I shouldn't have used the expression "a moment of silence" when the country is in mourning.

While the film was running, Goulam rushed up to me and urged me to apologise when the film finished, which I did. I said, "I want to apologise for the personal remark I made about Andy Gellis earlier on, and I want to apologise to all of you for using the term "a moment of silence" at a time when the country is still in mourning."

Live and learn!

I love you. Please write and tell me what is happening to you.
Daddy
XXXOOO

September 22, 2001
Subject: I awindow you!

My most precious daughters, Kim, Tina and Jen,

I just got off the phone with Tina. Tina, it was so lovely to reach you at last! You sounded deeply happy. I'm so glad you are enjoying guitar lessons!

Kim, I wish it was as easy to call you. It seems every time I get a break from meetings and speeches here in Chicago, I look at my watch, add 14 hours, and realize you are asleep so I can't call you!

Jen, I am so glad the sleep over last night was fun with your new Holton friends. And I am so proud of you for getting such high grades in your tests at school so far.

Did you all hear that we have bought a new car?!

Here is a good question that everyone should periodically ask themselves: What do you want to be remembered for?

I love you so much, and (ahem Kim) love receiving emails from you!

Buckets of love,
Dad
XXXOOO

September 23, 2001
Subject: Family Meeting #16

Gail wrote:
To my wonderful family,

Hello everyone! I will get this started!!

My rock this week: to juggle work and home and cory and jenny duties, with back-to-school night and tennis matches, with daddy away

Encouragements:

--Go Chris for making a lot of good contacts in Chicago and doing such a good job at your first conference

--Kim...for making the most of your time in Tokyo ... for coming up with feature ideas already that they like, for making friends, for having fun. All very exciting!!!

--Tina ... go Tina for doing SO MUCH to help your freshmen adjust to being at college. Being a freshman is really not easy for anyone, but this year's tragedy makes it especially challenging, and I think that your freshmen are VERY LUCKY TO HAVE YOU!!

--Jenny -- go Jen for settling in to Holton so well, for working so hard and doing well academically, for your trumpet successes, and your FIRST Holton tennis victory!

Well everyone ... have a great week!!! I love you madly!!!!
Happy 29th anniversary to Chris!!!!!! XXXXOOOO

love,
Mommy

September 23, 2001
Subject: Re: Family Meeting #16

To my precious family,
Kim, Tina and Jenny, did you realize that 29 years ago today, Mommy and I met at Harvard? I looked very cool in my green suit and purple shirt, but Mommy at first didn't realize how cool I was!

I am dying to come home but I have one more week to go in Jackson. Things are going really well here.

Gail, thanks for starting this virtual family meeting.

Kim, Tina and Jenny, I am so proud of you. I talk about you all the time here.

My rock is to give dazzling speeches this coming week as I promote conservation in wildlife films.

I love you each so much!
Chris/Dad
XXXOOO

September 25, 2001
Subject: I acurtain you!

My precious loves, Kim, Tina and Jenny,
I am now in Jackson Hole, one of the most beautiful places in the world. My room looks out on to the magnificent Grand Tetons (which rise sharply to about 14,000 feet). Tina, I am only a few miles from Lost Creek Ranch!!

I am here with about 700 or so other wildlife filmmakers. I am giving four speeches, and lots of old friends are here, so it is enormous fun while also very productive and exceedingly busy! I have back-to-back meetings throughout the day with filmmakers and others in the business.

Coming here by plane from Chicago (I flew through Denver) couldn't have been easier, and I was not concerned in the slightest. On the plane, I caught up on the news by reading Time magazine. (I haven't read a paper or watched TV since I left home a week ago.)

I came across this poignant little report:

"The search dogs digging through the World Trade Center crypt have become so discouraged by their failure, day after day, to find anyone alive that rescue workers have taken to burying themselves under blankets and allowing the dogs to sniff them out and "save" them, while others watch and cheer and pat the dogs on the back."

The inexplicable horror of the carnage in NY and the Pentagon finally hit me on the plane, and as I sat there reading Time magazine, I found myself overcome by tears.

I am completely safe, but were I to be caught up in anything like that and die, please know that I die happy, knowing that I leave behind three incredible daughters who are my proudest legacy.

Every day is a gift. I try to remember that. Every day is so special, and every moment in each day is unique and to be treasured.

I love you so much.
Daddy
XXXOOO

September 27, 2001
Subject: I can't wait to get home!

My darling Kimmie, Tina and Jenny,
Whew, this is tiring! All these presentations I am giving is wearing me out!

It can get overwhelming at these conferences. So much is going on. Many people want to talk to me. I have many responsibilities to fulfill on panels and in running meetings. Here is how I handle it: I keep reminding myself to go back to fundamentals. What are the fundamentals? They are my carefully thought out goals. Before I left home, I listed the key things I wanted to achieve at each conference. For example, for Jackson, I wrote:

--Make massive progress on my wildlife filmmaking book (collect ideas, talk to people, research themes, and so on)

--Cement and extend my network of contacts.

--Give brilliantly funny and substantive speeches

--Nail down the new deal we have with Animal Planet.

--Eat healthy food, exercise and run every day.

As all the "busyness" swirls around me, having these goals in mind helps me keep focused and not drawn into other people's agendas that don't concern me.

I also keep reminding myself of Jim Rohn's definition of success. He wrote that success is nothing more than a few simple disciplines (such as eating wisely and exercising rigorously) practiced every day; while failure is simply a few errors in judgement, repeated every day. It is the accumulative weight of our disciplines and our judgements that leads us to either fortune or failure.

Kim, Tina and Jenny, I love you so much!
Daddy
XXXOOO
PS Ahem, I enjoy getting emails from you! (Tina, great to hear from you today!)

October 08, 2001
Gail wrote:

To my precious family,

We are all so spread out, still!!! Hope that this finds everyone happy as you start this (shortened) week!!

My rock this week: to ship gifts to Mavis to try to bridge the big gap (of ocean) between us (since I didn't get to visit this week); to take the first steps to reach out to foundations with my prescription drug idea.

Encouragements:

--Chris -- go Chris for taking Cory to puppy school on Sunday ... GREAT!! I really think that Todd should charge for psychotherapy (Kim and Tina ... he tells us ALL ... just "relax"!!) Which is just what we need to do when we are with Cory!

--Kimmie -- GREAT essay you have written for grad school applications! You are so smart to start working away early on those! And congratulations for starting to work on features AND for becoming so domestic in your apartment a vacuum cleaner AND a washing machine, wow!!!!

--Tina -- for being so conscientious and thinking about the many challenges and decisions that you face, and for reaching out for help and taking steps to help you make your decisions. We are so proud of you!!!! And I marvel that you can be taking organic chem so far without any complaint ... are you sure you wouldn't want to major in chemistry??? :)

--Jenny -- for being SUCH good company! Did you know that when I am with you, you make me happy? I love sitting with you at breakfast as you chuckle over the comics. AND I am so proud of you for settling into Holton Arms, and for working so conscientiously, and for taking such very very good care of little Cory.

--Cory ... a big big happy happy birthday to you ... either Wednesday (says Cheryl) or Friday (real birthday, we think)..., you make us all so happy, too, just like your big sisters!!!

Tons of love and kisses to all. Daddy and I are so proud of you!!! Thank you for being you!!!

love,
Mommy
XXXOOO

October 8, 2001
Subject: Re: Family Meeting #17

Well done, Gail, for getting this started!

My rock is to make massive progress on my wildlife film book.

Encouragement:

Gail: for buying the new car all by yourself and for doing such a wonderful job of it! For looking after Jen, Cory and the house when I was away in Chicago and Jackson for two weeks.

Kim: for writing a terrific first draft of your essay for graduate school. For having dinner with Hardy Jones (how did that go, by the way?). For running and keeping fit.

Tina: for thinking so thoughtfully and proactively about your future so you make wise decisions, and for reaching out to people for help (which is the key sign of a smart, successful person...a willingness to constantly ask others for advice, guidance and coaching).

Jenny: for looking after Cory with such love and dedication. For being patient and tolerant with your boring old Dad, even though he drives you nutty with his bizarre and eccentric parent-like behavior. For staying in touch with special friends like Sarah and Maddie. I encourage you to invite your new Holton friends home so they know you want them as friends!

I love you all so much. The best thing I have ever done in my life is contribute to building our very special family.

Daddy/Chris
XXXOOO

October 9, 2001
Subject: Letter to Tina

FYI...Below is a recent letter sent to my middle daughter, Tina, who is facing a lot of tough decisions. She is a sophomore at Dartmouth. Her reply, and my response to her reply, is also below.

_____

My darling Tina,

You have a lot of decisions to make, including your major, whether to go abroad, how often, where to live next semester, getting an internship, who to live with, boyfriends, whether to reapply to be a UGA again, maximizing your Dartmouth experience, and so on.

Virtually everyone in your situation would feel stressed and even overwhelmed by the huge number of decisions that have to be made, often in the face of great uncertainty, i.e., not knowing much about something but having to make a decision anyway.

Here is an idea that might help you handle this situation while retaining an inner peace and tranquility.

Write each of the challenges/decisions you are facing down on a sheet of paper or even better in your laptop. Write as many down as you can think of. Maybe you'll have as many as 20 or 30. Be as specific as you can. Break them up into as many different units as possible.

You will find relief just by writing them down and seeing them "outside yourself" on a sheet of paper. Writing them down is a key step. If you don't do that, all these issues will continue to slosh around in your mind, fogging your judgement, impairing your resourcefulness and creativity, and pushing you into a mood of resignation and even despair.

Writing them down begins a process in which you can begin to look at the challenges and decisions you have to make as an outsider would look at them. As a UGA, you are always helping others with their problems. I am sure you have noticed how other people's problems never seem quite a intractable and severe to you as they do to the person who has the problem.

Now the real fun begins. For each of the discrete challenges/decisions you have written down, do the following:

1. Write down (and I do mean write...thinking about it in your head is totally insufficient) a list of resources (such as friends, advisors, organizations, books, family members, professors and so on) who might be able to help you. Pick up the phone and ask for a meeting, or talk to them over the phone. (Moving to some kind of action, however small, is crucially important.) Ideally you would hire a professional coach to help you. Many senior executives in the corporate world do this regularly.

2. Write down the names of mentors and role models whom you could use to inspire you. You might know them, or you might only know of them. They are people for whom you have huge admiration and respect. Ask yourself how they would solve this problem if faced by it. Perhaps they would be so focused on bigger goals that the problem would seem trivial to them. That is helpful to see that. What would Churchill, Gandhi, or Gloria Steinem do in the specific situation you are facing?

3. Begin to envision a "perfect' solution. Imagine how it might work out in an ideal world. Close your eyes, and make the vision strong and powerful in your mind's eye. See it large. See it in strong, bright colors. Hear the applause, the warmth, the security, the success, the deep satisfaction. Feel the plaudits, the rewards, the respect and the accolades you have won through making the right decision. Enjoy the new friendships and camaraderie from whatever it is you have done. See yourself rising to the challenge. Envision yourself succeeding beyond your wildest expectations. Remember, whatever you can imagine, you can accomplish. If you can imagine it, you can do it. You can find a way, or make a way. Write all this down.

4. You have described the "what" above in #3. Now you need to articulate the "why", i.e., the purpose. If you have a strong enough purpose, you can achieve any "what". For example, you might write down to achieve my full potential as a human being, to contribute something meaningful to society, to give back to society, to have children, to bring joy and laughter to friends, to earn money so I can live comfortably, to leave a legacy, to be a role model for others, to build up my resume so I will be in a position to earn enough money to support my children later on, or whatever.

5. Write down the disappointment and the pain you will feel later on if you fail, or if you procrastinate, or if you give up too easily. This is the "opposite" if you like to #3 where you envision the rewards.

Tina, there is more you can do but that is probably enough for now. If you even take small steps in the above direction, you will find yourself growing in self-confidence and taking actions you would otherwise hold back from taking. Other steps you could take beyond the above include writing down what you want to focus on, what questions to ask yourself, what questions not to ask yourself because they are disempowering (for example, suppose no one responds to my request for an interview to get an internship? That is a disempowering question. A better question is: what can I do to maximize my chances that an organization will be willing to give me an interview?)

Other steps beyond the above include writing down your values and your beliefs.

All this is simply planning. The basic idea is instead of drifting in uncertainty and in a miasma of unsettled, paralyzing overwhelm, you plan your "work", and then work your plan.

Lovebug, I hope this helps. Remember that all you are going through is making you stronger, more competent, and more powerful. But watch out for your moods. Surprisingly you can completely control them. You always want to be in moods of gratitude, enthusiasm, optimism and resourcefulness, and never in moods of resignation, despair and pessimism.

Finally, list (in writing of course) all the things for which you are grateful. It is easy to forget how lucky we are. Compare yourself to the women who live under the Taliban.

We are so proud of you Tina. You do have a lot of things to decide, so be gentle with yourself, keep fit and healthy (as I know you do), be patient, keep to the fundamentals (your values of courage, love, compassion, honesty, hard work, learning, and so on), and remember what a huge success you are. Look at what a great person you are, your academic success, your friends, your good judgement, how loved you are by so many people, how beautiful you are, all your accomplishments, parachuting out of planes, the Outward Bound course, the fact that you care about important issues and are not consumed with trivia, and so much more.

We adore you Tina! Good luck with everything. Hope this helps.

I love you.
Daddy
XXXOOO

Tina wrote:
Dear Dad,
Thank you so much for your email. I just printed it out and went through it all and did write some stuff out on my laptop. I do feel better! And I just emailed Career Services to make an appointment to talk about a bunch of these things.

I really appreciate you putting in all that time for that, dad!

love ya!!
love,
tina

_____

I responded:
Well done sweetie-pie! Way to go! Taking action is the key, and you did that by calling Career Services. Planning without action isn't worth squat. Every day take some action of some kind, and you'll begin to find making decisions an enjoyable challenge.

Many people never learn how to make decisions wisely. It is a vital skill to have in life. Well done lovebug.

It is very important to keep your mood up. Remember that your body has a huge effect on your mood. If you stand tall, smile, greet friends warmly, act totally self-confident in your body, walk like an athlete, act like Ms. Popularity, then you will feel that way too. That's one reason why exercise and keeping fit and healthy is so important. It has a giant influence on your attitude and your emotional balance.

I love you Tina!
Dad
XXXOOO

October 21, 2001
Subject: Virtual Family Meeting #18

My Darling Family,
Here are my rocks for this week: I will give two outstanding speeches next weekend in Missoula, Montana, and I will make huge progress on my book.

Encouragement:

Gail: Congratulations on your wonderful work on your report "A Pink Slip Away"; thanks for having a lovely dinner together at Thyme on Friday night; and thanks for finding a terrific film to watch: Chocolat.

Kim: Well done for giving that dinner party last Saturday a week ago. I am so proud of you for creating a network of friends and for getting to know so many Japanese people. You are taking advantage of every minute you are in Japan. You understand that the way you live each day is the way you live your life. I can't wait to visit you there. Thanks for your patience while we wait to see what ol' Binny boy is cooking up.

Tina: I am so proud of you for being so happy at Dartmouth with all your friends, and for reaching out to your econ, orgchem and Spanish professors for coaching when you find the going is tough (and what student doesn't?). By the way, if you are not sure what question to ask, a good one is: Can you please help me cope better? Congratulations on being a great UGA. I know I can't say that because I'm not up there, but just call it Dad's intuition! And well done for making pizza dough from scratch and playing the guitar with Greta. I can't wait for you to start writing and playing your own songs. Write about pain! People love to hear about suffering!

Jen: I am so proud of you for wanting to run the Edgemoor Classic 5K race on November 3. I love to see you and Cory running. Now that tennis is over (and congratulations on being on the JV team), I encourage you to start a regular regimen of enjoyable daily exercises to toughen and strengthen your body, and make it more powerful, durable and resilient. I am so proud of how well you are doing at Holton, and the high marks you are getting, and your participation in class discussions. And although you haven't yet started inviting any Holton friends over to our home, it is obvious that you have made good friends there and are very well liked. You have used your exceptionally good social skills to join the class in a way that they welcomed you. Those skills will be invaluable to you all your life.

Note to all: Don't we have a great Christmas family photo this year?!

I love you!
Daddy/Chris
XXXOOO

October 28, 2001
Subject: I love you from Missoula!

My darling Kimmie, Tina and Jenny,
How are all my loves?

Kim, I heard you enjoyed Disneyland! We can't wait to read your first article!

Tina, I am so proud of you for building relationships with your three professors. That is a great thing to do. Put them to work for you! That's why I did so well in college: the professors gave me more help than anyone else because I kept asking them questions.

Jen, I am delighted you have invited some Holton friends to study with you today. Aren't you lucky that I'm not there to meet them and embarrass you! I am so proud of you for the terrific grades you are getting at school.

I am in Missoula giving two speeches, meeting with people, raising money, and planning new projects. With regard to the speeches, I am resolved to try something new and different for me, something that requires me to exercise courage.

I am determined to get away from the lectern and from my written notes, and go physically into the audience to try and really connect with them. To leave the safety and security of the lectern and my carefully composed notes is not easy. Talk about getting away from my comfort zone! But it is good for me to do something that requires courage. Courage is like a muscle: the more you use it, the more courageous you become.

I realized the importance of this when I began to think about the audience and what they wanted instead of me and what I wanted. As soon as a speaker gets behind a lectern and uses notes, the audience is put at a distance. Of course, I am not talking about the terrible mistake of reading notes. It goes without saying that to read a speech is to invite disaster. But even if you don't read a speech, the lectern itself is a barrier.

So I intend to go into the audience, ask them a lot of questions, get them involved, use my body expressively, be spontaneously funny, and use names of people in the audience as much as possible. There is nothing like using names because everybody then becomes alert, thinking that they might be next!

I will still begin the whole process by carefully composing word-for-word the whole speech because that way I discipline myself to do fundamental preparation. But after that, I will practice and practice and practice without any notes at all. The goal is to deeply connect with the audience so I don't waste their time.

Kimmie, Tina and Jenny, I love you and miss you.
Daddy
XXXOOO

October 29, 2001
Subject: Letter from Daddy in Missoula

My Darling Kimmie, Tina and Jenny,
I am so tired that I'm not sure this letter will make a lot of sense. I must go right to bed after this. I am getting up very early in the morning to get a flight to Denver.

Everything here has gone very well. My speeches seemed to work OK, and I got out of my comfort zone and went without lectern or notes.

Let me briefly touch on something that Tina mentioned to me tonight. Tina said she felt like she was on a never-ending work treadmill, with labs, exams, tests, studying and so on stretching out seemingly forever in front of her in an oppressive and unappealing manner. This is very stressful for you, Tina, and I am sympathetic.

Here are some ways of helping to cope with this. You each might well think of better ways:

1. Celebrate victories. A mistake I have made over and over again is to reach a near-term goal, and then ignore that accomplishment and rush on to the next task even before the ink is dry on the last job. Take a minute to savor the accomplishment. Write it down in a notebook, or in your laptop, called Accomplishments. It is a fantastic feeling at the end of six months to look at a list like that. You'll be impressed at what you are getting done!

2. Find ways to associate hard work, learning, and creating probing questions with pleasure, rather than pain. This is key. I can easily resist the temptations of television because I instinctively associate it with the pain of boredom, near-death dullness, and a languid torpor that I loathe. If you can train your brain to associate deep pleasure with work and learning, then the treadmill will be transformed into a bed of roses. I was too tired to write this letter tonight, but my brain associates writing to you three as a critically important thing for me, something that not only gives me great pleasure, but also great pain if I don't do it. There are techniques for doing this that I can teach you.

3. Keep your lives balanced. Every day make progress in the four areas of the physical (that's keeping physically fit and powerful with lots of vitality and energy), mental (that's your school work and your own study program), spiritual (that's finding meaning and purpose in your lives), and emotional (that's spending time with friends, loved ones, your sisters, and so on, really connecting with them). If all you do is work (mental), your lives will become unbalanced and unhappy. I know you already know this.

Now, Tina, get back to that treadmill!

I love you, Kim. I love you, Tina. I love you, Jenny.
Your ol' Dad
XXXOOO

November 10, 2001
Subject: Virtual Family Meeting #19

A big warm loving hello to our dispersed and wonderful family! I love you!

My Rock this week: To carve out time on my calendar to make massive progress on my big strategic goals, and not let my day be frittered away and dominated by my email in-box.

Encouragement:

Gail: For the exciting new job interview! I am so proud of you for finding and pursuing this opportunity with such alacrity and skill.

Kim: For writing to Tina and Jenny. That was terrific of you. For your wonderful article on deodorants and smelling. For your camping trip… what a great thing to do! And we wish you all the luck in the world on your upcoming exciting trip to China. Good luck with the big speech (I am looking out for the draft to review). Will you be visiting my birthplace Hong Kong?

Tina: For being so appreciative and delighted on receiving Kim's letter. For being willing to give blood! (or at least half your blood!) A huge congratulations on getting an extraordinary 102 out of 110 on your organic chemistry exam!!!! You worked, you focused, you conquered. Good going on your geetar with Greta! That is wonderful you are learning to play well. And finally good luck on managing the TV in your life. I encourage you to make it your friend, and not be its victim. PLEASE assure me that you will never stoop to watching the local news! Don't worry about not having a boyfriend (I know you don't). You are so attractive, you can get a boyfriend any time you want to…remember what I wrote to you last week: You get good at whatever you focus on.

Jen: I wish you had done better in your first report card from Holton! I'm not sure three A+ and an A and a B+ (which Ms. Raverby said was almost an A-) is good enough…HA HA HA!! Congratulations on a superb report! When Mommy and I saw your teachers yesterday, they said glowing things about you. Congratulations on doing so well. I encourage you in Mrs. Raverby's class to be more vocal and active in class discussions. If you do, you will get an A+ in that class too!! The secret to success in class discussions is preparation before the class, and boldness in the class. Finally Jen, thanks so much for running in the Edgemoor Classic 5K race last Saturday. I loved running with you!

I love you Gail!
I love you Kim!
I love you Tina!
I love you Jenny!
Daddy/Chris
XXXOOO

November 21, 2001
Subject: Gift giving this Christmas

To my extraordinarily special family! This is a special family meeting bulletin!

Christmas is coming, and with it comes all that stress from shopping in crowded stores, parking in full parking lots, hordes of people competing to get served, long lines, wrapping presents for ever, never ending to do lists, and gifts that cost a lot but aren't that valuable.

Is this how holidays should be?! I don't think so! What we want is to be together (sorry Kim), to have fun, to relax, to have delicious meals together, to get renewed and re-energized, to plan, to think, to reflect, to have time to feel thankful, to read and to write, to see friends, and to catch up on some good movies. Oh yes, and get a lot of exercise so we after the holiday, we are strong, healthy and powerful, and ready for all the challenges which face us.

It sounds so simple. Yet so often we feel trapped by our frenzied rush of spending and shopping which have little to do with what we really want.

What we really want (and I talk for myself here) is more memorable moments, more meaning, and less "stuff".

I have a suggestion which I have made in the past (and to which you were all wonderfully responsive) and which I bring to your attention again now. Let's add to the joy of the holidays by putting less emphasis on spending money to give fancy gifts no one deep down really wants. Let's be less commercial and less consumer-oriented.

Let me know if you agree!

I still remember the shock I felt on first coming to this country in the early 70s and seeing the incredible lavish extravagance of Americans at Christmas. American children seem to be highly acquisitive, wasteful, and grossly over-indulged. Parents seemed to be on a consumer binge. Everyone seemed to be stressed, hassled, excessively busy, and preoccupied by things of little consequence. On top of all that, the environmental costs of all the trash produced and energy consumed by huge volumes of store-bought gifts was very high.

So let's simplify our lives and put a much reduced emphasis on buying gifts from shops (sorry Mr. President). This will help us feel less stressed and tired. The goal is to have more fun, and to give gifts which are more personal and meaningful. You are all already so good at giving gifts along those lines. The poems, letters, parodies, paintings, and other creative gifts you have given me over the years are among the most special gifts that anyone has ever given me in my whole life.

To set a good example, Mommy and I are giving each of you a "charitable certificate" for $40. Please decide by December 20 what good cause to give it to. We will give it your name. Mommy and I get the deduction, but you will get the thank-you note! This will remind us all how fortunate we are and help to spark in each one of us the joy of giving.

I love you Gail!
I love you Kim!
I love you Tina!
I love you Jen!
I love you Cory!
Happy Thanksgiving!!!!!!!!
Dad/Chris

December 6, 2001
Subject: Virtual Family Meeting #20

My Rock: To finish writing "Jenny's journal" for 2000-2001. It is a big job! But worth it. I feel I am creating a family heirloom. Each future generation will find it more interesting than the last.

From the Shearer-Palmer Complaints Department:

1. No one under 22 is acknowledging and responding to these virtual family meetings! Participation is markedly dropping off! I hereby register a complaint and request that each family member contribute something, even if it only to complain that they don't have time to contribute!

2. Oh, sorry, I only have one complaint, but it is a biggie so go back and read it again!

Encouragement:

Gail: Thanks for decorating the house so beautifully! It looks gorgeous. Good job on the job search. Well done for the great job on the family Christmas letter. And well done for calling Jim Guest. Happy birthday on the 16th!!!!

Kim: What a great trip you had to China! And it sounds like you did a superb job on the speech. I encourage you to build on that, and look for opportunities (or make opportunities) to give speeches like that in Japan. Well done for continuing to have a great year in Japan, and for making so many friends there. Happy birthday for the 12th! We'll be thinking about you love bug! Good girl for calling Tina at Dartmouth. And good luck with your article on the birth control pill.

Tina: Have a super trip to Boston, NYC and Philly if you decide to go. Good luck this week with your exams. It is a heck of an achievement to do as well as you is doing at a school of the caliber of Dartmouth. Well done on the test results you got over Thanksgiving on organic chemistry and econ. Thanks for acknowledging the package you received so I know you got it.

Jen: Thanks for draining me of money for all those A+s you got! I commend you for having the wisdom to look up and learn the names of girls at Holton by looking at previous years' Year Books. That is so smart. You showed great self-discipline in the last 24 hours as you worked on and prepared for the in-class history essay you wrote today. We are so proud of you playing in the jazz band tonight at Holton, and the music concert following the jazz band. To hell with the Holiday Ball. You do whatever you like.

To Kim, Tina and Jen: Don't forget (per my letter to you just before Thanksgiving) to pick a charity to which to give a gift of $40. I saw a wonderful idea the other day: there is a group in Berkeley called Seva (seva.org), and for $40 (that is just purely coincidental) you can buy the gift of eyesight for someone in India, Nepal or Tibet (the cost of cataract surgery). But you guys pick whichever good cause that appeals to you. I know Jen is leaning towards an animal shelter which would be wonderful.

I sent you all our New Year's Resolutions for this year (2001) recently. Look over them with fascination! Look how much you accomplished! And when you didn't do something you wanted to do, reflect on why that happened. I had a huge failure in that I failed to finish one of the books I am working on, but I don't worry about it in the slightest. I enjoy reflecting on how my plans changed and improved, and how I responded to advice and new information (in this case from my agent Lynn). It is fun to compare the reality with the dreams of 12 months ago.

I love you! (Now review complaint #1 again above!!!)
Daddy/Chris
XXXOOO

December 23, 2001
Subject: Virtual Family Meeting #21

My Rock To have a wonderful Christmas with the family, and not miss Kim too much!

Encouragement:

Gail: Great NYT quote! Well done my love! And good for you for not over-reacting to Trudy's self-absorbed memo to Jim Guest. And thanks for all the health insurance stuff you do for the family.

Kim: We are so proud of you for the two articles you wrote recently. One was about your China trip (for the Washington Post) and the other was on Japan/Afghanistan comparisons (for USA Today). Good luck in finishing up the birth control pill feature for the International Herald Tribune. I am so glad Laura is spending Christmas with you. We look forward to meeting her one day. Thanks for responding to the last VFM!

Tina: We are so proud of you for getting an A- in organic chemistry. I think that is an amazing achievement requiring hard work, tenacity and intelligence. Thanks for thinking of the idea and then taking Jen to the Britney Spears concert. Good for you for keeping fit and strong by running regularly. Well done for earning money by working at the pastry store for that old grouch Arthur! I think your proposals to the Dickey and Tucker Foundations to seek funding to support your work trip to Costa Rica next March are very strong. Well done lovebug. Thanks for responding to the last VFM!

Jen: We are so proud of you for getting 100 in your history test last week. That is excellent, especially considering it was extracted from the Raverby! Thanks for not running away to DC for 30 hours last week! Phew, I know it was a close call! Good for you for practicing softball with me. Your throwing and catching are outstanding. Let's buy some more balls, plus batting gloves, plus anything else you need. I encourage you to develop a rigorous daily habit of exercise, especially strength training, so you are totally prepared for those times when you need to reach a high level of physical performance. I want to encourage you to join in the family virtual meetings more. It may not seem important but it is. Thinking through what is most important for you to accomplish in the upcoming week is something everybody (except Bid Laden) should do. Also remembering (or trying to remember) all the things family members have done which are good and for which you are grateful is important, and a useful antidote to the natural tendency some people have (Ok, Ok, I referring to yours truly, I know, I know!) to focus excessively on the negative and what has gone wrong. In fact, that's what made me start family meetings when Kim and Tina were little, to create an action-forcing mechanism to make me catch family members doing something right. So, Jen, please do your best to contribute to family meetings. We NEED you!!!

Other points:

1. Kim, we will call you on Christmas Day, BUT it may be impossible to get through because everyone is calling. I remember I usually couldn't get through to Granny and Grandpa on Christmas Day because all the international lines were clogged with calls. You are traveling on Tuesday anyway with Laura. I just don't want you to worry or be disappointed if we don't connect.

2. Don't forget, everyone, to prepare your New Year's Resolutions and email them to me in the first week of January or earlier.

3. Don't forget to prepare Predictions. And remember it isn't a prediction if you predict an event in March and write your predictions in April!

4. Have you all chosen the recipients of your $40 charitable gift?

5. Constantly read and learn all you can. Keep a private learning journal like I do, and whenever you learn anything that interests you, put it in there so you don't forget it.

6. Jen, we need to start thinking about and planning for your activities this summer. Any thoughts on what you would like to do? Holton Creative Summer maybe?

I love you. Happy Christmas!
Dad/Chris
XXXOOO

2002

January 08, 2002
Tina wrote:
Mom that's great!!! It's funny cause it makes it sound like YOU individually are the publisher of consumer reports...hehe. Good job!

The audition was okay... kind of funny. We were SO nervous - I was looking at Greta as we were playing and her fingers were shaking!!! He basically told us we wouldn't get it, 'cause he only has space for 1 lesson... but he was really nice, and we can try again for the summer. And rush was pretty good - I'm really excited about this, but it is kind of scary - what if none of them want me?!?!!! last night and tonight we're going around to all the houses for 45 minutes and just talk to all the sisters. It's a pretty cool experience, I'm so glad I'm doing it. And all my friends are doing it.

I love you!
Love,
Tina

I replied:
My darling Tina,

I am so proud of you for going in for the audition. It would have been easy for you and Greta to have given in to the fear of rejection and not done it. But you did the right thing. You made yourselves vulnerable, made "an offer in the market place", and are stronger as a result. It doesn't matter that you didn't win. The important thing is that you showed character and courage by doing it.

Same for rush. Progress is only made by making yourself vulnerable to failure. If you don't make offers and put yourself out there, a person will lead a very dull and failed life. Naturally it is scary; who wants to be rejected? But that is where courage comes in. And the more you do these kind of things (volunteering, asking questions, making offers, going to Costa Rica, creating new possibilities for yourself and others) the easier it is, and the richer your life becomes. So it doesn't matter that you don't get invited to join a sorority because YOU HAVE ALREADY SUCCEEDED JUST BY GOING FOR IT!! If you can learn something from every life experience, then it is impossible to fail.

Like you, I am so glad you are doing rush! GO TINA!!!

I love you.
Dad
XXXOOO

January 12, 2002
My darling Kimmie, Tina and Jenny,
I went to NYC for one night on Thursday night and forgot to send you a letter! I don't think I've done that in 20 years! I actually didn't forget. I just failed to get it done. Anyway, I felt bad that I had broken my record of always leaving you a letter each night when I am away, so this letter is to apologize!

I love you!

Kim, it was wonderful to talk to you last night! Thanks for calling. I'm glad you and John had such a great time together. Can't wait to see your big article on birth control published today.

Tina, it was wonderful to receive all your emails this week about rush! Mommy told me you were ranked very high in all four lists, so that is great (although I feel for the girls who were ranked low). We are dying to know whether you picked Theta or Signa Del. Let us know!!

Jen, it is wonderful to see you so happy, so fit, so Cory-loving, so focused on doing well in your upcoming exams, and so here instead of in a tough boarding school out in the wilderness somewhere, taken there against your will! I hope you don't get too many A+'s so I don't go broke!

Kim, Tina and Jen, you are each unique and incredibly special and accomplished. Mommy and I are so lucky to have you as our daughters. We adore you.

Dad
XXXOOO

Sat, 19 Jan 2002
My darling Kimmie,
Thanks so much for your big, wonderful package! It arrived yesterday, and after I got home late from the office at 8 PM or so, I spent time reading all your articles and examining everything you sent us.

It was so thoughtful of you to send your ol' Mom and Dad all this "stuff". We loved getting it.

The photos were super! Were you able to find the plaque on the house in Hong Kong saying "Chris Palmer was born here in 1947"?! Keiko looks very nice. You orange picking!! (reminding me of picking peaches in Israel in a kibbutz in the late 60s).

The photo of you between Nicholas and Kevin is one of the best photos I've ever seen of you. You look beautiful. And as I told you last night when you called (BTW, thanks so much for calling!), the guy on the right has a faint resemblance to me, in that he looks graciously handsome, charmingly chivalrous and delightfully debonair!

The photo from your birthday party looks great, and the photos from your speech in China are intriguing! You look terrific! I wish someone had videotaped it. And the group photo of all the Luce Scholars is lovely.

Kimmie, your letters to Mommy were the nicest gift to her. Mommy was thrilled and honored to receive them.

Now the articles: Your most recent articles were published in the January 12/13, 2002 edition of the newspaper. Your writing is highly professional. Your review of Janet Jackson was good; not too effusive, not too obsequious, not too destructive; a well written collection of interesting observations.

Your article on the use of birth control pills in Japan (in the same Jan 12/13 issue) was absorbing and informative. That article performed a valuable public service.

The deodorant article (published Oct 27/28) about how different nationalities think they smell differently was provocative, amusing and well written. You had sent it to us earlier.

On Nov 17/18, you published "Racism Becomes a Lifelong Issue". It was a profile of Murphy-Shigematsu. Excellent writing and an engaging portrait.

Then on Nov 23, you published a book review "Let a hundred loves blossom". Hmmmm. I may pass on that book! Useful review though, because it allowed me to know enough about the book so I could judge whether or not I wanted to read it.

Your Nov 29 article on handmade quilts was charming and lovely! I particularly liked how women nurture their relationships and talk together while quilting in circles.

Finally your movie review of Shrek on Dec 15/16: a professional and admirable job. Well done lovebug. I want to see Shrek after reading your review.

Kim, we love you and we miss you. Thanks again for the wonderful package you sent us.

Buckets and oodles of love.
Yer ol' Dad
XXXOOO

January 20, 2002
Subject: Your big package!

Kim wrote:
Mom and Dad-
Thank you for that long e-mail dad, it was nice to know my package was appreciated!

And it was so nice to talk on the phone recently!

I got my haircut here for the first time - it was so different- she used these scissors that layer it. I really like it, and then you get a massage at the end, it's just how they do hair here - Dad you would love it!

I really miss you guys! I don't know, maybe it is the weather, but I really miss you more than I have this whole time now!

I spent the day with Keiko, we had lunch and then did some shopping, cool food shopping - I got special Japanese dried fish that has lots of calcium!

Now I am meeting Masato, we are going to an art museum. I don't know though, I am sort of not in the mood for the stress of a date!

LOVE you!
Kim

I replied:
My darling Kimmie,

Don't be saddish, eat a radish!

Your mood will inevitably move up and down. What helps is a steady focus on your goals, and lots of exercise. I know you do both those, which is why you are so happy most of the time, despite the vagaries of boyfriends, work pressures, etc.

Can you email us a photo of your new haircut?! I bet you look gorgeous!

Hang in there sweetie-pie.

We adore you.
Daddy
XXXOOO

January 23, 2002
Subject: A Love Letter From Cory

Woof, woof Jenny! I am dictating this to Dad just before he rushes off to the airport to go to Montreal to work on the post-production of his Tigers IMAX film.

I love you! In fact, the truth is, I adore you as much as a puppy can adore anyone. You are so special to me. You are the best puppy owner a puppy could ever yearn for. You love me, you feed me, you give me treats, you train me to roll over, you take me on walks, you take me on runs, you pick up (gingerly I've noticed) my #2s, you get so excited when I go #1 when you ask me to, you let me snuggle on your bed, you let me in your bedroom, you get Alice in to make sure I'm healthy, you play with me in just the way I love to play, you look at me admiringly, you boast about me to other people (which makes my tail wag), you cuddle with me, and you look after my EVERY need! I am so so so lucky! I love you.

Woof, woof, woof! Lick, lick, lick!

From you adoring, faithful, loving, loyal and devoted puppy,

Cory

PS Dad says he will be home tomorrow evening.

January 27, 2002
Subject: Virtual Family Meeting #22

My Rock: to give a dazzling speech next week in Alberquerque, NM.

Encouragement:

Gail: I am so proud of you for all your quotes in USA Today and other leading newspapers. Thanks for taking Cory to class today. And thanks for all the delicious meals you cook for Jenny and me. Your letter to Zechauser for Kim is great.

Kim: Congratulations again on Chicago! Good luck in the Philippines. I am looking for dates when I can visit you in Japan! Send us a picture of your new haircut! Your birth control article was excellent. Thanks for the big package with all the articles you've written, the photos and the letters. I hope Peggy publishes your China article.

Tina: Your recommendations on movies (Billy Elliot, A Wonderful Mind) are very good. Thanks! Well done for working so hard on your orgo exam and your stat exam. Sorry the latter was so hard. Well done to you and Greta for going in for the guitar audition. I am so proud of you for doing rush, and then getting into Sigma delt. And the wild west party last night sounded cornswagling good! Good luck if you go to Japan to see Kim. It is so nice that you want to go.

Jen: I commend you for the focus, self-discipline and determination you showed in preparing for your exams. Your results in Spanish, bio, math and English were terrific Thanks for practicing softball with me. I'm sure you'll get on the JV team. You throw and catch beautifully. I am so proud of you for having the courage and common sense to go and see Susan Springler to make sure you were accepted into Creative Summer. You'll be a great CIT2! I encourage you to start reading more. Please read voraciously. Television will rot your mind. Books will sharpen it and make it smart, flexible and confident. Do everything you can to absorb knowledge. I am very, very proud of you for getting into a routine of rigorous exercise. It makes you look like a winner in every way. I encourage you to continue building up your strength, endurance and flexibility to even higher standards. It will have amazing and positive effects on your life. Do we need to buy softball gloves and balls? What about roller blades?

One last thing Jen: here is a paragraph from the last Virtual Family Meeting which you must have overlooked!: I want to encourage you to join in the family virtual meetings more. It may not seem important but it is. Thinking through what is most important for you to accomplish in the upcoming week is something everybody (except Bid Laden) should do. Also remembering (or trying to remember) all the things family members have done which are good and for which you are grateful is important, and a useful antidote to the natural tendency some people have (Ok, ok, I referring to yours truly, I know, I know!) to focus excessively on the negative and what has gone wrong. In fact, that's what made me start family meetings when Kim and Tina were little, to create an action-forcing mechanism to make me catch family members doing something right. So, Jen, please do your best to contribute to family meetings. We NEED you!!!

For everybody:

1. Well done to everyone for doing their predictions (now safely stored away until next December 25) and their New Year's Resolutions.

2. Did everyone arrange to give a $40 charitable gift? If not, let me know what is holding you up.

3. Gail, let's set a date for our big April party!

I adore you Gail, Kim, Tina, Jenny and Cory!
Dad/Chris
XXXOOO

February 1, 2002
Subject: Letter from a Loving Dad in Albuquerque!

My Precious Loves, Kimmie, Tina and Jenny,
I love you so much! Tomorrow I give a big speech here in Albuquerque about bears and how we made

our new IMAX film *Bears*. I've been on the radio promoting the event and they are expecting the theater to be packed tomorrow night. I hope so! I like big audiences!

I flew here today very comfortably and with zero feelings of stress. I felt completely safe. As I came through the gates at Reagan National Airport, two US soldiers with guns were standing there on duty. I went up to them, and thanked them. They looked surprised and pleased by the compliment. I felt so grateful to them.

Oh how things change. When I was in my twenties, I would denounce spending on the military as wasteful and anti-social. Look at me now! I see an American soldier, and my little heart is filled with patriotic fever and tears of gratitude and pride!

Kim, Tina and Jen, you are three spectacular people. Mommy and I are so proud of you. You work hard, you keep healthy, and you choose wonderful friends. You design your lives instead of drifting aimlessly through your lives, and you constantly show initiative, enthusiasm, curiosity, and determination, as well as great consideration for others. You would each score extremely high marks on any emotional intelligence test.

I love you.
Dad
XXXOOO

February 3, 2002
Subject: Letter from a traveling Dad

My darling Kim, Tina and Jenny,
I wanted to write to you last night from Albuquerque, NM, but I couldn't because someone (with whom I wasn't very happy!) sent me a huge power point attachment that took over 24 hours to download!! This meant that my hotel phone line was tied up all that time, and I couldn't send any email. I am going to fix my laptop so that this won't happen again.

Anyway, my three loves, I am home safely after a hugely successful trip. The audience seemed to love my talk (which I had worked very hard on), and I was successful in making them laugh with gusto which I greatly enjoyed. It was lovely to get home to Mommy, Jenny and Cory.

Jenny told me today that she is going to get Cory a shirt which says, "Dog in therapy training". Wouldn't that be adorable? That would be like Cory going to Harvard!!! Tomorrow night, Jen and I take Cory to her first test in this area. I hope she passes!!

Tina, I heard about Danny! Would I like him, do you think?!

Big news: Jen responded to the last Virtual Family Meeting! Glory to life on earth and Amen! At least, that what Jen claims! Jen told Mommy and me that her computer ate her contribution! And now Jen says her laptop has lost it completely! At least Jen didn't attempt to claim that Cory ate her email!

I adore you!
Dad
XXXOOO

February 15, 2002
Subject: darn

Tina wrote:
I didn't get the Tucker funding. I just got a blitz about it. Hopefully I'll get the other one.

Happy Valentine's day!

love,
tina

I replied:
My darling Tina,
One of the most challenging times people face is when they get rejected. It is a real test of character.

Every successful person in the world faces rejection time and time again. In fact, the more successful they are, the more rejections they face because the only way to become successful is to make offers that might be rejected. The reason people succeed is that they keep putting themselves in situations where they are vulnerable to getting rejected. In other words, they make "offers in the market place", just like you have done by trying for the Tucker funding. If you don't make offers, then your life will never get going and be very dull.

Making offers is risky and takes courage, whether you are asking a boy out, attempting to get into Dartmouth, writing a book, asking for money, asking for advice from a professor, asking a group of strangers in the dining hall if you can join them for a meal, jumping out of an airplane, doing Outward Bound, or whatever.

The other reason successful people succeed is that they don't give up. So your reaction: "Hopefully I'll get the other one", is a great response. Always be optimistic, always look to turn every experience (especially the rejections) into learning experiences.

I remember feeling totally dejected over and over again from being rejected as I was growing up. It is part of life. It IS life! So sweetie-pie, don't get down because of Tucker. Instead give yourself a pat on the back for trying for it. As the saying goes, better to have tried and lost than never to have tried at all. Mommy and I are so proud of you, and we know you will keep trying, keep making new offers, keep greeting rejections with good humor, and we know you will have the resolve, creativity and courage never to give up trying to excel and do your best.

So hang in there! We adore you lovebug.
Dad
XXXOOO

February 21, 2002
Jenny wrote:
I'm so bored! I'm gonna be done with all my hw for tonight and most for the weekend in like an hour! ahhh

I replied:

Jenny, I'll say this in a whisper so you don't think I'm yelling: FIND A FANTASTIC BOOK IN THE LIBRARY, YOU MORON, AND ENJOY LEARNING AND GETTING EDUCATED!!!!!!!!!

You have an incredible library there. Explore it!!!! Exercise your curiosity!!!! Learn!!!!!!!!!!!!!! The person who has the ability to read but doesn't read might as well be illiterate. The world is a tough and rigorous place. It doesn't tolerate ignorance and incompetence. It is imperative that you be in constant mood of never-ending improvement. Just look around and see how much suffering and misery there is. These people have not learned the fundamentals of living. They keep making mistakes day after day. And one of the most common is to watch too much junk TV, and to stop reading and growing as a person. You should set yourself a goal of increasing your vocabulary by five good words a day. A rich vocabulary gives you the opportunity to be articulate, wise and persuasive. Here are some good words for you to learn and use (especially if you don't read widely): ignorant, stupid, short-sighted, dumb.. .ok, I'm only pulling your leg. Here really are some good words for you to learn and use: exciting, exuberant, inspirational, excellence, outstanding, talented, informed, articulate, passionate, determined, wise, far-sighted, ambitious, self-confident, energized, authentic, original, exhilaration, vitality, enthusiasm, transform, tranquil, curious, dynamic, powerful, strong, spirited, robust, strenuous, and diligently. Reading widely is fundamental to achieving success in life, how ever you measure success. SO GET GOING BUDDY!!! GO FIND SOME BOOKS THAT KNOCK YOUR SOCKS OFF!! (I was only joking when I called you a moron!)

I love you.
Dad
XXXOOO

March 4, 2002
Subject: Virtual Family Meeting #23

To my darling and most precious family:
My Rock this week: To give five effective and inspiring speeches this week in Atlanta at our big NWF Annual Meeting.

Encouragement:

Gail: Congratulations on being asked to speak before the House Health Task Force this Thursday. It is great CBPP is doing it with you!! Thanks so much for doing our taxes! Well done for being on the panel recently at the National Press Club. And well done for getting Richard Zechauser to inquire at Harvard on behalf of Kimmie (not that she needs any help). Let's set a date for our big April party.

Kim: So glad you have a steady stream of friends visiting you (like Katarina last week). We'll miss you on March 21 when we all go to see Bears. (I am so glad Mommy, Tina and Jen are coming.) Congratulations on your excellent China article in the Washington Post. (Just call me VP for Promotion at Kim, Inc.!) I am so pleased Alison is going to visit you, and Tina is thinking about it too!! I can't wait to see you May 2-7!!! Your dating articles in the IHT were excellent too. And thanks for all the great photos!

Tina: Congratulations for being awarded BOTH the Dickey funding (digression: Mommy has a funny Dicky-do joke about Gordon!) and the Nancy Boehm Policy funding. We are so proud of you. More importantly, I want to commend you for the way you handled the disappointment over the Tucker funding. You showed great resilience, and this is a sure sign of successful people. They feel the pain of defeat or rejection, think hard about what they can learn from the experience, talk to friends and coaches to extract every ounce of learning and wisdom from it, and then bounce back determined to carry on and not give up. Remember the secret of success is to fall down 19 times, and get up 20, and not the other way. I've told you this before, but one thing experts have noted about champion tennis players is their rapid speed of recovery from a bad shot or some other downer on the court. Within nanoseconds, they are back feeling optimistic, confident and resourceful. And this is what you did, Tina, when you were rejected by Tucker. You are all set for Costa Rica April 3 to June 5! Fantastic. I'll miss you by about three hours when you come home on the 13th! Darn and boo! My plane takes off from Dulles for Spain at 7 pm. I'm sure Dan likes you. How could he not? I am so pleased your social life is thriving. And I am so very proud of you for singing your song at the coffee house. That is marvelous!

Jen: I've noticed you are reading a little more, even if they are books that you have to read for school. Keep it up! I've also noticed that you are very selective and discriminating in what you watch on TV. That is good. I also love the way you are exercising more, and getting stronger and stronger. Thanks for practicing softball with me. I love doing that. Your Holton report at the a few weeks ago was outstanding. And I don't care whether you get in to JV softball or not; I am just very proud of you for wanting to get it and for working towards that goal by steady and regular practice (I don't think we'll be returning those cleats though!) You try so hard in history. You should be very proud of yourself for the effort you made on that recent history essay on which you got an 88 and you were frustrated you didn't do better. Whatever you focus on, you will get better at. Congratulations on achieving the highest score possible (a "1") on your solo and ensemble trumpet playing! Shall we buy you a printer for your room? And do you want roller blades?

Gail, I love you!
Kim, I love you!
Tina, I love you!
Jen, I love you!
Cory, you old pooper, I adore you too!
Dad/Chris
XXXOOO

March 09, 2002
Kim received this letter:
From: Crystal Johnson <ciohnso@midway.uchicago.edu>
To: kimberlyspalmerhotmail.com
March 6, 2002

Ms. Kimberly Palmer
Monarch, Shirogane
3-2-1 Minato-ku #502
Tokyo, 108-0072
Japan

Dear Ms. Palmer:

I am very pleased to inform you that you have been admitted to the master's program at the Irving B. Harris Graduate School of Public Policy Studies at the University of Chicago. The Committee on Admission and Aid accepted your application based on outstanding academic achievement, professional commitment, and personal motivation. Our decision reflects confidence in your continuing promise as a student. In turn, we are certain that you will contribute greatly to the intellectual vitality of the program.

This electronic message serves as official notification of both your admission to the program and any scholarship awarded to you by the Harris School. We are using e-mail to convey your news as quickly and efficiently as possible. There are several documents and forms attendant with an admission offer, so we have established a web site where you may review and download all the materials you will need to assist in your enrollment here. It is listed both here and at the conclusion of this message: www. harrisschool.uchicaco.edu/current/info.html

Further, the Committee has awarded you a Harris Fellowship, the School's most esteemed scholarship. The fellowship covers full tuition ($27,450 for the 2002-2003 academic year) and a stipend of $10,000. As a Harris Fellow, you will be invited to participate in several social and academic occasions during the year. I have enclosed specific information detailing the conditions of your award for the coming year and fellowship renewal procedures for future years; you should review it carefully.

You must inform us of your intention to enroll by April 15, 2002, the candidate reply deadline. To do so, sign and return the Admission Reply Form. Please include the $350 non-refundable deposit with your acceptance to assure your place in the 2002 entering class. The deposit will be credited toward your total costs.

The Admission and Aid Committee extends its warm and sincere congratulations to you. I hope this letter will be a subject of happiness and pride for you, your family and friends. We hope you will be joining us in the fall.

Sincerely,
Ellen Cohen
Director of Admission

P.S. You may find all the forms you need at:
www.HarrisSchool.uchicacjo.edu/current/info.html

Should you have any questions about the information in this message or at the site, feel free to contact me directly at (773) 834-2576, or via e-mail at cohen@uchicago.edu. I look forward to hearing from you.
==================
Crystal C. Johnson
Asst. to Dean of Students & Dir. of Admission
Harris Graduate School of Public Policy
1155 E. 60th Street
Chicago, IL 60637
Ph: (773) 702-8401
fax: (773) 702-0926
= = = = = = = = = = = == = = = = = = = = = = = = = = = =

Kim sent the letter to us and wrote:

Oh my goodness! This is so cool! That is so much money! What should I do?????
Love you!
Kim

I replied:

My Darling Kimmie,
I can't begin to tell you how proud Mommy, Tina, Jen, Cory and I are of you. I read this letter and almost burst into tears. I don't know why I felt so moved. Maybe because I am so exhausted from this week's intensive schedule and all my speeches, but the real reason is that I feel so incredibly proud of you three girls, and the letter from Chicago triggered a flood of appreciation for how accomplished you have become. I felt the same way when Tina got a letter from her host in Costa Rica a few days ago, commending her for taking 'the plunge' and deciding to go to CR. You three girls are wonderfully gifted, and all of you work hard to constantly improve yourselves so you can excel and be forces for good in the world. You probably don't fully appreciate the gift you give to society by your example, by your behavior, and by your accomplishments. I have been talking to literally hundreds of people over the last few days, and it is amazing how many of those conversations involve stories and observations about you three and Mommy.

Kimmie, you bring such honor to our family and such hope for the future of the world. Just imagine how society would be enriched if there were more people in the world like you three.

Congratulations sweetie-pie!
Dad (sniffle, sniffle)
XXXOOO

March 15, 2002
My darling Kim, Tina and Jenny,
I miss you! I love you!

I am in Spain, as you know, at a giant screen film conference. Lots of meetings. Very productive and useful. I leave tomorrow for England to see Granny, Tim and Jon.

I mentioned this to Tina and Jenny on the phone: Before I left home, I had been so busy getting prepared for this trip and so busy tying up all the hundreds of loose ends from our Annual Meeting in Atlanta (which only finished three days before I was due to leave to come here). All that frenetic busyness left me with four regrets that I reflected on during my flight to Spain:

1. A regret that I didn't spend nearly enough quality time with Jenny in the last few weeks.

2. A regret that I didn't make time to help Mommy more with her funny speech for Mark.

3. A regret that I forgot to leave a handwritten note hidden in Tina's bed like I did for Jen. I knew Jen was going to be climbing into bed that night, and forgot Tina would be as well! I felt terrible for that oversight

4. A regret that I forgot to bring any socks beyond the ones I was wearing!

Oh well. Live and learn.
I adore you!
Yer ol' Daddy
XXXOOO

March 21, 2002
Subject: Preparing for Costa Rica

My darling Tina,
In case we don't have a chance to talk at length before you go (since I got stood up for lunch today!) here are some thoughts off the top of my head to help you prepare:

1. Be prepared to be very homesick the first week or so. You'll have no friends, the family may be cold, where you work may be scary, and you may feel isolated and lonely.

2. As soon as you meet your family, give them a small gift, and learn their names. Keep a small notebook and write their names down. As you learn about them, jot notes down about them so you have questions to ask them and comments to make at meal times. Force yourself to take an interest in them. Mood follows action. Learn about the parents and grandparents and find out what they feel about historical events in CR that happened when they were alive.

3. Study Spanish all you can. Learn key phrases. Imagine the worst situation you might get in, and learn phrases to get you out of them. Make sure you know how to say things like: Get away from me! I need help! I am lost! Please call the police! I am scared, please help me! This is the crime of rape! Please stay with me until we are safe! And so on.

4. Act confident at all times, even if inside you are shaking. Never give away that you feel fearful.

5. Please re-read the booklet you wrote on self-defense at Holton.

6. Please take a piercing security alarm with you (with new battery).

7. Before you go, write out your prime goals while you are there in your notebook. Review them once a week to check you are keeping on track. I hope they will include having fun, making new friends, keeping a journal, speaking Spanish as much as possible, learning as much as possible about women's health issues, and acting brave at all times.

8. Try not to take anything to CR you are not prepared to lose. Try to leave irreplaceable things at home. One exception is the journal that I hope you keep. Write it as if for your grandchildren. Include vivid details.

9. As soon as you can after arriving, find out how to obtain emergency health care in CR in case you ever need it, and also how to call the police.

10. Resolve to be cheerful (even when miserable), to help others less well off than yourself, to be assertive, to create rapidly a network of friends and contacts in CR, to form a strong bond of friendship with Gail, to ask lots of questions, and to write down everything you learn so you don't forget it, especially things relating to health issues.

Sweetheart, we are so proud of you! I know you will have a fabulous time. By anticipating breakdowns, you can head them off before they occur.

I adore you!
Daddy
XXXOOO

April 2, 2002
Subject: Your great package!!

Darling Kimmie,
I loved your big package of articles and photos! Thanks so much Kimmie! And thanks for your sweet cover note.

All your photos are fun to see. Tatsuo looks very nice indeed. I am looking forward to meeting him. Nice pedicure! You looked fabulous in all your pictures, e.g., the one of you with purifying incense. Are those the hot baths I'll be trying out??! (with other men, I mean)

You are a very accomplished writer, Kimmie. I read all your articles carefully. I found ten of them:

1. Dec 29-30, 2001: Review of Don's Plum.

2. Jan 12-13, 2002: article on oral contraceptives.

3. Feb 1, 2002: Review of book Women on the Verge

4. Feb 9-10, 2002: Profile of performer Mark Oshima

5. Feb 16-17, 2002: The demand for Japanese males, plus the article at the bottom on nationality as a common come-on in personal ads.

6. Feb 23-24, 2002: Review of America's Sweethearts.

7. March 2-3, 2002: Review of Jeepers Creepers.

8. March 8, 2002: American born woman Buddhist priest

9. March 16-17, 2002: Profile of British entrepreneur Safia Minney.

10. March 23-24, 2002: Sales surge in diet products, plus another article on the bottom of the same page on obesity.

Whew!! You have been working so hard, and you have been very productive. Congratulations lovebug! I really enjoyed reading all your articles. You could make good money next year in Chicago as a movie critic or book reviewer! I very much liked your reviews of Jeepers Creepers, and of America's Sweethearts.

We adore you, and we all miss you. Cory says woof woof. Cory is sad today because Tina leaves early tomorrow morning for Costa Rica for two months and Cory will miss her.

Buckets of radishes (and to hell with Princeton!)
Daddy
XXXOOO

April 4, 2002
Subject: am so very proud of you

My darling Tina,
I am so very proud of you. Courage is overcoming fear. If you have no fear, there is no need of courage. Everybody is fearful of different things. The courageous person is like you; they face up to and recognize their fears, assess them in a grounded way, prepare carefully, and then they move forward with deliberate intentionality, with total alertness, and with their eyes wide open.

You left Dulles by yourself, to go to a third world county you have never visited before, to be greeted at the airport by a complete stranger, to go to a host family you have no idea about, to do a volunteer job that might (if you are unlucky) be anything from dangerous to boring, and you took a flight that scared the bejeezus out of you.

Despite all these uncertainties, you sucked it in, moved forward, prepared meticulously, saw the bigger vision that drove you forward, could see the long term advantages of making the trip to Costa Rica, and assumed a great attitude of optimism.

On top of that, you immediately started networking like crazy, for example, forming a friendship with that 26 year man who helped you when your pick up driver was late, and meeting those two other Dartmouth girls. Way to go Tina!

I am so very proud of you. You showed all the characteristics of people who are successful.

We are LONGING to hear more from you. Remember to teach. Remember to make requests. Remember to make offers.

I love you.
Your loving Dad
XXXOOO

April 07, 2002
Tina wrote:
Hi guys! Okay so the girls I'm with like checking their email a lot, that's why I can write you so much... they both have boyfriends, always want to call/write them. I'm so glad I don't, go me.

Sooo!!! I love it here!!!!! This morning we went on a hike in this ecological preserve, and saw a waterfall, and a banana plantation, and a cool little animal.

Last night was nice, we didn't do anything. They have elections here today, and it's so interesting cause they are not allowed to sell any alcohol yesterday or today or tomorrow, cause they don't want fights to break out. Isn't that cool!

So I sat in the hostel and read and wrote by candlelight, then learned how to fry a plantain! Those are those huge banana like things. And it was so good! I'll cook it for you when I get back.

Dad, what are you thinking about visiting? I don't know, just cause I'm going to be gone basically every weekend travelling with the volunteers, and then during the week I have to work. If you want to come, the best time would be during the week, and I could not work for a few days, and we could plan a fun little trip, or go stay with your friends or something. But I'm really happy and not lonely at all, so it's okay if you don't come. But if you want to I'd love to travel with you of course!

We're about to get on the long bus ride back to san Jose...

Please don't write me at this address, but to cpalmer519@hotmail.com

Thank you! I love you!
Kim - email me

love,
Tina

ps. Do you think there's any way you could send me some stuff here, or would it be too expensive? Cause I really want mase (I'm sure I won't need it but it'd be nice to have while walking places), and I don't know if I could buy it here. It's fine if you can't, I'll be fine! I have my screecher but I think mase would be more effective.

April 7, 2002
Darling Tina, how wonderful to hear from you!
Go you too Tina!!!!! (re boyfriends!)

You sound so happy lovebug. What experiences you are having! Please keep a detailed journal, even if it's only for your eyes.

Plantain, eh? Mmmmmmm.

Re visiting: Let's hang loose on it. I'd love to visit you if you wanted me too. If you were unhappy, I'd come immediately, but fortunately that isn't the case. If things continue to go well for you, if I were to visit, it would be in May after I return from seeing Kim in Japan on May 7. Let's see how things look for you in a few weeks' time. I'm happy not to come if you are doing just fine. So let me know how you feel in a few weeks' time.

Re mace (note spelling): Of course there are circumstances where it can be helpful and even life-saving. The companies that make them will have a zillion stories showing how useful they are. But anecdotes are not proof and they only tell part of the story. I have read other security experts who point out that mace has a downside: it gives an excuse to the mugger to get violent (after all, you attacked him), and they might seize the mace and use it on you. Better, I suspect, for you to use other strategies:

1. Never go anywhere without a buddy.

2. Always ask people if it is safe to go in the part of town or the street you are in or thinking of going in.

3. Always be assertive and ask appropriate strangers for help and assistance, even if it is only to say, "I am afraid of that person, and would you please walk with me until they leave me alone." (You should practice saying that in Spanish.)

4. Always walk with energy, alertness, vitality and strength. Never look vulnerable or weak. Let your body posture reflect resolution, determination, strength, invincibility and power.

5. As the situation deteriorates, your voice is an incredibly powerful weapon. Scream, shout, cause a scene. Women hate to do this. They much prefer to be polite. You have to overcome that cultural training. Emulate your flawless performance in the bathroom in the basement of the St. Barts a few months ago.

6. Use your piercingly loud alarm whistle.

7. Per your self-defense classes, get on the ground and use your legs to defend yourself.

Remember that prevention is better than a cure.

I don't think I would be allowed to send mace through the mail because it is a weapon. If you feel you need it, then ask around and buy it in Costa Rica.

Gail, Kim and Jenny, please comment if you have different ideas.

I love you sweetie-pie! I am so proud of you for making the most of your time abroad.
Dad
XXXOOO

April 7, 2002
Subject: Virtual Family Meeting #24

Hello my darling precious family:
My Rock: Make massive progress on my wildlife film book this week.

Encouragement:

Gail: Great work getting the tax rebate ($7,000 smackeroos!). Thanks for introducing me to financial whiz Suzy Orman. Well done for organizing the speech tomorrow night at Holton on stress, and getting journalist Laura Sessions Stepp to be there. Thanks for all your hours of work for Kim helping her with Harvard and Chicago. Thanks for coming to the book event today to listen to Jay Winik dazzle us with his presentation on his book April 1865.

Kim: If you decide to select Chicago, we will be so proud of you. If you select Harvard, we will be equally proud of you. They are both equally distinguished schools. Chicago REALLY wants you. So if it were my choice, I think I would go there. I like the idea of you going to law school, but Mommy is less enthusiastic, and you know how Mommy is usually right and I am usually wrong! Please move fast to get the University Housing you want in Chicago. And please find out why Princeton had the myopic audacity not to select you! I am totally baffled by that. Thanks for all your wonderful articles and photos. It amazes me that you are only 22 and writing major articles for the IHT in Japan. Sorry you felt homesick recently. Well done for rebounding from that so well and with your usual resilience. PLEASE take a whole month off in August at home to have some downtime. You will be working very hard at graduate school in the fall. Can't wait to see you on May 2 in Tokyo!!! So long Tatsuo...it was nice knownuo!!

Tina: What an incredible adventure you are having. And I don't mean just the zip lines in the Monteverde cloud forest and your dramatic and scary canopy tour, but just the adventure of being on your own, meeting the wonderful Costa Rican people, seeing a whole new culture, making new friends, speaking Spanish, taking care of yourself, and learning oh so many new and exciting things. Go Tina!! Robin and Jenny sound lovely. And your jobs (taking a blind, crippled girl who lives under a bridge to rehabilitation, working in a girl's shelter, and working in a shelter for pregnant teenagers) are extraordinary and challenging experiences in themselves.

Jenny: Mommy and I so loved watching you play JV softball on Friday. You looked so good out there... so athletic, so confident, so able, so alert, so cool. Thanks for practicing softball with me today in the garden. I love doing that, especially on such a beautiful, crisp, sunny and invigorating day. Well done on getting all A's on your report card. I love you getting such good grades, especially when I know that your focus is not on grades so much as it is on learning and questioning. And I love your Holton friends like Sarah Burgess.

Oh dear, I'm sure there is lots of things Iam forgetting! Help me out when you reply!!!

I adore you all!
Your loving and devoted Dad/Your loving and devoted husband
XXXOOO

April 14, 2002
Subject: Advice

My darling Tina,
You sounded a little down tonight. Let me see if I can help.

1. Re Laura: All you can do is "actively" listen. Show her you understand her feelings by articulating her feelings better that she can do so herself. For example, "I realize that you really wanted to go to Oxford, and you know that I was somewhat indifferent. Then I got in and you didn't. If I was in your place, I would be so angry at me for seemingly taking the place you so wanted. I feel terrible about it, etc.,) Apologize. Tell her how terrible you feel. Tell her you don't want to lose her as a friend. Tell her how much your friendship means to you. Tell her that if you were in her position, you wouldn't write to me either. Tell her how sad and distressed you are that she is not writing to you.

That's about all you can do. Having done that, relax knowing you've done the right thing, and focus on other things until she writes to you.

2. Re: a lousy weekend at the beach: Autonomy is one of your biggest goals in life. You were deprived of it this weekend. Constant learning should also be one of your biggest goals in life (assuming your goal

in life is to be happy) and this weekend you were also deprived of that. People are never really happy when they are drifting aimlessly without a deep purpose. So it is not surprising that your weekend was lousy. Look on it as a good learning experience, and try not to let it happen again!

3. Re: lack of friends: Jenny and Robin are emailing every two hours or so, and you wonder why they have so many friends and you don't. First, don't compare yourself to anyone except your own personal mission statement/New Year's Resolutions/Life Plan, or whatever you call your own vision of what you want your life to be. You are unique, and the way you design your own friendships will be unique to you.

Second, to have friends, you have to reach out to people, and so may be it would be good to email more and write to your friends more.

Third, focus on the people who have the potential to be lifelong friends i.e., the people of incredibly high caliber when it comes to integrity, courage and fundamentals like that.

Fourth, make yourself into a more interesting person by dedicating yourself to learning. Keep a "learning" journal in which you jot down everything you are learning, things you want to discuss with others, interesting things people tell you, fascinating facts, beliefs you want to challenge, authors you want to study, aphorisms, insightful jokes, biographical information, and so on. Keeping asking why. People will be drawn to you if you are an interesting person.

Fifth and finally, help others who need help. If you help people get what they want, they will help you get what you want, so constantly look out for ways to help people. You reap what you sow, but you have to be patient for the harvest. Understanding delayed gratification is the key. The greater the effort you make, the greater will be the reward.

4. Any other problems?! Just call me (aka Ann Landers!)

Tina, you are doing wonderfully! There are bound to be ups and downs. Mommy and I are so proud of you. On Wednesday, you would have survived two weeks down there! That is cause for celebration!

I adore you, Tina. Hang in there sweetie-pie.
Daddy
XXXOOO

Mon, 15 Apr 2002
Darling Tina,
We got your wonderful first letter today ... THANK YOU HONEY!!! I am so glad you found the letter I snuck in your suitcase ... I was afraid they would search your bag, find it, and when you didn't know what it was it would cause you problems (at the airport)!

Daddy says that you emailed today and he will share your note with me, can't wait! Your family sounds so wonderful... how very nice of Rita to take you into town your first day to show you around!!! So interesting that she said that you don't look American (right) ... but just don't talk!!:))) By the time you leave, maybe you'll be able to talk!! :)))

OH news flash from Holton-Arms.... 20 people in Jenny's class were nominated for class treasurer ...

they voted to narrow it down to 3 ... and Jenny is one of the three! Go Jenny!!!
We love you so much and miss you so!!

Love,
Mommy
XXXOOO

April 16, 2002
Tina wrote:
Hey Mom! I'm so glad the letter got to you! Sorry I forgot yesterday to reply to all of you to dad's note...

Things are so good. oh my gosh, I love this country. This morning was so nice. I went to the home for pregnant teens, did some computer with them, but then they had sewing so I came back to Santa Ana, went to the bank, and got coffee and wrote a few letters to friends, it was so nice, sometimes I really need time like that to think about everything.

Soon I'll go back home, eat lunch (which is always SO good - rice and vegetables or beans or chicken usually... so healthy too), then I'll take Scarlett to rehabilitation, then I'm going into San Jose with one of the volunteers, Robin, to explore, and i want to buy a little guitar.

Then I'll come back home, eat dinner with the family (which is always so fun too! They're so great), then I'll help Rita clean up (also so fun! they have great soap here, maybe I'll bring some home), then I'll go to my room, write and read, and around 9 I am so incredibly exhausted I can hardly move, so I sleep soundly from like 9 until 6:30 when the sun wakes me up, then I get up and have the amazing breakfast Rita has waiting on the table!!! What a life!

Jen -- GO YOU FOR GETTING NOMINATED FOR TREASURER!!! That's so great! did
you win???

I love you guys!
love,
Tina

April 16, 2002
Darling Tina, that is the nicest letter!! And we loved your handwritten letter to us which arrived yesterday. What a loving daughter you are.

Isn't that funny! I sent you a note an hour ago with this brilliant idea suggesting that you use your newly acquired skills of singing and playing on the guitar to break down barriers and create new friendships, and then I read your note below, and you are already way ahead of me!

To appreciate the simple things in life like you are now...that is the beginning of wisdom. Soap! Cleaning up the dishes! Sleeping soundly! Writing to a friend! These banal and humdrum activities are really sacred when you see the horror of what is going on in the Middle East. Pop Pop used to say, "Just give me a bird to look at, that's all I need to be happy." One of my goals in life is to simplify it and spend time only on projects which are important to me.

Please give a message to Rita and her husband "Gracias muchos amigos for taking such good care

426

yesterday, today and manana of our precious daughter Tina!!!! We deeply appreciate all that you are doing for her, and we gracias you muchos muchos for the bueno love and bueno care you are giving her!"

My Spanish is pretty darn bueno I think!

I love you.
Daddy
XXXOOO

April 27, 2002
Subject: Virtual Family Meeting #25

To my darling precious family:
Rock: to get ready for a great visit to Japan with Kim!

Encouragement:

Gail: for your great performance on C-SPAN!!! And what a nice note you received about that from Margy Heldring! For keeping everything together this week at home while I was away in Montana.

Kim: for recovering from food poisoning!! For incredible experiences in Vietnam ("the American War"!) and Laos. For all your observations about those countries (such as the ubiquitous sewage smell). For looking forward to seeing me next Friday!!!!! For responding to VFM #24.

Tina: for recovering from food poisoning!! (Did you and Kim coordinate the timing?! You both got sick at almost identical times!) For responding to VFM #24. For ordering a guitar! Rita and her family will love to hear you play. I am dying to learn more about your sea turtles experience. Do you remember the huge and magnificent loggerhead we saw on the beach in the middle of the night in the US Virgin Islands a few summers back? We watched it as it laid its eggs, seemingly oblivious to us watching her. What species of sea turtle did you see? All eight species are highly endangered. Tina, would you like me to visit you in Costa Rica? Let me know!!!!

Jen: For working hard on your Joan of Arc paper. For keeping your recent softball losses in perspective. For being so helpful to Mommy last Tuesday morning when Mommy was getting ready for her big C-SPAN debate. For getting a 92.66666666666666666666666666666666666 on your history essay, and 8 out of 10 on your bibliography. For being invited to play varsity softball. For your sweet and supportive email to me this week about my funny keynote speech.

I am scrambling to leave my hotel in Missoula now to get home, but wanted to get this VFM off to all of you. I should be home by 9 or 10 tonight. This week in Missoula has been tremendously successful for me. Wonderful people. At a big dinner last night, someone challenged me to stand on my hands! The trouble was I had just eaten a big meal! I did it anyway to much laughter and applause!

I adore you.
Your loving ol' Dad
XXXOOO

May 20, 2002
Darling Jenny,
I'm sure you will do great in your presentation on Joan of Arc, especially if you remember to:

1. Be enthusiastic! Let your passion shine through! Give the speech from your heart. Remember what an amazing person she was. Let your feelings of awe for her accomplishments radiate from your face, posture and body.

2. Enjoy yourself! Have fun! If you enjoy yourself, the chances are the audience will too.

3. Think about the needs of the audience. They want to be entertained!

4. Be physical! Move! Gesticulate! Put your body in motion! Point, laugh, smile, shake, rattle and roll! Wake up the class by being dynamic and powerful.

5. Get the class to interact with you by making them laugh, asking them a question, getting them to stand up, ANYTHING to keep them awake and eager to hear you talk.

Good luck lovebug. I know you'll do great!

I love you.
Dad
XXXOOO

May 25, 2002
My Darling Kimmie, Tina and Jenny,
One of my shortcomings as a father has been to fail to talk to you about sex and to fail to convey to you my standards in this important domain of life. it has been weighing on my conscience.

My parents didn't talk to me about sex, and I am sure their parents didn't talk to them.

The idea of talking to you fills me with dread, partly because I'm embarrassed, and partly because I haven't got the faintest idea of what to say. I know we often joke and laugh about sex, but that is very different from having a straightforward discussion on the topic.

All the books on this subject say that parents should talk to their children about sex. This letter is to compensate for my failure to do that. Apparently I am not unusual. According to a Kaiser Family Foundation study, over 50 percent of parents rarely or never talk to their teens about sex. That is shocking, and I am part of the problem.

I favor sex education in schools that teaches both abstinence and the use of contraceptives. I know this may seem like a contradiction, but so be it. I want you to be as knowledgeable as possible about sex, sexually transmitted diseases (STDs), and contraception. I want you to seek out information and ask questions. You have never asked me questions about sex, but that is almost certainly because I've unconsciously sent you signals that I'd be embarrassed if you did.

I favor abstinence until you are married or at least much older. I understand that if you marry late or decide not to get married, then that standard may be too high. By sexual behavior, I am including anal sex, oral sex, intercourse - - anything that is sexual "playing around".

As you know, kids are having sex at younger and younger ages. Apparently one in four sexually active teens will contract a STD. 20 percent of sexually active girls ages 15 to 19 get pregnant each year. STDs and risky "anything but intercourse" behaviors are rampant among teens, and there is an epidemic apparently of herpes, genital warts, gonorrhea, and gonorrhea of the throat (yuk!).

Apart from STDs, being actively sexual as a teenager or even in your early 20s, can lead to pregnancy, dependency on boys (yuk again), depression around breakups and cheating, and other suffering. These are burdens I'd rather you not have. You have much more important things to do with your time.

However, I don't want you to associate sex only with disease and suffering. It can also be warm, fun, life-affirming, and a wonderful way to express love — and, of course, it can be hugely enjoyable and relaxing. In the context of a loving relationship, it can be unforgettably very special. Heck, it can lead to the procreation of wonderful children and grandchildren!

When you eventually decide to have sex, I hope you will use contraceptives, and use safe sex practices. Premarital sex is always risky (television portrayals not withstanding) because of the risk of pregnancy and disease, and you should always be cautious. I'm not saying you should never have premarital sex because (as I've already noted) you may end up marrying late or never getting married, and such a standard might be absurd.

I wish for you a mutually faithful monogamous relationship in the context of a happy and loving marriage. As Debra Haffner says in her book *Beyond the Big Talk,* any moral sexual relationship should be consensual, nonexploitative, honest, mutually pleasurable, and protected against disease and unintended pregnancy. If you don't meet these criteria, then you can be subject to upsetting emotional trauma.

I am anxious to keep you safe from disease. What greater responsibility does a dad have than to keep his daughters safe? Condoms don't eliminate the risk of disease. Only abstinence can do that. The late stage ravages of sexually transmitted diseases are, as you know, ghastly.

I want you to get coaching on how to side-step unwarranted sexual advances, and how to say no in uncomfortable sexual situations. On the other hand, I want you to enjoy feeling beautiful and sexually attractive. Why should you be denied that? You have a right to feel good about yourselves. It is fun to flirt in an innocent Katie Couric-type of way. I think of it as making authentic contact with people. I do it all the time. It is vital for you to understand (as I know you already do) the importance of emotional intelligence and living your lives according to your deepest principles and beliefs.

I wrote you a letter on sex back in July 1997. Here is part of what I wrote:

> My darling Kim, Tina and Jenny,

> ...A recent article in the Washington Post reports that children in grades five through eight were told: "A nurse will be talking to your parents about sex. What questions would you like her to talk about?" The ten questions most frequently asked were (and I have added my comments in parentheses):

1. What changes might happen to me? (I will leave that one to Mommy.)

2. When do periods start and will it hurt? (I will leave that one to Mommy as well.)

3. Why do people have sex and how do you do it? (Oh brother.)

4. How come moms are so hard to talk to about sex? (I don't know why dads are left out of this question.)

5. What is the normal age for a kid to have sex? (I think the ideal for both men and women is not to have sex until you get married, and then to be totally monogamous.)

6. When do you know you are ready to have sex? (Oh brother.)

7. What is the most effective form of birth control? (Abstinence, I presume.)

8. Is it okay to be gay? (Of course.)

9. Is masturbation wrong? (Absolutely not -- it is perfectly normal and totally okay.)

10. What is HIV and how do you get it? (I need to be better educated on this myself)

Phew. I'm glad we had this little talk, girls. Now I can go back to watching the ball game!

I adore you.

Daddy
XXXOOO

I wrote that letter to you, as already noted, in July 1997! I remember Granny telling me it made her roar with laughter!

I hope you will talk to your kids (if you have any!) about sex so we break the family habit of not talking about it.

I love you more than I can say.
Your devoted and loving Dad
XXXOOO

May 26, 2002
Subject: Virtual Family Meeting #26

To My Darling Precious Family:
My Rocks: Make massive progress on my wildlife book, make massive progress on my projects at work, read five books, have fun at home with Gail, Jen and Cory.

Encouragement:

Gail: Great work on the exciting new, entrepreneurial idea you are developing at CU. Thanks for going to see The Importance of Being Ernest (Oscar Wilde is one of my favorite people). Thanks for playing tennis last night. Let's do that more! Thanks for fixing all the fallen trees. I love the colorful hanging plants on the porch, as well as the inspiring American flag you have put up there. I also love the colorful plants around the tree by the road you planted. Thanks for all the help you are giving Kim on her housing in Chicago.

Kim: Have fun in Mongolia, China, Tibet, and wherever else you are going in July. Please send us details so we know where to come looking for you if we need to. I encourage you to start packing NOW!!! Break the job into 20 or 30 subtasks, write them out and do at least one every day. In this way you can remain tranquil and at peace, and avoid a stressful panic at the end. I LOVED my visit to you in Japan! Thanks for being such a generous and loving host. Your article about Mommy in the Washington Post was wonderful and I encourage you to write more of them. What a great way to make money and do good at the same time! I'm sad you and Tina will miss each other most, if not all, of August; that makes your time together in Japan even more important. I encourage you to email Uncle Jon so he knows when to expect you. I've already given you his coordinates and I KNOW you are so well organized that you can retrieve that information from your filing system in under five seconds (if you can't, you have a problem that needs fixing immediately) but here it is again: jon.palmer@withyking.co.uk, and his phone number (which I have also already given you) is 1225 (that's Bath) 44 53 71. His number in the office is 425 731. (His two numbers are easily confused so Jon remembers them by the different groupings of numbers.) I'll copy Jon on this so he knows to expect your email. I'll also copy Tim because I know he would love to see you too. We'll see you (just after you've seen Jon, Tim and Granny) at 2:30 PM on Thursday August 1 at BWI.

Tina: Happy Birthday again for last Sunday lovebug! It is hard to realize you are now 20. Gail sounds such an interesting person. And that is exciting about those two boys spending a month in the US at a camp. What a wonderful thing for them. That sounds like a smart decision for you not to go on the turtle trip. I think you are learning to decline effectively! A lot of women never learn this because they are taught by society to say yes to requests so they please people. They end up over extended, exhausted and perplexed why they are not happy. I love to see you declining things after judicious reflection on what commitments you can and cannot make. (I note in passing, and for your amusement, how this advice directly contradicts another pearl of wisdom I have given you in the past, namely, "help others get what they want, and then they will help you get what you want".) I am so glad all your friends had a surprise birthday party for you! I'll meet you at 11:17 PM at Dulles on Wednesday June 5!

Jenny: Happy 15th Birthday again for last Wednesday lovebug! Well done for working so hard for your exams next week, and not just letting the work waft painlessly over your eyes, but actually simulating the exams so you are really learning. And well done for taking the SAT 2 Biology test. If you keep at it, and keep observing where you are falling short of 800, I know you will push your score higher. You have a lot of determination and tenacity. Well done for your Joan of Arc speech, and for scoring 100 in your math test. The concert was wonderful! We were so proud of you and your trumpet playing. Congratulations on winning MVP on JV softball! Wow!! Coach K said such complimentary things about you. Well done for playing on Varsity softball, and for acting as though you were pleased to be doing it. Thanks for all the love you lavish on Cory. And thanks for being such a delight to have at home. Thanks, too, for going to the Father/Daughter dinner with me. What the heck are we going to do now on Monday nights now that Boston Public is over?!

Cory: Well done for bringing such joy and happiness to the Nursing Home residents. You are the best therapy dog ever.

I adore you all.
Dad/Chris/Alpha
XXXOOO

June 8, 2002

My darling Jenny,

I miss you! And I miss Cory. The house is uncomfortably quiet without you both (and now without Tina too). Are you playing the trumpet? Are you using your laptop? Are you fitting in some exercise between romps with Cory, Henry, Erin and Leigh? Idea for you: Do exercises with Erin and Leigh! Put on music, make it fun, and teach them the distinction between stretching, strength and endurance exercises.

Here is what I miss about Cory: her wagging tail; her "please play with me" posture; her face when she goes weewee; her sweet nature; how she seizes the purple leash when we are walking/running and takes ME for a walk; how she suddenly gets a whiff of a scent and follows it with her nose glued to the ground; the exuberant, bouncy way she wakes up in the morning with her tail wagging, her nuzzles and kisses, and her wonderful doggy expressions of love and affection; her total living in the moment; her total lack of resentment when I won't let her grab something in her mouth; watching you train her and teach her tricks; and wrestling with her like I used to do with my brothers when we were kids.

Jenny, Cory is so lucky to have you as her devoted, caring, competent and loving "Mom".

I adore you and miss you.
Dad
XXXOOO

June 9, 2002

Subject: Letter to Cory!

Here is an extract from my journal. I love you! XXXOOO

Sunday, June 09, 2002
I sent the following letter to Cory today:

Darling Cory,

Please ask Jen to read this to you! I want Jen to know what you told me before you left home on Saturday morning when we went for our long run. You told me some of the many things you love about Jenny, including:

--The way Jen lets you snuggle up on her bed at night.

--The way Jen greets you when she gets home from school; she is so pleased and overjoyed to see you.

--The way you know with absolute certainty that Jen loves you, even on those rare occasions when Jen gets mad at you (e.g., when you are naughty in the garden and don't "come" when Jen says "come").

--The way Jen washes you so lovingly and thoroughly, and then tells everybody to feel you because you are so soft!

--The way Jen fastidiously picks up your poo with TWO bags! (You told me you'd still like to know why Jen thinks it's worth collecting!)

--The way Jen gently cleans your ears and your beautiful teeth.

--The way Jen clips your nails, and occasionally your gorgeous coat.

--The way Jen thoughtfully removes your collar when you eat so it doesn't disturb you by clanking against the bowl.

--The way Jen says goodbye to you so lovingly when she leaves for school.

--The way Jen teaches you new tricks and gives you treats when you do them right.

--The way Jen protects you from mean dogs (like Leonard's, although you told me you've never seen Leonard's mean dog because Leonard's body is always placed between his dog and you!)

--The way Jen lets you know every day that she is your best friend in the whole world and that she adores you.

--The way Jen lets you hide under her desk for comfort when there are scary noises outside that make you apprehensive.

There! I know Jen will be pleased to learn all these wonderful thoughts from you, Cory.

I love you too!
Please tell Jen I love her so much.
Alpha (and don't you forget it!) Dad
XXXOOO

June 9, 2002
Subject: Jason

Tina,
Jason called tonight.

He spoke virtually no English, so not much information was exchanged between us. From his tone of voice and mutterings, he was obviously (and understandably) deeply frustrated that he couldn't speak to me to tell me whatever message he wanted to convey to you.

Did you not tell him you'd be away? It seemed very unfair that he called you and spent a lot of money fruitlessly, money he doesn't have.

433

Please be careful not to give men expectations that cannot be fulfilled. It can trigger them into a rage. They can feel manipulated and cheated, even though you had the best of intentions, and manipulation was the farthest thing from your mind.

I know you'll dismiss these comments because I know nothing and I don't know Jason. But I do know that calling someone and expecting them to be there, and then finding them gallivanting off in NYC and Japan, can hurt terribly if it inconsistent with earlier behavior.

I just don't want anyone to get hurt. What if he unexpectedly turns up here, expecting you to be the same Tina he met in CR? I just don't want things to happen that you can't handle.

Sorry to be a pest and a pain.

I love you anyway.
Dad
XXXOOO

June 11, 2002
Subject: Love and kisses

My darling Kimmie and Tina,
I am thinking about you and hoping you are having a wonderful time together. What has happened to the boys, like Daniel??

Tomorrow is Granny's birthday. She will be 84. We have sent her flowers, gifts, cards, faxes, and I will call her. I don't know how she keeps going.

Today I had tears in my eyes driving home. I was listening to stories about the founding fathers. The friendship between John Adams and Thomas Jefferson (for many years they were alienated because of political differences) is a moving story of love and forgiveness. The profound affection between the young Lafayette (who gave up everything in France at age 19 to come to America to support the fight for freedom) and the father-like figure of George Washington (who was childless) is very touching. The tender, deep and enduring love between Abigail and John Adams is admirable in every way. I love the way Ben Franklin comforted Thomas Jefferson while the Continental Congress butchered his draft of the Declaration of Independence. I find so moving the description of Washington's goodbye to his fellow officers when the war was over and he resigned his commission.

I love learning about the founding fathers. They were an amazing group of men (and women like Abigail Adams) who lived by principles. We owe so much to their wisdom, compassion and courage.

One common characteristic of all of them, and which partly explains their greatness, is that they were voracious learners and readers. They loved to learn anything, to imbibe new knowledge, and to absorb new ideas. They hungered to know how the world worked.

It is nearly midnight, and I am tired.

I adore you Kim. I adore you Tina.
Dad
XXXOOO

June 20, 2002
Subject: classes! need advice

Tina wrote:
Hey,
Okay, so I can't take both anthropology and the American art class cause they're at the same time. So now I'm thinking I'll take a history class - history of warfare, and American art (cause I need those distributives...) and then Micro Econ. That means I won't be taking anthropology! What do you think? I don't know what to do! I could just wait and take an art class next year I guess... help!!!! The anthropology class looks so good... argh....

Thanks,
Love Tina

I replied:
Sweetie-pie, the first thing to remember is that anything you decide is great! It is hard to go wrong, as long as you work hard, have fun and love learning.

Second, give a little thought to skills you want to develop to help you later have a fulfilling and fun career.

Third, if it was me (which it isn't), I would consider taking an art class next year, and selecting anthropology, micro econ and history for this semester.

Good luck in your decision-making. Observe yourself during the process and see how you can strengthen your decision-making ability. It is a skill, something you can get good at. Ask yourself: Did I list the pros and cons for each combination of options? Did I list the criteria I wanted to use to evaluate the different options? Did I consult with enough people, and the right people? Did I think long term? Did I challenge myself enough?

Also remember that as soon as you've made your decision, forget about the turmoil of trying to decide, and don't keep questioning yourself. Instead, become filled with an inner tranquility knowing the decision is behind you, turn your total focus on the subjects you've selected, and fall in love with them. That is the path to success.

Good luck, Tina! I'll copy Mommy, Kim and Jen on this in case they have any thoughts on what I've said, or additional thoughts.

I adore you.
Dad
XXXOOO

June 24, 2002
Subject: Virtual Family Meeting #27

To my wonderful, precious family:
My Rock: To not get overwhelmed with my book and swept into a mood of resignation and despair, to not give up, to keep looking for ways to move forward, to look for ways to break a seemingly impossible

job into doable subtasks, and then get them done one by one.

Encouragement:

Gail: for keeping fit, for getting an outstanding job performance review, for being cheerful and optimistic at work even in the face of a pay cut, for developing a superb new project and building a powerful network of political support for it, for going to the Club party with me, for cooking delicious chili tonight and wonderful meals every night, and for being you.

Kim: for going to China with your fellow Luce scholars, for packing up your apartment in Tokyo without totally panicking and leaving it to the last moment, for letting us know your travel plans in China and Mongolia, for preparing what I am sure will be an excellent presentation to the other Luce scholars, for saying such nice goodbyes to all your wonderful friends in Japan, for enjoying the huge goodbye party for you in the office (which went on all night!!!), for welcoming Dean Couvares to Tokyo, and for being you. (BTW, Tim says he would love to see you in London. Any chance? You could stay with them in Wimbledon if you want.)

Tina: for being so happy in school, for taking on three challenging (and fascinating) subjects this semester (anthropology, physics and micro economics), for enjoying living in the basement with Greta, for getting along with all your new roommates, for loving Dartmouth, for all the adventures you've had this year, for pushing yourself like you do to get out of your comfort zone, for going to Oxford in the fall, for questioning whether you want to be a doctor, for not marrying Jason (just kidding), and for being you.

Jen, for playing tennis with me four times last week, for going boating with me and Cory on the Potomac, for enjoying Cory's headlong and totally unexpected plunge into the Potomac, for washing her afterwards thoroughly, for all the affection you lavish on Cory, for the job you have just started at Holton as a Counselor-in-Training at Holton's Creative Summer, for enjoying said job, for your stunningly good exam results last semester (virtually all A+s), for getting 740 in your SAT 2 Biology exam (terrific!), for sticking with your braces for the last 75 years and now you look gorgeous, for painting Mommy's nails so beautifully before the party at the Club last Saturday, for trying to be selective in the television programs you watch and for realizing that too much television in deadly to the spirit, and for being you.

To you all: a big thank you for my wonderful Father's Day! I appreciated all the warm loving thoughts, cards and other gifts from each of you.

Remember: a smooth sea never made a skilled sailor. Relish difficulties because they are what make life interesting. Every difficulty you face is an opportunity for character growth.

Kim, you've got a cold. I never got colds for two reasons: I stay away from people who have them, and I wash my hands with hot soapy water regularly, especially before eating. And I eat incredibly healthily so my immune system is always at its peak. My health is a gift I give to all of you as the father in our family. When I am fit, you never have to worry about me, and I am always there for you whenever you need me.

I adore you.
Dad/Chris
XXXOOO

436

PS: I received a lovely compliment from Delores yesterday. She took a course on diversity, and one of the discussions dealt with human relations. It contained advice on how to get along better with others, build team spirit, and so on. Delores Xeroxed this page and left it in my in-box with the following note: "Chris, you deserve my highest praise in this category... THANKS so much for ALWAYS behaving with good manners, thoughtfulness, dignity and respect."

Wasn't that nice? Delores and I have worked together for over 17 years now.

July 21, 2002
My darling Kim, Tina and Jenny,
After stretching, weight-lifting and exercising this morning, I took Cory for a run. Jenny put Cory's collar and leash on Cory, I grabbed a poop bag and off Cory and I went. At the end of the first block, Cory went #2, I praised her, and on we went with our run and one full poop bag.

When we were as far away from our house as we get on these 1 to 2 mile runs, Cory surprised me by going #2 again. I hadn't brought another poop bag, so I swore under my breath, and glared at it with frustration. I had two choices: run home and get another bag, or else pick it up with my hand and take it home. I chose the latter because I was eager to get home and swim laps in the pool before having breakfast.

So I gingerly picked up Cory's lovely poop (which would totally revolt me if it did not come from Cory) and started walking rapidly home (walking, not running, so the poop wouldn't fall out of my hands). I often see neighbors and friends as I run with Cory, and so had resolved, if I were to see anyone, to call out firmly, "Stay away from me; have stinky dog turds in my hand and you don't want to get too close to me!"

I had already planned out my next steps in my mind: get home, dump poop in lined bucket, wash hands in hot, soapy water, go for an energetic swim.

I got home and headed for the dog poop bucket. DARN! There was no liner so I couldn't dump it in!!! I felt immediately angry with Jenny. It is her responsibility to take care of that. I yelled for her, and was mean to her. Jenny said to me with some vehemence, "I don't like you Dad!"

During my swim, as I had a chance to reflect a little, I realized I had behaved badly to Jenny, and made up my mind to apologize to her as soon as I got home. I told her I was wrong and said I was sorry.

This little poopy incident reminded me that it is important not to let the big questions (my relationship with Jenny) get lost in the small questions (why am I walking around with dog poop in my hands? Jenny must be to blame for my aggravation!)

Everybody has "to do" lists. Most of them are not useful because they are not rooted in the "big picture" of their lives (am I living my dreams? am I smiling and laughing? am I contributing to society? am I loving? am I honest and honorable?). You want to derive your weekly "to do" list from your life plan, not the exigencies of the day.

I remember when I was young, I usually had a daily list of jobs I wanted to get done, but they were not consciously related to the bigger goals in my life (mainly because I had only the vaguest idea of what they were!)

To encourage me to get around the challenge of having a stronger congruence between by daily activities and my long term life goals, I don't call my daily "to do" list a "to do" list. Rather I call it a list of "commitments". I ask myself, "What am I really committed to get done today? What really matters to me?" And every Sunday evening, I review my Life Plan to see what I am neglecting, and to see what strategic goals I need to focus my energies on in the coming week.

I hope this is helpful lovebugs!

I love you Kimmie. I love you Tina. I love you Jenny. I love you Cory!
Dad XXXOOO

July 28, 2002
Subject: I love you (from Dartmouth)

My darling Kim, Tina and Jenny,
Mommy and I have had such a wonderful time at Dartmouth this weekend with you, Tina!!! From enjoying the wonderful communal lunch with everybody exuding camaraderie, to running through the verdant campus, to plunging into the cold Connecticut River, to canoeing in perspiring tranquility on the river, to the thrilling Indian headdress in the Hood Museum, to relishing the singing on Saturday night, to loving the lyrical songs you and Greta played to Mommy and me on your guitars, to seeing where you sleep in the basement, to seeing how determined you are to succeed at Dartmouth, to learning how you have introduced "family meetings" into your house with all your girlfriends, to seeing the bowl of "rocks" on the table which you use as a metaphor for "rocks", to seeing you wear the pants you got in Costa Rica, to seeing you imbibing books like Pirsig's (The Art of Motorcycle Maintenance...), to talking to you about being as intentional and design-oriented in your relationships as you are in your academic work, to seeing you keep fit, strong and in beautiful shape, to eating all those meals with you, to working at Borders with you, to seeing where you work on Friday nights at the Green Bean, to meeting all your delightful friends, to meeting the parents of your delightful friends, to running into Rufus, Heather, Kate, Justin and many other lovely friends of yours, and (most important of all) to seeing you so relaxed, self-confident and happy, it was a very special time for Mommy and me. I think Greta, Heather, Natalie, Betsy and Laura are all lovely people (Kern too, and I was sorry to miss seeing her), and I hope they will be lifelong friends of yours.

Thank Tina! And I am looking forward to having breakfast with you at 7:15 AM tomorrow morning before I return home!

I love you Kim (dying to hear all about your trip to England!!!!), I love you Tina, and I love you Jenny.

Good night, don't let the bedbugs bite, and if they do, Cory will go poo!!!
Dad
XXXOOO

August 4, 2002
Subject: Virtual Family Meeting #28

To My Precious Family:

Rocks: My rocks next week are to do whatever I can to help Ed, and to continue to keep very fit through daily stretching, weight-lifting, running and swimming so that I have the stamina and strength to write my book and give the many speeches I have coming up in the early fall.

Encouragement:

Gail: for all your creative and excellent work on the debate in the Senate on medicare prescription drugs, for your wonderful friendship with Jessica next door, for all the entertaining we are doing (thanks to you) with the Sugrues (last night with Tom, Pat, Erin, Kerry, Lloyd and Betty was a very special evening!), the Burgesses, and Kim's friends next Wednesday, for collecting Kim from BWI on Thursday and for taking Jenny and Maddie to BWI yesterday, for making all Kim's doctor's appointments, and for raising money (or beginning to start to) at work for your great project.

Kim: for returning safely home after a whole year of adventures in the far east, for visiting Granny in England, for seeing Tim, Jon, Jill, Mary, Clifford, Richard et al, for having cipro on you when you needed it, for camping out in Mongolia with all your Luce scholar friends for ten days, for giving your presentation in Bejing in the kimono Asoka's Mom so lovingly made for you, for staying in close touch with us this whole year while you have been on the other side of the world, for doing a great job writing for the International Herald Tribune over the last year, and for spending a month at home with us before going off to graduate school in Chicago (giving you a chance to catch your breath, see old friends, and relax).

Tina: for organizing a memorable Parents Weekend for Mommy and me at Dartmouth, for having great friends at Dartmouth (we so enjoyed Greta, Heather, Natalie, Betsy and Laura), for singing and playing your guitar (with Greta) so lyrically to Mommy and me, for being so determined to master physics, anthropology and economics even though these three topics are challenging, for earning money at the Green Bean (earning money is important), for introducing "family meetings" and "rocks" to your girlfriends in your house, for taking Mommy and me canoeing on the liquidly, languid waters of the Connecticut River, and for taking me swimming in the same river with its puzzling mini-eddies of warm and chilly water separating Vermont from New Hampshire.

Jenny, for completing conscientiously all your CIT responsibilities at Creative Summer at Holton even though it wasn't always electrifying work, for going to Sara's camp this week with Maddie, for unexpectedly painting that picture last week (I love you being creative like that), for enjoying the stars last night at camp (how magical to stare up into the night sky!), for being determined to improve your tennis skills and for taking lessons with Richard, for playing bridge with Mommy's group when they needed a fourth, for earning money baby-sitting and looking after Chauncy (it's great to earn money), for all the love and affection you lavish on Cory, for taking Cory to the nursing home every week and giving Lillian, Vivian, Mrs. Estrada and all our other friends there so much joy and pleasure, for coming to see my IMAX film Bears at the National Museum of Natural History, and for helping me get prepared for the Q&A session by asking me questions, and for putting up with your boring parents at home in such a good-natured way!

I love you Gail, I love you Kim, I love you Tina, I love you Jenny, and I love you Cory.
Chris/Dad
XXXOOO

August 14, 2002
Subject: Draft of a funny letter to Gus

OK Tina, here goes. You asked me to draft something. Treat this draft as a starting point.

The point is to break his pattern of behavior. A funny letter would catch him off guard. Jen says this letter would make you look like "such a loser", but if Gus isn't calling, what is there to lose? In my opinion, anything is better than being passive and not doing anything (unless you are making a proactive decision intentionally to do nothing). And surely a humorous letter is better (and more unexpected) than a more traditional letter asking him why he hasn't called.

So anyway, here is an idea for you to play with and either improve or else junk:

_____

To Gus's lawyer
Dear Mr. Attorney,

It has come to my intermittent attention that your client has failed to call me as promised. While gently bumfuddled by this, I hasten to tell you (so you may in turn inform your esteemed client) that this is not necessarily a bad thing. The pressure of exams weighs heavily on me, and phone calls from ardent suitors might distract me and diminish the high marks I would otherwise attain. Any relationship, however superficial, should start from the highest grades, don't you think?

So please convey to your client my appreciation for his procrastinating pokiness. Perhaps he and I learned a different set of seven habits, but regardless, I must take the bull by the tail and face the situation. Knowing the pressures on your client from being a counselor at a prestigious and exclusive boy's camp, I am sympathetic and empathetic (or at least one of those pathetics) with his lack of follow up.

Most Sincerely,
Christina M. Shearer

_____

Tina, I hope this inspires you to some kind of action. Gus has no idea how lucky he was when he met you.

I love you!
Dad
XXXOOO

August 17, 2002
Subject: I love you! (from old lonely Dad!)

My Darling Kim, Tina and Jen,
It is Saturday afternoon. The house is empty. Mommy, Cory and you three are all away. I'm in the study working. Sunshine is pouring in the window and splashing on the floor. The air-conditioning hums loudly in the background, and then suddenly stops, leaving a pleasant silence in the room.

I worked out for almost two hours this morning (stretching, weight lifting, running and swimming) and feel wonderfully healthy. I've been eating very healthily too. I made a great find at the Fresh Fields yesterday: scrumptious English peas! I love popping those big fat pods and finding those delicious green peas inside. Yummy!

I am not lonely. Jenny sweetly asks me this every time we talk on the phone, and I appreciate you asking Jenny. Tina, you just called me and asked me too. Thank you. But no, I'm not lonely. I am focused on getting through a ton of jobs, one of which is to write to my three precious daughters to tell them how much I love them! I am totally focused on my strategic goals, and I have the deep inner satisfaction of knowing that I am doing what I am meant to be doing.

I was struck recently by something Jenny said. She described Gus as likely one day to become President of the US. I've been thinking about that. It was a great compliment that Jenny paid him, and I think I know what Jenny meant. Here is my guess at what Jen perceived in Gus:

His bearing is characterized by an informal and self-confident dignity and grace. He is not caught up in superficial fads or temporary distractions. He seems to be comfortable with himself and to like himself a lot. He is driven by deep principles, not the exigencies of his environment, childhood or anything external to himself. He has integrity, and is a thoroughly decent, considerate and thoughtful person. He loves to laugh and has a great sense of humor.

He lives purposefully and with intention in all parts of his life. He doesn't drift. He is ambitious and has big goals to make a difference in the world, yet he is fundamentally a serene and calm person. He has the look and feel of success about him. Nobody intimidates him, and in that sense he is fearless. His mood is relentlessly optimistic and upbeat.

He is oriented to getting results and not wasting time. He lives with a sense of gratitude for all the wonderful things in his life. He dismisses the meretricious and trivial, and doesn't waste time on small things of little consequence. Things that would upset or irritate others, he lets flow by him without disturbing his equanimity. He has a vision for his life which he has thought through after much rigorous reflection. He views setbacks as temporary defeats that will be overcome by hard work, determination and tenacity.

Of course I'm not claiming that Gus is all these things because I don't know him. I am simply giving you my interpretation of what I suspect Jenny was driving at when she said she and the Wipflers think he has all the makings of a very successful person.

Come to think of it, if Gus is like that, I think he might even qualify to be my son-in-law!

Kimmie, Tina and Jenny, one of the smartest things you can do is to seek out successful people in the domains you want to succeed in yourself, and model yourself on those people. They do things that make them successful. Find out what those things are and do them yourself. Why waste time experimenting and making mistakes? Role models can radically reduce your learning time and can help you achieve your goals far quicker than you can ever imagine.

I adore you!
Dad
XXXOOO

August 31, 2002
Subject: Sorry

Darling Tina,
I apologize for last night. When you suddenly came down at 10 PM and said you felt "stifled" and wanted to borrow the car to go out, I got upset because I didn't understand why you felt that way, I always worry about your safety, and I don't want you to get into a car accident, especially late at night.

Now in retrospect, I wish Mommy and I had just said, "Go right ahead, here are the keys." You worked hard last semester and deserve some down time. You only have a month before you leave for Oxford. If I said last night (I can't remember if I did or not) that you should get a job, then I take that back. Your idea to join the exercise club, and your idea to read extensively and get mentally prepared over the next four weeks so you are in a position to more quickly grasp the distinctions you'll be learning at Oxford, is the smart and wise thing to do.

I forget sometimes what an extraordinary and unique person you are... going to Costa Rica, getting into Oxford, going to Japan to see Kim, doing well at one of the best Ivy League colleges in the country, challenging yourself in all kinds of ways, working at the Green Bean to bring in money, keeping fit and healthy choosing great friends, being such a wonderful sister and daughter, and so much more.

I realized, when I felt so miserable last night because of our conflict, that I don't appreciate you nearly enough. I love the way you follow your own drummer. For example, just because the family is watching "A Beautiful Mind", you don't feel you have to. It's great you design your own schedule and your own life.

So Tina, please take the big car whenever you want. All I ask is that you be sensitive (which you always are) to Mommy and me worrying about your safety.

Sorry again about last night. I love you.
Dad
XXXOOO

September 1, 2002
Subject: "Ode to Dad"

Kim sent me this funny poem for my birthday. I hope you enjoy it.

_____

Ode To Dad

When I left our cozy house to go to the foreign land of Japan
Before the year was over who came to visit? My favorite Man!
Not John or Joshu or Ned, but my dear father
Who flew across the world to visit his oldest daughter
As soon as he arrived, we had a whirlwind tour
To Asako's house, a Mexican restaurant, and more
He helped me with my problems, like he always does
Like when Tina has a basement chipmunk, just cuz

Or my shower overflows - he encouraged me to clean it out
So I took my chopsticks to it, and sure enough, it again could spout
Out of all our adventures, my favorite one occurred in my apartment
Early one morning, before I could even say, "What time is it?"
Dad was awake, busy writing out a list
I can't say it all, but I'll give you the gist
Before I could brush my teeth or drag myself sleepily into the loo
He started telling me how to improve me life, all that I should do
"Start your own company, dress for success, and publish a book
All before next year, come on, just give my list a look!
It will make you wealthy, successful and wise
Perhaps as much as me, If I dare surmise!"
While at first I admit as I was a tad overwhelmed at my new To Do list
I also saw it as n exciting challenge, "I accept!" I said, raising my fist
Dad you are inspiring and loving, I love our lunches in Bethesda
Happy 55th Birthday to you, we sure do love ya!!

I love you, Dad!!
Love,
Kim
XOXO

I looked back in my journal and found the following paragraph in the entry for May 6, 2002. This is the incident to which Kim is referring, It was my last night with her in Japan:

Last night at dinner, Kim said to me, "Dad, do you have any final advice for me?" At the time, I said what I felt, which is that she is doing so extraordinarily well in every way that I couldn't think of any advice to give her. But when I woke up early this morning, I thought of a few things which she might find useful, and I relayed them to her as we were getting ready to leave her apartment:

1. Let's write a book together!
2. Compose a Life Plan.
3. Network at high levels in society (see yourself as a mover and shaker).
4. Think about power and influence, and how to gain it.
5. Find a coach for every domain in your life where you intend to learn and improve.
6. Add public speaking to your list of skills you want to become good at.
7. Start your own company
8. Learn about money and how to manage and accumulate wealth.
9. Get really organized so you can retrieve and find anything you want in five seconds.
10. At Chicago, learn skills that are directly useful to people, and thereby sellable (to give you financial security).
11. Start planning your next books now.
12. You look beautiful but you need to focus on your appearance (clothes, posture, speaking, etc.) so you reflect most deeply who you want to be seen as.

September 28, 2002
Subject: Virtual Family Meeting #29

To My Darling, Most Precious Family in the Whole World,
My Rock this week: To stay in close touch with each of you even though I'll be away all week in Toronto, and to have a brilliantly successful GSTA giant screen film conference there.
Encouragement:

Gail: Thanks for going with Kim to Chicago and helping her settle in there so much. I know Kimmie appreciated it. Well done for the great proposal you've drafted to get that government grant, and well done too for skillfully managing the CU politics associated with creating your new program at CU. And I am so proud of you for being invited to meet with the Time magazine board of Economists!! September 23, 1972 was the luckiest day of my life!

Kim: Well done for keeping your resume up to date. Please send me the latest version so I can put it in the family journal. It was so good! And great to get it all on one page. Well done for getting your article on sexual harassment in Japan accepted for publication in USA Today. And congratulations again on your recent article in the Washington Post on living at home with your parents as an adult! Well done for making so many new and good friends in Chicago. I am so pleased you have found two delightful language exchange students from Japan. Well done for winning the LEAD competition this week during orientation. And I'm glad you were able to "make lemon out of lemonade" with regard to the bike you bought on eBay.

Tina: You sound so happy in Italy whenever we hear from you! That's wonderful. Happiness is not something that happens to you, but something you make happen, so I am proud of you for being happy and making your trip there a success. Dying to hear more details! We loved having you home! And I was so proud of the way your spent your time here. You kept so fit! Have a super time this week with Jon and Granny in Bath. And good luck on Friday when you arrive for the start of the semester at Oxford! I know you will do wonderfully well, although I'm sure it will be tough and challenging, and you will be forced outside your comfort zone. I know you will deep down relish that! Thanks for getting a gift (the blue scarf) for Granny. Mommy and I appreciate how you have kept in touch with us this week while you've been gallivanting around Europe.

Jen: Well done for getting on the JV Tennis team! All that self-discipline over the summer (keeping fit, playing tennis with me, taking lessons with Richard) is paying off. I am so glad you went to the "Flashback to the 80s" dance last night at Holton-Arms. You looked beautiful. Well done for your very good test scores so far this semester. I am so glad you are enjoying history more than last year. Mommy and I love it when you have friends around (like Sara, Sarah and Teddy last evening before the dance). And thanks, Jenny, for being such a lovely person to have at home with us. Mommy and I feel so lucky to have you!

For everyone: We need to start planning Thanksgiving, our Christmas vacation, the big party we are going to give this fall, and next summer.

Tina: I am coming to see you in Oxford!!! Are you free for dinner on Saturday October 19? Then I'd love to take you out for breakfast the next day before I leave for London to catch a 4 PM plane home from Heathrow. Let me know if that works for you! Or maybe I can join you for dinner where you normally have it.

BTW Tina, I talked to Jon yesterday and he is looking forward to seeing you. He is waiting to receive a call or email from you telling him when you are arriving in Bath.

I love you Gail!
I love you Kim!
I love you Tina!
I love you Jen!
I love you Cory!
Dad/Chris
XXXOOO

November 9, 2002
Subject: Virtual Family Meeting #30

To My Most Precious Wonderful Family in the whole world:
My Rock this coming week: To start work on a slew of exciting speeches I've got coming up, and to plan to deliver them with great passion and humor; and to continue doing the research needed for my book on wildlife films.

Encouragement:

Gail: thank you for going to England to see my mother and Tina, as well as Tim, Jon, Clifford, Richard, John Coles and all our other relatives and friends; thanks for having dinner out with Maddie's family and Sara's parents (two lovely evenings); thanks for coming with me on my surprise date for you at the London Tea House; you are doing a fantastic job at work and with Joel; well done for doing the 5K race last week in Edgemoor.

Kim: well done for applying for all those great internships for next summer; your Chicago Tribune article was great, as was the draft article I read last night on bachelorette parties for USA Today; good luck planning Alison's shower for January 4; I can't wait to visit you in Chicago after Christmas; well done for keeping up with the intense level of learning at graduate school.

Tina: I loved visiting you at Keble College in Oxford! Have fun with Mommy there this week; well done for decisively making a decision to live on campus next year (I'm sure that is a great decision, even though it wasn't an easy one); glad you had fun in London last weekend visiting the Tate Gallery and other places; Maya Lodish would love to talk to you this Christmas (she is almost a doctor now and would love to hear first-hand about your time in Costa Rica and about Gail); well done for working so hard and enjoying it (hard work is great because you get rewarded twice: first when you do it, and second later on when the rewards come in); sorry you are going to miss the Turkey Chase this Thanksgiving! We'll miss you terribly.

Jenny: what exceptional grades!! and only one teacher out of six said she wanted you to speak up more in class (the others all thought your level of participation was fine); thanks for coming to Maddie's for dinner; well done for keeping up your tennis skills on the backboard and for playing tennis with Sara Murray today; I'm so glad you volunteered to help the Van Hollen campaign (it was you and other volunteers like you who made the difference in that race); well done for getting up and running the

445

5K Edgemoor race with me last...oops, I misspoke on that one, hmmmm! Well done for learning to drive! I am proud of you for setting a goal of having your essay on constitutionalism be so good that the teacher select it as a model, and then actually achieving that goal ("Where there is no vision, the people perish" says the bible); thanks for your devotion to Cory; I want to encourage you to do weight-lifting, stretching and endurance exercises every day to keep fit, strong and powerful; good luck in thinking through what jobs you want to do next summer.

Cory: well done for being such a superb therapy dog at the nursing home; Jenny, Mommy, Kim, Tina and I are so proud of you.

To Kim, Tina and Jen: one of Mommy and my goals as parents is to make sure you always know that you are loved, you are cared for, and that you are important. We also hope to pass on to each of you the importance of you digging deeply into what matters most to you (as opposed to what others think should matter to you). Many people go through life and never take that journey. They end their lives not really knowing what their passions are. As you go through this adventure of self-discovery, you will learn incredible things about yourself and what you want to dedicate your life to. Don't forget you are multifaceted human beings and you want to succeed in many different domains, including being wives and mothers, as well as being successful professionals in fields that fascinate you. Uncovering all this and finding out what you care deeply about is not easy. And the process should never end. I wrestle with this issue for myself all the time, even though I'm 55. It is very healthy. I highly recommend getting a coach (or friend) to help you with this process of self-discovery. One of the keys to success in this process is writing. The palest ink is far more powerful than the loudest shout. Just thinking deep thoughts isn't good enough. I know you know that already. The important thing is not to give up, even though the journey is challenging and sometimes even painful. You want to tenaciously challenge everything you think you believe in, so you can reinvent yourself and feel totally authentic and have the incredible self-confidence which comes from that. Basically you are trying to find out what you care passionately about. It sounds easy but I know it isn't. Another thing that I have found very useful, as you know, is reading biographies and autobiographies of great people. Steven Covey's book "First Things First" is also very good and I strongly recommend it.

I love you Gail!
I love you Kim!
I love you Jen!
I love you Cory!
Dad/Chris
XXXOOO

2003

February 2, 2003
Subject: Virtual Family Meeting #31

To My Wonderful, Dispersed, Precious family:
I love you!

My Rock: To give a dazzling speech/workshop on Tuesday on how to give effective presentations!

Encouragement:

For Gail: for your wonderful performance on nationwide television on the Lehrer News Hour last Thursday on PBS! Fantastic! For the incredible job you are doing at CU. For turning lemon into lemonade at CU when it everything at CU looked like a scourge of lemons. For realizing that enthusiasm, creativity and highly professional work will eventually be recognized and rewarded. For your performance on Diane Rehm's radio show recently.

For Kim: for going on the retreat with the group you volunteer for (Literature For All). For the essay you wrote describing that experience. For working hard at Chicago and recognizing that you are getting a first class education that will help you all your life (and help those around you). For achieving that great education without having to go into awful debt. How smart is that?! For planning ahead and getting an apartment in NYC for this summer. For your "after midnight" beat with the Red Eye newspaper and the articles you are getting published as a result.

For Tina: for working hard to get on top and stay on top of your two very tough courses, Physics and Biology. And I know Anthropology is no walk in the park either! For finding a wonderful friend and roommate in Greta. For volunteering at the home for pregnant teenagers (the place you borrowed a car to get to). For all the great learning you are doing with Professor Baiker and Mommy on health issues. For realizing that progress is made by reaching out to others for help and not trying to do everything on your own. For realizing you have a great resource in Mommy and taking advantage of that opportunity.

For Jenny: for being a member of the wonderful Holton Jazz Combo and a member of the Upper School Wind Ensemble. For contributing to a wonderful evening of entertainment at last Thursday evening's Midwinter Instrumental Concert at Walt Whitman. For your excellent grades (earning you 95 buckaroos!) and, just as important, the complimentary comments made about you by your admiring teachers. For searching for other extracurricular activities to do at Holton so you can exercise leadership skills and excel outside of class too. For keeping calm and collected the other evening when water spilled throughout your book bag and threatened the sanctity of your books and papers. For being open to the idea of doing a self-defense course at Holton if I can organize it. For exploring with Sara the notion of going on an Outward Bound type course this summer. For exploring the possibility of attending a rigorous tennis training camp this summer. For wanting to get on the Varsity tennis team. For not taking your family for granted even though you think these virtual family meetings are weird. Try and see them for what they are: unique family letters which have a special focus on what is really important. Many families neglect to communicate and imperceptibly drift apart.

For everyone: well done for getting your Predictions done and your New Years Resolutions done. We had a wonderful Christmas together! Thank you for all my loving gifts (Kim for the Chicago running pants, Tina for the bow tie and Wild America tie, Jen for the scarf and soap holder). It was very, very special. I hope you are all enjoying the draft journal for the first few weeks of 2003 that I sent you each to read. (Thanks, Jen, I got your changes back today.) I think everyone is making good progress on their Easter plans and Summer plans.

I'm sure I've forgotten lots of things! Please let me know what I've forgotten!

I adore you!
Dad/Chris
XXXOOO

February 18, 2003
Subject: Great to talk to you!

Darling Tina,
You are under a lot of pressure, but good pressure. BTW, when you get in a mood of resignation when you see few possibilities, say to yourself, "This is fascinating! How fascinating that I have all I have compared to others and yet don't feel overjoyed with gratitude and excitement? This is fascinating!"

This will encourage you to look at yourself more objectively. Remember how other people's problems never seem quite as bad to you as they do to the other person? Try and see your problems as other people might view them.

This will help change the hidden assumptions on which you build the moods (or stories about yourself) you get in. Being able to shift your moods quickly is a skill you will develop if you write it down and work on it.

I've had a ridiculous story in my head this week about Ellen that was making me miserable. I realized after a bit that it had no grounding at all and I felt much better.

Some people try to alter their mood through drinks or drugs. This always backfires (and is dangerous too) and I know you would never do that.

Look out to help others who are worse off than you.

Act cheerful and resilient even if you don't always feel it.

Plan your work to include non-work activities, such as nurture a new friend, run for 20 minutes, ask Greta how she is doing and listen actively, talk to someone about the pros and cons of going to the AIDS conference, write a new poem, review your New Year's Resolutions, re-connect with your personal mission statement, and take steps to find a boyfriend.

By writing these down, and sprinkling them among your academic "to-do's", you can gain a sense of control over your life as well as a sense of balance.

Dartmouth is throwing a lot at you. Fortunately you are up to the challenge, even though it is tough.

An idea: send a brief letter to your college newspaper as follows: "Am I the only person at Dartmouth who feels overworked? I seem to do nothing else but work, work, work. Is this normal, or am I weird in some way?" I bet they'll print it and you'll be delighted by the firestorm of responses the paper will print!

I love you! You are wonderful! Thanks for talking to me tonight. Cory, my faithful spy, sends you a big woof!!!
Dad
XXXOOO

February 20, 2003
Subject: Love from LA!

My darling Kimmie, Tina and Jenny,
I intended to send you this note last night but I was so tired after a busy day of travel and meetings (and still being on east coast time) that I decided to write to you this morning. It's about 60 degrees here and no snow!

As I got on the plane yesterday, I looked down at my seat and saw a big dog next to me. I said to the person with the dog, "Are dogs allowed in the plane like that?" She replied that it was a seeing-eye dog and I immediately realized that the woman was blind. Of course my attitude changed instantaneously and I was thrilled to sit there.

Belle reminded me so much of Cory. She was a 2 year old lab and her owner was a middle-aged women who had been blind since she was five years old. Someone poked her in the eye with a stick and she lost both eyes.

She's led a normal life, been married 17 years and has two kids. Her husband has normal sight. She is a lobbyist for a national non-profit organization representing the interests of blind people. I asked her if she would rather be blind or deaf, and she replied blind. She was a lovely person and totally self-reliant. Imagine the courage and character it takes to do what she has done and accomplish what she has accomplished.

And Belle was a wonderful dog. At the end of the flight when the owner put Belle in her harness, I asked the owner if Belle liked the harness. The owner said, "Belle loves it. She loves to work and she loves to serve. That is when she is happiest." There is so much we can learn from dogs like Cory and Belle.

I love you! I miss you!
Dad
XXXOOO

February 21, 2003
Subject: Sending you all my love from LA

Darling Kimmie, Tina and Jenny,
Just a note to tell you I'm thinking about you and sending lots of love to each of you from LA. I hope you are each doing well and are happy and feeling fulfilled and full of purpose and joy.

As I was getting undressed tonight, I watched a compelling documentary on television about slavery as

450

told through slaves themselves. The horror and vileness of slavery was beyond comprehension.

You are each so incredible and special, and Mommy and I are so lucky to have three loving and successful daughters. I love you.
Yer ol' Dad
XXXOOO

February 21, 2003
Subject: Thinking of you in LA

My Precious loves: Kimmie, Tina and Jenny,
I can't wait to get home on Sunday. Delores told me today that it was rainy in the DC area today, but it is beautifully sunny here. Not that it makes any real difference to me because I am stuck indoors all the time in meetings.

You've heard of the Nobel Prizes for chemistry, physics, medicine, literature — and the famous Nobel Peace Prize that former President Jimmy Carter just won. (BTW, the only other American President to win the Nobel Peace Prize was Teddy Roosevelt for bringing peace to the Japanese/Russian conflict nearly 100 years ago.)

Well, did you ever hear the story of how those prizes got established? Alfred Nobel invented dynamite and spent his life amassing a fortune from the manufacture and sale of the stuff. Well one day in 1888, he woke up to read his obituary in the paper. Of course it was a terrible mistake. His brother had died and the reporter mistakenly wrote Alfred's obituary.

For the first time, Alfred Nobel saw himself as the world saw him — as a great industrialist who had made a fortune from explosives. As far as the general public was concerned, Alfred realized to his horror that this was the entire purpose of his live. He would be remembered as a merchant of death.

He was appalled. He himself perceived the true meaning and purpose of his life as being far more noble and decent. So he decided to show the world what kind of man he really was through his last will and testament. The final disposition of his fortune would reveal his true nature. And that's how the famous Nobel Prizes were established.

Kim, Tina and Jenny, I know you will live honorable, noble and decent lives. (Hey, and make a fortune too if you can!)

I love you.
Daddy
XXXOOO

PS: Kimmie, thanks so much for calling me today as you walked home from school. I appreciated you thinking of me.

February 22, 2003
Subject: Earthquake-sized love from LA!

My darling Kimmie, Tina and Jenny,

I was woken last night at 4:22 AM by the hotel shaking! I remember three big shakes. I immediately thought it must be an earthquake. I thought I heard a rushing sound but I probably imagined it. I lay in bed wondering if more jolts would follow. I didn't feel scared or fearful. I rolled over and went back to sleep. Hey, that's pretty exciting to experience an earthquake! Kim told me a moment ago that it was roughly the size of the one she experienced in Japan.

I am in Room 717 in the Hyatt in Irvine. My room is on the 7th floor. Here is something I always do now in hotels. I find the stairs and use them instead of the elevator. There is an exercise room here but I am so busy with meetings that I don't have time to go. Walking briskly up and down (especially up!) seven flights of stairs is a wonderfully bracing exercise. I love it!

One of the many reasons I exercise so much is because I realize it is important for me to think of myself as an athlete. I urge you to do this too. When you think of yourself as an athlete, you walk with power, with grace and with poise. You hold yourself like a champion. Your posture reflects an inner confidence which other people sense. You look agile, flexible and supple. You also — and I know this is important to each of you as it should be — look much more appealing to men. No man wants to date an unfit, unhealthy and weak person.

Physical fitness (in all three areas of strength, endurance and flexibility) is vitally important for another reason: "motion leads to emotion." In other words, if you have a good posture, toned muscles, flexible joints, gracious movements and an athletic look about the way you move, then that all leads to positive emotions and moods.

If you feel down about something, your shoulders sag, your mouth and face droop, and your voice loses its bounce. Here is the thing most people don't fully appreciate: if you straighten up, pull your shoulders back, smile (even though you don't feel like smiling), breathe deeply and stand tall, then you will begin to feel better and more self-confident. Try it next time you are feeling low! You can begin to reverse that downward spiral where the body feeds negative feelings to the mind and the mind feeds negative thoughts to the body, and on and on.

So always think of yourself as an athlete, carry yourself like an athlete and be proud of your athletic prowess.

I learned all this at the age of five or six. We lived at 89, Bloomfield Avenue. I was in a black mood for some reason. Despair filled my body. I felt trapped in something I can't even articulate fifty years later. Depression is the only word I can think of, although obviously something to do with my parents have triggered it. Maybe I felt neglected or something, who knows.

Anyway, Grandpa noticed that I couldn't move. The energy and motivation I normally had were gone. I was strangely still and motionless. He abruptly and brusquely ordered me into the garden to push a big heavy roller up and down the grass. I knew this was totally pointless, but when Grandpa gave a stern order, we four boys knew better than to disobey (unless we wanted to get cuffed).

So with my body filled with this despair and angst, I did as I was told. Up and down. Up and down. The heavy roller (a device to flatten the grass — you never see them nowadays although they were quite common when I was a child) was huge and it took me all my might just to roll it a few inches.

After about ten minutes of this exhausting work, with my father ordering me to work harder and push it more vigorously, I noticed the most amazing transformation in my body and in my mood. The black miasma of darkness clouding my mind and body lifted as if by magic, and I suddenly felt full of joy and enthusiasm. It was a magical transformation.

I realized that wise old Grandpa had done me a huge favor and found a way to rid me of my disabling depression. "Motion leads to emotion." I don't know how Grandpa has this wisdom but he did. He taught me a great lesson for which I will always be grateful.

Telling this story reminds me too of something else I have forgotten: how often (as a child and teenager) I thought of my father as incredibly wise and knowledgeable. I made the huge mistake later in life of not remembering that. Remembering it now makes me cry as I type this. Don't ask me why.

I love you so much. I hope you know how much you mean to me.
Dad
XXXOOO

PS: Jenny, thanks so much for helping Mommy with the flooding in the basement today. You and Maddie were a great help. I wish I was there to help. I'll be home tomorrow.

February 24, 2003
Subject: A treat for when you get home!

Darling Jenny,
I picked up delicious, scrumptious, delectable, mouth-watering, tasty, appetizing, flavorful, epicurean English (of course!) big, fat peas in their pods from Fresh Fields! A treat for when you get home!

I love you.
Dad
XXXOOO

March 1, 2003
Subject: Buckets of love from Chicago!

My darling Tina and Jenny,
As you know, I am spending the weekend with Kimmie in Chicago! It is wonderful to see her on her home "turf"! Kim looks wonderful. I've never seen her look healthier, happier, fitter, stronger or more full of energy and vitality.

She has "bloomed where she was planted" (as my friend in LA Mrs. Bernice Park likes to say) and is flourishing. Kim has made two or three very close friends, she loves her studies and especially loves the way she can put what she is learning in economics and statistics to work in her newspaper articles immediately, and she is liking the culture and feel of Chicago, one of the world's most vibrant cities.

I saw Kim's apartment tonight and could not believe how spacious and pleasant it was. I glimpsed through a cab window the Harris Graduate School where she is a student. We talked about John (who is doing really well in two jobs in NYC and who is going to teach me to tap dance!), her upcoming summer internship with the Wall Street Journal, her articles, her subjects this semester of micro economics, political institutions and statistics, and her dress for Alison's wedding!

It has been a wonderful weekend. I introduced Kim to Stephanie Truax (the daughter of a publisher friend of mine, Doug Truax) and Janet Ginsburg (a writer and film maker who lives in Skokie in the suburbs of Chicago).

We had dinner tonight at her favorite restaurant in Hyde Park (Calypso something) and then after seeing her apartment, I dropped her off at a party and returned to the hotel where I am writing this letter to you. Kim will get a cab back here at about midnight.

Tomorrow morning we will get up, exercise in the great little fitness room the hotel has on the second floor, have breakfast, and then I'll drop Kim off at her apartment before going on to the airport.

Tina and Jenny, I love you so much! Tina, I can't wait to visit you at Dartmouth and take you out for dinner up there! We'll work out a good date for that when you get home in a few weeks' time.

Buckets of love,
Dad
XXXOOO

March 2, 2003
I wrote:
Thanks, Tina! I love you! XXXOOO

PS: Mommy just told me what a tough and exhausting day you had last Thursday. You are becoming tough and resilient. Well done. XXXOOO

Tina replied:
Hehe, thanks dad :) I just could not take a physics lab and bio lab in one day, I felt numbed to life, and I got scared that that's what medical school would be like and I do not want to live a numbing life. AH! I want to be excited about what I'm learning and memorizing stupid biology terms is not what I call exciting.

It sounds like you had so much fun in Chicago! I'm so glad!

XOXO
Tina!

Then I replied:
I am so sympathetic, Tina. I remember studying biology at Dulwich, and it seemed like a big memory game. I didn't like it. It was one of my worst subjects. Yet health issues fascinate me now, and topics like nutrition, fitness, the relationship between mind and body, neuroscience, and the waste of resources by people who make recurrent life style misjudgments (like smoking and drinking) deeply interest me.

I suppose what you are going through now is equivalent to the basics of learning the guitar (which, as you know, can also be tedious). I think as you do more, it will become more interesting. I have sent you recently several articles on biology which are fascinating and more are on their way. So hang in there, and I think it will get better.

Also you now have good questions to ask people who have gone through biology and medical school: How did they deal with the numbing effect of having to memorize so many tedious and seemingly meaningless distinctions? What techniques helped them get through it? What advice do they have for you? What coping mechanisms can they recommend? Is medical school interesting or boring? If they found it interesting, why did they? Ask them to be specific.

I love you lovebug. Hang in there! See you on March 14! Can't wait!
Dad
XXXOOO

March 16, 2003
Subject: Lots of love from NYC

Darling Kim, Tina and Jenny,
Kim: Good luck with your microeconomics exam tomorrow. Congratulations on all the wonderful articles you've had published recently (and another one in USA Today tomorrow!)

Tina: It is so good to have you home! Thanks for the vegetarian meals you've cooked us two nights in a row! It's great to try new things like that. Thanks for reviewing my new workshop handout "Passions that fuel the American Dream." (Thanks to Gail and Jen who are also critiquing it.) Thanks for playing on the tennis backboard with me yesterday and for food shopping for me today. And that is so nice you are such good friends with Sirah.

Jenny: Sorry you didn't get into Varsity tennis. It's funny how personally hurt I felt by that. It was as if they had rejected me. Rejection is something all success people deal with over and over again. Stephen King got enough rejection slips when he was young to paper over his whole living room. Last year he earned $400 million dollars from his writing. Abraham Lincoln suffered multiple electoral defeats before becoming perhaps our greatest President. The difference between successful people and failures is that successful people receive more rejections (because they make more offers) and they never give up. You could have avoided that tennis rejection if you had not gone in for it. You did the right thing by trying. Now you need to look around to see what else you can go for i.e., not give up.

You want to get involved in extracurricular activities because it is an important way you grow as a person and grow in competence and confidence. You don't want to go through life resenting other people who boss you around and have more fun, autonomy, responsibility and compensation than you — all because they learned how to take initiative, be entrepreneurial, lead people, speak in public, make friends, get along with people and create new projects. You can learn that too. Anyone can if they get involved in (or create their own) extracurricular activities.

I'll arrange for you to visit BCC on March 27 and 28. I think that will be a very interesting experience for you. Whether you move from Holton to BCC for your final two years of high school will be governed by only one criterion, what is best for your long term happiness and fulfillment. I am eager to learn Kim's views about this issue. You are doing wonderfully well academically at Holton and that is a terrific accomplishment (which in our family we take as a given but really shouldn't). I know you think of yourself as a "grind" but it is the grinds of the world who run it and have the most satisfying and full lives (e.g., Margaret Thatcher, Thomas Jefferson, Bill Gates and Tony Blair). You'll soon get to the point where learning is not a grind but deeply satisfying, and in fact you will get to the point where you feel uncomfortable if you're not constantly learning (which doesn't mean just pouring over books for hours on end — there are many ways of learning).

I do think you may want to think about three things:

1. Broadening your learning beyond what you have to learn in school. You need to learn about things they don't teach you in school. You'll enjoy knowing things others don't know and you'll enjoy teaching others what you know. In fact, teaching might be something you might be very good at with your empathetic nature and your high intelligence.

2. Finding ways to feel more energetic and vital. You want to have a higher metabolism. Have you ever observed a bird? Their alertness and vitality is astonishing. That is one reason people find them so fascinating. I remember watching Jane Fonda once work a crowd. She exuded energy and vitality. Her smile was radiant. You might want to smile more, be more demonstrative, reach out to people more, think more about the concerns of other people, go out of your way to be warmer and friendlier to others.

(BTW, one thing I do every morning is when I get out of the shower, breathe in deeply and then I smile as I breathe out. If you want to smile more, you have to practice. I realized when I was in my twenties that my face in its default position was frowning and that this had a negative effect on the people around me. I have trained myself to smile more. At first it was an effort, but now it comes more easily.)

I know you are popular at Holton and well-liked but it is easy to get into a rut and into habitual ways of dealing with people which don't reflect the high level of "people-skills" of which you are capable.

Of course, the most essential step in becoming a more vital person is to exercise more regularly and pump up your muscles so your self-image is stronger. I have always had a poor self-image (probably because I was occasionally teased in school for being skinny) and one reason I work out is to overcome that problem. Anyway, I can't find the words to tell you how important it is that you strengthen your body by working out every day, increase your suppleness through yoga-type exercises, toughen your body through weight-training, and increase your endurance by running (or dancing, or whatever you enjoy). You will reap huge benefits from this, and if you fail to do it, you will reap great penalties health-wise, emotionally, in your relationships and in every part of your life. Being fit and healthy is foundational.

3. Getting to know the teachers at Holton better. I urge you to go out of your way to make better friends with the teachers. If you give them the chance to get to know you, they will love you and do anything for you. When you see a teacher in the hallway, catch their eye, smile at them and ask them how their weekend was. Act as if you care about them, and you <u>will</u> eventually care about them. They are wonderful people and you are so privileged to have the opportunity to be around them. Don't miss this opportunity. Look for chances to talk one-on-one with them. Go and ask them for advice. They will be thrilled to coach you. Tell them you want coaching in area X, and you will be amazed how they respond. Everyone loves to give advice! I know that some of your friends at Holton may not think it is cool to spend time with teachers, but you have never been one to go with the crowd and with the popular thing to do I know you can act independently and with an eye to your own long-term strategic interests. I would set yourself a specific, measurable goal of every day having at least one personal interaction with a teacher.

Kim, Tina and Jen and Mommy too of course, I welcome your reaction to these thoughts.

I love you!
Dad
XXXOOO

PS: Jen, great job driving today! Only two fender-benders was pretty good for you!

March 23, 2003
Subject: Virtual Family Meeting #32

To my precious family:
I love you! It was so wonderful to be together this last week! Thank you, Kim and Tina, for coming home. It was comforting to all be together when the country initiated Operation Free Iraq last week with a massive show of firepower against Baghdad.

I hope Gail, Kim and Jen have a great time in Florida this week and that Tina you have a great week back at Dartmouth.

My rock next week: to give four dazzling speeches at NWF's Annual Meeting.

Encouragement:

Gail: Thanks for doing the taxes. And thanks for writing the letter to Gary and Andrea about their noisy swimming pool pump. I've not heard from them yet! Congratulations on how well you are doing in your job and on receiving last week that encouraging letter from the government re that huge grant.

Kim: Congratulations on getting all those articles published! I'm glad you are enjoying the Jay Leno autobiography. All of us need to attach more importance to humor. I'm glad John's coming to visit next weekend. I'm glad you are enjoying economics.

Tina: Your grades are wonderful! I am so proud of you for getting an A-, an A, and a B+. Outstanding! By doing well, you open up new possibilities for yourself and more future choices. Thanks for playing tennis on the backboard with me. Well done for thinking about the possibility of doing a thesis. Good luck in deciding on whether or not to go to Costa Rica. And good luck in applying for money for your summer internship.

Jen: I am proud of you for exploring the option of attending BCC for your last two years of high school. By spending a day there on Thursday, you will be able to make the decision that is best for you. Well done for opening up some great ways to spend your summer. I know (because Mommy tells me) you are working hard on Chemistry SAT II. That's great. I was so delighted you and Eli went on a double date with Tina and Mauro. You are very special, Jenny. I don't tell you that enough.

Cory: You are wonderful to keep me company these few days! You are the most lovable doggy in the whole world.

I love you, Gail.

I love you, Kim.
I love you, Tina.
I love you, Jen.
I love you, Cory.
(whew, I didn't forget Tina this time!)
Lonely-old-Dad-by-himself-in-Bethesda
XXXOOO

PS: I'm so excited that Mommy, Kim (and John) and Jenny are coming to see Coral Reef Adventure next Friday. We'll miss you, Tina.

May 6, 2003
Subject: Home!

Darling Kimmie, Tina and Jenny,
I'm home from England! Has a great trip. Everything went according to plan.

Good luck to Jen for her big Spanish exam on Wednesday, good luck to Tina for any upcoming tests you have on genetics, and good luck to Kim for all your upcoming exams.

I am so proud of myself. For weeks now, I have been struggling to prepare an important speech I'm giving in NYC on June 12. (Kim, will you be in NYC then?). The burden of this unmet challenge has been weighing on me like Tina's gigantic suitcase weighed on her last year as she traveled around England.

Then, yesterday — Breakthrough!! In the seven hour plane ride from Heathrow to Dulles, I resolved to focus on nothing but that speech, and I worked non-stop the whole journey. First I brain stormed ideas, then I drafted an outline, then I wrote a first draft, and finally I finished writing — just as we landed — the second draft. This achievement threw me into a euphoric mood and made me wonder why doctors never recommend goal setting and achievement as a cure for depression. Anyway, I got off the plane feeling light as a bird and jubilant at my private success.

Make a super day!

I love you, Kim.
I love you, Tina.
I love you, Jenny.
Jet-lagged but happy Dad
XXXOOO

May 18, 2003
Subject: HAPPY 21st BIRTHDAY, TINA!!!!!!

Darling Tina,
Happy 21st Birthday, lovebug! We love you so much. You, Kim and Jenny are the best things (after meeting mommy!) that ever happened to me. You girls enrich my life like raisins in bread pudding, like salt on a boiled egg, like flippers on a diver's feet — no, no, those aren't good metaphors; you, Kim and Jen radically changed my life like water transforms to steam, like a caterpillar transforms to a butterfly, like the Wright brothers' aircraft transformed into a modern 747.

Mommy, Jenny and I can't wait to see you this coming weekend at Dartmouth.

Today I flew back from LA to Dulles. The person I sat next to was a 60 year old man and when he got out a notebook to write something, I noticed on the front of it, it said "Major General Larry Tayor."

Major General is a very high rank (equivalent to a Rear Admiral in the Navy). He and I were both absorbed in our reading, but when the meal came around, I asked him if he was in the military. He confirmed that he was. He was a marine and formerly flew Cobra helicopters. We talked about Tom Brokaw's books, James Bradley's book (Flag of our Fathers), and Iraq.

I felt very grateful to him for his service to our country and at one point I summoned up a little courage (not much was needed) and said to him, "I thank you for being a marine and for your service to this country." He commented that it was important to have the support of the public.

I asked him if his father had been in the military. No, he said, his father hadn't been in the military but he remembered as a small boy that his dad would go as often as he could (maybe every week or two weeks) and give blood to support the military. He took his son (the man I was talking to) every time he did this. His son didn't know why his dad took him to witness the father giving blood. His father never said much. He was a silent, taciturn man who communicated little.

One day, the small boy's face revealed some puzzlement about what was going on. His father only said three words: "You owe something." That's all he ever said about it. But the Major General never forgot it and has felt hugely privileged to serve his country as a Marine. He knows his dad would be proud of him.

Tina, we are so proud of you. Happy 21st Birthday!!!!!!

I love you.
Dad
XXXOOO

June 8, 2003
Subject: Virtual Family Meeting #33

To My darling and incredibly precious family:
My rocks this week: to give a dazzling speech in NYC on Thursday, and to warmly welcome Kim and Tina home next weekend! (And my rock last week was to do a super job emceeing the NWF staff picnic — mission accomplished!)

Encouragement:

Gail: Thanks for 28 years of married bliss! Well done on all your job successes, including the WSJ quote, your presentation to the Democratic Health Task Force, your negotiations with Congressman Allen, several speeches you've given, your talk this coming Wednesday at the National Press Club, your Evening Exchange appearance coming up this Friday on PBS, and your third interview on CNN coming up this week; thanks for meeting Greta at National airport yesterday (that was so nice for her), for all the delicious meals you make (like tuna yesterday and chicken tonight), for all the beautiful flowers you've planted in the garden, and for walking regularly to keep fit.

Kim: I am deeply enjoying your book on Japan; well done for producing your weekly column for Red Eye; I know you are doing well in your exams that you are right in the middle of now — I hope you don't arrive at the WSJ too exhausted; good luck in packing up everything in your apartment; so glad you love Sujay and we can't wait to meet him.

Tina: Did I ever congratulate you on the A-, A, and B+ you got at Dartmouth last March? Well done for winning that money ($2,000?) from DPCS for your volunteer internship this summer in DC; and congratulations for finding that job; so glad you love Tom and we can't wait to see him again; thanks for the wonderful weekend we had with you at Dartmouth to celebrate your 21st birthday. Have fun (I know you are having fun from your call today) this week at Dartmouth "working"! Well done for getting through the exams you've just completed.

Jen: Happy 16th birthday again! Your report card was superb; your 10th grade GPA was 99.40!! Thanks to your diligence and focus, I have a very good feeling about the SAT II Chemistry exam you took on Saturday morning. Well done for driving skillfully. Your internship with Congressman Van Hollen is going very well, and the health paper you prepared will be very useful to him (and well done for having the maturity to be willing to ask for advice on it from Mommy). Well done for organizing a memorable summer for yourself: Van Hollen, self-defense course, Costa Rica, Discovery Cove, tennis club, drivers license, and more. I'm glad you've made such good friends at Holton (as evidenced by the great lunch party you gave on your birthday for 15 or so of your Holton friends) and yet you've still held on in the most wonderful way to old friends like Maddie and Sara Wipfler. I want to encourage you to devote even more time than you do to getting stronger and more athletic. It will propel you forward in every area of your life, including your school work.

Cory: well done for having such a great time at Katie's when we all went to Dartmouth. That was such an adventure for you! Like you do so sensibly with everything in your life, you "bloomed where you were planted" and made the best out of it.

Question for the whole family: shall we go away for 5 or 6 days at Christmas to some exotic locale like Hawaii, the Keys or St. John's in the Caribbean? The pros are that it will be something the five of us will always remember, we'd have loads of fun, and with all the busy schedules you girls have; this may be the last chance for some time for all of us to go away together for a vacation.

The cons are the expense when we still have Jenny to get through college, we love being in our home in Bethesda, and it isn't so easy for Tom and Sujay to come and visit us in Bethesda.

Please give it some thought and let Mommy and me know what you think.

I'm sure I've forgotten lots of important things that I should have mentioned. In your replies please let me know what I have forgotten!

I adore you Gail, Kim, Tina, Jenny and Cory!
Your loving husband/father
Chris/Dad
XXXOOO

June 11, 2003
Subject: Love from NYC!

To my three precious daughters, Kimmie, Tina and Jenny,
I love you! I'm in NYC, as you know, getting ready to give a big speech tomorrow.

Kim, I picked up three copies of USA Today with your excellent op-ed article in it. Congratulations!

Kim, can't wait to see you tomorrow night (assuming I can get away from here); and Tina, can't wait to see you on Monday when you arrive home. Drive safely with Hilary.

Jen, have fun at your lunch on Friday with Joan. I have always found it best to prepare thoroughly for meetings like that. One very good tactic is to listen intently to what others are saying, and then at some appropriate point about half way through, say something like, "I'd like to go back to something Fred said about five minutes into the lunch: he made the point that the Democrats don't seem to have their act together. What does Chris think about that and how can he contribute to solving the problem?" Or whatever! The point is to refer back to a point someone else made that caught your attention.

This shows that you've been listening (very important and unusual) and you'll look like a star.

The other thing to do is to prepare questions and observations. It is important to do this in writing because you can then be more thoughtful and better prepared. For example, you might prepare questions along the following lines:

1. What is the worst crisis Chris has faced since becoming a Congressman? And what has he found to be the biggest challenge of the job?

2. There is only so much Chris can do in a day. Should his priority be with his constituents (visiting schools, holding town meetings, taking care of constituents' concerns, etc.) or should it be in taking a leadership role (in an appropriate way given his junior status) on creating path breaking legislation? Am I even right in thinking there is a tradeoff involved here?

3. Chris's job is very intense. He can't go anywhere without being "on duty." How does he relax? What does he do to get away occasionally from the relentless pressures?

Jen, I expect you'll be able to come up with better questions than those. The key point is for you to go into the lunch relaxed, smiling, sensitive to the concerns of others, and ready with some good questions and comments to put to Joan and the other interns. Brainstorm with mommy over breakfast and you'll come up with some great ideas to raise.

The main thing is to enjoy it. If you enjoy it, everybody will enjoy you too. If you're uptight and reticent, it's no fun for anyone. So have fun!!

Kim, Tina and Jen, I love you more than I can say.
Dad
XXXOOO

June 15, 2003

Dear Dad,

I did not want to talk about this last night because I am scared of what you will say. I want to make sure I explain everything I am feeling before you judge my decision. I want you to understand me, and I hope that if you understand me then you will accept my life choices and be happy for me, because I am happy.

I have thought about my life and my future a lot. I have followed your advice and kept open all possibilities. I have done as much as I can to figure out what I really want in life and what makes me deeply happy and fulfilled.

At this point in my life, I have decided that I do not want to continue on this path to becoming a doctor. I will not take the MCAT's in August. I have followed your suggestions my entire life, but I need to start making decisions for myself and create my own life.

I fear that you think this is the "easy" way out which I am making without careful consideration. You think I am giving up a good, rewarding career and stable income. But Dad, this has not been at all easy. This has been one of the hardest decisions I have had to make and I have talked to many many people about it. What I have realized is that it is *my* decision; it is me who is going to be living my life.

You came to America, you love America, because it is a land of the free. People are free to create the lives they want. And I will create the life I want. Yesterday in the car, I was thinking about you and mom when you were my age. You had a degree in Engineering, but you did not enjoy it. It did not fulfill you and you wanted something more. You found your way; you worked your way towards what you wanted to be doing. You did not have a stable, set path ahead of you. Both you and mom work for non-profit organizations! That is inherently unstable! You did not know what you would end up doing, but you figured it out. And so did mom. And along the way you have had a lot of adventures and experiences that have shaped and changed your life.

You raised Kim, Jen and me to be the best people we can be — to love, to give, to work hard, and to be passionate. I do not feel passionate about going to medical school and being a doctor. That is not what my heart wants. You always said I would be such a good doctor. Many people have told me that. I *know* I could be a good doctor. I know exactly what it would take to get there. For me, taking that path is the easy way. It is the weaker path because I know the road and I know the destination. It is the easier, more stable and sure path, but I *want* and I am *asking for* the more challenging, exciting, and rewarding path.

Your first reaction last night was to ask what am I going to do with my life then. I could not say anything then because anything I wanted to say would sound too small to your ears. There is so much I want to do in my life Dad that is the answer. I don't even know where to start. I know you can understand though, because you love life and you love learning. I have so many dreams and ideas. I want to do Americorps, Teach for America, the Peace Corps. I want to go back to Costa Rica and write a book about the street kids. I want to teach, to paint, to grow a garden, and to cook. Maybe one day I will get a Masters degree in education. Maybe I will go to culinary school. Maybe I *will* go to medical school one day.

I do not know exactly what I will do but I have dreams and ideas and that is what I LOVE and that is what gives me fire inside. To know that I can do anything and change and pick up something new is the life I want to live. And I want to be able to share my dreams with you and for you to understand.

I may not find success in the way that you define it. I may not be a top doctor with an M.D., I may not make a lot of money, but I will make enough. I know that I will find my way. I will figure it out, just like you and mom did, and just like everybody has to do. I will face challenges and I will suffer like everybody. But I will not regret anything because I will be fully living in the way I know how and the way that makes me happiest.

I need to know that you and mom will be proud of me no matter what I do. I think that is the greatest gift a parent can give a child: to let them create their own lives with them knowing that they are loved but they are free.

Thank you for understanding Dad.

Love,
Christina

Wednesday, July 02, 2003

Jenny wrote:
Hey guys! I'm in an internet cafe in Escazu. Last night we slept at a hostel in San Jose with all the rustic pathways people. This morning we drove to Escazu to our school and we had Spanish class in the morning and cooking class to make lunch. Our teachers nice. Me and Sara and Emma are in the same class with 2 other people. Then we walked around Escazu a little and that's how we ended up here. The internet is really slow, it's taken me like half an hour to get into my account and start writing this email. I haven't met my family yet, but i know me and Sara are with the same family.

We are going to meet them this afternoon. Is Cory Ok? Tell her I miss her. I don't know when I'll be able to email again.

byebye
Jen

Gail replied:
OH MY OH MY!!! How wonderful to hear from you love-bug!!! I'm glad you like your teacher! I wonder what the youth hostel was like! Do you like the kids?? Can't wait to hear about your family!

Cory is fine!! She slept "out" (in the hail) last night and was happy to see us in the morning! Daddy took her for a nice run this morning. She says, woof!

Love you!

Love and kisses,
Mommy
XXXOOO

July 03, 2003

Jenny wrote:

Hey Mom and Dad
My family is really really nice, there are 2 little girls, 5 and 7, the Mom is 28 and cooks us dinner and breakfast. The dad has 2 jobs so he's not home very often, but he's really nice too. Last night Sara and I played jump rope with the kids for like 2 hours. Oh and the family is really rich for Costa Rica, the kids even have a computer in their room. They have a dog whose really little and funny.

Right now we're in an internet cafe again, we just went out to ice cream during our break at school and we stopped here on the way back.

Adios
XOX

I replied:
Darling Jenny, how wonderful to hear from you. I'll keep this short because I know you don't like getting letters from me! Cory is wonderful and misses you.

I love you.
Dad
XXXOOO

July 04, 2003
Jenny wrote:
Hi Dad and Mom
I like getting letters from you!

Today we went to a 4th of July party for Americans. It was fun. Ok well I got to go a dance class now. Adios!

I replied:
Darling Jenny,

Wonderful to hear from you! I'm glad you told me you like getting letters!

Cory and I are at home by ourselves. Cory is resting and I am preparing a funny presentation I am giving on Tuesday to the whole NWF staff on spam (junk e-mail). I am dressing up as spam!

Mommy, Tina, Greta and Laura left at 7:30 AM this morning to go to the shore. Mommy called this afternoon and they were all on the beach. Kim arrives there this evening with Sujay. I'm very sorry to be missing meeting him.

I am so proud of you for doing that intensive self-defense course last week and am so pleased you want to take a more advanced class next summer. Mommy and I will happily pay for that with much pleasure. Please look for opportunities to teach others what you have learned. By doing that you give a gift to the world while reinforcing your own learning.

Kim had a tough but ultimately successful week at the WSJ. She had to fight hard to get accepted and respected among veteran WSJ journalists and editors there, putting in long hours and working with great productivity. She has two articles coming out under her byline in the next few days.

Tina also faced her own challenges this week at the clinic and, like Kim, is coming out on top through networking and making friends, and being diligent and conscientious. Tina really likes it there and loves the neighborhood which she is says is so totally different from Bethesda.

Today (Friday July 4) I have been working on my book, exercising, running with Cory, playing with her, watching a video on how to give an effective speech, watching a video on the Founding Fathers, swimming at the club — but mainly writing my book.

I love you, Jenny, and miss you. Cory misses you too. Please say hi to Sara from us all. It sounds like you are having a great time in Costa Rica. Are you speaking lots of Spanish? Hope so. Well done for "blooming where you are planted."

Love,
Dad
XXXOOO

July 5, 2003
Subject: **A** letter about our precious Cory

Darling Gail, Kim, Tina and Jenny,
Last night Cory could hear the far-away bangs and explosions of the fireworks celebrating July 4. She didn't like it at all and began to shake. All I could do was hug her tightly and tell her she was okay. Then I let her sleep next to me on the bedroom floor. Throughout the night she woke me periodically with her panting (I suppose she was trying to cool down). I often saw her sitting up in the dark looking at me, panting away. Then she would lie down and stop panting and I would drift off to sleep again. Occasionally in the night, she would lick my hands and push them with her nose as if to say, "Hiya Dad, isn't this fun sleeping together like this?!"

This morning I took her for a walk/run but under a mile because it was hot and humid. She went #1 and #2 quite normally. I put the air-conditioning on to help her feel more comfortable (and me too). Nothing I could do would induce her to eat breakfast though. I've been trying throughout the day. She occasionally nibbles on it but then gives up.

I went to the Giant to get her a toy, thinking that would cheer her up, and when I got back she was immediately excited but soon grew bored with it.

At the Giant, I also bought a brush and I took her into the garden to brush her. She rolled in the grass joyfully and loved it as I gave her a long and gently brush as she rolled gently on her back on the grass. I finished up brushing her on the deck. She looked beautiful. But she still wouldn't eat anything. In the process of trying to get her to eat, I gave her several treats so she is not starving.

Cory seems OK. It's hard to tell what is going on inside. She may simply be missing Jenny (and bored with me!) Let me know if you have any thoughts. I'm confident she will eat this evening. I'll let you know immediately.

I love you, Gail
I love you, Kimmie.

I love you, Tina.
I love you, Jenny.
Your devoted
Dad/Husband
XXXOOO

July 08, 2003
Subject: Chris and his Spam costume photo

I wrote:
Thanks, lovebug,

Are you enjoying your internship? Do you feel you are learning and growing professionally? XXXOOO

Tina replied:
Hey Dad,
Yeah I like my internship. It's kind of boring sometimes, but that's expected I guess. It's different each day, sometimes there's a lot to do and sometimes there's not really. But I'm definitely learning just by being there and seeing how it runs.

But I love the other people that work there -there are these women who are young and fun and I went to get lunch with them today.

Oh and we're planning a party for a fundraiser - It's august 23rd, at the clinic in the church, from 5-l0pm just dancing and stuff - would you and mom and Kim and Jen want to come maybe???

Love
Tina

I then replied:
Darling Tina, absolutely' I've put August 23 on my calendar. What can I do to help you with the fundraiser? How about if I ask colleagues at NWF if they want to go?

Why don't you suggest having an auction at the party to help raise extra money? People like me could donate items (in my case, videos and books). Then people bid on them, with all the money going to the clinic.

With regard to your internship, look for ways to suggest to Mimi they do things in a new and improved way.

For example, think about the flow of patients in the building and how that can be improved; think about the way mail is handled; the way decisions get made; what about morale issues?

How about starting a newsletter for patients full of "preventive medicine" ideas and ways to stay healthy (i.e., don't get sick in the first place); how about offering to give a yoga or stretching class? What about any special ideas for children so they don't get so scared when they come in?

What might Mimi delegate so she is not so stressed? How about finding ways to provide a warmer

466

welcome to patients as they enter? How about giving them useful things to do while they are waiting? (e.g., watching a health video)

How about promoting the accomplishments of the clinic better to donors and board members? And how about starting a membership program of some kind so patients feel a greater affinity/allegiance to the clinic and its mission?

How about articulating a new and inspirational mission statement for the clinic which is then put up with appealing signage by the entrance for all who enter to see? Having every staff person create their own mission statement consistent with the clinic's overall mission is another idea.

How about inviting in a management consulting firm to do pro bono work for the clinic by analyzing its operations with an eye to improving them?

You'll think of plenty more ideas I'm sure.

I think Mimi would welcome a memo from you with some fresh, interesting ideas; even if she turned them all down, she would have a new appreciation for you and your desire to excel and provide outstanding service to the clinic.

I'm so glad you like the other people that work there.

I love you sweetie-pie.
Dad
XXXOOO

July 13, 2003
Subject: Letter from Chicago!

Darling Kimmie, Tina and Jenny,
This is the letter I would have sent you from my hotel in Chicago on Thursday night if my plane had not been delayed by nearly three hours due to bad weather. BTW, it was wonderful to call you both, Kim and Tina, at Kim's apartment in NYC as I was heading to my hotel in the cab from O'Hare. I'm so glad you had fun together in NYC.

I recently received a hand-written letter from a young woman who had requested my help in finding a job. She wrote to thank me for my help and this is part of what she said: "It means so much to me that you took the time to review my resume. It has been so hard to get people to even look at my resume, let alone speak to me. Thank you for taking the time to encourage me to keep trying."

I tell you this not to indicate what a nice guy I am but to remind you how hard it is to find a job, especially a fun, satisfying job. Some people only manage to reach low level professional positions even though those positions are inconsistent with the identity they have for themselves and inconsistent with their personal mission statements.

Some people are unhappy in their jobs because all they do is what someone else tells them to do. They have no autonomy, no authority and little opportunity to be creative. You'll notice in my job how every day I create it myself. It is the very opposite of someone asking me to file a huge pile of papers between

9 and 5. My job consists of projects I have invented myself. My job never existed at NWF before I created it.

I'm saying all this not to boast but rather to remind you that you need to take your careers seriously. It is hard to be really happy if you don't. This is what I tell people (like that young woman who I mentioned at the start of this letter) who ask for my advice. If you want to be happy, then here is a fundamental six-point plan you need to follow:

1. <u>Focus on finding peace of mind.</u> This is foundational. Clearly to achieve this you need to rid yourself of all duplicity and lying, but you need to go way beyond that to think through what really matters to you. Developing a written personal mission statement that you reconnect with at least once a week (when you plan the upcoming week) is crucial. The greater your peace of mind, the more relaxed, positive, healthier and self-confident you will be.

2. **<u>Pay attention to what you want.</u>** You get what you focus on. Whatever you dwell on, focus your attention on and think about will grow and expand in your life. The more you pay attention to peace of mind, your relationships, the quality of your work, your health and physical fitness, your finances, and how to add meaning and purpose to your life, then the happier you will become. You will achieve what you focus on.

3. <u>Develop happy relationships.</u> You want to love and be loved by others. You want to have a happy, harmonious home life. You want to earn the respect of the people you respect. You want to get along with the people around you. Everything you do and accomplish is based on your relationships with other people. Learning how to listen, how to be assertive, how to make requests, how to manage promises and how to express appreciation, are all skills you need to develop happy relationships. It is important to realize that love is a verb, not an emotional state.

4. <u>Commit to interesting, challenging and enjoyable work.</u> Now we arrive at last at career considerations. You want to earn money of course so you have the freedom to buy essentials but to be happy you really want to enjoy your profession. The very best times in your life are when you are completely absorbed in your work. You can see examples of that over and over again in Mommy's professional work at Consumers Union. To achieve this requires you to be well educated and that requires hard work, determination, discipline and the courage to postpone gratification. The reason I have the job I now have is because I have made many sacrifices in the past. When I was young, my friends would be out partying while I would be working. (BTW, that young woman who I quoted at the start of this letter also wrote in her letter to me: "Though I'm sure there are plenty of hardships, it seems to me you have the perfect job." She is right but it has taken years of dedication to get there.) The key to success at work is continuous learning. Even though I have three degrees from London and Harvard, my education only began there, not ended. As you know, in the years since, I have continued learning through a wide range of personal and professional workshops and courses. Every day I read extensively and listen to tapes (Bill Bryson on cosmology and geology at the moment). I don't say this to brag but to encourage you to be absolutely passionate about ambitious and continuous learning. When you stop learning, you begin to atrophy and die. You need to keep your mind alert and your focus on constantly learning. Homework is one of the secrets of success that many people forget once they leave school. You should always go to a party with several things in mind you want to bring up with people for discussion and to get their views. Continuous learning will help you find enjoyable and challenging work, and will make your resume sparkle so that people <u>will</u> read it.

5. <u>Achieve financial independence.</u> You want to be free from worries about money. Financial independence frees you from poverty and a need to depend on others (like your husband) for your existence. If you save and invest regularly, and live within your means, you will do fine. Don't forget to read Mommy's wonderful and powerful multi-page letter to you on financial management.

6. <u>Enjoy high levels of health and energy.</u> You want to be free of pain and illness of course, but you want much more than that. You want to be flowing over with energy and vitality. You want to have endurance, strength and flexibility. There is only one way to achieve this incredible state, and that is invest in a daily regimen of exercise involving stretching, weight-lifting and aerobics, and to avoid all junk food. If you don't, you will eventually pay the price in lack of energy, poor vitality, physical weakness and vulnerability to infections and illness. You don't want to succumb to the miseries of a sedentary existence. Don't take good health for granted like so many people do. It is foundational to your ability to perform at your full potential as a human being and to be an innovative, high-flying, high-performing, results-oriented and oft-promoted professional. If you are fit and strong, then you will also be ready at all times to achieve that high-peak intensive performance needed when someone needs help and you are suddenly called upon to give an extraordinary physical performance to save someone's life, for example, by having to run miles to get help for someone.

Each of these six areas should be part of your written personal mission statement. Every week you should think about them, focus on them, think what would make you happy and satisfied in each of them, and set specific, measurable goals for improvement in each area.

Then resolve to schedule time on your calendar with activities that will increase the quality of those areas of your life that you have identified in your personal mission statement as important to you. And here is the key to success: keep that promise to yourself — feel the deep, profound pleasure of fulfilling a promise you made to yourself. That is what it means to have integrity.

My loves, I hope this is helpful to you as you continue the great journey of your lives. You have all been wonderfully successful so far. Mommy and I are so proud of you. We adore you.

Love from yer-still-learning ol' Dad
XXXOOO

July 13, 2003
Subject: Re: Letter from Chicago!

Kim wrote:
Dad,
Thank you so much for your letter! it helped calm me because I am so stressed about work now!

I will try to have inner peace.

It was good to talk to you just now!

Love,
Kim

I replied:
Darling Kimmie,
I'm sorry you are so stressed about work now. Hang in there love-bug. You are doing great. You are working for one of the greatest newspapers, if not the greatest newspaper, in the world, so it is bound to be stressful and challenging. Here are four things you can do:

1. Act totally confident and at peace with yourself, even if you don't feel it.

2. Talk to Nick and others who you like and confide in them that you need their help coping with the stress.

3. Keep your life in balance: eat well, exercise regularly, sleep well and keep things in perspective by regularly reviewing your personal mission statement.

4. Be highly efficient and productive, and continue to work diligently.

If you do all those things, then you'll get through this OK. And if you get through this, then you can get through anything in life.

I love you, Kimmie.
Dad
XXXOOO

July 14, 2003
Subject: Re: Letter from Chicago!

Tina wrote:
Thank you for those suggestions! i just wrote Mimi a letter (she is gone today) with the idea, so I will see what she says tomorrow. I'm scared she's going to say no! I really want to do it!

I know it is sad about Tom. I was sort of upset yesterday, cause i have these expectations and then they don't work out... It's not his fault cause he can't control when his practices are, but I get my hopes up and then it doesn't happen cause first it was he was going to live in DC, then he said he'd be able to come like every weekend, then he said he's be able to meet me in Cape Cod at the wedding, and none of that stuff is happening! I don't really know what to do about that. i don't want to be annoying about it, and he feels bad anyway.

I hope you're having a good day!

Love
Tina

I replied:
Darling Tina,
Re Mimi: be ready in case she says no. Try and understand what her concerns are so you can address them in a follow up offer. For example, she may be concerned that you are leaving in a few weeks, and then who would carry on the newsletter? Expectations would have been raised in her patients whom she can't fulfill. If that is the case, then here are a few ideas:

470

— Design an e-newsletter which is easily sent out electronically.

— Design a basic and simple template so that future issues can be produced by virtually "filling in the blanks".

— Scale back your offer to a one-time welcoming "letter" that everyone gets as they come in the door. It would still contain a lot of the same information as a newsletter but won't seem so intimidating to Mimi in terms of "keeping it up".

— Think through what Mimi's biggest concerns are (misbehaving patients? insufficient patients? not enough authority? unresponsive doctors? unsupportive board? inadequate compensation? no public recognition?) and make suggestions which help her with what is bugging her most.

Tina, whatever Mimi says, she will be pleased with your enthusiasm and good ideas, and that is important of itself. Keep thinking of new, innovative ideas which will help the clinic function better. For example, how about a "humor" board where people put up jokes, cartoons and anything funny? There is no greater therapy and patients will love it. It will take their minds off having to wait. Tell Mimi that you are willing to pay for the board and pins (I'll pay!).

Re Tom: don't play too easy to get. Be cool. Have a good time in DC with all your girlfriends. Be resilient and independent. Don't mope. Make him want you. Be cheerful. Be resourceful. Look for fun ways to get together. Plan for the future. Focus on your professional skills which will help you get the type of job you want in the future so you will have the power and freedom to choose wherever you want to live and work. For example, "Initiated and created a newsletter for the Free Clinic which reached X patients and led to a measurable increase in Y for the clinic" is the type of sparkle you want to be able to add to your resume which will enable you to get the kind of job you want — and hence the life you want to lead with (or without) Tom.

Good luck, treasure.

I love you.
Dad
XXXOOO

PS: I left work early this afternoon as a good dog Daddy should to get home to check on Cory to make sure she was OK and to put on Cortaid on her sore spot. She seems in good spirits. I will likely take her to the vet tomorrow morning just to get her looked at. I'm going to get Jenny from BWI tomorrow afternoon and Cory had better be in good shape for Jenny otherwise Mommy and I will be in deep guano!

Tina then replied:
Dad! Thank you for your advice again!!! It really helps me, thank you!

I stayed late and worked at the HIV clinic for a little tonight, it was really interesting. I helped set up, then worked at the front desk answering phones and checking people in. it was so good. I felt useful for once. And there were new volunteers there who I got to meet. So I feel good about everything.

And you're right about Tom. I will be independent and happy and not worry or get sad about it. I told him more how I feel and I feel better about it all now...

You're so good for taking such good care of Cory! I didn't know there was anything wrong! I hope she's okay!

Love
Tina

I then replied:
Darling Tina, yes, it is an incredible feeling to feel needed and useful. That is one of the worst things about getting old and frail. You stop feeling useful and needed. Someone (you!) ought to start an organization that provides ideas and services to nursing homes aimed at helping residents feel useful and needed instead of useless and a burden on society. I bet it would pay for itself in the money saved on drugs used to treat depression!

Well done for tonight at the clinic. That's the way. Create opportunities for yourself to be useful like you did tonight. See yourself as a "social entrepreneur" creating ideas and services that help people in need.

Here is another idea for you to propose to Mimi: you contact similar clinics in the area and go visit them. You find out their "best practices" and bring them back to Mimi for discussion and, if approved, implementation.

Another idea: you create a Listserv for all the clinics in the country so all of the clinics like yours can share ideas on the internet.

Another idea: when you meet people socially, tell them about a particular challenge the clinic faces and ask them for their advice. You'll be amazed at the good ideas you can invent with other people in conversations. Then take those ideas back to Mimi for discussion.

Re Tom: you are doing great. You don't want to give him the impression you are dependent on him in any way.

Hang in there, lovebug. Continue to be in an inventive and resourceful mood.

I love you.
Dad   XXXOOO

July 31, 2003
Subject: First day on my lonesome!

Darling Kimmie, Tina and Jenny,
I hope Alison and Paul's wedding is a happy time for everyone, especially you, Kimmie, as maid of honor! I am so sad about missing the toast you are giving but I know you will do an outstanding job.

I got home tonight and immediately played with Cory and took her out for a walk and exercise. She

472

went #1 and #2 in that order. Then while half-listening to NBC news, I had dinner — toast and cold fish (trout).

Plus I ate celery, a plum and a nectarine. It was perfectly satisfying (even though I sound like an abstemious monk!). Oh, and I had a glass of delicious iced water to go with it.

Then I turned the TV off, played with Cory, and as a wonderful calm and stillness suffused our home, got to work at my desk where I have been productively working all evening.

Cory seems very happy. She didn't want to come into the study with me so I check on her periodically and indulge in a monologue something along the following lines:

ohyou'resobeautifulyoubigbabyhowdidyougettobesowonderfulcoryyouusmellbutIloveyousomuch anyway youbigbabylookatthoseeyesandthatgorgeousnosehow'sthatsorebackohitssomuchbetter youcleverthingyoubigbabyohiloveyousomuch" and on and on. Cory closes her eyes and wonders what my problem is.

Sara Murray sent me the sweetest handwritten thank you letter today. Wow, does she have neat writing! She writes more neatly than I type.

Take care of each other and have the best fun together.

Love from lonesome Dad.
XXXOOO

August 1, 2003
Subject:　　　Second day on my lonesome!

My darling Kim, Tina and Jenny,
Dying to know how the wedding went, how your toast/speech went, Kim, and how beautiful you all looked! I was pleased to receive your e-mail this afternoon, Jenny, saying how excited you were about the wedding this evening. I hoped it lived up to everyone's expectations. Did you enjoy (I should say, are you enjoying) being maid of honor, Kimmie? I want to see photos of you all dressed up!

Everything here is great. I went to Fresh Fields on the way home and bought fresh English garden peas, raw brazil nuts, red pepper, freshly squeezed grapefruit juice, organic carrots, raisin bagel, black beans, peaches, pears, kiwi and apples. All that, plus lentil soup, was my dinner tonight.

I love you, Kim. I love you, Tina. I love you, Jenny. I love you moon. I love you air. I love you nothing. I love you box, I love you socks.

Sleep tight. You'll all be exhausted when you eventually get to bed tonight.

Lots of love from
lonesome Dad and Cory
XXXOOO

August 3, 2003
Subject: Third day on my lonesome!

Darling Kim, Tina and Jenny,
I'm so happy to hear Alison and Paul's wedding went so well and was so much fun. When Tina said to me on the phone today that it was an exuberant celebration of life, I suddenly wished that I had been there. I'm so glad you all had a super time.

Kim, I heard your speech was a huge success and that you delivered it without any notes!!! Congratulations for meeting that challenge head-on and for being such a winner. Maybe that experience will make you want to give more speeches and eventually that can be another source of income for you.

I'm so sorry about the 15 year old girl with lupus. That is so sad.

Cory and I have had a great day. This morning we went for a long run. It is very humid here so I got back sweating wonderfully. Then I went for a swim. What could be more delightful?

I spent the day working hard on a big speech I am giving in San Francisco on August 15 (about two weeks) and broke the back of it. So I am feeling very energized and pleased.

Tonight I had a delicious dinner of boiled eggs and toast, raw green peas, a red pepper, nuts and a kiwi.

I put on the book channel - C Span 3 - as I was cooking up my mouth-watering dinner and to my delight they were broadcasting an interview with Mary Higgins Clark, the author of "Mount Vernon Love Story."

She was being interviewed by the veteran journalist Roger Mudd. It was wonderful to listen to. Programs like this interview with Mary Higgins Clark, "It's Academic", and American Dreams (on tomorrow I noticed at 8 PM so get home by then!!!) redeem my faith in television as something that can be positive and valuable to society.

You would have loved to hear Mary Higgins Clark talk about George and Martha Washington. I found it fascinating. She first published the book in 1969 under the title "Aspire to the Heavens," which was the family motto of George Washington's mother (who, incidentally, George didn't get along with and was uncomfortable with).

No one bought the book. The public thought it was a religious-based inspirational book! Now she has reissued it under the title "Mount Vernon Love Story" and it is selling much better! She claimed the book is as historically accurate as she could make it. I thought it was a great book.

Kim, we'll call you tomorrow (Sunday) night. I'm dying to hear your take on the big wedding weekend In New England!

Tina and Jen, I can't wait to see you tomorrow. Safe journey home. Enjoy the beach in the morning! And please give my love to Nana, Gordon and Mark.

Love from lonesome Dad
XXXOOO

August 10, 2003
Subject: Letter #1 from dad on his lonesome!

Darling Kim, Tina and Jenny,
Where is Cory? I keep looking for her. Then I remember she is with Jen and Mommy in New Jersey. I'm so used to her being around!

Tina, great to talk to you a moment ago. Thanks for calling me. Glad you went to yoga today. That is a great thing to do. It was wonderful to have Tom visit this weekend. I like him very much. It was good to talk to his twin sister Carolyn this afternoon when she called to find out when Tom was getting home. Thanks to you and Tom for cooking that healthy meal for all of us on Friday night, Tina. Good luck with finishing the newsletter this week. I encourage you to put together a fundraising plan for the Free Clinic this week. What a great research project and what a great gift to leave the Clinic as you leave. (It also looks great, deservedly so, on your resume.) I can outline it for you if you want.

Kimmie, I've tried to call you twice this evening, without luck so far. Hope you got to Cat's apartment safely after leaving Nana's house at the shore. I'm sure you had a relaxing and lovely weekend with Nana and Gordon. When I went swimming yesterday afternoon, I talked to Bob Metzler who I know because he is Anne Marie's dad, and Ann Marie used to play soccer with Jen. Anyway, his wife is Mary Lou Carnivals (sp?) who, as you know, works for the WSJ. Bob said to me, with no prompting from me, that his wife had heard you were doing an excellent job, Kim! Your agent, Andrew Blauner, will arrive back from vacation tomorrow and find four copies of your book on his desk, ready for mailing to publishers. Kim, thanks for your comments on the Ted Turner chapter — oh, I forgot, those comments are "in the mail"! I am looking forward to meeting Sujay very much when I visit you in Chicago this fall.

PS to Kim: I just talked to you and to Mommy! Kim, *please* invite Sujay to visit us over Labor Day weekend. We won't go away (at one point we were thinking we would all go away for the weekend together) and would be delighted if he could come and visit. And then we'll have the Burgess's to dinner on Monday September 1. Is that OK for everyone?

Jenny, thanks for playing so much tennis with me. I love it. I am so proud of the way you are tenaciously and relentlessly building your vocabulary. That was wonderful you got a 1600 on a SAT practice test (thereby matching the 5 you got on Spanish AP and the 790 for.. .what was it? another SAT test you did a few months ago?) I am also delighted to see you stronger and fitter than you've ever been with your workouts in the basement. That will really help not only your tennis but also your academic performance (to say nothing of your self-image, posture and self-confidence). You've also been practicing the trumpet and reading — bravo. Thanks for coming to Discovery Cove and Blizzard Beach — I loved every moment of it, and you and Sara were great fun to be with. Thanks for helping Mommy buy our new car! (Gail, my love, superb job!!! Glad you went with my recommendation!!! (Ahem))

I love you, Gail.
I love you, Kim.
I love you, Tina.
I love you, Jenny.
I love you, Cory.

I love you, moon.
I love you, air.
I love you mittens and I love you kittens.
I love you socks lying in the box
I love you, nothing.
Good night moon, good night spoon, and good night kaboon!
Dad/Chris
XXXOOO

Monday, August 11, 2003
Subject: Letter #2 from dad on his lonesome

My darling precious daughters, Kimmie, Tina and Jenny,
You know that I am constantly searching for nuggets of wisdom (because, unlike Mommy, I didn't start my adult life with much of it so I am running to catch up!)

Just in the last few days, I have collected the following ideas and changed the wording on each to suit myself better. My hero, Ben Franklin, did this with the maxims he wrote for his Farmer's Almanac. Apparently very few of his adages were original.

So with thanks to the writers and sages who inspired me (and remembering that the essence of all these come from others, not me), please enjoy and reflect upon the following:

1. To climb steep hills requires a slow pace at first. (This reminds me of Steven Covey's metaphor of the plant that blossoms gloriously after seven years of patient care and watering.)

2. Time spent laughing is time spent in pure bliss.

3. One of the greatest gifts you can give others is a good example.

4. People often miss opportunities because they are disguised with hard work.

5. Our happiness depends on our attitude, not our circumstances.

6. Bravery is being the only one who knows you are afraid.

7. The greatest wisdom in the world in kindness.

8. To improve the world, first improve yourself.

9. It is more important to be fit and healthy than to have a good body. (I know that is a little self-serving on my part!)

10. Enthusiasm, tenacity and energy will eventually win every battle.

11. The winners in life, unlike the losers, are willing to take the first step.

12. A loving spouse is a masterpiece of nature (my tribute to Mommy!)

13. Avoid the easy and convenient life; rather seek out challenges and live to the edge of your possibility.

14. Every problem contains a hidden gift.

As I say, these were all inspired from things I have recently read and jotted down. I hope you find them as inspiring and provocative as I do.

I love you, Gail
I love you, Kim
I love you, Tina
I love you, Jenny
I love you, Cory
Don't be sadish, eat a radish
Goodnight air, goodnight moon, goodnight nothing.
Ol' Dad
XXXOOO

August 12, 2003
Subject: Letter #3 from Dad on his lonesome!

Darling Kimmie, Tina and Jenny,
Hey, I won't be lonesome any more in about 15 minutes because Tina is coming to visit! Yeehaahhh! Yessirreee Bill! Don't need no more of 'em radishes! Toodledoo kangaroo! I love you all. Goodnight moon, goodnight mittens, goodnight kittens, goodnight book about saying goodnight to the moon. Goodnight nothin'. Woof woof sand on the beach, running in the salty water, chasing down those tennis balls, rolling on my back, making Jenny laugh, and getting hosed down. Can't let Jen's new fancy car get dirty now, can we? Goodnight dirty socks in the box without any locks. Goodnight cat in the hat, goodnight green eggs and ham, goodnight Mr. Bartholomew. There's the bell and here's Tina.

Dad
XXXOOO

August 14, 2003
Subject: Letter #1 from San Francisco

Darling Kimmie, Tina and Jenny,
Kimmie, are you OK in the blacked-out northeast? I've been in close touch with Mommy monitoring the situation. Thanks for finding a phone and calling Mommy. Good luck on that 6 mile walk to Cat's house. Hopefully power will be restored soon. This country must move towards decentralized power sources (e.g., solar panels) so that we are not so vulnerable. Our infrastructure needs to be robust, not brittle.

Kim, is Sujay OK in Detroit? Detroit was also blacked-out.

Tina, I'm sure Tom will be OK too.

Tina, how is your memo going on fundraising? Good luck with it. Send it to me for feedback if you'd like to. It will be great to be able to add to your resume, "Initiated and created strategic fundraising plan for the clinic." Building your resume and real world skills in every way you can will open up new job possibilities for you in the future. Every leader of a non-profit needs to know how to raise money.

Jenny, I hope you are having fun on your trip to Pennsylvania!

On the plane here today, I used the four and a half hour flight to get through a ton of important reading, so I got off the plane feeling very happy.

I give a big speech here tomorrow and I am excited about it.

I love you.
Dad
XXXOOO

August 15, 2003
Subject: Letter #2 from San Francisco

My darling Kim, Tina and Jen,
My oh my, what an adventure you had in blacked-out NYC, Kimmie. That must have been very scary at first when all the power failed and you had no means of knowing if it was a terrorist action or what. Being right next door to the World Trade Center added to your anxiety. That was so thoughtful of Tina to call you right away on your cell phone to check you were OK. It is good she remembered Tom as an afterthought (hehehe. . .just kidding ... ow, stop hitting me Tina, ow, ow, stop it, was only ow kidding ow, ow, okay, okay, I know you love Kimmie and were concerned for her too!)

My speech today could not have gone better — oh, I wrote and told you that in an earlier e-mail today. Tomorrow I am giving another talk and really looking forward to it. (I can't write that without grinning because I immediately think of Steve Martin on that CD in the car..."really looking forward to it...")

Kim, Tina and Jen, you are so very special. I talk about you all the time on my travels. No Daddy could be prouder of his children than I am of you three (four, sorry Cory).

I adore you.
Dad XXXOOO

PS: There is no family rule saying you can't reply to my e-mails!!!

August 17, 2003
Subject: Letter #3 from LA

My loves,
Kim is in NC, Tina is home, Jenny is home, Mommy is home, Cory is home, and I'll be home late Wednesday.

I love you so much and miss you.
Dad
XXXOOO

August 18, 2003
Subject: Letter #4 from LA

My darling Kimmie, Tina, Jenny and Cory,
I have had another busy and productive day in LA. But I'm tired and must go to bed. Great to talk to you, Tina and Jen, today, and Mommy too of course. Kim, I was so glad you had such a great weekend in NC with Sujay. Is he coming to stay with us over labor day weekend?

None of you caught the error in my letter to you two nights ago. Ben Franklin wrote Poor Richard's Almanack (sic), not the Farmer's Almanac! Hey, is anyone reading my letters?!

I love you.
Dad
XXXOOO

August 18, 2003
Subject: Letter #5 from LA

My precious Kim, Tina and Jenny,
I love you and miss you! I can't wait to get home on Wednesday night. Traveling is like licking honey off a thorn — I have to do it for my job and I love my job but I don't like being away from home.

Kim, this is your last week at the WSJ! Tina, this is your last week at the Washington Free Clinic! Jen, this is your last week at...nothing!

I am reading with enormous fascination Edmund Morgan's gripping biography on Benjamin Franklin. It is beautifully written.

As a young man, he was very concerned with what constituted a good life. He thought long and hard about it and eventually articulated a list of the virtues he sought to attain in his own life. He didn't call it a personal mission statement, of course, but in effect, that's what it was.

Here (in my own words, not his) are those 13 virtues:

1. Eat and drink healthily.

2. Avoid trifling and gossipy conversation.

3. Everything should have its place so things are immediately retrievable (in other words, be organized).

4 Keep your promises and be reliable.

5. Don't be wasteful.

6. Be productive and diligent, and don't squander valuable time.

7. Never be deceitful, duplicitous or insincere.

8. Pursue justice and live justly.

9. Avoid extremes.

10. Be clean and hygienic.

11. Have inner peace and tranquility (don't be upset by minor upsets).

12. Be chaste.

13. Be humble and modest.

Edmund Morgan points out that what is missing from this list is charity, love of one's fellow man. And yet charity was the guiding principle of Franklin's life. Morgan speculates that Franklin left charity off the list because it was a virtue that Christians so often failed to exhibit while professing to hold it above all others.

I love you, Kim.
I love you, Tina.
I love you, Jenny.
I love Mommy of course too.

And I love Cory as well.

Can't wait to get home.
Dad
XXXOOO

August 20, 2003
Subject: Letter #6 from Denver

My darling Kimmie, Tina and Jenny,
I am now in Denver and have just come from a very successful dinner with Dr. Rick Smartt who heads up The Wildlife Experience Museum here in Denver. It has a large format theater.

Rick and I are working together to make a film about the early explorers of the west and the biomes here. (Biomes are habitats like mountains, forests, grasslands, wetlands, and canyons.) One of those early explorers was John Wesley Powell who lost his right arm at the elbow at the bloody Battle of Shiloh in the civil war. (He fought on the Union side.)

Despite that handicap, Powell in 1869 led a party of ten adventurers down the Green and Colorado rivers in four specially designed boats. It took them three months and they navigated some 900 miles of treacherous rapids and unknown waters. Remarkably, the only lives lost were those of three men who had given up near the end (the heat was terrible and they were short of food) and had climbed out of the canyon only to be waylaid and killed by Indians.

Every time I come out to the west, I am reminded of how fascinating a place it is. The history is amazing.

Did I ever tell you that one of my recurrent dreams as a little boy (3 or 4 years old?) was of being a cowboy out on the range. Where I got that idea from I have no idea. Hearing my father talk about it? Seeing a comic strip or cartoon? Seeing a movie? Anyway, I was obsessed by cowboys. I saw myself as a cowboy. I had barely heard of America, had no idea where it was, and yet something about it drew me to imagine my future there, I say myself careening down steep canyons, lassoing cattle, arresting law-breaking varmints, and galloping on my horse across the American plains chasing marauding Indians. It was a great life!

I think that is why when came across the Kennedy Scholarship, I jumped at the opportunity. I had always wanted to come to America — the land of the free, the untamed and the wild.

I love you.
Cowboy Dad
XXXOOO

August 20, 2003
Subject: Wonderful to get your call this evening!

I had written the evening before:
Darling Kimmie,
Wonderful to get your call tonight I was so glad you caught me before I left for dinner. All your conversations with the WSJ sound excellent. I think you are handling everything beautifully. Well done!

Question did Andrew receive the four copies of your book OK?

I love you, Kimmie.
Dad
XXXOOO

Kim replied:
Yes, Dad, He did -- Thank you! I am really glad I got to talk to you, too, it helps to calm me down when I am stressed.

Love,
Kim

I then replied:
Kimmie, we need to help give you ways of coping with stress. It is an important life skill that you already have, but you probably need to become even more skilled at dealing with stress.

You are only 23 and yet you are already working in a very high pressure environment which would be stressful for anyone at any age.

Some ideas: Yoga? Visioning? Anticipating breakdowns? Acting? Breathing? More exercise? Stronger reconnecting to your fundamental life goals so you keep things in perspective?

More ideas: Listing things you are grateful for every Sunday evening before the week starts? Developing a better comic vision so you more quickly see the humor in the ordinary and mundane? Keeping a journal in which you write about stress?

More ideas: Discussing it with friends to find out what coping mechanisms other people have developed? Take up a hobby like salsa dancing, painting or rock climbing which forces you to focus on something completely different?

You are doing incredibly well, Kimmie, and I am so proud of you. I'm confident you'll develop coping skills and learn how to deal with stress so you can feel a deep inner peace even while you are racing against a deadline. Hey, then you can write a book about it!

I love you.
Dad
XXXOOO

August 22, 2003
Subject: Re: Letter #5 from LA

I had written:
Isn't that funny? I could swear from reading other biographies that the number was 14 but I am evidently wrong. Or maybe it was 14 on an earlier list -- he attempted to articulate such a list of virtues on different occasions as he was struggling to get his life together."

Did you or Kim ask me re the meaning of "chaste"? I just wrote Kim a note about that but perhaps it was you, not Kim, who sent me that e-mail

Both your e-mails to me got caught in our anti-spam software and I didn't get them till I got into the office today.

Loveya Tina.
Dad

Tina replied:
nope that's right, Kim asked about "being chaste" but I think we were all wondering. hehe that reminds me of those funny emails you used to send on sex via email cause you didn't want to talk about it in person! re-send them! aahahaha! I'm LOL!!

I then replied to Kim, Tina, Jenny, and Gail:

OK, smarty pants who knows more about these things that yerol' dad!! Here it is, attached. I'm glad you didn't ask me at breakfast tomorrow morning otherwise your LOL would turn into HMCSOOYNAOTBTAMGBACLIU (half masticated cereal spewing out of your nose all over the breakfast table and Mommy going bonkers as Cory laps it up!) I love you. Dad XXXOOO

September 8, 2003
Subject: Virtual Family Meeting #34

To My Precious and Most Wonderful Family,
I love you. Thanks for a very special day yesterday rafting on the beautiful Shenandoah river in Virginia. It was the best fun!

My Rock next week: To have fun with Kim before she returns to Chicago, to support Jen at school, to keep in touch with Tina in the Grand Canyon, to work with Mommy on a "family security plan," and to prepare brilliant speeches for Jackson Hole.

Encouragement:

Gail: Thanks for wonderful meals, for buying the our new car so skillfully, for fixing the hoses, for building the bird houses, for fixing the dishwasher, for making the house and garden so pretty and beautiful with flowers everywhere, for getting quoted so frequently in the papers like the New York Times, for exercising every day, for that amazing press conference in June with Pelosi, Dingell, Rangel, Brown and other bigwigs, and thanks most of all for being an extraordinary mother and wife.

Kim: Well done for those two great ideas for articles for USA Today; great idea to take yoga classes to help you alleviate stress; well done for going with Tina to yoga classes this past month; well done for the great speech you made at Alison's wedding and for making it look so easy; we are so glad you love Sujay; he is a wonderful guy and we loved meeting him; I know you'll enjoy meeting his family next week; well done for the determination you showed yesterday getting back into the raft from the river; we are so proud of you for the success you made of your internship with the Wall Street Journal this summer; you have planned out a wonderful year of "building your intellectual capital" at the University of Chicago next year— good luck, Lovebug!

Tina: well done for the great experience you had this summer at the Free Clinic; you wrote a wonderful report on your experience too; what an exciting adventure you have planned for the Grand Canyon!; we are so glad you love Tom; he is a wonderful guy and we have loved getting to know him; tomorrow, relish getting to know his grandparents — I know you will: well done for taking yoga classes this summer, and for taking Kim whenever you could; great idea to think about learning how to teach it to others; the two essays you wrote for applying for scholarships were excellent; well done for going to the Library of Congress and taking advantage of all it has to offer; thanks again for your poignant and lovely letter about not wanting to be a doctor; well done for thinking so creatively and resourcefully about your future career plans; I know you'll have a great last year at Dartmouth!

Jen: Good luck on your history exam on Wednesday! And also good luck with your first Varsity tennis match on Tuesday! Well done for focusing on tennis this summer, improving your game with resolute determination, and then getting selected for the Varsity team; especially well done for supporting Sara through her ordeal re tennis — you have built a wonderful friendship with her; well done for getting a 5 on your AP exam on Spanish, and also the 790 on your chemistry SAT — wonderful! Well done for keeping fitter and stronger than you've ever been in your life; thanks for driving the Passat so well — you've had no fender-benders yet! What a great summer you had: working with Congressman Van Hollen and writing that paper on health care for him, swimming with Dixie the 29-year-old female dolphin at Discovery Cove in Orlando, spending two weeks in Costa Rica, taking an intensive self-defense course, and working for Richard at the tennis club; I also sense that you got some good reading done this summer too. Well done for practicing SAT tests this summer (and getting that 1600!)

To everyone: thanks for my wonderful, love-filled birthday on August 25! Gail, thanks for the Ben Franklin CDs; Kim, thanks for making me smell so good! Tina, thanks for the yoga class (ahem!); Jen, thanks for the lunch still to come! And thanks to everyone for taking me to the surprise outing to Wolf Trap to see "Thoroughly Modern Millie."

I am so lucky to have such a wonderful family. Thanks for making me so happy.

Love, Dad/Chris
XXOOO

October 08, 2003
Subject: Interesting replies to "Lovely article by daughter of a friend"

Michael Palmer <mpxxxii@btinternet.com> wrote:
Dear Chris, Here is another reaction to Christina's article. Would you be so kind as to drop her a brief e-mail? I am sure she (and others who have asked how Christina became so wise) would appreciate a response from "The Fathers Mouth"?

(You see what a demand there would be for "Lord Palmer's Letters to His Daughters"!! (All 10 Volumes.)

Cheers, Michael

Wednesday, October 08, 2003 2:47 PM
From: GalaFunctions@aol.com
To: mpxxxii@btinternet.com
Subject: Re: Interesting replies to "Lovely article by daughter of a friend"

Thank you for this beautiful e-mail, just what my children need, Inspiration. They are both teenagers going through a difficult time. How can we guide them to success? What it takes to be balanced? Accordingly to your experience in life what would be your advice for a young lady? Love to hear your opinions.

Carmen Triggers

I then sent this to Michael:

From "The Fathers Mouth"

Michael Palmer (no relation even though we both share the same last name) has asked me to respond to Carmen Triggers' delightful and charming e-mail, as well as several other lovely (and wise) e-mails that Michael has received because of my daughter's article in the Dartmouth College newspaper.

Christina is our middle daughter. She is 21 and a senior at Dartmouth in the U.S. Christina recently decided not to pursue a career as a doctor and her article was lamenting the uncertainty and quiet torment she was now experiencing as she wrestles with the issue of what to do with her life.

Michael asked me to comment on why Tina (as we call her) became so wise. I asked Tina for her reactions to Carmen's e-mail requesting advice for "young ladies," and she replied:

484

"I would say help them explore what is out there and help them to find their own way. Let them make their own decisions and mistakes."

I think that is good advice from Tina. Here are ten other ideas that I believe have helped our three daughters do well:

1. Marry a wonderful wife and mother.

2. Stay married and always put the family first.

3. Lead a decent and moral life, and thus set a good example.

4. Develop a family mission statement together and refer to it periodically.

5. Develop a personal mission statement (mine is attached) and live a designed, intentional life.

6. Hold weekly family meetings with a written agenda, and take it in turns to chair it.

7. Be affectionate and tell your daughters you love and admire them.

8. Everyday catch your daughters doing something right.

9. Teach them (by example) the foundational importance of being healthy, fit and strong.

10. Create memorable and joyful family traditions that your daughters count on and look forward to.

I hope this is helpful! Oh, one more thing: when you make a mistake (and I make lots of them) apologize!

Warmest wishes to everyone on Michael's list.
Chris Palmer (in Bethesda, MD, USA)
703 438 6077
palmer©nwf.org

Christopher N. Palmer
President and CEO
National Wildlife Productions
National Wildlife Federation
11100 Wildlife Center Drive
Reston, VA 20190-5362
703 438 6077
fax 703 438 6076
email: palmernwf.org
www.nwf.org

October 26, 2003
Subject: Virtual Family Meeting #35

To my wonderful, precious and totally-loved family,

My "Rock" next week is to have an optimistic, positive attitude at NWF and to rigorously implement the well-thought-out five-pronged strategy that Mommy and I have developed for dealing with the current situation (more on this below).

Encouragement:

Gail: Well done for doing the January editorial for Consumer Reports; that was so nice of you to send Kim and Tina home-made chocolate chip cookies; well done for all your work on the Medicare bill on the Hill; all your meetings on the Hill are great; your job is going so well!!; your friendship with Jessica is wonderful; that's great you made Alison and Paul feel so welcome when they spent two days with us last week; thanks for being so welcoming to Harrison and Ana Smith when we took them out to dinner on Friday night; the garden with all its flowers looks lovely and tranquil; and thanks for all your great wisdom, advice and help on my work situation — I feel back in the fight!

Kim: Well done for all your terrific articles for Red Eye (Arnold's groping and wedding expenses being the latest); so glad Sujay is looking for jobs in NYC, and congratulations on your six-month anniversary!; my friend, Harrison Smith (who now works for MacGillivray Freeman Films in Laguna Beach, CA) used to work for the Federal Reserve Board in NYC (he was there for six years) and I know would be delighted to talk to Sujay if that would be helpful to him; so glad you are loving your learning and studies at the Harris School in Chicago; I think you are handling your future job just fine — I'm sure WSJ will firm up its commitment, and in the meantime, their delay allows you to explore other options and most importantly, gives you a wonderful excuse to strengthen your network of contacts at other prominent newspapers.

Tina: That's great you had a question ready to ask Democratic candidate John Kerry! I'm so glad you are enjoying anthropology so much! ever think about doing a Ph.D and teaching?; good luck on Tuesday with your "case" interview with the Mercer consulting firm — remember they are looking for character, attitude, a sense of humor, and an ability to admit you don't know but you have ideas how you would go about finding the answer (the web, other organizations, books, experts and so on); and good luck on Friday at your interview for the Peace Corps; by the way, I'm sure whatever you wear to the interview on Tuesday (suit or no suit), you'll look great; I don't think a suit is as important as looking self-confident, together, and totally professional; remember smile and to act with unstoppable vitality and confidence (in other words, act yourself!); our best wishes to Tom!; I hope Homecoming was fun this weekend!

Jenny: Well done for earning money baby-sitting; earning money is very important — it gives you freedom and options; well done for getting mentioned in the Washington Post last week for your tennis prowess and for being virtually undefeated this season!!; thanks for introducing me to American Dream!; that is super you got a 93 in Mr. Tupper's class! I know that isn't easy to achieve and it is a great achievement; you work so hard and you are so conscientious; you are making an investment that will pay handsome dividends in the future for you — you are building intellectual capital that will be worth a lot of money one day and give you enormous satisfaction; that contribution you made yesterday to the school newspaper was great; I think Blue Baby is so lucky to have you dress her so lovingly; I'm so pleased that your PSAT seemed to go well; well done for practicing for the SAT test this morning; your upcoming road trip in early November with Mommy and Sara to see colleges is going to be fun — I'm glad you have Harvard as a backup!

To everybody: I had a fascinating experience last week at work (fascinating, as in "Isn't that fascinating?" when you face a breakdown, disappointment or failure).

Larry, our acting CEO, told me that while he was giving me a bonus, he had decided not to renew my contract because we have been sued by Primesco for $8.1 million. We are counter suing but it is a huge mess, and as the CEO of NWP, I'm responsible.

So my contract runs another two years, and although Larry went out of his way to say he had no intention of ending my employment then, I'm preparing for that, just in case. Please keep all this strictly to yourselves — this letter is for your eyes only and is confidential.

With Mommy's help, I have drawn up a detailed five-pronged strategy which I will show you (Kim and Tina) at Thanksgiving, and I am implementing it immediately.

I am deliberately modeling the behavior I want you to use when you face disappointments, whether in your private lives or in your careers. By creating a rigorously thought out strategy for proactively dealing with the situation (instead of being numbed into inaction) I have put myself into a mood of incredible resourcefulness and high-level energy.

At first I thought this would kill my chance of becoming CEO of NWF, and it still might, but I've thought of several things I can do to "get back in the fight" by sending, for example, a confidential letter to Craig Thompson who is Chair of the CEO Search Committee.

I see this development as a huge opportunity to elevate my professional life to a new level. For example, I am considering creating a new non-for-profit organization to further the causes I feel deeply about.

It is wonderful to have Mommy and Jen here to consult with and to share ideas with. They are an incredible support system for me and are helping see how I can make lemonade out of this lemon.

BTW, even though we still have huge bills to pay to get Jen through college and to pay off our mortgage on the house, Mommy has worked it out that we won't have to sell the house even if I completely stop earning money on October 2005 — a very unlikely scenario given that I have a minimum of two years to look for and plan my next career move.

Hey, Tina, we'll both be in the same boat — looking for work!!

I love you, Gail.
I love you, Kim.
I love you, Tina.
I love you, Jenny.
I love you, Cory.
Dad
XXXOOO

December 7, 2003
Subject: Letter #3 from LA

My darling precious Kimmie, Tina and Jenny,
Poor Mommy and Jen with new flooding in the basement. That is so frustrating. My love, I'm glad the Club party was fun tonight. I was so sorry to miss it.

I've driven about 400 miles this week to Santa Monica, Santa Barbara, Laguna Beach and other places for various meetings. Realizing this was going to happen, I planned ahead and took with me some CDs to listen to in the rental car so I wouldn't waste my time. One of them was by Mary Pipher who wrote the wonderful book "Reviving Ophelia" about girls growing up in a toxic, demeaning culture.

On this CD Mary Pipher was talking about her more recent book called "Another Country: Navigating the Emotional Terrain of our Elders." I loved it. She talks about what we can learn from listening to the life stories of the oldest people in our lives. She explains how to create a legacy of recorded stories and how this can build meaning into the lives of all family members.

Pipher quotes Alex Haley: "When an old person dies, a whole library is lost." I remember when little Granny died at age 98, I felt a sad regret that I didn't talk to her more about her life. I also felt grateful for the few stories that I did write down. You can read some of them in the book I wrote on the history of my side of the family.

Pipher also points out what a mistake it is when an elderly aunt comes, say, for tea, and the kids are shushed up and encouraged to go and watch a video because it is assumed the kids will find the elderly aunt boring. That elder (that's a good word, isn't it, compared to "old person" or "elderly aunt"!) has 80 years of living that is full of fascinating stories.

Pipher also says that the world in not held together by atoms but by stories. I think that is true in a very real sense. We try to make sense of the world by the stories we tell ourselves.

I'm having a wonderfully productive time here in LA. I love you and miss you. Good luck, Kim and Tina, in your exams next week.

Buckets of LA love,
Dad
XXXOOO

December 8, 2003
Subject: Letter #5 from Denver

Darling Kimmie, Tina and Jenny,
I can't wait to get home tomorrow! Today after landing in Denver airport, I accidently spilt (spilled?) soup on my trousers (most embarrassing!) and then my SUV and I got caught in a snow storm and took a wrong turn. I had to tell myself to keep calm as I slowly got myself "unlost." I had a terrific meeting at the Museum here south of Denver and so I'm glad I came despite the weather and the soup.

I was reading a book today and it mentioned the parable of the Good Samaritan. I remember that story from my childhood. It taught the importance of taking care of the downtrodden and rejected. I don't know how much it influenced me, but it gave me some minimal guidance I assume.

I worry that you three have not absorbed biblical parables like the one about the Good Samaritan (and so many others). From my point of view, this has nothing to do with religion but all to do with ethics. I wonder if we have taught you enough about right and wrong?

I suspect that parents generally don't think about this enough — even those parents who take their kids to church may not spend enough time teaching morality and how important it is to success and happiness. Do they teach you morality in school?

Of course the best thing parents can do is set a good example. But I am still left worrying that while you three decided that religion is not important to you, you also gave up the opportunity to imbibe some of the great biblical parables which have shaped and guided our culture for centuries. I can't help thinking that might be a loss.

I love you. I adore you.
Dad (in Denver)
XXXOOO

2004

January 16, 2004
Subject: Sorry, I wasn't much help

Darling Tina,
Sorry, I wasn't much help tonight on the phone.

Life will constantly throw challenges at you like this. Your best strategy I think is not to focus on what decision to make but instead focus on generating as many possibilities for yourself as possible. Leave the decision-making until later.

In other words, make a distinction between generating possibilities and making choices. They are two very different processes. Generating possibilities requires hustle and networking whereas making choices requires deep reflection. Both are exciting and enjoyable if you choose to make them exciting and enjoyable.

Whether to join the Peace Corps will be a slightly easier decision to make when you have some concrete alternative options. If you can't find a job in DC, it might be the way to go. Or if the only job you can find in DC is a boring one, then again the Peace Corps may be the way to go. But if you win a Wellstone Fellowship, then that option may be more appealing than the Peace Corps.

And you are right. It would be tragic for you to go through life regretting you never did something (in your case the Peace Corps) that you wish you had done. It would be like me dying without writing my book. To do something in life you regret is sad, but not to do something you feel passionately you want to do is a tragedy.

Good luck, treasure. Enjoy the process. You are incredibly privileged to have struggles like this. 99.999% of the world's population would die to have your problems!

Let me know how Mommy and I can support you as you wrestle with how to design your future.

Please say a big hello to Tom from me. I feel terrible about his tendinitis.

Buckets of love,
Dad
XXXOOO

January 23, 2004
Subject: Letter #1 from Charleston

Darling, precious Kim, Tina and Jenny,
What an incredible meeting Mommy had in NYC this morning!!!! Wow!!!!

It is interesting to reflect that success doesn't happen overnight or by chance. It takes years of diligence and hard work to achieve great things. The key is persistence and tenacity, and you can see that vividly illustrated in Mommy's professional life. Mommy had to put up with drudgery and all kinds of other unpleasant experiences over the last 30 years or so to accomplish what she accomplished today.

I'm in SC as you know. In about 30 minutes I am leaving my hotel room, where I am writing this, to go to a reception, then give a speech introducing Coral Reef Adventure, and then have dinner with three NWF Board members.

Then tomorrow morning, I am giving an hour-long workshop called "Adventures in Wildlife Filmmaking."

I adore you and miss you.
Dad
XXXOOO

January 24, 2004
Subject: Letter #2 from Charleston

My darling Kim, Tina and Jenny,
Last night was a huge success with everybody liking the film and also enjoying my humorous introduction of it. The dinner afterwards with staff and board members was a lot of fun. I sat next to Andy Brack who is joining the NWF board in March, so I was very glad to have a chance to get to know him.

Then this morning, I gave a workshop that everybody seemed to enjoy.

My letter to you yesterday about how the seeds of success are sown in long, quiet periods of dedication and hard work reminds me of the story of the Chinese Bamboo tree. I read this in one of Steven Covey's excellent books on personal development.

When you plant this tree, you have to keep watering it and caring for it continuously. Year 1, nothing happens. Keep watering. Year 2, again nothing. Year 3, nothing. Year 4, nothing. And again nothing happens in years 5 and 6. If during those six years, you stop watering or caring for the tree, it dies. You must never give up on it.

Then suddenly in year 7 it goes into galloping growth, blooms magnificently and becomes this huge and incredibly beautiful tree.

Life is like that too. You work away. Nothing much seems to happen. And then after years and years of work — like what is now happening with Mommy — amazing results start happening. It may seem sudden to other people. They may even think that the successful person had a lucky break. But luck (as Thomas Jefferson said) happens more often to those who work hard.

We all watch films and TV which show us stories where what counts is luck, or how pretty you are, or what men you know, or how rude and outrageous you are — but never show the fundamentals of success, which is tenacious hard work, having laser-clear goals, networking, finding mentors and role models, ridding your life of fluff and BS, choosing loving and decent people as friends, keeping fit and healthy, avoiding addictions like alcohol, never being duplicitous and so on. It is these fundamental things which really count in life — again as Mommy has shown.

You three are as successful as you are because you have already learned this. Kim's article for the Post on bringing boyfriends home to the parents, Tina winning the $2,800 grant for her work in Costa Rica, and Jen's very high grades this week for her mid-term exams are all things which outsiders might look at and say it was a lot to do with luck. But all three of you achieved those successes by hard work, being focused, meeting deadlines, giving up immediate pleasures to slog away at your projects, and having clarity about exactly what you wanted to achieve.

Mommy and I are so proud of you. We adore you.
Dad
XXXOOO

PS: Gail and Jenny, I hope you found the love letters I left under your pillows yesterday!

March 02, 2004
Subject: my speech :)

Kim wrote:
Here is my wedding speech!

Keiko-san to _____-san, Gokekkon omedetoo goziamasu. (Bow to couple)
(Kimberly to moosimasu.)

When I lived in Japan two years ago, I met Keiko when I interviewed her for work. She was the first person in Japan to invite me into her home, and she quickly became one of my best friends. Her family introduced me to eating around a kotatsu, sleeping on a futon, taking an ofuro, going to the onsen, picking mikans, and celebrating oshougatsu. I will always remember oshougatsu, when Keiko and her mom dressed me up in a kimono and even let me borrow special kimono shoes. Keiko taught me how to walk all the way up the steps to the shrine with them, which was not easy. She also tried to teach me how to walk in a kimono with the tight obi, which was even harder. But I loved every moment of trying to look as natural and graceful as Keiko.

I feel so honored and happy to be able to share this special day with Keiko, her family, and everyone here. My family also wanted me to tell you both to please come and visit us in Washington, DC whenever you can.

Toi America ni orimasu ga, Keiko-san to gokazoku no koto wa, totemo chikaku ni ommote imasu.

Ofutari no oshiawase o oinori itashite orimasu. (Bow to couple again)

I replied:
Darling Kimmie,

Your speech is a gem! So heartfelt, so sincere, so personal, so touching and so perfect. You have mastered the content and now your challenge is to master the performance. That's an important distinction.

Really try and connect with the audience. Take it slowly. Give them a chance to interact with you through smiles and eye contact. PAUSE. I mean it. Let the audience look at you for 5 to 15 seconds before starting (Napoleon paused for 45 seconds before addressing his troops and he seemed to grow in stature as his soldiers waited and their anticipation grew). It takes real courage and character to pause like that but the dividends are huge.

During the speech, give them time to react. Don't step on their smiles and laughter. You have a surprising number of laugh lines. Milk them for all they're worth. Don't let any word be wasted. They will be delighted by every word and phrase.

Smile! Look at specific audience members as you are speaking. Be emotionally expressive -- let your emotions show. In this way, your charisma will shine through and wow them.

Before you start, visualize the audience drinking in every word you say. See the delight in their faces as you entrance them with your lyrical tribute to Keiko. See them crowding around you afterwards to thank you and to touch the hem of your skirt in admiration!

Kim, you'll do great. I wish I could be there to see you.

I love you. Please say hi to Sujay from me. I know you'll miss each other terribly.
Dad
XXXOOO

P.S. Kimmie, I forgot one very important piece of advice. If you have notes in your hand (and I would encourage this because each word is perfect and you want to deliver it as you have written it) then it is vital NEVER to be talking when you are looking at your notes.

I can't emphasize the importance of this enough. If you talk when looking down, you'll immediately start disconnecting from the audience.

So this is how you do it: you look down and take in the line you are about to speak. Look up. PAUSE.

Then give the line with all the emotional sensitivity and power you have (think Martin Luther King on the Mall in his 1963 "I have a dream speech.")

Then look down and take in the next line. Look up. Pause (yes, I mean it). Deliver. Look down. Take in the line. Look up. Pause. Deliver. And so on. It takes courage to do this but it increases the impact of your speech ten-fold. And the pauses give the audience a wonderful opportunity to absorb and think about what you said.

XXXOOO

March 9, 2004
Subject: Letter #1 from St. Louis

Darling Kimmie, Tina and Jenny,
I arrived here this evening for NWF's Annual Meeting. The rumor is that the name of the new CEO will be announced tomorrow night at dinner. We'll see. Whoever it is had better be darn good!!!

Kim, congratulations for your big article in today's USA Today. That is a great accomplishment. Even though you have had many articles published now in major newspapers, I never want to take it for granted because I know how difficult it is. Great job!

Can you, Kimmie, please send me an electronic version of your article it so I can send it out to family and friends? Thanks (or perhaps you can, my love.) I also want to put it in my family journal.

Tina, we can't wait for you to get home tomorrow week! I think you've had a very valuable experience down there and it sounds from what you say that you'll be able to write up a good report for your Dartmouth professors. I am so glad you are getting home early so you have time to rehearse your five minute lesson.

Jen, I'll be dying to know tomorrow if you got on the tennis team or not. I'll be very sad if Sara doesn't get on. Hope you and Mommy liked the letters I left for you in your beds!

I love you!
Dad
XXXOOO

March 10, 2004
Subject: Letter #2 from St. Louis

My Precious Darling Daughters, Kim, Tina and Jen,
When I wrote yesterday about not taking Kim's outstanding accomplishments in her writing for granted, it reminded me how easy it is to take people we love for granted in general. That was one reason I added to our agenda for Family Meetings the item "Encouragement" because it is an action-forcing mechanism to make you think of positive things about somebody. Without such a mechanism, it is too easy to slip into just thinking about the things that are wrong.

For example, let's take Cory: in the old days, I would have thought of hairballs, noise, forced walks, buying food, clearing up poop, the heavy responsibility for her welfare, and so on.

Now, if it were Cory's turn to receive "encouragement," I would think about her joy, her playfulness, her love and affection for all of us, how she pokes her little nose around my desk and looks at me with those beautiful eyes that say, "Dad, come and play with me!!", her extraordinary athleticism, her living in the moment, her hiding under my desk when she's scared, her total devotion to Jen, her jumping up on Jen's bed to wake her, her natural beauty, her gorgeous coat, her curiosity, and so much more.

And don't forget, praise and encouragement are not the same. A person can fail at something but you can still extol the effort.

Kim, Tina and Jen, I love you and miss you.

Dad
XXXOOO

March 11, 2004
Subject: Letter #3 from St. Louis

My darling Kim, Tina and Jen,
Dealing with disappointment, rejection and setbacks (as I am now doing having failed to get the NWF CEO job) is a skill I am having to re-learn. It's good for me to re-learn it.

It is interesting to step outside myself, as it were, and observe what is going on. I don't show anything on the outside to the people here. It's all in the feeling in my stomach. The more upbeat I act, the more upbeat I will feel.

Larry Schweiger is an outstanding person so that is good.

I will think through what my fundamental goals are, what my career alternatives are, examine the pros and cons, and then pursue what makes the most sense. It will be fun and interesting.

Thanks for all your concern and love for me. I'll be fine.

Jen, well done for winning in tennis today. Kim, I'm glad your exam went well today. Tina, good luck as you begin to wrap things up in Costa Rica in your last week.

I love you.
Dad
XXXOOO

March 12, 2004
Subject: Letter #4 from St. Louis

My darling Kimmie, Tina and Jenny,
Last night at a reception, I met a husband and wife who represent one of NWF's affiliates, and we got talking about how great America is. They were so pleased and relieved to hear me say this because they feel that Americans aren't always appreciative of what a great country this is.

Then we started talking about the founding fathers and I told them one of my favorite stories about George Washington (which I was reminded of by reading Chris Matthews latest book, "American: Beyond Our Grandest Notions").

During the American Revolution, the artist Benjamin West was asked by King George III what he thought George Washington, the leader of the American revolutionaries, would do after the war. When West answered that Washington would return to his Virginia farm, the king replied, "If he does that, he will be the greatest man in the world."

Washington despised the pomp and opulence of the British royal court, and was determined from the beginning to set a new model. Chris Matthews points out that a heroic general could have made himself a dictator for life, but instead, "he calmly abdicated the spoils and laurels of victory for the freedom and dignity of private citizenship."

I loved telling this story last night to this husband and wife. Then we talked about Ben Franklin and Thomas Jefferson. We agreed they were all extraordinary men.

My workshop couldn't have gone better this morning. I had the audience participating immediately and I think (judging from the evaluation forms) everybody seems to have found it very stimulating and enjoyable.

Tonight we are all going to a Lewis and Clark exhibition at the Missouri History Museum. It will be wonderful, I am sure of it. And we are having dinner there too.

I adore you and miss you. I can't wait to get home on Sunday.
Dad
XXXOOO

March 13, 2004
Subject: Letter #5 from St. Louis

My darling Kim, Tina and Jenny,
I'll be home tomorrow by about six (if my plane is on time). I can't wait!

In a few hours, our big awards banquet begins. I have been practicing what I am going to say. Rehearsal is so important and it is a step many people don't do because public speaking is so painful for them that they keep postponing even rehearsals until it is too late. Then they wonder why they don't connect with the audience.

Remember this, Tina, next week as you work on your five minute lesson for Teach America. Aim to start rehearsing immediately you get home from Costa Rica. Look how much work actors put into rehearsals! There is a reason for that! Without it, the play or film will assuredly bomb.

I've seen some terrible speeches these last few days here at our Annual Meeting: speakers reading word-for-word their speeches with their heads down, speakers stuck behind a podium, speakers talking in dull voices with no energy, vitality or passion, and speakers who project themselves as nervous, weak and lacking in self-confidence.

It is vital to put on a big act, and then (like Teddy Roosevelt and Cary Grant) you'll become like that self-confident person.

Tonight the audience will look at me and say to themselves: How come he finds it so easy? How come he isn't nervous? How come he finds it so easy to be funny? They won't know about my heart beating at three times its normal speed, my sweaty armpits, the years of study and homework, or the hours of preparation and rehearsal.

Kim, I love you.
Tina, I love you.
Jenny, I love you.
Cory, I love you.
Gail, I love you too of course!

Dad/Chris
XXXOOO

April 8, 2004
Subject: Letter from Bath on the day we said goodbye to Granny

Darling Kimmie, Tina and Jenny,

We said goodbye to Granny today in a lovely, moving, celebratory ceremony. The service at St. Luke's just above Bear Flat (the same church where we said goodbye to Grandpa three years ago) was traditional (as I think she would have wanted).

I gave the tribute (or eulogy) that I had prepared and then handed out copies of a longer tribute as people left the church. Everybody seemed to like it. I managed to keep my composure pretty well — at least, until the very end.

About eighty people came. Georgina read a poem and Clifford (Granny's godson and nephew) read from Corinthians.

Mommy's idea of giving everybody a mauve/purple tulip or rose as they left the church so they would take a memory of Granny with them was a big hit. We had a big bowl of 100 mauve tulips. And another of Mommy's ideas was a big hit too — Jon and I took two big photos of Granny and Grandpa with us and displayed them during the tea party at the Rockery Tea Gardens where we all went after the cremation. One was of them at their wedding on August 11, 1941, and the other was of them celebrating their 50th wedding anniversary on August 11, 1991.

The whole event was also a wonderful reunion of the family. Tim and Lyson, Alexandra, Nick and Georgie; Carol, Andrew, Jenny, Adam and (oops, I can't recall their second boy's name) and Simon; Jon, Hannah, James, Ross; Yvette, Mary, Jill, Robin, Annabel (no Nicholas), Clifford, Lella, James; Toby; Lisa and her Mom; Maria, Rosemary and Ian, Dave and Pippa, Lou Rydill and Jessica, Arty and Leslie Bell, Naomie and Fay from the nursing home, Jane Cartwright, John and Jane Brownrigg, Elaine (Jon's girlfriend), Carol England. ..and many others.

After the funeral service, we had the brief cremation service (again, at the same place as Grandpa was cremated), and after mingling outside for a little, we all went to the Rockery for tea.

Tim, Jon and I all agreed that soon we will have a plot for Granny and Grandpa with their combined ashes buried underneath and their names on a tombstone (or whatever you call it) on top. We want there to be a place where they are remembered. Jon said he might well want his ashes put there too.

We all finished at the Rockery at about 6:30 PM. Jon and I went to Jon's house for a break. Then at about 8:30 PM this evening we went to the hotel where Carol, Andrew and his family and Simon were all staying and talked with them until about 11 PM.

All of us wondered when we would all see each other again. Jon said we should have a big reunion/ party in three years' time when Jon and I both turn sixty, but that seems a long way away.

I had interesting talks today with all the members of the extended family. Lyson is starting a new job, still in the cancer area. Tim and Lyson will sell their Wimbledon home at some point but will stay in Wimbledon. Alex is doing well (he now owns two properties) but has no girlfriend. Georgie has a great new job with Murdoch (Sky television) and is very excited. Nick is trying to decide what to do next.

Andrew works two jobs. He repairs computers and works as a doorman/bouncer. Jenny works in finance at a library. The two little boys are adorable. Andrew says that Adam (now eight) has a self-esteem problem.

Simon and Carol both live in the same house in Totness. She is on the floor below. Both have virtually no money. They each rent a "bed/sit." It is one room with a small stove in the corner and a small frig. They share bathrooms and loos with others. They see each other most days but live separate lives. Carol is trying to think of ways to make some money. Simon works 30 hours a week behind the counter at a gas station. He earns five pounds an hour (about seven or eight dollars an hour). He seems very happy. He has no computer, lives very simply and goes for walks/reads/watches television when not working. He says one day he might get married but he is in no hurry.

Toby has decided to go into the law (and give up geology). He smokes, as does Ross and I think Hannah does too.

Hannah got drunk tonight. Jon doesn't know how often it happens but worries it happens a lot. He worries that James will find it totally unappealing and leave her. When she gets drunk, she gets loud and angry (and uses the most foul language). James is not earning any money. He works hard at farming but it doesn't pay anything. Jon thinks that Hannah won't stick with him if he only earns a minuscule wage. Both James and Hannah are charming (when Hannah is sober). Hannah says she got very depressed last winter because she had nothing to do. She mainly cleaned the house and washed clothes for Lisa and Jeff, and she sad she didn't like being their servant. She feels better now that the spring is here and she can start her gardening job again.

Ross is wonderful. Such a good guy. He is working hard to pass his exams and will then spend a year traveling (a "gap" year) before deciding what career to follow.

There was so much talk of you three (and of Mummy too of course). All the people, Kim, who saw you on your recent trip with Sujay spoke so highly of you both. Everybody thought Sujay was wonderful. Everybody sends you three girls and Mommy their best love.

I told everybody how incredibly sad Mommy was not to be there because she was so close to Granny and Grandpa. Everybody praised Mommy for her ideas of the tulips and the photos.

Kimmie, safe journey home tonight as you fly from Chicago to BWI. Tina, safe driving to Cape Cod this weekend. I hope you have a super time. Jenny, I hope you found the love letter I left in your bed before I left on Tuesday. Please tell Cory I miss her.

I'm flying home tomorrow (Friday) and should be home by 9 PM if my flight is on time. It is United Airlines #925 departing Heathrow at 4:35 PM.

Kimmie, Tina and Jenny: I adore you. I love you. I miss you.
Dad
XXXOOO

April 29, 2004
Subject: Letter #2 from LA

My Precious Kim, Tina and Jenny,
I have had a busy day of meetings here but the highlight of my day was giving a workshop this morning to over 100 people (mainly IMAX filmmakers, distributors and theaters) on productivity. It could not have gone better and all my preparation really paid off. It created a real buzz in the hallways.

The workshop was completely different from the handout ("50 ways to triple your productivity") in that I made the audience do a lot of work. I worked them through half a dozen exercises in which they had to write and then work with a partner. I always thought I hated teaching, but in fact I love it - or at least this sort of teaching. I feel like a conductor of an orchestra!

Afterwards someone said to me that I should be a preacher. I didn't have the heart to tell them I was a secular humanist!

Here is the introduction I wrote for Paul Holliman (from Disney), who is the conference chair, to use when introducing me this morning:

"Chris Palmer, as you all know, heads the television, film and large format programs for the National Wildlife Federation, the nation's largest conservation group with over four million members and supporters. Chris is the President and CEO of National Wildlife Productions.

"Born in Hong Kong, Chris grew up in England and was a high school boxing champion. He earned three degrees from London University and from Harvard. He spent seven years in the British Royal Navy before emigrating to the United States in 1972.

"Chris has had a very different life from the one that he expected to have growing up in England in the 50s. He has been a Naval Officer, engineer, business consultant, energy analyst, Senate staffer, political appointee in Jimmy Carter's EPA, environmental lobbyist and wildlife film producer. He has been involved as producer or executive producer in six large format films.

"He is also a husband and father. Often away from his family on business travel, he has developed skills and techniques for keeping his life balanced, fulfilled, productive and happy. Chris will share with us this morning some of his ideas on increasing your productivity, a subject he has been studying for over 40 years.

"These ideas can change your life, increase your income, improve the quality of your relationships and lower your stress levels."

Do you like that? See any way to improve it for future occasions?

Jen, I hope you feel completely better soon. Lucky Cory, with you getting home at 12:30 PM tomorrow! Kim, good luck with your Albuquerque interview. Tina, sorry I missed you when I called you tonight. I had a nice talk with Greta.

I adore you.
Dad
XXXOOO

April 29, 2004
Subject: Letter #3 from LA

My darling Kimmie, Tina and Jen,
I love you. You are each, in your own unique ways, doing incredibly well.

Kim, you are finishing up a wonderfully rewarding and enjoyable two years at graduate school at one of the best universities in the world. Your intellectual prowess has grown tremendously. You met Sujay! And you have a great future ahead of you in journalism, authoring books and who knows what else. You also have some incredibly special friends like Alison.

Tina, you are finishing up a great four years at Dartmouth, one of the most prestigious colleges in the world, where you have surmounted all the challenges thrown at you by the anthropology Department. You have learned so much there and you are well prepared to take on the rigors of working at Booz Allen. You met Tom! You have a good job! That's a wonderful thing. You talk to anyone who is unemployed and can't find a job and you'll realize what an accomplishment that is. And you also have great friends like Greta.

Jen, you are finishing up four successful years at Holton. Your academic achievements are extraordinary, but more important, the character strengths you show in achieving those academic heights — self-discipline, a willingness to postpone gratification, hard work, focus, determination and shear intellectual horse power — will benefit you and all the people you love your whole life. And you've done this while volunteering with Cory, playing in the jazz band, having close friends like Sara Murray and Sara Wipfler, playing tennis and lots of other things.

Mommy and I are so proud of you. You are wonderful daughters — loving, affectionate and delightful. Mommy and I are so lucky.

I adore you.
Dad
XXXOOO

May 1, 2004
Subject: Letter #4 from LA

Darling Kimmie, Tina and Jenny,
I was watching a new IMAX film today (from National Geographic) called "Forces of Nature." It was part of the IMAX film festival I'm attending here in LA. "Forces of Nature" is about tornadoes, hurricanes, volcanos and other potentially devastating natural events.

I found it moderately interesting but dozed off a few times because I'm tired — until the credits. As I was watching the end credits, the filmmakers also ran a little "behind the scenes" video, i.e., some footage of the filmmakers making the film. Well for me, this turned out to be by far the best part of the movie.

On the screen we could see the cameraman behind the camera filming an on-coming tornado. The tornado was getting closer and looked menacing and dangerous. We weren't worried for them because a car was right there in the picture ready to whisk them away as the tornado got too close — which it was now doing.

You could see the people getting ready to flee to safety. The tornado was rapidly approaching and you could see it sucking up buildings and cars and throwing them about like paper wrappers.

The camera crew started disassembling the IMAX camera and moving with urgency towards the car in order to escape the danger. Suddenly panic broke out because they had locked the keys in the car and couldn't get in. We could see them shouting and swearing, and it was hilariously funny.

Oh well, you had to be there I suppose!

Kim, good luck in handling the Arizona job situation. Tina, I'll look out for articles relevant to your Booz, Allen work. Jen, I'm so glad you are excited to be a senior!

I adore you.
Dad
XXXOOO

May 2, 2004
Subject: Letter #5 from LA

My Precious and Loving Daughters, Kim, Tina and Jenny,
It is Saturday evening here in LA. I've just got back to my room after working out in the fitness center. I was the only one there. It is 8 PM here on the west coast. I ran, lifted weights, stretched and used several of the machines. Now I feel great. I have ordered room service (seafood noodle soup, a small salad and grapefruit juice). I have a list of a dozen jobs I want to get done before going to bed, the most important of which is this letter to you!

Tomorrow I fly to Missoula to the International Wildlife Film Festival. I have big presentations to do every day! But it is no problem because I am uber prepared! (That's the first time I've ever used the word "uber" — I may not be even be using it the correct way!)

You three are all winners in life. I say that because:

Winners always have goals (even if the goal is to rest and relax)
Losers don't have goals but drift around not sure what they are doing.

Winners are optimistic. They see opportunities for growth and learning everywhere, especially when facing challenges.
Losers are pessimistic. They see barriers and obstacles everywhere.

Winners take initiative. They try out new ideas. They make offers.
Losers are passive. They let others always take the lead and set the agenda.

Winners say, "It may be difficult but it is possible."
Losers say, "It may be possible but it is too difficult."

Winners hate squandering time. They realize that to waste time is to waste life.
Losers feel no remorse about wasting time and they wonder vaguely why they don't feel more fulfilled.

Winners take care of themselves — their health and their mental and emotional fitness. They also do things that give their lives purpose and meaning.
Losers don't think about these things and their lives are out of balance. They eventually get sick and

feel sorry for themselves, not realizing they have brought it on themselves through neglect.

So you can see why I say you three are winners. Mommy and I are so proud of you and we adore you.

Dad
XXXOOO

May 3, 2004
Subject: Letter #6 — now from Missoula

Darling Kim, Tina and Jen,
I'm now in Missoula. I left LA this morning and flew here with a stopover in Denver for about an hour. The crowds of people trying to get through security at LAX were horrendous. I was lucky to make my plane.

I sat next to a middle aged woman on the flight from Denver to Missoula and she told me that she was visiting her twin sister who is dying from a rare liver disease. She has been given less than six months to live. The woman I was talking to had offered to give half her liver to her twin sister to save her life, but when they did the necessary blood tests, doctors discovered that her liver was diseased too (but not nearly as badly as her sister's). It is impossible to me to imagine the trauma and pain that family is going through.

I love you and miss you.

This week here in Missoula is very (and delightfully) busy for me with big presentations and speeches every day.

Jen, good luck with you AP exams on Thursday and Friday. Tina, good luck with your big presentation to Mr. Goodman and the anthro department on Tuesday. I know you'll wow them with your passion for the subject. Kim, good luck with your finals this week (or were they last week?).

Kim, Tina and Jen, I talk about you all the time so your ears (as Granny used to say) should be burning. You are very special and I adore you.

Your loving ol' Dad
XXXOOO

May 4, 2004
Subject: Letter #7 from Missoula

My darling, precious Kim, Tina and Jen,
What a hectic week for each of us! Mommy has an emergency trip to Yonkers on Wednesday, Tina gives an important presentation tomorrow, Jen has four big exams on Thursday and Friday, Kim has big exams this week (is that correct, Kimmie?), and Cory has to go poop every bloomin' morning! Busy, busy, busy!

I'm sure the week will go well for all of us if we keep our eye on the prize. It is funny to think back five years and to think what we were worrying about then, and to realize that in retrospect it was no big deal. It's like that bit of wisdom that observes how we laugh our heads off when we think back over crises that happened ten years ago, and then asks, Why wait ten years to laugh about it?

It is beautiful out here in Missoula. The people are delightfully friendly and the weather is perfect. I went running this morning along the bike path on the bank of the Clark River, which runs right through the center of town.

We have an office here (our Northern Rockies Natural Resource Center) and today I visited there to say hello to my NWF colleagues. They are all terrific people. One of them is Dr. Sterling Miller, who is one of the world's leading bear biologists. He is one of my best friends in NWF and he has invited me out to meet with his family sometime this week.

Kim, Tina and Jen: good luck this week. Remember to keep adding to your joy list — all the things in your life you are grateful for and which give you great joy. I added one to my list this after lunch today. I had lunch with Chuck Bartlebaugh, an activist dedicated to getting people to behave better around wildlife. He told me about his dog, Lady, who is 16 and now blind. She loves to swim and Chuck threw a stick into a lake and directed Lady by voice commands where to find it. It was snowy and cold. After Lady found the stick in the water, she was elated and swam directly back to Chuck — except that because she is blind, Lady started swimming by mistake away from Chuck and into the middle of the lake. Without thinking for an instance, Chuck (who is about my age and not in all that good shape) dove into the freezing lake with all his clothes on to save Lady from drowning.

I added that story to my joy list.

Kim, Tina and Jen, I love you. You are the most wonderful daughters a Dad could have.

Your ol' loving, wisdom-spouting, maxim-emitting and grey-hair-a-coming
Dad
XXXOOO

May 5, 2004
Subject: Letter #8 from Missoula

Darling Kimmie, Tina and Jenny,
Congratulations, Jenny, on being elected captain of the tennis team! Abe Lincoln said late in his life that he never got as much satisfaction from any election than the time his company fighting Indians elected him as their captain. He was in his young twenties.

It's been a good day today for me with two big presentations. Tomorrow I give a workshop on how to give an effective presentation (Tina — you should be there to help you prepare for next Tuesday!!). I'm rehearsing with great determination — how embarrassing would it be to give a dull, insipid presentation on how to give a dynamic, inspiring presentation!

I can't wait to get home on Sunday.

My love, good luck in Yonkers tomorrow with $$$AI$$$!

I love you, Kimmie, Tina and Jen.
Dad

XXXOOO

May 6, 2004
Subject: Letter #9 from Missoula

Darling Kimmie, Tina and Jenny,
It is about 10 PM and I have just got back to my hotel room after the keynote speech (given by someone else, not me) and listened to Mommy's great message to me on my cell phone. I wish I could call now but it is midnight in Bethesda. Anyway, that is marvelous news about how well the day went with Al! I am so pleased!!! Well done, my love. I can't wait to get more details.

Jen, thanks for being so responsible and taking care of Cory and everything else at home.

Kim, did you send in your article on cliques to USA Today?

Tina, good luck with those rehearsals for next Tuesday!!!

I gave an exhausting workshop on "How to be a star presenter" today. It seemed to go very well. Now I am going to bed!

I love you, Kim, Tina and Jen.
Dad
XXXOOO

May 6, 2004
Subject: RE: Letter #9 from Missoula

Gail wrote:
To my wonderful family,
As I write this, Jenny is taking her AP English exam... let's all send her good vibes!!!!

Thanks for all of the notes ... and interest ... it really was a great meeting with Al.

Before the meeting, Jim Guest, Joel Gurin, Paige Amidon and I met briefly. Joel had briefed Jim in the am. Jim was good: he said that, like Al, he is a trial lawyer, and he urged us all to go in there with our heads held high as equal partners, and not be apologetic re the proposal. That was good advice!

I had prepared 3 pages of talking points for me (responding to all of his concerns) and working with Joel, talking points for him to open with basically saying that the model we were working on -- like other CR websites -- was a very sophisticated, state of the art gold standard (search optimization...) kind of model, and that costs a lot, but that we are now proposing a scaled back approach and lots of print stuff and outreach to key populations.

All this went well and is in line with what he wants.

SO we met for close to an hour and a half, we are back on track... And then we met afterwards... lots to do for sure, but all is going well.

506

Joel said that this reminded him of the quote about how the prospect of about to be hanged focuses one's mind! Well, that's what this was like: the whole project about to go down the tube made us focus intensely!!

ALSO ... as we rode up in the elevator to Al's 29th floor, Joel said that he hopes to meet you Chris ... he saw one of your films --- India/Tiger ... and thinks you have one of the most incredibly desirable jobs!!! This was nice, Jim and Paige were interested to hear what you do.

SO ... must go and respond to Al!!

Love to all!!!
Love,
Gail/mommyxxxooo

May 7, 2004
Subject: Letter #10 from Missoula

Darling Kim, Tina and Jenny,
I miss you. I can't wait to get home on Sunday. I still feel elated for Mommy's huge success yesterday. Jen, I'm glad your English AP exam went well today. Kim, I just picked up your message on my cell phone. Thanks so much. Unfortunately the connection was very poor and most of your message was undecipherable. Sorry! I'll try and reach you and Tina again tomorrow. I love you and miss you. Jen, good luck with your European History AP exam tomorrow afternoon. My love, how was the Holton meeting tonight? Tina, please say hi to Tom from me. Kim, please say hi to Sujay from me. Jen, please say hi to Cory from me (Hahaha!)

I adore you!
Dad
XXXOOO

May 8, 2004
Subject: Letter #11 from Missoula

My darling Kim, Tina and Jen,
I'll be home on Sunday and I can't wait. It has been a wonderful week out here and I've accomplished a lot, but I miss you all and want to come home!

After a keynote speech tonight from the famous wildlife biologist Dr. George Schaller, we were all taken by buses to a ranch in the mountains where we had a delicious dinner and a very good actor put on a performance of William Clark (of Lewis and Clark fame).

Tomorrow night I emcee a big awards dinner, which I am looking forward to.

Jen: Mommy said you were pleased how your European history AP exam went today. Great! Sorry I missed you when I called home tonight.

Tina, thanks for your e-mail tonight! I'll try and reach you tomorrow.

Kim, I love you too! I'll try and reach you again tomorrow.

Take good care. Have fun!

Buckets of love and hugs and kisses,
Dad
XXXOOO

May 9, 2004
Subject: Letter #12 from Missoula

My darling Kimmie, Tina and Jenny,
I don't want to be immodest but tonight my emceeing could not have gone better! I love being up on stage entertaining an audience. It was a great evening and everybody seemed to love it. The people attending the conference are delightful and I have many good friends here.

Kim, great to talk to you today. Tina, thanks for your loving message tonight — sorry we missed each other. Jen, great to talk to you today too. Well done for winning two matches in tennis! Good luck in the finals tomorrow!

OK, now let's see who gets the joke! (Mommy and Jen, pay close attention!) Kim, say hi to Sujay from me. Tina, say hi to Tom from me. Jen, say hi to Cory from me. Ha ha ha!!!! Good joke! Ahem, Jen, it is just a wee joke!!!

Sunday is Mother's Day. Mommy is so very, very special. There is a Jewish proverb: "God could not be everywhere and therefore he made mothers." Abe Lincoln said, "All that I am or ever hope to be, I owe to my angel Mother." And another person once said, "There was never a great person who had not a great mother."

I know how deeply each of you appreciates how lucky you are to have Mommy as your mother. There is no way to measure the love she has for you.

I can't wait to get home tomorrow.

I love you more than I can say.
Dad
XXXOOO

May 14, 2004
Subject: Letter #1 from Jackson Hole, WY

My darling Kim, Tina and Jenny,
I am so tired that I will only write a short note. The day here in Jackson Hole, WY has gone well. I got up at 4:30 AM to get a 6:25 AM flight so that's why I'm so tired.

Tina, I am so proud of the ambition, flair and drive you showed over your speech to the Anthropology Department yesterday. Well done! All three of you are doing so well. Mommy and I are so incredibly proud of you.

I adore you.
Dad
XXXOOO

May 14, 2004
Subject: Letter #2 from Jackson Hole

Darling Kim, Tina and Jenny,
One of the people I met with yesterday here in Jackson Hole was Rick Flory and his lovely fiancée Lee Robert. I would guess that Rick is in his late 30s.

When he was a teenager, he became a pizza delivery boy. He worked intensely hard, saved money, studied the business and decided to build a pizza house in Arizona. He did well and then built another. He went on to build 87 pizza houses and make a fortune.

Long before he made a fortune, he knew he was doing well enough that one day he could leave the pizza business and do something more in tune with what was really important to him. The way he put it to me yesterday when I asked him about this was that he "wanted to give something back."

He had always loved the outdoors and he knew that conservation of natural resources was of vital importance if our society is going to be healthy and flourish — so conservation was the area in which he chose to make a difference.

So long before he retired with significant wealth from the pizza delivery business, he made up his mind that he would start his own foundation and support conservation. In 1995, he sold everything he owned in the pizza business and founded Earth Friends, a non-profit organization dedicated to protecting wildlife and supporting other conservation organizations (like NWF) who share the same goals.

Now Rick works full-time on conservation and feels deeply satisfied that he is living his life to the full. And his fiancée Lee works very closely with him on this work. In fact, Lee is now the Executive Director of Earth Friends.

I love this story about Rick Flory because it is the American Dream. Rick has lived the life that Benjamin Franklin lived — starting at humble beginnings, and then through dint of hard work, astute planning, building relationships and alliances with great people (i.e., networking), being tenacious and determined, taking prudent risks, constantly making offers, being entrepreneurial and imaginative and so on, Rick Flory has designed and created a life that reflects what he and Lee feel most deeply about.

This is the way to create meaning and purpose in your life.

You three wonderful girls know all this already but I thought you might enjoy learning about Rick and Lee. I hope you'll have a chance to meet them one day.

I love inspirational stories like theirs' because it shows if we set bold and lucid goals, create a clear vision of where we want to end up, and then pursue that vision and those goals with determination and focus, we can achieve far more than we generally think we can.

Kim, Tina and Jen, I adore you and miss you. I can't wait to get home tomorrow. Jen, good luck in your trumpet competition tomorrow!

Buckets of love, kisses and hugs,
Yer ol' Dad
XXXOOO

June 26, 2004
Subject: Letter #1 from LA

My Darling Kimmie, Tina and Jenny,
Hi there from LA! I had an exhilarating and successful day. I started by attending a Board meeting in Santa Monica of the Large Format Cinema Association. The Board is facing a tricky decision about its future leadership. Should we continue to be led by Robert Dennis, who is currently the President and has done an outstanding job (and who would like to continue as President) or by Andy Gellis, who was led to believe by earlier Board discussions that he would take over as President when Robert's two-year term was up (and who is also a very good guy).

The room was seething with tense feelings and the Board asked me to chair this sensitive part of the meeting because it would obviously be a conflict of interest for Robert as President to chair it. In fact, I asked both Robert and Andy to leave the room while the Board deliberated. Anyway, it was a good and vigorous discussion and I enjoyed making sure everyone had a chance to speak (especially the less outspoken members of the Board) and enjoyed keeping the discussion focused, civil and constructive. Afterwards, I received the following e-mail from one of the LFCA Board members, Jonathan Barker:

"Chris, you did a masterful job chairing that difficult part of the meeting, as I knew you would. Thank you."

After the LFCA Board meeting, I drove 60 or so miles south on the 405 to beautiful Laguna Beach to spend the afternoon with MacGillivray Freeman Films. They had a sandwich lunch ready for me when I arrived. We had terrific discussions and it looks almost certain that I will join their staff in some part-time capacity. They are very eager to have me, as I am to join them.

I drove back and got to my hotel room feeling very tired (I'm still on east coast time). But then I went running in the exercise room, lifted some weights, stretched, and now I feel better and re-energized.

Kim, in the SPIRIT of fatherly advice, I would advise you not to fly that awful airline again. I cannot believe that they did not have the courtesy to apologize and explain what happened. You should tell them they should drop the middle two letters in their name in order to match their name with their level of service! (For any future readers of this letter, this morning, as Kim was returning from her five days with Sujay and his family on Lake Michigan, her plane came within ten feet of the runway and then suddenly took off again, rising rapidly and then suddenly dropping in a harrowing maneuver — and not once, even after the plane landed, did any one come on the speaker system and tell the passengers what was going on.)

By the way, I used Mapquest for the first time yesterday to find directions from my hotel at LAX to the LFCA Board meeting this morning in Santa Monica. I LOVE it! I had no idea how easy Mapquest was to do and how useful. Last time, I got hopelessly lost. This morning, I found my destination route de suite!

Jenny, please tell me how Cory is doing. Thanks.

Tina, re your car: what is the big hurry? You have no money to pay for it, we have no room to park it, your job may not start until September and you would be burdening yourself with two months of unnecessary insurance, maintenance, parking and other operating costs, which you have no money for either. This is what is called "living beyond your means"! I know my views are annoying, but that's the way it seems to me. If we co-sign the loan, we are simply encouraging you to ignore market signals.

I love you, Kim.
I love you, Tina.
I love you, Jen.

Dad
XXXOOO

June 26, 2004
Subject: Letter #2 from LA

My darling Kim, Tina and Jenny,
Did you buy the car, Tina?!

I was feeling overwhelmed this morning with a zillion jobs I had to do. I retrieved my serenity by listing everything I had to do — and I mean everything — and then putting them in order of importance (with "eating the frog" first, i.e., getting the most important and most challenging jobs done first). Then I steadily worked my way down the list, doing one after the other, feeling very focused and relaxed, enjoying the mounting feeling of success as the number of crossed-out jobs got longer and longer, and being able to totally focus with all my concentration and energy on whatever it was I was doing because I didn't have half my brain worrying if there is another task or project I should be doing instead.

Kim, Tina and Jen, I love you so much and I am so proud of each of you — your characters, your drive for success and happiness, your good judgement about things, your warm and generous natures, your choices in boyfriends and fiancés, your long-term thinking, and your desire to live good, loving and useful lives.

I fly to San Francisco tomorrow in the morning. I adore you. Thanks for looking after each other and Mommy (and Cory).

Yer 01' loving Dad
XXXOOO

June 28, 2004
Subject: Letter #3 from SF

Darling Kimmie, Tina and Jenny,
I love you! I adore you' I awindow you!

I've got one more meeting this evening with the James Foundation and then I fly to Seattle tomorrow morning for meetings and to give a big speech on Tuesday night.

Today as we flew into SF airport, the pilot suddenly said, "The whole SF airport has been closed down in an emergency. We are going to circle up here — we have a few minutes of fuel left." Then with no further messages from the pilot, we landed a few minutes later. It reminded me of Kim's experience yesterday with her flight with Spirit. No explanation, no apology, no reassurances. The carrier was United Airlines.

I started writing this letter at 6:30 PM local time here, and then broke away at the end of the last paragraph to have dinner with Laura James and her husband Neil Afford (Laura's family foundation is supporting our film on the Red Desert in Wyoming). Now I have just got back at 9:30 PM or so. It was a delightful dinner with Laura and Neil and I liked them very much.

Did you know that Winston Churchill said of Field Marshall Montgomery: "In defeat, indomitable. In advance, invincible. In victory, insufferable." Very witty.

And Adlai Stevenson said of Eleanor Roosevelt: "She would rather light candles than curse the darkness, and her glow has warmed the world."

Buckets and oodles of love and hugs.
Dad
XXXOOO

June 28, 2004
Subject: Letter #4 from Seattle

My darling Kimmie, Tina and Jenny,
The sun is out here and it is beautiful! But I believe it rains most of the time here. Someone said to me today, "We tell people it rains all the time here so they don't come here and crowd the place."

Tina: Kim and Mommy tell me you are stressed re the car. Sorry, lovebug. I know it is a pain for everyone. It will help to remind us all of the importance and wisdom of simplicity. If you need me at the bank on Thursday, of course I will go, but it is "rubbing salt in the wounds" for me because I am not happy with you getting a car in the first place. Having said that, I do appreciate the reasons you are buying it.

Tina and Jen, I hope you are having a great time at Wolf Trap this evening!

I am desperately trying to take my own advice and find time to rehearse my speech for tomorrow!

I adore you!
Dad
XXXOOO

June 30, 2004
Subject: Letter #5 from Seattle

My darling Kimmie, Tina and Jenny,
I just got back from my speech and it went very well. I felt very fatigued In the afternoon (as I told Kim and Jenny over the phone) but as guests started arriving and I started meeting and greeting them, my energy came flooding back and I felt on fire with vitality!

In my opening remarks, I had them all laughing over the dangers of three daughters (the segue was that Kass Sells, the President, who introduced me, also has three daughters) and I gave as an example your recent article, Kim, on bringing boyfriends home to meet the parents. I told them how it made me look like a looney eccentric and I gave examples of my looney behavior!

I'm so tired. I can hardly hold my head up. I adore you. Must go to bed.
Dad
XXXOOO

July 4, 2004
Subject:　　　Letter #1 when you are at the shore

Darling Kim, Tina and Jenny,
Here is a wonderful quote from Antoine de Saint-Exupery. I used it to good effect last Tuesday night in my speech in Seattle.

"If you want to build a ship, then don't drum up men to gather wood, give orders and divide the work. Rather, teach them to yearn for the far and endless sea."

It is a statement about the importance of dreaming big and keeping that dream in front of you as you work at the myriad mundane tasks that get you to achieve the vision embodied in the dream.

I am so proud of each of you. Here is one thing about each of you I love and admire:

Kim — I appreciate how you called Tina last week when you were in Michigan and Tina was by herself here at home to check that she was OK and not too lonely.

Tina — I appreciate how you had the political savvy to write to Booz Allen ahead of time and ask their advice on how best to prepare for your start with them in August.

Jen — I appreciate how you work on being physically active and strong even though virtually everything in our society and on television encourages teenagers to be lethargic, slothful, inert and sedentary.

I'm so glad you are all having such a super time at the shore with Nana. I'm working hard here and getting a lot done.

Buckets of love, hugs and kisses,
Yer lonely ol' greying Dad at home in the study,
XXXOOO

July 4, 2004
Subject:　　　Letter #2 to you at the NJ shore

My darling precious Kimmie, Tina and Jenny,

I am feeling euphoric! I set for myself certain goals today (including drafting an important letter to Greg MacGillivray, calling my brother Tim in England, and making major progress clearing out the books from my side of the study) and I am ahead of schedule and feeling very proud of myself.

I've not talked to anyone all day and the house has been deliciously quiet and peaceful. I've just been toiling diligently away in a very focused way.

I exercised extensively today when I got up — and watched a little of the Federa/Roddick Wimbledon men's final, but found it dull and colorless compared to the thrilling women's final yesterday between Maria and Serena.

I went running (it felt very odd not to have Cory with me) and then weeded the front path when I got back with drops of sweat landing beneath me like drops of rain at the beginning of rain shower (it was humid). What satisfying manual work that is! The goal is clear, one gets immediate feedback, and it is relaxing, useful and uncomplicated — and good stretching exercise to boot.

The running experience interests me. Kim and I were talking about this the other day. When I start off, I am tired and lethargic. The voice in my head wonders if I will even reach the end of the block without getting painfully fatigued. I keep going, and keep going. After half a mile or so, the fatigue begins to evaporate. I start to feel energized. It is counter-intuitive. After all, I've run some distance and should be tiring, not the reverse. After a mile or so, I am running quite hard. In fact, last week I was running with Cory towards the end of our run and someone (presumably a neighbor who knows me — I didn't see who it was) rolled down their car window and yelled out, "You're like an 18-year old!!" What a nice compliment!

I take this running experience as a great metaphor for life. If you keep trying and don't give up, your life will begin to be infused with vitality, vigor, strength and zingy pizzazz, rather than senility, feebleness, fatigue, anemic languidness and pooped-out wearied enervation.

Of course eating well has a lot to do with my energy level. I try to set a good example for you, but I also do it for myself. For your interest (I know you find this fascinating, especially Jenny!) I kept a record today of what I consumed just to show you how what an incredibly healthy diet I have. OK, here goes:

All Bran (OK, I added sugar, I admit it), 1% milk, blueberries, brazil nuts, walnuts, raisons, fresh OK, cherries, banana, toast (OK, I added generous portions of margarine, I admit it), baked beans, salmon, pear, apple, lots of cherry tomatoes, boiled eggs, fresh spinach, lentil soup, and (yes, I admit it!) ice cream.

OK, Jen, wake up, that exciting list is over and you can continue reading this letter now.

Are we all going canoeing next Sunday????!!!! Can't wait!

I had an interesting experience working on my books today. My goal is to move scores of them down to the shelves in the basement to free up space in the study for all my new post-NWF projects. I was worried that this was going to be painful because the question in my mind was, "What books do I enjoy having near me?" I didn't want to let any of them go!

Then I had the common sense to change the question and the job suddenly became a lot easier. The new question I asked myself was, "Over the next fifty years, what books do I really want to study that can make a direct contribution to the goals that I have set for myself?" When I posed that question, I found it a lot easier to move a lot of books to the basement (which was super exercise by the way — I made about 20 trips from the study to the basement with heavy boxes full of books.)

As I looked at each book, each one was like an old friend, evoking some period in my life and triggering interesting memories.

BTW, here is a new family rule I am promulgating unilaterally: There are now in the basement scores of my precious books. Borrow all you want but please put back any book you borrow in the exact same spot you took it from. (Same for the books in the study of course.)

I hope you have each had a rejuvenating day at the shore and that you got as much satisfaction and sense of fulfilment from your day as I did from mine. I adore you and miss you. See you all tomorrow!!!

Dad on his happy lonesome at home sweet home.
XXXOOO

July 19, 2004
Subject: Letter #2 from Phoenix

Darling Kimmie, Tina and Jenny,
Kim, I'm so sorry none of your friends will be there in NYC next weekend to greet you when you arrive there. Dang.

Tina, I'm so glad you and Kim have this last week together. I'm away. Mommy and Jen are both working — so I am so glad Kim will be there to hang out with you. It is great for Kim too to have you at home.

Jen, have a great last two weeks at HSUS. Make all the contacts you can. Learn all the names you can. Collect all the information you can about the organization so you can assess if there are other departments you'd like to work in if you ever work there again. I think you've done a great job of getting the most out of the experience.

Here is a story I recently read in a book. You three have already learned the important lesson in this story.

A girl and her father were walking along a road when they came across a large stone. The girl said to her father, "Do you think if I use all my strength, I can move this rock?" Her father answered, "If you use all your strength, I am sure you can do it." The girl began to push the rock. Exerting herself as much as she could, she pushed and pushed. The rock did not move. Discouraged, she said to her father, "You were wrong. I can't do it." Her father placed his arm around the girl's shoulder and said, "No, you didn't use all your strength. You didn't ask me to help."

I love that story.

Well, I had the time of my life here this evening. I don't know anyone here and, unlike other conferences I attend (relating to wildlife and films) where I am very well-known and a leader, I am pretty much a nobody. But I love it here at the National Speakers Association (NSA). I meet interesting people all the time (they are all speakers), I get to watch and learn from the greatest speakers in the world, and I get a ton of ideas for ways to improve my platform skills.

But tonight something special happened that made my day. I attended the National Speakers Association Foundation dinner. As usual, I didn't know anybody and sat with a group of people from South Carolina. As usual, I had very interesting and useful conversations with everybody around me. The guy on my left and his wife had three children about the age of you three, and the guy on my right and his wife (both hugely overweight) were charming and interesting too. I constantly quiz people about their speaking careers and learn a lot. So far, nothing unusual.

Then after dinner, the entertainment started. Because it was a dinner, the entertainment quotient was much higher than the rest of the conference (which is all serious discussions about how to speak more effectively) and one of the entertainers was a magician called Brad Montgomery who was brilliant and also very funny. He would come into the audience to get people to help him with his act. Well on his last trick, he came into the audience (about 1,000 or more people) and picked me!! I went up on stage to wild applause (Brad got them to do this), he found out my name, asked me a few questions with humor, and then asked me to remove my jacket (whispering to me first to check if it was OK for him to ask me to do that) and then asking me in another whisper to put my hands down firmly by my side and keep them there. He also whispered to me (between the patter to the whole audience) if I had any trouble with my knees or back. I said no.

I was hugely enjoying the whole process as was the audience. He then put something over us both and then proceeded (with great music blasting) to make the audience laugh hysterically as he stood hidden behind me and did things with his hands, juggled objects and generally pretended it was my arms doing all these funny things.

I was so admiring of the years of self-discipline and hard work it had taken to get his performance skills up to this level. What was also interesting was the difference in persona between the character he portrayed as the magician and humorist (diffident, jokey, a bit looney) versus the hardworking, highly professional performer I got glimpses of whenever he would whisper instructions or encouragement to me as he did his funny act.

At one point he had me bend over with him on my back to pick up a ring he had deliberately dropped, and another time, he had me bend my legs so he could reach something else — hence the questions about the health of my knees and back.

Anyway, I loved every moment of it, but the point I wanted to make is that I went from a nobody to somebody! Everyone at the convention suddenly knew me and congratulated me on doing a great job up there on the stage! It was funny how self-confident I suddenly felt!

So that is my story for tonight. I hope you enjoyed it.

Kim, Tina and Jenny, I hope you have a super week — or rather, I know you will each MAKE a super week.

I adore you.

Dad (magician's assistant!)
XXXOOO

Tue, Jul 20, 2004
Subject: Letter #3 from Phoenix

Darling Kimmie, Tina and Jenny,
I leave here tomorrow for Jackson Hole. It has a very rewarding and learning-filled time here at NSA in Phoenix. I hope you are all having a great week.

I have recently discovered what a wonderful poet former President Jimmy Carter is. He wrote this very moving poem about his relationship with his stern father:

This is a pain I mostly hide,
but ties of blood, or seed, endure,
and even now I feel inside
the hunger for his outstretched hand,
a man's embrace to take me in,
the need for just a word of praise.

I despised the discipline
he used to shape what I should be,
not owning up that he might feel
his own pain when he punished me.

I didn't show my need to him,
since his response to an appeal
would not have meant as much to me,
or been as real.

From those rare times when we did cross
the bridge between us, the pure joy
survives.

I never put aside
the past resentments of the boy
until, with my own sons, I shared
his final hours, and came to see
what he's become, or always was --
the father who will never cease to be
alive in me.

That, to me, is a beautifully moving poem, which resonates profoundly with me.

Kim, Tina and Jen: I adore you and I miss you.
Daddy
XXXOOO

July 21, 2004
Subject: Letter #4 (now from Jackson Hole)

My darling Kimmie, Tina and Jenny,
As I landed tonight at Jackson Hole and saw the Grand Tetons reaching so majestically into the ruddy evening sky, like (add your own vivid metaphor here please because I'm too exhausted to create one myself!), my whole mood was elevated. I remember how comforting I found them after 9/11 — solid, imperturbable, magnificent.

Jen, thanks so much for adding speed dial numbers to my cell phone. I love using them!!

Gail, thanks for all your hard work booking Woodend for that very special day on November 5, 2005.

Although Thomas Jefferson had slaves, he was always profoundly troubled by slavery. He wrote, "Nothing is more certainly written in the book of fate that these people are to be free." At another time, he wrote, "I tremble for my country when I reflect that God is just and that his justice cannot sleep forever." I also seem to remember he likened slavery to holding a wolf by the ears, i.e., the situation was very dangerous, unstable and unsustainable.

When I first learned this about Jefferson, I likened it my own mind it to the debate about hunting.

Kim, Tina and Jen, I adore you and can't wait to get home.
Dad
XXXOOO

July 21, 2004
Tina wrote:
Hi Dad!
So on Friday morning at 11am I am going in to meet with Kim Michienzi, my supervisor at Booz Allen. She is going to be my temporary supervisor because my real one is going to be on maternity leave when I get there.

I emailed Kim to ask to meet and she has been very professional in her emails -- not particularly friendly or warm. So I'm a little nervous about meeting, I don't want to be intimidated by her. I want to act professional, enthusiastic and confident and not be intimidated!

So I want your advice! On how to act? what to do? if she is intimidating and not very friendly. How I should act towards her. And what kinds of questions to ask her? I asked to come in to talk with her about what my role would be my first year at Booz Allen. Do you think she will think it is silly I am coming in to meet just about that? What other kinds of questions should I ask? I am starting in one month. I want to ask about what I can do to prepare and what my day to day tasks are. Do you have any advice on good questions/ how to act/ etc?

Thank you dad! you are so helpful!!
See you tomorrow!!
Love
Tina

July 22, 2004
Subject: Re: Booz Allen meeting

Darling Tina, you are going to do so well! I have total confidence in you. Practice with Kim. Ask Kim to simulate a cold person so you get used to it. You are doing everything right. It is great you are going in to see her. Smile. Shake hands. Look her firmly in the eye. Come with written questions. Start by thanking her for seeing you. Have good posture (shoulders back, stand tall). Be enthusiastic, even if you don't feel like it. Ask to see around the office. Ask to meet other members of the team. Ask for examples of REPs and proposals. Ask if there are any books she recommend you read. Ask for a list of the main clients they work with. Does she know what projects you will be working on when you start? At the start of the meeting, let her know why you asked for the meeting, e.g., "Thanks a lot for seeing me. I know you are busy so I appreciate it. I wanted to learn more about what I might be working on so I could do some background reading before starting on August 23."

Good luck treasure. Be strong. Be powerful. Be an example to others. Before going in, say to yourself over and over: "I will excel in this meeting with Kim M. and be the best I can be. I will smile, be enthusiastic, be likeable, and have unstoppable confidence. Above all, I will enjoy the meeting and enjoy meeting Kim M."

I love you.
Dad
XXXOOO

Mon, 29 Nov 2004
Subject: Professional Goals

My loves, have a hard copy at home of the attached for you to review (Mommy has it first) but here is an electronic copy. I warmly welcome your thoughts.

I love you.

Dad/Chris
XXXOOO

Kim replied:
Dad, this looks so good. How can I find my voice?

Kimberly S. Palmer
202.716.0181 (cell)
Kimberly.palmer@gmail.com

Thursday, December 09, 2004
Subject: RE: Professional Goals

Darling Kimmie,
Good girl for asking.

I think you find your voice by relentlessly searching for what really matters to you. If you can find issues and causes that are deeply important to you, and then work to solve them, you can find your voice because you will find meaning in your life.

You have to create meaning yourself. It isn't something that is given to you. Everybody has their own unique definition of what is meaningful to them anyway.

So find what is important and meaningful to you, work hard to master the skills that will enable you to contribute to the community working on that important issue, seek responsibility and leadership positions which give you a platform, make lots of offers in the marketplace (the more offers you make, the more skillful you become at making offers that trigger new, exciting possibilities for other people and the more appealing to other people your offers will become), network relentlessly, build a powerful network of friends and colleagues, write op-ed articles and books, and give speeches.

In short, use everything in your power to create programs and projects that you will be proud of and that will leave a legacy for future generations to benefit from and be inspired by.

That is one way to find your voice. I'm sure there are others.

I love you.
Dad
XXXOOO

2005

Tuesday, May 24, 2005
Subject: FW: Palmer Plays to SRO Crowd

My loves.. FYI. XXXOOO

Sent: Monday, May 23, 2005 10:22 PM
From: Film & Video Grad Students On Behalf Of John Douglass
To: AUFILM-L@LISTSERV.AMER1CAN.EDU
Subject: Palmer Plays to SRO Crowd

Crystal City, VA. Tonight, Chris Palmer, SOC's Distinguished Filmmaker in Residence, tested his mettle in the tough arena of stand-up comedy and triumphed. Zinging one liners about his experiences as a professor at American University and documentary filmmaker of IMAX Wildlife and environmental films, Palmer enthralled a packed house at Freddie's Beach Bar on S. 23rd St. in this Northern Virginia suburb. Palmer, having recently completed a course in stand-up comedy, took the challenge thrown down by family and friends to try out the material in public he normally reserves for his classes. He was an unqualified hit. Unavailable for comments after the performance, Palmer was, however, clearly pleased by the audience reception. What next? Wife Gail was clear. First it's Freddie's, next it will be Letterman. Those that missed this opportunity to see Palmer live can enroll in any of his summer classes or workshops in the Film and Digital Media Institute, which can be found under SUMMER@ AU.SOC on the web at http//wwwsoc.american.edu/.

John Douglass. Director
Film & Media Arts Division
School of Communication
American University
4400 Massachusetts Aye, NW
Washington. DC 20016-8017

(202) 885-2045

Kim replied:
Dad that's so awesome!

I then replied:
Thanks. love-dove. And thanks, too, for helping Tina prepare for her important 10:30 am meeting this morning. I love you. XXXOOO

Tuesday, May 24. 2005
Tina wrote:
Hi guys,
I just finished my meeting, it went well I think.

We talked about everything I wanted to -- promotion and salary.

She said I will be considered for a promotion. The one challenge I will face is that I look young and when my assessor, Ralph, meets me, he will say I have been there for a year, I look young. Why should I be promoted? So I need to be prepared for that and learn body language and delivery to gain respect.

Then we talked about salary, and Kim went through the different parts of a salary increase. She asked me what I expected, and I said I felt that I was performing at the level of a senior consultant and wanted to earn in that range. She calculated what I would earn if I earned the maximum percentages, and it was around 54. I said those percentages on my salary are low, and then she said they would look out for me and hopefully it would be in the high 50's.

What do you think???

love
Tina

Saturday, June 04. 2005
Darling Tina, it sounds great. Keep careful typed notes on what Kim said so that you can gently remind her in two months' time if nothing happens.

You will find excellent books at Barnes and Nobel about how to look more authoritative and eighty. Kim, your supervisor (as distinct from your wonderful sister) is being very helpful to you when she points out that if your body doesn't convey gravitas, wisdom and consequence, it will hurt you.

I will happily buy you those books if you can identify them.

There are specific things you can train your body to do that will convey to observers that you are not to be trifled with, and that if you don't get listened to, the consequences will he serious and possibly unpleasant.

Or, to put the same point more positively, that if you are listened to, new possibilities will he opened up for them personally and for Booz Allen in general.

This is very important! It involves eye contact, the tone of your voice, your posture, the expression on your face, your willingness to speak out, how you enter a room, how you greet people, how you shake hands, here you sit, how you sit, whether you take notes, whether you have an agenda and clear goals for meetings, the words you use and how you use them, how much research and preparation you do prior to meetings, whether you have the skIll to make a powerful request, the control you have over your moods, how focused you are, how distracted you get my trivial things, whether you refuse to engage in gossip, your loyalty to those not in the room, and many, many other things.

This is why I love reading about great people like Thomas Jefferson, John Adams, Abe Lincoln, Ben Franklin and George Washington. They had a mastery over life that we can all learn so much from.

I hope you can find some great books that will help you! You are already very strong in this area.

I love you
Dad
XXXOOO

Saturday, June 4, 2005
Tina, have you found any good books on this yet I'd like to buy them for you when you do. XXXOOO

July 05, 2005
Subject: hm

Tina wrote:
I sent an email over the weekend to everyone I work with about the marathon, and this morning Charlie (my boss), was like "Christina, you have to be careful with the memo's you send out. Now you are training for a marathon? People are going to think you are a perfect woman taking the MCATs, training for a marathon, working. .."

Sometimes he jokes around but it made me feel weird. Do you think it was okay to send out the email to the team about it and asking them to donate money? I want people to know, but I don't want to seem like I am bragging. Now I feel weird!

What do you think???

Love
Tina

I replied:
Darling Tina,
You have nothing to worry about at all. Charlie is just trying to be funny. You are doing great!

You should be aiming high with your life. You only live once and every day that passes means all the opportunities missed that day are gone. If you feel weird, it may because you lack confidence in your own judgment. I was the same way at your age (actually I totally lacked confidence at your age).

You are doing well and you should do well. You were born into a privileged life, you've worked hard to deserve such a life, and now you are determined to design and create a life that is worth living and worth celebrating.

Who cares what Charlie thinks? The only thing that really matters is what YOU think.

If you think running a marathon is a great goal (which it absolutely is -- it will put you into a elite of the special people who have done this) then it doesn't matter what anyone else thinks. If you are pursuing worthy and noble goals, what else matters? Nothing.

And people ask for contributions to worthy causes routinely. That is no big deal.

You have to watch out for people, especially men, who find successful women scary and will try and put you down in very subtle ways in order to make themselves look and feel superior.

I don't know Charlie but my best guess is that he was simply attempting to be harmlessly amusing. I wouldn't give it a moment's thought. Your mind should be focused on more important things, like developing new entrepreneurial business ideas for Booz Allen.

Remember, smile and act with unstoppable confidence. Every muscle in your body should reflect incredible self-confidence, ambition and inner tranquility. If you behave that way, you will become that person.

And keep setting and achieving inspiring goals for yourself which stretch and challenge you. You want to be a wonderful example to other people, and you are.

I love you.
Dad
XXXOOO

2006

October 12, 2006

PS Now I have a better idea of what my parents went through when they packed their four boys off to a bleak and forbidding British public boarding school in the early 1960s.

My Precious Loves,

As soon as the big, white vehicle taking Cory to Countryside Kennels pulled away from our house about half an hour ago, I burst into tears and wept uncontrollably.

She is going to be fine. I gave her Dramamine this morning to help calm her for when Christi would be coming. We had a routine morning together. I kept saying to her what Gail had told me to say: "Cory, you're going to camp today!" Gail had said to me that my outer attitude was pivotal and that I couldn't betray my own anxiety and grief. We went for a great run early this morning and I kept everything as completely normal as possible, even though I had a knot in my stomach. I felt better after talking this morning with Liz at the kennel place because I became convinced that they will take very good care of her. I told them she was easily scared and would need lots of TLC and Liz assured me they would give her lots of TLC.

Finally the dreaded front door bell went and it was Christi. She couldn't have been nicer or more understanding of Cory's concerns and feelings. Christi was very gentle and Cory went into the van without too much coaxing and into a very nice and roomy cage for the journey to the kennel. She was shivering with fright of course as I acted out my breezy and cheerful "you're going off to camp" act. Christi had treats ready for her.

I said goodbye to Cory, shook hands with Christi and thanked her, watched them pull away and, as I say, burst into sobs. I feel sad for her, even though I know she will be absolutely fine. We are purchasing the "pampered pooch" service for her (not "pampered poop" service as I said on the voice mail message I left for you this morning, Jenny!) so Cory will have a good time. There were two other dogs in the white van and they both looked delightful. I bet they and Cory become good friends and enjoy playing together.

Well, that's my story about our adorable Cory and I just wanted to share it with you. Bari just called so I'll copy her, Mark and Suzy on this too.

Love,
Dad/Chris
XXXOOO

Oct 14, 2006

Tina wrote:

cool im glad you guys goto there okay!

my exams were SO hard today, now i have to focus on anatomy all weekend! but tonight i sort of have a date... ill let you know how it goes :)

xoxo
tina

I responded:

Darling Tina,
I hope it goes well.

Kim, Sujay, Tina and Jenny: Mommy/Gail and I had a fun day today at an English tea with Clifford and Lella. Jill and Robin were there too. Everybody was dying to know all about what each of you is doing, so I expect your ears were burning, as Granny used to say. Ross now has a good job with a big law firm in London called Freshfields and looks very well groomed and grown up. It was great to see him. Lisa and Geoff have had a falling out with Hannah and Max over money, and now Geoff and Max refuse to talk to each other (this is confidential). Hannah and Max bought a house from Lisa and Geoff, but there was a dispute over how much was promised to be paid for it. Other than that, England is at peace!

We wish you were all with us here.

I love you.
Dad/Chris
XXXOOO

Jen then wrote the following e-mail:

Thanks for the update!

I got up at 9am today (saturday),worked for 3 hours on one econ problem set (this is after like 7 straight hours of it yesterday), had brunch with my friends, then spent the afternoon working on a religion paper (arguing that Paul was a feminist! hahaha), and then i went for a 3 mile run. I'm trying to get in shape for the turkey chase!

xox

And I responded at some length as follows:

Darling Jenny,
Your e-mail reminds me vividly of a passage from Thomas Jefferson's diary when he was about 16. He talked about getting up at 6 am, working on Latin for one hour, then science for one hour, then running "into the forest for about a mile," then reading some great book of literature for two hours, and so on throughout the day, not wasting one second. He is one of my heroes and I have learned a lot by studying his life.

Good luck with the econ problem set. I bet Jefferson couldn't have done it! When you say Paul, are you meaning Paul in the bible or one of your friends? I assume the former. What a great compliment to pay him! I'd love to read your paper if you're willing to share it with me when it's done.

Good for you, Jenny, for getting in shape for the Turkey Chase. I am so proud of you for wanting to meet that challenge. Sujay is thinking seriously of doing it too, which is super. I want you guys to keep terrifically healthy and fit so when I'm senile and decrepit, you are strong enough to push me around the Turkey Chase in my wheel chair! Maybe they don't allow that. If they do, Mommy can run alongside!

Mommy and I have saved an op-ed in the Post for all of you about Kim's Ten Mile Army race, which appeared on Friday morning as we were leaving DC to fly to England. Did you see it, Kim and Sujay? It was very poignant and moving. The writer focused on her feelings as she ran the race and saw the soldiers running with prosthetic legs, having had them blown off fighting in Iraq. Her article included the following wonderfully arresting phrase (the one in parenthesis): "As I passed each of the men (feeling oddly ashamed of myself for breezing by someone so clearly by athletic superior), it was..." I think that phrase in parenthesis is exquisite.

I think about Cory all the time, and wish I could cuddle her and tell her I love her and not to be sad.

I think I impressed Jill today (who as you all know is devotedly religious) because I quoted Proverbs ("a merry heart maketh a good life"). That's like her or Aunty Yvette quoting the atheistic secular humanist Richard Dawkins in conversation with me!

BTW, Richard Dawkins, another person I greatly admire, has a new book out attacking religion. He is the British scientist who created the concept of the "selfish gene," and the concept of "memes."

You are leading a great life, Jenny, and your future glows with promise. Kim, Sujay and Tina are exactly the same way. Cory too!

I adore you.
Dad
XXXOOO

PS My first big presentation is tomorrow (Sunday) morning at 10 am. I'm well prepared and raring to go! I'm pretty certain the room is going to be packed!

Oct 24, 2006

Dearest Kim, Sujay, Tina and Jenny,
Mommy/Gail and I met up yesterday in Bath after Mommy's successful time in London and my successful time at Wildscreen in Bristol. Jon drove the three of us to a country hotel called the Old Manor Hotel outside Bath deep in the rural west country of England. Tim and Lyson arrived from London at about the same time. The five of us had a great dinner together lasting about four hours!

We got up this morning to a sunny, breezy day with a forecast of possible rain. We put on our best clothes (in honor of Granny and Grandpa) and all drove to Haycombe Cemetery, Whiteway, Bath (about two miles south of 89, Bloomfield Avenue, where they lived for about 50 years). Haycombe Cemetery is where Granny and Grandpa are to have their final resting place. On the drive there, Tim took us over some wonderful country back roads. I can't think of anything in America which looks similar.

As we arrived a beautiful rainbow appeared in the sky as if to welcome us.

By about 11 am, about twenty of us had collected at the cemetery: Jon, Tim, Lyson, Hannah,

Max, baby Reina, Ross, Alex, Georgie, Nick, Carol, Simon, his barrister girlfriend Emma, Rosemarie Cunningham, Clifford, Lella, Richard, Sally, Mary, Mommy/Gail and me. Naturally there were lots of greetings and hugs. This was the first time I had met Max, and several people had not met other members of the party.

Very much missed were the four of you, Jill, Robin, Nicholas, Annabel, Yvette, Michael, Mary, Tim, Caroline, Lisa, Jeff, Andrew, Jenny, Adam, Nathaniel, James, Claire, Simon, Penelope, Seb, Daniel, Chris and Margaret Palmer, and Anna Sniffen. I'm sure I've left somebody out!

Tracy from the cemetery brought out a light brown wooden box weighing about 20 pounds containing Granny and Grandpa's ashes. On the box were their names and life spans on silver engravings. Granny: 1918-2004. Grandpa: 1913-2001. (Of course, it actually had their names, Mavis Palmer and Sidney John Palmer.)

To my surprise, I started to feel very emotional. I think this was true for Jon, Tim, Gail and several others. I carried the box containing my parents' ashes slowly towards their grave site. I was crying. Mary was by my side and very sweetly tried to comfort me. It was such a moving moment to be carrying Granny and Grandpa's ashes and saying a final goodbye to them. I was grappling with the idea that their full and eventful lives, with all the chaos, trauma, suffering, joy and laughter that goes with any full life, was finally coming to this extraordinary simple, stark and final end, and that each of us would end the same way, with this incredible finality.

We gathered around the grave site and I said the following:

"Jon and Tim have asked me to say a few words on behalf of the three of us. I want to thank Jon for bringing us all together today and arranging the lunch afterwards. We are all here today to say a final goodbye to Mummy and Daddy/Mavis and Sidney John. Each one of us here was enriched by their zest for life and by their love, affection, goodness and decency. We will never forget them. Let's be silent for a minute or so as we each remember them in our own way."

We had a minute or so of silence with the wind and sun playing all around us. We stood on graveside hill overlooking magnificent, verdant rolling countryside, each wrapped up in our own vivid and poignant memories. Jon put the box of ashes in the shallow hole in the ground by their gravestone. Then I went on:

"I want to tell you a story about Mavis and Sidney John. I welcome anybody else who would like to tell a story too. Please don't feel any pressure to say anything. We'll all be meeting for lunch afterwards at the Globe and can talk more about our memories of each of them then, but if anyone would like to say anything in a moment, that would be great.

"When I was 17, I was beginning a career in the Royal Corps of Naval Constructors as a Midshipman at the Royal Naval College in Manadon, Plymouth. Daddy was the head of the Corps. I was working averagely hard and felt pretty good about myself. After about the first two months at Manadon, I came home for a visit, proudly wearing my naval uniform. As I came in the house, Daddy was in bed upstairs because he had a sore throat and cold. I went into their bedroom to say hi, and he asked me how I was doing. I told him pretty well. He asked how I had done in the mid-term exams I had just taken, and I told him my marks were above average. He exploded with anger and shouted, "How dare you only get above average marks! You should be getting top marks! Nothing else is acceptable!" I left my parents' bedroom a little shaken. But from then on, I started working really hard, and this influenced, in a very positive way, my whole future career.

"The story I want to tell you about Mummy is that my mother, as a child, teenager and young adult, was reserved, shy, introspective and quiet. She was like that into her early 30s. Then one day she realized that life was passing her by, that she didn't like the person she was, and that she wanted to be expressive, colorful, exuberant and outgoing. She made a bold new choice— to have a different persona, one that would reflect a person determined to bring joy, happiness and comfort to other people. And this she did. This is the Mavis we all remember so well. It took an act of courage and speaks well of her strong character.

"On behalf of Tim, Jon and me, we thank you all for coming today. Would anyone else like to say anything?"

Clifford spoke first on behalf of all the Fountaines and spoke of his great affection for my parents. Then Mommy/Gail spoke and told everyone the funny story of Grandpa bumping his head on the sloping roof of our house in Bethesda and covering the ceiling with hanging tissues to warn him when his head was getting close to impact! Mommy also told the funny story of Grandpa dealing with an outbreak of flies in our house. He kept a record of how many he had swatted and created a bell shaped curve to show how when we could expect the problem to abate.

Mommy/Gail also spoke of how Granny and Grandpa would go for walks, hand-in-hand, often to meet you girls after school. And in later their later years would search for a bench so they could rest their weary legs.

Others also spoke about their memories of what warm, loving and caring people Granny and Grandpa were. I can't remember everyone who spoke but it also included Tim, Ross, Georgie, Carol, Sally, Mary and Rosemarie.

We said our final and silent goodbyes to Granny and Grandpa, and then all headed to the Globe pub for lunch together. It was a great chance for us all to catch up with each other's lives and share memories of Granny and Grandpa. Baby Reina cheered us all. Mummy brought pictures of Kim and Sujay's wedding. Carol shared photos of Nelope and Seb's baby, Daniel. Jon had arranged a perfect room and sandwiches. It felt a fitting way to celebrate the circle of life, lives well lived, and hope in the future.

As we drove out, believe it or not, there was another rainbow!

Georgie brought a local Southampton newspaper with a front page story about her starting with BBC South as a weather reporter. It was a great story and talked about Grandpa's long association with Gosport, Portsmouth and the surrounding area. The station is encouraging Georgie to do stories about her family's links to the local area. (Note to Georgie: in addition to the great material Tim has given you, you might also want to look at the book I wrote on our family history, and in particular page 53-62, as well as Appendix I. Your mum and dad should have a copy of it.)

Kim, Sujay, Tina and Jenny, I hope you've enjoyed this recounting of our final and moving goodbye to your wonderful grandparents. As I said at their graveside, we will never forget them.

I love you.

Dad/Chris
XXXOOO

PS to Emma: I'm missing Nelope's e-mail address. Would you please forward this e-mail to her? Thanks a lot. (And it was great to meet you, Emma!)

Tuesday, November 7, 2006

I sent the following e-mail to Jenny tonight:

Darling Jenny,

Mommy told me you were very disappointed today with your C grade in your economics test. C sounds pretty good to me!

Mommy also said you knew why you got it and knew the mistake you made. That's good! If the subject was gobbledygook to you, then that would be more of a worry for you, but it doesn't sound as if that's the case.

When I was your age, I took an important exam (to get into the British civil service). I thought at the time that my whole future career depended on getting an A. I got a C. (That's a pure coincidence that you also got a C today.) C wasn't a failing grade, but it wasn't an A, which would have given me the choice of the top jobs in the government, such as being a special assistant to a Cabinet Secretary.

I was at sea on HMS Hermes when the news came through. I was devastated. I couldn't believe it. It didn't sit well with the self-image I had of myself of always getting the top marks in exams. I felt angry, frustrated and helpless.

It turned out that it didn't matter because I came to America on a Kennedy Scholarship to study at Harvard, fell in love with Mommy, and didn't even want to go back to England!

None of this is relevant to your situation, but I thought I would share it anyway.

We are so proud of you, Jenny. And we adore you—even if you get an F in every exam you ever take!

Dad
XXXOOO

Friday, November 10, 2006

Jen's article on animal rights was published in *Prince* this morning. I am so proud of her!

I sent her an e-mail checking that she was going to send it to Dan Mathews at PETA. Jen responded:

Hmm... I'm not sure. I probably could since I did ask him about it but that might look like I'm bragging. What do you think?

I replied as follows:

Jenny,

Here is what I think. If you are to succeed in life, you need to get beyond this point! You've written a very important article. If no one sees it, you might as well not have written it. Sending it to people is not bragging. It is furthering the cause of animal rights.

You absolutely MUST send it to Dan Mathews! He would be annoyed if you didn't and wonder at your lack of thoughtfulness. You don't need any excuse to do this, such as "I asked him about it so I suppose it won't offend him to share it with him." You have a moral obligation to send it to him because he will share it with others, and you may end up changing someone's life. Bragging is irrelevant here! It is all about outreach and changing society. Your cover note to Dan could be along the following lines:

"Hi Dan, it was really super to meet you recently at AU.

"I wanted to share with you the attached article I wrote that was published on Friday in Princeton University's student newspaper, Prince. You might remember I mentioned this article when we were talking in my Dad's office.

"I hope you like it! Feel free to forward it to anyone else who might find it of interest.

"Keep up your inspiring work! I look forward to being the first in line to buy your book when it is published in April.

"I am also very excited about your willingness to come and speak at Princeton when we launch our new animal rights group, Princeton Animal Welfare Society (PAWS). I'll be back to you in the next month or so to discuss the details.

"All good wishes, Jenny Palmer."

Jen, you also MUST send your article to ALL your contacts at HSUS, especially the person you'll be working for this summer. They will all appreciate hearing from you and enjoy your article. If you feel you can't do this because you are bragging, then your career is facing some major hurdles! Protecting animals is too important for you to be worrying about that!

Take any steps you can to get your article reproduced and in front of new audiences. Offer it to HSUS for their publication.

Some of the e-mails you've received today from people wanting to join PAWS, and especially the e-mails you've received which are critical of you and your article, will be great raw material for your book! The harsher they are, the more your book benefits!

Them's my views!

I love you.
Dad
XXXOOO

2007

Sunday, August 26, 2007

What an incredible 60th birthday I had this weekend! On Saturday night (August 25), we invited 120 friends to come and celebrate. Gail organized everything beautifully. Tina and John drove down from Philly to be here with us. Gail and the girls came up with amazing gifts, which are described in my thank you letter to the whole family:

Dear Gail, Kimmie, Sujay, Tina, John, Jenny and Rob,
Thank you all for a wonderful and memorable 60th birthday! I am as happy as any man could be and the prime reason for that is all the love and affection I receive every day from my extraordinary family (and my daughters' boyfriends!). Thank you all for being such a source of joy and fulfillment.

Gail, my love, thank you for that incredible party last night!!! It was superlative in every respect and I had the time of my life! You thought of every detail and managed it as you manage everything, with impeccable competence and organizational skill.

Kim, Sujay, Tina, John, Jenny and Rob: Having you help last night added a new and lovely dimension to the party. Everyone who came loved meeting you, and you all worked hard to keep people fed and give them drinks. Gail and I appreciate how you conscientiously worked to keep the party moving. Thanks for being so warm to everyone.

Gail and I hope you all enjoy our little thank you gift for all your help.

Kim, Tina and Jen, I love the Treasure Hunt and "Dad's Ten Life Lessons." It is so funny, and clever, and true!!! You got me good!!! And from the beginning letter to the final word "lethargy," all eleven sheets were written beautifully. I will treasure it. (BTW, great material in there for laughs at my funeral!) Jen, please e-mail me everything so I can put it in the family journal. Thanks.

I will also treasure the t-shirt and the slide show. I'm seriously thinking of using the t-shirt, Kimmie, in my comedy set! It is really terrific, and all five lessons are excellent. I've been wearing it proudly today! It reminded me of the similarly clever t-shirt designs you did for me on occasions like Father's Day as you were growing up. I still have those t-shirts!!

And the slide show!! I love it!! What great memories!! And I love the Beatles music!! Jen you are so clever to do that. I can only imagine how hard it was to assemble all of the photos and edit them and line up the music. Thank you so much.

I also love the big poster board with the collage of all those family photos! That is so wonderful to have!

No father could be prouder of his three daughters than I am of you three. When I die, it will be my role as a father that will be my far the most important thing I have done in my life. Ow! Ow! Mommy just kicked me. Ow! Oh, I meant to write, "...the most important thing after being a husband..."

Sujay and Kim, thank you for the running outfit! I tried it on, Sujay, and it fits great! No need to change anything. The sizes you picked are good. I'm really pleased to have it. Thanks! As I told everyone at the party, Sujay, I feel incredibly lucky to have you for a son-in-law.

John, thanks for your card and for the warm message inside. Thanks, too, for bringing the movie for us to watch. I love those types of movies. Sorry I couldn't watch it all because of things I had to get done.

And a special thanks to John and Tina for taking the time from your intensive studies to be with us. I realize that this is hard to do.

Rob, thanks for the beautiful chopsticks you brought me back from my birthplace Hong Kong! That was very thoughtful of you.

Gosh, I'm sure I've forgotten to say thank you for something!

Gail, Kim, Sujay, Tina, John, Jen and Rob—thank you again for wonderful 60th birthday celebration!

Love,
Chris/Dad
XXXOOO

Sunday, September 23, 2007
I'm in Vancouver for a big IMAX meeting. I sent the girls the following e-mail tonight:

Darling Kim, Tina and Jenny,
Did you know that on this day (September 23) in 1972, Mommy and I met? So September 23 is a very special day for us and one we always remember and celebrate (in a quiet way).

I was reflecting today on how lucky I was on this day in 1972 to meet Mommy, and then I realized—although I had known it for a long time, but today it hit me with fresh force—that by far my biggest contribution to the world will always be you three girls. I'm certain Mommy feels the same way.

Yes, if anyone ever asks me what my biggest contribution has been to the world, there is only one answer. Mommy and I gave the world three amazing daughters, three loving sisters, and three incredible human beings.

I love you.
Dad
XXXOOO

PS Tina, good luck in your cardio exam tomorrow!!!!!

Tuesday, September 25, 2007
I sent the following letter to Kim, Tina and Jenny this evening:

Darling Kim, Tina and Jenny,

I leave here tomorrow and will be home late tomorrow night. We have a big awards dinner tonight (at which we hope some of our films will win—they've been nominated in several categories), and tomorrow morning, we are holding an event to show the all the theaters a rough cut of our latest film on fresh water (called *Grand Canyon Adventure*.)

Early on Monday morning, I fly to Jackson Hole for a week for the Jackson Hole Film Festival. I have to get there by 4 pm to give a workshop to everyone on networking.

Kim, congratulations again on your award today! That is really great!

Tina, Mommy told me you and John are going out tonight with friends to celebrate surviving your cardio exam on Monday! I hope you have a super time!

Jen, thanks for calling me back today. It was great to talk to you. All your plans for PAWS are very exciting. And that's great you got a good turn out last night. Your meetings remind me of what it must have been like in early 19th century New England as the abolitionist movement gathered steam and people met, seemingly against insurmountable odds, to combat deeply institutionalized slavery. Sometime in the future, eating meat, thanks to you and many others, will seem as disgusting to most people as, say, bear baiting does to us today (an activity which, in the past, was routine and perfectly acceptable).

Kim, Tina and Jenny, I love you and miss you.

Dad
XXXOOO

Tuesday, October 2, 2007
I'm in Jackson Hole for the wildlife film festival. I sent the girls the following e-mail:

Darling Kim, Tina and Jenny,
Every morning here at the Jackson Lake Lodge, I run under the Tetons. (Tina, do you remember them?!) They tower up to about 13,000 feet and look magnificently craggy. Wildlife is everywhere. As I ran this morning, a photographer pointed out a bull elk just 20 yards away.

Almost immediately after the terrorist attacks on September 11, I came out here for the wildlife film festival and found enormous comfort in these great mountains. The world may have been going crazy, but these mountains represented those things in life that were unchangeable and that really mattered. Just to look at them calmed my nerves and reassured me that everything was going to be OK.

Everything here is going great. It is super to see lots of old friends. I love you and miss you.

Dad
XXXOOO

Thursday, October 4, 2007
I sent the following e-mail to the girls today (with a copy to Gail and Sujay):

Darling Kim, Tina and Jen,
My e-mail came back up today so I'm able to write to you again!

One thing I've come to realize more and more strongly as I get older is that every little effort counts. For example, I exercised and went running this morning. No big deal. Yet it is a big deal because every extraordinary achievement results from thousands of routine achievements that no one thinks is a big deal. Thousands of little things done the right way every day can change lives and produce amazing results over time.

I adore you and miss you.
Yer ol' Dad
XXXOOO

Friday, October 5, 2007
I sent the following letter to the girls tonight:

Darling Kim, Tina and Jen,
I go home tomorrow! I'll get home very late—close to midnight I expect.

It's strange to me how seldom you hear people talk about the value of hard work. It is the basic building block of every achievement, yet people talk much more readily about things like stress, balance and relaxation.

If you look at the life of every great person, you'll find they worked hard and didn't waste time. In fact you can't achieve anything without hard work. The Sistine Chapel, Shakespeare's Hamlet, being physically fit, and nurturing successful, happy children all take hard work and perseverance.

You each have an outstanding work ethic. You are willing to make an intense effort to achieve your goals. I am so proud of you for that.

Mark Twain interests me. He was born in 1835 and died in 1910. He wrote 25 books and many articles. He worked very hard! He grew up in a slave-owning state (Missouri), his father owned a slave, but he came to see that slavery was wrong.

One funny incident is his life is that when the Civil War started in 1861 when Mark Twain was 26, some Missouri friends convinced him to join a Confederate volunteer militia. He and 14 others trained in the woods. Whenever they heard that Union troops might be coming, they retreated. He wrote later that when he retired from the rebel army, he knew "more about retreating than the man that invented retreating." He was a wonderfully funny man and spent his life fighting injustices.

Kim, Mommy told me tonight that you looked fabulous on TV today! I can't wait to watch a tape of it when I get home. BTW, how did your talk go at AU with Iris?

Tina, I hope your liver lessons are going well. BTW, why did cowboys say things like, "Why, you yellow livered son of a gun, I'll (and here some cowboyish threat would emerge related to guns in some way)". Or is the yellow liver reference something I just made up?!

Jen, I hope StARS and PAWS are doing well. I know you've got some big events coming up. I hope they go well.

I miss you all and adore you each. I told a ton of people this week all about you, so, as Granny used to say, your ears must have been burning.

I love you.
Dad
XXXOOO

Friday, November 23, 2007

I sent the following letter to the family today:

To my precious family:
It will be wonderful to all be together for the upcoming holidays!

I have a little suggestion: Let's all try to cut down on the stress we all feel every Christmas from having to buy gifts! I'm not saying to have no gifts, but let's try and avoid having to spend hours trudging through malls looking for something that the family member doesn't really need and that will just end up cluttering their lives. I have been as guilty of this as everyone else in previous years.

The holidays should be focused on companionship, silence, reflection, relaxation, reading, writing, laughing and spending time with each other, long-term planning, contemplation and exercise—not stressing painfully for hours and hours in an overcrowded mall.

I suddenly became very conscious of this today when I started listing what I wanted to get everyone for Christmas and realized that traditional gifts that help keep the economy going are basically unpleasant to me, and for the most part represent rampant consumerism. None of us is really lacking stuff! In fact the reverse is true—our lives are choking on too much stuff. I'll never forget how amazed and horrified I was back in 1972 when I came to this country and saw the volume and extravagance of the gift-giving at Christmas in American homes.

Now I know Jen needs a camera, Tina needs shoes and a treo for the hospital, Kim needs clothes I expect, and I love learning history on CDs in the car, and all those are great because they are all things we need. But let's try to reduce the busyness and stress of the holidays by reducing gift giving to a more modest level.

Let us know what you need and we'd love to give you that for Christmas. I'm thrilled to slog through a mall to find you something you need!

I love you!
Dad/Chris/Grinch
XXXOOO

PS I showed this e-mail in draft to Mommy and she says I shouldn't send it because I'm the only one who has this problem! Oh well—feel free to ignore!

2008

Wednesday, July 30, 2008

I received the following e-mail from Curt Shackelford yesterday. Curt runs the comedy club, Laugh Riot at the Hyatt, at the Bethesda Hyatt where I MC for him most Saturday nights:

> Hi Chris-
> I've got to start using professional comics to MC Hyatt shows--the Montgomery Drafthouse is opening next month in Silver Spring and will be competing with Hyatt.
> (they are using pro comics)
> Your sets have been inconsistent lately--some great, some not so great.
> I can afford inconsistency when nobody is on my turf, but not when I have to compete with another club who is using pros--
> I fully realize you helped me build the show to what it is, but the show has to change to meet the current threat.
> These Montgomery Drafthouse people are highly organized and have deep pockets, and are working from an existing successful model (Arlington Drafthouse).
> They know what they're doing and that scares me--I have to revamp the show to meet this challenge.
> They aren't going to shut down after a few weeks like the Bethesda Comedy Club did--these guys are planning to dominate all of Montgomery County.

> --------------------------------

I was upset and disappointed at first. I've been performing stand-up comedy for three or four years now and am on a steep learning curve. Ironically I was studying a book on stand up comedy by Judy Carter when his e-mail showed up in my in-box. After thinking it over and discussing the situation with Gail, I replied to Curt as follows:

> Hi Curt,
> I understand totally. Not a problem!
>
> It's been a wonderful experience working with you over the last three years or so. I've really enjoyed it and am grateful to you for letting me MC for you so much and giving me so much stage time.
>
> I wish you nothing but the best. You are incredibly professional at running comedy clubs. I'm confident you'll easily out-compete the Montgomery Drafthouse.
>
> If anyone shows up at a future show and asks for me, please tell them that I'm writing a book and taking a break from stand-up comedy.
>
> Take care and please say hi to Lia from me.
>
> Best, Chris

> ---

I also shared Curt's note with the family and sent it to them with the following cover note:

My loves,

As you can see from Curt's e-mail, he no longer wants me to MC for him. This is a blow!

When his e-mail first arrived this morning, I felt down. But this may be a blessing in disguise. I'm glad to have the extra time to put into writing my book, and strategically I'm probably wiser to focus more on giving speeches rather than doing stand-up. The typical audience at comedy clubs is not "my" audience (compared, say, to the audience at a film conference or big dinner).

When people ask me when I'm performing next, I'll just tell them that I'm taking a break to focus on my book. When the book is done, I'll examine my options then and decide whether to keep performing stand-up at other places or put my energy elsewhere.

It isn't fun watching one of your life's goals experience a setback, but it happens to everyone. All you can do is face the situation boldly, clearly understand what is going on, decide your options, and pursue a new set of goals with renewed optimism, vigor and energy.

I read somewhere that a winner is not someone who doesn't get knocked down, but someone who never stops getting up after being knocked down. (I think the original was more eloquent than that.) Anyway, I'll make lemon from this lemonade!

I love you!
Dad/Chris
XXXOOO

2009

August 2, 2009

Darling Tina,

I've just read your latest blog post, "A Superior State of Well-Being." It is wonderful! Here are a few thoughts inspired by what you wrote:

You can never be too attached to your To-Do list as long as your To-Do list is built from your personal mission statement and covers all aspects of it. So, for example, one of your tasks might be "Spend more time with friend X and help her feel less isolated," or whatever. In other words, the tasks shouldn't just be about "work."

All successful and fulfilled people are obsessed with their productivity. Like Ben Franklin, they don't want to waste precious time. They appreciate that every day that passes is one day less to live. But they also define productivity to cover everything in their personal mission statement, not just "work." Successful and happy people succeed in every part of their lives (emotional, mental, spiritual, physical, financial, family life, etc.), not only their professional work lives.

Writing all your tasks down and thus not having them clog up your mind as you focus single mindedly on the task at the top of your list, is exactly the way to do it. I think the time I spend planning my week, and then planning each day, is probably one of the best time investments I make.

I love the quote from *Surfwise*! I am in a constant superior state of well-being, but I can't help sadly noticing how rare good health is, even among young people who should be totally pain-free and in vibrant health. To achieve it takes hard work.

Your list of attributes which exemplify a superior state of well-being (at the end of your blog post) is terrific! Here are four ideas to add to it:

- Ridding your life of any duplicity so you have no stress from having to remember things to keep up deceptions
- Being autonomous to the maximum extent possible so you control your life and are not pushed around by anyone else or live your life according to someone else's agenda
- Keeping mentally fit by reading, writing, and thinking
- Having inspiring life goals that you constantly evaluate and reevaluate, and constantly rededicate yourself to achieving

I love you, treasure.
Dad
XXXOOO

August 8, 2009

Darling Tina,
I commend you for an outstanding blog post!

"The World that Men Don't Know" should be the title of a book and companion television documentary.

Men are blind to what you describe, just like lions on the savannah haven't a clue about the constant and unrelenting fear in which ungulates live from fear of predation.

This is why I attached so much emphasis to you girls learning about self-defense when you were young teenagers.

And it is why I attach great importance to women learning the Marine "buddy" system, so they keep an eye out for each other at all times. I'm sure you and Caitlin are doing that.

Men tend to be ignorant and clueless (unless they have daughters or are unusually empathetic) of the way women experience the world. Women have to be constantly alert to threats to their safety. It drains their emotional energy and puts them at a disadvantage in terms of competing with men for career advancement. Women are constantly distracted by worries about safety in a way that men never are.

I thank UPenn for the wisdom of your African "mothers."

I love you, treasure.
Dad
XXXOOO

2010

Monday, March 15, 2010

Simon's body was found yesterday on Dartmoor in a ditch. Very sad. Tim called today (his 66th birthday) to tell me. The police think Simon died the night he left his house on December 15.

I sent the following e-mail to the family:

Dear Kimmie, Sujay, Tina, and Jen,

Sad news re Simon. His body was found yesterday on Dartmoor in a ditch. My brother Tim called today to tell us. The police think Simon died the night he left his house on December 15 from exposure (a polite way of saying he froze to death). In a sense he committed suicide, but it's hard to say anything definitive like that because he was emotionally and mentally perturbed. Who knows the right way to describe why he died so tragically and in such a lonely way.

We'll never know what was going on in his mind. We know he was hearing voices and was troubled in some way. There was some early foreshadowing that something wasn't quite right with him when he changed his name to Jay (apparently because the letters in the name Palmer somehow resonated with the name Hitler) and he was burdened by parents who meant well but didn't always give him the help and guidance he needed.

I remember him as a lovely person. Mommy found some old Christmas cards he had sent us a few years ago, and they were warm and affectionate.

His death reminds us all that one never knows the suffering that goes on inside people. That's why it's important to be patient and sympathetic with people. People can wear masks of confidence, bluster, and serenity, when under the mask, very different moods prevail.

Let me know if you have any questions. I'll do my best to answer them.

I love you.
Dad/Chris
XXXOOO

Thursday, July 22, 2010

Tina sent me a lovely note yesterday asking if she could interview me for her blog. Here is her letter, and my replies to her questions in italics:

Hi Dad,
I want to do a blog post about you and your book at some point, would that be okay with you? *Sure!!!!*

I was thinking of starting a series of posts where I interview people I admire - including you! I will come up with some questions to ask you, for example:

Tell me about some of your daily habits. *I assiduously follow my Personal Mission Statement. I exercise daily for at least an hour, including standing on my hands for one or two minutes. I plan my day meticulously and always work on paper (not in my head). I never drink alcohol and like to live ascetically, simply, and with intentionality. My diet is vegetarian with lots of fruit and vegetables. I virtually never watch television.*

What are some things you do to stay healthy/energized while traveling? *I exercise daily when travelling (including swimming if the hotel has a pool), never waste time in the plane watching movies, avoid any foods that might upset my stomach (including coffee), eat black or white bean soup whenever I can get it, stay closely connected with my wife and three daughters by phone and e-mail, and keep careful track of my commitments so I build a deep trust with my colleagues and friends.*

What is your favorite meal? *Baked beans on toast*

What is your biggest fear? *My biggest fear is failing to achieve my goals as described in my Personal Mission Statement, and thereby dying with regrets and disappointments.*

What is one thing you want to accomplish in the next 5 years? *Write and get published a book on fathering daughters*

Who was your most influential mentor? *The author Stephen R. Covey*

What are your top 3 tips for a successful marriage? *Be kind, be considerate, be generous*

If you could tell a room of 10,000 young adults one piece of advice, what would it be? *Work hard, avoid indolence and idleness, be both serene and ambitious, and work on something that will improve society and help others.*

What is the key to achieving happiness, success and fulfillment: *Devote your life to helping solve one of society's great problems*

Tina, I'll improve these after I hear back from you. Not sure if the above is what you were expecting or seeking.   XXXOOO

What do you think about this idea? Are there any specific questions you would want me to ask you?

love,
tina

Sunday, August 22, 2010

Tina sent me the following e-mail this morning, and my answers are incorporated into her letter below.

Hi Dad!
I'm working on a blog post about you and your book and I think I'm going to focus it around the theme of non-violence (which is a big thing in yoga and also relates to your book).

Would you mind answering these questions?

1. Who are your greatest mentors on non-violence and why? **Gandhi because he was extraordinarily fearless in confronting violence with non-violence. And Congressman**

John Lewis because again he was incredibly brave when it came to facing down the vicious and violent tactics of the racist police departments in the segregated south.

2. What are 3 things people can do right now to minimize the harm we cause the environment? Stop eating meat. Buy organic fruits and vegetables. Live modestly and without ostentation.

3. What are some of your daily habits and routines that help keep you focused on your goals and purpose? I assiduously follow my Personal Mission Statement http://american. edu/soc/cef/upload/chris-palmer-mission-6-29-09.pdf . I exercise daily for at least an hour, including standing on my hands for one or two minutes. I plan my day meticulously and always work on paper (not in my head). I never drink alcohol and like to live ascetically, simply, and with intentionality. My diet is vegetarian with lots of fruit and vegetables. I virtually never watch television. I laugh smiling, laughing, being funny, and greeting everyone I meet with great warmth.

4. What is the key to achieving happiness, success and fulfillment? Devote your life to helping solve one of society's great problems (for example, environmental degradation, poverty, child abuse, and prejudice against women) so that your life has purpose, direction, and meaning.

5. What are some things you do to stay healthy while traveling? I exercise daily when travelling (including swimming if the hotel has a pool), never waste time in the plane watching movies (instead I read), avoid any foods that might upset my stomach (including coffee), eat black or white bean soup whenever I can get it, stay closely connected with my wife and three daughters by phone and e-mail, and keep careful track of my commitments so I build a deep trust with my colleagues and friends.

6. What is your biggest fear? My biggest fear is failing to achieve my goals as described in my Personal Mission Statement, and thereby dying with remorse, regrets, and disappointments.

7. If you could tell a room of 10,000 young adults one piece of advice, what would it be? Work hard, avoid indolence and idleness, be both serene and ambitious, avoid duplicity at all costs, and devote your professional lives to a cause that will improve society and help others.

Saturday, October 23, 2010
Kim spoke at AU last Wednesday about her new book *Generation Earn*. She did a wonderful job. Afterwards, I sent Kimmie the following e-mail:

Darling Kimmie,

You did a terrific job last night. You are a far better speaker than I was at your age, and you'll get better and better as you work hard to improve.

You really connected well with the audience and that is very important. Speaking is all about building a relationship with the audience.

I like the way you came out in front of the table so you were as close as possible to everyone in the room. I also liked the way you moved around the room and were not static. It's great when you walked up the middle. Audiences like to see energy, movement, and dynamism. They want to be entertained.

Your three questions at the beginning were great and got the audience to be active by raising their hands.

The credit/debit card story was excellent. Try to think of more stories like that.

Your voice projection was good.

It was great you didn't look at your notes much and instead "spoke from the heart." Well done!

I especially liked the "spending diary" section because you really interacted with the audience is a genuine way, as if you really *did* want to know their experiences.

Great having two handouts. This extends the learning and makes the audience feel they got something tangible out of the talk.

You were best when giving firm opinions. At one point someone asked you if paying rent was throwing away money, and you said it was a myth encouraged by the real estate industry. Excellent! Fun and interesting to listen to.

It was wonderful you encouraged and took so many questions. Audiences love that.

One thing I do is to say to the questioner after I've finished answering, "Does that answer your question? Are you satisfied?" Or words to that effect. It shows you really care about them and want to make sure they are satisfied.

I like how you mention the book regularly without overdoing it. It's a way of reminding them that you are a serious scholar and highly substantive. ("When I was researching for the book...." Or "I interviewed many people for the book to find out about....")

Good joke: "like dating." Terrific! The more you make them laugh, the better. In fact, the more you make them active in any way (asking questions, putting their hands up, laughing, taking notes, talking in pairs, etc) the better.

In terms of improving for next time, the biggest thing you can do is to stop saying "um." You want to completely rid your speech of any "ums," "you knows," etc. It's funny, you never do that on television! Great to bring some of your on-camera lessons to your speeches.

Linked to this is the power of pauses. Silence is golden. Not every second has to be filled with your voice. Dramatic pauses are wonderful.

Other ways to improve are to speak with more authority (as you do on television) and with a more authoritative voice.

I wouldn't say things like, "I don't feel qualified to talk about that," or "That's way beyond my expertise." Simply say that's an area where they need to seek specialized advice, or something like that. The audience is looking to you for guidance, and you don't want to give them any reason to doubt your abilities, authority, or competence.

You could milk the stories more and have some fun with them. The one about me helping you with salary negotiations is a good story, and people would love to hear you tell it in detail, imitating me, and making them laugh. It's important for the audience to really grasp the value of role playing and how it's done. Don't hurry through it. Relish the specific details (for example, how I made you practice over and over, how it made you feel uncomfortable, but how it ultimately helped you, etc). People love personal stories like that.

I would repeat the questions. That way you can be sure everyone in the back has heard it, and it also gives you time to think about your answer. I didn't catch some of the questions.

As people come in, I would greet and meet them. Audience members love that. They love to meet the speaker. And then when you get up to speak, they will all be rooting for you to succeed. You will have already established a warm bond with them. If you and Katherine had worked the room last night instead of chatting at the table, it would have provided you with a warmed-up audience.

In responding to questions, you often used the word "awesome." I would vary that a bit. Other words are excellent, insightful, wise, and savvy. Best not to praise the questions too much in case it comes across as condescending.

Take charge at the end: "I'll take two more questions, finish with a final comment, and then I'd be delighted to sign book for you." I think you may have said that, but I would say it with more authority.

I hope that helps, loveydovey. Overall, you did a really exceptional job. The more you give presentations and strive to improve, the better and more powerful you'll become, the more books you'll sell, and the more invitations you'll get to talk, and the more you can increase your fees and honorariums.

I love you and was so proud of you last night! Hope this feedback ("the breakfast of champions") is helpful.

Dad
XXXOOO

2011

Sunday, June 19, 2011

I sent Tina the following e-mail to thank her:

> Darling Tina,
> Dying to know how your first day on the job is going! I was so pleased when you called this morning after you'd been there for three and a half hours and you said you were loving it. Hope that continues!!!!!
>
> Thanks, treasure, for your wonderful letter for Father's Day! I loved it and I'm going to retype it into the family journal. It was very special and I deeply appreciate it. Thanks, too, for the three terrific photos from May 15 when you were awarded your MD. They are memorable family photos and I treasure them.
>
> We had a lovely tea this afternoon with Kim, Sujay, and Kareena. We missed you and Jenny!
>
> I love you.
> Dad
> XXXOO

Monday, June 20, 2011

Wonderful news! I've been so worried about Tina having to work 30 hours at UCSF non-stop, but we just received this e-mail from her (in reply to mine a few pages back):

> Hi Dad!
> I'm glad you had a good Father's Day! I wish I could've been there with you! Do you have any pictures from your visit with Kareena?!
>
> I'm great. I just woke up from a little nap after getting home at 1:30pm. It was an exhausting night but it was also really exhilarating. I was able to lie down twice for a little while (45min-1 hour each) and at 5am this morning brushed my teeth and acted like it was the start of the day. I got a coffee and was fine all morning!
>
> It's weird not being a med student anymore. I found myself automatically acting like one, and then would realize I'm actually the doctor! People called me when there was a problem, and everyone in the hospital called me "doctor"... it was amazing!
>
> I'm getting up to eat a little then will probably go to bed early for an early morning tomorrow.
>
> Love you!
> Tina

Monday, June 20, 2011

> Darling Tina,
> I was thrilled to receive your note! I am absolutely delighted you felt "exhilarated"! That is perfect! I can only imagine how exhausting it was for you, but you handled everything beautifully. It's so wonderful that you know (through yoga and the food you eat) what it takes to stay healthy, relaxed, and comfortable when getting through a very tough and grueling test like that. Mommy and I are incredibly proud of you. You acquitted yourself with high honors. That's

amazing you were fine all morning, and a great tribute to you.

I think it is also wonderful that at last you are in a position of real responsibility, and people (patients, nurses, others) look to you for leadership. I can see how you would love that. It is what everybody wants in their lives—autonomy, the ability to make your own decisions and to control your own life. You call the shots. Of course, I know you're just starting, but you got a flavor of it over the last 30 hours—people showing you respect by calling you doctor, asking for your guidance, and seeking your help on problems.

Projecting a high level of authority, influence, and charisma (through you body, your voice, your level of vitality and energy) is a good thing to aim for. The better you are at your job and the more you are able to help patients feel better and heal, the more respect you'll command, the more people will look up to you, and the more charisma and authority you'll naturally communicate and express. This is exactly the direction you are heading in. I am thrilled for you! Not that it will be easy and there won't be setbacks—but that goes with the territory when you're pursuing a noble and challenging mission.

Mommy and I were talking this evening how unbelievably successful you three girls are. You are role models for all your friends and for all who meet you.

I'll cc everyone on this because Kim, Jen, and Sujay are dying to know how you are doing!

Congratulations, treasure, for doing so much more than simply surviving those first tough and arduous 30 hours at UCSF.

Good luck tomorrow!

I love you.
Dad
XXXOOO

Monday, July 18, 2011
I sent to about five good friends in SF the following note about Tina (after getting her permission of course):

Dear Elizabeth,
My middle daughter Christina (www.prescribingyoga.com) has recently moved to SF to start her medical residency at UCSF. She is 29 and eager to meet people. I'll copy Christina on this by way of introduction. If you know anyone about her age (especially men!) who would like to meet her, please let Christina know!

Christina, Elizabeth is one of my best friends from NWF and a really wonderful person. She is an environmental activist, is married to Paul, and they have two young daughters called Zoe and Pia.

Elizabeth, thank you.

Best, Chris

From this initiative, Tina received a ton of warm invitations out. All my friends tried so hard to be responsive. As e-mails were flying about on this topic, at one point Tina wrote:

omg you guys this is a little out of control!

Sujay replied in his wonderfully humorous way:
Tina, I hope you don't mind, but I have placed several marital advertisements in Indian newspapers on your behalf. I'm sure we will have a number of suitor applicants in no time.

I responded to Sujay:
Sujay, that made me laugh out loud! Ha ha!

Earlier in the day, Kim had made us all laugh with the following funny comment:
Tina, maybe we should also take out a full page ad in the sf chronicle on your behalf :)

I responded to Tina in a more serious vein:
Tina, it isn't! Good men are hard to find, so you need to be very intentional and strategic. Typically women don't put nearly enough planning into this side of their lives. Women need to put as much effort into planning and succeeding in their personal lives as they do into planning and succeeding in their professional lives.

I know so many young women who can't find men worth marrying (or even worth dating), but most of them are not going about the challenge in an intentional, strategic way. They sort of sit back, perhaps try on-line dating, but basically they just cross their fingers and hope a man shows up. In my view, that's not being nearly proactive or resourceful enough. They end up getting mediocre men unless they're very lucky.

Danielle and my other SF friends have opened up a great opportunity for you! It doesn't mean you have to respond to every invitation. You're far too busy for that. But you can "interview" people over the phone and carefully pick the most promising opportunities.

Good luck, treasure. Don't forget to reply to all the people writing to you with a brief warm thank you.

BTW, your blog is really coming into its own in this arena because it's a wonderful way to separate the wheat from the chaff. People can get a very quick and accurate understanding of the kind of person you are—they can see that you are not only beautiful, but they can also see in a brilliant light your high moral values, humane outlook on life, and what your deepest concerns are.

I love you.
Dad
XXXOOO

Tina replied (a little mysteriously perhaps):
oh my gosh you guys. this is too funny.

And then she immediately sent another note:

>and omg I got over 300 hits on my blog today - i'm sure it's from that email chain you sent, dad. ahhh

I replied:

>Tina, is that good or bad?   XXXOOO

Tina responded:

>good I guess? depends on who's looking at it!

I replied:

>I think it's good, treasure. All the people I wrote to, including Danielle, are terrific, high caliber people, and many of them are interested in yoga. They'll find your blog highly engaging! They would all be good people to have in your network of friends and contacts.   XXXOOO

Thursday, August 11, 2011

Kim sent me the following request yesterday:

>Hi Dad!
>I was wondering where your ideas on family meetings, family mission statement, etc., originated from. Was there a particular book you read?
>Or did you come up with these ideas on your own? I am considering writing about the topic and am wondering where your theories came from... thank you!!!
>Love,
>Kim

I replied:

>Hi loveydove,
>I read a lot of books on fathering, as well as books by people like Stephen Covey on how to have a successful family, and from all those books I developed my own ideas on what might work and what might not work for us. So the ideas came from lots of different places. I took every opportunity to talk to other fathers about what they did or didn't do, and what they found worked or didn't work. And of course I observed other families and drew my own conclusions about what fathering behaviors produced good results and what ones didn't.

>The idea for the letters to you girls when I was away came from my desperate attempt to get your attention! You all loved Mommy so much that I had a hard time even being relevant (I was jealous of all the attention Mommy received from you girls!). So my nightly letters were an attempt to get your attention and not be "out of sight, out of mind" when I was away from home traveling and making films (which I often was). I soon realized of course that they were a wonderful way of telling you things and passing on information, knowledge, love, and wisdom that I would find difficult to do face to face. Like a lot of men, I wasn't very good at expressing my feelings, but I found it easier to do so when writing letters.

>Many of our other family traditions and rituals have come from fathering (or parenting) books, such as the Family Almanac. I have a whole collection of outstanding books on fathering daughters which I have found invaluable. One of my first insights into fathering was that it was a skill I could learn (like playing the piano), not something which just happened to a man when he

got children. Grandpa probably would have scoffed at that notion. To my parents, parenting was something you were, not something you did, and if that led to screaming, anger, and hitting, that was just part of the job.

Beyond my regular letters to you girls, Mommy and I created many other family rituals and traditions to help bring our family closer and bond us together. These included weekly family meetings, the creation of a family mission statement, annual goals or New Year's Resolutions, etc. To change the culture in our family from catching you girls doing something wrong to catching you doing something right (an idea I picked up from books on how to manage people effectively), I created the "encouragement" item on the agendas for our family meetings in which every member of the family would have to find something encouraging (not necessarily praising) to say about every other family member.

In summary, I knew that unless I intervened and took action, I would automatically tend to mimic my father's style of parenting and thus fail to be an outstanding Dad. Thus I undertook a deliberate, self-imposed program of study on the topic of fathering. I realized that parenting was a skill that I could actually learn if I studied and practiced it. Fathering was not something that one simply drifted into and did whatever came naturally. What came naturally and instinctively from me was often inferior and damaging. Mommy and I developed a number of family rituals and traditions, including weekly family meetings with a rotating chair and a written agenda (which you girls often resisted, but which I insisted on), always having "encouragement" as one of the agenda items, creating a Family Mission Statement, writing letters to you girls every night I was away traveling, hiding birthday dollars, holding birthday treasure hunts, your journals, annual predictions, science experiments, New Year's Resolutions, keeping a Family Journal, creating a Family Emergency plan, etc. (Some of my ideas never gained traction, such as a weekly "date with Dad" in which I and one of you girls would do anything you wanted together.) In an uncertain world, Mommy and I realized that it was important for you girls to have something that was certain, so we wanted to create a family where you three could be absolutely certain you could count on certain things to happen. Those traditions would be, like Mount Everest, unchangeable, reliable, and completely trustworthy. You three girls would feel anchored and secure. Mommy and I could die happy!

I'll cc Mommy in case she can think of anything else. Let me copy Tina and Jen in case they can think of anything else.

I love you. (BTW, that was something my parents never said to me, but I learned from a book on fathering that it was important for daughters to hear their Dads say that to them, so I forcefully disciplined myself to learn how to say it. It wasn't easy!)

Dad
XXXOOO

Kimmie responded:
Thank you Dad!!!! that helps and is very interesting!!! I think you definitely succeeded :)

Tuesday, August 16, 2011
We put Cory to sleep today. It was a hard, sad, heart-breaking day. Immediately afterwards, Gail and I called the girls (I was crying), and then I sent them the following letter:

Dear Kim, Sujay, Tina, and Jenny,
Mommy/Gail and I have just finished talking with you or leaving your voice mail messages about our precious and deeply loved Cory. She died peacefully about an hour ago, with Mommy and I hugging her and telling her how much we loved her and thanking her for sharing her exuberant and joyful life with all of us.

We all cherished her and adored her. She was an integral part of our family and we are so lucky to have had almost 11 years with her, full of play, laughter, and delight. We will miss her terribly.

Mommy and I asked for Cory's ashes so we can have a little ceremony next month when Jen is home to commemorate Cory and scatter her ashes in the garden.

I'm also going to buy a rose and put it on the floor in Jen's bathroom where she spent most of last couple of months as her health deteriorated.

I'm also composing a eulogy about her which I will send you in the next day or so.

Mommy and I are so sad to bring you the news of Cory's passing. She meant so much to each one of us. She had a good life and gave so much love and affection to so many people.

We love you.
Dad
XXXOOO

Later this evening, I sent another note to the family about Cory:
Tuesday night: This has been a heavy day, full of sad thoughts about our precious Cory. I instinctively keep looking for her in the house. She is everywhere, but nowhere. I bought some beautiful red roses today, put them in a vase, and placed them on the floor of Jenny's bathroom by the bath where Cory spent so much time recently. Mommy was out, so I was by myself. I placed them gently where she used to lie, and I cried. I miss her terribly. As I said in a note to Sujay earlier today, the house seems eerily and unnaturally empty without her. What a wonderful dog she was. Cory gave us everything. I hope you're all doing OK. I love you. Dad/Chris XXXOOO

Wednesday, August 17, 2011
I wrote the following tribute to Cory today:

Cory

October 9, 2000 -- August 16, 2011

We have lost our beloved dog Cory to cancer. We are grief stricken to lose her, but also deeply grateful for the beautiful life she shared with us. Cory died peacefully this morning at the vet, with Gail and me hugging her, telling her how much we loved her, and thanking her for sharing her exuberant and joyful life with us.

Cory was a totally loved and beloved member of our family. We all adored her and will miss her terribly. Her unstinting affection, love, and warmth brought us all enormous joy and happiness. All she ever knew was love. All she ever gave was love.

Ever since Jenny was about five years old, she had lobbied for the family to get a dog. We had decided against it because the house was already cluttered and disorganized, and Gail, I, and the girls had schedules which were already stressfully jammed packed. Adding the responsibilities of a dog would have been unwise, even irresponsible.

We eventually changed our minds when Jenny was about 12. Kim and Tina went off to college leaving Jen with the ghastly prospect (at least, that's how Gail and I imagined it) of being alone in a big house with her parents. We were worried that Jen would find our company so boring and the situation so detestable that she would be driven nuts. In fact, we were concerned that she would want to get out of the house and escape into the homes of school friends where there might be standards of behavior we weren't comfortable with.

When we told Jenny that we had decided to get a dog, we thought she would be deliriously happy, but in fact she responded by saying she wasn't sure she wanted a dog any more. When we asked her why she felt that way, Jen told us that she wasn't sure she wanted to go through the pain and grief she knew she would experience when the dog died. Anyway, Jen finally decided it was OK for the family to get a dog.

Born on October 9, 2000, Cory arrived in our home about seven weeks old. She spent her first night crying piteously because she missed her family. Jenny stayed up with her all night and slept next to Cory to give her whatever comfort she could.

One of the first things I noticed about Cory were her eye lashes—soft, beautiful, and human-like. It made her seem like one of us rather than a dog.

I never saw Cory more utterly contented and deeply serene as when she sat on Jenny's bed as Jenny was going to sleep while Jenny petted her. I swear I could see a smile on Cory's face from the sheer pleasure of it!

Whenever Kim came home, one of her special treats for Cory was to run around the lower floor of our house with a treat in her hand while Cory chased after her with her tail wagging. Cory loved that!

Tina gave us sound advice when Cory first showed signs of being sick. Tina said, "Just talk to her as if she's the healthiest dog in the world." That was good advice which we took to heart. Tina also remembers how Cory would always know when Tina was sad. Cory would follow Tina into her room and just sit and be with Tina while Tina cried. Tina says, "She knew."

To celebrate and commemorate Cory's 10th birthday last year, Gail arranged for Sara Wipfler, a gifted photographer, to come to our house to take scores of photos as Cory played like a puppy in our backyard chasing tennis balls and other toys. I'm grateful Gail did that. Cory was in peak form, so Gail and Sara captured her at her best in exquisite and gorgeous photos.

Cory had a special place in her heart for our family friend Betty. Whenever Betty arrived to help us in the house, Cory would go bananas with excitement, her whole body exploding in an ecstatic kaleidoscope of motion. She would make whimpering, bleating noises as she tried to express to Betty how thrilled she was to see her.

Cory would calm down after the initial excitement of Betty's arrival and would be lying on the study floor as I worked. When Betty came in to clean the study, Cory seemingly didn't move a muscle, except that her tail would start thumping really hard on the floor. Whack! Whack! Whack! Her tail was so expressive.

Gail and I are so pleased that Cory and Kareena spent some time together. I hope Kareena will retain a memory of Cory. I was always impressed by the way Cory behaved around Kareena. Cory could have easily knocked her over, but she seemed to know instinctively that this little person was precious beyond all words and that she had an obligation to be extra gentle around Kareena.

I could put my hand in Cory's mouth and she would never bite or hurt me in any way. While she had strong jaws, it was in her nature to be gentle and not hurt anyone. Affection poured out of her like sunrays pour out of the sun.

Cory was highly food motivated. One of our family traditions when celebrating birthdays is to hide single dollars around the house for the person being celebrated to search for and find (with the number of dollars equal to the birthday). We did this once, but made the mistake of hiding some of them on or near the floor and then leaving them there while we went out for a meal at a local restaurant. When we returned, we were baffled why some of the dollars were missing, but later realized that Cory had eaten them! They showed up the next day on our daily walk!

Some random memories: Cory loved to charge around the tennis backboard court chasing tennis balls. She loved to "sing" whenever Jenny played the trumpet. We loved her "play posture"—her rump thrust up into the air over stretched and dipping shoulders—and I could almost hear her saying, "Come on, Dad, let's play together and have the best fun!" She would love to roll over on her back to invite tummy tickles. As a puppy, she loved to rest on a small bookshelf in the kitchen. So cute! She hated thunder and lightning (and fireworks) and would hide under my desk shaking. She loved to roll in the grass. She loved it when Jenny took her to Norwood Park to play and run.

Cory was a really beautiful dog. Of course, she had no notion of this, but people were naturally drawn to her, and whenever we were out on walks, I would often receive compliments about her photogenic looks.

Thanks to Jenny, Cory was a therapy dog for about three years at the Carriage Hill Nursing Home. Jenny, Cory, and I would visit there on Sundays, and Cory brought her uninhibited playfulness, contagious high spirits, and loving joie de vivre to the residents.

Losing Cory leaves a huge hole in our lives. She was a devoted companion and friend. She was always in a good mood, always lived in the moment, and played at every opportunity. We all adored her and give profound thanks for her wonderful life.

2012

Tuesday, April 10, 2012
I sent the following letter to the family today:

> To my precious family,
> Two experiences to share:
>
> I've recently rediscovered a technique for finding serenity that I never should have forgotten. When I was 17, I had to have some teeth extracted. I suddenly realized to my surprise and consternation that my parents were going to leave me completely on my own for this with zero emotional support. Dentist visits back then were not as pain-free as they are now, and so, feeling quite apprehensive, I searched around desperately for something to help me deal with my fear and the anticipated trauma. I found a little book that told me one way to deal with pain was to focus on my breathing. I did this, and I noticed how it helped make the tooth extractions more bearable.
>
> I had forgotten that incident until I recently read *Spontaneous Happiness* by Dr. Andrew Weil. From him, I re-learned this technique and how to apply it in a situation in which I occasionally find myself. I sometimes lie in bed, or wake in the night, with frightening, loose, irrational worries floating seemingly uninvited into my mind. Usually these are absurd anxieties dealing with the safety of the family or some other thing that matters intensely to me. These ephemeral, extreme, and nutty thoughts keep me awake with worry, accomplish nothing, interfere with my sleep, and are negative and destructive with no redeeming features.
>
> By reading Andrew Weil's book and remembering my experience of getting some teeth extracted as a teenager, I have been practicing a new technique of helping rid myself of those nasty, upsetting, and nerve-wracking mental wisps that float creepily around the crevices of my mind when I least want them. I focus on my breathing! I can do this, even if I'm dog-tired, and it seems to be an effective way to block unwelcome thoughts. Of course, they teach this in yoga all the time! I find that if I'm focused on my breathing, my mind has no ability to entertain other thoughts.
>
> Second experience: do you remember how several weeks ago Melanie in AU's tech support unintentionally deleted everything on my calendar in my iPhone? At the time, although I reacted with equanimity and calmness, I felt it was a disaster and wondered how I would ever recover. Melanie literally deleted hundreds of commitments and meetings from my calendar which was not backed up anywhere else. The funny thing about this calamitous debacle is how in hindsight, it turned out to be not just a nugatory, trifling matter, but to actually be a good thing! I started keeping my calendar not in my iPhone, but in Outlook on my laptop, and I have discovered this to be a far faster and better method of keeping track of my commitments and promises than doing it on my iPhone. In short, Melanie's mistake turned out to be a blessing in disguise.
>
> I love you.
> Dad/Chris
> XXXOOO

July 28, 2012
    Darling Kimmie, here are my answers to your questions re my five-year stint dabbling in stand-

up comedy in local DC comedy clubs. I hope it helps your chapter on how to deal with setbacks and disappointments. I love you. Dad   XXXOOO

_____

When did you decide to explore stand-up comedy? How old were you? (Specific age when took first class?)

When I was 57 with a successful and jam-packed career as a professor and filmmaker, my oldest daughter Kimberly, then 26, came home one day from a class at the Bethesda Writing Center and gave me a flyer she had picked up for six classes on learning how to be a stand-up comic.

"Dad, you should do this—you like making people laugh," she said to me.

I looked at the flyer, my heart stirred, but I played coy. I replied, "Kim, I don't have time for that, but thanks for thinking of me."

The flyer stayed on my desk for a week or so and then I picked it up again. "Why not?" I said to myself. "If not now, when?"

The final class involved performing at a local comedy club. The challenge intrigued me. I signed up for the six evening classes and started trying to think of funny ideas.

Why? Was this a childhood dream? Can you be specific about what inspired it? When you were making films, were you dreaming of being a stand-up comic?

My first happy memory from my childhood is of making my family roar with laughter when I was about four years old. The power was intoxicating. I heard my mother say rhetorically to someone else in the family (my parents had four sons and I was the youngest), "I wonder how many famous people there are?"

I instinctively saw my chance. I sat down, put my hand under my chin in a "thinking" pose, feigned all the seriousness I could muster, and said, "Well let's see now. First, we have Sir Winston Churchill..." I knew I wouldn't need to go any further because I knew at that point the family would burst into laughter as the site of this little itty-bitty four year old acting like a knowledgeable professor.

Thinking back on it, I have no idea now if they were laughing *with* me or *at* me. All I knew was that I relished the power and delight of making them guffaw.

As I grew up, some of my most pleasurable memories were of making people laugh uncontrollably. Before becoming more serious in my late teens, I was the class clown and delighted in slapstick and verbal comedy, often at the expense of the teacher.

While I have those happy memories, becoming a stand-up comedian wasn't a childhood dream because my parents wouldn't have countenanced it. They wanted their boys to succeed in highly regarded professional careers. Stand-up comedy as a career wasn't on the family radar.

I never dreamed of becoming a stand-up comic because I was too obsessed with building my career. Besides, my career was deeply fulfilling to me, so I didn't feel anything was lacking.

Why hadn't you pursued it previously, earlier in your career?

See previous answer. It hadn't occurred to me until you gave me the flyer.

Could you send me a sample of the jokes you used in your routine- about mom, raising daughters, making films? If you have your old script I would love to quote from it!

I'll attach them.

When/who asked you to stop performing Saturday nights, or why did you stop? Were you crushed/very disappointed? How did you feel?

After working as a comic in local comedy clubs for about a year, Curt Shackelford, a guy who ran several local comedy clubs, saw me perform and invited me to give a set at one of his clubs. In this way, we got to know each other. He knew how to run a comedy club, and I had the high level contacts and social status to open doors and meet the right people. So after a lot of work, we founded a new comedy club at the Bethesda Hyatt in Bethesda, MD. We mutually agreed that if we pulled this off, I would be the resident MC.

This worked great for about four years. I would MC the Saturday night comedy nights regularly (while also performing occasionally at other comedy clubs on other nights) and he took care of setting up the stage and microphone, collecting the money at the door, and attending to many other logistical details.

Then one day he sent me an e-mail out of the blue. It read:

> Hi Chris-
> I've got to start using professional comics to MC Hyatt shows--the Montgomery Drafthouse is opening next month in Silver Spring and will be competing with Hyatt. (they are using pro comics)
> Your sets have been inconsistent lately--some great, some not so great.
> I can afford inconsistency when nobody is on my turf, but not when I have to compete with another club who is using pros--
> I fully realize you helped me build the show to what it is, but the show has to change to meet the current threat.
> These Montgomery Drafthouse people are highly organized and have deep pockets, and are working from an existing successful model (Arlington Drafthouse).
> They know what they're doing and that scares me--I have to revamp the show to meet this challenge.
> They aren't going to shut down after a few weeks like the Bethesda Comedy Club did--these guys are planning to dominate all of Montgomery County.
> Curt Shackelford

I felt wounded, angry, and indignant. I couldn't believe that Curt would have the nerve and temerity to fire me after all I'd done to create and promote the Bethesda Hyatt comedy club.

I was so embarrassed by this humiliation that I tried to hide the reality from others. I didn't admit to anyone what had really happened, except to my wife Gail and my daughters. I sent them the following e-mail: *(Kim, I'm still looking for it. I remember it contained advice on how to survive setbacks. Maybe you have a copy?)*

But to everyone else, I masked my failure by explaining (well, this was partially true) that I had a new book coming out and I needed to focus all my attention on marketing and promoting it. I tried to save face.

Did that cause you to shift gears in your career- focus less on standup, and more on other interests- book writing, teaching?

After Curt fired me as MC at the Bethesda Hyatt Comedy Club, I could have gone on performing comedy at other venues, but I lost my appetite for it.

So I focused intensely on giving speeches, teaching, making films, and promoting my new book.

I also found that I could use a lot more humor in my speeches and gain more satisfaction from that than by performing stand-up comedy.

Now, how do you think about that experience? Do you feel like your stand up helps you in the rest of your career—with your teaching, your speaking? Do you incorporate former jokes into that, or just use lessons learned?

I look back on my venture into stand-up comedy with great fondness. I learned a lot about performing on stage, which helps me in my speaking and teaching. And it gave me the chance to study comedy and joke-telling, skills that are important to me in all the endeavors in my life.

I failed at stand-up comedy because I never reached my goal of performing on a regional or national stage, the goal I had set for myself in my personal mission statement (attached). On the other hand, I succeeded in the sense that now I won't die regretting that I never tried my hand at stand-up comedy.

Are you glad that you pursued stand up or do you ever regret it, given the inevitable rejection in the industry? How do you think about the experience now, in retrospect?

I'm very glad and have no regrets. The pain of being fired has long gone. All I feel now is the pride in having succeeded as a local (and paid!) comic for five years in the DC area. I'm also writing a book about jokes, humor, and comedy, inspired by the experience.

July 29, 2012
Later I sent Kimmie the following PS:

PS Kimmie, I looked in the family journals and found that missing letter to the family in which I informed you I'd been fired by Curt. Here is an excerpt from my journal:

I also shared Curt's note with the family and sent it to them with the following cover note:

My loves,

As you can see from Curt's e-mail below, he no longer wants me to MC for him. This is a blow!

When his e-mail first arrived this morning, I felt down. But this may be a blessing in disguise. I'm glad to have the extra time to put into writing my book, and strategically I'm probably wiser to focus more on giving speeches rather than doing stand-up. The typical audience at comedy clubs is not "my" audience (compared, say, to the audience at a film conference or big dinner).

When people ask me when I'm performing next, I'll just tell them that I'm taking a break to focus on my book. When the book is done, I'll examine my options then and decide whether to keep performing stand-up at other places or put my energy elsewhere.

It isn't fun watching one of your life's goals experience a setback, but it happens to everyone. All you can do is face the situation boldly, clearly understand what is going on, decide your options, and pursue a new set of goals with renewed optimism, vigor and energy.

I read somewhere that a winner is not someone who doesn't get knocked down, but someone who never stops getting up after being knocked down. (I think the original was more eloquent than that.) Anyway, I'll make lemon from this lemonade!

I love you!
Dad/Chris
XXXOOO

Jen replied:

Thanks for setting such a good example about handling setbacks!! Sounds like it might be for the best at this point. And I bet mom will be happy to be able to have dates on Saturday nights again.

xox

I responded:

Thanks, Jen. It's no fun being rejected, but making as many offers in life as possible is what makes a great life, and that inevitably comes with lots of rejections. So paradoxically, the more rejections, the more successful you are. That's why I always say "welcome failure."

XXXOOO

Tina replied to my first letter (and adding to Jen's response):

Hey dad,
that is disappointing but I think your response is perfect. You have better things to focus your time and enegy on. Also, Curt does not seem very professional. I didn't like his

email.

And yes, more dates with mom!!! You can also start working on your book on being a father. and the children's book!

love
tina

Kim added to what Tina said:
Yes dad, that is a really good example for us on handling set backs!

Sujay wrote:
I agree with Christina - his e-mail was not very nice! Your response was great.

Sunday, July 29, 2012 (again)
Kim is hard at work on her second book and wrote to me with a request:

Hi Dad!
Would you be willing to be in my book for my chapter on how to deal with setbacks or disappointments? I would love to use the example of how you explored stand up and then stopped pursuing it to focus on your other interests instead- writing, teaching, etc... would that be possible??

If so, could you please answer these questions for me??

When did you decide to explore stand-up comedy? How old were you? (Specific age when took first class?)

Why? What this a childhood dream? Can you be specific about what inspired it? When you were making films, were you dreaming of being a stand-up comic?

Why hadn't you pursued it previously, earlier in your career?

Could you send me a sample of the jokes you used in your routine- about mom, raising daughters, making films? If you have your old script I would love to quote from it!

When/who asked you to stop performing Saturday nights, or why did you stop? Were you crushed/very disappointed? How did you feel?

Did that cause you to shift gears in your career- focus less on standup, and more on other interests- book writing, teaching?

Now, how do you think about that experience? Do you feel like your stand up helps you in the rest of your career—with your teaching, your speaking? Do you incorporate former jokes into that, or just use lessons learned?

Are you glad that you pursued stand up or do you ever regret it, given the inevitable rejection in the industry? How do you think about the experience now, in retrospect?

Saturday, October 6, 2012
I sent the following letter to the Kim, Sujay, Tina, and Jenny today:

Dear Kimmie, Sujay, Tina, and Jen,
I thought you might be interested in the following story.

As you know, I attended the BLUE Ocean Film Festival last week in Monterey, CA.

One of the people we honored was the film producer and explorer Jim Cameron (*Titanic*, *Avatar*). He received a Lifetime Achievement Award.

As you may know, Cameron recently dived to the deepest part of the ocean (the Marianas Trench), the only person ever to do this alone. It is over a mile deeper than Mount Everest is tall. It was a gutsy, brave thing to do. The pressures at those depths are crushingly high.

When he gave his acceptance speech at BLUE, he talked about how he did it, and we were all fascinated by his stories and how he overcame the challenges he faced.

He knew that all of us in the audience were filmmakers, environmentalists, and ocean conservation activists. He alerted us during his speech that he wanted to offer a challenge to us.

He told us that the biggest threat to the ocean came from climate change—loss of coral, acidification, rising levels, etc.

Then he said his wife Suzy about six months ago had made him sit down and watch the theatrical film *Forks Over Knives*.

Cameron said it had a radical and overwhelming influence on him. He said he immediately went to the kitchen and threw out everything related to animals---meat, dairy, etc.

The film taught him that big industrial agriculture was a far bigger contributor to greenhouse gases than the residential and transportation sectors combined (check). It is huge.

He said that anyone who is serious about ocean conservation and climate change has to be on a plant-based diet. Not to do this is to indulge in the most crass and flagrant hypocrisy.

He said that since going over to a plant-based diet six months ago, he has never felt so good. He runs twice as far as he used to, his cholesterol is way down, and he has much more energy and vitality.

He told us that a plant-based diet is good for everyone, including animals.

He went on to say that he was resolved now to spend his career making films on this topic which would make a difference and change the world. Raising awareness isn't enough he declared. He intends for his films to change society and create real action.

I was delighted to hear all this. It all made good sense to me.

The irony was that during the grand dinner following his speech, meat was served!

I was sitting one seat away from Jim Cameron during dinner and had the opportunity to talk to him about his speech. He was delighted to learn about the food preferences of Tina and Jenny! He and I both selected the vegetarian choice and both agreed it was delicious.

It was interesting to learn that a film can have such a dramatic impact on someone.

I thought you'd all be interested to hear about this. I liked him very much.

Love,
Dad/Chris
XXXOOO

Sunday, October 7, 2012

I called Tina last night to see how she was doing (she is in the middle of an intensive period of non-stop work at her hospital) and she told me that a cardiologist had been causing her trouble and was a bully. I immediately wrote her the following unsolicited letter:

Hi loveydove. Dealing with a bully is never easy, but you have to stand up to that cardiologist, otherwise he will continue to take pleasure in making you miserable.

Avoid him when you can.

If you can't avoid him, and he's rude, you might say, "Dr. Smith, unless you stop your flagrantly abusive rudeness, I intend to seek legal redress through HR." Or words along those lines. You might send him an e-mail to that effect and cc your department head or your attending.

Or you could say to his face, or in an e-mail, "I refuse to have anything to do with you while you persist in treating me so disrespectfully, nastily, and abusively."

I would also keep notes on exactly what he said and when (date and time), so that later you can put these telling details in a memo to your department head and/or HR. It is much more effective and powerful than saying something vague and amorphous like, "over the last month or so, he's been rude to me on several occasions."

Bullies like to pick on weak people, so don't act weak. Always smile, stand tall, be calm, and exhibit a strong demeanor and disposition.

Seek help from your attending physician. Everyone has had to deal with bullies, including your attending doctor, and so she will be able to give you sound advice.

If necessary, you may have to raise your voice to him to tell him you are reporting him for harassment, intimidation, and unprofessional behavior (or again, put words to that effect in an e-mail to him with a cc to your boss).

Other words that might be useful to you: arrogant, supercilious, cutting, acerbic, biting, undercutting, condescending, overly-critical, the exact opposite of collegial and collaborative, destructive, damaging to morale, not a team player.

Hope this helps, treasure. It is absolutely unacceptable and intolerable that another doctor should behave that way towards you and it has to stop immediately.

I love you.
Dad
XXXOOO

Sunday, October 28, 2012
I sent the following e-mail to Tina this evening:

Hi Tina,
Mommy tells me that you are not very happy because of understandable money worries and because you're not enjoying being a resident.

I totally understand.

When I was your age (and younger), I was often unhappy—stressed, overly-busy, adrift, frenetic, unsettled, ill-at-ease, without purpose.

I solved this problem by creating a personal mission statement which reflected, in great detail and with the most inspirational language I could muster, my vision for the life I wanted to lead and the values I wanted to live by.

Every week, I would reflect on this personal mission statement, and plan my week proactively around it.

This process helped me, over time, find peace and inner serenity. It helped keep me focused and to be purposeful, diligent, and energized—however enervating and stressful the circumstances I found myself in.

Above all, it gave my life purpose and meaning—which is the secret to finding happiness and fulfillment.

Sometimes well-meaning but naïve friends and family members would try to give me advice. "Take a vacation." "Take a break." "Have a drink." "Go to the pub of the evening." "Watch television and relax." "Buy yourself a nice car or some other luxury." "Take it easy and don't work so hard." "Be comfortable and relax." "Go to some fancy resort for a few days."

All this advice was worse than useless because none of it addressed the problem. The problem was that I lacked exciting goals and having projects that I was passionate about.

To be happy, I realized I needed to throw myself into one of the world's great social causes (in my case, energy conservation and environmental protection) so I could be involved in something that would outlast me and was bigger than I was.

Taking it easy and relaxing simply exacerbated the problem and didn't help at all.

I realized something that some people seemed to miss. Happiness came from inside me, not from what was going on around me.

This is why you find wealthy people who are miserable and all they do is whine and complain, and other people in concentration camps in unbelievably harsh and deprived conditions who are happy. (I think you know the famous book on that topic called *Man's Search for Meaning* by Viktor Frankl)

Happiness is something you can intentionally choose, however destitute and dispiriting your situation. For a start, there are always people around us who are worse off who need help.

Having scribbled these notes to you, I realize you know all this already. Your wonderful and inspiring blog posts, your yoga, the books you read, the guidance you seek from wise people, the maxims you collect, all speak to your wisdom in this area of finding happiness, fulfillment and success. You are *way ahead* of most other people! You have already dipped into, as I have, the wisdom literature, so I'm not telling you anything you don't already know!

Good luck, treasure, as you fight your way back to finding a fulfilling life. I hope these few reflections help.

You are a wonderful person with a great future ahead of you.

I love you.
Dad
XXXOOO

Tina replied:
Hi Dad!
I needed this tonight - your email came at a perfect time. I have lost some of my energy and inspiration and have been feeling drained and burned out.

I do need to draft a personal mission statement and reconnect with passions and projects that excite me.

You are right to be careful about trying to mask it with things like going away on vacation. I think I really need to reconnect with my basic values and passions and get back on track.

I found a draft of your mission statement and am borrowing some of your words since I don't have them right now... I hope you don't mind!

Do you mind if I share parts of your letter on my blog? It's so good!

love you!
tina

I immediately responded:

Darling Tina,

I am so happy to receive your note below! I am so proud of you for responding in that positive way! That says a lot about your character.

I'm attaching my personal mission statement. The copy you have may be out of date. I tweak and edit it constantly. So please use the attached.

Please borrow all the words you want from it. That's a great way to get started. Use anything you want in it and take it as your own.

I'd be honored for you to share my letter on your blog. That's a wonderful idea to help others.

I think you'd be amazed to find out how many other people are struggling like you. Many people are suffering far more acutely, although you'd have no idea by looking at them.

Would you mind if I pasted my letter to you, and your reply, in the Family Journal?

I'm also attaching a handout I wrote for a workshop I give four or five times a year (most recently a week or two ago, and before that in Monterey, CA, at the end of September) on success, fulfillment, and productivity. I hope you find it helpful. My students often tell me it's the most useful and inspiring class they've ever had. The Career Center at AU has asked me to give it to the whole university next semester!

By the way, I think one reason for my own profound happiness is I have rid myself of things that don't contribute to my goals—such as watching television. I manage my time with extreme care and don't waste a second. Whenever I'm in the car, I'm listening to biographies of famous people and learning from their lives. (I'm currently listening to Ron White's magnificent biography of Abraham Lincoln.) Of course, being a member of a loving family is the most important contributor to my happiness.

Hang in there, loveydove. You're doing great. Keep focused on what really matters to you.

I love you.
Dad
XXXOOO

2014

Thursday, July 24, 2014
I sent the following e-mail to the family today about Kimmie:

> To my precious family,
> I recently came across some private writing (not in the family journal) I did on July 15, 2001 and I thought I would share it with you because it reflects well on Kimmie!
>
> Here it is:
>
> > Daddy never said much to me. He never said "I love you". He never said, "I'm proud of you." I felt us drifting apart. We were always friendly on the surface, but there was no closeness. I missed that very much. Over the years, I got used to it, so much so, that when he died on April 14, 2001, I didn't feel the pain of much grief. It was as though he had died a long time ago. Kim intuitively knew the disappointment I felt and did her part to alleviate it. One day, showing a sensitivity that belied her years, she said to me, "You know, Dad, Grandpa is very proud of you. He is always talking about you and saying how proud he is of you." Kim wanted me to know that. She knew I needed to hear that. We are not all blessed with sensitive daughters like Kim. So don't wait. Don't hold back. Tell that son or daughter or parent how special they are to you. Every day that you delay saying "I love you" makes it harder to do because we get into habitual ways of behaving that are hard to change.
>
> I love you!
> Dad/Chris
> XXXOOO

Monday, November 17, 2014
I sent the following note to Kim and Sujay about Kareena:

> Dear Kim and Sujay,
> It was only yesterday evening when I suddenly remembered the following conversation I had with Kareena yesterday afternoon.
>
> Kareena and Neal were playing in the study with me, exploring Grandpa's Bag of Tricks.
>
> Kareena was getting a little miffed that Neal was diluting the attention I was hitherto giving solely to her.
>
> So I said to her that I had something very interesting to show her and that was my big dictionary. So while Neal played happily on the floor with various things from my bag, I helped Kareena stand up on a chair and take a look at my big dictionary on the music stand in my study. (I use it standing up.)
>
> She found it fascinating and loved turning the pages. When she saw something she recognized, like a map, she would point that out with enthusiasm.
>
> As this was going on, the following conversation ensued:

Kareena: If you had another granddaughter, would she be as special as me?

Me: Nana and I don't have another granddaughter. You're the only one.

K: Yes, but you might have another one in the future. If you did, would she be as special as me?

Me: (thinking quickly and carefully) She would be as special as you, and YOU would be as every bit as special as her.

K: If you don't have another granddaughter, would that make me the most special granddaughter in the world?

Me: You are so deeply special and Nana and we adore you. You couldn't be more special to us.

K: If another granddaughter didn't exist, then they would be invisible and I would be the most special.

Me (laughing) That is so true!

I thought you'd enjoy that!

I love you.
Dad/Chris
XXXOOO

2015

Sunday, August 23, 2015

We've had Kareena and Neal staying with us for the last 24 hours, while Kimmie and Sujay had a break in Berkley Springs, WVa.

I sent Kimmie and Sujay the following e-mail:

Dear Kimmie and Sujay,
So glad you had a happy time in Berkley Springs!

Kareena and Neal were wonderful. We had a super time with them. Here are some of the things we did:

1. Science experiment: keeping the tissue dry when you dip a glass under water because of the trapped air

2. Science experiment: catching a falling dollar

3. Science experiment: the magic pencil that turns to rubber

4. The big bath with the Jacuzzi jets of water (plus ice cubes, plus beach buckets and pool play things) (plus Kareena saying suddenly, "I don't want children!")

5. Rockets (Neal enjoyed it this time!)

6. Stories from my childhood

7. Hopscotch in the driveway (plus Kareena practicing writing numbers)

8. Sword fights

9. Big balloons on rubber bands, which you punch rapidly

10. Neal and Grandpa tossing a balloon back and forth

11. K, N, and Grandpa forming a triangle and throwing two big balloons around the triangle (Neal catching and throwing really well!)

12. Reading books (lots)

13. Building a big fort in the basement (plus reading about Bartholomew and Nelly inside it with a flashlight)

14. Sack races in the basement (plus wrestling on the big bed)

15. Spoon dangling from their noses

16. Put five objects selected randomly from Grandpa's Bag of Tricks, put them on table, close eyes, take one away. Which one is missing? (plus close eyes, put an object in hands, what is it?)

17. K and N doing exercises with me. (K is becoming athletic—so impressed)

18. The dinosaurs puppet show at Glenn Echo (plus riding on the carousel)

I'm sure Mommy/Gail will think of other things.

Thanks for letting K and N spend time with us! They are adorable!

We are feeling tired after an intense 24 hours. I joked to Mommy/Gail that we are suffering from Post-Traumatic Babysitting Disorder!

Love,
Dad/Chris
XXXOOO

2016

Wednesday, May 18, 2016
Tina sent us the following note today:

> Hi mom and dad!
> Dad, I hope you're still feeling better!
>
> I wanted to get your thoughts on this other idea I've been thinking about - doing the online/part time 2 year University of Arizona Integrative Medicine Fellowship -- this is Dr. Weil's program. Here is some info on it:
>
> http://integrativemedicine.arizona.edu/education/fellowship/index.html
>
> This I could start this fall on maternity leave, do part time online while still doing my current job, and become more specialized in this area/nutrition/integrative medicine.
>
> It would cost about $12,000 each year for 2 years (and no I don't think PAMF would pay but can always ask).
>
> What do you think?
>
> love
> tina

I replied (incorporating Gail's helpful edits):
> Hi Tina, I can see some positives in this, but my sense is that it is not a good fit for you now.
>
> Here are my thoughts about the pluses and minuses.
>
> I see that there are pluses. They are outlined persuasively on the website. It's also the perfect area for you to specialize in. I think you would be wonderfully successful. It taps into everything you are interested in and good at. AND what Dr. Weil teaches is so important, too.
>
> Here are some thoughts and questions that you should carefully research and probe. The website is good at its marketing job.
>
> After 7-8 years of study and your own personal interest, aren't you already up on this learning curve? Do you really need to take this degree? How about just declaring yourself an expert in this area and specializing in it without doing the degree? Just tell PAMF that's what you want to do and you want them to support you. Become an autodidact like Abe Lincoln and so many others. Study the issues on your own. Do your own online degree without paying all that money! Teach yourself what you need to know! When I got into television in my mid-thirties, I just learned on the job. I didn't go back to school to get a degree in filmmaking and get into heavy debt.
>
> $24K is a lot of money!
>
> Doing a degree online is lonely and very hard work. I'm currently taking a class at AU (I went to

the 2ⁿᵈ class this morning) on how to teach online. For students, it is very challenging. And the lack of F2F interactions can be very draining. Chase is doing an online course. You might ask him how he finds it. I know from Jenny he spends many exhausting hours working to get his Masters degree.

You are going to be constantly exhausted and sleep-deprived during your maternity leave. Doing the hard work required by the online degree will be very stressful.

You'd hate being away for 3 weeks from your children over the next 2 years. How would that work?

Is the degree worth $24K and all pain to get it? Does PAMF recognize the degree as worth anything? Would NIH or any respected health body recognize it? Would patients attach any value to it?

If you do decide to move forward with Arizona, only do it **after checking with former students to see if they think in it worth it.** You can't believe anything on the website just as you wouldn't believe a barber who recommends you need a haircut. Like AU, these organizations are fiercely determined to get your money.

If PAMF won't support you, it raises the question of why. Shouldn't PAMF be a leader in this area? Why haven't they established a Fellowship along these lines? Wouldn't they be able to generate a lot more business (attract more patients) if they trumpeted their expertise in this area? Of course they would. Why aren't they doing it and making you one of their leading doctors in this area? Is there a mentor (or your boss or someone) at PAMF with whom you could have a serious discussion of what alternatives PAMF might be able to consider to help you get this type of expertise without the 2 year course? I think you need to be a pioneer at PAMF on this and insist they do it. Don't take no for an answer. It sounds central to their mission. I would put together a plan for PAMF and present to your supervisors.

Good luck, treasure, in thinking this through. I hope the above comments are helpful and constructive.

I love you.
Dad
XXXOOO

Wednesday, May 18, 2016
It's Tina's birthday tomorrow and so I sent her the email below tonight:

Darling Tina,
Happy birthday for tomorrow, treasure! We'll be thinking about you all day—Mommy as she flies to Smith College, and me as I'm working away at home.

We adore you and are so incredibly proud of all you have accomplished.

You've gone to the best schools, done well in all of them, had the best medical training anyone can get, tenaciously persevered through very tough times (e.g., cycling in the rain through unsafe neighborhoods in the dark in the middle of the night to get to your job!), absorbed punishing schedules without giving up, survived mean doctors and mean patients, had to endure grueling conditions, sick and cranky patients, and goodness knows what else.

As I say, we are so proud of you—your courage, your tenacity, your intelligence, and your never giving up.

On top of all that you have created with CJ a fabulous family!!!!

You're like me in that you are constantly wondering if you are doing the right thing with your life, and relentlessly searching to elevate your life to a higher level. Good for you. Keep that up. Keep searching for what you really love to do. It took until I was in my late-fifties to realize what I really love to do is write and teach (and, of course, be a Dad!!!!).

Hang in there, sweetiepie. You are doing great and have so much to be thankful for.

Happy Birthday for tomorrow! Mommy and I will both call you tomorrow to say hi.

I love you.
Dad
XXXOOO

Saturday, May 21, 2016

Tomorrow is Jenny's birthday. I sent her the following email tonight:

Darling Jenny,
Happy birthday for tomorrow, treasure! We'll be thinking about you all day—Mommy as she flies home from Smith College, and me as I'm working away at home.

We adore you and are so incredibly proud of all you have accomplished.

You've gone to the best schools, done well in all of them, had the best legal training anyone can get, tenaciously persevered through very challenging and rigorous jobs, developed a deep love for all things healthy and fit, and have an abiding interest in animal welfare. And I'm so grateful for all the help you give me on my writing and websites.

As I say, we are so proud of you—your tenacity, your intelligence, your judgment, and your steady focus on your long-term goals.

I know you will keep searching for what you really want to do with your life. It took until I was in my late-fifties for me to realize that what I really love to do is write and teach (and, of course, be a Dad!!!!).

You are doing great and have so much to be thankful for. We can't wait to see you on Thursday! Please say hi to Chase from us!

Happy Birthday for tomorrow! Mommy and I will call you tomorrow to say hi.

I love you.
Dad
XXXOOO

2017

Sunday, September 24, 2017

Kareena and Neal spent the weekend with us, so Kim and Sujay could go away for a night to celebrate Sujay's 40th birthday.

We had a super time with Kareena and Neal. This afternoon, I sent the following email to Kim and Sujay:

Hi Kim and Sujay,

I hope you had a super time this weekend! Gail and I had a wonderful time with K and N. Here are some of the things we did with them:

1. Bubble bath
2. Cleared out and organized one of my desk drawers that contains scores of interesting things I collect to show K and N
3. Neal and I organized the table by the big TV
4. Read lots of books, including a bio on Jane Goodall with K
5. Neal did a quiz with me (like 2 + 2, 3+1, 4-1, etc.)
6. K practiced cartwheels
7. N did Geronimo, which involves jumping off our bed onto by back without getting eaten by all the sharks and crocodiles around my feet
8. Neal and I did some boxing and I showed him some of my boxing moves
9. K and N each wrote each other a letter, prepared the envelopes, added stamps, and we walked to the post box to mail them
10. I read them the well-known poem by Lewis Carroll called *Father William*
11. K and I discussed games for her birthday party at the club (I'll email you separately about that)
12. We did a great science experiment illustrating Bernoulli's Principle and how planes fly (the hair dryer keeping the ping pong ball in the air)
13. Neal did BrainQuest with me and enjoyed the learning
14. I did a relaxation session with K and N during which they have to relax every muscle in their body
15. We played the "glad/sad/mad" game where we each take turns to talk
16. I showed them how to meditate and say things like "May you be healthy and strong" to each other (it's called a "lovingkindness" meditation)
17. I showed K and N my school report from 1955 when I was just a few months older than K. I got a C in Art and a C in "Handwork" and my "Religious Knowledge" was assessed as "Satisfactory"!
18. I gave them a taste of falafels ("too salty"), lentils (didn't like), and beet juice (K thought okay, but N didn't like)

I'm sure Gail will think of things I've forgotten!

Love, Dad
XXXOOO

2018

January 1, 2018

To my precious family:

Dear Gail, Kimmie, Tina, Jenny, Sujay, CJ, Chase, Kareena, Neal, JJ, and Max,

If you are reading this, it means that I have died. Perhaps it will be suddenly and unexpectedly, or perhaps after a long illness, from something like prostate cancer.

I hope I had a chance to say goodbye to you all. If not, then this letter is designed to fill that sad omission.

For decades now, I've wrestled with the problem of how best to prepare Kimmie, Tina, and Jenny if I were to suddenly die. One worry was the thought that Mommy and I might perish together in, say, a plane crash. The chances are highly remote, but it could happen. Mommy and I periodically talk about it. As the years have gone by, this has become less of a worry for us, because you are all growing up and can take care of yourselves.

Back on October 12, 2006, I wrote the following letter, and whenever Mommy and I left home for a trip together, I placed it in the middle of my desk where it would be easily found. Mommy wrote a similar letter at about the same time, and I would always leave copies of both letters side-by-side on my desk. Okay, here is my letter: (I would include Mommy's letter too, but she has no electronic copy of it.)

> Darling Precious Kimmie, Tina and Jenny,
>
> If you are reading this, something terrible has happened. Whatever happened, remember that you made Mommy and me the happiest people in the world. We couldn't have died feeling any happier, more content, and more at peace.
>
> We are incredibly proud of each of you. You are strong, loving, resourceful, beautiful, courageous, bold, reflective, tenacious, caring, determined, intelligent, and wise. You are living honorable and wonderful lives. The world is a better and richer place for you being here.
>
> A few days ago, Mommy asked me, "What are you most proud of in your life?" Without hesitation, I said, "Kim, Tina and Jenny." I also now add Sujay to that list.
>
> You are all set to continue leading vibrant, optimistic and energetic lives, bringing joy and love to all those with whom you come into contact. Mommy and I know you will continue to live happy, rewarding, and fulfilling lives. We are the luckiest parents in the whole world and we will always adore you.
>
> Remember we will be at all the big events in your lives, in the same way Sujay's father and my parents were at Kim's wedding.
>
> Please tell your children that my biggest sadness in not having the opportunity to be a loving, mischievous, and wise grandfather.

I love you more than I can say.

Your loving Dad
XXXOOO

[Insert Gail's 2006 letter here.]

As I say, if you are reading this letter, it means that I have died. This letter (the one you are holding in your hand) is designed to update the one above from 2006. I have found inspiration from the Stanford Life Review project (https://www.nytimes.com/2016/09/07/well/family/writing-a-last-letter-before-you-get-sick.html). Here is another useful link (https://med.stanford.edu/letter/friendsandfamily.html).

If you are experiencing grief and sadness, then I hope you'll be okay. Grief is exacerbated by regrets, but I hope we've all lived in a way together that any regrets are insignificant or very minor.

I want to tell you how incredibly grateful I am to all of you for being the family that many husbands and fathers only dream about. I've been so extraordinarily lucky, especially meeting and falling in love with Gail back in 1972. You have all been so loving, so caring, so thoughtful, so generous, and so affectionate.

I am so proud of all of you:

- Gail for being such a loving, amazing, compassionate, and understanding wife, life partner, and mother.

- Kim for being such a loving and capable mom, wife, and professional, and for all the books you've written helping people, and for being a wonderful daughter.

- Tina for being such a loving and competent mom, wife, and professional, and for all the patients you've helped as a family doctor, and for being a wonderful daughter.

- Jenny for being such a loving wife and capable lawyer, and for all the pro bono clients you've helped, and for being a wonderful daughter.

- Sujay, for your love of reading (especially history!), your equanimity, your outstanding fathering, and your love and caring for Gail and me.

- CJ for your endless curiosity and love of learning, for your outstanding fathering, and the way you always make Gail and me feel so welcome when we visit you and Tina in Palo Alto.

- Chase for getting your job at Fitbit, for your determination to succeed, and for the touching way you talked to Gail and me about your desire to marry Jenny.

- Kareena, Neal, JJ, and Max for the indescribable joy you bring me, your love of games and play, your wonderful questions, and your inexhaustible love of learning.

Remember the vacation we all spent together in Monterey in August 2017? How much fun was that?! Here is an email I sent you all afterwards with some of our memories:

1. Surfing (Kim, Sujay, CJ, and Chase)
2. Swimming in Jen and Chase's pool with JJ
3. Whales lunge feeding and tail slapping
4. Anchovies jumping out of the ocean onto the beach in countless numbers
5. Birds flying in lyrical and lithe murmurations
6. Beach fire on the beach and fire pit
7. Reading the *Circus Ship* book to the grandkids
8. Train ride through the Redwoods
9. Visit to Monterey Aquarium
10. JJ playing tennis
11. Max's funny "old man" expressions
12. Neal doing exercises
13. Kareena showing how she can do two dances at the same time
14. Gift of a special book from JJ for my 70th birthday
15. Talking to K and N on beach
16. Sujay's 40th birthday and my 70th
17. Watching Wimbledon-level tennis at the Nordic Natural Challenger
18. Playing tennis with CJ
19. Watching Tina and CJ play tennis
20. Tina and me having a handstand competition
21. Happy Hour every day at 5 pm in our hotel room
22. Kim's branding: "Cousin Time"
23. Hide and seek with K, N, and JJ
24. Playing diving games in the pool at Dinah's with Kareena and Sujay
25. Planning for Jen and Chase's December 9 wedding
26. Kim and Sujay enjoying the Carmal Refuge water resort
27. Gail arranging everything (thank you, my love!)
28. Feeding ducks and fish at Dinah's
29. Neal and JJ holding hands as they walked together to the train station
30. JJ's 3rd Birthday party, all the neighbors and the piñata, plus the train ride
31. Seeing Mark and his five kids
32. Going to the Menlo Church with Tina, CJ, JJ, and Max for the evening service
33. Two dinners at Tina and CJ's
34. Babysitting K and N while the other grownups had a drink
35. "Ceej" and "Suj" joke
36. Talk of moving to Denver
37. Having Kareena, Neal, JJ, and Max spend time together
38. Having Kim, Tina, and Jen spend time together (as well as Sujay, CJ, and Chase)
39. Spike ball (thanks to Jen and Chase)
40. Chase and I agreeing that kids need moral education
41. Getting all of us together and realizing these times are special
42. Chase's top secret, and still secret, Fitbit project
43. Jenny trying on her wedding dress and having it sent back to China
44. Chase giving me Sangrias
45. Max in the process of learning to walk
46. Giving JJ and Max baths (and Gail washing their hair with no tears)
47. Dinner with Jen on the last night

48. Dinners at Sanderlings
49. Getting rides on golf carts to get to and from from the beach
50. Tina and CJ playing golf
51. Kareena and Neal showing JJ the red thimble magic trick
52. Kids playing Geronimo with me
53. Seeing Chance
54. Playing catch with a tennis ball on the beach.

I have so many happy and meaningful memories from my life. Here are just a small handful:

- Gail: dancing lessons, playing tennis, club parties, watching *The Crown*, StoryWorth questions

- Kim: when your first book was published

- Tina: when you finished your medical training

- Jenny: the trip you took with Mommy after taking the bar exam

- Sujay: sharing history books on tape

- CJ: playing tennis

- Chase: your personal training sessions

- Kareena: Admiral of the Fleet

- Neal: Geronimo

- JJ: the book you wrote for me for my 70th birthday

- Max: your smile

Thank you to all of you for everything you have done for me. I have so much to thank you each for:

- Gail for your profound love, your wisdom, your values, your empathy, and for teaching me so much.

- Kim, Tina, and Jenny for being fantastic daughters—so loving, so loyal, so affectionate, so generous, so capable, so wise. I learned so much from each of you.

- Sujay, CJ, and Chase for being fantastic sons-in-law. You are the sons I never had.

- Kareena, Neal, JJ, and Max, for letting me be the playful, loving grandpa I always dreamed of being.

I want you all to know that I love you very much

- Gail, I love you for being the most beautiful and wonderful wife a man could ever have.

- Kim, Tina, and Jenny, I love you for being incredible daughters.

- Sujay, CJ, and Chase, I love you for being the best husbands Kim, Tina, and Jenny could every marry.

- Kareena, Neal, JJ, and Max, I love you for being the most spectacular grandchildren a grandpa could ever wish for.

Thank you all for everything you have done for me. It has been an extraordinary honor to have been a part of your lives. I know you'll find peace, love, and joy in the years to come.

I want to end with a few specific goodbye messages:

- Gail, my love, do marry again if you'd like to!

- Kim, Tina, and Jenny, take care of each other and of Mommy. Never let anything come between you.

- Sujay, CJ, and Chase, thanks for taking care of Kim, Tina, and Jenny, and for loving them so profoundly.

- Kareena, Neal, JJ, and Max, I know you'll grow up to be strong, loving, successful, fulfilled, and resilient, that you'll bring joy and light to all those you connect with, and that you'll each leave a special and precious legacy that you can be proud of.

I love you.

Chris/Dad/Grandpa
XXXOOO

Appendix:
Family Stories

Shearer-Palmer Family Stories

By Chris Palmer

Updated November 22, 2017

Important note to the family

You are holding in your hands a first draft of a book on amusing or interesting family stories. It is unfinished—a work in progress. This first version is way out of balance because too many of the stories are about me or come from me. I'm eager to add more stories from everyone else in the family! Please send them to me as they occur to you and I will include them in the next edition. Thanks!

Why I started this project

I started this project because I wanted to find in one place all the best stories relating to our family. It is true that you can find them all in the official family journal and in the official family history books, but that's a lot to wade through to find these gems!

My parents (Mavis and Sidney John Palmer) were deft and skillful storytellers, especially my father. I often wished I had a written account of all their stories.

Author and family expert Bruce Fieler, who writes regularly for the New York Times, says that strong families know—and teach the next generation—their histories. This small book (as well as our family journals and books on our family history) is an attempt to help our children, grandchildren, and great grandchildren, know about their family. Fieler says this will help our progeny to have high self-esteem and more resilience.

Research at Emory University has shown that children who have the most self-confidence know they belong to something bigger than themselves.

The bottom line, says Fieler, is that if you want a happier family, create, refine, and retell the story of your family's best moments, as well as stories about your family's ability to overcome setbacks and disappointments. This small book you are holding is an attempt to do that.

Kimberly

Kim, age 3, and lots of weewee
Kim suddenly said to me, "I have seven vaginas." I replied, "Why do you say that?" Kim replied, "Because I have so much weewee."

Kim, age 5, when she sees a girl with freckles
Kim said, "Her has polka dots on her face!"

Kim, age 5, falls out of bed and then yells she wants to go back to bed
Kim falls out of bed with a big bump. I race around to make sure she is OK. She is crying. I pick her up and hold her tight. Suddenly Kim realized she was OK. She yells, "I WANNA GO BACK TO BED!"

Kim, age 5 or 6, gently reprimands PopPop for burping
We are having breakfast by ourselves at Nana and PopPop's house on the New Jersey shore. The intercom is on by mistake (we had one so we could listen to Tina when she was in her crib). We suddenly hear Ralph burp over the intercom. He is downstairs and doesn't realize the intercom is on. Kim and I laugh silently and go on eating our breakfast. Ten minutes later, Ralph comes upstairs. Kim says to him, "You burped, PopPop, and you didn't say excuse me!"

Kim, age 6, on sharing
In 1986 when Kim was six, I gave her a nature magazine to read (probably Ranger Rick). Kim said, "Is this mine?" I replied, "Yours and Christina's." Kim said, "I want it just to be mine." I responded, "But you are so good at sharing." Kim replied, "Maybe I'm good at it, but I hate it."

Kim and Becky, both 13, getting glued together
When Kim and her friend Becky were in 7th grade, they worked together on a science project at Westland which involved Super Glue. Well, purely by accident, or so they claimed, Kim and Becky got their fingers glued together. This quickly became an emergency and they had to be taken off to hospital where they were successfully separated. However, they were stuck together for over six hours and so this meant when nature called, they had an extra challenge navigating the bathroom.

Kim, age 14, supporting Jen in her petition to Gail and me for a dog
Kim wrote: "A dog will be a constant reminder (which we desperately need) that we need to be relaxed loving beings in order to get the most out of life — a prime goal of our family mission statement."

Kim, age 14, becoming a "changed woman,"
When Kim was about 14, she and her friend Emily went on a Teen Adventure with the National Wildlife Federation in North Carolina. This involved about ten days of hiking 10 to 14 miles a day up and down mountains with 30 pound backpacks. When they felt like complaining, they were encouraged to "suck it up". Kim also got mono, so by the time she and Emily got back, they were exhausted and Kim quite sick. When I met them at the airport, I asked Kim if she had enjoyed herself. She looked at me and said, "Dad, I am a changed woman!"

My awkward behavior when Kim first brought home a boy (Kim age 16?)

When Kim first brought home a boy to meet us, I found this a little awkward, but I always tried to be warm, friendly and relaxed. The first time this happened, in order to look relaxed and friendly, I sat on the end of the kitchen table as I started to say hello to them. I never usually did that but I was trying very hard not to be threatening. As I sat on the end of the table with my feet on a chair, the table became unbalanced, and, much to my embarrassment, the other end began to rise into the air. I dived off the table to stop the table from tipping over, and as I did so, I knocked a large salt shaker over. I then dived for the salt shaker, missed it, and knocked over a glass of water. I felt embarrassed. Kim and the boy were amused, as was Gail.

Kim, age 16, and funny birthday card

Kim, as well as Tina and Jen, has always been affectionate in their birthday cards to Gail and me, and enjoy poking fun at me. Here is one example. Kim has always asked me to review her draft essays and articles, and I have always been delighted to do that. I am deliberately as critical as possible in my feedback on the assumption that this is how I can be most helpful to her. When Kim was about 16, Kim gave me for my birthday a warm birthday letter she wrote to me, and then she pretended that I marked it up as though I were editing it. For example, at the bottom, she wrote (pretending I wrote it):

> Is that the best you could do? Maybe it has a chance of being published in the Bethesda Gazette if you totally rewrite it and get new topic. Give me the next draft when it is ready.

Kim, age 17, and Valentine's Day card

When Kim was 17, she sent me a Valentine's Day card in which she wrote, "Dear Dad, even though you are repressive and authoritarian, I still love you! You are a great dad!" I think we'd had a few fights that week!

Kim, age 17, giving an amusing reply about my enjoyment of working with celebrities

Sometimes I worry that people like me use celebrities more for their own ego satisfaction than to promote conservation. I get a huge kick out of working with famous people. I love to tell stories about camping with Isabella Rossellini on an African safari, about being caught in a blizzard in the Montana wilderness with Jane Fonda, and about being snared with Redford in a big New York City hotel by his tight security system when I was with him for a big dinner event. These stories are true and fun to talk about, but how large an impact celebrities make to the conservation cause when they appear in wildlife films is difficult to measure.

We had a dinner party at our home once, and Kimberly (then 17) was with us. One of our guests asked Kimberly questions about my job and what I enjoyed most. Kimberly responded, "I would have to say working with celebrities." Then she added, "I take that back, it is *telling* people that he has worked with celebrities!"

Kim, age 18, and her Washington Post article about our family journal

Kim's writing has always meant a great deal to Gail and me. This was one article she wrote for the Washington Post about the 300 plus page journal I wrote celebrating her last year at home.

This article meant a lot to me. I was in Denver airport when I called Gail and she told me this article was in the paper. Gail read it to me over the phone and people walking by me in the airport must have wondered why I was crying. Here is her article:

A Father's Journal, A Guide to Living
By Kimberly Shearer Palmer
Special to the Washington Post, Style, April 17, 1998

"What's this?" asked Ted, my football-player friend, pointing to a thick red book on the shelf above my desk.

"It's the journal my dad kept during my last year at home," I said.

"The Graduation Gift," Ted read from the cover. "'A Journal Celebrating Kim's Last Year at Home.' Can I see it?" he asked.

I was slightly hesitant about letting Ted read the journal. From briefly flipping through it, I knew It contained sensitive remarks from my dad ("It is a memoir to capture the wonderful humdrum events of our extraordinarily ordinary family") and revealed the serious nature of my family ("After leading our family meeting, Christina [my sister] reviewed the commitments that we had made . . . ").

Ted, a macho jock from Ohio, already got laughs out of the fact that my family held weekly family meetings while his family rarely had time to eat together.

He has become one of my best friends at college, but I wasn't sure I wanted to give him all this fresh ammunition.
Have you read it all yet?" he asked, after glancing over the first few of 500 pages.

I felt a twinge of guilt. "No, not quite yet." I know I was lucky to have a dad who devoted so much time to such a special gift, but right now, I wasn't motivated to read about Dad's record of our life when I could be out with my friends or should be studying.

Dad himself referred to his project as "the lonely journal" because, he would joke, he would be the only one to ever read it, along with maybe his grandchildren.

Ted was spending more time on the journal than I ever had. "Where did your dad get the idea to write this?"

"He wanted to give me something cool before I left for college," I explained.

"That's so awesome," Ted said, still reading.

"Look at this letter your dad wrote you." He shoved the book onto my lap. The letter included a story about Gandhi fasting in an attempt to stop the fighting with the British. Dad wrote: "A leader knows what she has to do and just goes ahead and does it." As a parent of three daughters, my feminist father is always careful to change the gender-pronouns so they apply to the female sex.

"That's sweet, Kim," Ted said, pulling the book back onto his lap.

"Wait," I said, pulling it back. "I want to read more."

"Kim, be careful with the book, please," Ted chastised. "You can read it when I'm done."

When he left and I had the journal to myself, I opened to the middle, around page 250, and started reading.

I was mesmerized by my dad's philosophical comments on life "By observing one's bodily sensations and one's mental reactions to them, one can stop becoming overwhelmed by emotions and realize that we have the freedom to *choose* how we design our lives."

I thought over my tension-filled week. My roommate and I had been feeling antagonistic toward each other, perhaps because of competitive feelings – we both want to be writers. Maybe if I refused to see her as a competitor (the chances that her success would influence my own or vice versa were slim) then I could avoid letting negative feelings into our dorm room and minimize the negativity in my life.

Dad continued. "I believe the secret to achieving inner peace lies in understanding our core values – those things that are most important to us – and then seeing that they are reflected in the daily events of our lives." I wanted to spend my time writing, reading, running, and appreciating my friends; not fighting with my roommate.

As I read the journal and remembered our family traditions, my mind began to clear and I put the issues in my life in perspective. With his reflections on our "ordinary life," my dad's writing was helping me to transcend my everyday life and concentrate on the things that I cared about most.

My family is one of those things. By recalling our interactions through Dad's writing, I was able to feel closer to my parents than I usually can at college. I read about a debate my dad and I had last year over whether or not animals feel pain. Another passage reminded me how similar I am to my father. He wrote, "Occasionally, I feel alone – not often, but now and then."

We probably wouldn't have discussed this "loneliness" we sometimes feel in a conversation. Through his writing, my dad told me that I wasn't really alone; he, at least, understands what it feels like to be misunderstood.

Near the end of his journal, he says, "Through this journal, I can get away from the busyness of daily life and talk to the girls in a way and with a depth that is not easy on a day-to-day basis. I can say things in this journal that are difficult to say face-to-face. I can talk to the girls about what I love, what I do, what I feel passionate about, and what principles, values and goals I think are important. I hope over time that this will come to mean a lot to them."

Actually, Dad, I didn't expect to care about your journal at first either, but it already means a lot to me and I thank you for it. I needed someone else – and it turned out to be the last person I would have expected to make me appreciate my family more – to make me realize how special this journal is and how special you are.

I am taking from it the purpose you intended it to serve. Your journal gives me another perspective, an important perspective – your perspective. Sometimes a parental perspective is exactly what I yearn for as I am here at college; removed from your daily guidance.
Kimberly Palmer is a freshman at Amherst.

Kim, age 18, and t-shirt

When Kim was 18, she gave me t-shirt on my 50th birthday on which she printed the words: "50 Years of Self-Improvement."

Kim, about 18, making a funny rejoinder after I commented that I worried that Gail and I make marriage look too easy

I wrote in the family journal the following: "If I could write to the girls tonight, I would write to them about how I hope Mommy and I haven't made being married look too easy. It has been easy for us because Gail is such a fabulous person but the truth is that most people don't find it easy and it takes a lot of dedication, good judgment and long-term thinking. So I would tell the girls (if I could write to them tonight) that being married is a constant challenge (and of course, being single is also very challenging.)"

Kim read that and then wrote amusingly in the margin: "Don't worry about that (it does not look easy to be married to you). ☺"

Kim, age 19, and her emotional maturity and my father

Fathers like me can sometimes forget to tell their grown children how proud they are of them, even though they will tell it readily to others out of earshot of their children.

My father was like that. I remember Kim realized this at one point when Granny and Grandpa were staying with us once. Kim was a teenager and mature way beyond her years. She went out of her way one day to tell me how proud Grandpa was of me. She knew I've never heard my father say that to me, even though I knew it intuitively, and Kim had heard him boasting about me to others at a party. She knew it was important for me to know and so told me. I was very grateful to Kimmie for telling me. I still remember her words: "Dad, you know that Grandpa is proud of you, don't you? He's always telling other people how great you are and how proud he is of you."

It's funny how I can't write that without crying, even though I'm almost 60. I had to stop typing to get a tissue.

My visit to Kim, age 22, in Tokyo

I went to visit Kim in Tokyo in 2001. Kim was spending a year there as a reporter working for a big newspaper. After I got home from the trip, she sent me a poem for my birthday and in it she described a true story. Here is part of her poem:

> When I left our cozy house to go to the foreign land of Japan
> Before the year was over who came to visit? My favorite Man!
> Out of all our adventures, my favorite one occurred in my apartment.
> Early one morning, before I could even say, "What time is it?"
> Dad was awake, busy writing out a list
> I can't say it all, but I'll give you the gist
> Before I could brush my teeth or drag myself sleepily to the loo
> He started telling me how to improve my life, and all that I should do
> "Start your own company, dress for success, and publish a book
> All before next year, come on, just give my list a look!
> It will make you wealthy, successful and wise
> Perhaps as much as me, if I dare surmise!"
> While at first I admit I was a tad overwhelmed at my new To Do list
> I also saw it as an exciting challenge, "I accept!" I said, raising my fist!

That birthday poem from Kim is a pretty accurate description of what actually happened!

Kim, age 25, complaining about the attention I was giving my students
Soon after I started teaching at AU, one of my students, Dan Gallagher, missed a deadline and he and I had a lengthy exchange of emails in which I talked about the importance of commitments, he was apologetic, and I was compassionate and didn't deduct any points from his grade.

I shared this exchange with the family and Kim responded as follows:
"Wait, this seems like a letter you would write to us. Are you still going to spend as much time writing to us? Are they like your new children? Don't care too much about them!

Sujay's first visit to us
The first time Sujay came to visit us, he said it felt like the movie Meet the Parents. He slept in the basement, he had to treat our dog Cory with great affection, and he had to deal with me, who I'm afraid may have reminded him of the Robert DeNiro character! In fact, Kim wrote an article last year called Passing the Dreaded Parents' Test about what it was like for Sujay to visit us for the first time. Kim wrote that one thing I do is to announce vocally the characteristics of the ideal "son-in-law."

Me comforting Kim, Kim comforting Kareena, 2012
Kim sent me the following letter in December 25, 2012

> Dear Dad,
> Every time I have to return upstairs to comfort Kareena after we've put her to bed, because she's upset or scared about something (like monsters or bad dreams), I remember this:
> When I was probably around 8 or 9 years old, I heard about the story of the Pied Piper, and it terrified me. The idea of a musician luring away children was one of the scariest things I'd ever heard. For some reason, one night, as I was trying to fall asleep in my bed, I couldn't stop thinking about this story. I couldn't sleep because I was so scared. So I called for you to come sit with me, and you did. I told you what was scaring me, and you explained that such a thing was not going to happen to me. That was very reassuring, but you didn't stop there, you stayed and sat on my bed and rubbed my back until I stopped feeling scared. Finally I was able to fall asleep.
> Now, when I am comforting Kareena because of some kind of similar scare, I think of that night. I think less about the dishes I need to do, or emails I need to send, or dinner I need to eat, and all of the other tasks calling me back downstairs. Instead, I think about how much better you made me feel that night, when I'm sure you had plenty of other grown-up things to do, too. And I take my time comforting her and am glad that I can make her feel better, just like you used to make me feel better.
> Love, Kim

Sujay's delay in calling us with the big news

After Kim and Sujay had been dating a fair amount of time, we received an e-mail from Sujay saying that he was going to call us to ask us about something highly confidential. Gail and I immediately anticipated that Sujay wanted to propose to Kim. We were so excited!

We waited for Sujay to call. An hour passed. Another hour passed. I couldn't wait any longer. I went to my computer and sent Sujay an e-mail: "Sujay, Gail and I are at home completely relaxed. Now would be a great time to call." Another hour passed. And then another. I went to my computer again and sent Sujay another e-mail: "Sujay, Gail and I are staying up late. We are totally relaxed. Now would be an excellent time to call us." What we didn't realize was that Sujay and Kim were watching a late night movie and so Sujay wasn't able to call us.

Sujay called the next day and we were elated with the news. A few days later, Sujay proposed to Kim in a wonderfully romantic way.

Kim's memory about me helping her deal with stress

"One night as a junior in high school, I had reached what was then my peak of stress: I had SATs to study for, a massive history exam, a swim meet and a poem to memorize. As I arrived home around 6 p.m., starving and cranky after an exhausting swim team practice, I just wanted to cry. I had no idea how I was going to get everything done.

"For some reason, my mom was out that night, so it was just my dad in charge, taking care of my two younger sisters and me. When I told him I was paralyzed with stress, he very calmly told me that everything would be fine: We would simply tackle one thing at a time. Starting with the poetry memorization, we did just that, crossing the tasks off our list as we accomplished them.

"I'm not sure how he managed to help me so much when he was also juggling dinner time and caring for two other children but, in my memory, I had his complete attention. My problems were important enough for him to focus on, and that alone helped me to relax and face them. Today, I still take the "one task at a time" approach when my to-do list feels overwhelming."

Kim's memory of my passion for work

"When I was young, my dad always worked in his study at home after we went to bed. I would hear him dictating into his phone or shuffling papers late into the night. He also brought us to his office and showed us what he was working on. Seeing his passion for his work, combined with his obvious enjoyment of it, helped show us that we could find work one day that we would find satisfying, too."

Kim's memory of me giving her feedback

"My dad did not give us overly positive feedback when we asked him to help us with writing assignments. In fact, I often dreaded showing him my written work because he would have dozens of suggestions for ways to improve it. At times, I found this quite frustrating, but it also made me commit to improving and not settling for thinking my work was "good enough." That kind of pursuit of excellence stuck with me, too."

Kim's memory of my positive approach to failing

Here is a story from Kim, which she sent me for me to include in my book on parenting (Raise Your Kids to Succeed):

"I was thinking recently about how it was so great how you taught us to embrace failure/rejection and that is such a key to our current ability to handle it - and of course failure is a necessary part of success. For example, do you remember how I used to submit essays to all the writing contests in Highlights magazine as an 8-year-old or something like that? They never wrote back but you never suggested that I should stop submitting them - and what good practice for dealing with rejection and continuing anyway."

Kim, age 30, interviewed in Ladies Home Journal in 2010, about negotiating salaries

Kim was asked, "What is the best advice you received on being a woman and/or being financially confident?" This is how she answered: "It actually came from my Dad. He always told me and my sisters to make sure we asked for what we deserved when it came to job promotions, salaries, or even in our personal lives. In fact, before job interviews, he made us practice how we would negotiate our salaries! He knows the whole process can be awkward, especially for women, and that's one reason women earn less money than men. His advice paid off. I'm sure my negotiating skills benefited from those practice sessions."

Tina

Tina getting comforted by Kim when Tina first started pre-school

When Tina first went to pre-school, she was miserably homesick and apprehensive. Kim, deeply feeling her pain, hid under a table in Tina's school room so she could be there to comfort her young sister.

Tina giving MacMac her name (Tina was about 2)

Dorothy McCormack looked after Kim, Tina and Jen when Gail and I went to work. When Dorothy first joined our family, Tina was about two years old. As she left on the first day, Gail said to Tina, "Say goodbye to Mrs. McCormack." Tina said, "Bye bye MacMacMac." From that day on, Dorothy became MacMac.

Tina, age 3, and Jay Johnson pulling her pants down

I wrote this story in early 1986 when Tina was 3: Jay Johnson came around to play with Christina yesterday. Christina came up from the basement where she had been playing with him and told Gail that Jay had pulled her pants down. Gail went downstairs and asked Jay if it were true and (he nodded) and she very gently said that that wasn't the right thing to do. Gail later called me to ask whether she should call Peggy about this and I told her absolutely. (Gail was worried that it might look like snitching!)

When I got home, Gail must have told Kimberly or indicated something had gone on because Kimberly kept saying to Christina "Christina, what did you and Jay do today?" And, "Christina, what happened today with you and Jay?" she was dying to get more information! Christina wouldn't tell her.

I had watched the excellent program with Mike Farrell on "Child Sexual Abuse" on PBS last year and had made some notes of the key points. So after dinner when we were up in the study, I beckoned Kimberly and Christina over to talk to me, got out my notes and talked with them about sexual abuse and the four golden rules:

- It's <u>your</u> body – you decide what happens to it. It's not fair for people to touch you when you don't want them to.
- If you get the "o-oh" feeling that something is wrong, then you are right.
- Tell someone.
- It is never your fault.

The girls and I had a nice talk and all of us felt comfortable.

Tina, age 4, asking Gail about going to the bathroom when you're dead

In 1986 when Tina was four, she asked Gail, "Do you go to the bathroom after you are dead?" Gail answered, "No." Tina replied, "That's good because you couldn't get up to go."

Tina, age 5, with premonitions of her future as a doctor

From Tina's journal April 1988 (she was almost six): "When I grow up I want to be a doctor to help people get better. When someone dies, and if someone needs a new heart, I'll have to hold it and put it in the sick person. And you have to write a list of who needs a heart."

Tina, age 6, from her diary January 15, 1988, with funny joke about sex

Here is what Tina wrote in her journal. It's in my handwriting, so I obviously helped a lot, but it is written as if from Tina:

Tonight, at dinner, I wanted a second helping. For fun I said, "May I please have secs?" Everybody laughed uproariously. So did I when they explained the joke! Daddy said I should tell this story for show-and-tell in school!

Tina, age 12, supporting Jenny's petition to Gail and me for a dog

Tina wrote: "Just imagine — it would be the perfect family. Two great loving parents, three wonderful kids, and a cute loving golden retriever to top it off! A little puppy — I know you're thinking "there's no way, the girls won't take care of it, it's not fair to the dog." BUT, how would you feel if Kim, Jen and I made a plan of how to take care of it? Think about it! A little golden retriever, at the door to welcome you home when your three daughters are neglecting you. Soon it may be the only thing you have!"

Tina tells the story about her dislike of show-and-tell

"I was a very shy child. I hated "show and tell" days in kindergarten and *never* wanted to participate in them. My dad knew this. He didn't get angry or make me feel bad, but got a big empty plastic box and starting collecting interesting things in it. Each week, the night before show and tell, he would take out the box and we would do a practice a show and tell. While I still didn't particularly enjoy doing show and tell, this helped me feel more prepared, so I could participate with more confidence."

Tina tells the story of family meetings and "teacher/student"

"Growing up, I remember Sundays being our day for both "family meetings" and "teacher/student" time. In our family meetings, we would take turns being in charge and would discuss our plans for the week, our biggest upcoming challenges, and any family conflicts. While we didn't always love going to family meetings, they were a vital part of our family ritual and taught us each a lot about leadership, working as a team, and setting goals.

"Later in the day, we did "teacher/student." We would have to a pick a topic to "teach" our dad about. It could be anything we had learned the week prior, but we had to make sure we knew it well enough to teach it. This helped me learn."

Tina tells the story of my "University on Wheels"

"When I was in high school my dad would drive me to school most mornings. As a moody teenager, this was not something I particularly enjoyed. My dad had a long morning commute and his car was piled up with books on tape: self-help books, books about the Civil War, biographies of Benjamin Franklin, and so on. Sometimes he would put these on and we would listen together. He called this his "University on Wheels," which for some reason made me laugh (and those days he had a hard time making me laugh). While I never would have told him this at the time, I found his University on Wheels secretly inspirational. Having him role-modeling constant learning and self-improvement made me want to do the same."

Tina, age 15, swimming in Tahiti in the ocean with a dangerous shark

When Tina was about 15, I took her to Tahiti to swim with whales and dolphins. A 10 to 12 foot white-tipped oceanic shark, one of the few sharks with a reputation for being dangerous, suddenly swam menacingly right at her. Tina got out of the water very fast! Gail was very upset with me when she found out about it later.

Tina, age 15, and me in a fight

Tina and I were fighting over something when Tina first started using a school laptop in about 2000. I sent her an email to make up. Later I received this email response written from her bedroom 25 feet away:

> Hey Dad! Thanks for your email!!! I'm in my room right now on my laptop!! Isn't that cool! We're in a fight now, but I still love you of course. Love, Tina

Tina, age 16, makes an amusing request for a bigger allowance

When Tina was about 16, she wrote Gail and me the following memo:

> After school, when I am waiting to get picked up, I often buy food from the vending machines when my stomach is rumbling. Often I cannot concentrate unless I put something in my hungry tummy, and I spend the afternoon looking for money and searching my entire backpack for a couple of quarters which I know are not there. By having a higher allowance, I will be able to satisfy this hunger and take care of my needy, growing body.

Tina, age 16, and a funny story from her tennis coach about her faith in him

At noon today, Gail, Tina and I went to Larry and Jan Mandel's house for a wrap-up tennis party with coach Fred Drilling. Fred gave Tina the Coach's Award, and told the following story about her. He said that during one game, Tina asked to talk to the coach. When Fred went to see her, Tina asked him, "Coach, what should I do?" Fred asked Tina what the score was, an Tina said she was losing 9-0! (In other words, Tina had lost every game so far, and there was only one more game to go.) Fred made everyone laugh by saying that Christina must have a lot of faith in Fred that she would ask him for help in those circumstances!

Tina, age 18, and her skydiving adventure

When Tina was about 18, she went skydiving. This caused huge tension in our family, just a day or two before Gail and I were to celebrate our 25th wedding anniversary! Gail was deeply upset whereas I thought it was extremely brave and plucky of her. Gail felt that after 18 years of devoted motherhood, not to mention natural childbirth, free falling from 11,000 feet was an unnecessary risk!

Tina, age 18, on a tough Outward Bound course and the letter she wrote

At age 18, Tina did an Outward Bound course. As part of the experience, she was left alone on an island to take care of herself for three days. While there, she wrote us this letter:

> Dear Mom, Dad, Kim, Jen,
> Hi!! How are you guys? I'm okay here, although IT'S REALLY HARD. Scarier than I thought it would be. Yesterday we took a boat to Hurricane Island & it was freezing cold & raining on the way here. First thing we did as we got to the island was JUMP IN THE 54 DEGREE WATER! Can you believe it? It was so cold. I could hardly breathe in it was so cold. My body was paralyzed. We had to swim forward, tread water as we said the alphabet, then swim back on our backs. It was horrible. Ten this morning we had to wake up at 6 a.m., go running, then get in the water again. This time just dip in & out. This morning it wasn't as bad.
> We have 2 instructors, Leslie and Fred. They're really good. Then there are 10 girls & 2 boys on the trip. Last night was hard. I felt lonely & cold & I was dreading getting up this morning. But I feel better today & I am working on having a good attitude. I'm so glad Serena's here with me. Oh my god it turns out we have a 3 DAY SOLO. I THOUGHT IT WAS 1 NIGHT & 2 DAYS, BUT IT'S 2 NIGHTS AND 3 DAYS – ALL ALONE! It'll be fine. I'm sort of excited, it'll be relaxing. I love you guys so much & I miss you. Kim – how's work going? And your DATE?? Jen – how was Disneyworld with Dad? I'm so jealous?
> Mom – I really miss you. I hope you aren't too lonely with Dad, Jen & me gone! I love you!
> Dad – How was your trip with Jen? You'd be really proud of me I think. It is hard here. You'd love it.
> I love you so much! I don't know how much I'll be able to write. Don't feel bad. Know I'm thinking about you.
> I love you.
> Love,
> Tina
> Xoxo

Tina's complaint about her "tyrannical parents"

Tina wanted to go to Florida, so she decided to write a memo to Gail and me laying out the arguments for why she should be allowed to do this. Part of her memo read:

> Out of all my friends, I am the only one who has had her progress of trip-taking harshly impeded by her tyrannical parents.

And she ended her memo by declaring:

> On May 19, I will be an adult: able to vote, to buy cigarettes, and GET MARRIED...I should start being treated as an adult.

Tina's poem about me at the Father/Daughter Dinner at Holton on April 30, 2000
The time has finally come when I have to stand up here,
And think about all the things I will miss about you next year.
I've begun to realize that this includes everything,
From your funny habits to the weekly family meeting.
Although I may complain or make fun of you.
I want you to know I will miss everything you do.

I will miss waking up to you yelling up the stairs "Wake up Teen!"
And the shouts of pain during your morning exercise routine.
I'll miss the kitchen in the morning before you have put on your suits,
When you point to your bowl bragging, "Look what I'm eating: All Bran and 5 kinds of fruits!"

I definitely will miss our trips to Holton each morning,
And I must say they never are boring.
I know I always complain about not having a car,
But the books on tape are more educating by far.
(My dad calls these books on tape his "university on wheels,"
And they've educated me on everything from the Civil War to how to make business deals.)
I apologize for those times Dad when I seem happy when you leave on trips,
But I must admit, driving your car does have its kicks.

I'll miss the family dinners we have each night,
Even the ones when we end up in a fight.
I'll miss the Charlotte Church cd you blast to keep you inspired,
And how you won't let me stay out late because you are tired.
I'll miss the jokes you tell at dinner that you find on the Internet every day,
And how even though I usually don't understand them, I laugh anyway.

I'll miss how for every night you're out of town you say, "There might be a letter!"
And how whenever I miss you this always makes me feel better.
Ever since I've been little and even still now when I'm a teen,
I've loved these letters you leave filled with wisdom, jokes, and the latest nature magazine.
I've gotten so used to your letters when you're far away,
Next year you might have to write one every day.

And I actually will miss you calling throughout the house each week "family meeting time!"
And how you notice if I take a pen off your desk – or, as I should say, off your shrine.
And I'll miss seeing you with the family meeting notebook, red pen, and gavel,
As we go through the agenda planning the day, the week, and plans to travel.
I'll miss being lectured each week on organizing my time and doing more chores,
And though I roll my eyes now next year I'll want you to do it more.

You've always tried to be the best father you could be,
By watching my tennis matches, giving me advice, and wanting to spend individual time with me.
Although I may complain about having an over-organized, health-freak controlling man of a father,
I must admit there's no one I would rather.
For the past 18 years of my life I've learned so much from you here,
I will miss you so much when I'm away next year.

I LOVE YOU DAD!!!

Tina's college essay on our family meetings

"Family Meeting," my dad yells throughout the house Sunday morning. My sisters and I roll our eyes as we walk into the study, where my mom and dad are. We sit on the blue carpeted floor in the space between their desks. My little sister Jen sits at the computer and clicks on America Online.

Kim looks at her watch. "This has to be quick," she says, "I have a lot of work to do and I'm meeting Clare at one."

"Okay, first on the agenda is to plan today," my dad says as he opens up our family meeting notebook and gets out a red pen. Jen starts IM-ing her friends online. My dad notices: "Jen, pay attention." We plan the day, then my dad says to my mom, "Gail, what chores do the girls have to do today?" This is one of his weekly complaints. There really aren't any chores, but he makes my mom think of a list anyway. "When I was growing up we worked for hours doing chores for the family. This isn't fair. Mummy and I end up doing everything."

"Who wants to do the food shopping today? He asks. No one answers. "I guess I'll be doing it again." He says this every week too. He always ends up doing it. "Who's going to make dinner tonight?" No one says anything again. My mom will do it.

"Plan the week," he says, as he moves down the agenda. We go through each day of the coming week, saying what each person has on, and who needs the car when.

"Next item: Family Outings. Girls, we need to have more family outings. We never do anything together." We all shift in our seats and I look at my watch. "Do you want to go to the circus? He suggests. We all have our own excuses of why we're too busy. Then he says, "We're going to start making it a weekly thing to go out to brunch every Saturday."

"Can we move on? This is a waste of time," I interrupt as I think of all the things I have to do. My sisters and I are all slouched down against the wall doodling on our paper.

"Okay, okay," he says. "Tina, you need to learn to balance your time better. You seem to have time for everything but your family."

My dad continues, "Alright, now, next item on the agenda is Mummy's birthday. Next year is her 50th birthday. We should do something special." We talked about this last meeting, and the meeting before.

"Dad," I say trying not to yell, "we've talked about this every meeting. It's more than a year away. We don't need to keep bringing it up." He marks a start next to it to remind himself to bring it up again next week.
"Next: Plan this summer." We talked about this one last week, too.

I tell him, "I still don't know my plans yet, Dad. Things haven't changed in a week." My sisters say the same. He marks a star next to that one too and moves on.

"Next thing is Rocks." This is when we go around the room and we all say the biggest thing we have this week. My dad got this idea from one of his many self-improvement books. That's also where he got the idea of these family meetings, not to mention our family mission statement. Today, and recently, my dad's rock has been to get along better with me since we've been fighting a lot. Jen's rock is "school" – the same as usual since she can't think of anything else. Kim's is to work on one of her articles, mine is my college applications, and my mom's is to work on her family history book.

"Next: Encourage each other." This is one we're supposed to come already prepared with. My dad goes first, with a list of things to praise each one of us for. I think them up as I go along "Mom, for working so hard on your book, Kim for your article, Jen for being such a good little sister (that's what I say when I can't think of anything else,) and Dad for ... uh ... come back to me."

Next is when we raise any issues we might have. Jen brings up her allowance policy. She wants a raise. My dad doesn't wait for her to finish and says, "Jen, write down as one of your commitments to write up a proposal and show it to the whole family. Then we can all sign it if we agree." Jen groans as she writes down to do it on her doodled paper.

I have something to bring up: "I think it's ridiculous that no one of the opposite sex can go into my room." I've brought this up before, but they still aren't convinced. Maybe if I wrote a proposal and had everyone sign it they would let me.

We all start getting antsy. "DAD, hurry up, we don't have all day," Kim says.

"Okay, now, does everyone know their commitments for the next meeting?" my dad asks.

"Yes" we say in unison.

I start walking away. "Hey, where do you think you're going? We're not done yet" my dad yells to us jokingly.

"Bye!" I say as I walk away laughing.

Tina's decision to become a doctor

When Tina was 21, she wrote me a letter saying she had decided not to become a doctor. It was very eloquent. Here is an excerpt:

> I know that I will find my way. I will figure it out, just like you and mom did, and just like everybody has to do. I will face challenges and I will suffer like everybody. But I will not regret anything because I will be fully living in the way I know how and the way that makes me happiest.
>
> I need to know that you and mom will be proud of me no matter what I do. I think that is the greatest gift a parent can give a child: to let them create their own lives with them knowing that they are loved but they are free.

She found her own way, and that's the way it should be. It was her doing, her decision to become a doctor, her working out what was the best way for her to move forward.

Tina, age about 21, in an email exchange with me over my letters to the girls about sex

Me: Did you or Kim ask me re the meaning of "chaste"? I just wrote Kim a note about that but perhaps it was you, not Kim, who sent me that e-mail.

Tina: Nope, that's right, Kim asked about "being chaste" but I think we were all wondering. Hehe that reminds me of those funny emails you used to send on sex via email cause you didn't want to talk about it in person! Re-send them! Aahahaha! I'm LOL!!!

Me: OK, smarty pants who knows more about these things than yerol' dad!! Here it is, attached. I'm glad you didn't ask me at breakfast tomorrow morning otherwise your LOL would turn into

HMCSOOYNAOTBTAMGBACLIU (have masticated cereal spewing out of your nose all over the breakfast table and Mommy going bonkers as Cory laps it up!) I love you. Dad XXXOOO

Jenny

Jenny, age 5, with an amusing rejoinder to Gail
Gail: "Are you ready to go, Jenny, to pick up Tina?"
Jenny: "I don't want to go. I want to continue to work at the computer. I know you'll be sad." She laughs, knowing she's being amusing.

Jenny's early sense of fairness, age 5
Jenny comes up to me with a Valentine's Day card she has designed and produced for Nana. Jen immediately says to me, "Dad, don't get all upset because I'm going to make one for Granny and Grandpa."

Jenny, age 5, attempts to write
Jenny asked me to write "Granny and Grandpa." I said, "Jenny, you can do that. Have a go. Here's some paper and a pen. Have a go and show me what you can do." A few minutes later Jenny came back. She had written on the piece of paper, "GRANE and GAPO."

Jenny, age 5, with snappy rejoinder
Jen: "I need a tissue." (she comes over)
Me: "May I have a kiss, too?"
Jen: "I'll skip that!"

Jenny, age 5, wanting to set a good example to her future kids
Me: (Writing Jen's diary with Jen) "Today I had a doughnut in church"
Jenny: "No no no! I don't want to give a bad habit to my children when I grow up!"

Jen, age 5, asking a question about death
Jenny asked me, "If I was 100 and I was dead, how old would you be if you were dead?"

Jen, almost 6, yelling out of character
I arrived home and Tina was hugging me. Suddenly we heard Jenny shout out, "GET OFF MY MAN!"

Jen, on the day she turned 6, talking philosophically about money
Jen: "I want that watch."
Gail: "If you spend money on everything, you won't have anything left."
Jen: "If you spend money on everything, there's nothing left to want."

Jen, age 6, commenting on truth
Sometime in 1993 when Jen was six, she said, when commenting on something that was true: "It's a real not mistake."

618

Jen, age 6, telling me she's too busy for a kiss
July 1993: Gail is hugging Jenny as she is waking up. I enter her bedroom to give her a kiss. Jenny says, "Hug baby blue—I'm already busy." Baby blue is her precious doll.

Jen, age 6, telling me to act like I really love her
Summer 1993 at the New Jersey shore: I'm carrying Jenny into the waves at the beach. The waves are big and Jen gets apprehensive. Jenny yells at me, "Hug me as though you really cared!"

Jen, age 6, getting her words mixed up
Summer 1993: Jenny, after a long, tiring drive to Nana's house: "Are we at Nana's almost house?"

Jenny, age 6, trying her best to be polite
At breakfast, my father and Jenny are sitting together:
Grandpa: "How was your night, Jenny?"
Jenny: "Good"
Gail: "Good what, Jenny?" (Meaning for Jenny to add "thank you")
Jenny: "Good morning"

Jen, age 6 and in 1st grade, and hiding the fact she didn't eat the lunch I made her
One evening we had this exchange:
Me: "Jenny, did you eat all the lunch at school that I made you?"
Jen: "Yes, I ate everything—the cheese sandwich, the raisons, the applesauce, the cucumber, and the OJ."
Me: "Great, Jen! Well done!"
Ten minutes later:
Me: "Jen, I can't find your lunch bag. Do you know where it is?"
Jenny: "I'll get it." (Jen gets it and starts heading for the garbage)
Me: "Hey Jen, let me see it." I look—and find most of her lunch in her bag!

Jen, age 7, making a witty remark about my intelligence
When Jen was seven, I was reading a joke book to her and I told her that I would explain the hard ones to her. She replied, "And I'll explain the easy ones to you, Dad."

Jen, age 10, lobbying for a puppy
When Jen was ten, she lobbied intensively for a puppy. I refused because I know how much work they involve. She never stopped lobbying for a puppy and about four years later, I gave in and we got Cory, a golden retriever.

Jen, age 11, responding sassily with "Carpe Diem" to my request to her
March 1999: Jen was about 11 and Gail and I were encouraging her to prepare a detailed plan on how she could make the most out of her spring break. I wanted to see a plan with all her goals, such as

reading, strength exercises, relaxing, playing with her hamsters, coming to the Naval Observatory with me, buying a trumpet, and so on. In response to my pressuring her, Jen sent me the following succinct, cheeky memo:

How to Make Spring Break Fun

1. Live spontaneously, don't plan out. Carpe Diem.

This made me LOL! She deftly put me in my place!

Jen, age 12, showing great maturity
I was demanding in a loud voice that Jen get ready for soccer and not leave everything to the last minute. I was lecturing her about this and cajoling her, when she interrupted me by saying, "OK, Dad, you don't have to yell at me." Then she paused before adding in a quiet voice, "but thanks for caring."

Jen, age 13, making funny remark about me being bossy (i.e., doing nothing)
When Jen was 13, I was telling Gail and the girls how my brothers and I were sharing responsibilities for looking after my elderly parents. My lawyer brother would take care of legal issues and my accounting brother would take care of financial issues. Jen said, "And that leaves you, Dad, to do the bossy stuff!"

Jen, age about 13, and her rejoinder to me when I criticized a popular comedic film
I took Jen to see an Austin Powers comedy. As it ended, I was full of scorn and contempt for how raunchy and unfunny it was. I derisively said to Jenny, "Charlie Chaplin must be turning in his grave." I told Jen I thought the film as miserable and pathetic. Jen looked at me and said, "Dad, every time I looked at you, you were laughing you head off!" Busted!

Jen, age 14, and her rebuttal to me about Reality Television
When Jen was 14, she fell in love with Reality Television. Jen rebutted all my complaints against them by cleverly saying, "Arguing against Reality TV is like arguing against non-fiction books."

Jen, age 14, putting me in my place when I complained she wasn't reading enough, and wishing that I was just a normal Dad
Here is what I wrote at the time in 2002: I think Jen is watching too much TV, and I have been teasing her about this to try to dissuade her from watching so much. I told her today that she should be reading 10 to 15 books a week on poetry, science, fiction, biography, or anything that she is curious about. Jenny replied:
"Oh Dad, why can't you just be a normal Dad?"
This made me laugh! Then I said to Jenny, "Jen, if you want to lead an interesting life, you have to read voraciously."
Jen responded (in a somewhat dismissive tone): "Do you think your life is interesting?"

Jen, age 17, and the funny things she said about me at the Holton Father/Daughter dinner
In April 2005, I emceed the Holton-Arms Father-Daughter dinner. This is a traditional yearly event at

which daughters say sentimental and often teary-eyed things about their Dads. This is what Jen said about me (the audience laughed uproariously):

Here is a top ten list of what I will miss about my dad next year:

#10: I'll miss his daily encouragement to eat a healthy breakfast like his – a huge bowel of nuts, oranges, apples, pears, and raisons – and All-Bran, which I am constantly reminded has 40% of your daily fiber needs.

#9: I'll miss how whenever my friends call me, he ends up talking to them longer than I do.

#8: I will miss him coming into my room at 9 o'clock on Saturday mornings when I'm deeply sleeping after a long week, putting my shades up and asking me if I'm awake yet.

#7: I'll miss him then telling me he's been up since 6 AM exercising, and I should do the same.

#6: I'll miss how after 3 daughters, he still doesn't understand the difference between APs, SATs, SAT 2s, or school exams – but he still tries to.

#5: I'll miss him doing handstands by the pool wearing only his speedo and seeing all the kids pointing at him, amazed at his talent.

#4: I'll miss the piles of articles he cuts out of newspapers for me to read, telling me "how to be a strong woman in the workplace" or encouraging me to learn pages of vocab from Reader's Digest.

#3: I'll miss the daily advice he gives me, which he has compiled on a handy bookmark for my sisters and me to take with us always. Some of "Dad's 70 Rules for Success" are:

   -Live passionately
   -Battle injustice
   -Cherish sisters
   -Read voraciously
   -And call home.

#2: I'll miss him telling me that him taping the O.C. for me when I am not home would be like bringing home Playboy for a son.

And The number 1 thing I'll miss about my dad next year are the daily detailed updates he emails me on our dog's bodily functions.

For example, the other day, I checked my email during break and saw this subject:
"Cory achieves a new world record!" The email from my dad said:

   "Oh my goodness! Cory did something this morning she has NEVER EVER done before. She went poop THREE times on our run this morning. Isn't that wonderful? I am so proud of her. This is a NEW WORLD RECORD!"

As you can see from all these things, my dad might be a little unusual but Dad, I really will miss you next year!

Jen tells story about my reliability and trustworthiness (originally written for my book on parenting

"I have always been able to count on my dad 100 percent to be there when I need him. When I was growing up, no matter how busy he was, he would always make time for me. If I ever asked him for anything, I knew I could count on him to help me right away or let me know when he would be able to help. He spent a ton of time, for example, reviewing draft after draft of my college admission essays and providing feedback. His reliability and trustworthiness made a huge difference to me."

Jen tells story of how I encouraged her math skills (originally written for my parenting book)

"My dad used to give me math problems while we were eating breakfast before school. He didn't care when I was "supposed" to learn things. I remember that he taught me how to solve algebra equations when I was in around third grade, putting me light years ahead of the other kids when we finally got to algebra class in seventh grade. These mornings were actually very fun for me! The math problems were games, and my dad was very encouraging."

Jen tells story of how I praised the effort she made and for working diligently (originally written for my parenting book)

"My dad definitely set high expectations, and was always happy when I did well. If I didn't have straight As, he would ask me what happened. But as long as I worked hard and tried my best, he would tell me that a B (or C!) didn't matter at all. And no matter the grade, he would still praise me for working hard and trying my best. This continued all the way through law school!"

Kim, Tina, Jenny, Gail, Chris, and Cory

When I boxed at school and how one day I met my match. I was about 13.

I was skinny and small but reasonably strong and fast for my weight. Boxing came easily to me. I always seemed to win. This was one of the few things I did well in school. Then I got too big for my britches. I went in the ring with a guy, Doug Robbins, in my class. We didn't particularly like each other. The way I boxed was to dance in and out, escaping blows aimed at me by scooting backwards and then swiftly stepping in to land a punch. Doug had a style that totally floored me – literally. He moved forward towards me aggressively, punching hard with both his fists. I didn't know how to handle this style of boxing and I quickly fell apart. I was knocked to the floor several times. My teeth got chipped (I wore a mouth guard after this bout), and I lost badly. I felt humiliated.

Kim and Tina and ice cream when Kim was 6 and Tina was 3

I wrote this story in early 1986: Gail and I occasionally like to have ice cream at night after dinner. (Now in 2017, I never touch the stuff!) We don't like Kimberly and Christina to see us eating ice cream because we try to discourage them from eating junk food. Sometimes after I kiss Kimberly and Christina good night and on my way downstairs Kimberly will call out "Daddy, is Mommy eating ice cream?" I have to tell her the truth!

Occasionally I will get myself some ice cream and then head upstairs to the study to eat it while I am working at my desk. Occasionally Kimberly is not asleep and as I sneak through her room to go up to the study on the top floor, a little voice (Kimberly's) will call out "Daddy, what have you got there?"!

How I first met Gail at Harvard on September 23, 1972

A small decision I made that ended up having a big impact on my life (more than big—massive!) happened on September 23, 1972.

I was 25 and had just arrived in the US on a Kennedy Scholarship to study at the Kennedy School of Government at Harvard to get another Master's degree.

I knew no one, and was eager to network and start making new friends and contacts.

My first chance to do this was at the orientation session before the semester got underway. I arrived wearing a green suit and purple shirt and tie.

I walked into the meeting room and surveyed the space wondering where to sit and decided to walk down the central aisle. As I did so, I looked to my left and there my gaze alighted on a beautiful young woman with an empty seat next to her. I decided to sit in that empty seat.

That beautiful young woman was Gail!

After the orientation, we talked briefly, and I—eager to meet new friends—said to her in my very pronounced English accent, "Would you like to pop around to my flat for a drink sometime?"

Gail declined.

I found out afterwards that she went home to her roommates and told them that she had met a "real mover from Great Britain" at the orientation.

A week later I was walking through Harvard Yard on my way to class when I bumped into Gail coming in the opposite direction. We chatted and after a bit, when I suggested we get dinner, she invited me back to her apartment for dinner and we had grilled tuna sandwiches.

And that's how we met.

I was clueless about my feelings for Gail at first

I loved Gail right away, but I had no idea how serious we were until two things happened.

The first was that after we'd been dating for a couple of months, one evening we were on a bus on our way to a party. We were chatting and thinking nothing of it. As we reached our destination, a complete stranger, who'd been sitting next to us, turned to us and said, "May I say something to you both? It's wonderful to see you both so happy and so much in love!"

I was totally clueless.

The second thing that happened was that early one morning I received a telegram from Western Union with a note of congratulations on our engagement from my parents, who had misinterpreted one of my letters. Later that morning we were having coffee at a little coffee shop just off Harvard Square. I nonchalantly said, "Who would want to get married? Marriage is ridiculous." Gail rose from her chair visibly upset and replied, "Then let's just forget it, right now!"

Again, I was totally clueless.

Anyway, we had a fantastic year together at Harvard, and then I moved to DC to work at Booz Allen, while Gail stayed in Boston to finish her Master's degree.

I went up to visit her in Boston on the first weekend after I started living in Bethesda. As she opened the door to greet me, I looked at her, and for the first time, realized I could never live my life without her.

My visceral reaction to the CEO of Booz Allen stating that our mission was to increase our profits

In 1975 at age 28, I attended the Annual Meeting of a huge management consultant firm, Booz Allen and Hamilton, at a downtown hotel in Washington DC. I was invited because I worked on the Booz Allen staff as a senior consultant, a position which carried little authority or power. It was my first job after leaving the Royal Navy and after completing graduate degrees at London and Harvard.

The President of Booz Allen stood up to inspire the troops. He said the past year had been good but that he was setting a new goal for the coming year, and that was to increase our profits by $10 million. I waited for him to give the reason. And waited. And waited. I suddenly realized to my dismay that he had no intention of giving any reason. In the President's mind, increasing profits was enough of a reason. That's when I realized I could never work for Booz Allen.

Me trying to obtain permanent residency in the US in 1973 and how rude a US official was about some nationalities

When I first arrived in the US, I had difficulty obtaining my permanent residency. Without it, I would have been forced to return to England. My boss at that time – a Vice President with Booz Allan & Hamilton, Peter Wood – generously suggested that he and I go and see the Administrator of the Immigration & Naturalization Service to see if my application could be expedited.

The official turned out to be a cold, brusque man who wasn't the slightest bit impressed by our visit. After a rather fruitless discussion, we were about to leave when my boss said to the immigration official, "You know, Chris is going to marry an American," and he went on to describe what a wonderful person Gail was.

Well, this had a softening effect on the guy – which shows not all bureaucrats are heartless – and he gradually became friendlier and eventually agreed to do what he could to expedite my application for permanent residency.

Of course, I was elated, but also somewhat puzzled. So I said to him, "But how do you know that my upcoming marriage to Gail isn't simply a marriage of convenience so I can obtain my permanent residency?"

"Oh", he said, "You're British. Brits never do that. Greeks, Italians, Irish, Germans, yes, but the British only marry for love."

"But surely," I said, "You need more proof than that."

"We do," he said, "The marriage must be consummated."
"But," I said, "How could you possibly know if the marriage is consummated?"
"Oh, that's easy, "he replied, "You can tell by the look in the guy's eyes."

The girls give me a memorable t-shirt on my 60th birthday

It was my 60th birthday and Kim, Tina, and Jen gave me lots of wonderful gifts, including a t-shirt. On the front, they wrote: "Happy 60th Birthday, Dad!" along with the date. On the back, they wrote:

Dad's Top Five Life Lessons:

1. Find a good husband
2. Welcome failure
3. Work hard
4. Write a personal mission statement
5. Stay regular – eat All-Bran

That *is* pretty much what I taught them!

Other wonderful t-shirts over the years

Kim, Tina, and Jenny have given me some great t-shirts over the years. Here are three from Kim:

1. #1 DAD: 50 Years of Self-improvement (my 50th birthday)

2. WHY DAD LOVES KIM: (Christmas 96)
   5. I take your clothes
   4. I leave cereal boxes open
   3. I take your money
   2. I make you stay up late while I go out
   1. I take your car
   BUT YOU LOVE ME ANYWAY!!

3. OBSTACLES I MUST OVERCOME TO LOVE DAD

   1. When you come to my softball games, you spend more time on your cell phone than watching me play.
   2. You still don't know what SATs stand for.
   3. You read books like *How to Talk to Your Teen* and *Living with Your Teenager*.
   4. I have to write a research paper every time I want something.
   5. You listen to so many self-improvement tapes in the car that I can't see out the back window.

Our family mission statement, November 1990

The mission of our family is to create a nurturing place of love, laughter, warmth, security, relaxation and happiness, and to provide opportunities for each of us to meet our full potential so that we can each make a positive contribution both to our own family life and to society.

Among these goals are to love each other, to help each other, to believe in each other, to encourage each other, and to wisely use our time, talents and resources.

We want to live our lives with integrity, courage, humility, love, justice, patience, humor, trust, loyalty, self-confidence, hard work and self-discipline.

We want our home environment to be warm and to provide a place where we all feel relaxed and happy and which warmly welcomes our friends and relatives.

As parents, we want our children to gain from their family life not only their roots but their wings. We want them to feel the special bond that pulls them back home to spend time with their family, but also to understand who they are, based on what we know and can learn about grandparents and relatives who went before them. We want them to develop faith in themselves so that they will work hard in school and know that, with hard work and self-confidence, the world is theirs and they can achieve great things.

Bringing these goals to a day-to-day level:

➢ We want to have time to be with our friends, but also to save time to spend together doing things as a family. And we should have some time to just relax and do things around the house;

➢ We want always to be loving to each other;

➢ We want to be happy;

➢ We want each of us to have a love of learning;

➢ We want each of us to remember people who are not as fortunate as we are, and to find concrete (even if small) ways to help them;

➢ We want to exercise wisdom in what we choose to eat, read, and see and how we spend our time;

➢ We should remember to be generous with our hugs (everyone needs at least 10 a day!);

➢ No matter how pressing our work or school challenges, we should always remember that a happy family life is of prime importance and demands a lot of our time and attention. "Quality time" isn't enough!

➢ We will have weekly family meetings, plan memorable and exciting vacations, and keep fit and healthy;

➢ We should all be patient with each other;

➢ We should all be sensitive to each other's feelings.

We are lucky to have each other. We should remember this each day!

Family traditions and rituals

One successful idea I came up with was to write letters to my daughters every night when I was away traveling and making films. I invested a lot of time and effort in these letters, and wrote hundreds of them over the years. I saw that my daughters really liked them and got a lot out of them.

The letters were a way I could build a meaningful connection with my children. I wrote to them about all sorts of things, such as how to give a dinner party, the importance of having a rich vocabulary, and stories about Abraham Lincoln and George Washington.

When I was away from home, my nightly letters were an attempt to get the attention of my daughters and not be "out of sight, out of mind." I soon realized that the letters were a wonderful way to tell my daughters things and pass on knowledge, love and wisdom that I might find difficult to do face-to-face. Like a lot of men, I wasn't very good at expressing my feelings. I found it easier to do in letters.

Another family ritual was to hold a weekly family meeting with a written agenda. Our family members took turns chairing and running the meetings, which usually lasted about half an hour. The agenda would contain perhaps 15 items relating to family matters, such as upcoming vacations, organizing the trips for the next day's multiple soccer games, deciding how to organize chores more fairly, going over New Year's resolutions, providing "encouragement" and sharing "rocks."

The "rocks" agenda item involved each family member stating the one or two most important projects she faced in the coming week, such as an exam, repairing a frayed relationship, or completing an unfinished task.

The "encouragement" agenda item was important. During "encouragement," everyone in the family, in turn, offered encouragement (not necessarily praise) to every member of the family for doing "something right."

For example, I might say, "Kim, you worked really hard on that calculus homework last night and I commend you for that." Or, "Tina, you lost the tennis match 0-8 but you didn't give up and kept focused until the end."

Encouragement is a mechanism to get everyone to focus on what is going *right* in the family. The point was to avoid the natural tendency in people and families to focus on what is going *wrong*.

My daughters often resisted these family meetings, but I insisted. They enabled us to communicate more effectively. They helped to maintain order in what otherwise could have been a chaotic household. And they gave our daughters the experience of organizing and leading meetings.

Here are 11 other successful rituals and traditions we developed:

1. Over about a nine-month period when my children were young, we created a Family Mission Statement (see above). Everyone contributed to it. We then framed it and hung it on the wall in a prominent place in the house, so it would be a constant reminder to us all.

2. Every year on January 1, we each wrote our goals for the coming year. I collected them all and made copies for everyone, so that we all knew each other's goals and could help each other achieve them. My daughters are in their late 20s and 30s now, but I still collect everyone's New Year's resolutions!

3. I keep a family journal, and every Christmas Day I give each member of the family a book of about 200-300 pages chronicling everything of interest that has gone on in the family that year.

4. We started a "predictions" tradition, in which every member of the family makes a secret prediction on January 1 for the coming year. On the following Christmas Day, we open the sealed envelopes and see how accurate the predictions have been. As we go around the table, smiles and laughter fill the room.

5. On each child's birthday, I hid dollars around the family room equal in number to their age, such as 12 dollar bills on a 12th birthday.

6. Also on their birthdays, I developed a treasure hunt for each birthday gift. Following funny, cryptic clues, often poems, the birthday girl went around the house to find the hidden gifts.

7. I often bought T-shirts for the whole family with a family photo on them, or with the words, "The Shearer-Palmer Family," emblazoned across the front.

8. I did science experiments regularly with my daughters. (More on that in Chapter 9.)

9. I took my daughters on filming trips to Alaska, Tahiti, Barbados, the Bahamas and other fun and educational places. While the "Date with Dad" idea may have fizzled, I found other ways to spend time one-on-one with the girls.

10. I instigated daily sessions of something I called "teacher/student," in which my kids and I would reverse roles and they became the teacher. They could pick any topic (usually something they had learned in school) and had to teach it to me.

11. Finally, a crucially important thing I had to learn was how to say, "I love you." I learned from a book on fathering that it was important for children to hear their dads say that to them. I disciplined myself to say it. It wasn't easy.

Asking for feedback from my daughters on how I was doing as their Dad

We ask for and obtain feedback and evaluations in our professional jobs all the time, but suggest this to fathers and they think there is something weird about it. Not at all. When my daughters were 9, 14, and 17, I sent them a letter in which I asked them three questions: What would you like me to continue doing as a father that I am already doing? What would you like me to stop doing as a father that I am now doing? What would you like me to start doing that I am not now doing? My daughters' answers to these questions were helpful and revealing. For example, I discovered that my middle daughter, Christina, didn't like me walking around the house dressed only in my booty (her word) underpants. This process of asking kids their opinions can't be taken too far. Children want parents to be parents and not exhibit bizarre psychological behavior, yet there is something to be said for listening to the "customer."

Dad's 70 Rules for Success
I wrote these for Tina when she started at Dartmouth in September 2000.

Work hard
Set goals
Pursue excellence
Discern fundamentals
Show up
Live passionately
Take risks
Smile easily
Pay attention
Help others
Make friends
Battle injustice
Obtain feedback
Love deeply
Write daily
Keep healthy
Stand tall
Study relentlessly
Get help
Be indomitable
Cherish sisters
Ask questions
Don't quit
Make offers
Stay focused
Laugh often
Have vitality
Be bold
Have fun
Read voraciously
Find meaning
Keep promises
Avoid TV
Find mentors
Be indefatigable
Enjoy jokes
Be honorable
Take initiative
Delay gratification
Listen actively
Welcome failure
Get coaching
Anticipate breakdowns

Manage moods
Practice courage
Show affection
Be considerate
Acquire role models
Practice self-discipline
Spend wisely
Show enthusiasm
Feel gratitude
Seize opportunities
Nurture friendships
Be joyful
Avoid gossip
Relish humor
Act fearlessly
Invent happiness
Appreciate nature
Dream big
Drink water
Exercise daily
Seek power
Have integrity
Value family
Celebrate success
Rebound quickly
Speak effectively
Praise specifically
Call home!!

A story from when I was about 19 and planned a visit to Russia

When I was about 19 and in the Royal Navy, I made plans to visit Russia. It was at the height of the Cold War and my father had a fit and called in the security people. I was called up to London for a meeting, heavy with gravitas, with top security officials and told in no uncertain terms not to go or suffer the consequences, which were left vague. I cancelled my plans. But much to my father's annoyance (and my pleasure), I got a story published about it in the Bath Chronicle (the local paper), where I had contacts because I wrote occasional articles for them.

My letter to girls on October 20, 1999 describing the desirable characteristics of their future husbands

My adorable loves, Kimmie, Tina and Jenny,

As you know, I am at the Liberty Science Center in New Jersey tonight for the opening of Wolves. I am delighted that Janet, Gordon, Suzy and Steve will all be there. I hope they don't fall asleep during my presentation!

I have been so interested to observe how you, Tina, and you, Jenny, have recently expressed your desire one day to have children. When I was your age, nothing was further from my mind!

Anyway, your comments have made me reflect on the kind of man I hope you will marry one day. Of course, you may decide never to marry, which is just fine.

In no particular order, your future husband should:

1. Have competent, loving parents.

2. Work hard because you want to marry someone who knows how to earn a living.

3. Have superior "people skills."

4. Be patient and forgiving.

5. Be playful.

6. Not be attracted to the pursuit of frivolous or inane activities.

7. Understand that love is a verb, not a noun. Love is something that you do, a sacrifice that you make. It is not a feeling - that notion comes from Hollywood and is selfish and immature. The feeling of love is the result of the action of love.

8. Attach little importance to physical beauty, realizing that this is genetic (in other words, mere chemistry), and that inner beauty is the only thing that really matters.

9. Have a humility and an uncertainty when it comes to religious matters. Marrying someone who is arrogantly dogmatic can be very unpleasant if you don't share their views. It is good to be skeptical of all dogma and authority.

10. Have values very similar to your own.

11. Be profoundly serious (but not solemn) about making his life mean something. He should want to leave the world a better place for his passage through it, to leave his footprints in the sands of time.

12. Be ambitious, but at the same time, have an inner tranquility.

13. Be optimistic, cheerful and positive.

14. Attach great importance to the concept of families being the basic building block of all healthy and vibrant societies.

15. Value family traditions and rituals.

16. Be responsible. By this I mean that your future husband should believe that his life is ultimately his responsibility, however many "bad" things happen (or have happened) to him.

17. Be able to take care of himself, and manage his time, space, commitments and health well, so that he has more to give and share with you and the children.

18. Have the capacity and ability to keep promises and honor commitments he makes to you and others.

19. Be dedicated to lifelong learning.

20. Have a good sense of humor and enjoy laughing out loud.

21. Be absolutely reliable and trustworthy.

22. Be physically fit.

23. Be courageous, fair, honest, loyal, devoted, compassionate, generous, creative, tenacious, and a person of sound judgement and wisdom.

24. Be relentless in his examination of his life to see how to redesign it so it is more effective, purposeful, and loving.

25. Be a highly competent and empathic listener.

26. Be ruthless about getting rid of clutter and have a strong desire to simplify his life so he has room for what really matters to him (you).

27. Not speak negatively of others when they are not present.

28. Be skillful in coordinating his actions with those of others.

29. Focus his efforts on things he can do something about rather than on things beyond his control.

30. Have a written plan for his life which he enjoys sharing with you.

31. Want to make you look good in front of other people.

32. Catch you and the children doing things right. And if he does criticize you, he should do it in private and in a loving way.

33. Be affectionate and loving, and want to "coddle" you (to use Granny's word.)

It goes without saying that when I married Mommy nearly 25 years ago, I measured up poorly against virtually every one of these criteria.

My loves, I do not claim this list of desirable attributes in a husband is complete, comprehensive, well organized, or even particularly insightful. I am sure it can be improved a lot. It is just what occurs to me as I sit writing this letter to you. By the way, he doesn't have to wear booty shorts!

Somerset Maugham said that, "American women expect to find in their husbands a perfection that English women only hope to find in their butlers." Don't expect too much of men, otherwise they are bound to disappoint you. Ann Landers said it best: "A successful marriage is not a gift; it is an achievement."

When I was young, someone silly told my fortune and claimed that I would be married three times. I still remember the revulsion I felt at that possibility and I resolved that I would be free of the dreary, painful banality of divorce.

So there, my treasures, are some quick thoughts on your future husbands! Whomever they turn out to be will be very lucky to marry you!

I adore you.

Dad (aka Mrs. Bennett!)
XXXOOO

How I loved making people laugh when I was a small kid
I loved making my family laugh. I'd overheard my mother ask another family member how many famous people there were in the world. It was a rhetorical question, but I saw my chance. "Well, let's see," I said, with as much mock seriousness as I could muster, as I sat down and put my hand under my chin. "First, we have Sir Winston Churchill...." I knew the sight of a five-year-old acting like an erudite professor who knew the answer would make my family laugh.

The first time I performed stand-up comedy
When I tried stand-up comedy (in 2006 at age 59), my first performance was in a tawdry bar in Crystal City. A ton of neighbors and friends came out to support me and I was too busy performing and greeting people to take much notice of my surroundings. I was oblivious to the fact that it was a gay bar.

Jon and I shaking creamy milk to make butter, under the watchful eye of my father
When Jon and I were four years old in 1951, England was still under strict rationing from the war. Although butter was in short supply, we had plenty of milk. Our father would make Jon and me stand on the verandah (we lived at 89 Bloomfield Avenue in Bath) and shake heavy bottles of creamy milk until the milk was transformed into butter. Our arms would ache painfully, but if we stopped to rest, he would shout at us to keep going.

My father's instinctive remedy for melancholy
When I was about six years old, I found myself one day in a deeply melancholy mood. My father saw that I was dispirited and depressed. He ordered me out to the garden, insisting that I push our heavy lawn roller up and down the yard until I was exhausted. Soon enough, the strenuous exercise transformed my mood from ennui to endorphin-driven optimism.

When I was about 3, I exhibited sagacity by giving away my Christmas gifts
One Christmas, after all the gifts had been opened, I looked at everything I had received and realized that it wasn't of much use to me and that others would benefit from them much more than I. I slipped out of the front door with my gifts under my arm and went to each neighbor's house, leaving a gift on the front step. This struck me as eminently sensible and rational. When my parents discovered what I had done, they were perplexed and flummoxed, and hurriedly went to each neighbor to apologize and retrieve the gifts. I often think that I reached my zenith of wisdom back then.

My father didn't believe in giving kids a false sense of self-esteem by mindlessly praising inferior work

One summer, there were races on the last day of school. Jon and I ran "the hundred yards" race. We did our best, but didn't win. We felt quite pleased with ourselves. My mother enthusiastically congratulated us. Then my father came over and abruptly told us in a hectoring tone that we hadn't tried hard enough, that we have to run with more determination and show more willpower, resolve, and grit. Later on I came to deeply appreciate his candor.

My father had a playful side when we were young, but it was often hidden by stress

One evening as we were getting ready for bed, my father said he was going to build an obstacle race for us. Jon and I were so excited! In our bedroom, he created tunnels, ladders, piles of pillows, and all sorts of other things for us to surmount and overcome. It was fun! And it inspired me when I became a dad and grandfather.

Gail's favorite t-shirt

"My next husband will be normal"

Cory, our wonderful golden retriever, ate some hidden birthday dollars when we weren't looking

Cory was highly food motivated. One of our family traditions when celebrating birthdays is to hide single dollars around the house for the person being celebrated to search for and find (with the number of dollars equal to the birthday). We did this once, but made the mistake of hiding some of them on or near the floor and then leaving them there while we went out for a meal at a local restaurant. When we returned, we were baffled why some of the dollars were missing, but later realized that Cory had eaten them! They showed up the next day on our daily walk!

Kim's story about me recommending against his daughters having kids, but then acting very differently

In one of Kim's articles for the Washington Post , she told the following story:

At a recent family dinner, the topic of children came up.

"Oh girls, you don't want children," my Dad said to me and my two younger sisters. "They'll take over your life." He started delving into the expense, time demands, and lifestyle changes brought on by babies.

My mom rolled her eyes—her usual response to his rants. Then she revealed what he had purchased at a recent school auction they attended: a book on how to be a more effective grandparent.

How my views have changed between 21 and age 70

Kim asked me, as part of her StoryWorth project, "What have you changed your mind about over the years?" Here was my reply:

Contrary to when I was 21, I now believe (at almost 70) the following 21 things:

1. Marriage is important

2. Children and grandchildren are adorable
3. A plant-based diet is crucial for good health
4. Daily vigorous exercise is vital
5. Adequate sleep is essential
6. Anger and irascibility are major character flaws
7. Listening is intense hard work
8. Teaching is a performance art
9. Dying is hard
10. Parenting is harder
11. My parents did a better job than I gave them credit for at the time
12. Knowing your family history is vital
13. My biggest success in life is my marriage and my family
14. TV is corrupting
15. Pop culture is decadent and degenerate
16. Wisdom only comes with age if you work at it
17. Relationships are everything
18. Loneliness and isolation are epidemic and deadly
19. Character is foundational
20. Handstands are easy
21. A sense of humor is vital

My celebration of Gail on her 50th birthday on December 16, 2000
To celebrate your 50th birthday, here are 50 reasons why I love you and you are so special:
1. For the three incredible daughters you (I!) produced.
2. For being a wonderful wife, mother, daughter, sister, daughter-in-law and aunt.
3. For your beauty, both on the surface, and deep down.
4. For the values we share as parents.
5. For the way you hug me every morning after we get out of bed.
6. For the gin-and-tonics you and my father enjoy together.
7. For the love and affection you shower unreservedly on my side of the family.
8. For the way you encourage me to be more sociable.
9. For your efforts to keep fit and healthy.
10. For your fascination with public affairs.
11. For helping me to be a good father to Kim, Tina and Jen.
12. For your expertise in health policy.
13. For the way you have made CU a leading and respected advocate in consumer-oriented health care.
14. For your unimpeachable honesty and integrity.
15. For the way you plan ahead.
16. For the great dinner parties you give.
17. For the way you don't let our different religious beliefs come between us.
18. For the extraordinary emotional stability you give me.
19. For the security of knowing you will always love and cherish me.
20. For the soundness of your advice.
21. For helping me complete my book on the Hallett/Palmer family history.
22. For the incredible job you did writing and publishing your book on the history of the Mellen/Shearer family.
23. For your natural beauty.

24. For the delicious and original soups you make.
25. For your financial planning acumen and for managing our finances so expertly.
26. For your enjoyment of the great game of tennis.
27. For the way you do your hair.
28. For marrying me (despite my purple shirt and green suit!)
29. For your wonderful ability and willingness to listen.
30. For the fantastic job you did on the house addition to create our dream home.
31. For the outstanding job you did as President of the Holton-Arms Parent Association.
32. For being tolerant of my shortcomings and idiosyncrasies.
33. For cherishing me more than I deserve.
34. For your warmth and love.
35. For your support and affection.
36. For your encouragement and wisdom.
37. For your patience and sense of humor.
38. For helping to create so many great family traditions, such as family meetings, "rocks," "encouragement," birthday treasure hunts, and Christmas Day predictions.
39. For setting a good example by catching family members "doing something right."
40. For helping me lead a more balanced life than otherwise would be the case.
41. For your taste in interior design.
42. For your competence in running our household and managing our family affairs.
43. For your ethical standards.
44. For how you bring Cory to the front door to say goodbye to Jenny when she (Jen) leaves for school.
45. For having such high emotional intelligence and good judgment.
46. For making me so proud to be your husband.
47. For your dedication to our family and to Kim, Tina and Jenny.
48. For reaching the age of 50 with such grace and beauty.
49. For still loving me after all these years together; and
50. **For making me the luckiest man in the whole world!**

I LOVE YOU!!!

When I was 10, a herd of aggressive cows trampled over our picnic

At age 10, picnicking with my mother way out in the beautiful countryside outside Bath, spreading out a rug on the field near a weir (a small waterfall), suddenly finding an aggressive herd of cows moving in on us, getting scared, finding a stranger rush to our rescue by boldly grabbing the cows by their horns and giving them a sharp slap on their behinds, sending the cows running, allowing us, relieved, to recapture our rug and picnic. Observing wryly at my sudden change of mood from fearful defeat to confident bravado, and my admiration for the audacity and boldness of our rescuer.

My discovery of books at age 16

At age 16, discovering the infinite joy of books when an inspired English teacher decided not to teach us formally, but rather give us the time in class to pick books to read from his large collection of Penguin books by authors like Andre Gide, JD Salinger, William Golding, Margaret Drabble, Thomas Hardy, CS Lewis, Aldous Huxley, PG Woodhouse, Albert Camus, George Orwell, Arthur Koestler, and Anthony Burgess. I discovered a new world.

At age 16, my intense effort to improve my vocabulary
At age 16, starting to collect and learn words I didn't know in a small A through Z notebook. I still have that little notebook today and showed it recently to Kareena (age 7). It is now worn, decrepit, and covered in scotch tape to stop it falling apart. An old friend.

At age 11, giving myself a knife wound while playing with my twin Jon
When Jon and I were about 11, we were playing with a penknife. While I held the knife in an attacking position, I tried to show him how I would escape from his grasp if he held both my wrists over my head. As I forcefully yanked both hands downwards, I unintentionally plunged the knife into my own thigh, requiring four stitches. The main thing I remember about the event was whimpering like a coward and showing nothing but fear and weakness, when my father said brusquely that it was no big deal, and I suddenly realized that I was feeling little pain and my father was quite correct. I stopped crying and immediately felt calm and composed! Nothing had changed except my perspective.

My brother Jeremy getting his fingers crushed when helping my father in the garden
My oldest brother Jeremy, when about 16, was helping my father in the backyard moving some massive concrete blocks. His fingers got caught between two blocks and crushed. He was rushed to the emergency room and eventually his fingers recovered with no permanent damage. I often wondered if Jeremy had unconsciously allowed this accident to happen in order to obtain some sympathy, attention, and compassion from my father, with whom he had a highly stressful, tenuous, and tense relationship.

A great aunt in the USA finding a large black snake in a bin of flour
A great aunt in the USA almost had a heart attack when in the 1920s, she reached into a barrel to get some flour for cooking, and, to her horror, found her hand touching a large black snake lying on top of the flour.

Kim asking me what surprised me about having children
I answered as follows: There were many aspects of having children that confounded my expectations. It was a topic I had given little attention as a young man. Children were not something I ever thought about. To the extent I thought about it, my attitude was quite negative. After experiencing my own childhood, I saw kids as vexing, onerous, frustrating, painful, and unrewarding.

It turned out that I was completely wrong. Kim, Tina, and Jen gave me exactly the opposite experience. They were delightful, diligent, loving, responsive, responsible, and deeply appreciative of our parenting efforts.

I feel—and I'm sure Gail feels the same way—that our greatest legacy when we die, and the thing we will be most intensely proud of, will be our three daughters and their families. If I die tomorrow, I'll die feeling at peace and fulfilled because of Kim, Tina, and Jenny. They are Gail and my gifts to a future we will not see ourselves.

There were five aspects of having children that surprised me:

First, one of the most profound surprises was how having children gave my life purpose. It gave a "why" to living. This was not something I expected. I thought kids would just give me constant migraines, but in fact they imbued my life with meaning. I was now responsible for something bigger than myself. Through my daughters, I became myself.

Second, grandchildren! I never imagined that Kareena, Neal, JJ, and Max would give me so much joy or would be so important to me. I think about them all the time and what their futures might hold. I worry about the world we are leaving them.

Third, sons-in-law! Who would have ever thought that through my daughters I would be given three amazing sons-in-law, who are like the three sons I never had.

Fourth, I never thought having daughters would lead to so much learning, but in wanting Kim, Tina, and Jenny to be fulfilled and happy, I felt compelled to study how people achieve their goals and then teach my daughters everything I learned.

Fifth, another surprise was how easy it was to be a half-decent parent once I started taking it seriously, realizing I was making mistakes, learning from them, and studying what effective, loving parenting means in practical terms. Early in my marriage, I was incredibly ignorant about the basics of being a good parent and what being a good parent entailed. It took me years to learn and I'm still learning. Being the youngest of four boys, I never had to take care of younger siblings. Parenting at first seemed like an impossibly challenging responsibility. But once I realized it was a something I could study and learn about, it started making more sense to me and became less intimidating. Family meetings, a family mission statement, "catch them doing something right," writing letters to them, staying calm, and all the traditions and rituals that I write about in the Preface to my parenting book, *Raise Your Kids to Succeed*, were not on my radar screen when I got married.

So those are five things that surprised me about having children. One thing that didn't surprise me was how brilliant Gail was as a mother. She took to it as if she'd been training for it her whole life. Gail was preternaturally gifted and skilled in that domain—loving, warm, empathetic, kind, giving, unselfish, generous, capable, astute, and perceptive. Gail's careful, prudent, and risk-averse approach to parenting was a bracing and healthy counterbalance to my more rambunctious, physical, and adventurous attitude.

Sujay

From my wedding toast in 2005
Let me tell you something about Sujay. Gail and I took an immediate liking to Sujay when we met him. He was evidently an ambitious person who would go far professionally, but it was his personal qualities that we especially loved – his wonderful sense of humor, his warmth, his genuineness, his inner serenity, his easy-going and relaxed attitude, and, above all, his deep love and caring for Kim.

Kim and Sujay met about three years ago at graduate school at the University of Chicago. We knew from Kim's e-mails that she had met someone extraordinarily special, and they both knew from their earliest dates that they were meant for one another.

The first time Sujay came to visit us, he said it felt like the movie *Meet the Parents*. He slept in the basement, he had to treat our dog Cory with great affection, and he had to deal with me, who I'm afraid may have reminded him of the Robert DeNiro character!

In fact, Kim wrote an article last year called *Passing the Dreaded Parents' Test* about what it was like for Sujay to visit us for the first time. Kim wrote that one thing I do is to announce vocally the characteristics of the ideal "son-in-law."

I want to tell you all that Sujay passed "the dreaded parents' test" with flying colors. We are so happy to welcome him into our family. If Gail and I searched the whole world, we couldn't find a more wonderful husband for Kim.

About 18 months ago, we received an e-mail from Sujay saying that he was going to call us to ask us about something highly confidential. Gail and I immediately anticipated that Sujay wanted to propose to Kim. We were so excited!

We waited for Sujay to call. An hour passed. Another hour passed. I couldn't wait any longer. I went to my computer and sent Sujay an e-mail: "Sujay, Gail and I are at home completely relaxed. Now would be a great time to call." Another hour passed. And then another. I went to my computer again and sent Sujay another e-mail: "Sujay, Gail and I are staying up late. We are totally relaxed. Now would be an excellent time to call us." What we didn't realize was that Sujay and Kim were watching a late-night movie and so Sujay wasn't able to call us.

Sujay called the next day and we were elated with the news. A few days later, Sujay proposed to Kim in a wonderfully romantic way.

CJ

From my wedding toast in 2014

Let me tell you something about CJ. Gail and I took an immediate liking to CJ when we first met him. We soon realized that he is highly intelligent and well-educated, is doing extremely well professionally having created his own law firm, and is an excellent athlete.

But as we got to know him better, we found out that he was also a person of great integrity, that he has a wonderful sense of humor, that he is a genuine, warm, and generous person, that he's devoted to his mom and dad, his brothers and sisters, and his nephews and nieces, and that, above all, he has a deep love and caring for Tina.

Tina and CJ met in San Francisco. We knew from Tina's e-mails that she had met someone extraordinarily special, and we think they both knew from their earliest dates that they were meant for one another.

Believe it or not, many years ago when Kim, Tina, and Jen were growing up, I had the nerve and temerity to write them a three page letter describing the character and habits of the men they should marry. Like Sujay before him, CJ met all the criteria with flying colors. We are so happy to welcome him into our family.

Before Christmas, CJ called me, and I was hoping he was calling to seek Gail's and my blessing for proposing to Tina. I was excited with anticipation as the conversation started! After a long talk, he finally said, "Oh, Chris, there's one last thing."

My heart leaped! At last! CJ went on to tell me how much he loved Tina and how they wanted to spend their lives together. As he talked, tears welled up, and so when he finally said, "So, Chris, I want to ask you for your blessing," I was overcome with emotion and had to ask him to wait for a moment while I got a tissue and regained my composure.

I told him how thrilled I was with the news and how Gail and I would feel honored to have him as our son-in-law. I told him I knew he would make an outstanding husband. A few days later in Hawaii, CJ proposed to Tina in a wonderfully romantic way.

Chase

From my wedding toast in 2017

Let me tell you something about Chase. Gail and I took an immediate liking to Chase when we first met him. He is an Air Force veteran and passionate about his career. He has two graduate degrees and has recently joined FitBit in operations and is responsible for new product introduction. He is, like Jenny, a health and fitness devotee.

One of the first stories we ever heard about Chase relates to his physical strength. He and Jenny were doing a Tough Mudder race, which for those of you who don't know, is an extraordinarily challenging 10-mile race full of obstacles designed to push your body to its limit. At one of these obstacles—a 20-foot wall they had to climb over—Chase paused at the top of the wall to lean down and help pull over an exhausted and heavy competitor who was struggling. The grateful man looked at Chase and said admiringly, "You're all kinds of strong!"

Chase was a personal trainer while he was getting his MBA. Whenever I get the chance, I take a training session with him... and I'm sore for days. Like Jenny, he knows a lot about fitness, health, and nutrition. If you haven't experienced one of his ginger shots, you're missing something!

After his first visit to our home, he wrote Gail and me a wonderful thank you letter in which he said, "I realize now where Jenny gets her 'towel on the floor' habit," He also wrote, "Visiting your home really helped me understand Jenny at a deeper level—her drive, passion, and motivation for life."

Chase is a person of great integrity, a wonderful sense of humor, and a warm and generous spirit. He is devoted to his family and he has a deep love for Jenny.

Many years ago, when Kim, Tina, and Jen were teenagers, I wrote them a long letter describing the character of the men they should marry. Like Sujay and CJ before him, Chase meets all the criteria with flying colors. We are so happy to welcome him into our family.

Our first inkling that Jenny and Chase might get married came last Christmas when they were staying with us for a few days. Just before they left, Chase asked if he could talk to Gail and me privately about something.

While Jen was busy doing something else, we sat in the lounge and Chase told us how much he loved, respected, and admired Jenny, and how he wanted to spend the rest of his life with her. He told us that Jenny had brought out the best in him, and he thought that he had brought out the best in her.

He asked us if he could have our permission to propose to her, and we said how we would be thrilled for him to do that and how he had become part of our family.

He was so gracious, and Gail and I were elated. We had been hoping that Chase was going to say something along these lines, but had not expected something so thoughtful, so well prepared, and something so wonderfully expressive.

We told Chase how thrilled we were and how Gail and I would feel honored to have him as our son-in-law. We told him we knew he would make an outstanding husband.

Kareena, Neal, JJ, And Max

JJ, age 0, responding to emails
"Thank you for your email. I will be unavailable for the next 5-6 years as I am just a newborn now. Should you require immediate assistance, please contact my parents. That's what I do. I suggest screaming. They really respond to that."

Kareena, age 4, asking Kim when I'm going to be an old man
Kareena came over to play. Afterwards, I received the following e-mail from Kim:
> Kareena just asked me, as I was helping her down the stairs, "when is grandpa going to be an old man?"
> I said I don't know, maybe in 20 years.
> Then she said, "maybe I will help him down the stairs when he's an old man."
> No idea where that came from!

I replied:
> Kimmie, that's so funny!
> Kareena and I were upstairs exercising and having fun, and then we decided to make a smoothie downstairs. As we started down the stairs, I said, "Do you want to hold my hand?"
> "No thanks, Grandpa, I can do it on my own."
> "OK," I said, "but hold on tight to the bannisters." And down we went slowly, with me going in front so I could catch her if she fell.
> As we got to the bottom, I said to her, "Kareena, I'm helping you now when you're little. Will you help me when I'm an old man?"
> "What do you mean, Grandpa?"
> "Well, when I'm an old man, I'll be frail and will need help getting up and down the stairs. Will you help me then, just as I'm helping you now?"
> Pause.
> "Grandpa, when will you be an old man?"
> Me, laughing: "I think I may be an old man now!"
> As this conversation unrolled, all I could think of was Bartholomew and the little girl in the book we all loved when you girls were little.
> That is so interesting that Kareena would remember this incident on the stairs and bring it up with you at home!
> I love you.
> Dad
> XXXOOO

My questionable advice to Neal, age 2 (via Kareena, age 5) about how to deal with bullies
Kim wrote to me as follows: "Today I heard Kareena explaining to Neal after he said his friend Oscar pushed him, 'Neal, Grandpa says you have to look tough, but then if that doesn't work, you can punch them.'" Kim added: "LOL! Nice lesson, Dad—now I know who to blame when Neal starts beating up the other 2-year-olds."

Kareena, age 5, checking that she will remain high up in my esteem
Kareena and Neal were playing in the study with me, exploring Grandpa's Bag of Tricks. Kareena was getting a little miffed that Neal was diluting the attention I was hitherto giving solely to her. So I said to her that I had something very interesting to show her and that was my big dictionary. So while Neal played happily on the floor with various things from my bag, I helped Kareena stand up on a chair and take a look at my big dictionary on the music stand in my study. (I use it standing up.) She found it fascinating and loved turning the pages. When she saw something she recognized, like a map, she would point that out with enthusiasm. As this was going on, the following conversation ensued:

Kareena: If you had another granddaughter, would she be as special as me?

Me: Nana and I don't have another granddaughter. You're the only one.

K: Yes, but you might have another one in the future. If you did, would she be as special as me?

Me: (thinking quickly and carefully) She would be as special as you, and YOU would be as every bit as special as her.

K: If you don't have another granddaughter, would that make me the most special granddaughter in the world?

Me: You are so deeply special and Nana and I adore you. You couldn't be more special to us.

K: If another granddaughter didn't exist, then they would be invisible and I would be the most special.

Me: (laughing) That is so true!

My Parents

See my family history book

Two stories about Little Granny (born in 1890) I recorded in 1971 when I was 24, presumably told to me by my father (Little Granny was his mother)
Granny's Uncle Robert (her mother's brother) took the exam for Inspector of Taxes (about 1895) and passed. He received a letter afterwards saying that it was only kept open for "gentleman's sons." This turned him into a rabid socialist. He had been rejected for a job simply because he was from the working class.

Also, Granny's father was a blacksmith in Pembroke Dock. When she was 18 months old (1891) his leg was crushed and his foot smashed when working in the Dockyard. Three months later he died of the wound. His family received no compensation, nor would he have done had he died when his injury occurred. That is outrageous.

One of my father's favorite stories he liked to tell about his mother (Little Granny) as she entered old age and got tinnitus

Granny had a hearing problem of tinnitus, so she had her hearing tested. She couldn't hear anything the doctor was saying. Then the doctor said, at the same voice level, "I hear you like a drink of Scotch every evening." Granny was a teetotaler, and replied indignantly, "No, I do not!"

My father at age 6 devastated by the death of his father

Daddy was born in 1913 in Pembroke Dock in Wales. As a child of six in 1919, he lost his father. My grandfather had, we now think, a duodenal ulcer, which burst. The country doctors were unable to save him. My father was devastated. He was very close to his Dad and adored him. Years later, in 1981, he wrote in a letter to my wife Gail and me, "My father died when I was six and I had loved him dearly. Afterwards I did not want anyone to talk about him – not for years – and when they did, my eyes filled with tears and I could not speak." It is impossible for me to imagine the pain, loss, and suffering my father had to confront as a child when his father was taken from him so suddenly and unexpectedly.

My father berating me for not working hard enough

When I was about 18 years old, I came home for leave after joining the Royal Navy. My father greeted me with a perfunctory handshake, and then immediately asked me about my grades. Rather pleased with myself, I told him they were above average—mostly As, with a few A minuses and B pluses. His face darkened. "For God's sake, you can do better than that," he snapped angrily. "You *have* to do better than that. You should be getting nothing but As. Your grades are unacceptable." I was shocked by his fierceness, but from that point on, I resolved never to get anything less than As. His demands pushed me to achieve what I'd previously assumed were impossible goals—and after that conversation, I always did my best and earned virtually perfect grades.

My father's secret order to go to America with a package if Hitler invaded the UK

The year before my parents were married in 1941, an unusual thing happened to my father. He was working at Haslar. One day the superintendent, Dr. Gawn, sent for him and said that if the Germans got a foothold on the south coast, which then seemed quite likely, my father was to drop everything and take a small secret package from Dr. Gawn's safe, and make his way to Liverpool. At Liverpool, he was to board a waiting cruiser which would sail to America, where he was to hand the secret package to the British Ambassador. In the meantime, nobody else was to know about this. My father believed the package contained reports of German magnetic and acoustic mines and ways to sweep them. Some months later, my parents were married and my father asked Dr. Gawn whether this changed anything. He was told firmly it did not! So, my mother was happily unaware that if the Germans invaded Britain, my father would have to abandon her and make his way to America.

My father put in charge of a Home Guard platoon to fight of a German invasion

In early 1940, Anthony Eden formed the Home Guard to repel a possible German invasion. Dr. Gawn called Daddy into his office and said, "I think you are the most aggressive member of our team. I'm putting you in charge of our Home Guard platoon." Daddy was made a second lieutenant and put in charge of the platoon of twelve men. They were issued Long Lee Enfields, which were ancient rifles from World War I!

My father's recollection of D-Day (June 6, 1944), in his own words

At the time, we were living in Alverstoke, a small seaside town near Portsmouth, and for a year or more we had not been allowed to go on the beach because there was tremendous activity there building the Mulberry Harbour which was later transported to France to make a sheltered harbour at Arromande, Normandy.

I was working in Portsmouth Dockyard, which then employed 20,000 men and was the key port for the D-Day adventure. I was a naval constructor and I was a senior member of the management because there were not many fully-trained constructors about.

I was in charge of the maintenance and repair of all landing craft, and we had hundreds of them by June 1944. They were mostly hidden in creeks and harbours, ready to transport our soldiers and their guns and tanks to France. If I remember correctly, the standard landing craft, called and L.C.T. (for Landing Craft, Tank) could carry 4 tanks and about 100 soldiers.

Like everybody else in the Dockyard I was listening to the radio every day (there was no T.V. of course.), and the great news came, very early in the morning of the 6th June, to tell us that our warships and planes were bombing the French coast and that an immense fleet of landing craft was sailing to Normandy. How excited this made us, and we all prayed that our troops would succeed in forming a bridgehead and not be driven back by the Germans.

As far as I was concerned there was not much to do on that day because the Dockyard was empty, but the next day the ships that had been damaged by the enemy started coming in, returning. They had all sorts of problems – holes in the sides and superstructure, damaged engines and equipment, torn plating and sometimes bodies lying amongst the wreckage. My job was to get the ships repaired as quickly as possible so that they could take more soldiers and tanks and guns to France.

The Dockyard workmen were magnificent. They worked as they had never worked before. I remember running from dock to dock telling the men what to do, and I did this for the whole of the 7th June and then on through the night and then on through the next day when I became too exhausted to go on, so I cycled home to Granny and our two little boys (Jeremy and Timothy). But the critical battle was won, the beachhead in Normandy was established, and there were plenty of landing craft to supply the troops because our men in the Dockyard were repairing all the damaged ships so quickly and sending them back like new just a few days after the enemy had thought they had destroyed them.

My mother's experience in WWII in the WAPC

On September 4, 1939, one day after World War II was declared, my mother, then 21, joined the Women's Auxiliary Police Corps as an interpreter working in the "Alien's Office" in Plymouth. Plymouth was brimming with aliens fleeing from Hitler. Many foreigners were interrogated and my mother's skill with languages was greatly valued. One of her duties in the Women's Auxiliary Police Corps was to man the telephones whenever an air raid warning sounded. She would run up to the police station as the bombs were dropping. At the police station, she handled calls about the bombing until the raids were over. Then she would go out with a mobile canteen to help victims and others who needed help. Large areas of Plymouth were devastated. My mother told me once, "Looking back at myself racing up to the Police Station in the pitch black with incendiaries falling relentlessly, it amazes me I wasn't scared to death."

My mother was sure she would have a little girl

With the war in Europe finishing, my father was appointed Constructor Commander with the British Pacific fleet, and he left for Australia in May 1945, leaving my mother and two small sons behind. The departure was traumatic. My parents wondered if they would ever see each other again, but after eighteen months, my mother traveled to Hong Kong and the family was reunited in December 1946.

My mother became pregnant as soon as she arrived in Hong Kong. She was excited because she desperately wanted a girl and thought her chances were good because she already had two boys. That wasn't thinking logically, but that is how her mind worked.

A few weeks before her due date, my mother fell down some stairs and was taken to the local hospital where she was X-rayed to check everything was okay. A few days later, the doctor sent the X-rays to my father (this was before *The Feminine Mystique*) with an attached cover note, which simply said "Ha Ha."

The reason for the "Ha Ha" was that the X-rays revealed that my mother was pregnant with twins. My mother was pleased because she thought that having twins doubled her chances of having a girl.

On August 25, 1947, my mother went into labor. Jon came out first and now my mother was convinced that the probability of the next baby being a girl was practically a certainty. I was born 45 minutes after Jon. When my mother saw that I was also a boy, she became hysterical with bitter disappointment and the doctors had to sedate her to calm her down.

I think my mother, because basically she was a sensible person, soon got used to the idea that she would never have a daughter, and dealt with her disappointment in a mature way. I certainly never experienced any sense from her that I was a disappointment to her because of my gender.

My mother's extraordinary propensity for writing warm and chatty letters

My mother's letter writing was legendary. I remember when Jeremy, Tim, Jon and I were boarders at Dulwich College as young teenagers. None of us were very happy. There was, however, one ray of comforting sunshine — the letters we received from my mother. She would write long, detailed and loving letters to us once a week, affirming each one of us with words of encouragement and affection.

Hannah, age 4 or 5, revealing how vibrant she thinks my mother is (her Granny)

Lisa (Hannah's mother) told my father this story in 1986:
Hannah said to her "Grandad (Graham) is very old, isn't he?"
Lisa. Yes, he's quite old.
Hannah. And Nanny (Toni) is old. And Grandpa (me) is old. And Little Granny is old.
Lisa. What about Granny? (Mavis)
Hannah. No! She isn't old. She's new!

My father writing about Admiral Beatty at the Battle of Jutland in 1916 in WWI

This was the one great naval battle of World War I, and Beatty & Jellicoe knew that if we were defeated we would lose control of the sea and lose the war.

The battle started badly as (I think) four of our leading battleships blew up when hit by German shells at 15-20 miles range. Beatty was on the bridge of his flagship (Lion?) with his flag captain Chatfield (later Admiral of the Fleet Lord Chatfield and the son of a constructor) and one can imagine his thoughts as he said quietly, "There's something wrong with our bloody ships, Chatfield." But he sailed on into the Germans and eventually they were driven back and never ventured out of Kiel again until they came out to surrender about 3 years later.

An exhaustive enquiry showed what was wrong. Our Gunnery experts had not realized that the flash from an exploding shell could travel down through the (open) gun hoists and detonate the hundreds of tons of ammunition in the magazines.

The solution was to make the gun hoists flashtight.

Incidentally, the reason the Germans did not go on blowing up our ships in this way was that we started hitting them, and their beautifully designed optical fire control was shaken to bits and they could no longer score direct hits on the British ships.

Love,

Daddy

A story Daddy used to love to tell about a smug student and how a teacher gave him his comeuppance

There was a student called Spanner and he had a famous father and a mother who was the daughter of a bishop. They were all terribly religious. Spanner was easily the top student in the Dockyard School exam for the Corps, and averaged about 90% in the 10 three hour paper. When his teacher in Naval Architecture congratulated him he said "I owe it all to God. He guides me & watches over me in everything I do." This sounded so smug that the teacher was stung to reply "Well he can't be much of a God if he only got 90%." … Perhaps the teacher was disappointed not be given some thanks for what he had done.

My father describing "culm" fires that "country folk" in Wales used for heat in the early part of the 20th century when he was a boy

My father wrote this in a letter to Gail and me in August, 1977: "I have a few enclosures from recent copies of the Times for you. The one about Ocean Sediments may be of interest. When I was a small boy my Granny & all the local country folk had what they called 'culm' fires. 'Culm' was the mud they dug off the river bed at low tide. I think they sometimes mixed a little coal dust with it. They rolled it into balls (in their hands) about 2" or 3" in diameter and stacked them on the fire. It burnt as a dull red glow for an incredibly long time. Indeed, the culm fires usually were kept burning right through the year."

My great grandparents

My mother's grandparents on her father's side were Richard Thomas Hallett (1843-1903) and Agnes Mary Stratton (1848-1937). They married in England in 1870 and the emigrated to America in 1871, six years after the Civil War ended. After a false start on the coast of Virginia, they moved inland to Nottoway County. In 1876, Richard became an American citizen. Agnes hated Nottoway County and returned to England in 1877. Richard then started spending half a year in the US and the other half in UK.

They must have been tough, robust, strong people. Imagine crossing the Atlantic all those times in the late 19th century! That was an arduous and dangerous journey. Richard must have been amazingly tough and hardy. And I remember my mother telling me that Agnes could still jump rope at 89. That has always inspired my handstands!

My father's grandfather on his father's side was William Palmer (1849-1934) and his grandmother was Ellen Letitia Rees (1852-1928). William was born in Llangwm in Wales and became a blacksmith (like many family members) in Pembroke Naval Dockyard and built warships for the Royal Navy. His nickname was "doctor," because, according to my father, people often came to him for advice and guidance. He had a reputation for wisdom.

The story my father told of how he hated beetroot, but came to love it

As a child, my father loathed the taste of beetroot. (That's what we call it in England. Americans may call it beets. It is a deep crimson vegetable.) One day he came home feeling famished. He looked everywhere for something to eat. Nothing. No food anywhere. He kept looking and eventually the only thing he could find was beetroot. His hunger compelled him to take a bite. To his amazement, he loved it. From then on, beetroot became one of his favorite foods.

Gail's Parents

See the family history book written by Gail.

Index

ballerina joke, 206

Barbados, 381, 385

Barker, Jonathan, 510

Bartlebaugh, Chuck, 505

Basinger, Kim, 76

Bath, England: family cemetery in, 530–31; hot mineral springs in, 280; Palmer, Mavis, funeral in, 498–500; Palmer, S., job in, 35, 177

Battle of Gettysburg, 195–96, 244

Battle of the Great Plains, 42

Beach, Carol, 174

The Beagle And Mr. Flycatcher, 150

bears: about, 157, 308; conference on, 305; IMAX film (*Bears*) on, 135, 209, 391, 412–13, 415, 439; Kodiak, 221, 231, 308

Beatty (admiral), 646

beauty, 155, 214

bed, falling out of, 604

bedtime rituals, 232

Beebe, Diana, 212–13

Beetroot, 647

beginners mind, 42–43

Bennis, Warren, 307–8

Berkeley Springs, 75

Berle, Lila, 66

Berle, Peter, 20, 61–62, 66–67, 71

Betty (family friend), 565

Beyond the Big Talk (Haffner), 429

Bickel, Glenn, 283

Big Apple Circus, 173

biomes, 480

birth: of Jen, 10; of Kim, 10, 356; of Palmer, Chris, 60, 409, 501, 539, 645; of Tina, 10

birthdays and celebrations: "dollar bills" hunt on, 565, 628, 634; Jen's, 385, 431, 590; JJ's, 598; Kim's 21st, 374, 375, 376; Palmer, Chris, 387, 442–43, 484, 538–39, 598, 605, 608; Palmer, Jeremy, 247, 320, 364; Palmer, Mavis, 215–16, 218, 300, 434; Palmer, T., 346; Shearer, G., 46, 47, 331, 374, 375, 376, 635–36; Sujay's, 594, 598; Tina's, 10, 295–96, 349, 350, 385, 431, 458–59, 589–90; treasure hunts on, 46, 199, 237, 349, 538, 628

bison, 162, 209, 271–72, 282

Bison, 209

Bits And Pieces, 289–90

blackout, power (2003), 477, 478

Blauner, Andrew, 475

blog (Tina's), 548–49, 552–54, 560, 561

BLUE Ocean Film Festival, 574

body weight, 87, 205, 242–43

Bohlen, Mary and Brent, 170

boldness: importance of, 248, 534; maxims on, 107, 266

Bombeck, Erma, 218, 287

books: on appearance, professional, 523; on breathwork, 568; childrearing, 123, 210–11, 227–28,

Bushell, Johnny, 221
business cards, 228
butter making, 633

California, 559–60; earthquakes, 451–52; gold rush, 196, 246; Hollywood, 42, 63, 78, 83, 140, 263, 283, 340
Cameron, Jim, 574–75
Camp Carysbrook, 236, 305, 307, 309
camping trips: with Jen, 85, 122; of Kim, 163, 170, 172, 176, 240, 242, 402; New England family, 75; with Rossellini in Africa, 605; in Saw Tooth Mountains, 97–98
Camp Letts, 40, 76, 85, 255
Canada, 169, 199, 214, 293, 411
cancer, 162, 382, 563, 596
career: advice to daughters, 481–82, 519–20, 523–25, 534, 575–76, 588–89, 611; appearance in, 522–23; bullying in, 575–76; celebrity stories in, 605; competition in, 192; control over, 350; enjoyment/fun in, 61, 65, 161, 210, 240, 286, 294, 467–69, 519, 605, 610; family balanced with, 7, 43, 61, 98, 104, 123, 206–7, 233, 315; gender considerations in, 524, 549; gratitude for, 207, 237, 239, 240, 313, 358, 361; insecurity in, 360; Jen's, highlights of and path to, 533–34, 622; Kim's, highlights of and path to, 309, 315, 390, 420, 460, 464, 479, 481, 483, 519–20, 611; learning from mistakes in, 167–68; modeling passion for, 610; over-scheduling in, 98–99, 206–7; Palmer, Chris, early, 61, 62, 110, 221, 351, 354, 501, 531–32, 533, 624; Palmer, Chris, promotion disappointment in, 487, 496–97; Palmer, Chris, shift into conservation, 61, 351–52; Palmer, Chris, teaching, 9, 522, 569, 578, 609; of Palmer, S., 35, 60, 177, 242, 291, 642–43, 644; praise in, 437; respect in, 559; salary negotiation skills in, 611; self-confidence in, environment, 524–25; service to others in, 360; of Shearer, G., 170, 371, 402, 415, 427, 439, 444, 448, 457, 459, 486, 492, 506–7, 533; Steinem on men balancing marriage and, 190, 233; success in, tips for, 324–26, 466–67, 469, 470–71, 472, 492; tenacity with, 492; Tina's, highlights of and path to, 296–97, 386, 388, 395, 465–67, 470–72, 475, 477–78, 479, 481–82, 483, 486, 492, 502, 513, 518–19, 523–25, 558–59, 575–76, 588–89, 617
The Caring Institute, 222, 224
Carpe Diem, 118–19, 619–20
cars, financial costs of, 213, 511, 512
Carter, Jimmy, 451, 501, 517
Carter, Judy, 544
Catholicism, 188
celebrities, working with, 605
cemetery, family (England), 530–31
cetaceans, about, 119–20
Character Above All, 117
charity: Christmas gifts of donations to, 403, 404; Franklin and, 480; joke, 113–14; Palmer, Chris, childhood Christmas, 633
Charles (prince), 162
Chase, 638; marriage proposal to Jen of, 640–41; memories of, 599; Palmer, Chris, life review letter on, 597–600; physical strength of, 640; wedding toast for Jen and, 640–41
chaste, 417, 482
Chatfield (admiral), 646
"Chauvinist Pigskin" (Garfield), 277

Cher, 234

Chicago, 391, 392, 416–17, 423–24, 453–54

Chicago Tribune, 445

childhood (Chris Palmer): boarding school in, 6, 35–36, 74, 85, 147, 151, 346, 528; books discovery and love in, 74, 636; boxing in, 501, 622; butter making in, 633; Christmas charity in, 633; cooperation lesson from, 37; cowboys fascination in, 481; cow herd memory in, 636; exam success in, 36; family time during, 82; humor appreciation and skill in, 290–92, 569, 633; letters from mother impact in, 6, 36, 645; math tutoring in, 147; nature in, love of, 291; science in, 37; self-assessment of, 278; sibling relationships in, 70, 74, 130, 148, 151, 342; speeches, first, 338; stuttering in, 291; teacher favorite from, 291; vocabulary skills self-study in, 139–40, 637; writing experience in, 36

childrearing: activity/play dates in, 40, 65, 74, 572, 573, 628; aphorisms and maxims on, 63, 107, 230; books, 123, 210–11, 227–28, 231–33, 260, 388, 561–62; career balanced with, 589; character training with, 96; communication skills in, 210–12, 227, 231; Covey on, 180–81; death discussed in, 372; diligence taught in, 91; eating habits "cheats" in, 622–23; Edison on, 34; family history importance in, 603; family traditions importance in, 485, 562, 627; gender/gender roles in, 6–7, 43, 123; gifts and benefits of, 53–54, 63, 70, 89, 107, 141, 160–61, 637–38; jokes and witticisms on, 85–86, 218, 223, 234, 277–78, 332; learning art of, 94, 227–28; letters significance in, 6–9, 615; materialism and privilege dangers with, 216–17, 323; mealtime conversations importance in, 153–54, 250–51; memory creation in, 356; mirroring parents', 609; mistakes in, 210–11, 217, 358; modeling enjoyment in, 93, 610; Palmer, Chris, book on, 7, 611, 622, 638; poems on, 339; praise in, keys to, 141–42, 232, 358, 485; regrets, 192, 418; success in, tips for, 231, 285–86, 485, 554, 627; surprises and gifts of, 637–38; Tina on strictness in, 614–15; Tina on women's sacrifice in, 347; two-parent benefits in, 170; vacations and, 227, 628; while traveling, tips for, 231, 554, 627. *See also* fatherhood and fathering skills; motherhood and mothering skills

China, 402, 404, 405, 409, 436. *See also* Hong Kong

Chinese bamboo tree metaphor, 106, 185, 493

Christian, T. C., 97

Christmas, 448, 460; charitable donations as gifts at, 403, 404; companionship focus during, 405, 542; gift-giving habits for, 314–15, 375, 376, 402–3, 404, 542, 633; journals for year gifted at, 628; Palmer, Chris, childhood charity at, 633; predictions tradition at, 286, 406, 412, 628; T-shift gifts for, 625

Christofferson, Lynn, 97

Churchill, Winston, 90; humor of, 159, 512; on marriage, 115, 159; overweight woman story of, 242–43; on service to others, 225; on success, 46, 373; in WWII, 25, 97, 322

circumcision, 199

circumstances, maxim on, 265

circus, 173

Civil War, 150, 195–96, 216, 244, 480, 541

CJ, 590, 638; marriage proposal to Tina of, 639–40; Palmer, Chris, life review letter on, 597–600; wedding toast for Tina and, 639–40

Clark, Barry, 283

Clark, Dave, 93

Clark, Mary Higgins, 474

Clark, William, 190, 195, 243, 507

classism, 642–43

Cleveland, 260

climate change, 574

61, 623

Haslar, 96, 643

Hawaii, 93, 119, 120; *aloha* meaning in, 116; Pearl Harbor attack in, 25, 116, 251

health: aphorisms and maxims on, 230, 479; as basic need, 127; in childrearing tips, 485; control over personal, 350, 436; gratitude for, 358; humor and laughter benefits for, 274; Palmer, Mavis, issues with, 193, 351; Palmer, S., issues with, 151, 162, 193, 382–83; self-assessment, 229; sexual, 429; traveling precautions for, 419. *See also* eating habits, healthy; exercise and sports

Hechinger, Debbie, 77

Heidenreich, Pat and Bill, 54

Height, Dorothy, 224

Heinz, Lynn, 161

Hemingway, Mariel, 54

Highlights newsletter, 212–13, 611

Hillel, 222

Hitler, Adolph, 25, 78, 96, 643

holiday, perpetual, 35

Holliman, Paul, 501

Hollywood: awards ceremonies in, 78, 140; Palmer, Chris, work in, 42, 63, 78, 83, 140, 263, 283, 340

Holocaust, 207, 213, 266

Holton-Arms: Creative Summer camp at, 125, 128, 229, 255, 406, 412, 436, 439; Father/Daughter Dinners at, 431, 615–16, 621–22; Jen's first year at, 390, 392, 396, 399, 402; mission of, 212–13; opportunities at, 155, 212–13; Palmer, Chris, as Peer Facilitator at, 182; Tina's acceptance to, 112, 122. *See also The Scribbler*

homesickness: in boarding school, 6, 35–36, 85; in college, 352, 424; in preschool, 611; while traveling, 20, 35, 419

honesty, 106, 311; Franklin on, 198, 479; importance of, 128, 161, 249, 548; joke about, 111–12

Hong Kong: Palmer, Chris, birth in, 60, 409, 501, 539, 645; Palmer, Mavis, in, 60; Palmer, S., in, 60, 242; trips to, 409, 501

honorable path, 171, 222, 267, 347

Hope, Bob, 208

Hopkins, Tom, 373

Horn, Alan, 283

hotel towel joke, 205, 310

Houdini, 333

housekeeping, 284; gratitude for, 239; issues, 30, 121, 123, 174, 437–38; joke, 234; sharing tasks of, 322–23, 375, 616

How To Talk So Kids Will Listen And Listen So Kids Will Talk (Faber and Mazlish), 210–11

Hugo, Victor, 267

hugs, 232; family mission statement on, 186, 626; gratitude for, 72; Jen as child and, 220, 618, 619

humanism, 274, 501

human relations, 92, 346; aphorisms and maxims on, 50, 267, 311, 347, 348; as basic need, 127; in college, 352–53; communication guidelines for authentic, 292–93; constructive criticism and, 168; cooperation in, 37; declining requests in, 368; family meetings aiding in, 44, 627; first impressions in, 301–2; Franklin on, 198; gratitude for, 37, 313, 365; happiness relationship to, 257, 468; humor and laughter and, 37, 554; importance of, 37, 43–44, 50, 130, 230, 343–44; key words exercise for, 353; listening skills impact in, 99, 293; networking and, 559–61; over-scheduling impact on, 98–99; practice in, 44, 84, 130, 309, 382, 456, 627; respect in, 128, 181; Shearer, G., skill in, 309;

journalism. *See* writing and journalism

journals/journal keeping: Christmas gift of year of, 628; communication skills aided with, 345; discipline for, 271; for family history/legacy, 9, 59, 271, 345, 403, 603; family meetings, story about value of, 179–80; feedback on, 88, 94, 135, 136, 143, 149, 166, 198, 244; goal setting aided with, 345; gratitude for, 237; Kim's article on, 214, 605–7; for Kim's last year at home, 135, 143, 149, 166, 606–7; on learning, 388, 406; as life essential, 131; memory integrity with, 260; Palmer, Mavis, inspiration for, 6, 36, 645; Palmer, T., appreciation of, 166, 167, 313; promotion of and tips for, 21–22, 59, 100, 101, 249, 286, 345, 360, 606–7, 618; stress management with, 306, 345; for unborn children, 12, 227; writing skills aided with, 59, 345

joy lists, 285; benefits of, 63; dog story on, 505; of Palmer, Chris, 71–72, 236–40, 365

The Joy of Sisters (Brown), 320

judgment, poor, 39, 167–68, 368

Judy (aunt), 167

July 4th. *See* Fourth of July

Kabat-Zinn, Jon, 168–69

Kapatkin, Rhoda, 371

Kareena: aging questions from, 641; Cory relationship with, 565; night fear of, 609; Palmer, Chris, life review letter on, 597–600; Palmer, Chris, relationship with, 580–81, 584–85, 594, 637, 638, 641–42; on "specialness," 581, 642

Keiko, 409, 410, 494, 495

Keller, Helen, 266

Kennedy, John F., 115, 283

Kenya, 20–21

Key Largo National Marine Sanctuary, 59

killer whales, 270

King, Martin Luther, Jr., 224

King, Stephen, 455

kisses, 230

Kissinger, Henry, 204

Kodiak Brown Bear, 221, 231, 308

Kodiak Island, 231, 233, 308

Kubler-Ross, Elisabeth, 225

Kuhn, Margaret E., 224

Ladies Home Journal, 611

Landers, Ann, 94, 336, 632

language: choices, impact of, 366–67; in declining requests, 368; distinctions, value of, 38, 202, 367; foreign, while traveling, 419; goal setting and choice of, 322; jokes, play on, 56. *See also* vocabulary words

Lao Tzu, 265

Large Format Cinema Association (LFCA), 209, 384, 510–11

Las Vegas, 108

lateral thinking, 200–201, 299

laughter. *See* humor and laughter; jokes

lawyers, 57–58, 332, 506

leaders/leadership: characteristics of good, 307–8, 441; family meetings and, 612; humor as skill for,

Palmer, Hannah, 499–500, 529, 645

Palmer, Jenny (Jen): academic highlights of, 117, 146, 252, 375, 385, 399, 402, 404, 405, 409, 412, 416, 425–26, 427, 431, 436, 445, 448, 455, 457, 460, 475, 483, 502; Alaska trip (1997) letters to, 155–58; animal rights work of, 533–34, 540, 542; Barbados trip with, 381, 385; birthdays, 385, 431, 590; birth of, 10; at Camp Carysbrook, 236, 305, 307, 309; camping trips with, 85, 122; career advice for, 534; career and career path highlights of, 533–34, 622; Chase marriage proposal to, 640–41; childhood reading habits, 43, 79; childhood speech patterns of, 618, 619; on church and confirmations, 174, 380; Conker and, 371, 372; Cory relationship with, 376, 378, 383, 396, 431, 432–33, 471, 564, 565; Costa Rica trip of, 463–64, 483; Creative Summer for, 125, 128, 229, 255, 406, 412, 436, 439; dog petition from, 619; drive, learning to, 446, 457; emotional intelligence of, 82, 278, 413, 620; exercise/sports highlights of, 166, 170, 252, 374, 383, 386, 392, 399, 402, 424, 427, 444, 464, 486, 505, 513; family meeting encouragements for, 373–76, 378, 380, 381, 383, 384, 385–86, 390, 392, 396, 399, 404–5, 412, 416, 424, 427, 431, 436, 439, 444, 445–46, 448, 457, 460, 483, 486–87; Father/Daughter Dinner speech of, 621–22; fathering skills feedback from, 620–22; 5th grade goals of, 162–63; Florida trips with, 314, 315, 351, 352, 358; friendship highlights for, 193, 445, 460, 473, 502, 564–65; Holton-Arms, first year at, 390, 392, 396, 399, 402; on hugs as child, 220, 618, 619; humor of, 125, 219–20, 618–22; interviewing questions advice for, 461; joy list items about, 236–38; learning/school advice for, 455–56; letters from, 414, 463–64, 529, 533–34, 572; math learning appreciation of, 622; memories of, highlighted, 219–20, 255, 599, 618–22; musicianship of, 178, 193, 373, 380, 381, 384, 385, 386, 392, 416, 431, 448, 502, 510, 565, 620; 1995 highlights of, 255; Palmer, Chris, life review letter on, 597–600; school opportunities for, 42, 55; school participation disagreement with, 328–30; school peer letters (1996) to, 126–27; sea glass memory with, 39–40; television watching in childhood of, 122, 620, 621; wedding toast for Chase and, 640–41; write, learning to, 618; writing/journalism of, 533–34

Palmer, Jeremy: birthday of, 247, 320, 364; childhood of, 82, 130, 148, 637; death of, 247, 320; Palmer, S., relationship with, 637

Palmer, Jon, 193, 279, 382, 431, 444, 445, 531; birth of, 60, 645; childhood of, 35, 74, 148, 291; humor of, 22; love life of, 167; at Palmer, Mavis, funeral, 499, 500; visits with, 387

Palmer, Kimberly (Kim): academic highlights of, 123, 374, 378, 380, 384, 385, 395, 416–17, 423–24, 502; advice list for, 443; Alaska trip with, 155–58; arguments with, 605; Australia trip of, 270, 274, 276; as baby, 7; birthday (21st) of, 374, 375, 376; birth of, 10, 356; camping trips of, 163, 170, 172, 176, 240, 242, 402; at Camp Letts, 40, 76; career advice for, 519–20, 611; career and career path highlights of, 309, 315, 390, 420, 460, 464, 479, 481, 483, 519–20, 611; China trips of, 402, 404, 405, 409, 436; college life of, 162–69, 170–76, 178–82, 384; college visits with, 332, 371, 380, 384; college writing of, 163, 164, 165, 170, 172–73, 175; confirmation of, 53; Cory relationship with, 564; Disneyland trip of, 400; dog petition from, 604; dolphins, swimming with, 58, 85; emotional intelligence of, 82, 278, 413, 580, 608; England visits of, 343, 346, 431; exercise/sports highlights for, 255, 530; family journal article by, 214, 605–7; family meeting encouragements for, 373–76, 378, 380, 383, 384, 385, 386, 390, 392, 395, 396, 399, 404–5, 411–12, 415, 423–24, 427, 431, 436, 439, 444, 445, 448, 457, 460, 483, 486; on father comforting nighttime fear, 609; fathering skills feedback from, 77; on father reaction to meeting boyfriends, 513, 605, 609, 639; on father's time spent with students, 609; on Florida trip (1993), 57–59; friendship highlights for, 240, 242, 254–55, 305, 409, 410, 415, 445, 483, 494, 495, 502, 604; *Generation Earn* by, 554–56; on grades, academic, 172; graduate school acceptance letter and decision for, 416–17, 423–24; graduate school life for, 444, 448, 453–54, 502; humor of, 560, 605, 608, 625; humorous T-shirt gift from, 625; Japan job and stay of, 383, 388, 389, 390, 392, 399, 409, 410, 422, 427, 431, 436, 443, 452, 608–9; journal for, last year at home, 135, 143, 149, 166, 606–7; journalism/writing of, 85, 111,

practice: at human relations, 44, 84, 130, 309, 382, 456, 627; mindfulness, 168–69; respect, 318; show-and-tell, with Tina, 612; smiling, 382, 456; tenacity/perseverance, 294, 318; trustworthiness and reliability, 318. *See also* preparation

praise: at bedtime, 232; in career, 437; in childrearing, keys to, 141–42, 232, 358, 485; for diligence/industriousness, 622; encouragement distinction from, 142, 312, 496; expressions of, 9, 23–24, 28–29, 31, 42–43, 53–54, 59, 71, 76, 79, 82, 111, 121–23, 125, 160–61, 285, 312, 597, 622; feedback on lack of, 328; habit of, 285; of maturity, 342; Palmer, S., on, 634; of progress, 141; self, 80; of students, 9; of tenacity/perseverance, 9, 52, 380, 381, 405, 431, 589–90; for Tina's wisdom, 484–85

predictions, annual, 286, 406, 412, 628

pregnancy, unintended, 429

prejudice, 25, 116, 132, 554; awareness, 292–93; family history experience of, 642–43; storiey about, 262, 624

preparation, 133, 267; for exams, 22, 354–55; for interviewing others, 461; for meetings, 518–19; for presentations/speeches, 77–78, 84, 237, 280–81, 301, 316, 378, 384, 394, 400, 428, 458, 498

presentations/speeches, 245–46; courage in, 400, 401; emcee work and, 507–8; at Environmental Media Association's Awards Dinner, 42; feedback on children's, 428, 494–95, 555–56; on *Generation Earn*, 554–55; goal setting for, 394; GSTA, 316; humor and laughter in, 55, 280–81, 428, 513, 571; IMAX, 135, 138, 176, 209, 233, 242, 333, 334, 348, 391, 412–13; at International Wildlife Film Festival, 503, 504; at Jackson Hole Film Festival, 90, 135, 322; Jen's Father/Daughter dinner, 621–22; Kim's ability for, 474, 494, 554–55; notes protocol with, 495; NWF, 152, 281, 286, 415, 464, 493, 498; Palmer, Chris, self-composed introduction for, 501; in Palmer, Chris, childhood, 338; preparation for, 77–78, 84, 237, 280–81, 301, 316, 378, 384, 394, 400, 428, 458, 498; self-confidence in, 498, 556; spam, 464; stand-up comedy experience impact on, 571; tips for, 428, 494–95, 555–56; at UN, 59; on wildlife filmmaking, 90, 135, 322, 393, 503, 504; workshop on giving, 505, 506. *See also* workshops

presidential history, 189, 190, 195, 243, 250, 451

The Price of Motherhood (Crittenden), 388

primates, 178

Primesco lawsuit, 487

Princeton Animal Welfare Society (PAWS), 534, 540, 542

Princeton University, 140, 376, 534

principles. *See* values

"The Private and the Toolbox" joke, 259

proactivity, 396; aphorisms and maxims on, 265–66; in childrearing, 562; Covey on, 263, 288; in dating, 560; failure relationship to, 52; in language choices, 367; in life path creation, 37, 343; modeling, 217; in problem assessment, 343; for success, 37, 199, 248; tips/guidelines for, 296–97; with visualizations, 296–97, 299–300

procrastination, 355

productivity: time management for, 93, 284–85, 290, 317–18, 340, 349, 354, 361, 479, 548; traveling, 283–84; workshops on, 500–501

prostate cancer, 162, 382, 596

proverbs: on discipline, 266; on fatherhood, 57; on life purpose, 266; on listening, 268; on mothers, 508; quiz on, 235; on self-reliance, 234; on time management, 290

Proverbs, biblical, 266, 268, 530

pseudoscience, 161, 274, 320–21, 324

Puppy and I, 241–42

About the Author

Chris Palmer is a teacher, author, speaker, and environmental filmmaker, but more importantly, he is a husband, father, and grandfather.

www.ingramcontent.com/pod-product-compliance
Lightning Source LLC
Chambersburg PA
CBHW080222270326
41926CB00020B/4111